The
Authoritarian
Moment

The Authoritarian Moment

How the Left Weaponized America's Institutions Against Dissent

Ben Shapiro

HARPER LARGE PRINT

An Imprint of HarperCollinsPublishers

HarperCollins books may be purchased for educational, business, or sales promotional use. For information, please e-mail the Special Markets Department at SPsales@harpercollins.com.

FIRST HARPER LARGE PRINT EDITION

ISBN: 978-0-06-309058-3

Library of Congress Cataloging-in-Publication Data is available upon request.

21 22 23 24 25 LSC 10 9 8 7 6 5 4 3 2 1

To my children, who deserve to grow up in
a country that values the freedoms promised
by the Declaration of Independence and
guaranteed by our Constitution

Contents

Introduction

According to the institutional powers that be, America is under authoritarian threat.

That authoritarian threat to America, according to the Democratic Party, establishment media, social media tech bros, Hollywood glitterati, corporate bosses, and university professors, is clear—and it comes directly from the political Right.

And that authoritarian threat, according to those who control vast swaths of American life, manifested itself most prominently on January 6, 2021.

On that day, hundreds if not thousands of rioters broke away from a far larger group of pro-Trump peaceful protesters and stormed the United States Capitol, many seeking to do violent harm to members of Congress and the vice president of the United States.

Their goal: to overturn the legally constituted results of the 2020 election.

The images from January 6 were indeed dramatic—and the rioters of January 6 did indeed engage in acts of criminal evil. Pictures of barbarians dressed in buffalo horns and idiots carrying Trump flags and military gear–clad fools carrying zip cuffs made the front pages globally. Sitting congresspeople and the vice president of the United States were rushed to safety, shielding themselves from the droogs beyond.

All Americans of goodwill—on all political sides—decried the January 6 riots. Vice President Pence personally oversaw the counting of the electoral votes; Senate Majority Leader Mitch McConnell (R-KY) condemned the rioters as vile cretins, then moved forward to the certification of the election.

But according to the Left, the January 6 riots weren't merely an act of universally condemned criminality. They were the culmination of right-wing authoritarianism. Jonathan Chait of *New York* magazine wrote, "We entrusted a sociopathic instinctive authoritarian with the most powerful office in the world. What did we think would happen?"[1] Paul Krugman of *The New York Times* suggested, "one of our major political parties has become willing to tolerate and, indeed, feed right-wing political paranoia. . . . The GOP has reached the culmination of its long journey away from democracy, and it's hard to see how it can ever be redeemed."[2] Greg Sargent of *The Washington Post* explained, "Trump's GOP has an ugly authoritarian core."[3] Lisa McGirr wrote in *The New York Times*, "Republicans will certainly seek to pivot from the riot, but the nativism, extreme polarization, truth-bashing, white nationalism and anti-democratic policies that we tend to identify with President Trump are likely to remain a hallmark of the Republican playbook into the future."[4]

"If you voted for Trump," said Don Lemon of CNN, "you voted for the person who the Klan supported. You voted for the person who Nazis support. You voted for the person the alt-right supports. That's the crowd that you are in. You voted for the person who incited a crowd to go into the Capitol and potentially take the lives of lawmakers."[5]

Score settling would be necessary. Charles Blow of *The New York Times* asked, "What do we do now as a society and as a body politic? Do we simply turn the page and hope for a better day, let bygones be bygones? Or do we seek some form of justice, to hold people accountable for taking this country to the brink?"[6] Joy Reid of MSNBC called for "de-Baathification," à la the post–Iraq War purge of Saddam Hussein's military.[7]

Indeed, the American Left argued, the greatest threat to America's future came from right-wing authoritarianism—which, naturally, the Left conflated with white supremacy and conservative philosophy. To fail in the quest of ridding America of this threat would spell the end of the republic.

Authoritarianism had to be stopped.

But what if the most dangerous authoritarian threat to America wasn't the several hundred evil conspiracists, fools, and criminals who breached the Capitol?

What if the most dangerous authoritarian threat to the country wasn't a properly despised group of agitators making asses of themselves by charging into the Hall of Democracy, variously dressed in military gear, animal skins, and buffalo horns?

What if the primary threat to American liberty lies elsewhere?

What if, in fact, the most pressing authoritarian threat to the country lies precisely with the institutional powers that be: in the well-respected centers of journalism, in the gleaming towers of academia, in the glossy offices of the Hollywood glitterati, in the cubicles of Silicon Valley and the boardrooms of our corporate behemoths? What if the danger of authoritarianism, in reality, lies with those who are most powerful—with a ruling class that despises the values of half the country, and with the institutions they wield? What if the creeping authoritarianism of those who wield power has been slowly growing, unchecked, for years?

What if authoritarianism has many strains—and the most virulent strain isn't the paranoia and fear that sometimes manifests on the Right, but the self-assured unearned moral virtue of the Left?

THE AUTHORITARIAN INSTINCT

Something there is in man that loves a dictator.

In the book of Samuel, the people of Israel, threatened from without by warring tribes and within by dissention, seek to end the age of judges: they want a king. They have been warned repeatedly about the disastrous consequences of such a choice. God tells Samuel that the people have "rejected Me"; Samuel excoriates the people, telling them that a king "will take your sons" and "take your daughters" and "take your fields and your vineyards" and "take the tenth of your flocks"—that, in the end, "you shall be his servants, and you shall cry out in that day because of the king you chose, and the Lord will not answer you in that day."

And the people answer: "No, there shall be a king over us; that we also may be like all the nations, and that our king may judge us, and go out before us, and fight our battles."[8]

Human nature does not change.

This is the unfortunate truth of human history: because man is a threat to man, human beings seek safety and satisfaction in authority; because man is a threat to man, human beings seek the possibility of a *remolding* of man, a remolding to be achieved through the exercise of power. Human beings, all too often, trust not in the moral authority of a God above, looking down benevolently on humanity, providing ethical guidelines for building fulfilling lives and rich communities. Instead, they look to the earthly authority of a king, a leader, an institution. It took just a few weeks from the splitting of the Red Sea for the Jews to embrace the Golden Calf.

Human beings are ripe for authoritarianism.

For most of human history, authoritarianism manifested in centralized governmental systems: monarchies, oligarchies, aristocracies. The widespread democracy of the post–World War II period is extraordinary, and extraordinarily fragile: human beings may be granted freedom, but freedom has a short shelf life.

Democracy is threatened chiefly by ochlocracy: the rule of the mob. Mob rule transforms freedom into authoritarianism in two ways: through reactionary brutality, in which citizens seek protection from the winds of change, without and within—a form of brutality largely associated with the political Right; and utopian brutality, in which citizens seek to escape present challenges through the transformation of mankind itself—a form of brutality largely associated with the political Left. Often, the two forms of brutality feed on each other, creating a downward spiral into tyranny. This is precisely what happened in Weimar Germany, where the utopian brutality of German communists came into conflict with the reactionary brutality of German Nazis. The winning side implemented the most vicious tyranny in the history of mankind; the losing side was an offshoot of one of the most vicious tyrannies in the history of mankind. Neither side sought the preservation of a democratic, rights-based system.

The Founding Fathers of the United States saw in mob rule the greatest danger to their nascent system— and they put in place governmental checks and balances in order to protect individual rights from the frenzied whims of the riotous mass. The Constitution was designed to check ambition against ambition, passion against passion. James Madison famously abhorred "faction"—by which he meant "a number of citizens, whether amounting to a majority or a minority of the whole, who are united and actuated by some common impulse of passion, or of interest, adverse to the rights of other citizens, or to the permanent and aggregate interests of the community." He posited two possible ways of preventing faction: one, "by destroying the liberty which is essential to its existence; the other, by giving to every citizen the same opinions, the same passions, and the same interests." Both ways would end in authoritarianism.[9] The solution, he suggested, lay in checks and balances, in creating such a diffusion of interests that combination would become nearly impossible.

For a while, it worked.

It worked for two reasons.

First, the checks and balances built by the founders were wondrous in their durability. The hopes of would-be authoritarians were routinely stymied by the balances of federalism, of separation of powers. Those checks and balances remain durable today: the constitutional system's series of speed bumps certainly blunt momentum. Despite the best attempts of members of both parties to completely override the constitutional order, excesses are often mitigated, at least in small part.

Second, and more important, the American people broadly rejected the impulses of the mob—they rejected both the utopianism of left-wing authoritarianism and the reactionary nature of right-wing authoritarianism. Core American freedoms—freedoms of speech and of the press, freedoms of religion and association—were widely perceived to be beyond debate. If oppression deeply marred American history—and, of course, it did—it did so against a backdrop of American liberty, more and more broadly applied to more and more Americans. The Founding Fathers were united in their support for a culture of freedom—particularly freedom of thought and speech.[10]

THE AUTHORITARIAN MINDSET

But beneath the surface, the authoritarian mindset always looms.

In 1950, Frankfurt School theorist Theodor Adorno, along with University of California, Berkeley, researchers Else Frenkel-Brunswik, Daniel Levinson, and Nevitt Sanford, authored a book titled *The Authoritarian Personality*. The book, an attempt to explore the origins of anti-Semitism, posited that people could be classified via the use of a so-called F-scale—F meaning "pre-fascist personality." Adorno et al. posited that such personalities were churned out by the American system. The authors suggested, "The modification of the potentially fascist structure cannot be achieved by psychological means alone. The task is comparable to that of eliminating neurosis, or delinquency, or nationalism from the world. These are the products of the total organization of society and are to be changed only as that society is changed."[11]

Because Adorno was a leftist and a Freudian, the analysis was deeply flawed; the very possibility of a left-wing authoritarianism was ignored by Adorno. Still, right-wing authoritarianism is quite real. Following in Adorno's footsteps, Harvard social scientist Robert Altemeyer utilized a "Right Wing Authoritarianism" (RWA) scale, attempting to detect three character traits:

"Authoritarian submission," or willingness to submit to established and legitimate authorities;

"Authoritarian aggression," or aggressiveness approved by the authorities against a particular "outgroup";

"Conventionalism," defined by adherence to approved social conventions.[12] Altemeyer found that right-wing authoritarianism was unnervingly common.

Surprisingly, Altemeyer found that left-wingers were not at all susceptible to authoritarianism. Altemeyer concluded that left-wing authoritarianism was "like the Loch Ness Monster: an occasional shadow, but no monster."[13] Perhaps that had something to do with the fact that the "Left Wing Authoritarianism," or LWA, scale-loaded the questions.[14] In fact, when University of Montana social psychologist Lucian Conway simply rewrote Altemeyer's exact questions, replacing only the right-wing premises with left-wing premises, he found that "the highest score for authoritarianism was for *liberals* on LWA." Conway explained, "Our data suggest that average Americans on the political left are just as likely to be dogmatic authoritarians as those on the political right. And those left-wing authoritarians can be just as prejudiced, dogmatic, and extremist as right-wing authoritarians."[15]

The *content* of the dogma is merely different: as sociologist Thomas Costello of Emory University et al. writes, left-wing authoritarianism is characterized by three traits that look quite similar to those of right-wing authoritarianism:

"Revolutionary aggression," designed to "forcefully overthrow the established hierarchy and punish those in power";

"Top-down censorship," directed at wielding "group authority . . . as a means of regulating characteristically right-wing beliefs and behaviors";

"Anti-conventionalism," reflecting a "moral absolutism concerning progressive values and concomitant dismissal of conservatives as inherently immoral, an intolerant desire for coercively imposing left-wing beliefs and values on others, and a need for social and ideological homogeneity in one's environment."[16]

In reality, there are authoritarians on all sides. Even Adorno came to take this view: during the student protests of the 1960s, Adorno, who taught at the Free University of Berlin, was confronted by student radicals. He wrote a plaintive letter to fellow Frankfurt School theorist Herbert Marcuse complaining about the left-wing authoritarianism he saw in the student protesters who occupied his room and refused to leave: "We had to call the police, who then arrested all those they found in the room . . . they treated the students far more leniently than the students treated me." Adorno wrote that the students had "display[ed] something of that thoughtless violence that once belonged to fascism." Marcuse, a strident left-wing authoritarian himself—he infamously proposed that "repressive tolerance" required that dissenting right-wing views be censored[17]—then chided Adorno, stating that "our cause . . . is better taken up by the rebellious students than by the police," and argued that violence by the Left was merely "fresh air."[18]

Authoritarians rarely recognize their own authoritarianism. To them, authoritarianism looks like simple virtue.

THE AUTHORITARIAN QUESTION

So, if there are authoritarians on the Right and on the Left—and if the two feed on one another, driving America ever deeper into a moral morass—where does the true risk lie?

To answer that question requires us to evaluate two more questions. First, which form of authoritarianism is more common in the halls of power?

Second, which form of authoritarianism is more likely to be checked?

Let's revisit January 6 and its aftermath with these questions in mind.

There is little doubt that the rioters of January 6 were right-wing authoritarians. They invaded the Capitol building in order to stop the workings of democracy, overthrow the constitutional process, and harm those seeking to do their legal duty. They participated in authoritarian submission—they believed they were doing the work of President Donald Trump against a corrupt and effete establishment. They participated in authoritarian aggression—they believed they were empowered to do harm in order to defend Trump and take on the legislative branch. And they were engaged in conventionalism—they felt they were defending established values (the flag, the vote, democracy itself) against a revolution from within.

On January 6, these right-wing authoritarians invaded the Capitol.

And, contrary to popular opinion, the system held.

As it turns out, authoritarianism on the right was checked, in large measure, by *members of the right.* It was Vice President Mike Pence who sent a letter to President Trump explaining that he would do his duty "to see to it that we open the certificates of the Electors of the several states, we hear objections raised by Senators and Representatives, and we count the votes of the Electoral College for President and Vice President in a manner consistent with our Constitution, laws, and history. So Help Me God."[19] It was Senate Majority Leader Mitch McConnell (R-KY) who congratulated Joe Biden on his victory immediately after the Electoral College vote. It was Republicans in the Senate who abandoned their electoral challenges immediately upon the reconvening of the electoral counting, after the Capitol building was cleared out. It was Republican governors and secretaries of state who certified their state votes.

The institutions held.

Many in the media termed January 6 a "coup," but it was never a coup in any proper sense: a coup requires institutional support. Certainly the rioters had no institutional support. In fact, Trump himself never explicitly called for the Capitol riot, stated in his speech that morning that he wanted the protests to be "peaceful," tweeted that he wanted everyone to go home in the midst of the riot (the vast majority of his supporters at the rally already had), and eventually—far too late, of course—put out a statement in which he acknowledged his defeat and told his supporters to remain peaceful. Trump might have authoritarian tendencies, but he did not wield authoritarian power. And beyond Trump himself, not a single major institution in American society supported the Capitol riots. Few even supported the president's efforts to challenge the election beyond the Electoral College vote.

As a matter of fact, whatever personal authoritarian tendencies Trump may have had were checked *throughout his administration.* Trump had certainly engaged in authoritarian rhetoric—he utilized violent language, he suggested weaponization of the legal system, he called for breaches of the Constitution. And *nothing happened.* His much-maligned attorneys general refused to violate the law. He didn't fire special investigator Robert Mueller. His anger at the press translated mostly into increased ratings for his enemies; CNN's Jim Acosta, who spent every waking minute proclaiming that he was endangered by Trump's over-heated talk, became a household name thanks to his grandstanding. At no point did Acosta fear arrest or even deplatforming. The shock of January 6 was that the guardrails collapsed for a brief moment in time after holding for years on end. And then the guardrails were re-erected, including by some of Trump's erst-while allies.

Now let's turn to the other side of the aisle.

In the aftermath of January 6, America's institu-tional powers swung into action on behalf of authori-tarian measures.

Establishment media broadly promoted the idea of deplatforming mainstream conservatives and conser-vative outlets. CNN reported that the Capitol riot had "reignited a debate over America's long-held defense of extremist speech." Naturally, the media quoted "ex-perts" like Wendy Seltzer, affiliate at Harvard's Berk-man Klein Center for Internet & Society, to the effect that free speech primarily benefited those who are white.[20] Nikole Hannah-Jones, the serial social media prevaricator and Pulitzer Prize–winning purveyor of historical fiction about the inherent evils of America, quickly asked for a "reckoning" in the media.[21] Max Boot suggested in the pages of The Washington Post that Fox News be removed from Comcast, or that the

Federal Communications Commission be empowered to censor cable networks, stating, "Biden needs to reinvigorate the FCC. Or else the terrorism we saw on Jan. 6 may be only the beginning, rather than the end, of the plot against America."[22]

This wasn't just talk. Nearly every social media company in America promptly removed President Trump's accounts, even while acknowledging that they could not justify that removal on the basis of their stated policies. Major corporations announced they would cut funding to any Republican who had challenged electoral votes, despite never having done so to Democrats.[23] Senator Josh Hawley (R-MO), who had supported challenging electors (without serious legal basis, it should be noted), had his publication contract pulled by Simon & Schuster.[24] Harvard Kennedy School of Government dropped Representative Elise Stefanik (R-NY) from its senior advisory committee for making "public assertions about vote fraud in November's presidential election that have no basis in evidence."[25] Godaddy.com kicked AR15.com, the biggest gun forum in the world, offline.[26]

The most dramatic and immediate reaction to the Capitol riot was the institutional move against Parler. Parler had been launched in August 2018 as an alternative to Twitter; conservatives had been complaining about Twitter's opacity and discrimination against conservatives relative to leftists. Parler was the supposed free market solution. Then, in the aftermath of the riot, Apple's app store removed Parler, as did the Google Play store. The excuse: supposedly, Parler users had coordinated with regard to the January 6 protests, and Parler had allowed inflammatory and threatening material to remain up. The final blow came when Amazon Web Services—a company that merely provides cloud-based web infrastructure for companies—canceled Parler altogether, taking it offline. AWS, Parler CEO John Matze wrote, "will be banning Parler until we give up free speech, institute broad and invasive policies like Twitter and Facebook and we become a surveillance platform by pursuing guilt of those who use Parler before innocence."[27]

As it turned out, Facebook and Twitter had been used by Capitol protesters to coordinate as well. Neither company lost its cloud infrastructure. But leftist members of the media didn't react to that hypocrisy by calling for Parler's restoration—they reacted to it by calling for *further censorship against Facebook and Twitter.* Joe Scarborough of MSNBC—who throughout the 2016 race spent inordinate time pumping up Trump—ranted, "Those riots would not have happened but for Twitter, but for Facebook. . . . Facebook's algorithms were set up to cause this sort of radicalism to explode. . . . Facebook and Twitter set up their business models in a way that would lead to the insurrection."[28] Other tech journalists mirrored that sentiment—a sentiment they had been pumping for years, hoping to shut down social media companies that distribute alternative sources of media.

Meanwhile, governmental actors talked of revenge—and of using the Capitol riots to achieve long-sought political goals. Representative Alexandria Ocasio-Cortez (D-NY) stated that Congress should put together a "media literacy" commission in order to "figure out how we rein in our media environment."[29] Representative Cori Bush (D-MO) called for every single member of Congress who "incited this domestic terror attack" to be removed from Congress.[30] Senator Ron Wyden (D-OR) averred at NBCNews.com that the only way to prevent another Capitol riot was the addition of Washington, D.C., as a state, a renewed Voting Rights Act (likely unconstitutional), and universal mail-in voting.[31] As Joe Biden entered office on January 20, Representative James Clyburn (D-SC), who had compared Donald Trump to Hitler and Republicans to Nazis,[32] said that Biden should simply act unilaterally via executive action to implement his agenda if Congress balked: "If they're going to throw up roadblocks, go on without them. Use your executive authority if they re-fuse to cooperate . . . you can do big things and you can do great things. You can do things that are lasting."[33] It is worth noting that there is no clause of the Constitu-tion whereby the president can simply implement his favored policies without congressional approval.

To sum up: on January 6, a group of radical extrem-ist Trump supporters—right-wing authoritarians—stormed the US Capitol, where they were quickly put down. The institutions survived; the insurrectionists were roundly derided, disowned, and prosecuted.

Immediately thereafter, left-wing authoritarians took full advantage of the situation to press forward revolutionary aggression, top-down censorship, and anti-conventionalism targeting not just the rioters, but conservatives and individual rights more broadly. This perspective was mirrored across nearly every powerful institution in American society.

So, let us repeat the question.

If there is a serious threat to free speech, does it come chiefly from right-wing authoritarians? Or does it come from the left-wing authoritarians in media, big tech, and government?

If there is a threat to democratic institutions, does it come chiefly from right-wing authoritarians? Or does it come from the left-wing authoritarians in government, who broadly disdain the Constitution and believe in the implementation of their worldview from the top down?

If there is a threat to our most basic liberties, whom should we most fear: the dumbasses in clown suits invading the Capitol on January 6? Donald Trump, a man who talked like an authoritarian but did not actually govern as one? Or the monolithic leftists who dominate the top echelons of nearly every powerful institution in American society, and who frequently use their power to silence their opposition?

LIFE UNDER LEFT-WING SOCIAL AUTHORITARIANISM

Deep down, Americans know the answer to this question.

More than six in ten Americans say they fear saying what they think, including a majority of liberals, 64 percent of moderates, and fully 77 percent of conservatives. Only self-described "strong liberals" feel confident in saying what they believe these days.[34] To be a left-wing authoritarian is to feel the certainty of anti-conventionalism, the passion for top-down censorship, the thrill of revolutionary aggression.

Tomorrow belongs to them.

For the rest of us, a society run by left-wing authoritarians is extraordinarily burdensome. It is to be surrounded by institutional hatred. If you are conservative—or merely non-leftist—in America, the hatred is palpable.

They hate you in academia. They hate you in the media. They hate you on the sports field, in the movies, on Facebook and Twitter. Your boss hates you. Your colleagues hate you—or at least have been told they should.

They hate you because you think the wrong way.

Perhaps the problem is that you attend church regularly. Perhaps it's that you want to run your business and be left alone. Perhaps it's that you want to raise your children with traditional social values. It could be that you believe that men and women exist, or that the police are generally not racist, or that children deserve a mother and a father, or that hard work pays off, or that the American flag stands for freedom rather than oppression, or that unborn children should not be killed, or that people should be judged based on the content of their character rather than the color of their skin.

Maybe the problem is that you won't post a black square on your Facebook page to symbolize your support for the Black Lives Matter movement. Maybe the problem is that you won't kneel for the national anthem or cheer for those who kneel. Maybe it's that you haven't put your preferred pronouns in your Twitter profile, or hashtagged with the latest pride symbol for the latest cause, or used the proper emoji in your text messages.

Or maybe it's just that you have friends, or family members, or even acquaintances who have violated any of the thicket of cultural regulations placed upon us by our supposed moral betters. Guilt by association is just as damning as guilt through action or inaction.

The reasons they hate you are legion. They change day to day. There's no rhyme or reason or consistency to them. One day, you might be a ballyhooed champion of justice for standing up for gay rights or feminist ideals; the next day, you might be told that you have been banished to the cornfield for your refusal to acknowledge that a man calling himself a woman is not in fact a woman (Martina Navratilova or J. K. Rowling). One day, you might find yourself a hero of the intelligentsia for your cynicism about religion; the next, you might find yourself a villain for the great sin of suggesting that cancel culture breeds radicalization (Sam Harris or Steven Pinker). One day, you might be a well-respected opinion maker, considered de rigueur reading for your complex take on economics and sociology; the next, you might be considered a privileged white male worthy of excommunication (David Shor or Matthew Yglesias).

This is not a question of Democrat or Republican. Not one figure named above would identify as a Republican, let alone a conservative. There is only one thing in the end that unites the disparate figures deemed worthy of the gulag in our ongoing culture war: refusal. Like Herman Melville's Bartleby, it is simple refusal that demands compulsion. The standards matter less than the simple message: you will comply, and you will like it.

The consequences for those who do not are quite real. As a prominent conservative, I always warn those who aren't prepared for social, cultural, and familial blowback not to associate with me publicly. There are consequences for treating conservatives as human. That's why every birthday, I'm amused but unsurprised to receive a bevy of kind wishes from liberals via text message—and none publicly in places like Twitter, where the mere recognition that a conservative was born of woman is enough to earn unending scorn.

Such situations are far from hypothetical. In June 2018, prominent Hollywood actor and producer Mark Duplass approached me about getting together— he was producing a film dealing with gun rights, and wanted to speak with someone on the Right to get a more accurate point of view. I thought that was shockingly decent of him, given Hollywood's permanent and thoroughgoing determination to caricature conservative positions; I told him so, and suggested he come by the office for a discussion.

We ended up spending about an hour and a half together. As he left, I gave him the usual warning: don't mention that we've met publicly, unless you're prepared for the fallout.

He didn't listen. In July, a couple of weeks later, he tweeted this shocking message: "Fellow liberals: If you are interested at all in 'crossing the aisle' you should consider following @benshapiro. I don't agree with him on much but he's a genuine person who once helped me for no other reason than to be nice. He doesn't bend the truth. His intentions are good."

The world fell in on poor Mark. After trending on Twitter publicly, and surely receiving a boatload of nasty notes privately, Mark quickly deleted his tweet, and then replaced it with a Maoist struggle session of hot-button social justice warrior thoughtvomit:

So that tweet was a disaster on many levels. I want to be clear that I in no way endorse hatred, racism, homophobia, xenophobia or any such form of intolerance. My goal has always been to spread unity, understanding and kindness. But I am going to make mistakes along the way. Sometimes I move too quickly when I get excited, or fail to do enough research, or I don't communicate myself clearly. I'm really sorry. I now understand that I need to be more diligent and careful. I'm working on that. But, I do believe deeply in bi-partisan understanding and I will continue to do my best to promote peace and decency in this world right now. That said, I hear you. And I want to say thank you to those who reached out with constructive criticism. I have genuinely learned so much and wish everyone all the best.[35]

Well, almost everyone.

Honestly, I felt rather sorry for him. Duplass has to work in this town. And Hollywood is a one-party ideological dictatorship. That said, I did warn him. And cowardice is indeed a form of sin.

Naturally, Duplass's craven apology to the world for having acknowledged that a conservative is indeed human brought cheers from the usual suspects (Vox's Zack Beauchamp headlined, "Duplass was right to take back his praise").[36] Order had been restored; the binary moral universe ruled by the woke priestly caste had been maintained.

And it *will* be maintained.

Because Duplass isn't alone. This sort of stuff happens *all the time*. Just about a year after the Duplass incident, I attended a rather tony political summit—perhaps the only real ritzy cocktail party I've ever gone to. One of the other attendees happened to be one of the more prominent left-wing podcasters in the country. After a few pleasantries, I suggested that perhaps we ought to do an election-year crossover podcast. "The numbers," I said, "would be extraordinary. And I know my audience would love it. We're always having on guests who disagree."

"I'm sure your audience would be cool with it," the podcaster answered. "But mine would murder me."

He wasn't wrong. Which is why when I meet prominent people, from conservative sports stars to libertarian tech magnates, from right-wing Hollywood creators to goodhearted liberals in the media world, I do so quietly. I'm not in the business of taking billions of dollars off the market capitalization of major corporations or getting studio heads fired simply by confirming with whom I lunch. Those who violate ideological quarantine risk being treated as lepers in this environment.

Now, I'm lucky. I speak my views for a living. But tens and tens of millions of people aren't so lucky. For them, the consequences of speaking non-leftist views publicly in our absolutist time are grave. The authoritarian Left seeks to quell dissent. And they use every means at their disposal to do so.

Every day, I receive dozens of letters and calls from people asking how to navigate the minefield of American life. It's easily the most common question I receive.

"My boss is forcing me into diversity training, in which I'm told that all white Americans are inherently racist. Should I speak up about it? I'm afraid I'll be fired."

"My professor says that anyone who refuses to use preferred pronouns is a bigot. What should I write on my final? I'm afraid he'll grade me down."

"My sister knows I voted for Republicans. Now she says she doesn't want to talk to me. What do I do?"

The consequences of woke cultural authoritarianism are real, and they are devastating. They range from job loss to social ostracism. Americans live in fear of the moment when a personal enemy dredges up a Bad Old Tweet™ or members of the media "resurface" an impolitic comment in a text message. And the eyes and ears are everywhere. One simple tip from someone on Facebook to a pseudo-journalist activist can result in a worldwide scandal. Your boss cares what you say. So do your friends. Cross the social justice warriors, and you will be canceled. It's not a matter of if. Only when.

The only safety from the mob is to become a part of

the mob. Silence used to be possibility. Now silence is taken as resistance. Everyone must stand and applaud for Stalin—and he who sits down first is sent to the gulag.

So repeat. And believe.

Perhaps the most galling aspect of our culturally authoritarian moment is the blithe assurance whereby Americans are informed that they are exaggerating. There is no such thing as cancel culture, our woke rulers assure us, while busily hunting down our most embarrassing political faux pas. There's nothing wrong, they say, with calling your boss to try to get you fired—after all, that's the free market just working! Why are you whining about social media censorship, or about social ostracism? People have a right to tear you to shreds, to end your career, to malign your character! It's all free speech!

In a certain sense, they're not wrong: your boss does have a right to fire you; your friends and family do have a right to cut you off. None of that amounts to a violation of the First Amendment.

It simply amounts to the end of the republic.

Free speech and free exchange of ideas die when the attitude of philosophical tolerance withers. Government authoritarianism isn't the only way to kill American freedom. Cultural authoritarianism works, too. It has always worked. Writing in 1831, the greatest observer of America and democracy, Alexis de Tocqueville, summed up the threat of democratic despotism in terms that sound shockingly, eerily prescient:

Under the absolute government of one alone, despotism struck the body crudely, so as to reach the soul; and the soul, escaping from those blows, rose gloriously above it; but in democratic republics, tyranny does not proceed in this way; it leaves the body and goes straight for the soul. The master no longer says to it: You shall think as I do or you shall die; he says: You are free not to think as I do; your life, your goods, everything remains to you; but from this day on, you are a stranger among us. You shall keep your privileges in the city, but they will become useless to you; for if you crave the vote of your fellow citizens, they will not grant it to you, and if you demand only their esteem, they will still pretend to refuse it to you. You shall remain among men, but you shall lose your rights of humanity. When you approach those like you, they shall flee you as being impure; and those who believe in your innocence, even they shall abandon you, for one would flee them in their turn. Go in peace, I leave you your life, but I leave it to you worse than death.[37]

This is the America we currently occupy. As Axios reporter Jim VandeHei writes, "Blue America is ascendant in almost every area: It won control of all three branches of government; dominates traditional media; owns, controls and lives on the dominant social platforms; and has the employee-level power at big tech companies to force corporate decisions . . . our nation is rethinking politics, free speech, the definition of truth and the price of lies. This moment—and our decisions—will be studied by our kid's grandkids."[38]

There is no respite: your employer requires your fealty to woke principles; corporations require that you mirror their political priorities; the media treat you as a crude barbarian. There are no distractions: Hollywood mocks your morals and damns you for adherence to them; the sports world requires that you mimic the popular perversities of the moment before being allowed to escape; social media controls the flow of information you can see, while preventing you from speaking your mind. And each day you wonder if today will be the day the mob comes for you.

This book is about how our authoritarian moment

came to be. It is about the takeover of our most powerful institutions by a core of radicals, and about the miasmatic hatred and dire consequences Americans face for standing up for heretofore uncontroversial principles.

But it is also about something more.

It is about how to fight back in the *right way*.

Because buried in authoritarianism is always one deep flaw: its insecurity. If authoritarians had broad and deep support, they wouldn't require compulsion. The dirty secret of our woke authoritarians is that *they are the minority*.

You are the majority.

It's not that everybody hates you. It's that millions of Americans are afraid to say that they *agree with you*.

We have been silenced.

And now is the time for the silence to be broken by one simple, powerful word, a word that has meant freedom since the beginning of time:

No.

Chapter 1
How to Silence a Majority

On November 8, 2016, a bombastic reality television star became president of the United States. Donald Trump became president despite months of media hysteria and extraordinary attacks on his campaign and his character; he became president despite the confident predictions of the pollsters and pundits that he had virtually no chance.

Most of all, the pollsters and pundits got Trump's level of support wrong because they got Trump supporters wrong. Trump's supporters, they believed, were a diamond-hard core of bigots, annoying but generally unthreatening—a set of "deplorables," in Hillary Clinton's phraseology.

Then Trump won.

This presented the political elitists with two possible choices: they could engage in some well-earned introspection, considering the possibility that they had missed something vital in American political life and reexamining their premises about the nature of the American public; or they could castigate tens of millions of Americans as moral and intellectual deficients.

They chose the latter.

After some initial media coverage, in which Brooklyn-based, Gucci-loafer-wearing would-be-journalistic–Jane Goodalls covered Trump supporters as mysterious, grunting gorillas-in-the-mist; in which graduates of the New York University School of Journalism, fresh-faced and bright-eyed after classes with Lauren Duca on how to bitch about Tucker Carlson in *Teen Vogue*, traveled to fabled primitive red state America—a chaotic and brutal place filled with chain restaurants and Walmarts and churches, and characterized by a serious lack of culturally sensitive vegan restaurants and artisanal coffee shops and Planned Parenthood facilities; in which said ace reporters talked to Poor Old Billy, a down-on-his-luck former factory worker merely aching for some Democratic subsidy programs . . . the journalistic establishment came to a conclusion: Trump voters were, as they had originally thought, and as Hillary Clinton had once said, deplor-

able. They were, as Barack Obama had once characterized them, bitter clingers, desperately clutching to God
and guns and racism, wearing their hard hats to decay-
ing factories, then turning them in for white hoods at
night to terrorize the neighborhood minorities. Trump
voters were poor white Americans in dying Rust Belt
towns, hoping to stop demographic shifts by voting
Trump. (It somehow escaped attention that some 2.8
million New Yorkers voted for Trump, or 4.5 million
Californians. There are lots of Republicans who don't
sit around in diners wearing trucker hats.)

This was a convenient narrative. It certainly relieved journalists of the obligation to leave their comfort zones, both literally and figuratively—no need
to spend a night in rural Ohio rather than the com-
forts of the Upper West Side, or to bother discussing
uncomfortable issues with the rubes. It also allowed
journalists to abandon the practice of journalism more
broadly. Now, instead of focusing on Trump's policies,
they could simply focus on his tweets, the id-driven
manifestations of their original thesis: every tweet
could be read as a confirmation of their hypothesis
about red-state Americans. Now, instead of examining
all sides of various political controversies, they could
simply assume the sinfulness of their opponents, and

demand surrender. Journalism became a search-and-destroy mission, directed not merely at Trump but at Trump's supporters.

This wasn't much of a change, as it turned out. Republicans of all stripes had always been the problem, not just Trump. Before Trump was a glint in the media's eye, the media had targeted a small-town plumber who had the temerity to ask Barack Obama a question about his tax policy; they dug up his tax record, his home address, his plumbing license. Mitt Romney, the most milquetoast human being of the modern era, had been castigated by the media as a racist and a bigot. John McCain, who would later be hailed as an anti-Trump hero, was hit with similar slander.

The media itself had shifted on Trump personally over the years. For years, he'd been treated as easy clickbait, a genial figure of comedy and an outsized figure of wealth and pomposity, an icon of garish frivolity and entertaining charlatanry . . . up until the point he declared himself a Republican candidate for the presidency. Even then, Trump received late night phone calls from Jeff Zucker and advice from Joe Scarborough. Then he won the Republican nomination. Overnight he became the fonthead of evil—because overnight he became the symbol of his supporters, not the other way around. After all, it wasn't as though the media would have treated Ted Cruz or Marco Rubio as anything but pariahs had either won the nomination. As Trump would later argue, they hated him mostly because they hated his supporters.

This created an extraordinary amount of loyalty to Trump among Republicans—Republicans felt that Trump had merely taken bullets otherwise aimed at them. And they weren't totally wrong. The political slings and arrows *were* aimed at them. Trump just made an easier, more convenient, and more justifiable target. The media wasn't the only institution committed to the narrative that all conservatives—or at least the ones who hadn't flipped and joined the Lincoln Project, earning Strange New Respect™—were vicious racists, know-nothing xenophobes, bigoted idiots. Nearly *every major American institution* was committed to the same idea.

Conservatives felt the left-wing authoritarianism. They understood it on a gut level. And they hated it.

They felt the top-down censorship from social media, which deemed their speech "hate speech" and their worldview "harassment." They felt the anti-conventionalism from Hollywood, which painted conservatives as the great threat to a more beautiful, tolerant, and diverse country, and from their bosses, who declared their fealty to tolerant, liberal ideals while not-so-subtly threatening to fire dissenters, and from their friends and family, who told them in no uncertain terms that they were not welcome at the table. They saw the revolutionary aggression of a radical Left directed against fundamental American ideas—and patted on the back by all of America's most powerful institutions.

Conservatives were to be treated as outsiders. Anyone who voted for Trump was to be banned from polite society, to be treated as a gangrenous limb. Better to lop them off from the body politic than allow their poison to fester. In fact, it wasn't enough merely to silence conservatives who didn't actively oppose Trump. Silence, as the nonsensical woke slogan went, was violence. Conservatives had to be *outed*. Even those who might not feel themselves sympathetic to Trump had to be outed if they so much as engaged in *conversation* with Trump voters, or even those open to engaging in conversation with Trump voters. Such discussions, the logic went, would serve to humanize the inhuman, to tolerate the intolerable. Excision of the occasional Trump supporter was utterly insufficient—*exorcism* of the very concepts that could lead to the presence of Trump support had to be undertaken. Confessions had to be forced. Purity tests had to be administered. Struggle sessions had to be initiated.

Symbols of loyalty would be demanded: properly self-righteous hashtags on Twitter; anti-Trump bumper stickers on cars; semantically overloaded, tautology-laden lawn signs plunked into well-manicured grass. Statements of dissociation would have to be undertaken: dissociation from newly identified code terms like "meritocracy" and "Western civilization" and "color-blindness." Dissenters would be lumped in with Trump supporters. The Overton Window—the window of acceptable discourse—would be smashed shut, then boarded over.

And, our cultural leftist authoritarians thought, it had worked.

In 2018, Democrats won an overwhelming electoral victory, swamping Republicans across the country and seizing control of the House of Representatives, flipping 41 seats blue. Support for Democrats washed through the suburban areas of the United States, flipping 308 state legislative races in favor of Democrats. That was without Trump on the ballot.

With Trump on the ballot—the symbol of evil himself, bigotry and racism and vulgarity and brutality made Orange Flesh—surely Democrats would usher in a never-ending Golden Era of dominance, and cement Republicans into minority status for a generation.

And sure enough, one week before the election of

2020, Joe Biden was apparently ahead in the polls by nearly double digits. Democrats had a generic ballot advantage in Congress of nearly seven points.

Triumph was at hand.

Except it wasn't.

It turns out that if the major cultural institutions in a society declare all-out war on a large percentage of the population, those people don't convert—they go underground. And that's precisely what they did. They fibbed to pollsters, or didn't pick up the phone at all. They didn't tell their friends and family how they were voting. They didn't post on Facebook or Twitter. They didn't tell their bosses their real thoughts about Joe Biden or Kamala Harris or Alexandria Ocasio-Cortez.

Then they entered the polling places, and they voted.

And they voted against those who had declared them the cultural enemy.

Donald Trump may have lost the election, but Republicans across the land didn't. Republicans outperformed the polls across the board. Many pollsters had projected that Trump would lose by double digits nationwide; instead, Trump personally won more votes than any other Republican in American history, and more votes than any candidate in American history outside of his opponent, Joe Biden. Some pollsters had suggested that Republicans would easily lose the Senate and drop a dozen seats in the House. Instead, Republicans nearly maintained the Senate (losing control only because of Trump's asinine intervention in two winnable Georgia Senate races), gained seats in the House, maintained their stranglehold on state legislatures in a redistricting year, and nearly retained the White House, too.

The elevation of a geriatric nonentity like Joe Biden was no endorsement of the Democratic agenda. It was far more likely a rejection of Trump's personality—which came as little surprise after years of erratic tweeting, bizarre personal behavior, and extraordinarily savage media coverage. Trump underperformed Republicans in nearly every state with a competitive Senate race; Republicans swept into power in New Hampshire, where Trump lost by nearly eight points. Trump bled in the suburbs; had he lost the suburbs by the same margins he did in 2016, he would have been reelected. So Americans may have rejected Donald Trump personally. But the silent majority—a majority the media, the pollsters, and the experts completely missed—broadly rejected the Democratic agenda, in truly shocking fashion.

Americans didn't vote in defiance of the polls because they were racists. They didn't vote in favor of Trump because they were bigots. They didn't vote for Susan Collins in Maine and Thom Tillis in North Carolina and Steve Daines in Montana because they were benighted rednecks committed to a vanishing demographic majority. Latinos didn't vote in outsized numbers for Trump because they were suddenly "white," even though Pulitzer Prize–winning prevaricator and much-ballyhooed mountebank Nikole Hannah-Jones of *The New York Times* declared them so. Black males didn't vote in surprising numbers for Trump because they had abandoned their race, as Joe Biden himself implied. Suburban white women didn't vote Republican because they had decided they were in love with Donald Trump's casual grossness with women.

These Americans voted the way they did because they are Americans, and because they demand to be heard. Because they refuse to surrender to the alliance of the authoritarian Left and their liberal enablers. Because they never agreed with the media or their bosses or their idiot nephews in college carrying around copies of unread Ta-Nehisi Coates books to get laid. Because they won't be bullied into putting up meaningless symbols on their social media pages, or into declaring that all police are racists, or into cheering on the idea that America ought to be denigrated.

They went quiet. They didn't go away.

And then they weren't quiet anymore.

That's why the pollsters got it wrong. It wasn't because pollsters are purely incompetent. It's because pollsters can't pry answers out of those who have been intimidated into silence. As Eric Kaufman, professor of politics at the University of London, observed, pollsters didn't actually get it wrong with white non-college-educated voters—those who are likely to feel the least peer pressure from the self-empowered newfangled cultural fascisti. They got it wrong with *precisely the people most likely to feel pressured*: white college graduates. As Kaufman concludes, "If America cannot reform its regime of speech discipline, it has no hope of overcoming its yawning cultural divide."[1]

In order to overcome that yawning cultural divide, however, we must first acknowledge the obvious: our divide *is* cultural. It is not economic. It is not racial. It is cultural.

THE CULTURE WAR

Our philosophical betters—the elitist opinion makers who claim to understand the deeper meaning in our politics—generally present two explanations for division in America: race and class. Both are utterly insufficient.

The Marxist theory of class-driven division has long provided a shoddy explanation for real-world phenomena. During World War I, Marxist theorists were firmly convinced that international warfare would certainly result in a revolution by the working class, only to find that workers of the world were actually Brits, Frenchmen, Germans, and Russians. Today, Thomas Piketty explains Trump by appealing to rising income inequality[2]—but can't understand just why Trump voters continue to reject the overt redistributionism of the Democratic Party. By Marxist theory, Trump voters should have become Bernie voters over time. They aren't.

The racial theory of American politics is similarly non-explanatory. That theory supposed that Trump's outsized white support in 2016 was evidence of a white majoritarian backlash to an ascendant minority coalition. But that theory was firmly debunked in 2018, when white suburban voters handed a majority to Democrats in Congress, and in 2020, when Trump increased his vote share among minorities but *lost vote share* among white voters, and white men particularly. If racial animus were the driving force behind Trumpism, or Republicanism more broadly, that wouldn't have manifest itself in a 55 percent Cuban vote for Trump in Florida, or in Trump closing the gap in majority-Latino Rio

Grande Valley districts like Starr and Hidalgo counties from 60 and 40 points in 2016 to 5 and 17 in 2020.

Trump didn't overperform estimates among Latino and black voters because he was a racist. He overperformed because the elitists in our institutions *declare things racist even when they aren't*. Joe Biden suggested that Trump engaged in full-time dog whistling, despite Trump's repeated denunciations of white supremacy and his unprecedented outreach to minority communities, including a criminal justice reform program largely opposed by many in the grassroots conservative community. But as it turns out, elitist white Americans and woke "anti-racism" advocates who largely overpopulate the media, corporate America, social media halls of power, and Hollywood don't have a read on broader minority viewpoints. When these elitists declare that standing with the police is a "dog whistle," voters of all stripes tune out.[3]

In fact, that sort of labeling—the attempt to turn all political opposition into evidence of personal malevolence, the mainstreaming of anti-conventionalism, combined with top-down censorship and incentivization of revolutionary aggression—is the reason for the backlash against down-ballot Democrats.

Our culture wars aren't about anything so mundane as marriage, policing, or even abortion. Our culture wars are about a simple question: Can we agree that freedom of speech is more important than freedom from offense? Can we hire, work with, and break bread with people who may differ on the nature of the good life, but agree on the individual freedoms that come along with being an American?

If the answer is no, you're probably a leftist. If the answer is yes, you're part of the silent majority.

And perhaps you're only silent because you don't know that you're *in the majority.*

Why don't you know that?

Because for three generations, there's been an on-going, successful attempt to wrest institutional control from the apolitical, and to weaponize those institutions on behalf of the authoritarian Left. Most Americans tend to think individually, both philosophically and strategically: they spend their time attempting to convince friends and family of their viewpoints, rather than infiltrating institutions and using the power of those institutions for mass marketing. Leftists have no such qualms. Most Americans, trusting in the free market and free speech, insist that people be left free to make choices they don't like, and oppose the exercise of institutional power; leftists militarize powerful forces in a variety of fields to achieve their political ends.

The authoritarian Left has successfully pursued a

three-step strategy to effectuate their takeover of the major institutions in our society. The first step: winning the emotional argument. The second step: renormalizing the institutions. The third step: locking all the doors.

CONVINCING AMERICANS TO SHUT UP

The Left has spent decades gradually suppressing most Americans—and encouraging conservatives to suppress themselves. The process began with an appeal to politeness; that appeal became a demand for silence; then the demand for silence became an order to comply, repeat, and believe.

This was a heavy lift, and it didn't happen overnight. The Left began with a simple recognition that both conservative and liberal philosophies have soft underbellies. For conservatives, the soft underbelly is a militant insistence on *cordiality*. Conservatives were, until Donald Trump, deeply concerned with personal *values* in their politicians—but they were insistent on them in daily life. One of those virtues was peacefulness, affability, treating thy neighbor as thyself. As philosopher Russell Kirk suggested, conservatives believe in peace and stability, in human imperfectability and in community.[4] If we believe in peace and stability, that requires tolerance; if we believe human beings are imperfectible, we shouldn't be too quick to judge; if we believe in the value of community, we must be willing to forgive small slights. These are nuanced ideas, but all too often conservatives boil them down to *being proper*. And by being proper, conservatives all too often mean being *inoffensive*.

But being inoffensive is a bastardization of the call to decency. Conservatism doesn't merely believe in anodyne cordiality—a cordiality that looks the other way at cruelty, or requires silence in the face of sin. Conservatism promotes certain values that come into conflict with leftist values. Conservatism relies on moral judgment, too. Conservatism believes that friendship relies on willingness to steer those we love away from sin: as the Bible states, "You shall not hate your brother in your heart. You shall surely rebuke your fellow, but you shall not bear a sin on his account."[5]

Nonetheless, leftism identified in conservatives a fundamental willingness to go along to get along—to see cordiality as virtue itself. And it wasn't difficult for leftists to transmute some conservatives' desire to be cordial into a political principle: anything considered offensive ought to be barred. This principle—we can call it the Cordiality Principle—manifested in ways directly contrary to the conservative ability to speak freely. Conservatism believes in standards of right and wrong, of good and bad. Distinguishing between good and bad requires the exercise of judgment. The Left suggested that judgment was itself wrong, uncivilized, vulgar. Judgment was, of course, *judgmental*. And this was bad. To be judgmental was to offend someone, and thus to violate the Cordiality Principle.

"Equality" and "inclusion" and "diversity" and "multiculturalism" became the bywords of the day. As conservative philosopher Roger Scruton writes, "In place of the old beliefs of a civilization based on godliness, judgment and historical loyalty, young people are given the new beliefs of a society based on equality and inclusion, and are told that the judgment of other lifestyles is a crime. . . . The 'non-judgmental' attitude towards other cultures goes hand-in-hand with a fierce denunciation of the culture that might have been one's own."[6]

This Cordiality Principle gained serious traction in arenas ranging from arguments over religion to pornography to abortion to same-sex marriage. Many conservatives became uncomfortable standing up for their own principles in polite company, or in moral terms—better not to be perceived as *Not Very Nice*.

The soft underbelly of liberalism to the Cordiality Principle was obvious. For liberals, compassion isn't merely a principle: it is an ersatz religion. Where conservatives define virtue in accordance with religious precepts or natural law, liberals define virtue *as empathy*. Liberals see themselves as compassionate, at root; they see themselves through the lens of kindness. And it simply isn't "nice" to quarrel with others, no matter how demanding. Niceness lies at the core of everything; better to bite one's tongue than to start a fight, which might be seen as intolerant.

The Cordiality Principle was just the beginning. The second step came when leftists began to contend that judgmentalism wasn't merely a violation of the Cordiality Principle, it was an actual harm. The argument shifted from "Just Be Nice" to "Silence Is Required."

Now, traditionally, offense has not been considered a serious harm. J. S. Mill famously posited the so-called harm principle—the notion that activity that actually harms someone ought to be condemned, or even legally barred. But Mill himself rejected the conflation of harm and offense—just because someone found something offensive, Mill argued, didn't mean that it ought to be regulated or socially banned.

The distinction between harm and offense, however, can be murky. Philosopher Joel Feinberg points out that few of us believe that people should publicly have sex with one another; that's a crime against our sense of cordiality. Offensiveness, he says, can in fact be a harm. To that end, Feinberg posited a balancing test: on one hand, society would balance the "seriousness of an offense"; on the other hand, society would balance "reasonableness of the offending conduct." If offensive conduct did not seriously offend anyone, for example, and was personally important to the offender, the conduct would be allowed. If, however, the offense is "profound," the balance could shift, and shift precipitously.[7]

The authoritarian Left has artificially shifted Feinberg's balance. Every offense to particularly "vulnerable groups"—meaning groups defined as vulnerable by the Left in a kaleidoscopically changing hierarchy of victimhood—represents the possibility of profound offense. Those who engage in such offense must be silenced.

Thus, the Left has posited that even minor offense amounts to profound damage—hence the language of "microaggressions," which posit by their very nature that verbiage is an act of violence. Microaggressions range from the utterly anodyne ("Where are you from?" is apparently a brutal act, since it presupposes that the subject of the question is of foreign extraction) to the extraordinarily counterproductive (references to "meritocracy" are deeply wounding, since they presuppose that free systems reward hard work, thus condemning the unsuccessful by implication).

Microaggressions require no intent—intent is not an element of the crime, since we may not be aware, thanks to our "implicit bias," of our own bigotry. They do not even require actual evidence of harm. Subjective perception of offense is quite enough. The culture of microaggression is about magnifying claims of harm in order to gain leverage. That leverage can grow to astonishing proportions: woke staffers got a reporter for *The New York Times* fired for using the n-word to explain why and when using the n-word was wrong. *Times* executive editor Dean Baquet even repeated the authoritarian Left's favorite mantra: "We do not tolerate racist language regardless of intent." *Regardless of intent*.[8] If you can be racist without intent, silence becomes the only protection for most Americans. After all, as Berkeley leftists chanted when I spoke there in 2017, "Speech is violence."

But now the Left has gone even further. Now, *silence* is violence. This idiotic, self-contradictory slogan has been picked up by a myriad of politicians and thoughtleaders. The idea is that if you remain silent in the face of an evil—an evil defined by the Left, naturally—then you are complicit in that evil. It's no longer enough to oppose racism, for example; you must carry around a copy of Robin DiAngelo's *White Fragility*, announce your white privilege for the world to hear, and prepare for your inevitable atonement. If you don't, you will be deemed an enemy.

Now, don't mistake the slogan "silence is violence" as a call for open speech. Far from it! "Silence is violence" means that you *must* remain silent, but only after "doing the work"—learning why your point of view is utterly irrelevant, ceding all ground to woke leftists, and becoming a crusader on behalf of their point of view. If you refuse, you will be targeted. Abject apologies will be demanded. The only way to escape the social media brute squads is to become a member, baying in unison.

THE RENORMALIZATION OF AMERICAN INSTITUTIONS

All of this might remain a fringe phenomenon relegated to the wilds of Twitter and college campuses, but for a simple fact: the culture of authoritarian leftism has now hijacked nearly all of Americans' major institutions and cultural touchstones.

Universities, once bastions of free thought, are now philosophical one-party systems dedicated to the promulgation of authoritarian leftism. Corporations, petrified of legal liability—or at least hoping to avoid accusations of insensitivity or bigotry—have caved to this culture. They have enforced a culture of silence in which tens of millions of employees fear speaking their minds for fear of retaliation. Social media have banned people who refuse to abide by social justice dictates, and social mobs, egged on by eager activists in the media, mobilize daily to target the un-woke. Culturally apolitical spaces ranging from sports to entertainment have been mobilized on behalf of the Left, weaponized in pursuit of the cultural revolution.

How did this happen? How did colleges, supposedly protectors of open inquiry and free speech, turn into the bleeding edge of censorship and ideological compulsion? How did the media, supposedly committed to the business of facts and First Amendment freedoms, fall prey to the iron grip of the woke? How did corporations, oriented toward apolitical profit making, turn away from the vast majority of their audience and toward pleasing a vocal but small minority?

The answer lies in a process that author Nassim Nicholas Taleb labels "renormalization." This process allows a motivated minority to cow a larger, largely uninterested majority into going along to get along. Taleb gives a simple example: a family of four, including one daughter who eats only organic. Mom now has a choice:

she can cook two meals, one for the non-organic family members and one for her daughter; or she can cook one meal with only organic ingredients. She decided to cook only one meal. This is *renormalization* of the family unit, which has converted from majority non-organic to universally organic. Now, says Taleb, have the family attend a barbecue attended by three other families. The host has to make the same choice mom did—and the host chooses to cook organic for everyone. This process of *renormalization*—the new normal—continues until broader and broader numbers have been moved by one intransigent person.

The process applies in politics as in life. "You think that because some extreme right- or left-wing party has, say, the support of ten percent of the population," Taleb writes, "their candidate will get ten percent of the votes. No: these baseline voters should be classified as 'inflexible' and will always vote for their faction. But some of the flexible voters *can* also vote for that extreme faction. . . . These people are the ones to watch out for, as they may swell the number of votes for the extreme party."[9]

It's not enough, though, to have a lone stubborn person. You need a tipping point—a certain number of people within a whole in order to create a renormalization cascade. While each minor demand made of the broad majority might seem reasonable, or at least low-cost, over a long enough period of time, people fight back. It's one thing to hold one block party with organic ingredients. It's another to demand, day after day, that everybody in the neighborhood turn in their hamburgers for organic tofu. At a certain point, a long train of minor demands amounts to a major imposition. Even the American Founding Fathers were willing to tolerate a "long train of usurpations and abuses" for a while. Only after it dawned on them that those demands pursued "invariably the same Object, evinc[ing] a design to reduce them under absolute Despotism," did they declare independence.

The process of renormalization can only go so far unless a tipping point is reached. That tipping point, however, does not require a majority. Not even close. If *all* the intransigent actors get together, a core can be formed, which triggers the tipping point. Physicist Serge Galam has posited that in some cases, only about 20 percent of a population is needed to support an extreme view in order to cause radical renormalization. One way of creating such an intransigent minority coalition: the activation of what Galam has called "frozen prejudices," at the risk of appearing intolerant or immoderate to a broad majority, while still maintaining a solid core base.[10] In other words, start with a motivated core group; don't worry about who you alienate; appeal to the prejudices of vulnerable groups, who are then forced to choose between the core group and its most ardent enemies. Make the choice binary.

This is, in a nutshell, the strategy for the authoritarian Left. By putting together an intersectional coalition of supposedly dispossessed groups motivated by a common enemy—the system itself—they can move mountains. They can build a coalition of people who look the other way at revolutionary aggression, who endorse top-down censorship, who believe deeply in anti-conventionalism. And when the ascendant authoritarian leftist coalition uses its momentum against those who populate the highest levels of institutional power, offering job preservation or temporary absolution in return for surrender, institutions generally surrender. And then those institutions cram down these authoritarian leftist values. That's how you get Coca-Cola, a company with over 80,000 employees, training its workforce to be "less white" in fully racist fashion, noting that to be "less white" means to be "less arrogant, less certain, less defensive, less ignorant, and more humble"—and claiming that this discriminatory content was designed to enhance "inclusion."[11]

SHUTTING THE OVERTON WINDOW

Within institutions, the authoritarian Left's incremental demands have been taken up, one by one: from diversity training to affirmative action hiring, from charitable donations to internal purges. But for the generalized impact of institutional takeover to be felt requires one final step: the renormalization of our societal politics in favor of censorship.

Those who work within hijacked institutions remain a small fraction of the general population—but they can renormalize the society more broadly if they can convert liberals into leftists. American politics is, broadly speaking, divided into three significant groups: conservatives, leftists, and liberals. Liberals may share redistributionist goals with leftists, but can be distinguished from leftists with a simple test: asking whether those who disagree ought to be silenced. The American Civil Liberties Union, for example, used to be liberal—it stood up for the right of Nazis to march through Skokie, Illinois. Now, however, the ACLU is fully leftist—in 2018, the ACLU promulgated an internal memo explaining, "Our defense of speech may have a greater or lesser harmful impact on the equality and justice work to which we are also committed . . . we should make every effort to consider the consequences of our actions. . . ."[12]

The bulk of mainstream Democrats—and the vast majority of Americans—don't stand in favor of top-down censorship. But increasingly, the Democratic Party leadership has shifted from liberal to leftist. This means threatening action against social media companies for allowing dissemination of nonliberal material, or seeking regulation targeting corporations who do not mirror the liberal agenda.

Renormalization takes place by inches. Instead of simply calling for outright bans on broad swaths of speech, leftists have insisted that the Overton Window—the window of acceptable discourse, in which rational discussion can take place—ought to be gradually closed to anyone to the right of Hillary Clinton. This means savaging conservatives as racists and penalizing liberals who deign to converse with conservatives.

This means that liberals are left with a choice of their own: they can either choose to form a coalition with leftists, with whom they agree on most policy goals, but with whom they disagree on fundamental freedom principles; or they can form a coalition with conservatives, with whom they disagree on policy goals, but with whom they agree on fundamental freedom principles.

That choice is, so far, up in the air.

On the one hand, there are liberals who still stand for free speech—or at least appear to do so. In June 2020, 153 liberals ranging from J. K. Rowling to Noam Chomsky signed a letter decrying the rise of "the intolerant climate that has set in on all sides." These prominent thinkers explained, "The free exchange of information and ideas, the lifeblood of a liberal society, is daily becoming more constricted. . . . . The way to defeat bad ideas is by exposure, argument, and persuasion, not by trying to silence or wish them away."[13] This was a heartening development. But not one Trump supporter appeared on the letter. Which meant that the question remained an open one: did these liberals mainly seek to avoid the radical Left's censorious purges themselves, or did they truly hope to open up the Overton Window beyond themselves?

Whether liberals side with conservatives in defense of free speech and individualism or they side with leftists in pursuit of utopia remains an unanswered question. The jury is still out. But time is running out for liberals to decide. Matthew Yglesias, one of the signatories on the *Harper's Weekly* letter and a cofounder at Vox, was berated by members of his own staff for deigning to join up with the likes of Rowling, who has been unjustly accused of transphobia. Unsurprisingly, Yglesias stepped down from his position at his own website just a few months later, citing that incident: "It's a damaging trend in the media in particular," Yglesias told Conor Friedersdorf of *The Atlantic*, "because it is an industry that's about ideas, and if you treat disagreement as a source of harm or personal safety, then it's very challenging to do good work."[14]

The threat to core American values is only increasing.

CONCLUSION: WILL AN AGE OF HEALING EMERGE?

On the night the media announced their projection that Joe Biden would be president-elect of the United States, Biden sought to put the culture war genie back in the bottle. This was, in and of itself, rather ironic, given Biden's role in stoking the culture wars, from destroying the Supreme Court hopes of Robert Bork to suggesting that Mitt Romney wanted to put black Americans back in chains. Still, Biden expressed that the way forward for the country lay in unity rather than recrimination. "Now," Biden intoned, "let's give each other a chance. It's time to put away the harsh rhetoric. To lower the temperature. To see each other again. To listen to each other again. To make progress, we must stop treating our opponents as our enemy. We are not enemies. We are Americans."[15]

This was undoubtedly a nice sentiment. But conservatives remained suspicious; time and again in politics, unity has been used as a club to wield against those who disagree. There are two types of unity: unity through recognition of the fundamental humanity of the other and unity through purification. Given their long experience of watching the Left's political quest to cleanse the country of conservatism and conservatives, conservatives remained wary.

They were right to be wary.

The same day Biden gave his "unity" speech, former first lady Michelle Obama—a supposedly unifying figure in her own right, according to her media sycophants, despite her long record of divisive statements—claimed that Trump's 70 million voters were motivated by love for the "status quo," which meant "supporting lies, hate, chaos, and division."[16]

Biden, naturally, said nothing.

Meanwhile, Democrats and media members called for political de-Baathification of Trump supporters. Former Clinton labor secretary Robert Reich called for a "Truth and Reconciliation Commission" to root out

Trump supporters. Democratic National Committee press secretary Hari Sevugan tweeted that "employers considering [hiring Trump staff] should know there are consequences for hiring anyone who helped Trump attack American values," and pushed the Trump Accountability Project—a list of Trump employees and donors to be held accountable for Trump's presidency. Representative Alexandria Ocasio-Cortez (D-NY) suggested "archiving these Trump sycophants for when they try to downplay or deny their complicity in the future."[17] Members of the Lincoln Project, a group of former Republicans-cum-Democrats who raked in tens of millions of dollars in donations to attack Trump and Republicans during the 2020 cycle, called on members of the law firm Jones Day to be inundated with complaints for the great crime of representing the Trump campaign in court.[18]

Meanwhile, Democrats with the temerity to call out the woke, militant wing of their own party were subjected to claims of racism and bigotry. Even elected Democrats, it turned out, were deplorables. When moderate Democrats complained that they had nearly lost their seats thanks to the radicalism of fellow caucus members pushing "defund the police" and socialism, Representative Rashida Tlaib (D-MI) called them bigots seeking to silence minorities.[19] Progressive groups including the Justice Democrats, the Sunrise Movement, and Data for Progress issued a memo declaring that fellow Democrats who wished not to mirror the priorities of the woke were participating in "the Republican Party's divide-and-conquer racism."[20]

The battle to silence the silent majority remains ongoing. It is likely to accelerate, not to decelerate, as time goes on.

To understand how to combat it, we must first understand the history and program of our new cultural fascisti; next, we must understand how deeply our core institutions have been weaponized; and finally, we must understand our own weaknesses, and seek to correct them.

Chapter 2
How the Authoritarian Left Renormalized America

In 2012, President Barack Obama won reelection. He did so despite winning 3.5 million fewer votes than he did in 2008, and 33 fewer electoral votes; he did so despite winning the same percentage of the white-vote-losing Democrat John Kerry did in 2004; dropping support from 2008 among Americans across all age groups and education groups; and losing voters who made above $50,000 per year.

Obama had barely gotten his head above water in the approval ratings by the time of the election, the economy had stagnated (in the two quarters just prior to the election, the gross domestic product had grown just 1.3 percent and 2.0 percent)[1], and Obama had performed in mediocre fashion in the presidential debates. Nonetheless, he became the first president since

Ronald Reagan to win two elections with a majority of the popular vote.

So, what did Obama do to work this magic? He put together a different sort of coalition. Obama won because he held together a heavily minority-based, low-income coalition: 93 percent of black voters, 71 percent of Hispanic voters, 73 percent of Asian voters, 55 percent of female voters, 76 percent of LGBT voters, 63 percent of those making below $30,000 per year, and 57 percent of those making between $30,000 and $50,000 per year.[2] Obama became the first president since FDR in 1944 to drop electoral and popular vote support and win reelection anyway.

The story of Obama's 2012 victory is the story of the transformation of American politics. In 2008, Obama had been a different sort of candidate running a quite familiar campaign: a campaign of unification. Ronald Reagan had run on "morning in America"; Bill Clinton had run on a "third way" eschewing partisanship; George W. Bush had run on "compassionate conservatism"; Obama ran on the terms "hope" and "change," pledging to move beyond America as a collection of "red states and blue states" and instead to unite Americans more broadly. In fact, Obama's personal story was part and parcel of this appeal: he could justifiably claim to unite the most contentious strains of America in his own background, being the child of a white mother and a black father, raised in Hawaii but ensconced in the hard-knock world of Chicago, born to a single mother and raised by grandparents but educated at Columbia and Harvard Law School. Obama was, as he himself stated, a "blank screen on which people of vastly different political stripes project their own views."[3]

By 2012, however, Obama had cast aside those ambiguities. He was the architect of Obamacare, the creator of Cash for Clunkers and "shovel-ready jobs," a critic of police departments across the country, a newfound expositor of same-sex marriage, a defense-cutting, tax-increasing, big-spending progressive. His progressivism had prompted an ardent response from the American Right: the Tea Party movement and Obama's loss of Congress in 2010. No longer could Americans of various political stripes project onto him their own views, or their hopes and desires for the nation.

Obama's personal popularity—his eloquence, camera-readiness, lovely family—certainly buoyed him. But none of that would have been enough to get him reelected. No, what Obama needed was a new strategy. That strategy—the shift away from appealing to broad bases of Americans with common themes and toward narrowcasting to fragmented audiences, cobbling together ostensibly dispossessed groups—was transformational. It pitted Americans against Americans, race against race, sex against sex. Obama domesticated the destructive impulses of authoritarian leftism in pursuit of power.

Before Barack Obama, the American Left had been split by dueling impulses: on one hand, the impulse toward top-down government control, complete with its implicit faith in the unending power of the state to solve individual problems; and on the other hand, the impulse toward destruction of America's prevailing systems, which the American Left believed were, in essence, responsible for disparities in group outcome— systems rooted in individual rights, ranging from free markets to free speech to freedom of religion. Each of these impulses—the Utopian Impulse and the Revolutionary Impulse—carries certain aspects of authoritarian Leftism. The Utopian Impulse reflects a desire for top-down censorship, and reflects anti-conventionalism; the Revolutionary Impulse believes in revolutionary aggression, and reflects a similar anti-conventionalism. But the two impulses are in conflict.

Obama rectified that split by embracing the power of government—and acting as a community organizer within the system itself, declaring himself the revolutionary representative of the dispossessed, empowered with the levers of the state in order to destroy and re-constitute the state on their behalf.

And it worked.

In building his coalition, Obama no doubt worked a certain political magic. It just so happened that Obama's brew of identity politics and progressive utopianism emboldened an authoritarian leftism that poisoned the body politic. America may not recover.

THE RISE AND FALL OF UTOPIAN GOVERNMENT IN AMERICA

The American Left has always been attracted by the promise of power.

The power of the state is an aphrodisiac: it warms the heart and fires the mind with the passion of utopian change. Utopians of the Left are generally advocates for anti-conventionalism; they believe that their moral system is the only decent moral system. They're also quite warm toward top-down censorship, designed to stymie those moral opponents.

American progressives in the early twentieth century felt the euphoric intoxication of the Utopian Impulse. The early American progressives identified the state as the solution to a variety of social ills: income inequality and exploitation of labor, under-education and even intellectual deficiency. Concerns about individual rights were secondary; the Declaration of Independence and its guarantees of natural liberty were hackneyed; the Constitution itself was a mere constraint on the possibility of utopia.

Woodrow Wilson suggested that the state was the repository of all possibility, championing the notion that "all idea of a limitation of public authority by individual rights be put out of view, and that the State consider itself bound to stop only at what is unwise or futile in its universal superintendence alike of individual and of private interests." Such a notion, Wilson thought, did not preclude democracy—after all, democracy was merely about "the absolute right of the community to determine its own destiny and that of its members. Men as communities are supreme over men as individuals." Given the challenges of modern life, Wilson asked, "must not government lay aside all timid scruple and boldly make itself an agency for social reform as well as political control?"[4]

John Dewey, perhaps the most influential early progressive, believed similarly that the state could act as the moving force behind utopian ambition. "The State," wrote Dewey, "is then the completed objective spirit, the externalized reason of man; it reconciles the principle of law and liberty, not by bringing some truce or external harmony between them, but by making the law the whole of the prevailing interest and controlling motive of the individual."[5]

Indeed, progressives reveled in the limitless nature of ambition given a powerful state. As president, Wilson activated the state to persecute his political opponents, including antiwar socialist Eugene V. Debs; Wilson's attorney general, Thomas Gregory, turned a blind eye toward the American Protective League, a vigilante group a quarter of a million strong, raiding their neighbors' mail for proof of antiwar activity.[6] Justice Oliver Wendell Holmes, a fellow progressive, explained that the state had the ability to restrict reproduction of those with Down syndrome, since "It would be strange if [the public welfare] could not call upon those who already sap the strength of the State for these lesser sacrifices, often not felt to be such by those concerned, in order to prevent our being swamped with incompetence."[7] Margaret Sanger, founder of Planned Parenthood, called for the sterilization or quarantining of some "fifteen or twenty millions of our populations" in order to prevent the supposed poisoning of the gene pool.[8]

With the end of World War I, however, America grew tired of the progressive vision of state as sovereign; the Utopian Impulse had been humored and found wanting. The triumphant election of Warren G. Harding ushered in an era of smaller government, and a return to the traditional vision of individual freedoms guarded by a constitutionally limited state. Calvin Coolidge, Harding's successor and the winner of 54 percent of the popular vote and 382 electoral votes in the 1924 election, expressed his view of business with reverence toward the free markets. "[I]f the federal government should go out of existence, the common run of people would not detect the difference in the affairs of their daily life for a considerable length of time," he stated. "We live in an age of science and of abounding accumulation of material things. These did not create our Declaration. Our Declaration created them."[9]

The restoration of constitutional normalcy did not last. With the Great Depression, the Utopian Impulse—and the crushing hand of government—once again gained the upper hand. Crisis was, as always, an excellent opportunity for a renewed love affair with democratic socialism. While today's intelligentsia likes to bask in the glow of President Franklin Delano Roosevelt's accomplishments—most obviously, the creation of massive new welfare state programs—his actual record was dismal. FDR implemented massive new regulations, manipulated the currency, and attacked private property. Individualism once again fell out of vogue, with FDR stating, "I believe in individualism in all of these things—up to the point where the individualist starts to operate at the expense of society."[10] Which, of course, meant that he didn't actually believe in individualism.

FDR declared that the fundamental freedoms guaranteed by the Constitution—free speech, freedom of the press, trial by jury, freedom of religion—were utterly insufficient. "As our Nation has grown in size and stature," FDR declared, "these political rights proved inadequate to assure us equality in the pursuit of happiness." Instead, he proposed, America had to embrace a "second Bill of Rights," which would guarantee the rights to a job, to food, to clothing, to a decent profit for farmers, to housing, to medical care, to social security, and to education. "All of these rights spell security," FDR trumpeted. He went so far as to suggest that should the economic policies of the 1920s—a time of limited government and free markets—return, "even though we shall have conquered our enemies on the battlefields abroad, we shall have yielded to the spirit of Fascism here at home."[11]

FDR combined his utopian government programs with top-down censorship, including fascistic crackdowns on dissenters. As Jonah Goldberg describes in his book *Liberal Fascism*, "it seems impossible to deny that the New Deal was objectively fascistic. Under the

New Deal, government goons smashed down doors to impose domestic policies. G-Men were treated like demigods, even as they spied on dissidents. Captains of industry wrote the rules by which they were governed. FDR secretly taped his conversations, used the postal service to punish his enemies . . ." FDR aide Harry Hopkins openly suggested, "we are not afraid of exploring anything within the law, and we have a lawyer who will declare anything you want to do legal."[12]

The result of all of this government utopianism was catastrophic for everyday Americans, besotted though they were with the overpowering personal appeal of FDR. According to University of California, Los Angeles, economists Harold Cole and Lee Ohanion, FDR's policies—particularly his attempt at top-down organization of industry via cartelization, curbing free market forces in favor of centralized control—made the Great Depression great again, lengthening the depression by fully seven years. Consumption dropped dramatically; work hours dropped dramatically.[13]

With the rest of the world lying in ruins at the end of World War II, America could afford the bloat and inefficiency associated with larger government programs. But the added ambitions of the LBJ administration taxed the resources of the American democratic socialist ideal to the breaking point. President Lyndon

Baines Johnson doubled down on FDR's commitments, now suggesting that America could become a "Great Society" only by launching a multiplicity of major government spending initiatives, fighting a "war on poverty." Government encroached into nearly every arena of American life, offering subsidies and threatening prosecutions and fines. Government promised housing; it offered instead government-run projects, which quickly degraded into dystopian hellholes. Government promised welfare; it offered instead the prospect of intergenerational poverty through sponsorship of single motherhood. Government promised educational opportunity; it offered instead forced busing and lowered public schooling standards.[14]

This was a bipartisan affair—former conservative Richard Nixon, as president, re-enshrined LBJ's economic programs, including unmooring the American dollar from the value of gold and setting prices, wages, salaries, and rents.[15] And once again, as with FDR's response to the Great Depression, economic stagnation set in, with the percentage of people living in poverty stopping its decrease in 1970 and the stock market topping out in January 1966 around 8,000 . . . and dropping steadily until July 1982 in inflation-adjusted terms.[16]

By the end of the Jimmy Carter presidency, America had fallen out of love with the utopian government schemes. The Utopian Impulse had waned. "Fixing the world" through government measures had been reduced to gas lines, inflation, unemployment, and a president bemoaning an American malaise, admitting that "all the legislation in the world can't fix what's wrong with America."[17] Ronald Reagan took up that baton, declaiming in his First Inaugural Address, "government is not the solution to our problem; government is the problem. . . . It is time to check and reverse the growth of government which shows signs of having grown beyond the consent of the governed."[18]

In reality, Reagan didn't reduce the size and scope of government—government continued to grow. But in the minds of Americans, the progressive agenda had failed. By 1996, the Democratic president, Bill Clinton, was mirroring Reagan's rhetoric on the role of the government, explaining, "the era of big government is over," sounding almost Reagan-esque in his suggestion that a "new, smaller government must work in an old-fashioned American way," calling for a "balanced budget" and an end to "permanent deficit spending."[19] In his 2000 Republican National Convention acceptance speech, George W. Bush echoed that language, suggesting "big government is not the answer."[20] And in 2004, a young black Senate candidate from Illinois named Barack Obama suggested, "The people I meet—in small towns and big cities, in diners and office parks—they don't expect government to solve all their problems."[21] A consensus had formed in the minds of most Americans: government was not a panacea, the cure to all human problems. Often, government was the obstacle to human success and flourishing. Yes, Americans were happy to accept taxpayer-sponsored programs that benefited them, and reacted with anger to proposals that would implement change to those programs. But Americans now sounded more like Reagan than Wilson in terms of what they thought government could accomplish.

THE RISE AND FALL OF REVOLUTIONARY IDENTITY POLITICS

While progressives argued throughout the twentieth century that government was the solution to all of humanity's ills—and as Americans were gradually disabused of that notion—another, somewhat contradictory idea began to take root on the American Left. This idea agreed with the progressive thesis that the Declaration of Independence and Constitution were past their sell-by dates. But it went further: it suggested that virtually every system in America had to be torn to the ground in order to achieve true justice. Where progressives had believed that the power of government could be harnessed to a redistributive agenda in order to achieve utopian ends, this new brand of radicalism—animated by the Revolutionary Impulse—argued that the American governmental system was itself inherently corrupt, and that it needed to be torn out at the root. Revolutionary aggression was justified, the radicals argued, in order to tear down the hierarchies of power acting as a barrier to the triumph of moral anti-conventionalism.

An early influential form of this argument came from the scholars of the so-called Frankfurt School, European expatriates who escaped to America to avoid the Nazis. Max Horkheimer (1895–1973), one of the leaders of this school of thought, suggested that since all human beings were products of their environments, all evils in America could be attributed to the capitalist, democratic environment; as he put it, "the wretchedness of our own time is connected with the structure of society."[22] Erich Fromm, another member of the Frankfurt School, posited that American freedoms didn't make human beings free. "*The right to express our thoughts, however, means something only if we are able to have thoughts of our own,*" he stated. American consumerism, however, had deprived

Americans of that ability—and thus made them ripe for proto-fascism.[23] To liberate individuals, all systems of power had to be leveled.

This meant that traditional American freedoms would have to be curbed. Freedom of speech would have to die so that freedom of subjective self-esteem could flourish. As Herbert Marcuse explained, "Liberating tolerance, then, would mean intolerance against movements from the Right and toleration of movements from the Left . . . it would extend to the stage of action as well as of discussion and propaganda, of deed as well as of word." This held true *especially* for minority groups, who could assert their power only by striking back against the system.[24]

While the Frankfurt School thinkers were Marxist in orientation, their argument made little sense as a matter of class. After all, economic mobility has long been the hallmark of American society, and free markets grant opportunities to those of all stripes. But when the argument for American repression was translated from economic into racial terms, it began to bear fruit. America *had* allowed and fostered the enslavement of black people; America had allowed Jim Crow to flourish. While America had abolished slavery and eventually eviscerated Jim Crow—and done so, as former slave Frederick Douglass suggested in 1852, *because* of the ideals expressed in the Declaration of Independence and Constitution—the argument that America was at root racist and thus unfixable had some plausibility.

This was the contention of so-called Critical Race Theory (CRT). CRT transmuted the class-based argument that America is rigged into a race-based one. According to CRT, every institution in America is rooted in white supremacy; every institution is "structurally" or "institutionally" racist. This idea was first put forth by Stokely Carmichael, then the head of the Student Nonviolent Coordinating Committee, in 1966 (later, Carmichael would become a black separatist and the head of the Black Panther Party). Hot on the heels of the Civil Rights Act of 1965, Carmichael posited that while the federal government had barred discrimination on the basis of race, racism could not be alleviated by such action: inequality in outcome could be chalked up to historic racism and the structure of institutions built in a time of racism. Carmichael wrote, "It is white power that makes the laws, and it is violent white power that enforces those laws with guns and nightsticks." The predictable result: institutions would have to be torn down to the ground.[25]

Carmichael was not arguing that the system could be mobilized on behalf of those it had victimized. He was arguing that the *definition of racism* would have to itself change: from now on, actions would be considered prima facie racist if they produced racially disparate results, rather than if they were *actually racist* in intent or content. This made disparate impact the test of racism—a logically unsupportable proposition, since literally every policy ever crafted by humankind has resulted in disparate results for some groups. In fact, many of the Left's favorite policies—see, for example, minimum wage—exacerbate disparate outcomes rather than vitiating them. To treat disparate outcomes as a result obtained *only* through racist systems is to ignore all of human history in pursuit of a mythical utopia. Instead of arguing that some measures would have to be taken to level the playing field, Carmichael was arguing that the playing field would have to be dynamited.

This was the Revolutionary Impulse given an intellectual framework: revolutionary aggression, combined with anti-conventionalism.

Carmichael's intellectual heirs formally launched the CRT project in the late 1970s and early 1980s. Expositors Richard Delgado and Jean Stefancic set out the basic principles of CRT: first, that "racism is ordinary, not aberrational"; second, that "our system of white-over-color ascendancy serves important purposes, both psychic and material." The system, in other words, is designed to *create* racially disparate outcomes; any proof of racially disparate outcomes is evidence of the malignancy of the system.[26]

Critical Race Theory pioneer Derrick Bell wrote that "the whole liberal worldview of private rights and public sovereignty mediated by the rule of law needed to be exploded . . . a worldview premised upon the public and private spheres is an attractive mirage that masks the reality of economic and political power."[27] According to Bell, even purportedly *good outcomes* may be evidence of white supremacy implicit within the system—white people are so invested in the system that if they have to do something purportedly racially tolerant to uphold it, they will. But in the end, it's all about upholding white power. No wonder Bell posited that white Americans would sell black Americans to space aliens in order to alleviate the national debt if they could—and suggested *in 1992* that black Americans were more oppressed than at any time since the end of slavery.[28]

This argument gained little ground in the mainstream for decades. The confidence of Lyndon Baines Johnson–era progressives stymied it. LBJ believed the power of government could bridge gaps between white and black. And the government *did* engage in effort after effort to level the playing field, spending trillions on anti-poverty programs designed to act as a form of soft reparations for the evils of American racism. Because LBJ believed that the gap between identity politics and utopian progressivism could be papered over by the power of government, he created massive new governmental tools, rewriting the essential bargain between Americans and their government. As Christopher Caldwell writes, "The changes of the 1960s, with civil rights at their core, were not just a major new element in the Constitution. They were a *rival* constitution with which the original one was frequently incompatible."[29] The system of law in the United States radically changed, with the federal government given extraordinary power to end discrimination, both real and imagined, both in the public sector and the private sector. As Caldwell writes, there was a successful attempt by government to "mold the whole of society—down to the most intimate private acts—around the ideology of anti-racism."[30] And when instances of racism couldn't provide a proper pretext for government interventionism, the rubric of anti-discretion was expanded to include any supposedly victimized minority group. Coercion by government—and support for such coercion—became a sign of morality rather than a violation of freedom:

The civil rights model of executive orders, litigation, and court-ordered redress eventually became the basis for resolving every question pitting a newly emergent idea of fairness against old traditions. . . . Civil rights gradually turned into a license for government to do what the Constitution would not previously have permitted. It moved beyond the context of Jim Crow laws almost immediately, winning what its apostles saw as liberation after liberation.[31]

In pursuit of these liberations, trillions of dollars were spent; millions of Americans were made more dependent on government; hundreds of thousands of Americans ended up working for the government directly. Even though the programs did little overall to alleviate the standing of black Americans relative to white Americans, the programs *did* paradoxically shore up the moral credibility of the American governmental system: it was difficult to claim that systems that had now been turned *in favor* of black Americans—systems from affirmative action to anti-discrimination law—were designed to make black Americans subservient. The legitimacy of the system, ironically, had been upheld by efforts to overhaul the system in the name of

race-neutral progress. The Utopian Impulse had stymied the Revolutionary Impulse.

Thus, by the early 1990s, the radical arguments had
been put aside. While critical race theorists continued
to blame "the system" for racial gaps, and called for
race-specific discrimination on behalf of victimized
groups, Americans of all stripes instead maintained the
notion that race-neutral legal systems were indispensable. When hip-hop artist Sister Souljah defended the
Los Angeles riots, suggesting, "I mean, if black people
kill black people every day, why not have a week and
kill white people?,"[32] candidate Bill Clinton called her
out, comparing her to David Duke.[33] When crime rates
soared out of control, particularly in minority communities, a bipartisan coalition came together in Washington, D.C., to pass a tough-on-crime bill designed
to lengthen sentencing. That bill was supported by 58
percent of black Americans, including most black may-
ors.[34] It passed the Senate by a 94–5 vote.

In the battle over whether to utilize the government
to pursue utopia, or to tear down the government in
the name of radicalism, the utopians had won. Calls
to destroy the system from within were rejected, not
merely by the political Right but by the political Left.
Identity politics had been roundly defeated.

In fact, in 2004, a young Barack Obama confirmed that thesis in his Democratic National Convention speech rejecting the central tenets of identity politics and Critical Race Theory. "I stand here knowing that my story is part of the larger American story, that I owe a debt to all of those who came before me, and that, in no other country on earth, is my story even possible," Barack Obama stated, to wild cheers. He would go on to chide the myth, pervasive in inner-city neighborhoods, "that says a black youth with a book is acting white." And he would conclude with his most famous dictum, one he repeated—in increasingly hollow fashion—over the course of his subsequent career:

There is not a liberal America and a conservative America—there is the United States of America. There is not a Black America and a White America and Latino America and Asian America—there's the United States of America.[35]

HOW BARACK OBAMA FUNDAMENTALLY TRANSFORMED AMERICA

This general consensus—that right or left, the government could not solve all problems, but that the American system was inherently good—held through 2008.

Barack Obama campaigned on that promise. He promised hope. He suggested that Americans were united by a common vision, and by a common source.

But simmering under the surface of Obamaian unity was something philosophically uglier—something deeply divisive. As it turned out, Obama was no devotee of either founding ideology, LBJ-style government utopianism, or even a Clintonian Third Way. Obama's philosophy was also rooted not in the racial conciliation of Martin Luther King Jr., but in the philosophy of Derrick Bell, a man Obama himself had stumped for during his Harvard Law School days. It was no surprise that Obama gravitated to Jeremiah Wright, attending his church for twenty years, listening to him spew bile from the pulpit about the evils of the United States. Furthermore, Obama was a believer in his own messianic myth—that he was the embodiment of everything good and decent. Michelle Obama summed up the feeling well during the 2008 campaign: she suggested that "our souls are broken in this nation," and that "Barack Obama is the only person in this race who understands that . . . we have to fix our souls."[36] Obama himself said his mission was to "fundamentally transform[] the United States of America" in the days before the 2008 election.[37]

That combination led Obama to a revised political

position, after his overwhelming election in 2008: all criticism of him, it turned out, was *actually* racially motivated, because Obama—as America's first black president—represented the best hope of transforming America's systems from within. To be fair, the signs of Obama's racially polarizing stance were clear even in the 2008 race. Early on in that race, Obama explained his lack of working-class support in Rust Belt areas by referencing their supposed racism: "They get bitter, they cling to guns or religion or antipathy to people who aren't like them or anti-immigrant sentiment or anti-trade sentiment as a way to explain their frustrations."[38] Throughout his 2008 campaign, Obama made reference to his race as a sort of electoral barrier, despite the fact that but for his race, he never would have been nominated; he even said that his opponent, John McCain, was scaring voters by suggesting Obama didn't "look like all those other presidents on those dollar bills."[39]

But that racially polarizing undertone didn't fully surface until after the election. In Obama's view, the only reason for Americans to oppose any element of his agenda was subtle—or not-so-subtle—racism. As Obama revealed in his memoir in 2020, he believed "my very presence in the White House had triggered a deep-seated panic, a sense that the natural order had been disrupted . . . millions of Americans [were] spooked by a Black man in the White House." Obama saw McCain's running mate, Sarah Palin, as an avatar for this viciously bigoted America: "Through Palin, it seemed as if the dark spirits that had long been lurking on the edges of the modern Republican Party—xenophobia, anti-intellectualism, paranoid conspiracy theories, an antipathy toward Black and brown folks—were finding their way to center stage." Obama even wrote that he deployed Vice President Joe Biden to Capitol Hill to negotiate with Senate Minority Leader Mitch McConnell (R-KY) instead of doing so directly because of his awareness that "negotiations with the vice president didn't inflame the Republican base in quite the same way that any appearance of cooperation with (Black, Muslim socialist) Obama was bound to do." Obama and Michelle both chalked up Tea Party opposition to Obamacare to racism as well.[40]

Given Obama's personal rejection of opponents as benighted racists, it was no wonder that in 2012 he charted a different course than in 2008. Instead of running a campaign directed at a broad base of support, Obama sliced and diced the electorate, focusing in on his new, intersectional coalition, a demographically growing agglomeration of supposedly victimized groups in American life.

Practically speaking, this was a strategy long used by community organizers—as Obama well knew, since he had been one. Obama was trained in the strategies of Saul Alinsky, himself the father of community organizing—and as the Marxist Alinsky wrote in 1971, "even if all the low-income parts of our population were organized—all the blacks, Mexican-Americans, Puerto Ricans, Appalachian poor whites—if through some genius of organization they were all united in a coalition, it would not be powerful enough to get significant, basic needed changes. It would have to . . . seek out allies. The pragmatics of power will not allow any alternative." But while Alinsky encouraged radical organizers to use "strategic sensitivity" with middle-class audiences in order to "radicalize parts of the middle class,"[41] newer community organizers spotted an opportunity to jettison the lower-middle class—people Alinsky himself disdained as insecure and bitter (language Obama himself echoed in 2008). They would focus instead on college graduates, on the young, as potential allies.

This coalitional strategy would eventually be elevated into a philosophy, termed intersectionality by law professor Kimberlé Crenshaw. Crenshaw posited, correctly, that a person could be discriminated against differently thanks to membership in multiple historically victimized groups (a black woman, for example, could be discriminated against differently from a black man). But she then extended that rather uncontroversial premise into a far broader argument: that Americans can be broken down into various identity groups, and that members of particular identity groups cannot understand the experiences of those of other identity groups. This granted members of allegedly victimized identity groups unquestionable moral authority.[42] Identity lay at the core of all systems of power, Crenshaw argued; the only way for those of victimized identity to gain freedom would be to form coalitions with other victimized groups in order to overthrow the dominant systems of power.

The biggest problem with the intersectional coalition, however, remained practical rather than philosophical: the coalition was itself rift by cross-cutting internal divisions. Black Americans, for example, were no fans of same-sex marriage or illegal immigration—so how could a coalition of black Americans and gay Americans and Latino Americans be held together? And how could that coalition unite with enough white voters to win a majority again?

Obama did so in his very person. Essentially, Obama used his own identity as the wedge point in favor of policies black Americans *didn't especially like*—then used his popularity with black Americans in order to glue together the coalition. Every group in the intersectional coalition would receive its goodie bag during the 2012 cycle: in May, gay Americans were thrilled to learn that Obama had flipped on his 2008 position and now supported same-sex marriage;[43] the following month, Obama announced the Deferred Action for Childhood Arrivals program, unilaterally vowing not to enforce immigration law despite his own promises not to do so;[44] Obama, along with a compliant press, labeled Republican policies a "war on women" and vowed to fight for women's rights. As for the black community, Obama largely took it for granted that he would earn their support—and, as it turned out, he was right.[45]

To hold together his intersectional coalition, Obama had to raise the specter of something powerful and dangerous. That "something powerful" couldn't be the government, since Obama was the head of that government. Instead, Obama would unify the coalition against the past. Obama's brilliant slogan was the simple mandate, "FORWARD." Biden suggested to a black audience that opponent Mitt Romney wanted to put black Americans "back in chains."[46] Obama stated that Romney would "turn back the clock 50 years for women, gays and immigrants," stating that he would instead "move us forward."[47] Attacks on Barack Obama's political program wasn't a mere difference of opinion—it was now an attack on the *identities* of blacks, women, gays, Latinos.

The new Obama coalition successfully squared the circle: it knit together the Utopian Impulse, which put ultimate faith in government, and the Revolutionary Impulse, which saw tearing down the system as the answer. Obama united these two ideas with one simple notion: perpetual revolution from *within the government*. Democrats would campaign on revolutionary aggression designed to tear down hierarchies of power, both external to government and within the government itself; top-down censorship of all those who would oppose that agenda; and an anti-conventionalism designed to castigate opponents as morally deficient—indeed, as bigots.

And the strategy worked.

The election of 2012 marked the victory of the Obama coalition. Dan Balz of *The Washington* Post observed that Obama's campaign relied heavily on demographic change: "against the obstacles in Obama's path was a belief in Chicago in the glacial power of demographic change. . . . Obama's advisers were certain that the electorate would have fewer white voters." Obama received the same level of white support as

Michael Dukakis in 1988—but won the election because of changing demographics, since he won 80 percent of nonwhite voters. In fact, as Balz observed, Obama's team "invested in what it called Operation Vote, which was aimed exclusively at the key constituencies that make up Obama's coalition: African Americans, Hispanics, young voters and women (particularly those with college degrees)." The campaign communicated directly with these groups, targeting specific gathering places and advertising to niches.[48]

The Obama coalition strategy was forged. And progressives cheered wildly. As Ruy Teixeira and John Halpin wrote for the Center for American Progress (CAP), "Obama's strong progressive majority—built on a multi-racial, multi-ethnic, cross-class coalition in support of an activist . . . is real and growing and it reflects the face and beliefs of the United States in the early part of the 21st Century. The GOP must face the stark reality that its voter base is declining and its ideology is too rigid to represent the changing face of today's country." As CAP noted, the Obama coalition "marks the culmination of a decades-long project to build an electorally viable and ideologically coherent progressive coalition in national politics."[49]

Democrats had long hoped for that culmination. All the way back in 2002, Teixeira penned a book with journalist John Judis titled *The Emerging Democratic Majority*, positing that an increased number of minority Americans could come together to bring forth a permanent progressive utopia.[50] In 2016, NPR championed "the browning of America," suggesting that the country "is at a demographic inflection point," with Democrats reliant on their intersectional coalition buttressed by a majority of college-educated whites. "The Democratic Party," NPR concluded, "has adapted to this demographic change, and is more diverse, more urban, and more liberal than at any time in its history."[51]

Then came 2016. Trump shocked the world, winning a slim majority in the swing states. This created a choice for Democrats in 2020: either they could rethink the Obama intersectional coalition that Hillary Clinton had been unable to replicate or they could double down on it. They chose to try to remake the Obama coalition. As *Politico* noted during the Democratic primaries, "The rhetoric has shifted the debate about electability from an ideological plane—where moderates and more progressive Democrats argued for months over policy—to one based more on identity, and which candidate is best positioned to reassemble the Obama coalition of young people, women and nonwhite voters that proved instrumental to Democratic successes in the 2018 midterm elections."[52]

Biden successfully mobilized that coalition against Trump, largely by suggesting that Trump presented a unique historic threat to identity groups within the coalition. In his victory speech, Biden name-checked the identity groups in his coalition: "Gay, straight, transgender. White. Latino. Asian. Native American." He pledged, especially, support for the "African-American community" who "stood up again for me." "They always have my back," Biden stated, "and I'll have yours."[53] In homage of his coalition, Biden then doled out cabinet positions based on intersectional characteristics. This was overt racial pandering. The coalition was back in power. And that coalition had learned the main lesson of the Obama era: uniting the Utopian Impulse of progressivism with the Revolutionary Impulse of identity politics could achieve victory.

USING THE SYSTEM TO TEAR DOWN THE SYSTEM

In July 2020, in the midst of the George Floyd protests alleging widespread and systemic American racism, the National Museum of African American History and Culture—a project of the Smithsonian Museum, a taxpayer-funded entity—put up an online exhibit condemning "whiteness." The exhibit, titled "Aspects

& Assumptions of Whiteness & White Culture in the United States," explained that Americans had internalized aspects of white culture. What were these terribly white cultural barriers posing challenges to nonwhites? According to the exhibit, "rugged individualism" was a white concept, rooted in nasty ideas like "the individual is the primary unit," "independence & autonomy highly valued + rewarded," and "individuals assumed to be in control of their environment." "Family structure" represented another white concept, with "the nuclear family" condemned as an aspect of whiteness, along with the notion that children "should be independent." Other irrevocably white ideas included an "emphasis on scientific method," complete with "cause and effect relationships"; a focus on history, including "the primacy of Western (Greek, Roman) and Judeo-Christian tradition"; a belief that "hard work is the key to success" and encouragement of "work before play"; monotheism; placing emphasis on "delayed gratification" and following "rigid time schedules"; justice rooted in English common law and intent and private property; "decision-making" and "action orientation"; and, of course, "be[ing] polite."[54]

One moment's thought would betray the fact that assuming that such commonsense pathways to success as delayed gratification, being on time, being polite, and forming stable family structures has nothing to do with racism—and that to call such excellent notions "white" actually degrades nonwhite Americans by assuming them incapable of making decent life decisions. The NMAAHC exhibit was a textbook case of the soft bigotry of low expectations. To find it in a taxpayer-funded exhibit was indeed shocking.

But not all that shocking. The argument put forth by the new intersectional coalition—the argument that any failures within the American system are due to the inherent evils of the system, not to individual failures within that system—now predominates throughout instruments of politics, government, and law. Joe Biden's unity agenda with Bernie Sanders pledged, "On day one, we are committed to taking anti-racist actions for equity across our institutions, including in the areas of education, climate change, criminal justice, immigration, and health care, among others." By anti-racist policy, of course, Biden means policy designed to level all outcomes, no matter the individual decision making at issue. The 2020 Democratic Party platform makes that point even clearer: "Democrats are committed to standing up to racism and bigotry in our laws, in our culture, in our politics, and in our society, and recognize that race-neutral policies are not sufficient to rectify race-based disparities. We will take a comprehensive approach to embed racial justice in every element of our governing agenda."[55]

The federal government controversially was, until ordered to cease, inculcating Critical Race Theory inside the executive branch, with training sessions telling participants that "virtually all White people contribute to racism," and in which employees were required to explain that they "benefit from racism."[56] Companies have been threatened with loss of federal contractor status for failure to abide by woke ideological standards. Anti-discrimination law has been radically extended to include everything from transgender identification to same-sex marriage, clashing dramatically with freedom of association and freedom of religion; it remains an unsettled legal question whether failure to use a proper biological pronoun could be considered a violation of federal anti-discrimination law. Parents now have to fear the predations of state and local governments seizing control of their child rearing; churches fear loss of tax-exempt status; police departments are cudgeled into non-enforcement.

Advocates of this perverse ideology are dedicated to using the revolutionary tools of government created in the 1960s not to fix the system, but to tear it down. The tools of the system will be turned against the system. There is a reason that Ibram X. Kendi, ideological successor to Derrick Bell and Stokely Carmichael, has openly called for a federal Department of Anti-Racism, empowered with the ability to preclear "all local, state and federal public policies to ensure they won't yield racial inequality, monitor those policies, investigate private racist policies when racial inequality surfaces, and monitor public officials for expressions of racist ideas." The DOA would have the ability to punish "policymakers and public officials who do not voluntarily change their racist policy and ideas."[57] This is as pure an expression of fascism as it is possible to imagine.

We're not there yet. But the battle is under way.

WILL THE AUTHORITARIAN LEFTIST COALITION HOLD?

For progressives, the importance of the Obama coalition lies in its purported ability to cram down policy on a large minority—or even a majority—of Americans. By cobbling together supposedly dispossessed minorities and woke white Americans desperate for psychological dissociation from America's alleged systemic bigotry, Democrats hope to leave behind the era of broad public appeals and simply renormalize the American political system. Mainstream Democrats hope to cement the Obama coalition through concessions to "anti-racist" philosophy; in return, they demand fealty to a traditional progressive set of policy proposals.

The new governing power in America, so the theory goes, will be the intersectional-progressive coalition. This coalition is authoritarian in orientation: it promotes revolutionary aggression against the system itself, from both within and without; it seeks top-down censorship of those who disagree; and it sets itself up as an unquestionable moral system, superior to its predecessors.

Democrats banked on that strategy in 2020. They claimed that Donald Trump was a unique, shocking, and direct threat to black Americans, to women, to Latino Americans, to gay Americans. Trump represented all that was worst about America, and it was up to the intersectional coalition and their goodhearted allies to strike a blow on behalf of a new, transformed, *better* America.

Just three weeks after the 2020 election, Professor Sheryll Cashin of Georgetown University called on Democrats to continue to double down on the Obama coalitional strategy. She called on Democrats to ignore Trump voters, silence them, and focus on appeasing all the other members of the intersectional coalition. "A more viable strategy for progressives than trying to win over Trump's supporters right away would be to continue to win elections powered by energized majorities of Black Americans in critical states, in coalitions with other energized people of color rightfully taking their place in American politics and the critical mass of whites willing to see and resist racism," Cashin wrote. Progressive priorities could be allied to "anti-racist" priorities in order to solidify a coalition of the woke.[58]

But, as it turned out, things are not quite that simple.

First, demographics are not destiny. Trump's gains among various identity groups demonstrate that Americans think for themselves, and will not be relegated over time to the boundaries of racial, ethnic, or sexual orientation–based solidarity.

More pressingly, however, the practical problems of intersectionality remain: not all members of the coalition get along. The more radical members of the coalition are unlikely to sit idly by while the more moderate members shape policy. The tension between the Utopian Impulse and the Revolutionary Impulse has not dissipated. And without Barack Obama to paper over those differences—or, just as important, to wave the wand of race and magically deem friends anti-racist and foes the opposite—the coalition cannot hold. Moderate members are unlikely to watch their jobs disappear because radicals have taken the reins. In the aftermath of Biden's 2020 victory, moderate Democrats in Congress fretted that they'd nearly lost their House majority, and were unable to gain a Senate majority. Those moderates blamed radicals pushing idiotic positions for the tenuous Democratic grip on power: Representative Abigail Spanberger (D-VA) lit into her radical colleagues for their sloganeering about "defunding the police" and "socialism," pointing out that Democrats had "lost good members" because of such posturing.[59] Meanwhile, radical members of Congress—members such as Representative Alexandria Ocasio-Cortez (D-NY), Representative Ayanna Pressley (D-MA), Representative Rashida Tlaib (D-MI), and Representative Ilhan Omar (D-MN)—joined forces to savage Democrats like Spanberger, arguing in an open letter to colleagues, "The lesson to be learned from this election cannot and should not be to lean into racist resentment politics, or back away from the social movements that pushed Democrats to power."[60]

Because the Democratic coalition *is* so fragile, representing at best a large minority or bare majority of Americans, it can be fractured. The most obvious way to fracture the Democratic coalition is through generalized resistance to individual elements of the intersectional agenda. And each element of the intersectional agenda is becoming increasingly more radical. During the 2020 election cycle, Democrats, afraid of alienating black Americans, ignored the rioting and looting associated with Black Lives Matter protests; embraced the ideological insanity of CRT; indulged mass protests against police in the middle of a global pandemic; and fudged on whether they were in favor of defunding the police as crime rates spiked. Afraid of alienating LGBT Americans, Democrats embraced the most radical elements of gender theory, including approval of children transitioning sex; they pressured social media companies to punish Americans for "misgendering"; they vowed to crack down on religious practice in the name of supposed LGBT rights. Afraid of alienating Latino Americans, Democrats began treating the term *Latino* itself as insulting, instead embracing the little-known and little-used academic terminology, *Latinx*; more broadly, they advocated decriminalizing illegal immigration itself.

As each intersectional demand grows more radical, however, the Democrats' coalition is threatened. The renormalization of American politics that Democrats seek can only occur in the absence of majoritarian backlash. If, for example, a majority of Americans—including members of the Democratic coalition—said no to the radical transgender agenda, the coalition would have to choose between jettisoning transgender interest groups (perhaps fracturing the coalition) or losing the soft moderates who join their coalition (probably losing its slim majority in the process).

In order to solve these problems, the Left can't rely on pure renormalization through democratic means. It must stymie its opponents in order to prevent the fracture of its coalition. The Left must increase the size of its coalition by intimidating its opponents into inaction, or by browbeating them into compliance. The Left must engage in institutional capture, and then use the power of those institutions in order to compel the majority of Americans to mirror their chosen political priorities. Without control of the commanding cultural heights, the leftist coalition cannot win. That is why they've focused all their energies on taking those commanding heights.

Chapter 3
The Creation of a New Ruling Class

On March 12, 2019, federal prosecutors revealed a bombshell case involving at least fifty defendants, a case spanning from 2011 to 2018. Dozens of the defendants were extraordinarily wealthy; many were preternaturally famous. The two biggest names were Lori Laughlin, star of *Full House*, and Felicity Huffman, Oscar-nominated actress. Their crime: trying to bribe their children's way into college, by either paying someone to cheat on tests, paying someone to create fake résumé enhancers and bribe college administrators, or other means. Laughlin, according to prosecutors, "agreed to pay bribes totaling $500,000 in exchange for having their two daughters designated as recruits to the USC crew team—despite the fact that they did not participate in crew";[1] Huffman paid

$15,000 to inflate her daughter's test score by paying a proctor to correct her answers.[2]

College officials involved in the scheme hailed from some of the most prominent schools in the country: Yale, Stanford, UCLA, and USC, among others.[3] For her crime, Laughlin did two months in prison, two years of probation, 100 hours of community service, and paid a $150,000 fine; Huffman did 14 days in prison, 250 hours of community service, and paid a $30,000 fine.[4]

The scandal made national headlines. Those on the political Left suggested that the story smacked of white privilege—after all, these were all people of means, paying hundreds of thousands of dollars to game the system on behalf of their children. Those on the political Right suggested that the story was just more evidence that the college system itself had become a scam.

All of this missed the real point: why in the world did rich, famous parents—millionaires and billionaires—feel the need for their children to go to "good schools"? That question was particularly pressing with regard to Laughlin's daughter, Olivia Jade, already a social media celebrity with millions of followers. And after the scandal broke, Jade lost sponsorships with makeup companies like Sephora.[5] So why, exactly, was it vital for Laughlin and her husband, Mossimo founder Mossimo Giannulli, to drop half a million dollars to send their daughter to the second-best school in Los Angeles?

The question becomes even more puzzling when we reflect that Jade had no great aspirations for college. It's not as though she was looking forward to a career in genetic engineering. In fact, Jade drew outsized criticism when she posted a social media video describing her hopes for her university career to her 2 million followers, explaining, "I don't know how much of school I'm gonna attend. But I'm gonna go in and talk to my deans and everyone, and hope that I can try and balance it all. But I do want the experience of like game days, partying . . . I don't really care about school, as you guys all know."[6]

But here's the thing: Jade was right.

The real reason many Americans go to college—particularly Americans who aren't majoring in science, technology, engineering, and math fields—is either pure credentialism, social cachet, or both. College, in essence, is about the creation of a New Ruling Class. It's an extraordinarily expensive licensing program for societal influence.

Americans simply don't *learn very much* if they're majoring in the liberal arts. Yes, Americans may have a higher career earnings trajectory if they attend a good college and major in English than if they stop their educational career after high school. But that's because employers typically use diplomas as a substitute for job entrance examinations, and also because college graduates tend to create social capital with other college graduates. College, in other words, is basically a sorting mechanism. That's why Olivia Jade's massively wealthy parents would risk jail time and spend hundreds of thousands of dollars to get her into a good-but-not-great school like USC.

Begin with credentialism. In 1950, only 7.3 percent of American men and 5.2 percent of American women had gone to college; in 1980, that number was 20.9 percent of men and 13.6 percent of women, a nearly three-fold increase. As of 2019, 35.4 percent of men had gone to college, and so had 36.6 percent of women.[7] This trend, which relies on the simple fact that Americans on average earn more with a college degree than without, has led to tremendous inflation in the credential market: where you could get a job as a dental lab technician or medical equipment operator just a few years ago without a college degree, that's no longer true. You now have to outcompete others who have graduated from college for the same job—and this means that colleges have an interest in churning out as many degrees as possible, given that employer demand for college graduates continues to increase.

One October 2017 study from Harvard Business School professors Joseph Fuller and Manjari Raman found that "degree inflation is undermining US competitiveness and hurting America's middle class." Fuller and Raman explained that "[p]ostings for many jobs traditionally viewed as middle-skills jobs (those that require employees with more than a high school diploma but less than a college degree) in the United States now stipulate a college degree as a minimum education requirement. . . . Our analysis indicates that more than 6 million jobs are currently at risk of degree inflation." Damage from degree inflation particularly targets those who disproportionately don't go to college—namely, low-income students, many of whom are minority. During economic downturns, those trends are only exacerbated as newly unemployed college graduates crowd out those who don't have college degrees in middle-skills professions.[8]

Naturally, the demand for college graduates has led to a massive increase in the number of Americans pursuing postgraduate degrees. According to the Census Bureau, the number of Americans over twenty-five with a master's degree *doubled* between 2000 and 2018, and the number of Americans with a doctorate increased 125 percent. Overall, while only 8.6 percent of Americans had a postgraduate degree in 2000, 13.1 percent did in 2018.[9]

Degree inflation doesn't necessarily mean that Americans are better qualified for work than they were when they didn't go to college—nothing about a queer studies theory bachelor's degree will make anyone ready for an entry-level position as a dental assistant. In fact, top high school graduates who don't attend college tend to do just as well as college graduates. As a recent Manhattan Institute study found, high schoolers who graduate within the top 25 percent of their class but don't go on to college routinely outperform college graduates who finish in the bottom 25 percent of their class. And as the study authors point out, "more than 40 percent of recent college graduates wind up in jobs that do not require a degree . . . on top of the roughly half of college attendees who fail to earn a degree at all."[10]

College, then, may grant an undue advantage to graduates based on credentials. But that's not the only advantage. The other advantage is access to a new class hierarchy.

In *Hillbilly Elegy*, J. D. Vance writes of his ascension from growing up poor in Appalachia to graduation from Yale Law. For Vance, the transition wasn't merely economic or regional—it was cultural. As Vance writes, "that first year at Yale taught me most of all that I didn't know how the world of the American elite works." Vance was embarrassed to find at a formal dinner that he didn't know what sparkling water was, how to use three spoons or multiple butter knives, or the difference between chardonnay and sauvignon blanc. But this was all part of a test: "[law firm] interviews were about passing a social test—a test of belonging, of holding your own in a corporate boardroom, of making connections with potential future clients."[11]

That test of belonging separates college graduates from everyone else. As Charles Murray notes in his seminal 2012 work, *Coming Apart*, Americans—he focuses on white Americans particularly—have separated into two classes: an elite, "the people who run the nation's economic, political and cultural institutions," those who "are both successful and influential within a city or region" . . . and everyone else.[12] Murray calls the former group the new upper class, "with advanced educations, often obtained at elite schools, sharing tastes and preferences that set them apart from mainstream America." They are better termed the New Ruling Class, given that economic strata are not the main divider.

The members of the New Ruling Class have almost nothing in common with the "new lower class, characterized not by poverty but by withdrawal from America's core cultural institutions." Members of the New Ruling Class are more likely to be married, less likely to engage in single parenthood, less likely to be victimized by crime. They are also more likely to be political liberal. Murray describes their viewpoint as "hollow"—meaning that they refuse to promulgate the same social standards they actually practice. They stand firmly against propagating and encouraging adherence to the life rules they have followed to success. Left-leaning historian Christopher Lasch says the New Ruling Class (he calls them the "new elites) "are in revolt against 'Middle America,' as they imagine it: a nation technically backward, politically reactionary, repressive in its sexual morality, middlebrow in its tastes, smug and complacent, dull and dowdy. . . . It is a question whether they think of themselves as Americans at all."[13]

The ticket to membership in the New Ruling Class is often credential-based. Members of the New Ruling Class know this. In December 2020, Joseph Epstein, who taught at the University of Chicago, wrote a column pointing out that incoming first lady Jill Biden was not in fact a doctor—her doctorate was in education from the prestigious University of Delaware. "A wise man once said that no one should call himself 'Dr.' unless he has delivered a child," Epstein wrote. "Think about it, Dr. Jill, and forthwith drop the doc."[14] The media reacted with unmitigated scorn and fury. Dr. Jill, they said, was not merely a doctor—she was the greatest doctor since Jonas Salk.

Michelle Obama posted in umbrage on Instagram: "All too often, our accomplishments are met with skepticism, even derision. We're doubted by those who choose the weakness of ridicule over the strength of respect. And yet somehow, their words can stick—after decades of work, we're forced to prove ourselves all over again." Second Gentleman Douglas Emhoff tweeted that Biden "earned her degrees through hard work and pure grit. She is an inspiration to me, to her students, and to Americans across this country." Dr. Jill herself went on Stephen Colbert's propaganda hour, where he cloyingly read from her book and nodded along as she intoned, "One of the things I'm most proud of is my doctorate. I've worked so hard for it."[15]

There is only one problem. Dr. Jill is not a doctor in any meaningful sense. That's not just because her supposed hard work amounted to receiving a degree for a dissertation from a university with a public policy school named after her husband in a state represented by her husband for decades (although one could make the case that such a degree is a tad . . . well . . . unearned). It has to do with the fact that only actual doctors—you know, people you'd call if your kid had an ear infection—should be called doctor. I have a juris doctor from Harvard Law School. I am not a doctor. My wife has a medical degree from UCLA. She is a doctor. There is, in fact, a terribly simple test of whether someone ought to be called doctor in daily life: if you're on a plane and the pilot asks if there is a doctor available, do you raise your hand? (Note: if you raise your hand because you have a doctorate in education, your fellow passengers should be allowed by law to send you through the exit door at 30,000 feet.)

So, what was the big deal? Why, in fact, does Dr. Jill insist that everybody call her doctor, when she is about as much of a doctor as Dr. J, and boasts a significantly lower lifetime PPG average? (Dr. J does have an honorary doctorate from the University of Massachusetts.) She insists on being called "doctor" because it's a mark of membership in the New Ruling Class. As Dr. Jill once told her husband, Joe Biden, "I was so sick of the mail coming to Sen. and Mrs. Biden. I wanted the mail addressed to Dr. and Sen. Biden."[16]

This is, technically speaking, the height of obnoxious silliness. My wife—again, an actual doctor—is frequently referred to as Mrs. Shapiro. And as she told me, she doesn't care one whit, since she knows what she does for a living, and her identity isn't wrapped up in whether others know her degrees.

Credentialism, in other words, isn't generally about recognition of merit. It's a way of signaling commonality with the patricians of our society.

But something has happened since Murray's book came out that has deepened cultural divides even further: members of the New Ruling Class aren't merely constituted by educational history. They must now *speak the language of social justice*. There is a parlance taught at America's universities and spoken only by those who have attended it, or adopted by those who aspire to membership in the New Ruling Class. That parlance is foreign both to non–college graduates and to those who graduated from college years ago. It sounds like gobbledygook to those who haven't attended universities; it's illogical when rigorously examined. But the more time you spend in institutions of higher learning, the better you learn the language.

Quibbling with that language earns you a ticket to the social leper colony. While from the 1990s to the 2008 election, the voting gap between high school and college graduates was "small, if not negligible," it opened wide between 2008 and 2012. As Adam Harris of *The Atlantic* observes, "white voters without a college degree were distinctly more likely to vote Republican than those with college degrees." In 2016, 48 percent of white college graduates voted for Trump, compared with 66 percent of those who didn't graduate from college.[17] In 1980, the 100 counties with the highest share of college degrees went Republican, 76 to 24; in 2020, Democrats won top college-graduate counties 84 to 16.[18]

Naturally, leftist commentators attribute this emerging voting gap to both Republican stupidity and Republican racism. But that's not the story. The story is the creation of an elitist group of Americans who speak the Holy Tongue of Wokeness—a language built for internal solidarity and designed for purgation of unbelievers.

LEARNING THE WOKABULARY

Wokeism, of course, is rooted in identity politics. It takes cues from intersectionality, which suggests a hierarchy of victimhood in which you are granted credibility based on the number of victim groups to which you belong. But it doesn't stop there. Wokeism takes identity politics to the ultimate extreme: it sees *every structure of society* as reflective of deeper, underlying structures of oppression. Reason, science, language, and freedom—all are subject to the toxic acid of identity politics.[19] To stand with *any* purportedly objective system is to endorse the unequal results of that system. All inequality in life can be chalked up to systemic inequity. And to defend the system means to defend inequity.

This argument, which fell out of favor over the course of the 1970s and 1980s, suddenly roared back in full force in the 2010s in the universities. To be fair, the philosophy had never truly disappeared—even when I attended UCLA in the early 2000s, calls for mandatory "diversity courses" steeped in intersectionality were commonplace. But in the 2010s, wokeism moved from a prominent but minority philosophy to the dominant philosophy of America's major universities. Suddenly, discredited theories of inherent American evil sprang back to the forefront.

But these theories don't constitute another mere trend. They represent an entire *religious*, unfalsifiable worldview. To deny that an inequality means an inequity has taken place became sinful and dangerous: by suggesting that perhaps inequality resulted from luck, natural imbalances, or differential decision making, you are a *threat* to others, a victim-shamer. As Boston University professor of history Ibram X. Kendi, perhaps the most popular of the woke thinkers, states,

"Racial inequality is evidence of racist policy and the different racial groups are equals."[20] Robin DiAngelo, Kendi's white woke counterpart and a professor at the University of Washington, summarizes: "if we truly believe that all humans are equal, then disparity in condition can only be the result of systemic discrimination."[21] In other words, all decisions should create the same result—and if you disagree, you are racist.[22]

"Social justice" dictates that you sit down and shut up—that you listen to others' experiences, refrain from judgment, and join in the anarchic frenzy at destroying prevailing systems.

And it is a cult. It is a moral system built on anti-conventionalism—on the belief that its expositors are the sole beacons of light in the moral universe, and therefore justifiable in their revolutionary aggression and top-down censorship.

To be deemed anti-racist, for example, one must take courses with Robin DiAngelo, participate in Maoist struggle sessions, and always—*always*—mirror the prevailing woke ideas. To fail to do so is to be categorized as undesirable. All "microaggressions" must be spotted. All heresies must be outed. And all logical consistency—even basic decency itself—must be put aside in the name of the greater good. As Kendi puts it, "The only remedy to racist discrimination is antiracist discrimination. The only remedy to past discrimination is present discrimination. The only remedy to present discrimination is future discrimination."[23]

Repeat and believe. Or be labeled evil. For Ibram X. Kendi, America has two souls. One is the soul of justice, which "breathes life, freedom, equality, democracy, human rights, fairness, science, community, opportunity, and empathy for all." The other is those who disagree, who breathe "genocide, enslavement, inequality, voter suppression, bigotry, cheating, lies, individualism, exploitation, denial, and indifference to it all."[24] Notice the inclusions of the terms "individualism" and "denial" in Kendi's litany of evil. If you believe that individuals have rights, that in a free country you are largely responsible for your own fate, or if you deny the clearly false proposition that all inequality is evidence of inequity, you are inhabited by the soul of evil.

If this sounds cultish, that's because it is. "Social justice" has indeed become a cult. As Helen Pluckrose and James Lindsay, both liberal scholars, write:

Social Justice Theorists have created a new religion, a tradition of faith that is actively hostile to reason, falsification, disconfirmation, and disagreement of any kind. Indeed, the whole postmodernist project now seems, in retrospect, like an unwitting attempt to have deconstructed the old metanarratives of Western thought—science and reason along with religion and capitalist economic systems—to make room for a wholly new religion, a post-modern faith based on a dead God, which sees mysterious worldly forces in systems of power and privilege and which sanctifies victimhood. This, increasingly, is the fundamentalist religion of the nominally secular left.[25]

The religion of wokeism requires more than adherence. It requires *fluency* in the wokabulary. This isn't an attribute unique to wokeness—all religions contain elements of signaling, the use of unique signifiers to identify members of the group. Social groups often rely on signifiers in order to create solidarity, thus forming bonds across larger numbers of people: religious Jews wear yarmulkes, for example, not only to symbolize fealty to something higher, but in order to signal to other religious Jews a level of commitment to the religion. As evolutionary anthropologists Richard Sosis and Candace Alcorta write, this sort of activity is true even in the animal kingdom: "Ritual signals, by allowing clear communication of intent, were seen as promoting coordination and reducing the costs of agonistic encounters, thus laying the foundation for the development and stability of social groups." In order to deter those trying to imitate group signals in order to gain improper social entry, groups often require sacrifice—signaling that becomes costly to fake. The most effective signaling includes an aspect of the sacred: "The ability of religious ritual to elicit emotions makes it difficult for nonbelievers to imitate and renders it a powerful tool for social appraisal."[26]

This is what the wokabulary is all about. It is not about convincing others. It is about demonstration of belief in the cult. As Lasch writes:

> The culture wars that have convulsed America since the sixties are best understood as a form of class warfare, in which an enlightened elite (as it thinks of itself) seeks not so much to impose its values on the majority (a majority perceived as incorrigibly racist, sexist, provincial, and xenophobic), much less to persuade the majority by means of rational public debate, as to create parallel or "alternative" institutions in which it will no longer be necessary to confront the unenlightened at all.[27]

Membership in the New Ruling Class comes with clear cultural signifiers—it is easy to tell whether someone is an initiate into the New Ruling Class. Do they use pronouns in their public bio to show solidarity with the transgender agenda, nodding gravely at patent linguistic abominations like ze/hir, ze/zem, ey/em, per/pers—ridiculous terms meant to obscure rather than enlighten? Do they use the word *Latinx* rather than *Latinos* in order to show sensitivity to Latinas, despite the gendered nature of Spanish? Do they talk about "institutional" or "systemic" or "cultural" discrimination? Do they attach modifiers to words like *justice*—"Environmental justice," "racial justice," "economic justice," "social justice"—modifiers that actually undercut the nature of individual justice in favor of communalism? Do they worry about "microaggressions" or "trigger warnings"? Do they use terms like "my truth" rather than "my opinion"? Do they "call out" those who ask for data by castigating them for "erasure" or "destruction of identity," or dismiss their beliefs by referencing their opponents' alleged "privilege"? Do they talk about "structures of power," or suggest that terms like "Western civilization" are inherently bigoted? Do they speak of the "patriarchy" or "heteronormativity" or "cisnormativity"?

It's a complex language. Adherence requires constant attention to the changing dictionary of norms. What was absolutely inoffensive yesterday can become deeply offensive today, without warning—and ignorance is no defense. There is no set system for changing the wokabulary—changes can emerge, fully formed, nearly instantaneously.

The wokabulary is facially absurd. Two decades ago, New York University mathematician Alan Sokal published a gobbledygook word salad of deconstructionism in a postmodern academic journal. Its title: "Transgressing the Boundaries: Towards a Transformative Hermeneutics of Quantum Gravity." In 2018, scholars James Lindsay, Helen Pluckrose, and Peter Boghossian repeated the feat, but on a far larger scale. The left-liberal scholars submitted a series of hilariously farcical articles to prestigious academic journals—and a bevy of those articles were accepted. Of the twenty papers submitted, seven were accepted and four were published. Only six were rejected outright.[28] *Gender, Place, and Culture* published a paper titled, "Human Reaction to Rape Culture and Queer Performativity at Urban Dog Parks in Portland, Oregon." The journal *Fat Studies* published a paper titled, "Who Are They to Judge? Overcoming Anthropometry and a Framework for Fat Bodybuilding." *Sex Roles* approved a paper titled, "An Ethnography of Breastaurant Masculinity: Themes of Objectification, Sexual Conquest, Male Control, and Masculine Toughness in a Sexually Objectifying Restaurant."

The content of these papers was no less absurd. One of the articles argued against "western astronomy," since that field of inquiry was allegedly rooted in bigotry; instead, the authors suggested "[o]ther means superior to the natural sciences . . . to extract alternative knowledges about stars," which would include such wonders as "modern feminist analysis" of "mythological narratives" about stars and perhaps "feminist interpretative dance (especially with regard to the movements of the stars and their astrological significance)." Another accepted paper took on the important topic of whether masturbation while thinking about someone makes you a sexual abuser, since the object hasn't given her consent.[29] Yet another paper discussed whether transphobia and homophobia from straight males could be overcome through "receptive penetrative sex toy use." One paper was a rewrite of a section of *Mein Kampf* using women's studies terminology.

The hoax worked because Lindsay, Pluckrose, and Boghossian were fluent in the wokabulary: they understood that simply by characterizing every problem as a critique of societal victimization, they owned the skeleton key to academia. The professors themselves explained, "Scholarship based less upon finding truth and more upon attending to social grievances has become firmly established, if not fully dominant" in many areas of higher education.[30]

It is this language—the wokabulary—that universities now teach. Outside of the sciences, universities no longer exist in order to train you for a job. They exist to grant you a credential and usher you into the broader world of the New Ruling Class via your new bilingualism in the wokabulary. David Randall of the National Association of Scholars notes that over the last twenty years a new generation of academics and administrators has taken power, seeking to "transform higher education itself into an engine of progressive political advocacy, subjecting students to courses that are nothing more than practical training in progressive activism." So dominant is the wokeism that in many major university departments, not a single conservative can be identified on the staff. Professors leverage social justice into their curricula, into their research, into their writings; administrators use their power to push social justice in all aspects of both academic and social life, from residential life to public events.

To that end, the New Ruling Class in charge of our universities aims at maximizing the budgets allocated to social justice–oriented courses; overall, colleges spend tens of billions of dollars on such pursuits.[31] One of the not-accidental by-products of wokeism is the dramatic increase in college budgets directed toward useless fields—diversity studies directed not toward broadening minds but narrowing them. As Heather Mac Donald writes in *The Diversity Delusion*, "Entire fields have sprung up around race, ethnicity, sex, and gender identity. . . . A vast administrative apparatus— the diversity bureaucracy—promotes the notion that to be a college student from an ever-growing number of victim groups is to experience daily bigotry from your professors and peers." Even departments supposedly disassociated from social justice activism are often rife with it. Wokeism completely dominates our institutions of higher education.[32]

HOW UNIVERSITIES WERE RENORMALIZED

The universities represented the first line of attack for cultural radicals. In the 1960s, a liberal consensus still prevailed, a belief in the freedoms guaranteed by the Constitution, as well as a commitment to the very notion of truth-seeking itself. By the end of the 1960s, that consensus had completely collapsed on campus. The renormalization of the universities occurred because that liberal consensus was hollow—because enlightenment ideals of open inquiry and the pursuit of truth are not self-evident, and die when disconnected from their cultural roots.

The soft underbelly for Enlightenment liberals lay in an inability to rebut what Robert Bellah termed "expressive individualism." Expressive individualism is the basic idea that the goal of life and government ought to be ensuring the ability of individuals to explore their own perception of the good life, and to express it as they see fit.[33] Enlightenment liberalism was still unconsciously connected to old ideas about reason and virtue. By contrast, expressive individualism obliterated all such limits. If you found meaning in avoiding responsibility for others, including children, that was part and parcel of liberty; if you found meaning in defining yourself in a way directly contrary to reality or decency, that was simply liberty, too.

What's more, according to philosopher Charles Taylor, expressive individualism requires the *approval* of others. As O. Carter Snead of the University of Notre Dame relates, Taylor "identified a new category of harm that emerges in a culture of expressive individualism, namely, the *failure to receive, accept, and appreciate* the expression of others' inner depths. . . . To fail to recognize the expression of other selves is a violation and a harm to them." We must all cheer for others' ideas, decisions, and proclamations, no matter how bad, how perverse, or how untrue.[34]

The critique provided by deconstructionism was, at heart, merely a radical version of expressive individualism. Where Enlightenment liberalism had taken for granted certain ideas about human rights, the value of objective truth, and the ability for human beings to understand the world around them—ideas borrowed from Judeo-Christianity—and then built on those ideas by questioning long-held but unproven axioms about science and power, deconstructionism bathed *everything* in the acid of questioning, hence "deconstructing" everything. The postmodernists made the case that all knowledge was the result of preexisting narratives that had to be questioned, and that none of those narratives could rebut any other narratives. Postmodernism could be used to tear down any attempt to establish truth—even scientific facts could be rebutted by critiquing the way we define truth based on our cultural context.

Postmodernism carved the heart out of the liberal project. Enlightenment liberalism pushed reason and logic to the center of discourse; postmodernism dismissed reason and logic as just, like, your opinion, man.

The resulting hollowness spelled disaster for the universities, where postmodernism had become heavily influential. Colleges were ripe for the picking. Instead of dedicating themselves to teaching the long-held truths of Western civilization, they dedicated themselves to "thinking critically"—which, in practice, meant critiquing Western civilization while asking "who are we to judge?" about other cultures. While pure deconstructionism, however, would have pointed out the frailty of *all* cultural structures, the deconstructionism adopted in American universities applied *only* to the West. To apply deconstructionism to others would violate the tenets of expressive individualism. Identity groups quickly took advantage of this weakness, suggesting that membership in a victimized group lent special knowledge and status to their critiques of the prevailing ideological systems. And those in charge of the universities—crippled by their inability to rebut criticisms of Western systems of inquiry and knowledge, and too "nice" to use the tools of deconstructionism against other cultures—simply collapsed.[35]

In practical terms, the universities imploded because in the name of the Cordiality Principle, those who should have fought back did not; because in the name of liberalism, those who should not have tolerated illiberalism did; because the radicals were simply intransigent, and built coalitions large enough to hold institutions hostage. The authoritarian leftists took over the university because they successfully renormalized the institutions themselves.

To take but one example, the 1964 Berkeley Free Speech Movement (FSM), now championed as a glorious American moment of liberty, was actually a mere pretense designed at gaining power and control. As author Roger Kimball notes, the controversy began when students began using a strip of university-owned land for political purposes. The university objected, pointing out that the students had plenty of areas designated for such activity. Nonetheless, the students rallied to the call—and that call went far beyond time and place restrictions on political activity. One 1965 FSM pamphlet pointed out that "politics and education are inseparable," and that the university should not be geared toward "passing along the morality of the middle class, nor the morality of the white man, nor even the morality of the potpourri we call 'western society.' "[36]

During the same period, Harvard students seized buildings; Columbia students held a dean hostage and occupied the president's office. At Cornell, armed students took professors hostage, invaded college buildings, and forced the faculty to reverse its own penalties placed on offending students. The president of the university then proceeded to call the incident "one of the most positive forces ever set in motion in the history of Cornell." Professors with spines, including Walter Berns and Allan Bloom, resigned. Later, one of the ringleaders of the entire affair, Tom Jones, would be appointed to the Cornell board of trustees. Bloom wrote that students now knew that "pompous teachers who catechized them about academic freedom could, with a little shove, be made into dancing bears."[37]

The students knew it. Shelby Steele, who would later become conservative, recalls attending college in the late 1960s, leading black students into the president's office with a list of demands. As Steele narrates, "with all the militant authority I could muster, I allowed the ashes from my lit cigarette to fall in little grey cylinders onto the president's plush carpet. This was the effrontery, the insolence, that was expected in our new commitment to militancy." Steele fully expected the college president, Dr. Joseph McCabe, to chastise him. But, says Steele, it simply didn't happen:

I could see that it was all becoming too much for him. . . . There was no precedent for this sort of assault on authority, no administrative manual on how to handle it. I saw something like real anger come over his face, and he grabbed the arms of his chair as if to spring himself up. . . . But his arms never delivered him from his seat. I will never know what thought held him back. I remember only that his look turned suddenly inward as if he were remembering something profound, something that made it impossible for him to rise up. Then it was clear that the cigarette would be overlooked. . . . In that instant we witnessed his transformation from a figure of implacable authority to a negotiator empathetic with the cause of those who challenged him—from a traditional to a modern college president.

As Steele states, it was McCabe's understanding of the evils of racism that allowed such outrageous behavior by students. His own "vacuum of moral authority," springing from knowledge of American sins, stopped him cold.[38] Authoritarian leftists, relying on an anti-conventionalism that castigated traditional liberalism as morally deficient, silenced McCabe, as they did most college administrators.

Liberalism's separation from its values-laden roots left it unable to defend itself. The dance of renormalization had occurred. First, they silenced those in power. Then they forced them to publicly repent. Then they cast them aside. That's the authoritarian Left's process in every country and in every era.

THE PURGE

The universities have now become factories for wokeism. There are few or no conservatives in the faculty and staff of most top universities; a 2020 *Harvard Crimson* survey found that 41.3 percent of the faculty members identified as liberal, and another 38.4 percent as very liberal; moderates constituted just 18.9 percent of the faculty, and 1.46 percent said they were conservative.[39] A similar *Yale Daily News* survey of faculty in 2017 found that 75 percent of faculty respondents identified as liberal or very liberal; only 7 percent said they were conservative, with just 2 percent labeling themselves "very conservative." In the humanities, the percentages were even more skewed, with 90 percent calling themselves liberal; overall, 90 percent of all faculty said they opposed Trump.[40] One liberal Yale professor told *The Wall Street Journal*, "Universities are moving away from the search for truth" and toward "social justice."[41]

Overall, for over 2,000 college professors spanning thirty-one states and the District of Columbia who donated to political candidates from 2015 to 2018, contributions to Democrats outpaced those to Republicans by a 95:1 ratio.[42] Another study published in *Econ Journal Watch* in 2016 found that of the 7,243 professors registered to vote at forty leading universities, Democrats outnumbered Republicans 3,623 to 314.[43] The Carnegie Foundation surveyed professors about their political affiliations in 1969, and found 27 percent were conservative; by 1999, just 12 percent were. Samuel Abrams of the Higher Education Research Institute suggested that since 1984, the ratio of liberals to conservatives on college faculty has increased 350 percent. By one study, just 2 percent of political science professors were estimated to be conservative; just 4 percent of philosophy professors; just 7 percent of history professors; and just 3 percent of literature professors.[44] These are political identification numbers that would make Fidel Castro blush in envy.

It's not only that conservatives have been weeded out at America's top universities. It's that even old-school, rights-based liberals have now been marginalized. Former head of the American Civil Liberties Union Ira Glasser recently told *Reason* about visiting one of America's top law schools:

[T]he audience was a rainbow. There were as many women as men. There were people of every skin color and every ethnicity . . . it was the kind of thing we dreamed about. It was the kind of thing we fought for. So I'm looking at this audience and I am feeling wonderful about it. And then after the panel discussion, person after person got up, including some of the younger professors, to assert that their goals of social justice for blacks, for women, for minorities of all kinds were incompatible with free speech and that free speech was an antagonist. . . . For people who today claim to be passionate about social justice to establish free speech as an enemy is suicidal.[45]

But the suicide of the academy is well under way. Even moderate liberals now find themselves on the chopping block. When liberal professor Bret Weinstein refused to leave the Evergreen State College campus after black radicals demanded that white teachers not teach on a particular day—and when he added to that sin by stating that faculty jobs should be rooted in merit rather than skin color—authoritarian leftist students called him racist and took over campus buildings.[46] Students walked out on a class taught by his wife, evolutionary biologist Heather Heyer, when she pointed out that men are, on average, taller than women.[47] Professor Nicholas Christakis and his wife, Erika, were shouted out of their positions as Yale faculty-in-residence at Yale's Silliman College after Erika committed the grave sin of asking students to be less sensitive about Halloween costumes. Students confronted Nicholas on the quad and screamed at him. "Who the f*** hired you?" screamed one black female student. "You should step down! . . . It is not about creating an intellectual space! It is not! Do you understand that? . . . You are disgusting!"[48]

Such incidents have terrified dissenters into silence or, worse, compliance. But it's not just student intimidation at issue. It's the self-perpetuating nature of the New Ruling Class at our universities. According to sociologist George Yancy, 30 percent of sociologists openly admitted they would discriminate against Republican job applicants, as well as 24 percent of philosophy professors; 60 percent of anthropologists and 50 percent of literature professors said they would discriminate against evangelical Christians. But just as important, once wokeism has been enshrined as the official ideology of higher education, conservatives self-select out of that arena. How often will a dissertation adviser take on a PhD student in political science who posits that individual decision making rather than systemic racism lies at the root of racial inequalities? How often will a college dean hire an associate professor who maintains that gender ideology is a lie? As Jon Shields, himself an associate professor of government at Claremont McKenna College, notes at *National Affairs*, "the leftward tilt of the social sciences and humanities is self-reinforcing."[49]

CONCLUSION

The religion of the New Ruling Class—as well as the ritualistic pagan activities surrounding it—is an intellectual virus. And it has infected broad strains of American life. In fact, wokeism is so incredibly virulent that in February 2021, French president Emmanuel Macron stated that the country's unity was threatened by "certain social science theories imported from the United States." Macron's education minister warned that the "intellectual matrix from American universities" should not be imported.[50]

For decades, conservatives scoffed at the radicals on campus. They assumed that real life would beat the radicalism out of the college-age leftists. They thought the microaggression culture of the universities would be destroyed by the job market, that paying taxes would cure college graduates of their utopian redistributionism, that institutions would act as a check on the self-centered brattishness of college indoctrination victims.

They were wrong.

Instead, wokeism has been carried into every major area of American life via powerful cultural and governmental institutions—nearly all of which are composed disproportionately of people who graduated from college and learned the wokabulary. Growth industries in the United States are industries dominated thoroughly by college graduates. In fact, between December 2007 and December 2009, the Great Recession, college graduates actually *increased* their employment by 187,000 jobs, while those with a high school degree or less lost 5.6 million jobs. Over the course of the next six years, high school graduates would gain a grand total of just 80,000 jobs during the so-called Obama recovery, compared to 8.4 million jobs for college graduates.[51]

Instead of postgraduation institutes shaping their employees, employees are shaping their institutions. It turns out that corporate heads and media moguls are just as subject to renormalization as colleges ever were. As we will see, corporate titans are now afraid of their woke staff, and have turned to mirroring their priorities; old-school liberals in media have turned over their desks to repressive wokescolds; even churches have turned over their pulpits, increasingly, to those who would cave to the new radical value system.

One area of American life, though, should have been immune to the predations of authoritarian leftism: science. After all, science has a method, a way of distinguishing truth from falsehood; science is designed to uncover objective truths rather than to wallow in subjective perceptions of victimization. Science should have been at the bleeding edge of the pushback.

Instead, science surrendered, too. Next, we'll take a look at why.

Chapter 4
How Science™ Defeated Actual Science

Two thousand twenty was a banner year for science. In the midst of a global pandemic caused by a novel coronavirus, scientists in laboratories across the world stepped into the breach. They researched the most effective methods of slowing the virus's spread. They developed new therapeutics designed to reduce death rates, and researched new applications of already-existent drugs. Most incredibly, they developed multiple vaccines for Covid-19 within mere months of its exponential spread across the West. Most of the West didn't shut down until March 2020. By December, citizens were receiving their first doses of vaccine, immunizing the most vulnerable and flattening the infection curve.

Meanwhile, in hospitals, doctors and nurses labored

in perilous conditions to care for waves of the sick. Physicians were called upon to be resourceful with limited resources; nurses were called upon to brave danger to themselves to treat others. As they learned more about the nature of the disease, those medical workers saved tens of thousands of lives.

And the public took measures, too. Across the West, citizens socially distanced and masked up; they closed their businesses and took their children out of school and told their parents to stay home in order to protect others.

The historic scourge of disease challenged humankind. Science emerged victorious.

And yet.

While laboratory scientists did unprecedented work creating solutions for an unprecedented problem, while doctors worked in dangerous conditions to preserve the lives of suffering patients, public health officials—the voices of The Science™, the politically driven perversion of actual science in the name of authoritarian leftism—proceeded to push politically radical ends, politicize actual scientific research, and undermine public trust in science itself. Unfortunately, because science is such an indispensable part of Western life—it is perhaps the only arena of political agreement left in our society, thanks to the fact that it has heretofore remained outside the realm of the political—it is too valuable a tool to be left unused by the authoritarian Left. And so the authoritarian Left has substituted The Science™ for science.

Science itself is a process of gathering knowledge through painstaking trial and error, through gradual development of a body of knowledge through observation and data collection, through falsification. Science requires that we believe in objective truths about the world around us, and that we believe in our own capacity to explore the unknown to uncover those truths. Most of all, science provides the final word where it speaks.

The Science™ is a different story. The Science™ amounts to a call for silence, not investigation. When members of the New Ruling Class insist that we follow The Science™, they generally do *not* mean that we ought to acknowledge the reality of scientific findings. They mean that we ought to abide by their politicized interpretation of science, that we ought to mirror their preferred solutions, that we ought to look the other way when they ignore and twist science for their own ends. The Science™ is never invoked in order to convince; it is invoked in order to cudgel. The Science™, in short, is politics dressed in a white coat. Treating science as politics undermines science; treating politics as science costs lives. That's precisely what the authoritarian Left does when it invokes The Science™ to justify itself.

We saw The Science™ prevail over science itself repeatedly during the pandemic, to ugly effect.

Perhaps the most robust finding with regard to Covid—a finding replicated across the globe—was that large gatherings involving shouting and singing were inherently more dangerous than sparsely populated, socially distanced situations. The media quickly seized on this fact, for example, to chide anti-lockdown protesters for their irresponsibility, claiming that even outdoor protests could be unsafe.[1] Meanwhile, local officials in many areas went beyond the science itself, closing beaches, hiking trails, and even public parks—areas that were in no way chief vectors for transmission.[2] Republicans who refused to close beaches in largely unaffected areas, like Governor Ron DeSantis of Florida, were heavily criticized.[3] All of the pro-lockdown policy and rhetoric was justified with appeals to science.

As it turned out, public health officials weren't concerned about science. They were merely using science as a tool to press for their preferred policies. They were, in short, more interested in The Science™ than in science itself.

That became perfectly clear at the end of May.

On May 25, George Floyd, a forty-six-year-old black man, died in the custody of Minneapolis police. Floyd was a career criminal with a serious record; the police were called because he had passed a counterfeit twenty-dollar bill while buying cigarettes; his autopsy found that he had a "fatal level" of fentanyl in his system. Selectively edited tape of Floyd on the ground for nearly nine minutes, saying he couldn't breathe as a police officer put his knee on the back of Floyd's neck, went viral. The officer restraining Floyd was charged with second-degree murder.

Floyd's death generated massive protests and riots around the country. Those protests and riots were driven by the false notion that police across the nation routinely murdered black men—an evidence-free untruth.[4] Led by the radical Black Lives Matter movement, these "racial justice" gatherings—in the midst of a deadly pandemic—were unprecedented in size and scale. According to polling, somewhere between 15 and 26 million people in the United States attended a protest.[5] The protests were certainly not socially distanced; some wore masks, but certainly many did not. Often, the protests devolved into violence, including mass looting and property destruction; major cities across America were forced to declare curfew for the law-abiding. More often, the protests turned into party-like atmospheres, including dancing and singing and shouting.

And the same public health professionals who decried anti-lockdown protests, who urged Americans to do their part to socially distance, who cheered as businesses were told to close and schools to board up, ecstatically endorsed the mass gatherings. Apparently, the virus was itself woke: it would kill Republicans who opposed economy-crippling lockdowns, but would pass over anyone chanting trite slogans about defunding the police.

Politicians from the Left—devotees of wokeism— appeared in the midst of mass protests personally. Governor Gretchen Whitmer (D-MI) attended a civil rights march in Highland Park with hundreds of others, standing "shoulder-to-shoulder with some march participants." She did so just days after explaining that protests could in fact endanger lives.[6] Even as the National Guard policed Los Angeles in the wake of widespread rioting and the law-abiding were confined to their homes, Mayor Eric Garcetti took a knee with the Black Lives Matter crowd and "pulled down his blue Los Angeles Dodgers face mask to speak."[7] Speaking on CNN, New York mayor Bill de Blasio openly stated that only BLM marches would be allowed in his city:

"This is a historic moment of change. We have to respect that but also say to people the kinds of gatherings we're used to, the parades, the fairs—we just can't have that while we're focused on health right now."[8]

Leaving aside the First Amendment implications of such statements, none of this could be remotely justified by the science itself. But authoritarian leftist politicians could count on members of the public health establishment to back their play, manufacturing antiscientific narratives in the name of science. More than one thousand "public health specialists" signed an open letter supporting the largest protests in American history *in the middle of a global pandemic*, claiming that such protests were "vital to the national public health," and adding, "This should not be confused with a permissive stance on all gatherings, particularly protests against stay-at-home orders." Infectious-disease expert Ranu S. Dhillon of Harvard Medical School told *The New York Times*, "Protesting against systemic injustice that is contributing directly to this pandemic is essential. The right to live, the right to breathe, the right to walk down the street without police coming at you for no reason . . . that's different than me wanting to go to my place of worship on the weekend, me wanting to take my kid on a roller coaster, me wanting to go to brunch with my friends."[9]

The social science simply does not support the contention that the police are, writ large, targeting Americans of color based on racial animus. But even if such a wild accusation could be substantiated, it is absolutely absurd to suggest that mass protests over such a systemic issue—protests capable of spreading a highly transmissible deadly disease—represent a net positive for public health. Yet precisely that contention became commonplace in the world of The Science™.

Julia Marcus, epidemiologist at Harvard Medical School, and Gregg Gonsalves, epidemiologist at Yale School of Public Health, penned an article at *The Atlantic* claiming, "Public-health experts are weighing these same risks at a population level, and many have come to the conclusion that the health implications of maintaining the status quo of white supremacy are too great to ignore, even with the potential for an increase in coronavirus transmission from the protests."[10]

The University of California, San Francisco, hospital gave doctors of color a day off after Floyd's death; many of those doctors joined protests. One, Dr. Maura Jones, explained, "I would argue that, yeah I'm a doctor and I encourage you to social distance and I care about coronavirus and I know that it's a real threat, but racism is, to me to my family, the bigger threat right now and it has been for hundreds of years." Dr. Jasmine

Johnson joined a protest by the University of North Carolina Student National Medical Association with a sign reading, "Racism is a pandemic too!" She claimed that racism was the root cause of racial disparities in death statistics from Covid—and therefore suggested that protest was actually a public health *good*.[11] Ashish Jha, dean of the Brown University School of Public Health, made the most insane case of all: that the protests would fuel Covid spread, but that this didn't matter. "Do I worry that mass protests will fuel more cases? Yes, I do. But a dam broke, and there's no stopping that," he stated.[12] Based on The Science™, liberal figures in government began promoting declarations that racism represented a "public health crisis."[13]

The science said that gathering in large numbers was a bad idea. To that end, thousands of Americans watched from afar as parents, brothers and sisters, family and friends died alone in hospitals; funerals were held by Zoom. Businesses shut by the hundreds of thousands.

The Science™ said that health concerns were secondary, and political concerns were primary.

And then our scientific establishment wonders why Americans have trust issues.

As it turned out, we may never know whether the mass protests spread Covid. We do know that the summer saw radical increases in viral transmission—increases the media quickly chalked up to Memorial Day gatherings, which occurred the same week protests broke out. But cities like New York actually told their contact tracers *not to ask* whether those diagnosed with Covid had attended a protest.[14]

The public health community's willingness to extend its area of supposed expertise to problems of alleged racial injustice highlights one very serious problem for the scientific establishment: the Ultracrepidarian Problem. Ultracrepidarianism is weighing in on matters outside one's area of expertise, or pretending that one's area of expertise extends to questions in different subject areas. Suffice it to say, our public health experts—and the doctors who weigh in on the political matter of policing and race relations—are certainly operating in uncharted waters for them. Simply slapping the label "science" on a political opinion doesn't make that opinion scientific any more than calling a man a woman makes that man a biological woman. The Ultracrepidarian Problem extends the reach of science into areas of pseudo-science, claiming the mantle of the objective and verifiable on behalf of subjective conjecture.

There is a second related, perhaps even more serious problem for scientific institutions in the United

States, however: what we can call the Bleedover Effect. Whereas the Ultracrepidarian Problem comes from the scientific community speaking outside its area of expertise, the Bleedover Effect occurs when outside political viewpoints bleed over into scientific institutions themselves. This, predictably, restricts the actual reach of science, supplanting anti-scientific ruling ideologies for scientific inquiry.

Take another example from the world of Covid policy: the decision making surrounding vaccine distribution. Now, this would seem to be a simple scientific question: who is most vulnerable to Covid? The most vulnerable obviously ought to be given the Covid vaccine first. And, as it turns out, that question has an obvious answer: the elderly, who are most susceptible to multiple preexisting conditions. Covid risk is heavily striated by age: according to the Centers for Disease Control, the death rate of Covid for those above the age of eighty-five is 630 times the death rate for those between the ages of eighteen and twenty-nine; for those between seventy-five and eighty-four, the death rate is 220 times higher; for those between sixty-five and seventy-four, the death rate is 90 times higher.[15] So it should have been an easy call for the Centers for Disease Control to set out vaccine distribution guidelines based on age.

That, however, was not what happened. Instead, wokeism bled into the scientific process, turning science into The Science™.

On November 23, 2020, CDC public health official Kathleen Dooling presented her recommendations for tranching out the vaccine to the Advisory Committee on Immunization Practices. Dooling explained that essential workers—some 87 million people—should receive the vaccine *before* the elderly. Yes, Dooling's modeling acknowledged, this would increase the number of deaths somewhere between 0.5 percent and 6.5 percent. But such differences were "minimal," Dooling stated, when compared with the fact that racial equity could be pursued through her recommended policy. After all, Dooling pointed out, "racial and ethnic minority groups are underrepresented among adults > 65." Because white people have a longer life expectancy than black and Hispanic Americans, Dooling was arguing, there were too many old white people. Why not prioritize younger black and Hispanic people *at lower risk of dying from the disease* as a sort of reparative measure?

This proposal was not merely morally idiotic. It was evil. Statistically speaking, even if white people are overrepresented as a percentage of the population among those over sixty-five, placing that group after essential workers would kill *more black people*—it would tranche black Americans more likely to die (those over age sixty-five) behind black Americans who were less likely to die (twenty-year-old grocery workers, for example). Thus, even if fewer black Americans would die as a percentage, more black Americans would die in *absolute numbers*.[16]

This perspective was not fringe. It was well respected and well reported. On December 5, *The New York Times* reported that the committee had unanimously supported Dooling's proposal. At least eighteen states had decided to take into account the CDC's "social vulnerability index" in tranching out vaccines. As the *Times* acknowledged, "Historically, the committee relied on scientific evidence to inform its decisions. But now the members are weighing social justice concerns as well, noted Lisa A. Prosser, a professor of health policy and decision sciences at the University of Michigan." The *Times* quoted one Harald Schmidt, an alleged expert in ethics and health policy at the University of Pennsylvania, expressing himself in blatantly eugenic terms: "Older populations are whiter. Society is structured in a way that enables them to live longer. Instead of giving additional health benefits to those who already had more of them, we can start to level the playing field a bit."[17] All it would take to level that playing field was to bury some disproportionately white bodies in the low-lying areas.

Public blowback to the CDC's standards led them to revise—but only somewhat. After medical workers were treated, the CDC recommended that the elderly and frontline workers be placed in the same tranche. This approach, too, will cost lives. As Yascha Mounk, a liberal thinker who often writes for *The Atlantic*, points out, "America's botched guidance on who gets the vaccine first should, once and for all, put the idea that the excesses of wokeness are a small problem that doesn't affect important decisions to bed." Furthermore, as Mounk pointed out, the *Times*—which was so eager to cheer on the infusion of wokeism into scientific standards—barely reported that the committee had changed its recommendations based on public pressure. "A faithful reader of the newspaper of record would not even know that an important public body was, until it received massive criticism from the public, about to sacrifice thousands of American lives on the altar of a dangerous and deeply illiberal ideology," Mounk wrote.[18]

When science becomes The Science™, Americans rightly begin to doubt their scientific institutions. They begin to believe, correctly, that the institutions of science have been hijacked by authoritarian leftists seeking to use white coats to cram down their viewpoints in top-down fashion.

"LISTEN TO THE EXPERTS"

The Ultracrepidarian Problem crops up regularly in the realm of policy making, when scientists determine that they are not merely responsible for identifying data-driven problems and providing data-driven answers, but for answering all of humanity's questions. The Ultracrepidarian Problem is nothing new in the realm of science. Indeed, it is an integral part of Scientism, the philosophy that morality can come from science itself—that all society requires is the management of experts in the scientific method to reach full human flourishing. Scientism says that it can answer ethical questions without resort to God; all that is required is a bit of data, and a properly trained scientist.

The history of Scientism is long and bleak—it contains support for eugenics, genocide, and massively misguided social engineering—but the popularity of Scientism hasn't waned. Modern Scientism is a bit softer than all of that, but maintains the same premise: that science can answer all of our moral questions, that it can move us easily from the question of what is to the question of what *ought* to be done.

Steven Pinker, a modern Scientism advocate, writes, "The Enlightenment principle that we can apply reason and sympathy to enhance human flourishing may seem obvious, trite, old-fashioned . . . I have come to realize that it is not."[19] The phrase "human flourishing" comes up a lot in the philosophy of Scientism. But the question of what "human flourishing" constitutes is indeed a moral question, not a scientific one. The debate over whether a human being should live a socially rich life filled with commitment to others or a hedonistic life filled with commitment to self-fulfillment is literally as old as philosophy.

On a less philosophical level, the Ultracrepidarian Problem undermines science by undercutting the credibility of scientists who insist on speaking beyond their purview. Take, for example, the problem of climate change. In the scientific community, there is a set of well-established facts and well-accepted principles: first, that climate change *is* happening, and that the world has been warming; and second, that human activity, particularly carbon emissions, are contributing significantly to that warming. There is serious debate over how much the world will warm over the course of the next century—the Intergovernmental Panel on Climate Change estimates that the global climate will warm somewhere between 2°C and 4°C above the mean temperature during the 1850–1900 period. That's a rather large range.[20] There is also significant uncertainty about sensitivity of the climate to carbon emissions; as NASA's Goddard Institute of Space Studies director Gavin Schmidt explains, climate sensitivity "has quite a wide uncertain range, and that has big implications for how serious human-made climate change will be."[21] Furthermore, there is wide uncertainty about the *impact* with regard to climate change—will human beings be able to adapt? How many "shock" events will occur?

These uncertainties lie at the heart of climate change policy. How much should we sacrifice current economic well-being and future economic growth for the sake of stabilizing the environment? What level of probable future risk justifies real-world, real-time policy making in the present?

True scientists are modest about their recommendations on such questions. They speak in terms of risk assessments and quantifiable metrics. William Nordhaus, for example, who won the Nobel Prize in Economics for his work on climate change, has suggested that people ought to accept that a certain amount of global warming is baked into the cake, and that we will be able to adapt to it—but that we ought to work on curbing global warming outside of that range.[22]

Experts in The Science™, however, have no problem proposing radical solutions to climate change that just coincidentally happen to align perfectly with left-wing political recommendations. Those who disagree are quickly slandered as "climate deniers," no matter their acceptance of IPCC climate change estimates. Thus the media trot out Greta Thunberg, a scientifically unqualified teenaged climate activist who travels the world obnoxiously lecturing adults about their lack of commitment to curbing climate change, as an expert; they ignore actual scientific voices on climate change. After all, as Paul Krugman of *The New York Times* writes, "there are almost no good-faith climate-change deniers . . . when failure to act on the science may have terrible consequences, denial is, as I said, depraved." He then lumps together those who deny outright the reality of global warming with those who "insist that nothing can be done about it without destroying the economy."[23]

But here's the thing: very little can be done about climate change in terms of regulation without seriously harming the economy. To abide by the Paris Agreement guidelines would cost, by Heritage Foundation estimates, at least $20,000 income loss per family by 2035 and a total aggregate GDP loss of $2.5 trillion.[24] And as even the UN Environment Programme found in 2017, if every major country kept to its pledges under the much-ballyhooed Paris Agreement, the earth will *still* warm at least 3°C by 2100.[25] In fact, even if the United States were to cut its carbon emissions 100 percent, the world would be 0.2°C cooler by 2100. To reach net zero carbon emissions worldwide by 2050 via Representative Alexandria Ocasio-Cortez's (D-NY) infamous Green New Deal would cost the typical family of four $8,000 *every single year.*[26]

This is not to suggest that nothing can be done about climate change. We should be investing in adaptive measures like seawalls, and be looking to new technologies like geoengineering. We should be cheering on America's fracking industry, which has redirected energy use from more carbon-intensive industries; we should be pushing for the use of nuclear energy; we should be promoting capitalism, which increases living standards around the globe, thus making people in poverty less vulnerable to the ravages of climate change. Yet those who promote these policies are treated as "deniers"; those who shout that the world is ended and the only solution is massive economic redistributionism are treated as truth speakers.

Behind closed doors, those who truly know about climate change understand the complexity of the problem and the foolishness of many of the publicly proposed solutions. Several years ago, I attended an event featuring world leaders and top scientific minds. Nearly all acknowledged that climate change was largely baked into the cake, that many of the most popular solutions were not solutions at all, and that the alternatives to carbon-based fossil fuels, particularly in developing countries, were infeasible. Yet when one actress then stood up and began cursing at these prominent experts, screaming that they weren't taking climate change seriously enough, they all stood and applauded.

That wasn't science. That was The Science™.

But the attempt to claim solutions for all problems in the name of science—the Ultracrepidarian Problem—quickly shades over into an even deeper problem: the Bleedover Effect, in which those with the politically correct opinions are deemed experts, and in which science finds itself at the mercy of these so-called experts.

THE BLEEDOVER EFFECT

Perhaps the greatest irony of the Ultracrepidarian Problem is that by enabling scientists to speak outside their area of expertise—to allow them to engage in the business of politics while pretending at scientific integrity—scientists create a gray area, in which politics and science are intermingled. This gray area—the arena of The Science™—then becomes the preserve of leftist radicals, who promptly adopt the masquerade of science in order to actively prevent scientific research.

In recent years, postmodernism has entered the world of science through this vector, endangering the entire scientific enterprise. Postmodernism claims that even scientific truths are cultural artifacts—that human beings cannot truly understand anything like an "objective truth," and that science is merely one way of thinking about the world. In fact, science is a uniquely Western (read: racist, sexist, homophobic, transphobic, etc.) way of thinking about the world, since it is a theory of knowledge that has historically perpetuated systems of power.[27] Again, this is nothing new in human history—the Nazis rejected "Jewish science" just as the Soviets rejected "capitalist science." But the fact that the Western world, enriched to nearly unimaginable heights by science and technology, has even countenanced the postmodern worldview is breathtakingly asinine.

This philosophy obviously hasn't infused all of our scientific institutions, but it doesn't have to do so in order to endanger the enterprise. Renormalization must merely occur in terms of *setting boundaries* to research—science must be curbed in the most sensitive areas when it conflicts with authoritarian leftist thought. That is precisely what has happened. Where the Ultracrepidarian Problem widens the boundaries of science beyond the applicable, the Bleedover Effect narrows the boundaries of science to the "acceptable." By infusing social justice into science, science must now meet with the approval of the New Ruling Class. Those who speak in contravention of established left-wing theology are outed and ousted, in truly authoritarian fashion. As theoretical physicist Lawrence Krauss writes, "academic science leaders have adopted wholesale the language of dominance and oppression previously restricted to 'cultural studies' journals to guide their disciplines, to censor dissenting views, to remove faculty from leadership positions if their research is claimed by opponents to support systemic oppression."[28]

That left-wing theology dictates that all groups ought to achieve equal results in every area of human life; if science suggests differently, science must be silenced. Thus, conversations about IQ and group differences will be met with exorbitant outrage, as Sam Harris found out, even when the participants explicitly denounce racism in all of its forms;[29] conversations regarding differences between men and women in terms of aptitudes and interests must be punished, as Lawrence Summers found out;[30] studies questioning whether women do better with male mentors in academia rather than female mentors are retracted, based not on faulty research but on "the dimension of potential harm." In fact, *Nature*—perhaps the most prestigious science publication on the planet—quickly issued a policy stating that editors would be seeking outside opinions on the "broader societal implications of publishing a paper," an open invitation for political interference into the scientific process.[31] This means the death of scientific inquiry at the hands of the woke.

The overt politicization of science is most obvious with regard to gender dysphoria. Gender dysphoria is a condition characterized by the persistent belief that a person is a member of the opposite sex; it is an exceedingly rare phenomenon. Or, at least, it was—rates of reported gender dysphoria have been increasing radically in recent years, particularly among young girls, a shocking phenomenon given that the vast majority of those diagnosed with gender dysphoria have historically been biologically male. That unexplained phenomenon became the subject of research from Brown University assistant professor Lisa Littman, who released a study on "rapid-onset gender dysphoria," documenting the fact that teenage girls were becoming transgender in coordination with others in their peer group. Brown pulled the study, with Brown School of Public Health dean Bess Marcus issuing a public letter denouncing the work for its failure to "listen to multiple perspectives and to recognize and articulate the limitations of their work."[32] Something similar happened to journalist Abigail Shrier: when she wrote a book on rapid-onset gender dysphoria, Amazon refused to allow her to advertise it,[33] and Target temporarily pulled the book from its online store. Chase Strangio, the ACLU's deputy director for transgender justice, suggested "stopping the circulation of this book"—a fascinating take from an organization literally named for its defense of civil liberties.[34]

There is no evidence whatsoever that gender is disconnected from biological sex. Yet scientists have given way to gender theorists, whose pseudo-science is inherently self-contradictory. This leads directly to absurdity. Doctors have claimed that gender identity is "the only medically supported determinant of sex," despite the fact that biology clearly exists.[35] In 2018, the American Medical Association announced that it would oppose any definition of sex based on "immutable biological traits identifiable by or before birth," instead favoring language stating that doctors "assign" sex at birth—a laughable assertion.[36] The AMA even outlined legislation that would ban therapists from suggesting to children that they ought to become more comfortable with their biological sex rather than acting in contravention to it.[37]

The *New England Journal of Medicine*, likely the most prestigious scientific journal in America, printed an article in December 2020 recommending that sex designations on birth certificates be moved below the line of demarcation, since they "offer no clinical utility."[38] Despite the lack of longitudinal data on transgender surgeries and the high rate of desistance from gender dysphoria over time from young people, much of the scientific community has rejected "watchful waiting" as somehow transphobic; blacklisted doctors and journalists who refuse to encourage gender transition for those who are underage; and stated without evidence that the solution to gender dysphoria is a radical redefinition of sex itself, whereby children ought to be taught that they can freely choose their own gender, and adults ought to be socially cudgeled into using biologically inapposite pronouns. "Your truth" now matters more than objective scientific truth. And those who know better are forced to denounce the objective science, engaging in top-down censorship of other viewpoints while proclaiming their adherence to the new moral code.

Scientific inquiry is forbidden. Now authoritarian leftism, citing The Science™, rules.

How far has this insanity gone? In June 2020, the American Physical Society, an organization of 55,000 physicists, closed down its offices as part of a "strike for black lives," recommitting itself to "eradicate systemic racism and discrimination, especially in academia, and science." *Nature* put out an article titled "Ten simple rules for building an anti-racist lab." Princeton faculty—more than one thousand of them—issued a letter to the president proposing that all scientific departments create a senior thesis prize for research that "is actively anti-racist or expands our sense of how race is constructed in our society."[39]

In December 2020, a group of professors of computer science felt it necessary to write an open letter to the Association for Computing Machinery—the world's largest computing society—decrying cancel culture. "We are a group of researchers, industry experts, academics, and educators, writing with sadness and alarm about the increasing use of repressive actions aimed at limiting the free and unfettered conduct of scientific research and debate," the group of professors wrote. "Such actions have included calls for academic boycotts, attempts to get people fired, inviting mob attacks against 'offending' individuals, and the like. . . . We condemn all attempts to coerce scientific activities into supporting or opposing specific social-political beliefs, values, and attitudes, including attempts at preventing researchers from exploring questions of their choice, or at restricting the free discussion and debate of issues related to scientific research."[40]

The fact that such a letter was necessary in *computer science* demonstrates the depth of the problem. But it was necessary: earlier in 2020, NeurIPS, the most prestigious AI conference on the planet, required authors to submit papers only with a statement explaining how the research could impact politics—a question decidedly outside the bounds of science, but firmly within the bounds of The Science™.[41]

THE "DIVERSIFICATION" OF SCIENCE

If science is supposed to be about the pursuit of truth via verification and falsification, the scientific community is supposed to be a meritocracy: those who do the best research ought to receive the most commendations. But when wokeism infuses science, the meritocracy falls by the wayside: the composition of the scientific community becomes subject to the same anti-scientific demand for demographic representation. To prove the point, in 2020, the Association of American Medical Colleges hosted professional racists Ibram X. Kendi and Nikole Hannah-Jones to explain that the standards for entrance into the scientific community ought to be changed in order to achieve demographic parity. Hannah-Jones explained to the annual meeting of the AAMC that when she requires a doctor, she tries to "seek out a black doctor"; Kendi explained that the lack of black doctors overall is a result of "stage 4 metastatic racism." Kendi told the AAMC—which administers the Medical College Admissions Test—that standardized tests are racist, because standardized tests tend to weed out black and Latino students. "Either there's something wrong with the test, or there's something wrong with the test-takers," Kendi said. And of course to suggest that not all individuals perform equally well on tests is to suggest that there is something wrong with some of the test takers—which would make you racist. All of this supposedly "anti-racist action," Hannah-Jones agreed, is part and parcel of choosing "to undo the structures that racism created."[42]

This is insulting tripe. It's insulting to those who achieve in the meritocracy; it's even more insulting to those who are assumed victims of the system. More than insulting, however, such ridiculous race-based thinking is *dangerous*. After all, if the alternative to a meritocracy is wokeism, wouldn't that necessarily mean the admission of less-than-qualified people to the highest ranks of science?

Yes. But it's happening nonetheless. According to Claremont McKenna professor Frederick Lynch, between 2013 and 2016, medical schools "admitted 57 percent of black applicants with a low MCAT of 24 to 26, but only 8 percent of whites and 6 percent of Asians with those same low scores." Meanwhile, the National Science Foundation, a federal funding agency for science, says that it wants to pursue a "diverse STEM workforce"—not the best scientists of all races, but a specifically diverse group.[43]

There is no evidence that a more diverse demographic research body should impact the findings of science. Science is not literature; personal experience should be of little relevance in chemistry. But to point this out is to meet with the rage of the mob. In June 2020, Brock University chemist Tomáš Hudlický printed an essay in Wiley's *Angewandt Chemie*, a prominent chemistry journal. He argued that the push for diversity over merit in chemistry had damaged the standards of the field, stating that diversity training had "influenced hiring practices to the point where the candidate's inclusion in one of the preferred social groups may override his or her qualifications." He also explained the patently obvious truth that "hiring practices that suggest or even mandate equality in terms of absolute numbers of people in specific subgroups is counter-productive if it results in discrimination against the most meritorious candidates."[44] Chemists emerged from the woodwork to condemn the essay and its author; the Royal Society of Chemistry and the German Chemical Society penned a statement calling the essay "outdated, offensive and discriminatory," adding "We will not stand for this. Diversity and equality are fantastic strengths in workplaces, in culture and in wider society. This is not only demonstrated by overwhelming evidence from decades of research, but we also hold it is morally the only acceptable position."

What overwhelming evidence suggests that prioritizing racial diversity over scientific ability is a fantastic strength? The statement cited no such evidence. But the moral statement—an unscientific statement, to be sure—was clear. The journal deleted the article, and added a statement: "Something went very wrong here and we're committed to do[ing] better." Two editors were suspended. Sixteen board members, including three Nobel Prize winners, resigned. They put out a joint statement lamenting the "journal's publishing practices," which they said had "suppressed ethnic and gender diversity." Fellow scientists called for Hudlický to be fired.[45]

CONCLUSION

In October 2020, the politicization of science—and its replacement with The Science™—became more obvious than ever before. *Scientific American*, perhaps the foremost popular science publication in America, issued the first presidential endorsement in its 175-year history. Naturally, they endorsed Joe Biden. "We do not do this lightly," the editors intoned. "The evidence and the science show that Donald Trump has badly damaged the U.S. and its people—because he rejects evidence and science." Joe Biden, by contrast, was providing "fact-based plans to protect our health, our economy and the environment." Those fact-based plans were, of course, simply liberal policy prescriptions, open to debate. But *Scientific American* spoke in the name of The Science™.[46] Not to be outdone, *Nature* similarly endorsed Joe Biden. "We cannot stand by and let science be undermined," the editorial board explained. Among their reasons: Trump's rejection of the Iran nuclear deal, a decidedly ultracrepidarian concern.[47] The *New England Journal of Medicine*, another prominent medical journal, suggested that Trump be booted from office for his Covid response. Yes, Trump's Covid rhetoric was wild and inconsistent. But even Trump's most ardent critics, were they honest, would recognize that Biden provided no actual Covid plan of his own. "Reasonable people will certainly disagree about the many political positions taken by candidates. But truth is neither liberal nor conservative," *NEJM* stated.[48]

No, science is neither liberal nor conservative. But The Science™—the radicalized version of science in which scientists speak their politics, and in which political actors set the limits of science—is certainly a tool of authoritarian leftists. And it predominates across the scientific world. Americans still trust their doctors to tell them the truth; they still trust scientists to speak on issues within their purview. But increasingly, they reject the automatic institutional legitimacy of the self-described scientific establishment. And they should. We can only hope that scientists realize that scientific credibility relies not on membership in the New Ruling Class but in the pure legitimacy of the scientific process before the entire field—a field that has transformed the world in extraordinary ways—collapses.

Chapter 5
Your Authoritarian Boss

In December 2020, I received an email from a fan. The fan explained that she worked at a Fortune 50 company—a company that had "quotas on who they want to hire and put into position of leadership based solely on skin color." At a company meeting, this fan voiced her opinion that the company should not support programs rooted in racial composition. "All 5 of the participants in the meeting immediately called my manager and their managers to voice deep concerns," she related. "My manager asked if I was still a good fit and I came close to losing my job." Her question, she wrote, was simple: "Should I immediately start looking for another role outside the company?"

I receive these sorts of emails daily. Multiple times a day, in fact. Over the past two years, the velocity of such emails has increased at an arithmetic rate; whenever we open the phone lines on my radio show, the board fills with employees concerned that mere expression of dissent will cost them their livelihood.

And they are right to be worried.

America's corporations used to be reliably apolitical. If anything, the business world trended toward conservatism. From 2000 to 2017, executives at the biggest public companies gave overwhelmingly to Republicans: according to the National Bureau of Economic Research, 18.6 percent of CEOs routinely donated to Democrats, while 57.7 percent donated to Republicans. Yet over time, while the percentage of Republican CEOs remained far higher than that of Democratic CEOs, more and more CEOs began preferring political neutrality to Republican giving. And the disparity between Republicans and Democrats in the West and Northeast—read California and New York—is far lower than in other regions of the country, with those who are neutral comprising a heavy percentage.[1]

Now, today's corporations are bastions of authoritarian leftism. During the Black Lives Matter summer, nearly every major corporation in America put out a statement decrying systemic American racism, mirroring the priorities of the woke Left. What's more, nearly all of these corporations put out internal statements effectively warning employees against dissent. Walmart, historically a Republican-leaning corporation, put out a letter from Doug McMillon pledging to "help replace the structures of systemic racism, and build in their place frameworks of equity and justice that solidify our commitment to the belief that, without question, Black Lives Matter." McMillon pledged more minority hiring, "listening, learning and elevating the voices of our Black and African American associates," and spending $100 million to "provide counsel across Walmart to increase understanding and improve efforts that promote equity and address the structural racism that persists in America."[2] The fact that Walmart had to close hundreds of stores due to the threat of BLM looting went unmentioned.[3]

Major corporations tripped over themselves to issue public statements denouncing racism—and, more broadly, America's supposed systemic racism. Many of the corporations pledged to fund their own quasi-religious indulgences, which would alleviate their supposed complicity in the racist system. Tim Cook of Apple issued a letter stating that America's racist past "is still present today—not only in the form of violence, but in the everyday experience of deeply rooted discrimination," and offered funding for the Equal Justice Initiative,[4] a progressive organization that blames historic racism for nearly every modern ill. Satya Nadella, CEO of Microsoft, issued a letter stating, "It's incumbent upon us to use our platforms, our resources, to drive systemic change";[5] the company stated that it would spend $150 million on "diversity and inclusion investment," aiming to "double the number of Black and African American people managers, senior individual contributors, and senior leaders in the United States by 2025."[6] Netflix issued a statement commanding, "To be silent is to be complicit," and pledged $100 million to build "economic opportunity for Black communities." That commitment followed CEO Reed Hastings announcing he would donate $120 million to black colleges.[7]

Even the most tangential and irrelevant companies chimed in. Ice cream company Ben & Jerry's issued a statement: "We must dismantle white supremacy. . . . What happened to George Floyd was not the result of a bad apple; it was the predictable consequence of a racist and prejudiced system and culture that has treated black bodies as the enemy from the beginning."[8] And it would be remiss not to mention that Gushers partnered with Fruit by the Foot to fight systemic racism, trumpeting, "We stand with those fighting for justice."[9]

These statements and actions weren't merely meaningless public breast-beating. Corporations began taking internal actions to cram down the radical Left's viewpoint on American systemic racism. Corporation after corporation mandated so-called diversity training for employees—training that often included admonitions about the evils of whiteness and the prevalence of societal white supremacy. Dissent from this orthodoxy could be met with suspension or firing. Employees at Cisco lost their jobs after writing that "All Lives Matter" and that the phrase "Black Lives Matter" fosters racism;[10] Sacramento Kings broadcaster Grant Napear lost his job for tweeting that "all lives matter";[11] Leslie Neal-Boylan, dean of University of Massachusetts Lowell's nursing school, lost her job after stating, "BLACK LIVES MATTER, but also, EVERYONE'S LIFE MATTERS"—which, after all, is the hallmark of nursing;[12] an employee at B&H Photo lost his job for writing, "I cannot support the organization called 'Black Lives Matter' until it clearly states that all lives matter equally regardless of race, ethnicity, religion or creed, then denounces any acts of violence that is happening in their name. In the meantime, I fully support the wonderful organization called 'America' where EVERY life matters. E pluribus unum!"[13]

Even corporate heads weren't immune from the pressure: CrossFit CEO Greg Glassman was forced to resign from his company after controversial comments about George Floyd; two officials from the Poetry Foundation stepped down after their pro-BLM statement was considered too mealy-mouthed; the editor in chief of *Bon Appétit* was forced out after an old photograph circulated of him dressed in Puerto Rican garb.[14]

To be clear, none of these corporations—all beneficiaries of a free market in hiring, firing, and customer base—actually believe that America is "systemically racist" in the same way the authoritarian leftists mean. These corporations merely mirror what most Americans think when they hear the term "systemic racism"—that racism still exists. And they say that "black lives matter" because, of course, black lives *do* matter. But the very term "black lives matter" is semantically overloaded: it's unclear, when used, whether it signifies a belief in the value of black lives (undeniable), the evils of the American system that supposedly devalues black lives today (an extreme notion lacking serious evidence), or support for the Black Lives Matter organization (which pushes actual Marxist radicalism).

Corporations, then, merely do what they do in order to make money. As always.

And herein lies the problem.

As we've examined, the authoritarian Left believes that America's systemic racism is evident in *every aspect of American society*—that all inequalities in American life are traceable to fundamental inequities in the American system. That means that for the authoritarian leftists who promote the "systemic racism" lie, systemic racism is evidenced by the *simple presence of successful corporations.* Successful corporations, in supporting the notion that America is systemically racist, are chipping away at the foundations of their own existence.

There is something undeniably ironic about corporations pretending support for a worldview that sees their very presence as evil. Black Lives Matters cofounder Patrisse Cullors infamously proclaimed, "We do have an ideological frame. Myself and Alicia [Garza], in particular, are trained organizers; we are trained Marxists. We are superversed on, sort of, ideological theories. And I think what we really try to do is build a movement that could be utilized by many, many Black folks." Black Lives Matter DC openly advocated for "creating the conditions for Black Liberation through the abolition of systems and institutions of white supremacy, capitalism, patriarchy and colonialism."[15]

Yet corporate employees fear speaking up about the decency of America, against racial preferences, against racial separatism. When corporations began posting black squares on Instagram to signify support for

BLM, employees often did the same, seeking safety in symbolic virtue signaling. Failure to abide by the increasingly political diktats of the corporate overlords may risk your job.

What's more, everyone lives in fear of retroactive cancellation. It's not merely about you posting something your employer sees. It's about a culture of snitching, led by our media, that may out a ten-year-old Facebook post and get you canned from your job. In internet parlance, this has become known as "resurfacing"—the phenomenon whereby a person who doesn't like you very much finds a Bad Old Tweet and then tells your employer, hoping for a firing. It works. Resurfacing has become so common that NBC News ran a piece in 2018 guiding Americans on how to "delete old tweets before they come back to haunt you."[16]

All of which is a recipe for silence.

The nature of the business world requires adherence to top-down rules, the threat of expulsion, and fear of external consequences. Counterintuitively, then, the institutional pillar thought to guard most against the excesses of authoritarian leftism crumbled quickly and inexorably once the stars aligned.

And align they did.

THE CONFLUENCE OF INTERESTS

To understand the corporate embrace of authoritarian leftism, it's necessary to first understand a simple truth: corporations are not ideologically geared toward free markets. Some CEOs are pro-capitalism; others aren't. But all corporations are geared toward profit seeking. That means that, historically, corporate heads have not been averse to government bailouts when convenient; they've been friendly toward regulatory capture, the process by which companies write the regulations that govern them; they've embraced a hand-in-glove relationship with government so long as that relationship pays off in terms of dollars and cents. Government, for its part, loves this sort of stuff: control is the name of the game.

What's more, corporations are willing to work within the confines provided by the government—in particular, in limiting their own liability. Since the 1960s, the framework of civil rights had been gradually extended and expanded to create whole new categories of legal liability for companies. The Civil Rights Act and its attendant corpus of law didn't merely outlaw governmental discrimination—it created whole new classes of established victim groups that had the power to sue companies out of existence based on virtually no evidence of discrimination. Those companies, fearful of lawsuits and staffed increasingly by members of the New Ruling Class—people who agreed with the idea that society could be engineered in top-down fashion by a special elect—were all too happy to comply with the de rigueur opinions of the day. As Christopher Caldwell writes in *The Age of Entitlement*:

> Corporate leaders, advertisers, and the great majority of the press came to a pragmatic accommodation with what the law required, how it worked, and the euphemisms with which it must be honored. . . . "Chief diversity officers" and "diversity compliance officers," working inside companies, carried out functions that resembled those of twentieth-century commissars. They would be consulted about whether a board meeting or a company picnic was sufficiently diverse.[17]

Second, it's important to note that businesses cater to their customer base—and, in particular, their most passionate customer base. This provides a catalyst for renormalization via market forces: if enough customers can form an intransigent core, dedicated to one ideology, they can direct corporate resources toward appeasing them. Studies show that as we've become more polarized, more and more Americans now say they want their brands to make political stands. One research group found that 70 percent of American consumers say they want to hear brands' stands on social and political issues—this despite the fact that a bare majority of consumers say that brands only do so for marketing purposes. Some 55 percent of respondents claimed they would stop shopping with brands that didn't mirror their political preferences; another 34 percent said they would cut their spending to such brands.[18]

Such desire for politics from corporations resides almost solely with the Left. One study found that survey participants dinged a fake company, Jones Corporation, 33 percent for conservative politics, and said they were 25.9 percent less likely to buy its products, 25.3 percent more likely to buy from a competitor, and 43.9 percent less likely to want to work there. For companies perceived as liberal, no penalty accrued. As James R. Bailey and Hillary Phillips observed in *Harvard Business Review*, "That a company engaged in conservative or liberal political activity did not affect Republicans' opinions of that company, but it did for Democrats . . . the 33 percent drop in opinion with Jones Corps engaged in a conservative agenda was entirely driven by participants who identified as Democrats." In the end, consumers thought that companies being liberal was "merely normal business." Being conservative? That was punishable activity.[19]

Third, corporations seek regularity in their day-to-day operations. They seek to avoid controversy at nearly all costs—whether via legal liability, frustrated consumers, or even staffers. Concerns about trouble-some staffers used to manifest in what was called "the company man"—the man in the gray flannel suit, rigid in his outlook, cookie-cutter in his type. Conserva-tives and liberals alike used to fret about the enforced conformity of corporate life. But corporations have now discovered the magic of quaffing from the well of wokeism: by following the diktats of political correct-ness in hiring, they can escape censure for the "cor-porate culture." After all, they have Diversity™—an amalgamation of various people of different races, genders, heights, ages, and hair colors . . . all of whom think precisely the same way, and who raise holy hell if anyone different is discovered among them. Corporate heads are now petrified of their own woke staffers, and cater to their every whim. Where old-style bosses used to tell quarrelsome, peacocking employees to sit down at their desks or find themselves standing on the bread lines, today's bosses seek to comply with every woke demand, up to and including days off for mental health during politically fraught times.

Finally, all three of the aforementioned factors— the legal structures that provide liability for violating the tenets of political correctness; a motivated and politicized customer base; and authoritarian staffers unwilling to countenance dissent—mean that the true power inside corporations doesn't lie in their own hands at all: it lies with the media, which can manipulate all of the above. All it takes is one bad headline to destroy an entire quarter's profit margin. Corporations of all types are held hostage to a media dedicated to the proposition that the business world is doing good only when it mirrors their priorities. It isn't hard for a staffer to leak a lawsuit to *The New York Times*, which will print the allegations without a second thought; it isn't difficult to start a boycott campaign on the back of a clip cut out of context, and propagated through the friends of Media Matters; it isn't tough to generate governmental action against corporations perceived to violate the standards of the authoritarian Left.

And so corporations live in fear.

THE SECRET COWARDICE OF
CORPORATE DO-GOODERISM

That corporate fear used to manifest as unwillingness to court controversy. But as the authoritarian Left moved from "silence is required" to "silence is violence," corporations went right along. They declared themselves subject to the authoritarian Left structure—and were consolidated by the Borg. That's most obvious in corporate America's willingness to engage in every leftist cause, from climate change to nationalized health care to pro-choice politics to Black Lives Matter, on demand.

In fact, corporate leaders have determined that they will clap loudest and longest for the authoritarians, in the hopes that they will be lined up last for the guillotine. They know that capitalism is on the menu. They just hope that they'll be able to eke out a profit as the chosen winners of the corporatist game. Centuries ago, governments used to charter companies and grant them monopolies. Today, corporations compete to be chartered by the authoritarian Left, to be allowed to do business, exempted from the usual anti-capitalism of the Left. The only condition: mirror authoritarian leftist priorities.

Thus, in December 2020, NASDAQ, a stock exchange covering thousands of publicly traded companies, announced that it would seek to require those listed on its exchange to fulfill diversity quotas on their boards. According to the *Wall Street Journal*, NASDAQ told the Securities and Exchange Commission that it would "require listed companies to have at least one woman on their boards, in addition to a director who is a racial minority or one who self-identifies as lesbian, gay, bisexual, transgender or queer." Any company that did not do so would be called on the carpet by NASDAQ and made to answer for its lack of diversity or be subjected to delisting. Smaller companies would be hardest hit by the requirements, of course, but NASDAQ had no problem putting its boot on their neck. The New York Stock Exchange similarly set up an advisory council to direct "diverse" board candidates toward publicly traded companies. Goldman Sachs stated it would not help roll out initial public offerings for companies without a "diverse" board member. The civil rights movement that once sought to treat people by individual merit rather than group identity has been turned completely on its head—and corporations, which supposedly used to stand for the meritocracy, are pushing that moral inversion.[20]

Many are doing so under the guise of so-called stakeholder capitalism. In late 2020, Klaus Schwab, founder and executive chairman of the World Economic Forum, laid out his support for what he called "the Great Reset." Schwab explained in *Time* that the Covid pandemic had pushed forward a key question: "Will governments, businesses and other influential stakeholders truly change their ways for the better after this, or will we go back to business as usual?" Now, this was truly an odd question. Prior to the pandemic, the world economy was in the midst of a boom time. Unemployment rates in the United States had dropped to record lows; economic growth was strong. What, then, was the impetus for corporations "changing their ways for the better"? Indeed, what did "the better" even *mean*?

According to Schwab, the problem was free markets. "Free markets, trade and competition create so much wealth that in theory they could make everyone better off if there was the will to do so," wrote Schwab. "But that is not the reality we live in today." Free markets, he said, were "creating inequality and climate change"; international democracy "now contributes to societal discord and discontent." Yes, the time had come to move beyond the "dogmatic beliefs" that "government should refrain from setting clear rules for the functioning of markets," that "the market knows best."

Instead, Schwab recommended a "better economic

system" rooted not in doing the bidding of shareholders, but in acting in the interest of "stakeholders"— acting "for the public good and the well-being of all, instead of just a few." What would metrics of success look like? Not profitability. Oh no. The success of companies would revolve around their "gender pay gap," the diversity of their staff, the reduction of greenhouse gas emissions, the amount of taxes paid. Corporations would no longer be so low-minded as to focus on producing goods and services at the best possible price for the most possible consumers. Now corporations would be in the do-gooding business.[21]

This commitment to "stakeholder capitalism" versus "shareholder capitalism" has become increasingly popular in the business world. That's because it allows business leaders to retain control over the levers of power—they're Platonic philosopher-kings, sitting atop vast empires but acting for the benefit of the masses—without being answerable to lowly shareholders, those greedy investors who have actually put their own savings and faith into the company. Such nonsense is also pleasant to the ears of the authoritarian Left, which can now—with the permission of the business community, no less!—dump regulations and commitments on corporations in the name of the so-called public good. No wonder Joe Biden has called for "an end to the era of shareholder capitalism," suggesting his antipathy for the dreaded stock market.[22] And the US Business Roundtable agrees—in an August 2019 statement, they explained, "While each of our individual companies serves its own corporate purpose, we share a fundamental commitment to *all* of our stakeholders."

Putting shareholders second sounds kind and nice. It isn't. It's sinister. It's placing unnamed, uninvested interests in charge of corporations, and placing corporate heads in positions of untrammeled power—so long as they please the *true* powers that be: members of government, members of the press, and their politically like-minded peers. Capitalism creates wealth and prosperity for all because it is rooted in a fundamental truth: your labor belongs to you, and you have no right to demand the products of my labor without giving me something I want in return. Stakeholder capitalism doesn't create wealth or prosperity. It just traffics in unearned moral superiority, turning the engine of growth into a second quasi-government, unanswerable to those it is supposed to represent in the first place—and it simultaneously forwards the lie that corporations that *do* seek to do business alone are somehow morally suspect.

DESTROYING DISSENTERS

In October 2020, CEO David Barrett of Expensify, a corporation that specializes in expense management, sent a letter to all of the company's users. That letter encouraged them all to vote for Joe Biden. "I know you don't want to hear this from me," Barrett wrote, quite correctly. "And I guarantee I don't want to say it. But we are facing an unprecedented attack on the foundations of democracy itself. If you are a US citizen, anything less than a vote for Biden is a vote against democracy. That's right. I'm saying a vote for Trump, a vote for a third-party candidate, or simply not voting at all—they're all the same, and they all mean: 'I care more about my favorite issue than democracy. I believe Trump winning is more important than democracy. I am comfortable standing aside and allowing democracy to be methodically dismantled in plain sight.' "[23]

What were Expensify employees supposed to think of the letter? If they signaled their support for Trump, certainly they could expect to lose their jobs. But Barrett obviously didn't care. His politics were the right politics. His opponents were wrong.

Yet few concerns about the power imbalance between Barrett and his employees materialized. Instead, praise came pouring from the rafters.

In reality, Barrett wasn't taking a business risk in issuing this letter. He was doing the opposite. He was signaling that he and his company were members of the righteous coterie of right-thinking corporations.

Such signaling isn't merely done via external public relations. It's enforced in rigorous fashion internally. Employees are subjected to bouts of "diversity training" with "experts" like Robin DiAngelo, who maintain that white supremacy pervades all of American life; that it is impossible for members of victimized groups to be racist; that meritocracies are themselves representative of racist hierarchical thinking; that believing you aren't racist is excellent evidence that you're racist; that white women's tears are a form of racism; that racist intent is absolutely unnecessary in order to label action racist, since only impact and harm matter.[24] All it costs them is $20,000 a pop to both indoctrinate their workers into the requisite politics and to ensure against the possibility of a discrimination lawsuit![25]

This garbage is wildly ineffective. A controlled study of one diversity training course found that there was "very little evidence that diversity training affected the behavior of men or white employees overall—the two groups who typically hold the most power in organizations and are often the primary targets of these interventions."[26] Actually, diversity training tends to drive *more* anger and discrimination, because people don't like being told they are racists or that they must follow a set of prescribed rules in order to alleviate their supposed racism.[27]

But effectiveness isn't the point. Preventing blowback is the point—and creating an environment of conformity on controversial issues. And corporations pour billions into doing both. As of 2003, corporations were spending $8 billion per year on diversity efforts. And in America's biggest companies, the number of "diversity professionals" has increased dramatically over the past few years—by one survey, 63 percent between 2016 and 2019. Nearly everyone now has to sit through some form of indoctrination designed by the authoritarian Left—indoctrination that requires struggle sessions, public compliance with the new moral code, and kowtowing to false notions of racial essentialism. All of this is designed to cram down false notions of systemic privilege and hierarchy.[28]

Meanwhile, for those corporations that refuse to comply, the cudgel is available.

When Goya CEO Robert Unanue appeared at a Trump White House event to tout his work during the pandemic, leftists began a nationwide boycott. Something similar happened when LGBT activists targeted Chick-fil-A over founder Dan Cathy's support for traditional marriage, encouraging local Democratic politicians to try to stop the chain's expansion into their cities.[29] When billionaire investor Stephen Ross held a fund-raiser for Trump in 2019, leftists launched a boycott against Equinox and SoulCycle, both companies in which Ross had investments. Chrissy Teigen tweeted, "everyone who cancels their Equinox and Soul Cycle memberships, meet me at the library. Bring weights."[30]

No one would want to be Goya or Equinox. So when, in June 2020, leftist organizations including Color of Change, NAACP, ADL, Sleeping Giants, Free Press, and Common Sense Media called for Facebook advertisers to pause their spends to pressure Facebook into restricting content on its platform, more than a thousand companies complied. Those companies included the brands REI, Verizon, Ford, Honda, Levi Strauss, and Walgreens.[31]

And that's the goal for the authoritarian Left: to cow everyone into silence, except those who agree with them. Corporations generally survive boycotts— statistics demonstrate that most boycotts are wildly unsuccessful at removing revenue. But boycotts can impact the overall health of a brand, and can certainly generate sleepless nights for the companies targeted. As Northwestern Institute for Policy Research professor Braydon King argues, "The no. 1 predictor of what makes a boycott effective is how much media attention it creates, not how many people sign onto a petition or how many consumers it mobilizes."[32] Companies *hate* media attention they can't control. Which is why they so frequently apologize, back down, and beg for mercy.

Which, of course, only starts the cycle anew.

The purging of the public square has now reached epidemic proportions. All it takes is one bad story about your business to put you squarely in the authoritarian leftist cultural crosshairs. And it's now easier than ever to manufacture and spotlight such stories. In October 2020, Yelp—a site that allows members of the public to review businesses—announced that it would place an alert on a business if "someone associated with the business was accused of, or the target of, racist behavior." That means that if someone resurfaced a Trump-supporting post from a janitor, you could find yourself on the wrong end of a Yelp alert. And if there was "resounding evidence of egregious, racist actions from a business owner or employee, such as using overtly racist slurs or symbols," such evidence being "a news article from a credible media outlet," the business would be hit with a "Business Accused of Racist Behavior Alert." Yelp had now created a Stalinesque system of woke snitching, in which all it would take to forever destroy a business would be an account of racism about an employee, a twenty-two-year-old reporter looking for clicks, and an email address. Between May 26 and September 30, more than 450 alerts were placed on business pages accused of racist behavior related to Black Lives Matter alone.[33]

THE DEATH OF BUSINESS NEUTRALITY

The final consequence of corporate America going woke isn't merely internal purges—it's corporate America's willingness to direct its own resources against potential customers guilty of such heresy. As the authoritarian Left flexes its power, wielding pusillanimous corporations as its tool, those corporations will increasingly refuse to do business with those who disagree politically. The result will be a complete political bifurcation of markets.

In fact, this is already happening. In 2016, North Carolina passed a bill that would ensure separate bathroom facilities for men and women throughout the state, in contravention of a local Charlotte ordinance that would allow transgender people to access the bathroom of their choice. The business world reacted with universal outrage, and big business vowed not to do business *at all* in the state: PayPal dumped plans for a facility, as did Deutsche Bank; Adidas decided to hire in Atlanta rather than Charlotte; the NCAA vowed to cancel championship games; Bank of America CEO Brian Moynihan stated, "Companies are moving to other places, because they don't face an issue that they face here." According to the Associated Press, North Carolina was slated to lose some $3.75 billion over a dozen years if the state didn't dump the bathroom bill.[34] In March 2017, the bathroom bill was duly repealed.

The same pattern has held true in a variety of states. In 2010, businesses began boycotting Arizona after the passage of a law that allowed local law enforcement to enforce federal immigration law.[35] After Georgia passed a pro-life law, Hollywood production companies announced they wouldn't do business in the state—even while doing business in human-rights-abusing China.[36]

And corporations are beginning to target private citizens based on political belief, too. In August 2017, Visa and Discover announced they would not allow "hate groups" to process their credit card payments; PayPal, too, announced its app would be barred from use for those groups. MasterCard, by contrast, said it doesn't ban merchants "based on our disagreement with specific views espoused or promoted."[37] In February 2018, the First National Bank of Omaha dropped its National Rifle Association credit card, stating, "Customer feedback has caused us to review our relationship with the

NRA."[38] That same month, American Airlines and United Airlines announced they would pull all discount benefits for NRA members.[39]

In March 2018, Citigroup announced it would limit retail clients' firearm sales; one month later, Bank of America announced the bank would no longer give loans to manufacturers of guns for civilians. Leftist interest groups immediately began pressuring other major banks to do the same: American Federation of Teachers president Randi Weingarten said the union would not recommend Wells Fargo's mortgage lending program to its members because of ties to the gun industry.[40] In May 2019, Chase Bank began closing bank accounts for customers deemed radical, including Enrique Tarrio of the Proud Boys and radical activist Laura Loomer. Jamie Dimon, CEO of Chase Bank, said, "Very directly, we have not and do not debank people because of their political views."[41] For now, presumably.

This threat extends beyond the financial services industry. When Amazon Web Services, whose sole job is to provide cloud services, decides to deplatform Parler, that's polarizing. When Mailchimp, an email delivery service, refuses to do business with the Northern Virginia Tea Party, that's polarizing.[42] When PayPal announces that it uses slurs from the Southern Poverty Law Center to determine which groups to ban, that's polarizing.[43] When Stripe announces it will not process funds for the Trump campaign website after January 6, that's polarizing.[44]

The question here isn't whether you like any of these groups. The question is whether neutral service providers should be removing access to their business based on political viewpoint. The hard Left demands that religious bakers violate their religious scruples and bake cakes for same-sex weddings . . . and then turn around and cheer when credit card companies decide not to provide services for certain types of customers. There's a solid case to be made that private businesses should be able to discriminate against customers based on their right to association. But our corpus of law has now decided that such freedom of association is largely forbidden, unless it targets conservatives. Anti-discrimination law in most states bars discrimination on the basis of sex, sexual orientation, gender identity, religion, race, medical disability, marital status, gender expression, age, and a variety of other categories. But there is no anti-discrimination protection for politics. Since the Left is particularly litigious, this means that businesses are wary of avoiding business with anyone of the Left—but when it comes to the right, businesses have acted to protect themselves from rearguard attacks by the woke authoritarians.

The result will be two separate systems of commerce in the United States. We won't eat at the same restaurants. We won't go to the same hotels, theme parks, or movies. We won't use the same credit cards.

All of which makes it rather difficult to share a country.

THE MONOLITH

The chances are that you, the reader, know all of this already. That's because the chances are quite good that if you work, you're working for a giant company that's part of the authoritarian monolith. Decades ago, you probably would have worked for a company with fewer than 100 workers; today, you likely work for a massive company with rigorous, top-down policies that mirror the prevailing political notions of the day. According to *The Wall Street Journal*, nearly 40 percent of Americans now work for a company with more than 2,500 employees, and about 65 percent work for companies with more than 100 employees.

And the big companies are growing. The arenas in which big companies thrive—the services sector, finance, the retail trade—are also the fastest-growing areas in the American economy.[45] Unsurprisingly, these are also the areas in which employers are most likely to lean to the Left, or at least to mirror leftist priorities.

The Covid-19 pandemic has only exacerbated the advantage for large companies. Between March 2020 and September 2020, more than 400,000 small businesses closed. Meanwhile, big companies got bigger. As economist Austan Goolsbee wrote in *The New York Times*, "Big Companies Are Starting to Swallow the World."[46]

Small businesses are generally tied to the communities in which they exist—they know the locals, they trust the locals, and they work with the locals. Large companies cross boundaries of locality—they're national in scope and orientation. This means that they are far more concerned with enforcing a culture of compliance than in preserving the local diversity that typically characterizes smaller outfits. Large companies have huge HR departments, concerned with the liability that innately accrues to deep pockets; they have legislative outreach teams, concerned with the impact of government policy; they have corporate CEOs who are members of the New Ruling Class.

And there's something else, too. Entrepreneurs believe in liberty, because they require liberty to start their businesses. But as those businesses grow, and as managers begin to handle those businesses, managers tend to impose a stifling top-down culture. Managers prefer order to chaos, and rigidity to flexibility. And these managers are perfectly fine with the rigid social order demanded by the authoritarian Left.

Which means that our corporations aren't allies of free markets—or of the ideology that undergirds free markets, classical liberalism. They've now become yet another institutional tool of an ideology that demands obeisance. And so long as their wallets get fatter, they're fine with it. Better to lead the mob, they believe, than to be targeted by it.

There's only one problem: sooner or later, the mob will get to them, too.

Chapter 6
The Radicalization
of Entertainment

In September 2020—in the midst of the supposed racial "reckoning" sweeping the nation after the death of George Floyd—the Academy Awards announced it would shift the standards for its golden statuettes. No longer would films be selected on the basis of quality. Instead, studios would be given a choice of fulfilling one of four criteria. First, the film could itself contain certain woke prerequisites: either a lead or significant supporting actor from an "underrepresented racial or ethnic group"; or at least 30 percent of all actors in secondary roles would have to be from such a victim group or a woman or LGBTQ or have a disability; or the main story line would have to center on such an underrepresented group. Second, the film could be staffed by members of those underrepresented groups. Third, the film company could provide paid apprenticeship and internship opportunities for such victimized groups. Finally, those participating in the marketing could be from one of those victimized groups. Academy president David Rubin and CEO Dawn Hudson explained, "We believe these inclusion standards will be a catalyst for long-lasting, essential change in our industry."[1]

The standards were superfluous: Hollywood has long dedicated itself to the simple proposition that prestige pictures must fulfill leftist messaging requirements, and moneymakers must please the public. Sometimes prestige pictures *are* moneymakers. Generally, they aren't: superhero movies bring in the dollars, and *Moonlight* brings the critical plaudits. The last four Best Pictures winners are, in reverse chronological order, a morality tale about the evils of income inequality (*Parasite*); a morality tale about racism and homophobia (*Green Book*); a morality tale about the evils of the military, and discrimination against the disabled, blacks, homosexuals, communists, and fish (*The Shape of Water*); and a morality tale about racism and homophobia (*Moonlight*). None of this means all these movies are necessarily bad (although *The Shape of Water* is indeed one of the worst movies ever committed to film). It just means that Oscar voters aren't typical representatives of the American entertainment audience. It isn't difficult to handicap the odds of Oscar victory by tallying woke talking points beforehand.

But the Academy's new standards weren't about a change of heart. They were about ass covering. In 2015, on the back of massive racial unrest after the shooting of Michael Brown in Ferguson, Missouri, and the death of Freddie Gray in Baltimore, Hollywood's woke contingent began complaining that Hollywood had marginalized black creators. In 2015, the Academy hadn't nominated a single black actor in any of its categories. This, obviously, meant that Hollywood had to get woke. Thus the hashtag #OscarsSoWhite was born. Cheryl Boone Isaacs, president of the Academy, said that as soon as she saw the nominations, "my heart sank." Spike Lee later commented, "When black Twitter gets on your black ass . . . ooh, it ain't no joke." Ana Duvernay, who directed *Selma*—which was indeed nominated for Best Picture that year—said, "It was a catalyst for a conversation about what had really been a decades-long absence of diversity and inclusion."

Decades-long. Never mind that literally the year before, in 2014, *12 Years a Slave* had won Best Picture, Chiwetel Ejiofor had been nominated for Best Actor, Barkhad Abdi had been nominated for Best Supporting Actor, and Lupita Nyongo had won Best Supporting Actress. Never mind that *Selma* is, in fact, a rather mediocre movie. *Selma*'s lack of awards attention meant that discrimination had reared its ugly head.

And no dissent would be brooked. As Duvernay said, "I would do it all again. If you cannot be respectful of our alignment with that cause, with that protest, with that rallying cry, then there was nothing I wanted from you anyway."

Naturally, the Academy responded the next year with an emergency meeting and sought to radically shift the Academy membership through affirmative action directed at women and minorities. When other members of the Academy complained that political correctness had taken control of the institution—when, for example, Dennis Rice, a member of the Academy's public relations branch, explained that he was "color- and gender-blind when it comes to recognizing our art," and added, "You should look purely and objectively at the artistic accomplishment"—Boone Isaacs shot back, "Are you kidding me? We all have biases. You just don't see it if it doesn't affect you."

In 2017, *Moonlight,* a little-known film among audiences, revolving around a black gay man growing up in gang-infested Miami, won Best Picture. As Barry Jenkins, director of the film, said, "If *Moonlight* had come out three years earlier, I'm not sure how many people would have picked up that screener."[2]

Hollywood had embraced woke politics as the sine qua non for art.

And Hollywood would continue to chest-thump its own wokeness in spite of the evidence that Hollywood is, in many ways, insanely regressive.

Later that year, sexual abuse allegations against mega-producer Harvey Weinstein began to resurface. Hollywood celebrities began hashtagging #MeToo, pointing out the exploitation of women that ran rife through the industry. And they weren't wrong. The Hollywood casting couch—the sexist and disgusting practice by which females were subjected to sexual harassment and assault by powerful men in Hollywood in exchange for job advancement—had been a feature of the industry since the very beginning: the intersection of Hollywood and Highland featured, for years, a fiberglass structure widely known as the "casting couch" in town. But it was Hollywood's decision not to look internally but to pronounce judgment on the *rest of America* that spoke to the new wokeness. Instead of recognizing its own complicity in #MeToo, Hollywood celebrities began lecturing the rest of America about the country's inherent sexism.

The cause quickly morphed from the universally praised attempt to end sexual harassment and assault into broader left-wing talking points: criticism of the supposed gender pay gap, for example, or attempts to lecture Americans about heteronormativity. At the Oscars, Jimmy Kimmel—who used to star on a television show, *The Man Show*, featuring women bouncing on a trampoline, and who infamously wore blackface on Comedy Central—lectured America, "the truth is if we are successful here, if we can work together to stop sexual harassment in the workplace, if we can do that, women will only have to deal with harassment all the time at every other place they go." Magically, Hollywood was transformed from moral pariah to moral leader.[3]

It was merely an ironic shock, then, when the Oscars ended up canceling a black host, Kevin Hart, for violating woke tenets. After Hart was named the host of the 2019 Oscars, the woke internet went to work, digging up Bad Old Tweets™—in this case, a tweet from 2011 suggesting, "Yo if my son comes home & try's 2 play with my daughers doll house I'm going 2 break it over his head & say n my voice 'stop that's gay.'" In 2010, it turns out, Hart did a routine about how he would prefer his son not to be gay, too. Hart responded to the burgeoning scandal correctly: "Our world is becoming beyond crazy, and I'm not gonna let the craziness frustrate me . . . if you don't believe people change, grow, evolve as they get older, [then] I don't know what to tell you."[4] Within a few days, Hart announced he would be stepping down from the Oscars gig. He then kowtowed to the mob: "I'm sorry that I hurt people. I am evolving and want to continue to do so. My goal is to bring people together not tear us apart." When Ellen DeGeneres tried to encourage Hart to come back and do the show in January, even Ellen was slammed by the woke Left.[5]

With all that controversy, it was no shock when the Academy moved to formalize woke standards, largely as a preventative measure designed at buying time and space from the woke mob. Just as in the universities, the liberals gave way to the radicals.

HOLLYWOOD'S LONG HISTORY OF PREENING

More broadly, the Academy's move to formalize its heretofore-voluntary politics was merely the culmination of a long-lasting movement in Hollywood to propagandize on behalf of leftism, slap at flyover country, undercut traditional values, and excise those who disagree. Hollywood has been the preserve of political liberals for decades: the artistic community in the United States has typically leaned to the Left, a phenomenon that can be attributed to the counterculturalism that characterizes art itself. Pushing the envelope is often the name of the game in art, and in the United States—a traditional values country with a solid religious streak—the artistic community has historically bucked hard against traditional values. And when it comes to film and television, artistic media predominantly located in the echo chambers of New York and Hollywood, such attitudes are amplified radically. That echo chamber routinely reflects the self-absorbed notion of liberal elites that they have a monopoly on decency. As Allan Burns, co-creator of *The Mary Tyler Moore Show*, told me years back, "Writers have always had a social conscience. That's no surprise. I don't mean to sound arrogant about it, because I don't consider myself to be an intellectual, but I do consider myself to be a person who empathizes and thinks about what's going on in the world."[6]

Hollywood has long believed itself better than the common rabble.

That disconnect was evident early. The Hollywood films of the 1920s were so racy, for example, that local authorities began passing laws censoring theaters. Hollywood responded with the so-called Production Code, a set of standards meant to prevent films from promoting sundry moral no-nos of the time. The Production Code held, "No picture shall be produced which will lower the moral standards of those who see it. Hence, the sympathy of the audience should never be thrown to the side of crime, wrongdoing, evil or sin. . . . Law, natural or human, should not be ridiculed, nor shall sympathy be created for its violation."[7] By the 1960s, the American people had stopped boycotting films on the basis of Code violations, and adherence quickly collapsed. Television made a similar move during the 1960s, moving away from more values-oriented programming like *Bonanza* and toward politically oriented material like *All in the Family.* Hollywood both reflected and drove forward America's generalized move toward liberal causes. And as that liberalism set in, Hollywood closed itself to outside voices and creators: As Michael Nankin, producer on *Chicago Hope* and *Picket Fences,* told me, "People generally like to work with people they've worked with before or with whom they're comfortable. . . . And that mindset, which is entirely appropriate, makes it hard for new people to get in."[8] Fred Silverman, former head of NBC, ABC, and CBS, was blunter when I spoke with him a decade ago: "Right now, there's only one perspective. And it's a very progressive perspective."[9]

Hollywood is the land of liberal renormalization, the chief outlet for a political minority making emotional appeals to a broader country. As television's top creator Shonda Rhimes stated in her book, *Year of Yes*:

> I am NORMALIZING television. You should get to turn on the TV and see your tribe. . . . If you never see openly bisexual Callie Torres stare her father down and holler (my favorite line ever), "You can't pray away the gay!!!" at him . . . If you never see a transgender character on TV have family, understand, a Dr. Bailey to love and support her . . . If you never see any of those people on TV . . . What do you learn about your importance in the fabric of society. What do straight people learn?[10]

In 2017, she added, "I get really offended at the concept that what came out of the [2016] election was that—how do I say this?—impoverished people who are not of color needed more attention. . . . I don't think any [of the audience that watches my shows] are [Trump supporters], because I'm a black, Planned Parenthood–loving, liberal feminist."[11] So perhaps Rhimes should have explained that you should be able to turn on the TV and see your tribe . . . unless your tribe disagrees with Rhimes. In that case, your tribe will be represented by stand-ins for John Lithgow in

Footloose, glowering at the joy and wonder of liberal moral culture.

That attitude toward conservatives in both movie and television content is nothing new. Conservatives exist in dramas as foils for more open-minded and tolerant liberals; in comedies, they generally take the form of wrong-thinking incompetents. Occasionally, a stray libertarian may be portrayed as a cynical life guide (see, for example, Ron Swanson in *Parks and Recreation* or Jack Donaghy in *30 Rock*), but it is an absolute certainty that no mainstream television show or movie will ever portray an advocate for traditional marriage as anything but a bigot, or a thoroughly pro–life woman as anything but a sellout.

Why does this matter? It matters because, as my old mentor Andrew Breitbart used to say, culture is upstream of politics. Americans engage with the culture *far more* than with politics: political feeling is just the manifestation of underlying feelings people have about compassion and justice, about right and wrong. And *those* feelings are shaped by the cultural sea in which we all swim.

Netflix has 195 million global subscribers; Disney+ has over 70 million; Hulu has another 32 million. HBO Max has in excess of 30 million subscribers. Apple TV has over 42 million subscribers. Amazon Prime has over 140 million.[12] According to Nielsen, Americans over the age of eighteen spend at least four hours per day watching TV; they spend more than twelve hours a day on average engaged with TV.[13]

And that cultural sea is dominated by the Left, from top to bottom. There is a reason Netflix has green-lit a multiyear slate of projects from Barack and Michelle Obama;[14] that Obama administration alum and now Biden staffer Susan Rice was on the Netflix board;[15] that 98 percent of all donations from Netflix employees went to Democrats in 2016, and 99.6 percent in 2018;[16] that Netflix announced it would not invest in making film or television in Georgia if the state's pro-life law stood[17] (Netflix has no problem doing business with China, of course).[18] There is a reason Disney said it would have a tough time doing business in Georgia, too[19] (and yes, *Mulan* was filmed in Xinjiang, where the Chinese government has been stuffing Muslim Uighurs in concentration camps).[20] There is a reason that during the Black Lives Matters riots of summer 2020, Amazon Prime recommended left-leaning films and television to those who chose to log on. Hollywood is thoroughly leftist, and that is reflected from top to bottom. Its bias is inescapable.

The product is obvious: more people thinking along

leftist lines. A study from the Norman Lear Center found that conservatives watch far less television than either "blues" or "purples," and are also "least likely to say they have learned about politics and social issues from fictional movies or TV"; both "blues" and "purples" are more likely to discuss politics based on entertainment and to take action based on entertainment; 72 percent of all political shift measured since 2008, not coincidentally, was toward liberal perspectives. Naturally, the Lear Center concluded that television creators should place "more emphasis on raising awareness of discrimination and its profound social impact."[21]

But Hollywood's progressivism isn't enough. Not anymore. Not for the authoritarian Left. The Hollywood Left used to decry McCarthyism. Now they are its chief practitioners.

THE CANCEL CULTURE COMES FOR EVERYONE

Cancel culture is the order of the day in Hollywood. And you need not be a conservative to be canceled. The mere passage of time may subject you to the predations of the authoritarian leftist mob. It's become a truism to state that classics of the past simply wouldn't be made today—movies like *Airplane!* and shows like *All in the Family* would never make the cut. And that's obviously true. Hollywood studios regularly prescreen their shows for activist groups like the Gay and Lesbian Alliance Against Defamation; GLAAD brags that its media team "work closely with TV networks, film studios, production companies, showrunners, scriptwriters, casting directors, ad agencies, and public relations firms" to ensure "fair and accurate representation" of LGBT people. By "fair and accurate," GLAAD presumably means reflective of GLAAD's agenda.[22] It's unlikely that GLAAD would let slide any joke about sexual orientation.

In fact, most jokes are now off-limits. *The Office* retconned its own content, removing a scene in Season 9 in which a character wore blackface (never mind that the scene was about how insane and inappropriate it was to wear blackface). Executive producer Greg Daniels intoned, "Today we cut a shot of an actor wearing blackface that was used to criticize a specific racist European practice. Blackface is unacceptable, and making the point so graphically is hurtful and wrong. I am sorry for the pain that caused." Meanwhile, *Community* cut an entire episode from the Netflix library because an Asian character dressed in blackface, prompting a black character to fire back, "So, we're just gonna ignore that hate crime, uh?" Even *condemning* blackface is offensive now. Episodes of *Scrubs* and *30 Rock* were also disappeared.[23]

Movies of the past have been taken down to provide "context," most famously when HBO Max removed *Gone with the Wind* from its library, explaining that the film was "a product of its time" that contained "ethnic and racial prejudices" that were "wrong then and are wrong today."[24] Never mind that Hattie McDaniel, who was accused of embodying that prejudice in playing Mammy, became the first black actress to win an Oscar for her role. Disney+ has now updated old movies with a warning: "This program includes negative depictions and/or mistreatment of people or cultures. These stereotypes were wrong then and are wrong now. Rather than remove this content, we want to acknowledge its harmful impact, learn from it and spark conversation to create a more inclusive future together. Disney is committed to creating stories with inspirational and aspirational themes that reflect the rich diversity of the human experience around the globe." Movies tagged with this pathetic mewling include *Aladdin, Fantasia, Peter Pan, Lady and the Tramp, The Jungle Book*, and *Swiss Family Robinson*.[25]

And if content is perceived as un-woke—no matter how apolitical—it may be targeted for cancellation as well. In the midst of the Black Lives Matter protests and riots of 2020, the reality series *Cops* was canceled from Paramount Network after a thirty-one-year run—all because of fears that the show might show police officers in a positive context. The leftist activist group Color of Change cheered the decision, stating, "Crime television encourages the public to accept the norms of over-policing and excessive force and reject reform, while supporting the exact behavior that destroys the lives of Black people. *Cops* led the way. . . . We call on A&E to cancel *Live PD* next."[26] Days later, it was.[27]

It's not a matter of merely canceling shows or movies, either. Artists who cross the woke mob find themselves targeted for destruction. In July 2018, Scarlett Johansson dropped out of production on a movie titled *Rub and Tug*, about a transgender man. The radical Left suggested that *only* a transgender man could play a transgender man—a biological woman who did not identify as a man could not. Now, this is one of the most absurd contentions in human history: actors literally act like other people. And verisimilitude shouldn't have been an issue here: a biological human female was playing a biological human female who believes she is male. Yet the woke community decided it was better that the film, starring one of Hollywood's biggest stars, be canceled outright rather than starring a non-transgender person. Johansson duly performed her penance: "I am thankful that this casting debate . . . has sparked a larger conversation about diversity and representation in film."[28] This illogical proposition creates some awkward moments: when Ellen Page announced she was a transgender man, the series in which she stars, *Umbrella Academy*, announced it would be fine for "Elliot Page," a transgender man, to continue to play a non-transgender woman.

This puritanism regarding woke standards represents a serious career threat to comedians, who make their money off willingness to mock hard-and-fast rules. Hilariously, this has led to the specter of top comics tearing into the woke. After Sarah Silverman, a radical leftist, revealed that she had lost a film role thanks to a blackface sketch from 2007 (again, the sketch was about racism faced by black Americans), she tore into cancel culture: "Without a path to redemption, when you take someone, you found a tweet they wrote seven years ago or a thing that they said, and you expose it and you say, 'this person should be no more, banish them forever.' . . . Do we want people to be changed? Or do we want them to stay the same to freeze in a moment we found on the internet from 12 years ago."[29] Dave Chappelle has slammed cancel culture, calling it "celebrity-hunting season."[30] Bill Burr ranted on *Saturday Night Live*, "You know, how stupid is that 'canceled' thing? They're literally running out of people to cancel. They're going after dead people now."[31] Rowan Atkinson recently and correctly compared the cancel culture to the "digital equivalent of the medieval mob, roaming the streets, looking for someone to burn." He added, "It becomes a case of either you're with us or against us. And if you're against us, you deserve to be 'canceled.' "[32]

HOW HOLLYWOOD GOT RENORMALIZED

All of this raises a serious question: if woke culture quashes compelling entertainment, wrecks comedy, and generally makes entertainment worse, why cave to it? Why not simply make entertainment for the broadest possible swath of Americans?

The answer lies, once again, in renormalization. All it takes to renormalize an institution is a solid minority of intransigent, inflexible people: catering to that base, while preying on the innate compliance of the majority, can lead to a complete reorientation. That's precisely what's happened in Hollywood. Where Hollywood used to broadcast—emphasis on *broad*—searching for the biggest possible audience, they now narrowcast in order to appease the inflexible leftist coalition. Practically, this means catering to critics, who are near universal in their reflection of woke priorities; it also means superserving intransigent subsets of the audience, then counting on the rest of the audience to go along.

Hollywood critics are monolithically adherents to authoritarian leftism. This authoritarian leftism has infused film criticism to an extraordinary extent: films, if perceived as political, are no longer judged broadly on their merits. Instead, they're judged on checking woke boxes. RottenTomatoes—the one-stop-shop for movie criticism—demonstrates a clear bias in favor of leftist films.[33] For critics, RottenTomatoes' aggregation of opinion also exacerbates confirmation bias: critics don't want to stand out from the crowd. As Owen Gleiberman of *Variety* writes, "The sting of the pressure to conform is omnipresent."[34] When one *Variety* critic recently had the temerity to suggest that Carey Mulligan was miscast in the left-wing-oriented *Promising Young Woman*, *Variety* went so far as to tar its own critic as a crypto-misogynist and offer an *apology* for his review.[35] The top-down censorship of the authoritarian Left is in full swing among the critics. The goal isn't just silencing dissent, but forcing public confession and repentance.

There's a reason critics are, all too often, wildly out of touch with movie audiences. It's not rare for audiences to reject a film based on its lack of quality, but for critics to praise it to the skies for political reasons. For example, *Ghostbusters* (2016), the female-cast reboot of the original Bill Murray classic, met with tepid audience response—a 50 percent positive score among audiences on RottenTomatoes, and a brutal box-office run that cost the studio $70 million. That's because the film happens to be a mediocre piece of annoying crap. But according to critics, the movie was *important*—and it was important because it supplanted male leads with female leads. Megan Garber of *The Atlantic* wrote, "For a moment, it seemed, the future of women in Hollywood—and the future of feminism itself—would be riding on the shoulders of Paul Feig, Ivan Reitman, Melissa McCarthy, and some CGI-ed ghosts." And—surprise!—Garber found the movie to be "pretty great," balancing "ghosts and guns and gags and girl power."[36]

When critics come into conflict with audiences, there can be only one explanation: Americans are a bunch of bigots. So naturally, *Ghostbusters'* failure became evidence that Americans simply couldn't handle powerful females. And the film's failure was laid at the feet of these fans, who were merely frustrated manbabies incapable of expressing a thought about a mediocre film.

This phenomenon has been invoked over and over again to explain just why critics like movies the public often doesn't. If fans think that *Star Wars: The Last Jedi* was an incoherent mishmash of bad plotting, destruction of beloved and iconic characters, addition of new and boring characters, with a side plot of animal rights silliness, that's not because maybe they're right—it's because they are "toxic fans." If, in particular, *Star Wars* fans found Rose (Kelly Marie Tran) to be an absolutely superfluous and soporific character (she was), that was because they were racist and sexist. The critics spoke, and loved *The Last Jedi* (90 percent fresh); the audience spoke and hated it (42 percent fresh). Obviously, the audience was wrong. As Matt Miller of *Esquire* put it, *Star Wars* fans "have tragically become synonymous with hate, bigotry, and pervasive assholeness in 2018. . . . *The Last Jedi* inspired the worst impulses of a far-right movement that's taking hold of the internet and extending its influence into the real world."[37] Toxic fans can be used as a constant excuse for the fact that critics are out of touch with the unwashed masses.

Meanwhile, critics can be as toxic as they like with reference to work they perceive as insufficiently woke.

Dave Chappelle's *Sticks and Stones* comedy special took on cancel culture and wokescolding—so critics excoriated it, giving it a 35 percent fresh score, complaining that Chappelle had become "a man who wants it all—money, fame, influence—without much having to answer to anyone."[38] When Chappelle reverted to rants about the nature of systemic American racism, the critics reverted to type: "Can a comedy set win a Pulitzer? . . . theater at its most powerful,"[39] "not funny . . . but the comedian was in top form."[40] (Chappelle, it should be noted, survived in large measure because his entire shtick had been built around opposition to cancel culture.) When *Hillbilly Elegy* premiered, the critics savaged it (27 percent fresh)— not primarily because of its moviemaking, but because between 2016 and 2020, it became un-woke to take seriously impoverished white protagonists, or to champion the power of individual decision making. The movie review for *The Atlantic*, which deemed the film "one of the worst movies of the year," found it worthy of note that the original book, which sold several million copies, "often appears uninterested in interrogating deeper systemic issues."[41] Audiences, by the way, loved the film—the audience rating was 86 percent fresh on RottenTomatoes.

Critics help kill entertainment projects they oppose

politically. But most Americans don't sit around waiting for takes from the critics. The biggest factor cutting in favor of the woking of Hollywood, ironically enough, is the fragmentation of the market itself. For decades, the rule in Hollywood was to try to cater to the largest available audience—to *broad*-cast. The biggest tent-pole movies—think of the Marvel Universe—still do. But as the distribution mechanisms for entertainment fracture, it becomes more plausible to narrowcast toward particular audiences, or to cater to the most intransigent audiences. Narrowcasting automatically breeds renormalization.

Hollywood relies on conservative or apolitical Americans to ignore being offended, and superserves those most likely to raise a stink—or to consume products enthusiastically based on ideology. That's why Netflix has categories like "Black Lives Matter Collection" alongside "Drama," and announced just before launching the "Black Lives Matter" genre, "To be silent is to be complicit."[42] The industry is no longer about producing blockbuster films geared toward drawing massive audiences. It's about pleasing the loudest, cudgeling everyone else, and hoping nobody will tune out. Most of the time, that hope is justified. After all, it's not as though there are tons of conservative-friendly alternatives out there. Even if you're offended by Netflix mirroring the woke dictates of BLM, you can't exactly switch over to Hulu or Amazon: those companies put up their own propagandistic film categories designed to respond to America's racial "reckoning," and announced their own solidarity with Black Lives Matter.[43] Renormalization of Hollywood, combined with closing the door to dissent, has created an entertainment monolith.

HOW SPORTS WENT WOKE, THEN WENT BROKE

The radicalization of entertainment is most obvious in the context of sports. Sports is the ultimate broadcasting entertainment: it is designed to hit all subgroups. It's pure competition, merit against merit, winners and losers. The narratives are generally apolitical and the plot lines perfectly simple. Sports is about taking on the competition, muscling through adversity, working with teammates. Sports unifies.

Or at least it used to. Yes, politics played a crucial role in sports narratives—from Jackie Robinson breaking the color line in Major League Baseball to Muhammad Ali giving up his boxing career for refusing the Vietnam draft to the American Olympic hockey team defeating the Soviets. But once the game began, all exterior conflict was telescoped *into the sport*. Americans had strong rooting interests, often politically oriented, but the primary concern was the exhibition of skill *on the field.*

Sports leagues worked to keep politics off the field or court entirely. When Denver Nuggets star Mahmoud Abdul-Rauf refused to stand for the national anthem in 1996, NBA commissioner David Stern, a committed liberal, suspended him without pay. Rauf had violated a league policy requiring players and trainers to "stand and line up in a dignified posture."[44] When asked why he had remained apolitical in a contentious 1990 North Carolina Senate race, Michael Jordan explained, "Republicans buy sneakers, too." Years later, he explained, "I wasn't a politician when I was playing my sport. I was focused on my craft."[45]

This sentiment was considered relatively uncontroversial. But then something changed.

What changed was the renormalization along racial and political lines.

ESPN, the top sports channel on the planet by a vast margin, began losing money hand over fist. The network cleared cash in two ways: through advertising, which was viewer-reliant, and through carriage fees. Fully 75 percent of ESPN's money comes from cable and satellite subscribers; cable and satellite companies pay ESPN to carry the network. ESPN takes that money and pays sports leagues in order to carry *their* content.

Now, the vast majority of cable and satellite subscribers don't watch the vast majority of content on ESPN. So as people cut their cable and carriage fees dropped, and as other sports cable competitors got into the business and bid up the price of sports programming, ESPN found itself in a world of hurt. As sports journalist Clay Travis describes, "Its business model was under attack on two fronts. The cost of sports it rented and put on the air was surging just as its subscriber revenue was collapsing. . . . In 2011, at the height of its business, ESPN had 100 million subscribers. [By 2018], they'd lost 14 million subscribers."[46] ESPN responded by putting more hot talk, more cheap-to-produce, guaranteed-to-create-controversy hot takes on the air. As Travis points out, ESPN "was elevating the talent that most fervently connected left-wing politics and sports. Jemele Hill, Max Kellerman, Sarah Spain, Bomani Jones, Michelle Beadle, Pablo Torre— the more left-wing your politics, the more you got on television."[47]

This was a reflection of both the political culture of the sports journalists themselves, who voted overwhelming Democrat, and the desire to superserve a customer base that skewed disproportionately to the

Left. Demographic composition of fan bases varies widely based on the sport. NBA fans are disproportionately black, for example; NHL fans are disproportionately white. And ESPN spends a disproportionate amount of time on sports viewed by minority audiences. As of 2012, according to Deadspin, *SportsCenter* spent 23.3 percent of its coverage on the NFL, 19.2 percent of its time on the NBA, and just 2.1 percent of its time on NASCAR. Yet according to a 2015 Harris poll, just 5 percent of Americans said that basketball was their favorite sport, compared to 6 percent who said auto racing.[48] ESPN isn't skewing its coverage out of a weird sense of diversity, however—they're doing so because black Americans watch more TV than white Americans,[49] and have historically spent more money per capita on "visible goods" like footwear, clothes, cars, and jewelry.[50]

And superserving a disproportionately left-leaning population means catering to their political belief system—which just happens to reflect the values held by the higher-ups at ESPN. By catering to a small subsection of the population—a population that preferred its sports with a heavy dose of politics—the sports world renormalized itself around woke propositions.

Sports leagues began catering to their political audiences, allowing politics to spill over onto the field.

In 2014, a white police officer shot to death eighteen-year-old Michael Brown; Brown had assaulted the officer, attempted to steal his gun, fired it in the officer's car, and then charged the officer. Members of the media repeated the lie that Brown had surrendered to the officer with his hands raised. The slogan "Hands Up, Don't Shoot" became shorthand for the accusation that Brown had been murdered, and for the broader proposition that police across America were systematically targeting black Americans. And the sports world followed suit: five players on the St. Louis Rams walked out during the pregame introductions with their hands raised in the "Hands Up, Don't Shoot" pose.[51] The NFL quickly announced there would be no consequences, with NFL vice president Brian McCarthy explaining, "We respect and understand the concerns of all individuals who have expressed views on this tragic situation."[52] This wasn't out of a generalized respect for free speech values, however—it was about catering to wokeness. In 2016, after a Black Lives Matter supporter shot to death five police officers, the NFL rejected the Dallas Cowboys' request to wear a decal paying tribute to the victims.[53]

Over the course of the ensuing years, sports media's and leagues' embrace of on-field wokeness only increased. When Abdul-Rauf protested the national anthem, it was utterly uncontroversial for David Stern to suspend him. When Colin Kaepernick, after being benched as starting quarterback for the San Francisco 49ers in favor of the immortal Blaine Gabbart, decided to kneel for the national anthem in protest at the police shooting of armed stabbing suspect Mario Woods,[54] the media rushed to his defense. ESPN covered the millionaire Kaepernick as a hero, blanketing its network in worshipful praise for the benched QB, even as he declared that he would not "stand up to show pride in a flag for a country that oppresses black people and people of color."[55] The sports media then spent years propping him up as a civil rights icon. Eventually the quarterback, who had once donned socks depicting police officers as pigs, was given millions of dollars by Nike—also attempting to superserve leftist populations—in order to sell shoes with the slogan, "Believe in something. Even if means sacrificing everything." In reality, Kaepernick sacrificed nothing— he had already been benched when he made his protest, would later avoid even the most basic preconditions for rejoining an NFL team, and has cleared millions of dollars in advertising. Nonetheless, Kaepernick is now treated as a hero in the sports world; in 2020, the NFL itself tried to leverage a team into signing him. For good measure, EA Sports named Kaepernick a "starting-caliber" quarterback in its *Madden NFL 21* game, despite the fact that Kaepernick hadn't played for years and wasn't very good the last time he did.[56]

The politicization of sports had dire ramifications for its audience numbers. Ratings, which were already in recession, went into steep decline. The most popular league in America, the NFL, saw ratings declines of nearly 10 percent during the 2017 regular season.[57] ESPN saw such dramatic drop-off that ESPN president John Skipper, who had overseen the politicization of his network, admitted in late 2016, "ESPN is far from immune from the political fever that has afflicted so much of the country over the past year. Internally, there's a feeling among many staffers—both liberal and conservative—that the company's perceived move leftward has had a stifling effect on discourse inside the company and has affected its public-facing product. Consumers have sensed that same leftward movement, alienating some." Jemele Hill, an outspoken and censorious leftist, immediately shot back, "I would challenge those people who say they feel suppressed. Do you fear backlash, or do you fear right and wrong?"[58]

In 2018, Skipper was replaced by Jimmy Pitaro, chairman of its consumer products. He quickly admitted that ESPN had strayed from its core mission: "uniting people around sports." Pitaro stated, "We have to understand we're here to serve sports fans. All sports fans." ESPN's internal research showed that all fans, liberal and conservative, didn't want to hear politics on ESPN.[59]

But the network—and the leagues—had already been renormalized. It was simply too late to pull out of the tailspin. By 2020, after the killing of George Floyd in police custody resulted in nationwide protests, virtually every sports league *mandated* wokeness. The NBA festooned its sidelines with the phrase "BLACK LIVES MATTER"—a semantically overloaded phrase suggesting that America was irredeemably bigoted against black Americans. That was in and of itself a rather shocking contention coming from an 80 percent black league[60] in which the average salary is $7.7 million per season.[61] NBA players were told they could emblazon woke slogans on the back of their jerseys, limited to: Black Lives Matter, Say Their Names, Vote, I Can't Breathe, Justice, Peace, Equality, Freedom, Enough, Power to the People, Justice Now, Say Her Name, Si Se Puede, Liberation, See Us, Hear Us, Respect Us, Love Us, Listen, Listen to Us, Stand Up, Ally, Anti-Racist, I Am a Man, Speak Up, How Many More, Group Economics, Education Reform, and Mentor. Thus, it became a common sight to see Group Economics blocking Justice, and I Can't Breathe throwing up an alley-oop to Enough.[62] How any of this had anything to do with sports was beyond reasonable explanation. (The NBA's newfound commitment to political issues apparently stopped at calling America systemically racist—Houston Rockets general manager Daryl Morey was forced to apologize for tweeting "Free Hong Kong" as the Chinese government subjected that formerly free city to complete subservience. LeBron James, the most celebrated politically oriented athlete in America, called Morey "misinformed." After all, LeBron, Nike, and the NBA make bank in the Chinese market.)[63]

Major League Baseball opened its season with "BLM" stamped onto pitchers' mounds, universal kneeling before the national anthem, and Morgan Freeman voicing over, "Equality is not just a word. It's our right." The Tampa Bay Rays tweeted out, "Today is Opening Day, which means it's a great day to arrest the killers of Breonna Taylor"[64] (Taylor was accidentally killed during crossfire when police knocked on her apartment door to serve a no-knock warrant and were met by gunfire from her boyfriend inside). The NFL followed suit, with Roger Goodell admitting he was "wrong" by not overtly siding with Kaepernick in 2016,[65] and the league painting social justice warrior slogans in the end zones during games—phrases like "It Takes All of Us" and "End Racism."[66]

Racism, as it turns out, was not ended. But at least the leagues had pleased their most ardent customers.

Unfortunately for the leagues, there weren't that many of them anymore. The NFL's ratings dropped 10 percent in 2020;[67] the NBA Finals declined 51 percent year-on-year;[68] MLB's World Series was the least watched of all time.[69] To be sure, not all of that decline had to do with politics. Sports viewership dropped across the board due to the pandemic. But the long downward trend of sports as a unifying factor in American life continued at record rates in 2020.

CONCLUSION

When it comes to the politics of our entertainment, many Americans prefer to remain in the dark; better not to think about politics being pushed than to turn off the TV. The result: large-scale emotional indoctrination into wokeism, courtesy of censorious, authoritarian leftists in our New Ruling Class. Americans now float atop a tsunami of cultural leftism, from movies to television shows, from streaming platforms to sports games. And all of this has an impact. It removes an area of commonality and turns it into a cause for division. It turns the water cooler into a place of abrasive accusation rather than social fabric building.

We are told by our New Ruling Class that worrying about culture is a sign of puritanism. Meanwhile, they practice witch burning, insist that failure to abide by certain woke standards amounts to heresy, and use culture as a propaganda tool for their ideology and philosophy, renormalizing our entertainment in order to renormalize us. Our entertainment can reflect our values, but it can also shape them. Those in positions of power know this. And they revel in it.

If entertainment is where Americans go to take a breath—and if the authoritarian Left seeks to suck all the oxygen out of the room—we begin to suffocate. America is suffocating right now. And as our entertainment becomes more and more monolithic, less and less tolerant, more and more *demanding*, we become a less fun, less interesting, and less tolerant people.

Chapter 7
The Fake News

Authoritarian Leftism pushes revolutionary aggression; it calls for top-down censorship; it establishes a new moral standard whereby traditional morals are considered inherently immoral.

If there is one institution that has, more than any other, engaged in the cram-downs of the authoritarian Left, it is our establishment media. That media often cheers revolutionary aggression; participates in censorship of dissenting views, and seeks to have it cemented by powerful institutions; and promotes the notion that there is only one true moral side in American politics.

In the summer of 2020, that truth became crystal clear.

In response to the death of George Floyd while in police custody, massive protests involving millions of

Americans broke out in cities across America. Never mind that even the circumstances surrounding Floyd's death were controversial—the police had been called to the scene by a shop owner after Floyd passed a counterfeit bill, was heavily drugged on fentanyl, resisted arrest, asked not to be placed in the police vehicle, and was in all likelihood suffering from serious complicating health factors.[1] Never mind that there was no evidence of racism in the actual Floyd incident itself. The impetus for the protests was rooted in a false narrative: the narrative that America was rooted in white supremacy, her institutions shot through with systemic racism, that black Americans are at constant risk of being murdered by the police (grand total number of black Americans, out of some 37 million black Americans, shot dead by the police while unarmed in 2020, according to *The Washington Post*: 15).[2] That narrative has been pushed by the media for years, in incidents ranging from the shooting of Michael Brown (the media pushed the idea that Brown had surrendered while shouting "hands up, don't shoot," an overt lie) to the shooting of Jacob Blake (the media portrayed Blake as unarmed even though he was armed with a knife).

The narrative didn't just result in protests. It resulted in violence, rioting, and looting. In Los Angeles, my hometown, the city shut down its iconic Rodeo

Drive at 1 p.m. in the aftermath of looting.[3] Melrose Avenue was systematically looted as well, and police cars were left to the tender mercies of rioters, who promptly set them on fire and spray-painted them with the slogan "ACAB"—All Cops Are Bastards.[4] Looters attempted to break into the Walgreens a few blocks south of our home; a few blocks north of us, the Foot Locker was looted. For days on end, in the middle of a pandemic, the authorities informed law-abiding citizens to lock themselves in their homes at 6 p.m. Santa Monica and Long Beach saw looting as well. The *Los Angeles Times* labeled the events "largely peaceful."[5] Similar scenes took place in Washington, D.C., Chicago, and New York, where days of rioting resulted in "jarring scenes of flaming debris, stampedes and looted storefronts," according to *The New York Times*. Police officers were injured and hundreds were arrested. The *Times* labeled the events "largely peaceful."[6] So did *The Washington Post*, which used the hilarious phraseology "mostly peaceful displays punctuated by scuffles with police."[7] The media's desperate attempts to downplay the violence reached comical proportions, with reporter after reporter explaining that the protests were "mostly peaceful." Ali Velshi of MSNBC stood in front of a burning building while intoning, "This was mostly a protest, it is not generally speaking unruly, but fires have been started."[8] All of this came to its sadly hilarious culmination during riots in Kenosha, Wisconsin, in August: a CNN reporter stood in front of a flaming background, the chyron reading, "FIERY BUT MOSTLY PEACEFUL PROTESTS AFTER POLICE SHOOTING."[9]

Overall, the protests were "mostly peaceful" only in the sense that many protests took place that didn't break into explicit violence. But riots and looting related to the BLM movement cost somewhere up to $2 billion, making them the most expensive riots and civil disorder in American history.[10] The rioting hit some 140 cities.[11] At least 14 Americans died in violence linked to the BLM unrest[12]; more than 700 police officers were injured; at least 150 federal buildings were damaged.[13]

Many in the media went further than merely downplaying the violence: they fully excused it, cheered it, and justified it. They indulged their own Revolutionary Impulse. Now was a time to celebrate the revolutionary aggression inherent in their left-wing authoritarianism.

Nikole Hannah-Jones of *The New York Times* explained, "Destroying property, which can be replaced, is not violence."[14] She also cheered that some had termed the riots the "1619 Riots," in honor of her pseudo-history of the United States, *The 1619 Proj-*

ect.[15] "Nobody should be destroying property and that sort of thing, but I understand the anger," explained CNN's Don Lemon. "Our country was started . . . The Boston Tea Party, rioting. So do not get it twisted and think that 'Oh this is something that has never happened before, and this is so terrible, and these savages,' and all of that, that's how this country was started."[16] Fellow CNN anchor Chris Cuomo wondered, "Now, too many see the protests as the problem. No, the problem is what forced your fellow citizens to take to the streets: persistent, poisonous inequities and injustice. And please, show me where it says protesters are supposed to be polite and peaceful. Because I can show you that outraged citizens are what made the country what she is."[17] Harvard associate professor Elizabeth Hinton explained to *Time* that "rioting" didn't really capture the essence of the events—instead, the mob violence should have been termed an "uprising," since it "really captures the fact that the violence that emerges during these incidents isn't meaningless, that it is a political expression, and it is communicating a certain set of demands." *USA Today* printed an article tendentiously explaining, " 'Riots,' 'violence,' 'looting': Words matter when talking about race and unrest, experts say."[18] NPR printed the commentary of Marc Lamont Hill, who declared the riots "acts of rebellion."[19]

And the media didn't stop with mere rhetorical flourishes. The overall narrative—that America was evil, and that its police were systemically racist—led to practical efforts across the country to defund the police, cheered on by the media. Police officers, realizing that even a proper arrest, if effectuated by a white officer against a black suspect, could result in a media-led crusade against them and their departments, stopped proactively policing. As a result, thousands of Americans died in 2020 who simply wouldn't have died in 2019. As Heather Mac Donald observed in *The Wall Street Journal*, "The year 2020 likely saw the largest percentage increase in homicides in American history. . . . . Based on preliminary estimates, at least 2,000 more Americans, most of them black, were killed in 2020 than in 2019."[20]

The media's desperate attempts to portray the Black Lives Matter movement as both legitimate and nonviolent led them to legitimize both untruth and violence. So when the media—quite properly—expressed outrage at the insanity of the January 6 Capitol invasion, Americans with an attention span longer than that of a guppy could see the hypocrisy and double standard a mile off. The media, it seems, is fine with political violence when it is directed at one side.

When asked about their perfectly obvious shift from

riot-cheerleaders to riot-chastisers, members of the media have reacted with pure outrage. To even compare the media's tolerance for BLM violence rooted with their rage over January 6 meant that you were engaging in intellectual hypocrisy. Anyone who pointed out the double standard was hit with the charge of "whataboutism," even though the entire basis for the double standard accusation was *condemnation of violence across the board*—condemnation in which the media had refused to engage itself.

CNN's Lemon, for example, sputtered, "I'm sick of people comparing, you can't compare what happened this summer to what happened at the Capitol. It's two different things. One was built on people, on racial justice, on criminal justice, right, on reform, on police not beating up—or treating people of color differently than they do Whites. OK? That was not a lie. Those are facts. Go look at them."[21] Lemon presented no such facts. But his opinion was good enough. After all, Lemon says that he has "evolved" as a journalist:

Being a person, a black man—let's put it this way: being an American who happens to be Black, who happens to be gay, from the south, I have a certain lens that I view the world through and that's not necessarily a bias. That's my experience . . . if

I can't give my point of view, and speak through the experiences that I have had as a man of color who has lived on this earth for more than 50 years, who happens to have this platform, then when am I going to do it? I'd be derelict in my duty as a journalist and derelict in my duty as an American if I didn't speak to those issues with honesty. . . . I think, in this moment, journalists realize that we have to step up and we have to call out the lies and the BS and it has nothing to do with objectivity.[22]

Lemon's statement encapsulates the media's breathtaking dishonesty. On the one hand, media members want to be free to express their politics in their journalism, which would cut directly against their purported objectivity. On the other hand, they want to maintain the patina of objectivity so as to maintain an unearned moral superiority over supposed partisan hacks on the other side. How can today's pseudo-journalism—or those who engage in Journalisming™, as I often term it—square this circle? They simply do what Lemon does: they suggest that their opinions are actually reflections of fact, that those who disagree are dishonest, and that objectivity doesn't require you to listen to other points of view or report on them. Journalists make themselves the story—and if you doubt them, you are anti-truth and anti-journalism.

This skewing of journalism makes its purveyors, quite literally, Fake News. They pretend to be news outlets but are actually partisan activists. It would be difficult to find a single bylined staffer at *The New York Times* who voted for Donald Trump. The same holds true at *The Washington Post.* Certainly, CNN, MSNBC, ABC News, CBS News, the *Los Angeles Times,* the Associated Press—none of them are hot-beds of Republican activity. According to a 2020 report in *Business Insider,* a survey of political donations from establishment media members found that 90 percent of their donated money went to Democrats (the survey included names from Fox and the *New York Post*).[23] In 2013, a survey of journalists showed that just 7 percent identified as Republican. And by 2016, according to *Politico,* "more than half of publishing employees worked in counties that Clinton won by 30 points or more," with just 27 percent of employees working in a red district. As Jack Shafer and Tucker Doherty acknowledged, "On such subjects as abortion, gay rights, gun control and environmental regulation, the *Times*' news reporting is a pretty good reflection of its region's dominant predisposition. . . . Something akin to the *Times* ethos thrives in most major national newsrooms found on the Clinton coasts." Our Journalisming™ superiors don't just occupy a bubble. They occupy an isolation tank.[24]

Americans aren't blind. They distrust the media for a reason. Members of the media frequently blame Trump for endemic American mistrust of the fourth estate. They neglect the simple fact that Americans, particularly on the right, had justified trust issues long before Trump ever rose to prominence in politics. In 2013, for example, only about 52 percent of Americans trusted traditional media. Today, that number is 46 percent; only 18 percent of Trump voters trust the media, compared with 57 percent of Biden voters. Six in ten Americans believe "most news organizations are more concerned with supporting an ideology or political position than with informing the public."[25]

They happen to be correct. The only real question is why four in ten Americans still believe in the veracity of a media that openly disdains—and often seeks to target—one entire side of the American political conversation.

THE RISE AND FALL OF
MEDIA OBJECTIVITY

From the outset, the American press has been a contentious lot, vying for supremacy and arguing passionately about right and wrong. The notion of a political objectivity in journalism would have seemed bizarre to the Founding Fathers: Thomas Jefferson employed journalist James Callendar to muckrake on behalf of his favored causes and to undermine his enemies.[26] For well over a century, newspapers openly identified with political parties. The era of yellow journalism was markedly free of concerns about objectivity. Only in the aftermath of World War I, with America's intelligentsia falling out of love with democracy itself, did the press begin to conceive of itself as "objective"—as guardian of a unique fact-finding process that could provide audiences with information beyond the realm of political debate.

Leading the charge for "objectivity" was *New Republic* editor Walter Lippmann. Lippmann began life as a progressive activist, a political critic of "the old individualism, with its anarchistic *laissez-faire*," an advocate of Great Leaders "acting through the collective will of the nation." Lippmann disdained "Georgia crackers, poverty-stricken negroes, the homeless and helpless of the great cities," and called for a "governing class." He fretted about the ability of those who disagreed to peddle dissenting ideas—after all, they might be leading the public astray: "Without protection against propaganda, without standards of evidence, without criteria of emphasis, the living substance of all popular decision is exposed to every prejudice and to infinite exploitation." The solution to all of this, Lippmann decided, was to curb free expression in favor of "freedom from error, illusion, and misinterpretation." To this end, Lippmann proposed the notion of journalistic objectivity, explaining that editors were to act as a priestly caste—newspapers were, said Lippmann, "the bible of democracy."[27]

To achieve this objectivity meant shifting the notion of what a journalist *was*. Instead of the sardonic, chain-smoking, flattened-hat-type working the streets, journalists were now transformed into scientific specialists, inculcated in the latest methods, protected from the heresies of the hoi polloi. Many in the press began to see themselves as a class apart; they viewed the freedom of the press guaranteed by the Constitution not as a guarantee that government refrain from infringing on Americans' right to engage in reporting and public debate generally, but as a *specific* protection for a *specific and special group*—people who have the title "reporter" next to their bylines, who work for certain prestigious publications.

Lippmann's idea of regularizing a journalistic process wasn't bad, of course: facts do exist, and we should use rational, scientific methods to suss them out. Where Lippmann went wrong was in assuming that journalists wouldn't use their newfound sense of superiority to *re-embrace* their bias, while presenting themselves as "objective."

And that's precisely what happened. Establishment institutions declare themselves objective, and thus trustworthy. But in reality, sometimes partisan hacks can print truth, and self-appointed "objective" outlets can print lies; "objective" journalists can lie through omission, favor allies through contextualization, focus on stories most flattering to their own political priors. Bias is simply inseparable from journalism. Some journalists do a better job than others at attempting to remove their own biases from the stories they cover. Virtually all fail—and over the past few years, they have begun to fail more and more dramatically. The establishment media's slavish sycophancy for Barack Obama, followed by their rabidly rancorous coverage of Donald Trump, followed again by their absurd ass kissing for Joe Biden, has ripped the mask away.

Lippmann insisted on at least a façade of nonpartisanship, despite his own elitism: "Emphatically [the journalist] ought not to be serving a cause, no matter how good. In his professional activity it is no business of his to care whose ox is gored. . . . As the observer of the signs of change, his value to society depends upon the prophetic discrimination with which he selects those signs."[28] Our New Ruling Class journalists don't bother. These journalists argue that they are actually *better* journalists than the forebears who attempted to provide a variety of viewpoints in any controversy. *Real* journalists, they say, don't engage in "false balance"— meaning, respect for a side other than their own. *Real* journalists, they say, bring their own experiences to bear. *Real* journalists, they say, are crusaders rather than passive observers.

Real journalists are activists. *Real* objectivity is allegiance to refracting facts through the prism of leftism.

The mask is off.

In 2014, *The Washington Post*'s Wesley Lowery found himself under arrest in a McDonald's during the Ferguson, Missouri, riots in the aftermath of the shooting of eighteen-year-old Michael Brown by Officer Darren Wilson. He claimed that he had been a victim of police brutality; the police claimed that Lowery had trespassed and refused orders to clear an area from the police.[29] Lowery's perspective on endemic American racism was obvious. Later, he would write about Ferguson that reporting on the details of the shooting itself was irrelevant—instead, the media should have focused on the broader narrative, contextualizing the riots and violence by referring to America's history of racial discrimination.[30]

Lowery was an opinionated fellow, and routinely took to Twitter to disparage his critics. In fact, Lowery's Twitter habit eventually ended with *Washington Post* editor Marty Baron threatening to fire him; Lowery had tweeted that the Tea Party was "essentially a hysterical grassroots tantrum about the fact that a black guy was president." Baron suggested that Lowery ought to work for an advocacy organization or write an opinion column. Lowery eventually quit, complaining, "Should go without saying: reporters of color shouldn't have their jobs threatened for speaking out about mainstream media failures to properly cover and contextualize issues of race. What's the point of bringing diverse experiences and voices into a room only to muzzle them?"[31] Lowery ended up at CBS News.

Lowery is now widely viewed as the future of mainstream journalism. In June 2020, Ben Smith of *The New York Times* observed, "Mr. Lowery's view that news organizations' 'core value needs to be the truth, not the perception of objectivity,' as he told me, has been winning in a series of battles, many around how to cover race . . . The shift in mainstream American media—driven by a journalism that is more personal, and reporters more willing to speak what they see as the truth without worrying about alienating conservatives—now feels irreversible." Lowery believes that the "American view-from-nowhere, 'objectivity'-obsessed, both-sides journalism is a failed experiment. We need to rebuild our industry as one that operates from a place of moral clarity."[32]

Of course, moral clarity is generally a matter of opinion. When you maintain that your opinion is fact, and then declare yourself an objective news source *rooted in that opinion,* you are a liar. And our media are, all too often, liars.

THE MEDIA'S WOKE INTERNAL RENORMALIZATION

The religious wokeness that infuses our newsrooms is enforced daily. It turns out that "moral clarity" often looks a lot like the Spanish Inquisition. Nobody expects it. But at this point, everybody should.

The battles in America's newsrooms these days aren't between conservatives and liberals. As we've seen, there *are* no conservatives at most establishment media outlets. The battle is truly between authoritarian leftists and liberals—between people who may largely agree on policy preferences, but who disagree on whether robust discussion should be allowed. The authoritarian Left argues no. The liberals argue yes. Increasingly, the authoritarian leftists are successfully wishing the liberals into the cornfield—or at least intimidating them into dropping any pretense at bipartisanship. The authoritarian Left is only tangentially interested in canceling individual conservatives who occasionally write for liberal outlets. Their true goal is to browbeat liberals into *preemptively* canceling conservatives, thus establishing a total monopoly, assimilating liberals into the woke Borg or extirpating them.

That's what *New York Times* op-ed editor James Bennet found out the hard way when he had the temerity to green-light a column from sitting senator Tom Cotton (R-AR). Cotton's column, written in the midst of the BLM riots, suggested that President Trump invoke the Insurrection Act and use the National Guard to quell violence if state and local officials failed to do so. Not only was this a plausible argument—the argument would later be used by those on the Left to call for more federal presence in Washington, D.C., following the January 6 riots—but at the time, Cotton's comments were considered not merely foolhardy, but *dangerous*. Dangerous, as we know, is one of the predicates used by political opponents to stymie dissent: if your words pose a "danger" to me, they must be banned.

That's precisely what *New York Times* staffers claimed: that because of Cotton's op-ed, they were now under existential threat. This made no sense, given that *Times* staffers presumably weren't engaged in rioting. But the mere idea that law enforcement ought to crack down on violent activity was enough to send these woke staffers into spasms of apoplexy. Staff writers including Jenna Wortham, Taffy Brodesser-Akner, and Kwame Opam tweeted the same message: "Running this puts Black @NYTimes staff in danger." Reporter Astead Herndon messaged out support for coworkers, "particularly the black ones." Columnist Charlie Warzel tweeted, "I feel compelled to say that I disagree with every word in that Tom Cotton op-ed and it does not reflect my values." The company's Slack channel blew up with staffers whining over their discomfort.

Initially, Bennet defended the move. He tweeted that while many opinion writers and the editorial board had defended the protests and "crusaded for years against the underlying, systemic cruelties that led to these protests," the newspaper "owes it to our readers to show them counter-arguments, particularly those made by people in a position to set policy."[33] Within three days, Bennet resigned, with publisher A. G. Sulzberger blaming a "significant breakdown in our editing process," without noting any actual problems with the Cotton piece. Bennet didn't leave without a Maoist struggle session—he apologized to the staff. The newspaper added an editorial note to the Cotton piece suggesting that it carried a "needlessly harsh tone"[34]—a bizarre accusation coming from a newspaper that routinely prints the vile, vitriolic, woke word vomit of columnists ranging from Paul Krugman to Charles Blow to Jamelle Bouie. This was a full authoritarian leftist defenestration: revolutionary aggression against the powers that be; top-down censorship; and a sense of moral superiority.

Bennet's ouster was merely the latest shot in the ongoing war to oust traditional liberals from positions of power—or to cow them into silence. In March 2018, *The Atlantic* hired iconoclastic *National Review* columnist Kevin Williamson. When Jeffrey Goldberg, editor of *The Atlantic*, hired Williamson, he informed Williamson that he'd stand by him—he even defended Williamson publicly by stating that he would not judge people by their "worst tweets, or assertions, in isolation." That stance lasted just a few days. Goldberg backtracked after staffers told Goldberg they felt threatened by Williamson's pro-life viewpoint, expressed in jocular fashion on a podcast. "[T]he language used in the podcast was callous and violent," said Goldberg. "I have come to the conclusion that *The Atlantic* is not the best fit for his talents, and so we are parting ways."[35] Goldberg, the supposed liberal, became yet another tool of the authoritarian Left, unwilling to challenge their dominance, even at the risk of editorial self-castration.

Something similar happened at *Politico* when that publication asked me to guest-host its prestigious *Playbook* in late December 2020. The publication was, an editor explained, having a series of guest editors including MSNBC's Chris Hayes, PBS's Yamiche Alcindor, and CNN's Don Lemon, among others. I thought the project might be fun. But, as always, I warned the editor that the blowback he received would be immense.

My day to write the *Playbook* fell the day after Trump was impeached for the second time in the House of Representatives. I wrote about the generalized Republican unwillingness to vote to impeach, and explained that unwillingness by pointing to the belief by most conservatives that impeachment was merely a way of lumping together Trump supporters more broadly with the Capitol rioters: conservatives correctly saw impeachment as merely the latest club for the Left to wield against an opposing political tribe.

The blowback was, predictably, immense. Within minutes, *Politico* was trending on Twitter. Within hours, *Politico* leadership was hosting a conference call for some 225 staffers enraged over my name sullying the sacred *Playbook*.[36] Some of those participants compared me to Alex Jones and David Duke, adding that to print my words cut against their journalistic mission—which was to shut me up. "I'm spending all this time trying to convince them that we're here for them, and that there's a difference between what Ben Shapiro is doing and what Alex Jones is doing and what Politico is doing," one *Politico* staffer fumed. "I don't even know how to go tell them now not to listen to Ben Shapiro because we published Ben Shapiro."[37] Two weeks later, the staff at *Politico* was still fuming. More than one hundred staffers wrote a letter to the publisher, demanding an explanation for why I had been platformed.[38]

Most of the establishment media agreed: as Erik Wemple of *The Washington Post* sneered, "You know, if you want to hear Shapiro's opinions, there's a place to go for that."[39] Karen Attiah wrote in *The Washington Post* that platforming me in *Politico* granted legitimacy to white supremacy, and called it "willful moral malpractice," adding, "I am reminded that in this country White people once gathered to watch the public lynching of Black people, and even made souvenir postcards of the events. I am reminded that, in America, White racism against minorities is titillating, not disqualifying—because it is profitable."[40] Less than three months before writing those words, Attiah was joking with me on Twitter about grabbing drinks and finding new common ground.

She couldn't have proved my point better.

Now, this little hubbub had no effect on me. I *do* have an outlet, with extraordinarily high traffic. But the goal of such public shaming rituals is to prevent adventurous editors from even conversing with conservatives. And, as it turns out, that's precisely what happened: I later found out that Guy Benson and Mary Katherine Ham, both mainstream conservatives who had been asked to guest-write the *Playbook* after me, were ghosted by the editors. In effect, they were preemptively canceled.

Liberals are being ousted or cowed into submission across the media.

The same week James Bennet resigned, Stan Wischnowski, top editor of the *Philadelphia Inquirer*, stepped down from his position for the great sin of having published an op-ed titled "Buildings Matter Too," complaining about BLM rioting and looting. The *Inquirer*'s editors issued a groveling apology, mewling,

"We're sorry, and regret that we [printed it]. We also know that an apology on its own is not sufficient." That apology followed staff members calling in sick to protest the editorial, and issuing an overwrought letter stating, "We're tired of being told of the progress the company has made and being served platitudes about 'diversity and inclusion' when we raise our concerns. . . . We're tired of being told to show both sides of issues there are no two sides of."[41]

One month later, as the fallout from the BLM purge continued, opinion writer and editor Bari Weiss, a traditional liberal, resigned from *The New York Times*. Her parting letter was a Molotov cocktail tossed in the middle of the *Times* editorial structure. Weiss stated that she had been hired to usher in a variety of viewpoints to the *Times*, but that the newspaper of record had surrendered to the woke. At the *Times*, Weiss wrote, "truth isn't a process of collective discovery, but an orthodoxy already known to an enlightened few whose job is to inform everyone else." Calling Twitter the "ultimate editor" of the paper, she tore into her colleagues—colleagues who had labeled her a Nazi and a racist, and some of whom had publicly smeared her as a bigot. "[I]ntellectual curiosity," Weiss wrote, "is now a liability at *The Times* . . . nowadays, standing up for principle at the paper does not win plaudits. It puts a target on your back." Weiss concluded, "The paper of record is, more and more, the record of those living in a distant galaxy, one whose concerns are profoundly removed from the lives of most people."[42]

The newspaper's lack of defense for Weiss stood in stark contrast to its vociferous defense of woke authoritarian leftist thoughtleader Nikole Hannah-Jones, creator of the *1619 Project*. That effort billed itself as a journalistic attempt to recast American history—to view the country as being founded not in 1776 but in 1619, the year of the first importation of an African slave to North American shores. That idea was in and of itself egregiously flawed: America was founded on the principles of the Declaration of Independence. While chattel slavery was a deep, abiding, and evil feature of America during that time and before—as it was, unfortunately, in a wide variety of countries around the world—it did not provide the core of America's founding philosophy or institutions. But the *1619 Project* not only insisted that slavery lay at the center of America's philosophy and that its legacy inextricably wove its way into every American institution—it lied outright in order to press that falsehood forward. The project compiled a series of essays blaming slavery and endemic white supremacy for everything from traffic patterns to corporate use of Excel spreadsheets to track employee time.

Then there were the blatant errors, ignored or defended by the *Times*. Five historians, including Pulitzer Prize winner James McPherson and Bancroft Prize winner Sean Wilentz, as well as famed founding-era historian Gordon S. Wood, wrote a letter to the *Times* blasting the accuracy of the project, including its mischaracterizations of the founding, Abraham Lincoln's views of black equality, and the lack of support for black rights among white Americans. The historians asked that the *Times* correct the project before its distribution in schools.[43] Hannah-Jones then derisively referred to McPherson's race in order to dismiss the criticism. Jake Silverstein, editor in chief of the *New York Times Magazine*, then acknowledged that "we are not ourselves historians," but added that Hannah-Jones "was trying to make the point that for the most part, the history of this country has been told by white historians."[44] Similarly, historian Leslie Harris of Northwestern University wrote that she had warned Hannah-Jones that her contention that the American Revolution was fought in large part to preserve slavery was simply false. Hannah-Jones and the *Times* ignored her.[45]

In the end, after the *Times* spent millions of dollars to publicize the *1619 Project*, the Pulitzer Prize committee gave the pseudo-history its highest honor. After all, the narrative had been upheld, and its critics chided. When the *Times* printed a piece from its own columnist Bret Stephens critical of the *1619 Project* in October 2020, the publisher of the newspaper weighed in to call the project a "journalistic triumph that changed the way millions of Americans understand our country, its history and its present," and called the project "one of the proudest accomplishments" of the *Times* generally. *The New York Times* guild actually attacked Stephens personally, stating that "[t]he act, like the article, reeks."[46] Hannah-Jones is currently in a development deal with Oprah Winfrey and LionsGate to develop the *1619 Project* into multiple feature films, TV series, and documentaries.[47]

JOURNALISTS AGAINST FREE SPEECH

Authoritarian leftists often claim that "cancel culture" isn't real—that deplatforming isn't a problem, because conservatives and traditional liberals can simply present their ideas elsewhere. That argument is the height of gaslighting. It also happens to be utterly specious on its face: it is indeed a cancellation to be barred from participation in the most widely read outlets thanks to dissent. But consigning conservatives and traditional liberals to non-establishment outlets has a rather unfortunate side effect for the authoritarian leftists: conservatives and traditional liberals begin consuming nontraditional media at record rates. In the days when the media had a monopoly on the distribution of information—three TV networks, a few national print newspapers—cleansing conservatives would have been the end of the story. But with the rise of the internet, podcasts, and cable news, conservatives have been able to construct media of their own. Websites like the Daily Wire generate enormous traffic *because* the media have silenced conservative voices.

And so the authoritarian leftists must go one step further: they must destroy conservative and traditional liberal voices *outside traditional media.* They first force those they hate into ideological ghettos. Then, when it turns out the ghettos create their own thriving ecosystem, they seek to level them.

To that end, our journalistic New Ruling Class have become full-scale activists. Instead of reporting on the news, they generate it by working with activist groups to motivate advertisers, neutral service providers, and social media platforms to downgrade or drop dissenting media. They claim that the very presence of conservative ideas in the public square ratchets up the possibility of violence—and then they seek to blame advertisers, neutral service providers, and social media platforms for subsidizing the unwoke or allowing them access to their services. When that fails, they call for outright government regulation of free speech. The Founding Fathers would have been astonished to learn that the greatest advocates for curbing free speech in the United States are now members of the press.

The authoritarian leftist activist journalists pick their targets well.

They begin with advertisers. For nearly two decades, Media Matters, a pathetic hit group started by unstable grifter David Brock and backed by Hillary Clinton's team, has spent every waking minute monitoring conservative media for opportunities to push advertiser boycotts. That generally involves cutting conservatives out of context, then letting media allies know about those out-of-context quotes, spinning up controversy—and then creating a fake groundswell of outrage directed at advertisers, who generally wish to be left alone. The tactic has been sporadically successful when directed at hosts ranging from Rush Limbaugh to Sean Hannity to Tucker Carlson, and over time other groups have joined in the game as well. Major media outlets routinely use Media Matters as a source for coverage;[48] an ex-employee of Media Matters bragged in February 2012 that the activist group was "pretty much writing" MSNBC's prime time, and coordinating with *The Washington Post's* Greg Sargent, and reporters from the *Los Angeles Times,* *Huffington Post,* and *Politico,* among others. (Media Matters also reportedly held weekly strategy calls with the Obama White House communications director, and now Biden chief spokeswoman, Jen Psaki.)[49]

Members of the media don't merely crib off of Media Matters' out-of-context clips—they then target advertisers, asking them why they are continuing to spend their dollars with conservatives. Naturally, such questions aren't designed to elicit a response. They're designed to elicit a cancellation of the advertising dollars. And the media cheer when they start an advertiser cancellation cascade against a conservative. Their glee is fully evident.

Members of establishment media cheer on this tactic. In fact, they go further: they call for anyone who provides services to the unwoke to stop doing so. They call for Comcast to stop carrying Newsmax, One America News, and Fox News. Nicholas Kristof of *The New York Times* recently wrote that in order to dampen the extremism of the Republican Party, "advertisers should stop supporting networks that spread lies and hatred, and cable companies should drop channels that persist in doing so. As a start, don't force people to subsidize Fox News by including it in basic packages." Sure, Kristof acknowledged, this could create a slippery slope. But the slippery slope was a lesser risk than Kristof's opponents being able to make a living.[50] Margaret Sullivan of *The Washington Post* agreed, calling Fox News a "hazard to our democracy," and demanded that "[c]orporations that advertise on Fox News should walk away, and citizens who care about the truth should demand that they do so."[51] Max Boot of *The Washington Post* believes that "large cable companies . . . need to step in and kick Fox News off."[52] CNN's Oliver Darcy joined the chorus, stating that "TV companies that provide platforms to networks" like Fox News ought not escape scrutiny: "it is time TV carriers face questions for lending their platforms to dishonest companies that profit off of disinformation and conspiracy theories." Darcy even called up cable platforms to attempt to pressure them.[53]

This stuff is fully delusional: were conservatives to be deprived of Fox News, they'd seek similar conservative outlets. But that delusion is consistent with the authoritarian Left's true goal: a reestablishment of the media monopoly it had before the death of the Fairness Doctrine and the rise of Rush Limbaugh. Many on the authoritarian Left celebrated when Limbaugh died, declaring him "polarizing." The reality is that *they* were polarizing, but they had a monopoly . . . and Limbaugh broke that monopoly. Now they want to reestablish it, at all costs.

This is why the media grow particularly vengeful when it comes to distribution of conservative ideas via social media. A shocking number of media members spend their days seeking to pressure social media platforms into curbing free speech standards in order to reinstitute an establishment media monopoly. Now, blaming social media platforms for violence is sort of like blaming free speech for Nazis: yes, bad people can take advantage of neutral platforms to do bad things. That doesn't mean the platforms should be restricted. But for pseudo-journalists like Joe Scarborough of MSNBC, the platforms bear primary responsibility for violence: "Those riots would not have happened but for Twitter, but for Facebook . . . Facebook's algorithms were set up to cause this sort of radicalism to explode."[54]

By citing the danger of free speech, our establishment media can close the pathways of informational dissemination to those outside the New Ruling Class. These media members consider anyone outside their own worldview an enemy worth banning. Mainstream media members simply lump in mainstream conservatives with violent radicals—and *voilà!*—it's time for social media to step in and get rid of them. Kara Swisher of *The New York Times* spends her column space, day after day, attempting to pressure Mark Zuckerberg of Facebook to set restrictive content regulations in violation of free speech principles. "Mr. Zuckerberg," Swisher wrote in June 2020, "has become—unwittingly or not—the digital equivalent of a supercharged enabler because of his enormous power over digital communications that affect billions of people." And, Swisher added, Zuckerberg shouldn't worry about free speech as a value—after all, the First Amendment doesn't mention "Facebook, or any other company. And there's no mention of Mark Zuckerberg, who certainly has the power to rein in speech that violates company rules." Free speech is *the problem.* Corporate censorship is *the solution.*[55]

And what sort of content should be restricted? The tech reporters believe the answer is obvious: anything right of center. That's why, day after day, Kevin Roose of *The New York Times* tweets out organic reach of conservative sites, trying to pressure Facebook into changing its algorithm. It's why *The New York Times* ran a piece by Roose in June 2019 titled "The Making of a YouTube Radical," linking everyone from Jordan

Peterson, Joe Rogan, and me to Alex Jones and Jared Taylor. Roose lamented, "YouTube has inadvertently created a dangerous on-ramp to extremism."[56] The goal is obvious: get everybody right of center deplatformed. And threaten the platforms themselves in order to do so.

It won't stop there. Media members have now decided, in the post-Trump age, that it's time to rewrite the First Amendment bargain altogether. Jim VandeHei of *Politico* acknowledges that Blue America hopes desperately to rethink "politics, free speech, the definition of truth and the price of lies."[57] The First Amendment must be rethought. In 2019, Richard Stengel—now the head of Joe Biden's transition team for the US Agency for Global Media—contended that America ought to embrace hate speech laws, since free speech should not "protect hateful speech that can cause violence by one group against another." New York University journalism professor and MSNBC contributor Anand Giridharadas questions, "Should Fox News be allowed to exist?" Steve Coll, dean of Columbia Journalism School, now believes that those in journalism "have to come to terms with the fact that free speech, a principle we hold sacred, is being weaponized against the principles of journalism." Bill Adair, founder of the highly biased news fact-checking source PolitiFact, now believes that the government should use "regulations and new laws" to fight the "problem of misinformation."[58]

Curbing free speech has two particular benefits for the establishment media: first, it boots their competitors; second, it purges the public sphere of views they dislike. It's a win-win. All they require is ideologically authoritarian control.

CONCLUSION

On January 18, 2019, during the March for Life, something frightening happened: a group of high school boys wearing MAGA hats swarmed around an innocent Native American man, taunting him, laughing and dancing. Reports suggested that four black protesters had also been harassed by the cruel white students. The Native American man told the media that he had confronted the students while they shouted, "Build the Wall!" And the journalistic world went to work, journalisming as hard as they could. Kara Swisher tweeted, "[T]hose awful kids and their fetid smirking harassing that elderly man on the Mall: Go f★★★ yourselves." Joe Scarborough tweeted, "Where are their parents, where are their teachers, where are their pastors?" *The New York Times* headlined, "Boys in 'Make America Great Again' Hats Mob Native Elder at Indigenous People's

March." CNN called the incident a "heartbreaking viral video."[59]

There was only one problem.

It wasn't true.

In reality, as Covington Catholic student Nick Sandmann—the kid in the MAGA hat—stated, the white students were accosted by four black members of the Black Hebrew Israelites—a radical group of nut cases who had called them "racists," "bigots," "faggots," and "incest kids." The students were also accosted by the Native American man, who strode into their group and began banging a drum in their faces. Sandmann stood still, smiling awkwardly. As Sandmann related:

I was not intentionally making faces at the protestor. I did smile at one point because I wanted him to know that I was not going to become angry, intimidated or be provoked into a larger confrontation. I am a faithful Christian and practicing Catholic, and I always try to live up to the ideals my faith teaches me—to remain respectful of others, and to take no action that would lead to conflict or violence.[60]

Sandmann was telling the truth. Nearly every element of the story as reported by the establishment media was false. "[T]he elite media have botched the story so completely that they have lost the authority to report on it," wrote Caitlyn Flanagan of *The Atlantic*. Flanagan went further, slamming *The New York Times*: "You were partly responsible for the election of Trump because you are the most influential newspaper in the country, and you are not fair or impartial. Millions of Americans believe you hate them and that you will casually harm them."[61]

Nothing has changed.

If anything, the problem has grown worse.

The establishment media have declared themselves the heroes of the past four years—the bravest, the most noble, the guardians of our democracy. They weren't, and they aren't. They are willing to attack everyone from commoners to kings to advance their agenda. Doubt them, and they'll cast you out. Compete with them, and they'll work to silence you.

Within days of Joe Biden's ascension to the White House, our Journalisming™ experts reverted from watchdogs to lapdogs. CNN's Dana Bash swooned, "The adults are back in the room."[62] CNN's White House reporter Jim Acosta tweeted a picture of himself with NBC News' Peter Alexander: "Just a couple of guys covering the White House on the last full day of Trump admin. Think we will finally have time for that drink now @PeterAlexander?"[63] CNN's Brian Stelter, host of the ironically named *Reliable Sources*, wrote a glowing chyron about White House press secretary (and former CNN contributor) Jen Psaki's assurance that she would only speak truth: "Psaki promises to share 'accurate info' (how refreshing)."[64] Margaret Sullivan of *The Washington Post* praised the "Biden White House's return to normalcy," and warned against media members being too *harsh* on the new administration.[65]

It's all fine. Trust them.

This is dangerous stuff. It's dangerous that the guardians of our democracy—the media—aren't guardians but political activists, dedicated to their own brand of propaganda. It's even more dangerous that they now work on an ongoing basis to stymie voices with whom they disagree, and use the power of their platforms to destroy their opponents at every level. A thriving marketplace of ideas requires a basic respect for the marketplace itself. But our ideologically driven, authoritarian leftist media seek to destroy that marketplace in favor of a monopoly.

Every day, they come closer to achieving that goal.

Chapter 8
Unfriending Americans

One month before the 2020 election, the *New York Post* released a bombshell report—a report that could have upended the nature of the election. That report centered on Hunter Biden, son of Joe Biden, the Democratic presidential nominee. According to the *Post*'s report, "Hunter Biden introduced his father, then–Vice President Joe Biden, to a top executive at a Ukrainian energy firm less than a year before the elder Biden pressured government officials in Ukraine into firing a prosecutor who was investigating the company, according to emails obtained by the *Post*." A board member of Burisma, the company on whose board Biden sat, sent Hunter Biden a note of appreciation to thank him for the introduction.

The bombshell rebutted Joe Biden's consistent statements that he knew nothing about his son's business activities abroad, and that Hunter's activities had all been aboveboard. The *Post* even reported the provenance of the emails: Hunter Biden's laptop had been dropped off at a computer repair shop in Delaware in 2019, and Hunter had never returned to pick up that computer. The *Post* further reported that "both the computer and hard drive were seized by the FBI in December, after the shop's owner says he alerted the feds to their existence."[1]

It was no surprise to find that Hunter had been trafficking in his father's name—members of Biden's family have been doing that for years. In 2019, *Politico* reported, "Biden's image as a straight-shooting man of the people . . . is clouded by the careers of his son and brother, who have lengthy track records of making, or seeking, deals that cash in on his name."[2] Hunter admitted publicly in October 2019 that he certainly wouldn't have been selected to sit on the board of Burisma were his last name different—he has a long history of self-destructive behavior, zero experience in Ukraine, and zero experience with natural gas and oil. ABC News' Amy Robach asked Hunter, "If your last name wasn't Biden, do you think you would've been asked to be on the board of Burisma?" Hunter responded, "I don't know. I don't know. Probably not, in retrospect. But that's—you know—I don't think that there's a lot of things that would have happened in my life if my last name wasn't Biden. Because my dad was Vice President of the United States. There's literally nothing, as a young man or as a full grown adult that—my father in some way hasn't had influence over."[3] For his part, Joe Biden suggested that it was unthinkable that Hunter shouldn't have taken the position, and absurd to believe that Hunter had been given the position because the company wanted access to Joe.[4]

Hunter's willingness to use his father's name became a front-page issue that same year when Donald Trump, suspicious of corruption in Ukraine, held a controversial phone call with Ukrainian president Volodymyr Zelensky in which he stated, "There's a lot of talk about Biden's son, that Biden stopped the prosecution and a lot of people want to find out about that so whatever you can do with the Attorney General would be great. . . . It sounds horrible to me." Trump's political opponents accused him of blackmailing a foreign power into digging up dirt on Biden by threatening to withhold aid; the phone call resulted in Trump's impeachment in the House of Representatives for the first time.[5]

Now, a year later, the *Post* was reporting that Biden's

Ukrainian associates had been promised a meeting with Biden himself. Follow-on stories in the *Post* quoted Hunter Biden's ex–business associate Tony Bobulinski accusing Joe Biden himself of lying about his knowledge of Hunter's activities: "I have heard Joe Biden say he has never discussed his dealings with Hunter. That is false. I have firsthand knowledge about this because I directly dealt with the Biden family, including Joe Biden," Bobulinski alleged.[6]

The Biden campaign and its media allies responded by calling the Hunter Biden story "Russian disinformation."[7]

The story, needless to say, was not Russian disinformation; there was no evidence that it was in the first place. In fact, about a month after the election, media reported that Hunter Biden had been under federal investigation for *years*—CNN reported that the investigation began as early as 2018, and that it had gone covert for fear of affecting the presidential election.[8]

The Hunter Biden story never fully broke through into the mainstream consciousness. According to a poll from McLaughlin & Associates, 38 percent of Democratic supporters weren't aware of the story before the election; by contrast, 83 percent of Republicans were aware of the story.[9]

There was a reason for that: social media companies such as Twitter and Facebook simply shut down the story cold.

When the *Post* tweeted out the story, Twitter itself *suspended* the *Post*'s account. The company went so far as to prohibit users from posting a link to the story itself. Twitter tried to explain that it would not disseminate stories based on hacked materials—even though the *Post*'s story was *not based on hacked materials*. If Twitter had followed the same policies consistently, virtually every major story of the past several decades would have been banned on the platform.

Then, a few days later, Twitter did the same thing with the *Post*'s follow-up story. Those who attempted to post the links were met with the message, "We can't complete this request because this link has been identified by Twitter or our partners as being potentially harmful."

Later, Twitter CEO Jack Dorsey would admit that the "communication around our actions . . . was not great." Spin regarding censorship rarely is.[10]

Meanwhile, Andy Stone, the policy communications director at Facebook—and an alumnus of the Democratic House Majority PAC, former press secretary for Senator Barbara Boxer (D-CA), and former press secretary of the Democratic Congressional Campaign Committee[11]—tweeted, "While I will intentionally not link to the New York Post, I want to be clear that this story is eligible to be fact checked by Facebook's third-party fact checking partners. In the meantime, we are reducing its distribution on our platform."[12] He added, "This is part of our standard process to reduce the spread of misinformation. We temporarily reduce distribution pending fact-checker review."[13] In other words, Facebook *admitted* to curbing the reach of the *Post* story *before it had been fact-checked at all.* It had no evidence the story was false—as it turns out, the *Post* story was true. But Facebook restricted the reach of the *Post* piece anyway.

Facebook actually had moderators *manually intervene* in order to shut down the *Post* story, as the company admitted: "[W]e have been on heightened alert because of FBI intelligence about the potential for hack and leak operations meant to spread misinformation. Based on that risk, and in line with our existing policies and procedures, we made the decision to temporarily limit the content's distribution while our factcheckers had a chance to review it. When that didn't happen, we lifted the demotion."[14]

Just in time for Joe Biden to cruise to the presidency.

FROM OPEN AND FREE TO THE
NEW GATEKEEPERS

The *real* story of the Hunter Biden saga, as it turned out, was not about Hunter Biden per se: it was about the power and willingness of an oligopoly to restrict access to information in unprecedented ways. Social media companies were founded on the promise of broader access to speech and information; they were meant to be a marketplace of ideas, a place for coordination and exchange. They were, in other words, the new town square.

Now social media are quickly becoming less like open meeting places and more like the town squares in Puritan New England circa 1720: less free exchange of ideas, more mobs and stocks.

The saga of the social media platforms begins with the implementation of the much-maligned and misunderstood Section 230 of the Communications Decency Act in 1996. The section was designed to distinguish between material for which online platforms could be held responsible and material for which they could not. The most essential part of the law reads, "No provider or user of an interactive computer service shall be treated as the publisher or speaker of any information provided by another information content provider." *The New York Times*, for example, can be held liable as a publisher for information appearing in its pages. *The New York Times'* comments section, however, does not create liability—if a user posts defamatory material in the comments, the *Times* does not suddenly become responsible.

The purpose of Section 230, then, was to open up conversation by shielding online platforms from legal liability for third parties posting content. Section 230 itself states as much: the goal of the section is to strengthen the internet as "a forum for a true diversity of political discourse, unique opportunities for cultural development, and myriad avenues for intellectual activity."[15] As the Electronic Freedom Foundation describes, "This legal and policy framework has allowed for YouTube and Vimeo users to upload their own videos, Amazon and Yelp to offer countless user reviews, craigslist to host classified ads, and Facebook and Twitter to offer social networking to hundreds of millions of Internet users."[16]

There is one problem, however: the stark divide between platforms for third-party content and publishers who select their content begins to erode when platforms restrict the content third parties can post. Thus, for example, a New York court found in 1995 that Prodigy, a web services company with a public bulletin board, became a publisher when it moderated that board for "offensiveness and 'bad taste.' "[17] In reaction, Section 230 created an extremely broad carve-out for platforms to remove offending content; bipartisan legislators wanted to protect platforms from liability just for curating content in order to avoid seamy or ugly content. Thus Section 230 provides that no platform shall incur liability based on "any action voluntarily taken in good faith to restrict access to or availability of material that the provider or user considers to be obscene, lewd, lascivious, filthy, excessively violent, harassing, or otherwise objectionable, whether or not such material is constitutionally protected."[18]

At the beginning, our major social media companies understood full well the intent behind Section 230. In fact, they celebrated it. Facebook's mission statement for its first decade was "to make the world more open and connected."[19] Twitter said that its goal was "to give everyone the power to create and share ideas and information instantly, without barriers."[20] Google's working motto was simple: "Don't be evil."

For a while, it worked.

The social media giants were essentially open platforms, with a light hand in terms of censorship. Then the 2016 election happened.

The shock that greeted Trump's victory in 2016 fundamentally altered the orientation of the social media platforms. That's because, up until that moment, the personal political preferences of executives and staffers—overwhelmingly liberal—had meshed with their preferred political outcomes. But with Trump's win, that math changed dramatically. Members of the media and the Democratic Party began looking for a scapegoat. They found one in social media. If, the logic went, Americans had been restricted to viewing news the New Ruling Class wanted them to view, Hillary Clinton would have been installed as president rather than Trump. The dissemination of information was the problem.

Media elites and Democratic Party members couldn't make that argument explicitly—it was simply too authoritarian. So instead, they designed the concept of "fake news"—false news that Americans had apparently been bamboozled by. Post-election, the term gained ground in rapid fashion, with left-wing sites like PolitiFact explaining, "In 2016, the prevalence of political fact abuse—promulgated by the words of two polarizing presidential candidates and their passionate supporters—gave rise to a spreading of fake news with unprecedented impunity." Predictably, PolitiFact blamed Facebook and Google.[21] After the election, President Barack Obama—a man who certainly was no stranger to dissemination of false information, often with the compliance of a sycophantic press—complained about the "capacity to disseminate misinformation, wild conspiracy theories, to paint the opposition in wildly negative light without any rebuttal—that has accelerated in ways that much more sharply polarize the electorate and make it very difficult to have a common conversation."[22] In November 2017, Senator Dianne Feinstein (D-CA) openly threatened the social media companies, growling, "You created these platforms . . . and now they're being misused. And you have to be the ones who do something about it—or we will. . . . We are not going to go away, gentlemen. . . . Because you bear this responsibility."[23]

Initially, Facebook rejected the idea that as a platform it had somehow shifted the election to Trump—or that it bore responsibility for the material on its platform. That, of course, was the basic supposition of Section 230: that platforms *do not bear responsibility for material placed there by third parties.* Zuckerberg correctly countered the criticisms: "I do think that there is a certain profound lack of empathy in asserting that the only reason why someone could have voted the way that they did was because they saw some fake news. I think if you believe that, then I don't think you have internalized the message that Trump supporters are trying to send in this election."[24]

But the tsunami of rage at social media continued.

And, faced with the combined power of staff unrest, media manipulation, and Democratic Party threats, the social media companies shifted. They began to jettison their roles as the guardians of open and free discourse and began to embrace their new roles as informational gatekeepers.

In February 2017—just weeks after the inauguration of President Trump—Zuckerberg redefined Facebook's mission. Now, he said, the goal of the company was to "develop the social infrastructure to give people the power to build a global community that works for all of us." This was a far more collectivist vision than the original vision. And it called for new content standards to help reach this utopian goal, designed to "mitigat[e] areas where technology and social media can contribute to divisiveness and isolation."[25]

Facebook would no longer stay on the sidelines. Facebook would get involved. In a congressional hearing in April 2018, Zuckerberg went so far as to state that "we are responsible for the content" on the platform—a direct contravention of Section 230.

On a personal level, Zuckerberg continued to maintain his allegiance to free speech principles. In that

April 2018 hearing, Zuckerberg stated, "I am very committed to making sure that Facebook is a platform for all ideas. . . . We're proud of the discourse and the different ideas that people can share on the service, and that is something that, as long as I'm running the company, I'm going to be committed to making sure is the case."[26] Speaking at Georgetown University in 2019, Zuckerberg maintained, "People no longer have to rely on traditional gatekeepers in politics or media to make their voices heard, and that has important consequences. I understand the concerns about how tech platforms have centralized power, but I actually believe the much bigger story is how much these platforms have decentralized power by putting it directly into people's hands." He then correctly noted, "We can continue to stand for free expression, understanding its messiness, but believing that the long journey toward greater progress requires confronting ideas that challenge us. Or we can decide the cost is simply too great. I'm here today because I believe we must continue to stand for free expression."[27]

That allegiance to free speech principles—principles commonly held by the tech bros at the launch of their companies—didn't extend to other tech leaders. These tech leaders suggested that the very basis for their companies—free access to speech platforms—had to be reversed. Their companies would no longer be about free speech, but about free speech for the approved members of the New Ruling Class. Jack Dorsey, the new darling of the media establishment, slammed Zuckerberg for pledging himself to traditional liberalism: "We talk a lot about speech and expression and we don't talk about reach enough, and we don't talk about amplification," said Dorsey. The tech companies, Dorsey suggested, should decide which posts deserved amplification.[28] (Dorsey, it should be noted, is no critic of authoritarian wokeness—in fact, he's one of its biggest proponents. In 2020, Dorsey cut a $10 million donation to Ibram X. Kendi's "Center for Antiracism Research,"[29] which has to date presented no actual research. Kendi's website explains, "Our work, like our center, is in the process of being developed.")

This angle—free speech is not free reach—has become the new standard in establishment media, of course: Kara Swisher, the activist masquerading as a tech reporter for *The New York Times*, says, "Congress shall make no law. There's no mention of Facebook, or any other company."[30] That's easy for her to say, considering she's paid to write repetitive, censorious garbage by an establishment media company given favorable treatment by the social media companies.

This perspective, not coincidentally, mirrored the

prevailing view in the Democratic Party: the tech companies should simply censor the views of political opponents. Representative Alexandria Ocasio-Cortez (D-NY) browbeat Zuckerberg about even meeting with conservative figures, labeling them "far-right" and calling the Daily Caller "white supremacist." Representative Maxine Waters (D-CA) lambasted Zuckerberg's commitment to open discourse, stating that he was "willing to step on or over anyone, including your competitors, women, people of color, your own users, and even our democracy to get what you want."[31] In January 2020, Joe Biden personally ripped Zuckerberg, stating, "I've never been a big Zuckerberg fan. I think he's a real problem." In June 2020, the Biden campaign circulated a petition and open letter to Mark Zuckerberg, calling for "real changes to Facebook's policies for their platform and how they enforce them" in order to "protect against a repeat of the role that disinformation played in the 2016 election and that continues to threaten our democracy today."[32]

The social media companies have increasingly taken heed.

And they've moved right along with the clever switch made over the course of the past several years from "fighting disinformation" to "fighting misinformation." After 2016, the argument went, Russian "disinformation" had spammed social media, actively undermining truth in favor of a narrative detrimental to Democratic candidate Hillary Clinton.

There was some evidence of this—although the amount of actual Russian disinformation on Facebook, for example, wasn't overwhelming in the grand scheme of things. According to a Senate report in 2018, for example, the last month of the 2016 campaign generated 1.1 billion likes, posts, comments, and shares related to Donald Trump, and another 934 million related to Hillary Clinton.[33] In total, according to a report from New Knowledge, of Russian-created posts from 2015 to 2017, 61,500 posts from the Russian influence operation garnered a grand total of 76.5 million engagements. Total. Over two years. That's an average of 1,243 engagements per post—an extremely low total.[34]

But put aside the relative success or unsuccess of the Russian manipulation. We can all agree that Russian disinformation—typically meaning overtly false information put out by a foreign source, designed to mislead domestic audiences—is worth censoring. Democrats and media, however, shifted their objection from Russian disinformation to "misinformation"—a term of art that encompasses everything from actual, outright falsehood to narratives you dislike. To declare something "misinformation" should require showing its falsity, at the least.

No longer.

In December 2019, according to *Time*, Zuckerberg met with nine civil rights leaders at his home to discuss how to combat "misinformation." Vanita Gupta, CEO of the Leadership Conference on Civil and Human Rights—and now associate attorney general of the United States for Joe Biden—later bragged that she had cudgeled Facebook into changing informational standards. "It took pushing, urging, conversations, brainstorming, all of that to get to a place where we ended up with more rigorous rules and enforcement," she later told *Time*.[35]

The result: our social media now do precisely what government could not—act in contravention of free speech, with members of the Democratic Party and the media cheering them on. They follow no consistent policy, but react with precipitous and collusive haste in group-banning those who fall afoul of the ever-shifting standards of appropriate speech. That's what happened with the domino effect of banning the Hunter Biden story, for example.

Section 230, designed to protect open discourse by allowing platforms to prune the hedges without killing the free speech tree, has been completely turned upside down: a government privilege granted to social media has now become a mandate from the government and its media allies to take an ax to the tree. The iron triangle of informational restriction has slammed into place: a media, desperate to maintain its monopoly, uses its power to cudgel social media into doing its bidding; the Democratic Party, desperate to uphold its allied media as the sole informational source for Americans, uses threats to cudgel social media into doing its bidding; and social media companies, generally headed by leaders who align politically with members of the media and the Democratic Party, acquiesce.

COVERING FOR CENSORSHIP

So, how is material removed from these platforms—the platforms that were originally designed to foster free exchange of ideas? In the main, algorithms are designed to spot particular types of content. Some of the content to be removed is uncontroversially bad, and should come down—material that explicitly calls for violence, or pornographic material, or, say, actual Russian disinformation. But more and more, social media companies have decided that their job is not merely to police the boundaries of free speech while leaving the core untouched—more and more, they have decided that their job is to foster "positive conversation," to encourage people to click on videos they wouldn't normally click on, to quiet "misinformation."

In the first instance, this can be done via algorithmic changes.

Those changes are largely designed to reestablish a monopoly on informational distribution by establishment media. The internet broke the establishment media's model; just as cable wrecked network television, the internet wrecked cable and print news. Originally, consumers went directly to websites in order to view the news—they'd bookmark Drudge Report or FoxNews.com, and go straight there. But then, as social media began to aggregate billions of eyeballs, people began to use social media as their gateway to those news sources. By 2019, according to the Pew Research Center, 55 percent of adults got their news from social media either "sometimes" or "often," including a plurality of young people.[36]

Establishment media saw an opportunity. By targeting the means of distribution—by going after the social media companies and getting them to down-rank alternative media—they could reestablish the monopoly they had lost.

And so the establishment media went to work. As we've already discussed, it's rare to find a voice in the establishment media dedicated to the proposition that dissemination of information on social media ought to be *more* open.

Social media companies have complied. So, for example, in 2019, in response to media reports blaming YouTube for violent acts supposedly inspired by viral videos—the media actually went further, blaming nonviolent, non-extremist videos for creating a "pipeline" to more violent and extremist content, all based on the flimsiest of conjecture[37]—YouTube changed its algorithm. As CBS News reported, "YouTube started re-programming its algorithms in the U.S. to recommend questionable videos much less and point users who search for that kind of material to authoritative sources, like news clips."[38] Facebook infamously did the same, demoting "borderline content" that supposedly trafficked in "sensationalist and provocative content." The goal was to manipulate what people could click on by deliberately making it more *difficult* to click on clickable stories.[39] The month after the 2020 election, in an attempt to tamp down speculation about voter fraud and irregularity, Facebook gave more algorithmic weight to sources that had higher "news ecosystem quality" scores.

Who were these mystical "authoritative sources" that ranked highly in terms of "news ecosystem qual-

ity"? Why, establishment media sources, of course—
the same exact outlets attempting to browbeat social
media platforms into censoring their competitors. As
The New York Times reported, "The change was part
of the 'break glass' plans Facebook had spent months
developing for the aftermath of a contested election.
It resulted in a spike in visibility for big, mainstream
publishers like CNN, *The New York Times* and
NPR, while posts from highly engaged hyperpartisan
pages . . . became less visible." And, added the Very
Authoritative *New York Times*, all this was a "vision
of what a calmer, less divisive Facebook might look
like." The *Times* also reported that Facebook's "idealist" employees wanted Facebook to maintain the
system; only its presumably corrupt, greedy "pragmatists" wanted to maintain an open standard in terms
of informational dissemination. And, lamented the
Times, if the pragmatists continued to win, "morale"
within the company would continue to drop.[40]

In establishing which sources ought to be "trusted,"
social media have outsourced their judgment to left-
wing pseudo-fact-checkers. In December 2016, Facebook announced that it would partner with a slate of
fact-checkers to determine which sources were most
trustworthy. According to BuzzFeed, Facebook would
verify "participating partners"; those participating

partners would then have access to a "special online queue that will show links Facebook determined may be suitable for a fact-check." How do links end up in the queue? Users report them as false, or the link goes viral. It's easy to see how such a system can be gamed: just put together an action response team, email them to spam Facebook's system, and then refer conservative links to fact-checks by left-wing organizations.

And that's precisely how the fact-checking business works. Facebook's original "participating partners": the Associated Press, PolitiFact, FactCheck .org, Snopes, *The Washington Post*, and ABC News. That would be three mainstream media outlets, and three left-wing fact-checking organizations. These pseudo-fact-checkers spent most of their time checking "misinformation"—which means, in many cases, declaring claims false based on "lack of context," even if the claims are overtly true. PolitiFact, for example, rated President Obama's lies about keeping your health-care plan if you like your health-care plan "half-true" *twice* before labeling it their "lie of the year."[41] Snopes.com recently rated "Mostly False" the claim that Representative Alexandria Ocasio-Cortez (D-NY) exaggerated "the danger she was in during the January 6, 2021, Capitol Riot, in that she 'wasn't even in the Capitol building' when the rioting occurred." That fact-check included the astonishing acknowledgment that it was true that Ocasio-Cortez "wasn't in the main Capitol building." Which, as it turns out, was the basis for the statement they were also calling "mostly false."[42]

The fact-checkers are certainly not unbiased. "When it comes to partisan fact-checking about complex issues—which describes much of the fact-checking that takes place in the context of political news—the truth as stated is often the subjective opinion of people with shared political views," says Professor Stephen Ceci of Cornell University.[43] And social media companies know that. They just happen to agree with the political leanings of the fact-checkers to whom they outsource their responsibilities.

Algorithmic censorship doesn't stop there. According to *The Washington Post* in December, Facebook made the decision to begin policing anti-black hate differently than anti-white hate. Race-blind practices would now be discarded, and instead, the algorithm would allow hate speech directed against white users to remain. Only the "worst of the worst" content would be automatically deleted—"Slurs directed at Blacks, Muslims, people of more than one race, the LGBTQ community and Jews, according to the documents." Slurs directed at whites, men, and Americans would be "deprioritized." The goal: to allow people to "combat systemic racism" by using vicious language.

Facebook would now apply its algorithmic standards differently "based on their perceived harm." Thus, woke standards of intersectional victimhood would be utilized, rather than an objective standard rooted in the nature of the language used. "We know that hate speech targeted toward underrepresented groups can be the most harmful," explained Facebook spokeswoman Sally Aldous, "which is why we have focused our technology on finding the hate speech that users and experts tell us is the most serious."[44] All hate speech is bad, except for the hate speech the experts say is nondamaging.

The so-called community standards put forward by the tech companies follow the same pattern: originally designed to protect more speech, they have been gradually ratcheted tighter and tighter in order to allow broader discretion to companies to ban dissenting material. As Susan Wojcicki, the head of YouTube, explained in June 2019, "We keep tightening and tightening the policies."[45] The ratchet only works one way.

These policies are often vague and contradictory. Facebook's "hate speech" policy, for example, bans any "direct attack" against people on the "basis of race, ethnicity, national origin, disability, religious affiliation, caste, sexual orientation, sex, gender identity and serious disease." What, exactly, constitutes an "attack"? Any "expression of . . . dismissal," or any "harmful stereotypes," for example.[46] So, would Facebook ban members for the factually true statement that biological men are men? How about the factually true statement that women generally do not throw baseballs as hard as men? Are these "stereotypes" or biological truths? What about jokes, which often traffic in stereotypes? How about quoting the Bible, which is not silent on matters of religion or sexuality? Facebook is silent on such questions.

And that's the point. The purpose of these standards *isn't* to provide clarity, so much as to grant cover when banning someone for *not* violating the rules. That's why it's so unbelievably easy for big tech's critics to point to inconsistencies in application of the "community standards"—Alex Jones gets banned, while Louis Farrakhan is welcomed; President Trump gets banned, while Ayatollah Khamenei is welcome.

When President Trump was banned from Twitter, Facebook, Instagram, and YouTube in the aftermath of January 6, none of the companies could explain precisely what policy Trump had breached to trigger his excision. Zuckerberg simply stated, "We believe the risks of allowing the President to continue to use our service during this period are simply too great."[47] Twitter explained that it had banned Trump "due to the risk of further incitement of violence." The tweets that supposedly created additional danger: "The 75,000,000 great American Patriots who voted for me, AMERICA FIRST, and MAKE AMERICA GREAT AGAIN, will have a GIANT VOICE long into the future. They will not be disrespected or treated unfairly in any way, shape or form!!!" and "To all of those who have asked, I will not be going to the Inauguration on January 20th." Twitter did provide a strained explanation of how those two rather benign tweets would incite further violence. It remains unconvincing.[48]

For the authoritarian Left, none of this goes far enough. The goal is to remake the constituency of companies themselves, so that the authoritarians can completely remake the algorithms in their own image. When Turing Award winner and Facebook chief AI scientist Yann LeCun pointed out that machine learning systems are racially biased only if their inputs are biased, and suggested that inputs could be corrected to present an opposite racial bias, the authoritarian woke critics attacked: Timnit Gebru, technical co-lead of the Ethical Artificial Intelligence Team at Google, accused LeCun of "marginalization" and called for solving "social and structural problems." The answer, said Gebru, was to hire members of marginalized groups, not to change the data set used by machine learning.[49]

CROWDSOURCING THE REVOLUTION

For most Americans, the true dangers of social media don't even lie in the censorship of news itself: the largest danger lies in the roving mobs social media represent. The sad truth is that the media, in their ever-present quest for authoritarian rule, use social media as both their tip line and their action arm. They dig through the social media histories of those they despise, or receive tips from bad actors about "bad old tweets," and proceed to whip the mob into a frenzy. Then they cover the frenzy. The same media that declaim their hatred for misinformation and bullying engage in them regularly when it comes to mobbing random citizens with the help of social media.

In December 2020, a recent high school graduate, Mimi Groves, found herself the subject of an interminable hit piece from *The New York Times*. Groves had, back in 2016, just received her learner's permit to drive. She took a video of herself on Snapchat, jocularly exclaiming, "I can drive, n***ah." As the *Times* reported, the video "later circulated among some students at Heritage High School," but it didn't raise any hackles—after all, she was a fifteen-year-old girl mimicking the tropes of rap.

But one student—an utterly despicable douche bag named Jimmy Galligan—held on to the video. Galligan, who is black, decided to post the video "publicly when the time was right." That time came in 2020, by which time Groves was a senior, headed to the University of Tennessee, Knoxville, to be part of the cheer team. During the Black Lives Matter protests, Groves made the critical error of *supporting* BLM; she posted to Instagram urging comrades to "protest, donate, sign a petition, rally, do something."

And so Galligan struck. He posted the old video to Snapchat, TikTok, and Twitter. Groves was booted from the University of Tennessee cheer team, then withdrew from UT altogether thanks to the social media frenzy. An admissions officer said that the university had received "hundreds of emails and phone calls from outraged alumni, students and the public."

The *Times* reported this story, not as a horrific attempt by a vicious grandstander to destroy a girl's life, but as a referendum on the "power of social media to hold people of all ages accountable." Galligan is portrayed as a hero, standing up to the threat of endemic white supremacy.[50]

This story should raise two questions, one about social media, and one about the media. First, why has social media become such a flaming dumpster fire of visceral hatred? Second, why have the media degraded themselves to the point where nonstories about individual *high school students* are worthy of national coverage?

For social media, the answer lies in virality. Social media companies *encourage* such activities, treating them as a source of traffic and news. Twitter's trending topics are a perfect example of how minor issues can quickly snowball; Twitter highlights the most controversial stories and elevates them, encouraging minor incidents to become national stories; velocity of attention matters more than sheer scope of attention. Thus, for example, topics that garner tons of tweets day after day don't trend; topics that spike in attention from a low baseline do. So if there's a random woman in a city park who says something racially insensitive and garners two thousand tweets for it, she's more likely to trend than President Biden on any given day. And it's not difficult for two thousand tweets to become 20,000, once a topic starts to trend: social media rewards speaking out, and devalues silence. On social media, refusal to weigh in on a trending topic is generally taken as an indicator of apathy or even approval.

It doesn't take much to form a mob, either. Social

media mobs form daily, with the speed of an aggressive autoimmune disorder. Where in the past, people had to find commonality in order to mobilize a mob, now social media provides a mob milling around, waiting to be mobilized. The cause need not be just. All it must do is provide an evening's entertainment for several thousand people, and a story for the media to print. Justine Sacco, a thirty-year-old senior director of corporate communications at IAC, watched her life crumble after sending a tweet joking about AIDS in Africa to her 170 followers. The tweet read, "Going to Africa. Hope I don't get AIDS. Just kidding. I'm white!" The tweet was apparently supposed to be a joke about the insufficiency of Western aid to Africa. Nonetheless, when she got off her eleven-hour flight, she had been targeted with "tens of thousands of tweets." She lost her job. She experienced PTSD, depression, and insomnia.

Which brings us to the second question: why do the media cover this stuff?

The answer: they are, in large measure, social authoritarians who use social media as a cheap and easy way of both creating traffic and finding stories.

Sacco's tweet only became a worldwide trend because a tipster sent it to Sam Biddle, a writer for Gawker Media. He promptly retweeted it. Biddle later explained, "It's satisfying to be able to say, 'OK, let's make a racist tweet by a senior IAC employee count this time.' "[51] Too many in the media have the same perspective. Twitter has enabled our journalistic establishment to play at both crusader and reporter with a single retweet. That's why whatever the latest Twitter trend, it's likely a media member will have the top tweet.

Singular events that chart on social media also allow members of the media to manipulate the narrative. The media overwhelmingly believe the woke tale that America is systemically racist—but the data for such contentions are vanishingly hard to find. In America, the demand for racism from authoritarians seeking social control wildly outstrips the supply of actual racism. To that end, media members seek out individual, non-national stories and then suggest they are indicative of broader trends, citing social media attention as the rationale for the story in the first place.

In the real world, Twitter trends rarely used to matter. But as social media becomes our new shared space, and as our media treat the happenings on social media platforms as the equivalent of real life, social media mobs become real mobs with frightening momentum.

THE NEW INFORMATIONAL OLIGOPOLY

Our social media oligopoly—cudgeled, wheedled, and massaged into compliance by a rabid media and a censorious Democratic Party—threatens true social authoritarianism at this point. In a free market system, the solution would be to create alternatives.

Parler attempted to do just that.

Angered at the capricious nature of Twitter's management, Parler began as an alternative. In 2020, as big tech began to unleash its power in the election, Parler steadily gained adherents: in late July, Parler saw over a million people join in one week. After the 2020 election, as big tech moved to stymie alternative media, conservatives jumped to Parler: Parler hit the top spot in Apple's App Store, and jumped by more than 4.5 million members in one week. Parler's chief selling point: it would not ban people based on political viewpoint. Parler's CEO, John Matze, said, "We're a community town square, an open town square, with no censorship. If you can say it on the street of New York, you can say it on Parler."[52]

Until you couldn't.

After the January 6 riots, based on vaguely sourced reports that Parler had been an organizing place for the rioters, Apple, Amazon, and Google all barred Parler. Apple's App Store barred Parler on the basis that Parler's processes were "insufficient" to "prevent the spread of dangerous and illegal content." Amazon Web Services used its power to kick Parler off the internet entirely, denying it access to its cloud hosting service. Amazon's excuse: Parler had allowed "posts that clearly encourage and incite violence," and that it had no "effective process to comply with the AWS terms of service."[53]

None of the big tech companies could explain what, precisely, a minimum standard would have looked like. And none of them could explain why Parler was supposedly more dangerous than the far larger platforms Facebook and Twitter—especially since, as Jason King has reported, nearly one hundred people involved in the January 6 riot used Facebook or Instagram, twenty-eight used YouTube, and only eight used Parler.[54]

The informational monopoly is being reestablished in real time. And alternatives are being actively foreclosed by social media companies determined to invoke their standard as the singular standard, a media that knows it can co-opt those standards, and Democrats who benefit from those standards. After having killed Parler, members of the media have turned their attention to Telegram and Signal, encrypted messaging services. All streams of dissent—or uncontrolled informational streams—must be crushed.[55]

Perhaps the only good news is that most Americans know they're being manipulated by the gatekeepers in social media. Fully 82 percent of adults told Pew Research that social media "treat some news organizations differently than others," 53 percent said that one-sided news was a "very big problem" on social media, and 35 percent worried about "censorship of the news." Some 64 percent of Republicans said that the news they saw on social media leaned to the Left; 37 percent of Democrats agreed. Just 21 percent of Democrats said that the news they saw via social media leaned to the Right.[56]

The bad news is that social media will remain the biggest players on the stage so long as they have the most eyeballs—and with alternatives increasingly foreclosed, that means for the foreseeable future. Facebook has 2.8 billion monthly active users;[57] more than 90 percent of all web searches happen via either Google or its subsidiary YouTube;[58] fully 70 percent of digital ad spending goes to Google, Facebook, and Amazon.[59] Building competition in the face of that oligopoly won't be easy.

What's more, our government actors have an interest in upholding the oligopoly: it's easy to control a market with just a few key players. And our media have an interest in upholding the oligopoly, too: these companies are run by like-minded allies, all of whom are either committed to or can be pushed into support for woke authoritarianism.

And these companies, as it turns out, aren't the only ones.

The Choice Before Us

In early February 2021, actress Gina Carano made a fateful decision.

She posted a meme on Instagram.

Carano, who played popular character Cara Dune on Disney+'s hit series *The Mandalorian*, had been verging on the edge of cancellation for months. That's because Carano is conservative. She'd jokingly posted that her pronouns were beep/boop/bop in order to mock woke authoritarians pressuring strangers to list their gender pronouns. In the aftermath of the 2020 election, she'd posted on Twitter, "We need to clean up the election process so we are not left feeling the way we do today." She'd posted a meme challenging the elite consensus on Covid by suggesting that Americans were putting masks over their eyes.[1]

All of this had already made Carano persona non grata with Disney+ and Lucasfilm. According to *The Hollywood Reporter*, citing a person inside the companies, the bosses had been looking to can Carano for two months; Disney+ and Lucasfilm had scrapped plans for Carano to star in her own spin-off inside the *Star Wars* universe in December.[2]

Carano's fatal error came in posting a meme citing the Holocaust. The picture showed a Jewish woman running away from a crowd of Germans, and carried this caption: "Jews were beaten in the streets, not by Nazi soldiers but by their neighbors. . . . even by children. Because history is edited, most people today don't realize that to get to the point where Nazi soldiers could easily round up thousands of Jews, the government first made their own neighbors hate them simply for being Jews. How is that any different from hating someone for their political views?"[3]

Now, comparisons to the Holocaust are generally overwrought. But Carano's post certainly was *not* anti-Semitic (as a recipient of more anti-Semitic memery than perhaps any person alive, I can spot anti-Semitism a mile off). The post was making the point that oppression of others doesn't start with violence. It starts with dehumanization of the other. That's a fairly generic and true point, even though Carano—as she herself acknowledged—shouldn't have invoked the Holocaust.

The blowback was immediate and final.

Disney+ and Lucasfilm fired her outright. They stated, wrongly, that she had "denigrat[ed] people based on their cultural and religious identities."[4] They could not explain precisely how she had denigrated anyone, particularly Jews. But authoritarian leftism requires only an excuse for cancellation, not a real justification.

One might think that Disney was merely setting a standard that overwrought Holocaust comparisons were forbidden on social media. Not so. Pedro Pascal, star of *The Mandalorian*, tweeted in 2018 comparing the Trump border policy with regard to children to Nazi concentration camps. To the sound of crickets.[5]

Normally, in our authoritarian culture, this is where the story would end.

But that's not where the story ended.

As soon as I heard what had happened to Carano— we'd never met before—I reached out to her personally; my business partner reached out to her business manager. And we offered Gina a job. To push back against Hollywood's absurd cancel culture, we would partner with her in producing a film, to star her. Gina's statement tells the tale:

The Daily Wire is helping make one of my dreams—to develop and produce my own film—come true. I cried out and my prayer was answered. I am sending out a direct message of hope to everyone living in fear of cancellation by the totalitarian mob. I have only just begun using my voice which is now freer than ever before, and I hope it inspires others to do the same. They can't cancel us if we don't let them.[6]

They can't cancel us if we don't let them.

This should be our rallying cry. Because if we say it together—liberals, centrists, conservatives—the authoritarian Left loses.

Our institutions have been remade in the mold of authoritarian leftism by elites who deem themselves worthy of holding the reins of power. But we don't have to acquiesce in that power grab.

We can say "no."

After announcing our partnership with Gina, tens of thousands of Americans joined Daily Wire as members. I personally received hundreds of emails from people asking how they could help—and hundreds more from people in Hollywood asking if they could escape the system. Americans recognized not just that we were attempting to challenge Hollywood on its own terms, but that we must all act in solidarity—that while we are individualists by ideology, cohesive action is necessary if we wish to make a consolidated counterattack on the authoritarians.

So, how exactly do we go about wresting control of our institutions away from an authoritarian Left hell-bent on American renormalization? We begin with an educational mission. And then we get practical.

EDUCATING AMERICA, REDUX

The authoritarian Left has successfully pursued an educational project: inculcating Americans into embarrassment at America's founding philosophy, her institutions, and her people. Their argument—that America is systemically racist, that her institutions fundamentally broken—has won the day on an emotional level. To even challenge this argument is deemed vicious. But the argument is fundamentally wrong.

America is not systemically racist. Racism does exist; slavery was one of history's greatest evils; history does have consequences. It's terrible and sad that gaps between white and black success remain a feature of American life. All of those things are undeniably true. And the solution to all of those evils is *not* the overthrow of all existing American systems. In fact, the "anti-racist" policies the authoritarian Left loves so much have been tried—and they have failed miserably. That won't stop the authoritarian Left from calling you a racist for pointing that out.

The solution is the same as it was in 1776: a government instituted to protect the preexisting rights of its citizens, and a commitment to both virtue and reason. America was not founded in 1619; it was founded in 1776. The principles of American liberty are eternal and true. The fact that America has not always lived up to those principles isn't a referendum on the principles themselves. And the greatness of America—the greatness of her individual freedom, of her powerful economy, of her moral people—represents the unique outgrowth of those principles.

The sins of 1619—the sins of brutality, of bigotry, of violence, of greed, of lust, of radical dehumanization—are sins that adhere to nearly all of humanity over the course of time. Human beings are sinful and weak. But we are capable of more. It is not a coincidence that America has been history's leading force in favor of human freedom and prosperity. The great lie of our time—perhaps of all time—is that such freedom and prosperity are the natural state of things, and that America's systems stop us from fulfilling their promise. Precisely the opposite is true.

So, how do we—the new resistance—fight back against an authoritarian Left that has embedded itself at the top of our major institutions? How do we stop an authoritarian Left dedicated to revolutionary aggression, top-down censorship, and anti-conventionalism?

We reverse the process begun by the authoritarian Left so long ago: we refuse to allow the authoritarian Left to silence us; we end the renormalization of our institutions and return them back to actual normalcy; and we pry open the doors they have welded shut.

OUR REFUSAL IS A WEAPON

The first step in unraveling authoritarian leftist dominance of our institutions is our refusal to abide by their rules. The authoritarian Left engaged in a three-step process directed toward cudgeling Americans into supporting their agenda. First, they relied on the Cordiality Principle—the principle that Americans ought to be cordial, and thus inoffensive—to make Americans uncomfortable about dissenting from prevailing social views of the New Ruling Class. Next, they made the argument that to speak up against the New Ruling Class amounted to a form of violence. Finally, they argued that failure to *echo* the New Ruling Class was itself a form of harm—"Silence is violence."

We must reject each one of these steps, in reverse order.

First, we must reject the imbecilic notion that "silence is violence." It isn't. All too often, it's sanity. When it comes to children—whom radical authoritarian leftists all too often resemble—bad behavior should be met with a simple response: ignoring them. This is a tough principle for parents to learn (I know, I've had to practice it routinely): the natural tendency when faced with radical behavior is to *engage*. But it's precisely our attention that often gives radicals their power. Imagine if, instead of rushing to respond to the pseudo-urgent needs of the latest establishment media–driven mob, we simply shrugged. Imagine if, next time someone declared that they had been harmed by mere dissent, we chuckled at them and moved on. Their power would be gone. We don't have to engage. And we certainly don't have to echo.

Second, we must firmly reject the notion that speech is violence. Dissent isn't violence; disagreement isn't harm. That's because politics *isn't an identity*; it isn't a denial of someone's identity to disagree with them. We know this in our everyday personal relationships—we disagree with those we love most of all, on a regular basis. They don't feel that we're "denying their humanity" or "doing them violence." They understand that if they wish to be treated as adults, they ought to subject their views to the scrutiny of others. Anyone who utters the phrase "speech is violence" should be immediately discounted as a serious human being.

Finally—and most carefully—we must deny the conflation of cordiality and inoffensiveness implicit in the Cordiality Principle. To be cordial does not mean to be inoffensive. As I'm fond of saying, facts don't care about our feelings. That doesn't mean that we should be deliberately rude. It does mean, however, that we shouldn't allow others' subjective interpretations of our viewpoints to rule our minds. We cannot grant others an emotional veto over our perspectives. To oppose same-sex marriage, for example, should not be considered prima facie offensive—one can make a perfectly plausible argument for the superior societal importance of traditional marriage over same-sex marriage without insulting those who are homosexual. To go silent in the face of important societal issues out of fear that you might offend is to grant unending power to those who are quickest to rise to offense. And that's a recipe for emotional blackmail.

In rejecting the Cordiality Principle, we need not give cover to those who deliberately offend. To be politically incorrect means to say that which requires saying, not to be a generic, run-of-the-mill jackass. There is a difference between making an argument against same-sex marriage and calling someone an ugly name. In fact, conflating the two grants the authoritarian Left enormous power: it allows them to argue that non-liberal points of view ought to be quashed in order to prevent terrible behavior. Fighting political correctness requires a willingness to speak truth and the brains to speak the truth in cogent, clear, and objectively decent language.

When we fight back in this way, we win. We win because bravery draws followers; we win because honesty without vile behavior draws admirers. Once again, this isn't an issue of Left versus Right. It's an issue of upholding values dear to a pluralistic democracy—values that should be held in common across the political spectrum, and in direct opposition to the authoritarian Left.

RENORMALIZING OUR INSTITUTIONS

As I've argued throughout this book, our institutions have been steadily renormalized by an intransigent minority, making common cause with other "marginalized" populations in opposition to the majority. But this process can be reversed. It's time to renormalize—return normalcy—our institutions.

To do this requires the creation of an intransigent minority. Because too many Americans have allowed the authoritarian Left to cudgel them into silence or agreement, the key here is *courage*. Americans must be willing to stand up, speak out, and *refuse to acquiesce to the power hierarchy.*

Take, for example, the case of Donald McNeil Jr., a science reporter for *The New York Times*. In February 2021, McNeil was forced out of his job. It turns out that two years before, in 2019, McNeil acted as an expert guide on a *Times* student trip in Peru. During that trip, a student asked McNeil whether he thought a twelve-year-old ought to be canceled for using the n-word. In the process of explaining contextual differences in using the n-word, McNeil uttered the infamous slur. Some of the students complained. And some woke staffers at the *Times* demanded action; they sent yet another in their endless stream of whining letters to the editors, demanding action. The editors quickly acquiesced, thanking the authoritarian leftist brute squad for their input. So McNeil lost his job.[7] Executive editor Dean Baquet went so far as to state, "We do not tolerate racist language regardless of intent"—a standard so insanely authoritarian that Baquet later had to walk it back.[8]

But here's the thing: a *lot* of New York Times staffers

thought McNeil should have retained his job. McNeil was a member of the NewsGuild, a union of 1,200 *Times* employees. As *Vanity Fair* reported, "McNeil is not without sympathy or support, both inside the *Times* and out. Some people feel that he was the latest victim of cancel culture run amok, forced out of his job by a public pressure campaign."[9]

So, here's the question: *where were they?*

What would have happened if the *Times* staffers, instead of allowing intellectual authoritarians like Nikole Hannah-Jones to rule the roost, stood up in favor of McNeil? There are 1,200 employees at the *Times.* Just 150 staffers signed the letter to the editors. What if 400 employees had signed a letter *the other way*? What if instead of caving to an intransigent minority, the *Times* employees who backed McNeil had formed their own intransigent minority—or even an intransigent majority? What if those staffers had forced the editors into a binary choice: side with free speech and non-authoritarianism or side with a relatively small group of malcontents?

The same logic holds throughout American life. What if employees banded together and simply refused to go along with the latest cancellations, or the latest demand for "diversity training," or the latest Maoist struggle session? What if religious Americans, who comprise a plurality of Americans in nearly every organization, said that they would not go along with attempts to force them into silence?

The answer has been shown time and time again: authoritarian leftists back down when faced with an intransigent majority. That's why they are authoritarians in the first place: if they could convince others of their arguments, they wouldn't need to create social stigma around their opponents, or militarize weapons of power against them.

In December 2020, Pedro Domingos, professor emeritus of computer science and engineering at the University of Washington, wrote publicly about the standards for scientific research at the Conference on Neural Information Processing Systems (NeurIPS). NeurIPS now suggests that "[r]egardless of scientific quality or contribution, a submission may be rejected for ethical considerations, including methods, applications, or data that create or reinforce unfair bias." This means that good research cannot be conducted under the NeurIPS auspices so long as such research challenges prevailing leftist politics.

Domingos wrote that this was a terrible idea. This prompted a backlash, naturally, with authoritarian leftists labeling Domingos a racist; as Domingos wrote, his own department distanced itself from him. Other professors suggested that anyone who cited Domingos's work was, by definition, a bigot.

But once again, that wasn't the end of the story. Domingos writes: "as the days passed, and it became clear who the real radicals were, something interesting happened. Many of the usually reticent moderates in our community began to speak up, and denounce the unhinged and ruthless tactics applied against me and my supporters. In the end, I suffered no professional consequences (at least not in any formal way). And the cancel crowd's ringleader even issued a public apology and promised to mend her ways."

So what happened? According to Domingos, solidarity kicked in: a network of like-minded people willing to speak up actually spoke up. Activate when you're on solid ground—and try to pick fights in which you can knock off the authoritarian Goliath. Never apologize. And direct your resistance not merely at authoritarian leftists, but at those *in charge of the institutions.* As Domingos writes, "Even companies that posture heavily in the area of social justice don't actually want to be stained by the disgraceful behavior of mob leaders."

If an intransigent minority can be activated, then renormalization can occur. Those in the middle rarely like the authoritarian Left. They're just afraid to speak out against them. So form a core group of intransigent people who share your values. And then build.[10]

PRYING OPEN THE INSTITUTIONS

All of this may work for institutions that are still up for grabs. But what do you do if the heads of these institutions aren't merely going along to get along, or blowing with the wind—what if the heads of these institutions are dedicated authoritarian leftists themselves, invulnerable to intransigent minorities, fully willing to utilize every power they have to silence dissent?

At this point, Americans are left with three options. And they should exercise all three.

First, the legal options. The authoritarian Left is extraordinarily litigious. When they can't win victories in the court of public opinion, they seek victory in the courts themselves. In fact, authoritarian leftists frequently use the mere threat of lawsuit to force compliance from those in power. Other Americans are generally reluctant to invoke the use of courts to force their employers to do their bidding.

That's usually the right instinct. But it's precisely the wrong instinct when it comes to fighting the authoritarian Left.

When it comes to the authoritarian Left's desire

to cram down "diversity training" that discriminates based on race, for example, lawsuits are fully merited. If companies force employees to attend training sessions segregated by race, or in which white employees are taught of their inherent privilege, white employees ought to seek legal redress. So-called anti-racism training often violates the provisions of the Civil Rights Act of 1965 by explicitly discriminating on the basis of race. Make your employer pay the price for doing so—or threaten to do so if the company doesn't stop its legal violations.

Another option is available politically for those who wish to fight the authoritarian Left: the formal expansion of anti-discrimination law to include matters of politics. Many states bar discrimination on the basis of sex, sexual orientation, gender identity, race, religion, age, and disability, among other standards. Yet you can still be discriminated against based on your politics. If we wish to hold the authoritarian Left to its own standards—if we wish to use the bulwark of the law to prevent "discrimination" by limiting free association—then why give the authoritarian Left a monopoly on anti-discrimination law? Why not *force* the authoritarian Left to back down by using the same legal tools they have utilized themselves to silence dissent? If you're a traditionally conservative baker who doesn't want to violate his political precepts by catering a same-sex wedding, you'll find yourself on the wrong end of a lawsuit. If you're a leftist caterer who doesn't want to violate his political precepts by serving a Republican dinner meeting, you're off the hook. Perhaps that should change.

This is an ugly option, particularly for those of us who still believe in core freedoms like freedom of association. I happen to believe that people should be able to hire and fire whomever they want to. But the authoritarian Left disagrees. And not only do they disagree, they've captured the legal system to the extent that you can *only* be targeted for having the wrong politics today.

All of this raises a broader strategic possibility: the possibility of mutually assured destruction. Before I founded the Daily Wire, I ran an organization called Truth Revolt. The goal of the organization was to act as a sort of reverse Media Matters: to use a team of activists to encourage advertisers *not* to spend their money with left-wing outlets. In launching Truth Revolt, we openly acknowledged that we didn't like our own tactics. In fact, as my business partner Jeremy Boreing stated at our founding, we'd happily dissolve our organization if Media Matters did the same. But if the authoritarian Left was going to utilize nasty tactics in order to force institutions to cave to them, we'd have to make clear that the Right could do the same. Either organizations would begin to ignore both sides—a preferable outcome—or they would simply stop engaging with the political universe generally. In our view, there was only one strategy worse than arming up against the authoritarian Left: unilateral disarmament.

Americans can engage in the same tactics as the Left when it comes to our most powerful institutions. We can withhold our money from Hollywood, refuse to shop at the wokest corporations, remove our endowments from authoritarian-run universities. We can stop subscribing to media outlets, and we can pressure advertisers to stop spending their money there. Either these institutions will learn to tune out all the insanity—which they should—or they can remove themselves from the business of politics.

Then there's the final option: building alternative institutions.

At the Daily Wire, we call ourselves alternative media, because that's what we want to be: a place for people who have been ignored by institutional media to access information they want to see. We're building up an entertainment wing to serve the needs of Americans who are tired of being lectured about the evils of their non-woke politics. This is necessary, because the authoritarian Left hasn't just captured most of our major institutions, they've closed the doors behind them. It would be nice if real conservatives wrote regularly at *The New York Times* or *The Atlantic*, but that seems like a pipe dream. Exclusion is the order of the day.

In shutting the doors of our most powerful institutions, the authoritarian Left has left those of us outside with one option: build it ourselves.

The outcome, unfortunately, will be a completely divided America. We might patronize different coffee brands, wear different shoes, subscribe to different streaming services. Our points of commonality might disappear.

That's not our preferred outcome. But it may be the most realistic outcome: two separate Americas, divided by politics.

None of these options are mutually exclusive. In fact, all of them should be pursued simultaneously. Our institutions must be opened up again. If they aren't, the social fabric of the country will continue to disintegrate.

FOR OUR CHILDREN

These days, I find myself worried for America on a bone-deep level.

I grew up in an America that made room for different points of view, an America that could tolerate political differences. I grew up in an America where we could attend ball games together without worrying about who voted for whom, where we could attend different schools and recognize our differences without trying to beat each other into submission. I grew up in an America where we could make the occasional offensive joke—and then apologize for it—and not have to worry about our livelihoods being stolen, because we all understood that we were human. Most of all, I grew up in an America where we could all participate in a search for truth, without fear that the mere searching would end in our societal excommunication.

That America is simply disappearing.

And that scares me for my kids.

I'm afraid that by the time they become adults, they'll take their lack of freedom for granted. I'm afraid that they'll already know not to speak out, because they'll have seen too many others lose their heads for doing so. I'm afraid that they won't explore interesting and diverse ideas, because to do so might mean social ostracizing or career suicide.

It's my job to protect my kids from this authoritarian culture. But as the institutions of America mobilize against families like yours and mine, we lose options.

What happens if my kids are *required* to reject my

values—to dishonor their father and mother, the tradition they've been taught—as a ticket into approved society?

What happens if my kids are told they can't speak truth about the nature of the world—and what happens if I fight back against the untruth?

What happens if I lose my job tomorrow because the authoritarian mob puts a target on my back?

Millions of Americans are asking these questions. Tens of millions.

Most of us.

That's the problem. But that's also the solution.

The authoritarian moment relies on the acquiescence of a silent majority.

We must no longer be silent.

When we stand up to the institutional dominance of an intransigent minority of Americans; when we announce that our values matter, that our ideas matter; when we speak out together, recognizing the diversity of our politics but cherishing our common belief in the power of liberty—the authoritarian moment finally ends.

And a new birth of freedom begins.

Acknowledgments

Every book is the work of dozens, not merely the author. That's certainly true of this book, too. To that end, thank you to Eric Nelson, my intrepid editor at HarperCollins, whose good humor, bravery, and nuanced thinking help me hone my own thinking and writing.

Thanks to my business partners, Jeremy Boreing and Caleb Robinson—both of them brilliant businessmen, true friends, and the guys with whom you'd want to walk into battle. Thanks to the entire staff at the Daily Wire, without whom our movement would be utterly debilitated, whose hard work makes my own possible, and whose constant sense of mischief enlivens every day and reminds me that the culture war is supposed to be fun. Thanks to our partners at Westwood

One, who don't just help us keep the lights on but stand with us when the going gets tough. Thanks to my long-time syndicators at Creators Syndicate, who discovered me two decades ago and have stood by that odd and incredible decision ever since.

Thanks to my parents, who are bulwarks for our family and for me personally, whose first response is always "How can we help?," and who instilled in me the values I hope to pass on to my children.

Speaking of which, thanks to my kids: my inspiration, my joy, and the source of my lack of sleep. Their hilarity, inventiveness, and imagination never fail to amaze.

Finally, thanks to my wife, who isn't just the world's greatest mom but the only person in the world with whom I'd want to forge forth on this adventure of a lifetime. I'm so glad I asked. And I'm more ecstatic every single day you said yes.

Notes

Introduction

1. Jonathan Chait, "Trump Authoritarianism Denial Is Over Now," NYMag.com, January 12, 2021, https://nymag .com/intelligencer/article/trump-authoritarianism-capitol -insurrection-mob-coup.html.
2. Paul Krugman, "This Putsch Was Decades in the Making," NYTimes.com, January 11, 2021, https://www .nytimes.com/2021/01/11/opinion/republicans-democracy .html.
3. Greg Sargent, "Trump's GOP has an ugly authoritarian core. A new poll exposes it," WashingtonPost.com, January 15, 2021, https://www.washingtonpost.com/opinions /2021/01/15/new-poll-trump-gop-approval-authoritarian/.
4. Lisa McGirr, "Trump Is the Republican Party's Past and Its Future," NYTimes.com, January 13, 2021, https://

www.nytimes.com/2021/01/13/opinion/gop-trump
.html.

5. CNN, January 14, 2021, https://twitter.com/tomselliott
/status/1349672644455575554.

6. Charles M. Blow, "Trump's Lackeys Must Also Be Punished," NYTimes.com, January 10, 2021, https://www
.nytimes.com/2021/01/10/opinion/trump-republicans
.html.

7. Joseph Wulfsohn, "MSNBC's Joy Reid suggests GOP
needs a 'de-Baathification' to rid support for Trump,"
FoxNews.com, January 15, 2021, https://www.foxnews
.com/media/msnbcs-joy-reid-suggests-gop-needs-a-de
-baathification-to-rid-support-for-trump.

8. 1 Samuel 8:7–20.

9. James Madison, *Federalist No. 10* (November 22, 1787).

10. John Adams, *The Political Writings of John Adams* (Washington, DC: Regnery, 2000), 13.

11. Theodor Adorno, Else Frenkel-Brenswik, Daniel J. Levinson, and R. Nevitt Sanford, *The Authoritarian Personality*
(London: Verso, 2019).

12. Bob Altemeyer, *The Authoritarian Specter* (Cambridge,
MA: Harvard University Press, 1996), 13–15.

13. Ibid., 216.

14. Ibid., 220–21.

15. Ronald Bailey, "Tracking Down the Elusive Left-Wing
Authoritarian," Reason.com, March 8, 2018, https://
reason.com/2018/03/08/tracking-down-the-elusive
-leftwing-autho/.

16. Thomas H. Costello, Shauna M. Bowes, Sean T. Stevens, Irwin D. Waldman, Arber Tasimi, and Scott O. Lilienfeld, "Clarifying the Structure and Nature of Left-Wing Authoritarianism," ResearchGate, May 11, 2020, https://www.researchgate.net/publication/341306723 _Clarifying_the_Structure_and_Nature_of_Left-Wing _Authoritarianism.

17. Herbert Marcuse, "Repressive Tolerance" (1965), https:// www.marcuse.org/herbert/pubs/60spubs/65repressive tolerance.htm.

18. Theodor Adorno and Herbert Marcuse, *Correspondence on the German Student Movement*, February 14, 1969, to August 6, 1969, https://hutnyk.files.wordpress.com/2013 /06/adornomarcuse_germannewleft.pdf.

19. https://twitter.com/Mike_Pence/status/134687981115 1605762.

20. Elliott C. McLaughlin, "Violence at Capitol and beyond reignites a debate over America's long-held defense of extremist speech," CNN.com, January 19, 2021, https:// www.cnn.com/2021/01/19/us/capitol-riots-speech-hate -extremist-first-amendment/index.html?utm_content =2021-01-19T14%3A35%3A03&utm_source=twCNN& utm_term=link&utm_medium=social.

21. https://twitter.com/nhannahjones/status/13483829480 05982208.

22. Max Boot, "Trump couldn't have incited sedition without the help of Fox News," WashingtonPost.com, January 18, 2021, https://www.washingtonpost.com/opinions/2021/01

/18/trump-couldnt-have-incited-sedition-without-help
-fox-news/.

23. Judd Legum and Tesnim Zekeria, "Major corporations
say they will stop donating to members of Congress who
tried to overturn the election," Popular.info, January 10,
2021, https://popular.info/p/three-major-corporations-say
-they.

24. Elizabeth A. Harris and Alexandra Alter, "Simon & Schuster Cancels Plans for Senator Hawley's Book," NYTimes
.com, January 7, 2021, https://www.nytimes.com/2021/01
/07/books/simon-schuster-josh-hawley-book.html.

25. Jazz Shaw, "The Cancel Culture Comes for Elise Stefanik," HotAir.com, January 13, 2021, https://hotair.com
/archives/jazz-shaw/2021/01/13/cancel-culture-comes
-elise-stefanik/.

26. Jordan Davidson, "The Biggest Gun Forum on the Planet
Was Just Kicked Off the Internet Without Explanation,"
TheFederalist.com, January 12, 2021, https://thefederal
ist.com/2021/01/12/the-biggest-gun-forum-on-the-planet
-was-just-kicked-off-the-internet-without-explanation/.

27. Brian Fung, "Parler has now been booted by Amazon,
Apple and Google," CNN.com, January 11, 2021, https://
www.cnn.com/2021/01/09/tech/parler-suspended-apple
-app-store/index.html.

28. https://twitter.com/tomselliott/status/135114085547894
7844.

29. Robby Soave, "No, AOC, It's Not the Government's Job
to 'Rein in Our Media,'" Reason.com, January 14, 2021,

https://reason.com/2021/01/14/aoc-rein-in-our-media
-literacy-trump-capitol-rots/.

30. https://twitter.com/coribush/status/134698514091284
4805.

31. Senator Ron Wyden, "The Capitol riots prove we need
to strengthen our democracy. That begins with voting rights," NBCNews.com, January 11, 2021, https://
www.nbcnews.com/think/opinion/capitol-riots-prove-we
-need-strengthen-our-democracy-begins-voting-ncna125
3642.

32. Eric Lutz, "Clyburn compares GOP bowing to Trump to
Nazi Germany," VanityFair.com, March 13, 2020, https://
www.vanityfair.com/news/2020/03/clyburn-compares
-gop-bowing-to-trump-to-nazi-nazi-germany.

33. "Representative Clyburn: Biden Should Use Executive Authority if the Other Side Refuses to Cooperate," Grabien
.com, January 18, 2021, https://grabien.com/story.php?id
=321515.

34. Emily Ekins, "Poll: 62% of Americans Say They Have Political Views They're Afraid to Share," CATO.org, July 22,
2020, https://www.cato.org/publications/survey-reports
/poll-62-americans-say-they-have-political-views-theyre
-afraid-share.

35. https://twitter.com/MarkDuplass/status/1019946917176
881152?ref_src=twsrc%5Etfw%7Ctwcamp%5Etweet
embed%7Ctwterm%5E1019946917176881152%7Ctwgr
%5E%7Ctwcon%5Es1_&ref_url=https%3A%2F
%2Fwww.vox.com%2Fpolicy-and-politics%2F2018%2F7

%2F19%2F17593174%2Fmark-duplass-ben-shapiro
-apology.

36. Zack Beauchamp, "Actor Mark Duplass apologizes for
praising conservative pundit Ben Shapiro," Vox.com,
July 19, 2018, https://www.vox.com/policy-and-politics
/2018/7/19/17593174/mark-duplass-ben-shapiro-apology.

37. Alexis de Tocqueville, *Democracy in America* (Chicago:
University of Chicago Press, 2000), 244–45, trans. Harvey
C. Mansfield and Delba Winthrop.

38. Jim VandeHei, "Our new reality: Three Americas," Axios
.com, January 10, 2021, https://www.axios.com/capitol
-siege-misinformation-trump-d9c9738b-0852-408d-a24f
-81c95938b41b.html?stream=top.

Chapter 1: How to Silence a Majority

1. Eric Kaufman, "Who are the real Shy Trumpers?,"
Unherd.com, November 6, 2020, https://unherd.com/2020
/11/meet-the-shy-trumpers/.

2. Thomas Piketty, "Thomas Piketty on Trump: 'The main
lesson for Europe and the world is clear,'" BusinessInsider
.com, November 16, 2016, https://www.businessinsider
.com/thomas-piketty-on-trump-the-main-lesson-for
-europe-and-the-world-is-clear-2016-11.

3. Nate Cohn, "The Election's Big Twist: The Racial Gap
Is Shrinking," NYTimes.com, October 28, 2020, https://
www.nytimes.com/2020/10/28/upshot/election-polling
-racial-gap.html.

4. Russell Kirk, "Ten Conservative Principles," KirkCenter .org, https://kirkcenter.org/conservatism/ten-conservative -principles/.

5. Leviticus 19:17.

6. Roger Scruton, *The West and the Rest: Globalization and the Terrorist Threat* (Newburyport, MA: Intercollegiate Studies Institute, 2014).

7. Joel Feinberg, *Offense to Others: The Moral Limits of the Criminal Law* (New York: Oxford University Press, 1985).

8. https://twitter.com/marcatracy/status/135780432142188 1348.

9. Nassem Nicholas Taleb, *Skin in the Game: Hidden Asymmetries in Daily Life* (New York: Random House, 2018), 75–77.

10. Rachel Brazil, "The physics of public opinion," Physics world.com, January 14, 2020, https://physicsworld.com/a/ the-physics-of-public-opinion/.

11. Christina Zhao, "Coca-Cola, Facing Backlash, Says 'Be Less White' Learning Plan Was About Workplace Inclusion," Newsweek.com, February 21, 2021, https:// www.newsweek.com/coca-cola-facing-backlash-says-less -white-learning-plan-was-about-workplace-inclusion -1570875.

12. "ACLU Case Selection Guidelines: Conflicts Between Competing Values or Priorities," WSJ.com, June 21, 2018, http://online.wsj.com/public/resources/documents /20180621ACLU.pdf?mod=article_inline.

13. "A Letter on Justice and Open Debate," *Harper's Weekly*, July 7, 2020, https://harpers.org/a-letter-on-justice-and -open-debate/.

14. Conor Friedersdorf, "Why Matthew Yglesias Left Vox," TheAtlantic.com, November 13, 2020, https://www .theatlantic.com/ideas/archive/2020/11/substack-and -medias-groupthink-problem/617102/.

15. "Read Joe Biden's President-Elect Acceptance Speech: Full Transcript," NYTimes.com, November 9, 2020, https://www.nytimes.com/article/biden-speech-transcript .html.

16. Ryan Saavedra, "Michelle Obama Demonizes 70 Million Americans Who Voted for Trump: Support 'Hate, Chaos, Division,'" DailyWire.com, November 7, 2020, https:// www.dailywire.com/news/michelle-obama-demonizes-70 -million-americans-who-voted-for-trump-support-hate -chaos-division.

17. Editorial Board, "Canceling Trump Alumni," WSJ .com, November 9, 2020, https://www.wsj.com/articles /canceling-trump-alumni-11604962923.

18. Harriet Alexander, "Lincoln Project urges 2.7m follow-ers to bombard law first trying to overturn Pennsylvania election result," Independent.co.uk, November 10, 2020, https://www.independent.co.uk/news/world/americas/us -election-2020/lincoln-project-election-pennsylvania-law -firm-linkedin-b1720710.html.

19. Laura Barron-Lopez and Holly Otterbein, "Tlaib lashes out at centrist Dems over election debacle: 'I can't be si-

lent,'" Politico.com, November 10, 2020, https://www
.politico.com/news/2020/11/11/rashida-tlaib-progressives
-election-435877.

20. Memo from New Deal Srategies, Justice Democrats, Sunrise Movement, Data for Progress re: What Went Wrong
for Congressional Democrats in 2020, November 10, 2020,
https://www.politico.com/f/?id=00000175-b4b4-dc7f
-a3fd-bdf660490000.

Chapter 2: How the Authoritarian Left Renormalized America

1. Josh Bivens, "Inadequate GDP growth continues in the
third quarter," Economic Policy Institute, October 26, 2012,
https://www.epi.org/publication/gdp-growth-picture
-october-2012/.
2. "President Exit Polls," *New York Times*, https://www
.nytimes.com/elections/2012/results/president/exit-polls
.html.
3. Barack Obama, *The Audacity of Hope* (New York: Crown,
2006), 11.
4. Ronald J. Pestritto, ed., *Woodrow Wilson: The Essential
Political Writings* (Lanham, MD: Rowman & Littlefield,
2005), 77–78.
5. John R. Shook and James A. Good, *John Dewey's Philosophy of Spirit, with the 1897 Lecture on Hegel* (New York:
Fordham University Press, 2010), 29.
6. Erick Trickey, "When America's Most Prominent Social-

ist Was Jailed for Speaking Out Against World War I," Smithsonianmag.com, June 15, 2018, https://www .smithsonianmag.com/history/fiery-socialist-challenged -nations-role-wwi-180969386/.

7. *Buck v. Bell* (1927), 274 US 200.

8. Margaret Sanger, "My Way to Peace," January 17, 1932, https://www.nyu.edu/projects/sanger/webedition/app /documents/show.php?sangerDoc=12 9037.xml.

9. Calvin Coolidge, "Speech on the 150th Anniversary of the Declaration of Independence," July 5, 1926, https://teaching americanhistory.org/library/document/speech-on-the -occasion-of-the-one-hundred-and-fiftieth-anniversary -of-the-declaration-of-independence/.

10. Franklin D. Roosevelt, "Campaign Address," October 14, 1936, https://teachingamericanhistory.org/library /document/campaign-address/.

11. Franklin D. Roosevelt, "State of the Union Message to Congress," January 11, 1944, http://www.fdrlibrary.marist .edu/archives/address_text.html.

12. Jonah Goldberg, *Liberal Fascism: The Secret History of the American Left, from Mussolini to the Politics of Change* (New York: Broadway Books, 2007), 158–59.

13. Samuel Staley, "FDR Policies Doubled the Length of the Great Depression," Reason.org, November 21, 2008, https://reason.org/commentary/fdr-policies-doubled-the -lengt/.

14. Amity Shlaes, *Great Society: A New History* (New York: Harper Perennial, 2019).

15. Alan Greenspan and Adrian Woolridge, *Capitalism in America: A History* (New York: Penguin, 2018), 306.

16. Alex J. Pollock, "Seven decades of inflation-adjusted Dow Jones industrial average," RStreet.org, April 18, 2018, https://www.rstreet.org/2018/04/18/seven-decades-of-the -inflation-adjusted-dow-jones-industrial-average/.

17. Jimmy Carter, "Energy and the National Goals," July 15, 1979, https://www.americanrhetoric.com/speeches/jimmy cartercrisisofconfidence.htm.

18. First Inaugural Address of Ronald Reagan, January 20, 1981, https://avalon.law.yale.edu/20th_century/reagan1.asp.

19. President William Jefferson Clinton, State of the Union Address, January 23, 1996, https://clintonwhitehouse4 .archives.gov/WH/New/other/sotu.html.

20. George W. Bush, "Full Text of Bush's Acceptance Speech," NYTimes.com, August 4, 2000, https://movies2.nytimes .com/library/politics/camp/080400wh-bush-speech .html.

21. "Barack Obama's Remarks to the Democratic National Convention," July 24, 2004, https://www.nytimes.com /2004/07/27/politics/campaign/barack-obamas-remarks -to-the-democratic-national.html.

22. Rolf Wiggershaus, *The Frankfurt School: Its History, Theories, and Political Significance* (Cambridge, MA: MIT Press, 1995), 135.

23. Erich Fromm, *Escape from Freedom* (New York: Henry Holt, 1941), 240.

24. Herbert Marcuse, "Repressive Tolerance" (1965), https://

www.marcuse.org/herbert/pubs/60spubs/65repressive tolerance.htm.

25. Stokely Carmichael, "Toward Black Liberation," *Massachusetts Review*, Autumn 1966, http://national humanitiescenter.org/pds/maai3/segregation/text8/car michael.pdf.

26. Richard Delgado and Jean Stefancic, *Critical Race Theory: An Introduction* (New York: New York University Press, 2012), 7–8.

27. Derrick A. Bell Jr., "Racial Realism," in George Wright and Maria Stalzer Wyant Cuzzo, eds., *The Legal Studies Reader* (New York: Peter Lang, 2004), 247.

28. Fred A. Bernstein, "Derrick Bell, Law Professor and Rights Advocate, Dies at 80," *New York Times*, October 6, 2011, https://www.nytimes.com/2011/10/06/us/derrick-bell -pioneering-harvard-law-professor-dies-at-80.html.

29. Christopher Caldwell, *The Age of Entitlement* (New York: Simon & Schuster, 2020), 6–7.

30. Ibid., 10.

31. Ibid., 34.

32. David Mills, "Sister Souljah's Call to Arms: The rapper says the riots were payback. Are you paying attention?," *Washington Post*, May 13, 1992, https://www.washingtonpost .com/wp-dyn/content/article/2010/03/31/AR20100 33101709.html.

33. Thomas B. Edsall, "Clinton Stuns Rainbow Coalition," *Washington Post*, July 14, 1992, https://www .washingtonpost.com/archive/politics/1992/06/14/clinton

-stuns-rainbow-coalition/02d7564f-5472-4081-b6b2
-2fe5b849fa60/.

34. Rashawn Ray and William A. Galston, "Did the 1994
    crime bill cause mass incarceration?," Brookings Institu-
    tion, August 28, 2020, https://www.brookings.edu/blog
    /fixgov/2020/08/28/did-the-1994-crime-bill-cause-mass
    -incarceration/.

35. "Barack Obama's Remarks to the Democratic National
    Convention," July 24, 2004, https://www.nytimes.com
    /2004/07/27/politics/campaign/barack-obamas-remarks
    -to-the-democratic-national.html.

36. Jonathan V. Last, "Michelle's America," *Weekly Standard*,
    February 18, 2008, https://www.washingtonexaminer.com
    /weekly-standard/michelles-america.

37. Victor Davis Hanson, "Obama: Transforming Amer-
    ica," RealClearPolitics.com, October 1, 2013, https://
    www.realclearpolitics.com/articles/2013/10/01/obama
    _transforming_america_120170.html.

38. Ed Pilkington, "Obama angers midwest voters with
    guns and religion remark," TheGuardian.com, April 14,
    2008, https://www.theguardian.com/world/2008/apr/14
    /barackobama.uselections2008.

39. Mark Preston and Dana Bash, "McCain defends charge
    that Obama playing race card," CNN.com, July 31, 2008,
    https://www.cnn.com/2008/POLITICS/07/31/campaign
    .wrap/index.html.

40. Dan Merica, Kevin Liptak, Jeff Zeleny, David Wright, and
    Rebecca Buck, "Obama memoir confronts role his presi-

dency played in Republican obstructionism and Trump's rise," CNN.com, November 15, 2020, https://www.cnn .com/2020/11/12/politics/obama-memoir-promised-land /index.html.

41. Saul D. Alinsky, *Rules for Radicals: A Practical Primer for Revolution* (New York: Vintage Books, 1989), 184–86.

42. Kimberle Crenshaw, "Why intersectionality can't wait," *Washington Post*, September 24, 2015, https://www .washingtonpost.com/news/in-theory/wp/2015/09/24/why -intersectionality-cant-wait/?noredirect=on&utm_term= .179ecf062277.

43. Josh Earnest, "President Obama Supports Same-Sex Marriage," ObamaWhiteHouse.Archives.gov, May 10, 2012, https://obamawhitehouse.archives.gov/blog/2012/05/10 /obama-supports-same-sex-marriage.

44. Julia Preston and John H. Cushman Jr., "Obama to Permit Young Migrants to Remain in US," NYTimes.com, June 15, 2012, https://www.nytimes.com/2012/06/16/us /us-to-stop-deporting-some-illegal-immigrants.html.

45. Shannon Travis, "Is Obama taking black vote for granted?," CNN.com, July 13, 2012, https://www.cnn .com/2012/07/12/politics/obama-black-voters/index.html.

46. Rodney Hawkins, "Biden tells African-American audience GOP ticket would put them 'back in chains,'" CBSNews .com, August 14, 2012, https://www.cbsnews.com/news /biden-tells-african-american-audience-gop-ticket-would -put-them-back-in-chains/.

47. Ewen MacAskill, "Obama steps up criticism of Romney in

battle for women voters," TheGuardian.com, October 17, 2012, https://www.cbsnews.com/news/biden-tells-african -american-audience-gop-ticket-would-put-them-back-in -chains/.

48. Dan Balz, "Obama's coalition, campaign deliver a second term," WashingtonPost.com, November 7, 2012, https:// www.washingtonpost.com/politics/decision2012/obamas -coalition-campaign-deliver-a-second-term/2012/11/07 /fb156970-2926-11e2-96b6-8e6a7524553f_story.html.

49. Ruy Texiera and John Hapin, "The Return of the Obama Coalition," Center for American Progress, November 8, 2012, https://www.americanprogress.org/issues/democracy /news/2012/11/08/44348/the-return-of-the-obama -coalition/.

50. Yoni Appelbaum, "How America Ends," *Atlantic*, December 2019, https://www.theatlantic.com/magazine/archive /2019/12/how-america-ends/600757/.

51. Domenico Montanaro, "How the Browning of America Is Upending Both Political Parties," NPR.org, October 12, 2016, https://www.npr.org/2016/10/12/497529936/how-the -browning-of-america-is-upending-both-political-parties.

52. David Siders, Christopher Cadelago, and Laura Barron-Lopez, "To defeat Trump, Dems rethink the Obama coalition formula," Politico.com, November 26, 2019, https://www.politico.com/news/2019/11/25/race-identity -democrats-2020-electability-072959.

53. Matt Stevens, "Read Joe Biden's President-Elect Acceptance Speech: Full Text," NYTimes.com, November 9, 2020,

https://www.nytimes.com/article/biden-speech-transcript
.html.

54. Byron York, July 15, 2020, https://twitter.com
/ByronYork/status/1283372233730203651?ref_src=twsrc
%5Etfw%7Ctwcamp%5Etweetembed%7Ctwterm
%5E1283372233730203651%7Ctwgr%5E%7Ctwcon
%5Es1_&ref_url=https%3A%2F%2Fwww.foxnews.com
%2Fus%2Fdc-museum-graphic-whiteness-race.

55. Ben Weingarten, "Would a President Joe Biden Institute
Systemic Racism in Our Legal System?," TheFederalist
.com, October 22, 2020, https://thefederalist.com/2020
/10/22/would-a-president-joe-biden-institute-systemic
-racism-in-our-legal-system/.

56. Russell Vought, "Memorandum for the Heads of Executive
Departments and Agencies," September 4, 2020, https://
www.whitehouse.gov/wp-content/uploads/2020/09/M-20
-34.pdf.

57. Ibram X. Kendi, "Pass an Anti-Racist Constitutional Amendment," Politico.com, 2019, https://www
.politico.com/interactives/2019/how-to-fix-politics-in
-america/inequality/pass-an-anti-racist-constitutional
-amendment/.

58. Sheryll Cashin, "A Blueprint for Racial Healing in the
Biden Era," *Politico Magazine*, November 21, 2020,
https://www.politico.com/news/magazine/2020/11/21
/biden-era-racial-healing-blueprint-438900.

59. Associated Press, "Spanberger to House Dems: Never
'use the word "socialist" or "socialism" again,'" Novem-

ber 6, 2020, https://wjla.com/news/local/house-democrats
-blame-losses-on-polls-message-even-trump-11-06-2020.

60. Open Letter from New Deal Strategies, Justice Democrats, Sunrise Movement, Data for Progress, November 10, 2020, https://www.politico.com/f/?id=00000175
-b4b4-dc7f-a3fd-bdf660490000.

Chapter 3: The Creation of a New Ruling Class

1. Graham Kates, "Lori Loughlin and Felicity Huffman
among dozens charged in college bribery scheme," CBS
News.com, March 12, 2019, https://www.cbsnews.com
/news/college-admissions-scandal-bribery-cheating-today
-felicity-huffman-arrested-fbi-2019-03-12/.

2. Kate Taylor, "By Turns Tearful and Stoic, Felicity Huffman Gets 14-Day Prison Sentence," NYTimes.com, September 13, 2019, https://www.nytimes.com/2019/09/13/us
/felicity-huffman-sentencing.html.

3. Graham Kates, "Lori Loughlin and Felicity Huffman
among dozens charged in college bribery scheme," CBS
News.com, March 12, 2019, https://www.cbsnews.com
/news/college-admissions-scandal-bribery-cheating-today
-felicity-huffman-arrested-fbi-2019-03-12/.

4. Kate Taylor, "By Turns Tearful and Stoic, Felicity Huffman Gets 14-Day Prison Sentence," NYTimes.com, September 13, 2019, https://www.nytimes.com/2019/09/13/us
/felicity-huffman-sentencing.html.

5. Lisa Respers France, "Brands distance themselves

from Lori Laughlin and daughter Olivia Jade," CNN .com, March 14, 2019, https://www.cnn.com/2019/03/14 /entertainment/olivia-jade-cheating-scandal/index.html.

6. Kerry Justich, "Celebrity kid called 'spoiled' and 'privileged brat' after saying she's going to college for 'game days' and 'partying,'" Yahoo.com, August 17, 2018, https://www.yahoo.com/lifestyle/celebrity-kid-called -spoiled-privileged-brat-saying-shes-going-college-game -days-partying-190101738.html.

7. "Percentage of the US population who have completed four years of college or more from 1940 to 2019, by gender," Statista.com, March 2020, https://www.statista .com/statistics/184272/educational-attainment-of-college -diploma-or-higher-by-gender/.

8. Joseph B. Fuller and Manjari Raman, "Dismissed by Degrees," Harvard Business School, October 2017, https:// www.hbs.edu/managing-the-future-of-work/Documents /dismissed-by-degrees.pdf.

9. "Number of People with Master's and Doctoral Degrees Doubles Since 2000," Census.gov, February 21, 2019, https://www.census.gov/library/stories/2019/02/number -of-people-with-masters-and-phd-degrees-double -since-2000.html#:~:text=Since%202000%2C%20the %20number%20of,from%208.6%20percent%20in %202000.

10. Connor Harris, "The Earning Curve: Variability and Overlap in Labor-Outcomes by Education Level," Manhat-

tan Institute, February 26, 2020, https://www.manhattan -institute.org/high-school-college-wage-gap?utm_source =press_release&utm_medium=email.

11. J. D. Vance, *Hillbilly Elegy: A Memoir of a Family and Culture in Crisis* (New York: HarperCollins, 2016).

12. Charles Murray, *Coming Apart* (New York: Crown Forum, 2012), 16–19.

13. Christopher Lasch, *The Revolt of the Elites and the Betrayal of Democracy* (New York: Norton, 1995), 6.

14. Joseph Epstein, "Is There a Doctor in the White House? Not if You Need an M.D.," WSJ.com, December 11, 2020, https://www.wsj.com/articles/is-there-a-doctor-in-the -white-house-not-if-you-need-an-m-d-11607727380.

15. Bryan Alexander, "Dr. Jill was blindsided by Wall Street Journal call to drop 'Dr.' title: 'It was really the tone of it,'" USAToday.com, December 17, 2020, https://www .usatoday.com/story/entertainment/tv/2020/12/17/jill -biden-speaks-out-wall-street-journal-column-drop-dr -title/3952529001/.

16. Paul A. Gigot, "The Biden Team Strikes Back," WSJ.com, December 13, 2020, https://www.wsj.com/articles/the -biden-team-strikes-back-11607900812.

17. Adam Harris, "America Is Divided by Education," *Atlantic*, November 7, 2018, https://www.theatlantic.com /education/archive/2018/11/education-gap-explains -american-politics/575113/.

18. Thomas Edsall, "Honestly, This Was a Weird Election,"

NYTimes.com, December 2, 2020, https://www.nytimes
.com/2020/12/02/opinion/biden-trump-moderates
-progressives.html.

19. Helen Pluckrose and James Lindsay, *Cynical Theories*
([Durham, NC]: Pitchstone, 2020), 57.

20. Ibram X. Kendi, *How to Be an Antiracist* (New York: One
World, 2019), 84.

21. Robin DiAngelo, *White Fragility* (Boston: Beacon Press,
2018), 17.

22. Ibram X. Kendi, "Pass an Anti-Racist Constitutional Amendment," Politico.com, 2019, https://www
.politico.com/interactives/2019/how-to-fix-politics-in
-america/inequality/pass-an-anti-racist-constitutional
-amendment/.

23. Ibram X. Kendi, *How to Be an Antiracist* (One World,
2019), 19.

24. Ibram X. Kendi, "A Battle Between the Two Souls of
America," TheAtlantic.com, November 11, 2020, https://
www.theatlantic.com/ideas/archive/2020/11/americas-two
-souls/617062/.

25. Helen Pluckrose and James Lindsay, *Cynical Theories*
([Durham, NC]: Pitchstone, 2020), 210–11.

26. Richard Sosis and Candace Alcorta, "Signaling, Solidarity, and the Sacred: The Evolution of Religious Behavior,"
Evolutionary Anthropology 12 (2003): 264–74, http://sites
.oxy.edu/clint/evolution/articles/SignalingSolidarityand
theSacredTheEvolutionofReligiousBehavior.pdf.

27. Christopher Lasch, *The Revolt of the Elites and the Betrayal of Democracy* (New York: Norton, 1995), 21.

28. Mike McRae, "A Massive Hoax Involving 20 Fake Culture Studies Papers Just Exploded in Academia," Science Alert.com, October 4, 2018, https://www.sciencealert.com /cultural-studies-sokal-squared-hoax-20-fake-papers.

29. Yascha Mounk, "What an Audacious Hoax Reveals About Academia," TheAtlantic.com, October 5, 2018, https:// www.theatlantic.com/ideas/archive/2018/10/new-sokal -hoax/572212/.

30. Christine Emba, "The 'Sokal Squared' hoax sums up American politics," WashingtonPost.com, October 10, 2018, https://www.washingtonpost.com/opinions/what -do-the-kavanaugh-confirmation-and-the-sokal-squared -hoax-have-in-common/2018/10/10/f7efabf8-ccc6-11e8 -a3e6-44daa3d35ede_story.html.

31. Heather Mac Donald, *The Diversity Delusion* (New York: St. Martin's, 2018), 2.

32. David Randall, "Social Justice Education in America," NAS.org, November 29, 2019, https://www.nas.org /reports/social-justice-education-in-america/full-report #Preface&Acknowledgements.

33. O. Carter Snead, *What It Means to Be Human* (Cambridge, MA: Harvard University Press, 2020), 68–70.

34. Ibid., 84–85.

35. Helen Pluckrose and James Lindsay, *Cynical Theories* ([Durham, NC]: Pitchstone, 2020).

36. Roger Kimball, *The Long March* (New York: Encounter Books, 2000), 106–11.

37. Ibid., 112–18.

38. Shelby Steele, *White Guilt* (New York: HarperCollins, 2006).

39. Jon Street, "Less than 2 percent of Harvard faculty are conservative, survey finds," CampusReform.org, March 4, 2020, https://www.campusreform.org/?ID=14469.

40. Rachel Treisman and David Yaffe-Bellany, "Yale faculty skews liberal, survey shows," YaleDailyNews.com, September 14, 2017, https://yaledailynews.com/blog/2017/09/14/yale-faculty-skews-liberal-survey-shows/.

41. James Freeman, "Yale Prof Estimates Faculty Political Diversity at '0%,'" WSJ.com, December 9, 2019, https://yaledailynews.com/blog/2017/09/14/yale-faculty-skews-liberal-survey-shows/.

42. Jon Street, "STUDY: Profs donate to Dems over Republicans by 95:1 ratio," CampusReform.org, January 22, 2020, https://www.campusreform.org/?ID=14255.

43. Bradford Richardson, "Liberal professors outnumber conservatives nearly 12 to 1, study finds," WashingtonTimes.com, October 6, 2016, https://www.washingtontimes.com/news/2016/oct/6/liberal-professors-outnumber-conservatives-12-1/.

44. Jon A. Shields, "The Disappearing Conservative Professor," NationalAffairs.com, Fall 2018, https://www.nationalaffairs.com/publications/detail/the-disappearing-conservative-professor.

45. Nick Gillespie, "Would the ACLU Still Defend Nazis' Right to March in Skokie?," Reason.com, January 2021, https://reason.com/2020/12/20/would-the-aclu-still-defend-nazis-right-to-march-in-skokie/.

46. Scott Jaschik, "Who Defines What Is Racist?," Inside-HigherEd.com, May 30, 2017, https://www.insidehighered.com/news/2017/05/30/escalating-debate-race-evergreen-state-students-demand-firing-professor.

47. Tom Knighton, "Leftists Storm Out of Lecture Over Claim Men, Women Have Different Bodies," PJMedia.com, March 16, 2018, https://pjmedia.com/news-and-politics/tom-knighton/2018/03/16/leftists-storm-lecture-claim-men-women-different-bodies-n56793.

48. Conor Friedersdorf, "The Perils of Writing a Provocative Email at Yale," TheAtlantic.com, May 26, 2016, https://www.theatlantic.com/politics/archive/2016/05/the-peril-of-writing-a-provocative-email-at-yale/484418/.

49. Jon A. Shields, "The Disappearing Conservative Professor," NationalAffairs.com, Fall 2018, https://www.nationalaffairs.com/publications/detail/the-disappearing-conservative-professor.

50. Norimitsu Onishi, "Will American Ideas Tear France Apart? Some of Its Leaders Think So," NYTimes.com, February 9, 2021, https://www.nytimes.com/2021/02/09/world/europe/france-threat-american-universities.html?action=click&module=Top%20Stories&pgtype=Homepage.

51. Joseph B. Fuller and Manjari Raman, "Dismissed by De-

grees," Harvard Business School, October 2017, https://www.hbs.edu/managing-the-future-of-work/Documents/dismissed-by-degrees.pdf.

Chapter 4: How Science™ Defeated Actual Science

1. Adam Gabbatt, "US anti-lockdown rallies could cause surge in Covid-19 cases, experts warn," TheGuardian.com, April 20, 2020, https://www.theguardian.com/us-news/2020/apr/20/us-protests-lockdown-coronavirus-cases-surge-warning.

2. Michael Juliano, "Some LA parks are closing until further notice after a busy weekend on the trails," Timeout.com, March 22, 2020, https://www.timeout.com/los-angeles/news/some-l-a-parks-are-closing-until-further-notice-after-a-busy-weekend-on-the-trails-032220.

3. Bruce Ritchie and Alexandra Glorioso, "Florida won't close its beaches. Here's exactly what DeSantis said about that," Politico.com, March 19, 2020, https://www.politico.com/states/florida/story/2020/03/19/florida-wont-close-its-beaches-heres-exactly-what-desantis-said-about-that-1268185.

4. Heather Mac Donald, "The Myth of Systemic Police Racism," WSJ.com, June 2, 2020, https://www.wsj.com/articles/the-myth-of-systemic-police-racism-11591119883.

5. Larry Buchanan, Quoctrung Bui, and Jugal K. Patel, "Black Lives Matter May Be the Largest Movement in

US History," NYTimes.com, July 3, 2020, https://www
.nytimes.com/interactive/2020/07/03/us/george-floyd
-protests-crowd-size.html.

6. Craig Mauger and James David Dickson, "With little social distancing, Whitmer marches with protesters," De-
troitNews.com, June 4, 2020, https://www.detroitnews
.com/story/news/local/michigan/2020/06/04/whitmer
-appears-break-social-distance-rules-highland-park
-march/3146244001/.

7. Jaclyn Cosgrove, Tania Ganguli, Julia Wick, Hailey
Branson-Potts, Matt Hamilton, and Liam Dillon, "Mayor
Garcetti takes a knee amid chants of 'Defund police!' at
downtown LA protest," LATimes.com, June 2, 2020,
https://www.latimes.com/california/story/2020-06-02
/mayor-garcetti-takes-a-knee-amid-chants-of-defund
-police-at-downtown-l-a-protest.

8. Vincent Barone, "NYC Black Lives Matter marches can
continue despite large-event ban, de Blasio says," NYPost
.com, July 9, 2020, https://nypost.com/2020/07/09/nyc
-allows-black-lives-matter-marches-despite-ban-on-large
-events/.

9. Rachel Weiner, "Political and health leaders' embrace
of Floyd protests fuels debate over coronavirus restrictions," WashingtonPost.com, June 11, 2020, https://
www.washingtonpost.com/health/political-and-health
-leaders-embrace-of-floyd-protests-fuels-debate-over
-coronavirus-restrictions/2020/06/11/9c60bca6-a761-11ea
-bb20-ebf0921f3bbd_story.html.

10. Julia Marcus and Gregg Gonsalves, "Public-Health Experts Are Not Hypocrites," TheAtlantic.com, June 11, 2020, https://www.theatlantic.com/ideas/archive/2020/06/public-health-experts-are-not-hypocrites/612853/.

11. Terrance Smith, "White coats and black lives: Health care workers say 'racism is a pandemic too,'" June 12, 2020, https://abcnews.go.com/Politics/white-coats-black-lives-health-care-workers-racism/story?id=71195580.

12. Michael Powell, "Are Protests Dangerous? What Experts Say May Depend on Who's Protesting What," NYTimes.com, July 6, 2020, https://www.nytimes.com/2020/07/06/us/Epidemiologists-coronavirus-protests-quarantine.html.

13. Joseph P. Williams, "Pandemic, Protests Cause Racism to Resonate as a Public Health Issue," USNews.com, July 8, 2020, https://www.usnews.com/news/healthiest-communities/articles/2020-07-08/racism-resonates-as-public-health-crisis-amid-pandemic-protests.

14. Isaac Scher, "NYC's contact tracers have been told not to ask people if they've attended a protest," BusinessInsider.com, June 15, 2020, https://www.businessinsider.com/nyc-contact-tracers-not-asking-people-attend-george-floyd-protest-2020-6.

15. "COVID-19 Hospitalization and Death by Age," CDC.gov, August 18, 2020, https://www.cdc.gov/coronavirus/2019-ncov/covid-data/investigations-discovery/hospitalization-death-by-age.html.

16. Yascha Mounk, "Why I'm Losing Trust in the Institutions," Persuasion.community, December 23, 2020, https://www.persuasion.community/p/why-im-losing -trust-in-the-institutions.

17. Abby Goodnough and Jan Hoffman, "The Elderly vs. Essential Workers: Who Should Get the Coronavirus Vaccine First?," NYTimes.com, December 5, 2020, https://www.nytimes.com/2020/12/05/health/covid-vaccine-first .html.

18. Yascha Mounk, "Why I'm Losing Trust in the Institutions," Persuasion.community, December 23, 2020, https://www.persuasion.community/p/why-im-losing -trust-in-the-institutions.

19. Stephen Pinker, *Enlightenment Now: The Case for Reason, Science, Humanism and Progress* (New York: Viking, 2018), 4.

20. M. Collins, R. Knutti, J. Arblaster, J.-L. Dufresne, T. Fichefet, P. Friedlingstein, X. Gao, W. J. Gutowski, T. Johns, G. Krinner, M. Shongwe, C. Tebaldi, A. J. Weaver, and M. Wehner, "2013: Long-term Climate Change: Projections, Commitments and Irreversibility," in *Climate Change 2013: The Physical Science Basis. Contribution of Working Group I to the Fifth Assessment Report of the Intergovernmental Panel on Climate Change* (Cambridge and New York: Cambridge University Press, 2013), https://www.ipcc.ch/site/assets/uploads/2018/02/WG1AR5 _Chapter12_FINAL.pdf.

21. Alan Buis, "Making Sense of 'Climate Sensitivity,'" Climate.NASA.gov, September 8, 2020, https://climate.nasa.gov/blog/3017/making-sense-of-climate-sensitivity/.

22. "Economics Nobel goes to inventor of models used in UN 1.5C report," ClimateChangeNews.com, October 8, 2018, https://www.climatechangenews.com/2018/10/08/economics-nobel-goes-inventor-models-used-un-1-5c-report/.

23. Paul Krugman, "The Depravity of Climate-Change Denial," NYTimes.com, November 26, 2018, https://www.nytimes.com/2018/11/26/opinion/climate-change-denial-republican.html.

24. Nicolas Loris, "Staying in Paris Agreement Would Have Cost Families $20K," Heritage.org, November 5, 2019, https://www.heritage.org/environment/commentary/staying-paris-agreement-would-have-cost-families-20k.

25. Michael Greshko, "Current Climate Pledges Aren't Enough to Stop Severe Warming," NationalGeographic.com, October 31, 2017, https://www.nationalgeographic.com/news/2017/10/paris-agreement-climate-change-usa-nicaragua-policy-environment/#close.

26. Kevin D. Dayaratna, PhD, and Nicolas D. Loris, "Assessing the Costs and Benefits of the Green New Deal's Energy Policies," Heritage.org, July 24, 2019, https://www.heritage.org/sites/default/files/2019-07/BG3427.pdf.

27. Helen Pluckrose and James Lindsay, Cynical Theories ([Durham, NC]: Pitchstone, 2020), 37.

28. Lawrence Krauss, "The Ideological Corruption of Science,"

WSJ.com, July 12, 2020, https://www.wsj.com/articles/the
-ideological-corruption-of-science-11594572501?mod=ar
ticle_inline.

29. Richard Haier, "No Voice at VOX: Sense and Nonsense
    about Discussing IQ and Race," Quillette.com, June 11,
    2017, https://quillette.com/2017/06/11/no-voice-vox-sense
    -nonsense-discussing-iq-race/.

30. Lawrence H. Summers, "Remarks at NBER Conference on
    Diversifying the Science & Engineering Workforce," Office
    of the President of Harvard University, January 14, 2005,
    https://web.archive.org/web/20080130023006/http://www
    .president.harvard.edu/speeches/2005/nber.html.

31. Editorial Board, "Science Eats Its Own," WSJ.com, De-
    cember 23, 2020, https://www.wsj.com/articles/science
    -eats-its-own-11608765409.

32. Ben Shapiro, "A Brown University Researcher Released
    a Study About Teens Imitating Their Peers by Turning
    Trans. The Left Went Insane. So Brown Caved," Daily-
    Wire.com, August 28, 2018, https://www.dailywire.com
    /news/brown-university-researcher-released-study-about
    -ben-shapiro.

33. Abigail Shrier, "Amazon Enforces 'Trans' Orthodox,"
    WSJ.com, June 22, 2020, https://www.wsj.com/articles
    /amazon-enforces-trans-orthodoxy-11592865818.

34. Abigail Shrier, "Does the ACLU Want to Ban My
    Book?," WSJ.com, November 15, 2020, https://www
    .wsj.com/articles/does-the-aclu-want-to-ban-my-book
    -11605475898.

35. Kathleen Doheny, "Boy or Girl? Fetal DNA Tests Often Spot On," WebMD.com, August 9, 2011, https://www .webmd.com/baby/news/20110809/will-it-be-a-boy-or -girl-fetal-dna-tests-often-spot-on#1.

36. "AMA Adopts New Policies at 2018 Interim Meeting," AMA-Assn.org, November 13, 2018, https://www.ama -assn.org/press-center/press-releases/ama-adopts-new -policies-2018-interim-meeting.

37. "AMA Adopts New Policies During First Day of Voting at Interim Meeting," American Medical Association, November 19, 2019, https://www.ama-assn.org/press-center /press-releases/ama-adopts-new-policies-during-first-day -voting-interim-meeting.

38. Vadim M. Shteyler, M.D., Jessica A. Clarke, J.D., and Eli Y. Adashi, M.D., "Failed Assignments—Rethinking Sex Designations on Birth Certificates," NEJM.org, December 17, 2020, https://www.nejm.org/doi/full/10.1056 /NEJMp2025974.

39. Lawrence Krauss, "The Ideological Corruption of Science," WSJ.com, July 12, 2020, https://www.wsj.com/articles/the -ideological-corruption-of-science-11594572501?mod=ar ticle_inline.

40. "An Open Letter to the Communications of the ACM," December 29, 2020, https://docs.google.com/document /d/1-KM6yc416Gh1wue92DHReoyZqheIaIM23fkz0KwO pkw/edit.

41. "Yann LeCun Quits Twitter Amid Acrimonious Ex-

changes on AI Bias," SyncedReview.com, June 30, 2020, https://syncedreview.com/2020/06/30/yann-lecun-quits -twitter-amid-acrimonious-exchanges-on-ai-bias/.

42. Bridget Balch, "Curing health care of racism: Nikole Hannah-Jones and Ibram X. Kendi, PhD, call on institutions to foster change," AAMC.org, November 17, 2020, https://www.aamc.org/news-insights/curing-health-care -racism-nikole-hannah-jones-and-ibram-x-kendi-phd -call-institutions-foster-change.

43. Heather Mac Donald, "How Identity Politics Is Harming the Sciences," City-Journal.org, Spring 2018, https:// www.city-journal.org/html/how-identity-politics-harming -sciences-15826.html.

44. Philip Ball, "Prejudice persists," ChemistryWorld.com, June 9, 2020, https://www.chemistryworld.com/opinion /viewing-science-as-a-meritocracy-allows-prejudice-to -persist/4011923.article.

45. Katrina Kramer, "*Angewandte* essay calling diversity in chemistry harmful decried as 'abhorrent,' 'egregious,'" ChemistryWorld.com, June 9, 2020, https://www .chemistryworld.com/news/angewandte-essay-calling -diversity-in-chemistry-harmful-decried-as-abhorrent -and-egregious/4011926.article.

46. Editors, "*Scientific American* Endorses Joe Biden," *Scientific American*, October 1, 2020, https://www .scientificamerican.com/article/scientific-american -endorses-joe-biden1/.

47. Editorial, "Why Nature supports Joe Biden for US president," Nature.com, October 14, 2020, https://www.nature.com/articles/d41586-020-02852-x?utm_source=twitter&utm_medium=social&utm_content=organic&utm_campaign=NGMT_USG_JC01_GL_Nature.

48. Editors, "Dying in a Leadership Vacuum," *New England Journal of Medicine*, October 8, 2020, https://www.nejm.org/doi/full/10.1056/NEJMe2029812.

Chapter 5: Your Authoritarian Boss

1. Alma Cohen, Moshe Hazan, Roberto Tallarita, and David Weiss, "The Politics of CEOs," National Bureau of Economic Research, May 2019, https://www.nber.org/system/files/working_papers/w25815/w25815.pdf.

2. Doug McMillon, "Advancing Our Work on Racial Equity," Walmart.com, June 12, 2020, https://corporate.walmart.com/newsroom/2020/06/12/advancing-our-work-on-racial-equity.

3. Rachel Lerman and Todd C. Frenkel, "Retailers and restaurants across the US close their doors amid protests," WashingtonPost.com, June 1, 2020, https://www.washingtonpost.com/technology/2020/06/01/retailers-restaurants-across-us-close-their-doors-amid-protests/.

4. Tim Cook, "Speaking up on racism," Apple.com, https://www.apple.com/speaking-up-on-racism/.

5. Mitchell Schnurman, "'Silence is not an option': What CEOs are saying about racial violence in America," Dal-

lasNews.com, June 7, 2020, https://www.dallasnews.com /business/commentary/2020/06/07/silence-is-not-an -option-what-ceos-are-saying-about-racial-violence-in -america/.

6. "Addressing racial injustice," Microsoft.com, June 23, 2020, https://blogs.microsoft.com/blog/2020/06/23/addressing -racial-injustice/.

7. Joseph Guzman, "Netflix pledges $100 million to support Black communities in the US," Thehill.com, June 30, 2020, https://thehill.com/changing-america/respect/equality /505229-netflix-pledges-100-million-to-support-black -communities-in.

8. Mitchell Schnurman, "'Silence is not an option': What CEOs are saying about racial violence in America," Dal- lasNews.com, June 7, 2020, https://www.dallasnews.com /business/commentary/2020/06/07/silence-is-not-an -option-what-ceos-are-saying-about-racial-violence-in -america/.

9. https://twitter.com/gushers/status/1269110304086114304.

10. Katie Canales, "A 'handful' of Cisco employees were fired after posting offensive comments objecting to the compa- ny's support of the Black Lives Matter movement," Business Insider.com, July 17, 2020, https://www.businessinsider .com/cisco-employees-fired-racist-comments-black-lives -matter-2020-7.

11. Associated Press, "Sacramento Kings broadcaster Grant Napear fired after 'all lives matter' tweet," Detroit News.com, June 3, 2020, https://www.detroitnews.com

/story/sports/nba/pistons/2020/06/03/sacramento-kings
-broadcaster-grant-napear-out-after-all-lives-matter
-tweet/3132629001/.

12. Vandana Rambaran, "Dean fired after saying 'BLACK
LIVES MATTER, but also, EVERYONE'S LIFE MAT-
TERS' in email," FoxNews.com, July 2, 2020, https://
www.foxnews.com/us/dean-fired-after-saying-black-lives
-matter-but-also-everyones-life-matters-in-email.

13. Dunja Djudjic, "B&H Employee 'removed' after publicly
opposing Black Lives Matter movement," DIYPhotogra
phy.net, June 11, 2020, https://www.diyphotography.net
/bh-employee-removed-after-publicly-opposing-black
-lives-matter-movement/.

14. Jemimi McEvoy, "Every CEO and Leader That Stepped
Down Since Black Lives Matter Protests Began,"
Forbes.com, July 1, 2020, https://www.forbes.com/sites
/jemimamcevoy/2020/07/01/every-ceo-and-leader-that
-stepped-down-since-black-lives-matter-protests-began
/?sh=595688765593.

15. Brad Polumbo, 'Is Black Lives Matter Marxist? No and
Yes," FEE.org, July 7, 2020, https://fee.org/articles/is
-black-lives-matter-marxist-no-and-yes/.

16. Alyssa Newcomb, "How to delete old tweets before they
come back to haunt you," NBCNews.com, August 3, 2018,
https://www.nbcnews.com/tech/tech-news/how-delete
-old-tweets-they-come-back-haunt-you-n896546.

17. Christopher Caldwell, *The Age of Entitlement* (New York:
Simon & Schuster, 2020), 169.

18. "#BrandsGetReal: What consumers want from brands in a divided society," SproutSocial.com, November 2018, https:// sproutsocial.com/insights/data/social-media-connection/.

19. James R. Bailey and Hillary Phillips, "How Do Consumers Feel When Companies Get Political?," HBR.org, February 17, 2020, https://hbr.org/2020/02/how-do-consumers -feel-when-companies-get-political.

20. Alexander Osipovich and Akane Otani, "Nasdaq Seeks Board-Diversity Rule That Most Listed Firms Don't Meet," WSJ.com, December 1, 2020, https://www.wsj .com/articles/nasdaq-proposes-board-diversity-rule-for -listed-companies-11606829244.

21. Klaus Schwab, "A Better Economy Is Possible. But We Need to Reimagine Capitalism to Do It," Time.com, October 22, 2020, https://time.com/collection/great-reset /5900748/klaus-schwab-capitalism/.

22. Jesse Pound, "Biden says investors 'don't need me,' calls for end of 'era of shareholder capitalism,'" CNBC.com, July 9, 2020, https://www.cnbc.com/2020/07/09/biden -says-investors-dont-need-me-calls-for-end-of-era-of -shareholder-capitalism.html.

23. Biz Carson, "Expensify's CEO emailed users to encourage them to 'vote for Biden,'" Protocol.com, October 22, 2020, https://www.protocol.com/bulletins/expensifys-ceo -emailed-all-of-his-users-to-encourage-them-to-protect -democracy-vote-for-biden.

24. Robin DiAngelo, *White Fragility* (Boston: Beacon Press, 2018).

25. Benjamin Zeisloft, "UConn agrees to pay 'White Fragility' author $20k for 3.5 hour anti-racism lecture," Campus Reform.org, August 12, 2019, https://www.campusreform .org/?ID=15430.

26. Edward H. Chang et al., "Does Diversity Training Work the Way It's Supposed To?," *Harvard Business Review*, July 9, 2019, https://hbr.org/2019/07/does-diversity -training-work-the-way-its-supposed-to.

27. Frank Dobbin and Alexandra Kalev, "Why Diversity Programs Fail," *Harvard Business Review*, July–August 2016, https://hbr.org/2016/07/why-diversity-programs-fail.

28. Pamela Newkirk, "Diversity Has Become a Booming Business. So Where Are the Results?," Time.com, October 19, 2019, https://time.com/5696943/diversity-business/.

29. Emily Heil, "The Goya boycott could impact the brand, experts say—just not the way you think," Washington Post.com, July 28, 2020, https://www.washingtonpost.com /news/voraciously/wp/2020/07/28/the-goya-boycott-could -impact-the-brand-experts-say-just-not-the-way-you -think/.

30. Meera Jagannathan, "Equinox could experience lasting damage from the anti-Trump boycott, despite other companies escaping unscathed," Marketwatch.com, August 14, 2019, https://www.marketwatch.com/story/equinox-could -experience-lasting-damage-from-the-anti-trump-boycott -while-other-companies-have-escaped-unscathed-2019 -08-13.

31. Steven Overly and Laura Kayali, "The moment of reck-

oning for the Facebook advertiser boycott," Politico.com, July 29, 2020, https://www.politico.com/news/2020/07/29/facebook-advertiser-boycott-zuckerberg-385622.

32. "Do Boycotts Work?," Northwestern Institute for Policy Research, March 28, 2017, https://www.ipr.northwestern.edu/news/2017/king-corporate-boycotts.html.

33. Noorie Malik, "New Consumer Alert on Yelp Takes Firm Stance Against Racism," Yelp.com, October 8, 2020, https://blog.yelp.com/2020/10/new-consumer-alert-on-yelp-takes-firm-stance-against-racism.

34. Emery P. Dalesio and Jonathan Drew, "Exclusive: 'Bathroom bill' to cost North Carolina $3.75B," APNews.com, March 30, 2017, https://apnews.com/article/e6c7a15d2e16452c8dcbc2756fd67b44.

35. Peter O'Dowd, "Cities, Businesses Boycott Arizona Over New Law," NPR.org, May 4, 2010, https://www.npr.org/templates/story/story.php?storyId=126486651.

36. Lisa Richwine, "Disney CEO says it will be 'difficult' to film in Georgia if abortion law takes effect," Reuters.com, May 29, 2019, https://www.reuters.com/article/us-usa-abortion-walt-disney-exclusive/disney-ceo-says-it-will-be-difficult-to-film-in-georgia-if-abortion-law-takes-effect-idUSKCN1T003X.

37. Kevin Dugan, "Credit cards are clamping down on payments to hate groups," NYPost.com, August 16, 2017, https://nypost.com/2017/08/16/credit-cards-are-clamping-down-on-payments-to-hate-groups/.

38. Associated Press, "First National Bank of Omaha drops

NRA credit card," CBSNews.com, February 22, 2018, https://www.cbsnews.com/news/first-national-bank-of -omaha-drops-nra-credit-card/.

39. Chase Purdy, "Even America's worst airline couldn't stomach the National Rifle Association," QZ.com, February 24, 2018, https://qz.com/1215137/the-nra-loses-the -support-of-united-americas-most-hated-legacy-airline/.

40. Zachary Warmbrodt, "GOP split as banks take on gun industry," Politico.com, April 22, 2018, https://www.politico .com/story/2018/04/22/banks-guns-industry-gop-split -544739.

41. John Aidan Byrne, "JPMorgan Chase accused of purging accounts of conservative activists," NYPost.com, May 25, 2019, https://nypost.com/2019/05/25/jpmorgan-chase-accused -of-purging-accounts-of-conservative-activists/.

42. Dana Loesch,"Mailchimp Deplatforming a Local Tea Party Is a Hallmark of Fascism," Federalist.com, December 16, 2020, https://thefederalist.com/2020/11 /16/mailchimp-deplatforming-a-local-tea-party-is -a-hallmark-of-fascism/.

43. Caleb Parke, "Conservatives call for PayPal boycott after CEO says Southern Poverty Law Center helps ban users," FoxNews.com, February 28, 2019, https://www.foxnews .com/tech/conservatives-call-for-paypal-boycott-after-ceo -admits-splc-helps-ban-users.

44. "US businesses cut Republican party donations in wake of riot," DW.com, https://www.dw.com/en/us-businesses-cut -republican-party-donations-in-wake-of-riot/a-56189263.

45. Theo Francis, "Why You Probably Work for a Giant Company, in 20 Charts," WSJ.com, April 6, 2017, https://www.wsj.com/graphics/big-companies-get-bigger/.

46. Austan Goolsbee, "Big Companies Are Starting to Swallow the World," NYTimes.com, September 30, 2020, https://www.nytimes.com/2020/09/30/business/big-companies-are-starting-to-swallow-the-world.html.

Chapter 6: The Radicalization of Entertainment

1. "Academy Establishes Representation and Inclusion Standards for Oscars Eligibility," Oscars.org, September 8, 2020, https://www.oscars.org/news/academy-establishes-representation-and-inclusion-standards-oscarsr-eligibility.

2. Reggie Ugwu, "The Hashtag That Changed the Oscars: An Oral History," NYTimes.com, February 6, 2020, https://www.nytimes.com/2020/02/06/movies/oscarssowhite-history.html.

3. Anna North, "#MeToo at the 2018 Oscars: The good, the bad, and the in between," Vox.com, March 5, 2018, https://www.vox.com/2018/3/5/17079702/2018-oscars-me-too-times-up-frances-mcdormand-jimmy-kimmel.

4. Casey Newton, "How Kevin Hart tweeted himself out of a job hosting the Oscars," TheVerge.com, December 8, 2018, https://www.theverge.com/2018/12/8/18131221/kevin-hart-oscar-hosting-homophobia-twitter-tweets.

5. Stephen Daw, "A Complete Timeline of Kevin Hart's

Oscar-Hosting Controversy, from Tweets to Apologies," Billboard.com, January 13, 2020, https://www.billboard.com/articles/events/oscars/8492982/kevin-hart-oscar-hosting-controversy-timeline.

6. Ben Shapiro, *Primetime Propaganda* (New York: Harper-Collins, 2011), 71.

7. "The Motion Picture Production Code (as Published 31 March, 1930)," https://www.asu.edu/courses/fms200s/total-readings/MotionPictureProductionCode.pdf.

8. Ben Shapiro, *Primetime Propaganda* (New York: Harper-Collins, 2011), 59.

9. Ibid., 62.

10. Shonda Rhimes, *Year of Yes: How to Dance It Out, Stand in the Sun, and Be Your Own Person* (New York: Simon & Schuster, 2015), 235–37.

11. Jim Rutenberg, "How to Write TV in the Age of Trump: Showrunners Reveal All," NYTimes.com, April 12, 2017, https://www.nytimes.com/2017/04/12/arts/television/political-tv-in-age-of-trump-shonda-rhimes-scandal-veep-madame-secretary-house-of-cards-hbo.html?_r=0].

12. Elaine Low, "Disney Plus Subscribers Surpass 73 Million as of October," Variety.com, November 12, 2020, https://variety.com/2020/tv/news/disney-plus-subscribers-surpass-73-million-subscribers-as-of-october-1234830555/.

13. "The Nielsen Total Audience Report: August 2020," Nielsen.com, August 13, 2020, https://www.nielsen.com/us/en/insights/report/2020/the-nielsen-total-audience-report-august-2020/.

14. John Koblin, "The Obamas and Netflix Just Revealed the Shows and Films They're Working On," NYTimes .com, April 30, 2019, https://www.nytimes.com/2019/04 /30/business/media/obama-netflix-shows.html.

15. Todd Spangler, "Susan Rice Will Leave Netflix Board to Join Biden Administration," Variety.com, December 10, 2020, https://variety.com/2020/biz/news/susan-rice-exits -netflix-board-biden-administration-1234850756/.

16. Ari Levy, "The most liberal and conservative tech companies, ranked by employees' political donations," CNBC .com, July 2, 2020, https://www.cnbc.com/2020/07/02 /most-liberal-tech-companies-ranked-by-employee -donations.html.

17. Megan Graham, "Netflix says it will rethink its investment in Georgia if 'heartbeat' abortion law goes into effect," CNBC.com, May 28, 2019, https://www.cnbc.com /2019/05/28/netflix-would-rethink-investment-in-georgia -if-abortion-law-stands.html.

18. Sherisse Pham, "Netflix finally finds a way into China," CNN.com, May 3, 2017, https://money.cnn.com/2017/04 /26/technology/netflix-china-baidu-iqiyi/.

19. Lisa Richwine, "Disney CEO says it will be 'difficult' to film in Georgia if abortion law takes effect," Reuters .com, May 29, 2019, https://www.reuters.com/article/us -usa-abortion-walt-disney-exclusive/disney-ceo-says-it -will-be-difficult-to-film-in-georgia-if-abortion-law-takes -effect-idUSKCN1T003X.

20. Amy Qin and Edward Wong, "Why Calls to Boycott

'Mulan' Over Concerns About China Are Growing," NYTimes.com, September 8, 2020, https://www.nytimes .com/2020/09/08/world/asia/china-mulan-xinjiang.html.

21. Johanna Blakley et al., "Are You What You Watch?," LearCenter.org, May 2019, https://learcenter.org/wp -content/uploads/2019/05/are_you_what_you_watch.pdf.

22. "GLAAD works with Hollywood to shape transgender stories and help cast trans actors," GLAAD.org, May 12, 2020, https://www.glaad.org/blog/glaad-works-hollywood -shape-transgender-stories-and-help-cast-trans-actors.

23. Dave Nemetz, "*The Office* Edits Out Blackface Scene, *Community* Pulls Entire Episode," TVLine.com, June 26, 2020, https://tvline.com/2020/06/26/the-office-community -blackface-cut-removed-streaming/.

24. "Gone with the Wind removed from HBO Max," BBC.com, June 10, 2020, https://www.bbc.com/news /entertainment-arts-52990714.

25. Samuel Gelman, "Disney+ Updates Offensive Content Disclaimer for Aladdin, Peter Pan and More," CBR .com, October 15, 2020, https://www.cbr.com/disney-plus -update-disclaimer-aladdin-peter-pan/.

26. "*Cops* TV series canceled after 31 years in wake of protests," EW.com, June 9, 2020, https://ew.com/tv/cops -canceled/.

27. Sarah Whitten, " 'Live P.D.' canceled by A&E following report that the reality show filmed police custody death," CNBC.com, June 11, 2020, https://www.cnbc.com/2020

/06/11/live-pd-canceled-over-report-that-show-filmed -police-custody-death.html.

28. "Scarlett Johansson quits trans role after LGBT backlash," BBC.com, July 13, 2018, https://www.bbc.com/news /entertainment-arts-44829766.

29. "You would say that wouldn't you! Sarah Silverman says progressives should allow cancel-culture victims a 'path to redemption'—after she was fired from film role for black-face," DailyMail.co.uk, October 26, 2020, https://www .dailymail.co.uk/news/article-8880547/Sarah-Silverman -slams-non-forgiving-cancel-culture-progressives-warns -digging-mistakes.html.

30. Nick Vadala, "Dave Chappelle defends Kevin Hart in con-troversial new Netflix comedy special 'Sticks & Stones,'" Inquirer.com, August 28, 2019, https://www.inquirer.com /entertainment/tv/dave-chappelle-netflix-comedy-kevin -hart-louis-ck-michael-jackson-20190828.html.

31. Christian Toto, "Bill Burr: Cancel Culture Made Me a Bet-ter Stand-up Comedian," HollywoodInToto.com, https:// www.hollywoodintoto.com/bill-burr-cancel-culture-stand -up-comedian/.

32. Ben Cost, "'Mr. Bean' actor Rowan Atkinson equates cancel culture to 'medieval mob,'" NYPost.com, January 5, 2021, https://nypost.com/2021/01/05/mr-bean-rowan-atkinson -says-cancel-culture-to-medieval-mob/.

33. Center Is Sexy, "Graphing Rotten Tomatoes' Political Bias," Medium.com, September 18, 2019, https://medium

.com/@centerissexy/graphing-rotten-tomatoes-political -bias-957e43986461.

34. Owen Gleiberman, "Healthy Tomatoes? The Danger of Film Critics Speaking as One," Variety.com, August 20, 2017, https://variety.com/2017/film/columns/rottentomatoes -the-danger-of-film-critics-speaking-as-one-1202533533/.

35. Peter Bradshaw, "Variety's apology to Carey Mulligan shows the film critic's ivory tower is toppling," TheGuard ian.com, January 28, 2021, https://www.theguardian.com /film/2021/jan/28/variety-apology-carey-mulligan-film -critics.

36. Megan Garber, "Hey, Look, the New Ghostbusters Didn't Kill *Ghostbusters*," TheAtlantic.com, July 15, 2016, https://www.theatlantic.com/entertainment/archive /2016/07/hey-look-ghostbusters-didnt-kill-feminism /491414/.

37. Matt Miller, "The Year *Star Wars* Fans Finally Ruined *Star Wars*," Esquire.com, December 13, 2018, https:// www.esquire.com/entertainment/movies/a25560063/how -fans-ruined-star-wars-the-last-jedi-2018/.

38. Hannah Giorgis, "The Fear in Chappelle's New Special," TheAtlantic.com, August 28, 2019, https://www .theatlantic.com/entertainment/archive/2019/08/dave -chappelle-doubles-down-sticks-and-stones/596947/.

39. Jordan Hoffman, "Dave Chappelle Releases a Passionate and Raw Comedy Set, Making George Floyd Protests Personal," VanityFair.com, June 12, 2020, https:// www.vanityfair.com/hollywood/2020/06/dave-chappelle

-releases-a-passionate-and-raw-comedy-set-making -george-floyd-protests-personal.

40. Lorraine Ali, "Review: Dave Chappelle's new special isn't stand-up. It's an anguished story of violence," June 12, 2020, https://www.latimes.com/entertainment-arts/tv/story /2020-06-12/dave-chappelle-846-youtube-netflix-george -floyd.

41. David Sims, "*Hillybilly Elegy* Is One of the Worst Movies of the Year," TheAtlantic.com, November 23, 2020, https://www.theatlantic.com/culture/archive/2020/11 /hillbilly-elegy/617189/.

42. Todd Spangler, "Netflix Launches 'Black Lives Matter' Collection of Movies, TV Shows, and Documentaries," Va riety.com, June 10, 2020, https://variety.com/2020/digital /news/netflix-black-lives-matter-collection-1234630160/.

43. Kiersten Willis, "Netflix, Amazon and Hulu spotlight black stories with film collections," AJC.com, June 11, 2020, https://www.ajc.com/entertainment/netflix-amazon -and-hulu-spotlight-black-stories-with-film-collections /vMxIsfPV3ksp7x2W7AtlQM/.

44. John Mossman, "Abdul-Rauf Suspended Over National Anthem," Associated Press, March 13, 1996, https://ap news.com/article/0a244b7bf3d7c3882229d7f0e84587d6.

45. Tim Bontemps, "Michael Jordan stands firm on 'Republicans buy sneakers, too' quote, says it was made in jest," ESPN.com, May 4, 2020, https://www.espn.com/nba/story /_/id/29130478/michael-jordan-stands-firm-republicans -buy-sneakers-too-quote-says-was-made-jest.

46. Clay Travis, *Republicans Wear Sneakers, Too* (New York: HarperCollins, 2018), 41–49.

47. Ibid., 55.

48. "Pro Football Is Still America's Favorite Sport," The HarrisPoll.com, January 26, 2016, https://theharrispoll .com/new-york-n-y-this-is-a-conflicting-time-for-football -fans-on-the-one-hand-with-the-big-game-50-no-less -fast-approaching-its-a-time-of-excitement-especial/.

49. "Average daily time spent watching TV per capita in the United States in 2009 and 2019, by ethnicity," Statista.com, https://www.statista.com/statistics/411806/average-daily -time-watching-tv-us-ethnicity/.

50. Kerwin Kofi Charles, Erik Hurst, and Nikolai Roussanov, "Conspicuous Consumption and Race," *Quarterly Journal of Economics* 124, no. 2 (2009): 425–67, https://repository .upenn.edu/fnce_papers/413/.

51. "St. Louis police officers angered by Rams' 'hands up, don't shoot' pose," SI.com, November 30, 2014, https://www.si .com/nfl/2014/11/30/st-louis-rams-ferguson-protests.

52. "NFL won't discipline Rams players for 'hands up, don't shoot' gesture," SI.com, December 1, 2014, https://www.si .com/nfl/2014/12/01/nfl-discipline-st-louis-rams-players -hands-dont-shoot.

53. "NFL denies Cowboys' request to wear decal honoring fallen Dallas officers," Foxnews.com, August 12, 2016, https://www.foxnews.com/sports/nfl-denies-cowboys -request-to-wear-decal-honoring-fallen-dallas-officers.

54. David K. Li, "Colin Kaepernick reveals the specific po-

lice shooting that led him to kneel," NBCNews.com, August 20, 2019, https://www.nbcnews.com/news/us-news/colin-kaepernick-reveals-specific-police-shooting-led-him-kneel-n1044306.

55. Christopher Ingraham, "What Colin Kaepernick means for America's racial gap in patriotism," WashingtonPost.com, September 23, 2016, https://www.washingtonpost.com/news/wonk/wp/2016/09/23/what-colin-kaepernick-means-for-americas-racial-gap-in-patriotism/.

56. Jenna West, "Colin Kaepernick Returns to 'Madden' for First Time Since 2016," SI.com, September 8, 2020, https://www.si.com/nfl/2020/09/08/colin-kaepernick-returns-madden-nfl-ea-sports-2020.

57. Darren Rovell, "NFL television ratings down 9.7 percent during 2017 regular season," ESPN.com, January 4, 2018, https://www.espn.com/nfl/story/_/id/21960086/nfl-television-ratings-97-percent-2017-regular-season.

58. Ben Shapiro, "ESPN Admits They Mistreat Conservatives, and It's Killing Their Ratings," DailyWire.com, November 17, 2016, https://www.dailywire.com/news/espn-admits-they-mistreat-conservatives-and-its-ben-shapiro.

59. Ben Strauss, "As ESPN tries to stick to sports, President Jimmy Pitaro must define what that means," WashingtonPost.com, July 26, 2019, https://www.washingtonpost.com/sports/2019/07/26/jimmy-pitaro-espn-president-politics/.

60. Nikole Tower, "In an ethnic breakdown of sports, NBA takes lead for most diverse," GlobalSportMatters.com, December 12, 2018, https://globalsportmatters.com/culture

/2018/12/12/in-an-ethnic-breakdown-of-sports-nba-takes -lead-for-most-diverse/.

61. Tom Huddleston, "These are the highest paid players in the NBA right now," CNBC.com, October 22, 2019, https://www.foxnews.com/sports/nfl-denies-cowboys -request-to-wear-decal-honoring-fallen-dallas-officers.

62. The Undefeated, "Social Justice Messages Each Player Is Wearing on His Jersey," TheUndefeated.com, July 31, 2020, https://theundefeated.com/features/social-justice-messages -each-nba-player-is-wearing-on-his-jersey/.

63. Dan Wolken, "Opinion: LeBron James undermines values he's espoused in most disgraceful moment of career," USAToday.com, October 15, 2019, https://www .usatoday.com/story/sports/columnist/dan-wolken/2019 /10/14/lebron-james-daryl-morey-china-hong-kong-tweet /3982436002/.

64. Paul P. Murphy, "Baseball is making Black Lives Matter on Opening Day," CNN.com, July 24, 2020, https://www .cnn.com/2020/07/23/us/opening-day-baseball-mlb-black -lives-matter-trnd/index.html.

65. Associated Press, "Baltimore Ravens' Matthew Judon blasts NFL Commissioner Roger Goodell's 'Black Lives Matter' speech," USAToday.com, June 15, 2020, https:// www.usatoday.com/story/sports/nfl/ravens/2020/06 /15/roger-goodells-black-lives-matter-speech-blasted -matthew-judon/3196057001/.

66. Scott Polacek, "NFL Plans to Include Social Justice Messages in End Zone Borders for Week 1," BleacherReport

.com, July 27, 2020, https://bleacherreport.com/articles /2901950-nfl-plans-to-include-social-justice-messages-in -end-zone-borders-for-week-1.

67. Rick Porter, "NFL Ratings Slip in 2020, Remain Dominant on Broadcast," HollywoodReporter.com, January 6, 2021, https://www.hollywoodreporter.com/live-feed/nfl-ratings -slip-in-2020-remain-dominant-on-broadcast#:~:text= The%20league%20drops%20about%2010,draw%20on %20ad%2Dsupported%20television.

68. "NBA Ratings Decline Points to Broader Trouble in TV Watching," Bloomberg.com, October 13, 2020, https://www.bloomberg.com/news/articles/2020-10-13 /nba-ratings-decline-points-to-broader-trouble-in-tv -watching.

69. Chris Haney, "TV Ratings: MLB 2020 World Series Least-Watched of All-Time," Outsider.com, October 29, 2020, https://www.bloomberg.com/news/articles/2020-10 -13/nba-ratings-decline-points-to-broader-trouble-in-tv -watching.

Chapter 7: The Fake News

1. Richard Read, "Attorney for Minneapolis police officer says he'll argue George Floyd died of an overdose and a heart condition," LATimes.com, August 20, 2020, https:// www.latimes.com/world-nation/story/2020-08-20/george -floyd-derek-chauvin-defense.

2. "988 people have been shot and killed by police in the past

year," WashingtonPost.com, Updated January 26, 2021, https://www.washingtonpost.com/graphics/investigations /police-shootings-database/?itid=lk_inline_manual_5.

3. "Groups March into Beverly Hills, Loot Stores on Rodeo Drive," CBSLocal.com, May 30, 2020, https://losangeles .cbslocal.com/2020/05/30/rodeo-drive-protest-looting -george-floyd/.

4. Jonathan Lloyd, "Dozens of Businesses Damaged at Flashpoint of Violence in the Fairfax District," NBCLos Angeles.com, May 31, 2020, https://www.nbclosangeles .com/news/local/fairfax-district-melrose-damaged-looting -grove-fire-natioal-guard-lapd/2371497/.

5. Alejandra Reyes-Velarde, Brittny Mejia, Joseph Serna, Ruben Vives, Melissa Etehad, Matthew Ormseth, and Hailey Branson-Potts, "Looting hits Long Beach, Santa Monica as countywide curfew goes into effect," LATimes .com, May 31, 2020, https://www.latimes.com/california /story/2020-05-31/looting-vandalism-leaves-downtown -l-a-stunned.

6. "NYC Protests Turn Violent," NYTimes.com, May 31, 2020, https://www.nytimes.com/2020/05/31/nyregion/nyc -protests-george-floyd.html.

7. Isaac Stanley-Becker, Colby Itkowitz, and Meryl Kornfield, "Protests mount and violence flares in cities across US, putting the nation on edge," WashingtonPost.com, May 30, 2020, https://www.washingtonpost.com/national /protests-gain-force-across-us/2020/05/30/fccf57ea-a2a8 -11ea-81bb-c2f70f01034b_story.html.

8. Tim Hains, "MSNBC's Ali Velshi Downplays Riot in Front of Burning Building: 'Mostly a Protest,' 'Not Generally Speaking Unruly," RealClearPolitics.com, May 28, 2020, https://www.realclearpolitics.com/video/2020/05/28/msnbcs_ali_velshi_downplays_riot_in_front_of_burning_building_mostly_a_protest_not_generally_speaking_unruly.html.

9. Joe Concha, "CNN ridiculed for 'Fiery but Mostly Peaceful' caption with video of burning building in Kenosha," TheHill.com, August 27, 2020, https://thehill.com/homenews/media/513902-cnn-ridiculed-for-fiery-but-mostly-peaceful-caption-with-video-of-burning.

10. "Costliest US civil disorders," Axios.com, https://www.axios.com/riots-cost-property-damage-276c9bcc-a455-4067-b06a-66f9db4cea9c.html.

11. Ariel Zilber, "REVEALED: Widespread vandalism and looting during BLM protests will cost insurance $2 billion after violence erupted in 140 cities in the wake of George Floyd's death," DailyMail.co.uk, September 16, 2020, https://www.dailymail.co.uk/news/article-8740609/Rioting-140-cities-George-Floyds-death-cost-insurance-industry-2-BILLION.html.

12. Lois Beckett, "At least 25 Americans were killed during protests and political unrest in 2020," TheGuardian.com, October 31, 2020, https://www.theguardian.com/world/2020/oct/31/americans-killed-protests-political-unrest-acled.

13. Ebony Bowden, "More than 700 officers injured in George

Floyd protests across US," NYPost.com, June 8, 2020, https://nypost.com/2020/06/08/more-than-700-officers -injured-in-george-floyd-protests-across-us/.

14. https://twitter.com/CBSNews/status/12678774439117 78306.

15. Virginia Allen, "New York Times Mum on '1619 Project' Creator Calling '1619 Riots' Moniker an 'Honor,'" DailySignal.com, June 22, 2020, https://www.dailysignal .com/2020/06/22/new-york-times-mum-on-1619-project -creator-calling-1619-riots-moniker-an-honor/.

16. https://twitter.com/theMRC/status/12678186038075 67872.

17. "Chris Cuomo demands to know where it says protests must be 'peaceful.' Then he gets a lesson on the Constitution," TheBlaze.com, June 3, 2020, https://www.theblaze .com/news/chris-cuomo-protests-peaceful-constitution.

18. Andrew Kerr, "Here Are 31 Times the Media Justified or Explained Away Rioting and Looting After George Floyd's Death," DailySignal.com, September 4, 2020, https:// www.dailysignal.com/2020/09/04/here-are-31-times-the -media-justified-or-explained-away-rioting-and-looting -after-george-floyds-death/.

19. Tonya Mosley, "Understand Protests as 'Acts of Rebellion' Instead of Riots, Marc Lamont Hill Says," WBUR.org, June 2, 2020, https://www.wbur.org/hereandnow/2020/06 /02/protests-acts-of-rebellion.

20. Heather Mac Donald, "Taking Stock of a Most Violent

Year," WSJ.com, January 24, 2021, https://www.wsj.com /articles/taking-stock-of-a-most-violent-year-11611525947.

21. Brian Flood, "CNN's Don Lemon says anti-police violence of 2020 built on 'facts' so 'you can't compare' to Capitol riot," FoxNews.com, January 13, 2021, https://www .foxnews.com/media/cnns-don-lemon-2020-built-facts -riot.

22. Lindsey Ellefson, "Don Lemon on His Journalistic Approach: My 'Lens' Is 'Not Necessarily a Bias,' but 'Experience,'" TheWrap.com, July 7, 2020, https://www.thewrap .com/don-lemon-on-his-journalistic-approach-my-lens-is -not-necessarily-a-bias-but-experience/.

23. Paul Bedard, "90% of media political donations to Biden, Sanders, AOC, Democrats: Report," WashingtonExaminer .com, October 28, 2020, https://www.washingtonexaminer .com/washington-secrets/90-of-media-political-donations -to-biden-sanders-aoc-democrats-report.

24. Jack Shafer and Tucker Doherty, "The Media Bubble Is Worse Than You Think," Politico.com, May/June 2017, https://www.politico.com/magazine/story/2017/04/25 /media-bubble-real-journalism-jobs-east-coast-215048.

25. Keith Griffith, "American trust in the mainstream media hits an all-time low with just 18% of Republicans saying they believe journalists after the 2020 election," Daily Mail.co.uk, January 21, 2021, https://www.dailymail.co .uk/news/article-9173711/American-trust-media-hits-time -low.html.

26. "James Callendar," Monticello.org, https://www.monticello
.org/site/research-and-collections/james-callender.

27. Amy Solomon Whitehead, "The Unattainable Ideal: Walter Lippmann and the Limits of the Press and and Public
Opinion," LSU master's thesis, LSU.edu, 2015, https://
digitalcommons.lsu.edu/cgi/viewcontent.cgi?article=3281
&context=gradschool_theses.

28. Walter Lippmann, *Liberty and the News* (New York:
Harcourt, Brace & Howe, 1920), 88–89.

29. Ravi Somaiya and Ashley Southall, "Arrested in Ferguson Last Year, 2 Reporters Are Charged," NYTimes.com,
August 11, 2015, https://www.nytimes.com/2015/08/11
/us/arrested-in-ferguson-2014-washington-post-reporter
-wesley-lowery-is-charged.html?_r=0.

30. Wesley Lowery, *They Can't Kill Us All* (New York: Ha-
chette Book Group, 2016), 37.

31. Maxwell Tani, "Washington Post Threatened Another
Star Reporter Over His Tweets," DailyBeast.com, February 3, 2020, https://www.thedailybeast.com/washington
-post-threatened-another-star-reporter-wesley-lowery
-over-his-tweets.

32. Ben Smith, "Inside the Revolts Erupting in America's
Big Newsrooms," NYTimes.com, June 7, 2020, https://
www.nytimes.com/2020/06/07/business/media/new-york
-times-washington-post-protests.html.

33. Oliver Darcy, "New York Times staffers revolt over publication of Tom Cotton op-ed," CNN.com, June 4, 2020,

https://www.cnn.com/2020/06/03/media/new-york-times
-tom-cotton-op-ed/index.html.

34. Marc Tracy, "James Bennet Resigns as New York Times
Opinion Editor," NYTimes.com, June 7, 2020, https://
www.nytimes.com/2020/06/07/business/media/james
-bennet-resigns-nytimes-op-ed.html.

35. Michael M. Grynbaum, "The Atlantic Cuts Ties with
Conservative Writer Kevin Williamson," NYTimes.com,
April 5, 2018, https://www.nytimes.com/2018/04/05
/business/media/kevin-williamson-atlantic.html.

36. Kyle Smith, "Politico Staff in Uproar over Ben Shapiro Appearance," NationalReview.com, January 14, 2021, https://
www.nationalreview.com/corner/politico-staff-in-uproar
-over-ben-shapiro-appearance/.

37. https://twitter.com/ErikWemple/status/13499006144703
93864.

38. Maxwell Tani, "100+ Politico Staffers Send Letter to Publisher Railing Against Publishing Ben Shapiro," TheDaily
Beast.com, January 25, 2021, https://www.thedailybeast
.com/more-than-100-politico-staffers-send-letter-to-ceo
-railing-against-publishing-ben-shapiro.

39. https://twitter.com/ErikWemple/status/13498048434398
94532.

40. Karen Attiah, "The media had a role to play in the
rise of Trump. It's time to hold ourselves accountable," WashingtonPost.com, January 20, 2021, https://
www.washingtonpost.com/opinions/2021/01/20/media

-had-role-play-rise-trump-its-time-hold-ourselves-accountable/.

41. Marc Tracy, "Top Editor of Philadelphia Inquirer Resigns After 'Buildings Matter' Headline," NYTimes.com, June 6, 2020, https://www.nytimes.com/2020/06/06/business/media/editor-philadephia-inquirer-resigns.html.

42. Bari Weiss, "Resignation Letter," BariWeiss.com, July 14, 2020, https://www.bariweiss.com/resignation-letter.

43. Victoria Bynum, James M. McPherson, James Oakes, Sean Wilentz, and Gordon S. Wood, "RE: The 1619 Project," *New York Times Magazine*, December 29, 2019, https://www.nytimes.com/2019/12/20/magazine/we-respond-to-the-historians-who-critiqued-the-1619-project.html.

44. K. C. Johnson, "History Without Truth," City-Journal.org, December 31, 2019, https://www.city-journal.org/1619-project-history-without-truth.

45. Leslie M. Harris, "I Helped Fact-Check the 1619 Project. The Times Ignored Me," Politico.com, March 6, 2020, https://www.politico.com/news/magazine/2020/03/06/1619-project-new-york-times-mistake-122248.

46. Brian Stelter and Oliver Darcy, "1619 Project faces renewed criticism—this time from *The New York Times*," CNN.com, October 12, 2020, https://www.cnn.com/2020/10/12/media/new-york-times-1619-project-criticism/index.html.

47. "Oprah Winfrey, Nikole Hannah-Jones to Adapt '1619 Project' for Film, TV," HollywoodReporter.com, July 8,

2020, https://www.hollywoodreporter.com/video/oprah
-winfrey-nikole-hannah-jones-adapt-1619-project-watch
-1302506.

48. Jacques Steinberg, "An All-Out Attack on 'Conservative Misinformation,'" NYTimes.com, October 31,
2008, https://www.nytimes.com/2008/11/01/washington
/01media.html.

49. Tucker Carlson and Vince Coglianese, "Inside Media Matters: Sources, memos reveal erratic behavior, close coordination with White House and news organizations,"
DailyCaller.com, February 12, 2012, https://dailycaller
.com/2012/02/12/inside-media-matters-sources-memos
-reveal-erratic-behavior-close-coordination-with-white
-house-and-news-organizations/.

50. Nicholas Kristof, "A Letter to My Conservative Friends,"
NYTimes.com, January 27, 2021, https://www.nytimes
.com/2021/01/27/opinion/trump-supporters-conspiracy
-theories.html.

51. Margaret Sullivan, "Fox News is a hazard to our democracy. It's time to take the fight to the Murdochs. Here's
how," WashingtonPost.com, January 24, 2021, https://
www.washingtonpost.com/lifestyle/media/fox-news-is
-a-hazard-to-our-democracy-its-time-to-take-the-fight
-to-the-murdochs-heres-how/2021/01/22/1821f186-5cbe
-11eb-b8bd-ee36b1cd18bf_story.html.

52. Max Boot, "Trump couldn't have incited sedition without
the help of Fox News," WashingtonPost.com, January 18,
2021, https://www.washingtonpost.com/opinions/2021/01

/18/trump-couldnt-have-incited-sedition-without-help
-fox-news/.

53. Oliver Darcy, "Analysis: TV providers should not escape
scrutiny for distributing disinformation," CNN.com, January 8, 2021, https://www.cnn.com/2021/01/08/media/tv
-providers-disinfo-reliable-sources/index.html.

54. https://twitter.com/tomselliott/status/135114085547894
7844.

55. Kara Swisher, "Zuckerberg's Free Speech Bubble," NY
Times.com, June 3, 2020, https://www.nytimes.com/2020
/06/03/opinion/facebook-trump-free-speech.html?action
=click&module=RelatedLinks&pgtype=Article.

56. Kevin Roose, "The Making of a YouTube Radical," NY
Times.com, June 8, 2019, https://www.nytimes.com
/interactive/2019/06/08/technology/youtube-radical.html.

57. Jim VandeHei, "Our new reality: Three Americas," Axios
.com, January 10, 2021, https://www.axios.com/capitol
-siege-misinformation-trump-d9c9738b-0852-408d-a24f
-81c95938b41b.html?stream=top.

58. Armin Rosen, "Journalists Mobilize Against Free
Speech," TabletMag.com, January 24, 2021, https://www
.tabletmag.com/sections/news/articles/jounalists-against
-free-speech.

59. Caitlin Flanagan, "The Media Botched the Covington Catholic Story," TheAtlantic.com, January 23, 2019,
https://www.theatlantic.com/ideas/archive/2019/01/media
-must-learn-covington-catholic-story/581035/.

60. "Statement of Nick Sandmann, Covington Catholic High

School junior, regarding incident at the Lincoln Memorial," CNN.com, January 23, 2019, https://www.cnn.com/2019/01/20/us/covington-kentucky-student-statement/index.html.

61. Caitlin Flanagan, "The Media Botched the Covington Catholic Story," TheAtlantic.com, January 23, 2019, https://www.theatlantic.com/ideas/archive/2019/01/media-must-learn-covington-catholic-story/581035/.

62. https://grabien.com/story.php?id=321993.

63. https://twitter.com/Acosta/status/1351649797820862465.

64. Isaac Schorr, "Jen Psaki Is Living Her Best Life," National Review.com, January 25, 2021, https://www.nationalreview.com/2021/01/jen-psaki-is-living-her-best-life/.

65. Margaret Sullivan, "The media can be glad for the Biden White House's return to normalcy. But let's not be lulled," WashingtonPost.com, January 21, 2021, https://www.washingtonpost.com/lifestyle/media/the-media-can-be-glad-for-the-biden-white-houses-return-to-normalcy-but-lets-not-be-lulled/2021/01/20/ea444ac6-5b81-11eb-a976-bad6431e03e2_story.html.

Chapter 8: Unfriending Americans

1. Emma-Jo Morris and Gabrielle Fonrouge, "Smoking-gun email reveals how Hunter Biden introduced Ukrainian businessman to VP dad," NYPost.com, October 14, 2020, https://nypost.com/2020/10/14/email-reveals-how-hunter-biden-introduced-ukrainian-biz-man-to-dad/.

2. Ben Schreckinger, "Biden Inc.," Politico.com, August 2, 2019, https://www.politico.com/magazine/story/2019/08/02/joe-biden-investigation-hunter-brother-hedge-fund-money-2020-campaign-227407.

3. Tim Marcin, "Hunter Biden Admits His Last Name Has Opened Basically Every Door for Him," Vice.com, October 15, 2019, https://www.vice.com/en/article/a35y9k/hunter-biden-admits-his-last-name-has-opened-basically-every-door-for-him.

4. Mark Moore, "Joe Biden's testy response to NBC question about Hunter's dealings in Ukraine," NYPost.com, February 3, 2020, https://nypost.com/2020/02/03/joe-bides-testy-response-to-nbc-question-about-hunters-dealings-in-ukraine/.

5. "Read Trump's phone conversation with Volodymr Zelensky," CNN.com, September 26, 2019, https://www.cnn.com/2019/09/25/politics/donald-trump-ukraine-transcript-call/index.html.

6. Ebony Bowden and Steven Nelson, "Hunter's ex-partner Tony Bobulinski: Joe Biden's a liar and here's the proof," NYPost.com, October 22, 2020, https://nypost.com/2020/10/22/hunter-ex-partner-tony-bobulinski-calls-joe-biden-a-liar/.

7. Natasha Bertrand, "Hunter Biden story is Russian disinfo, dozens of former intel officials say," Politico.com, October 19, 2020, https://www.politico.com/news/2020/10/19/hunter-biden-story-russian-disinfo-430276.

8. Evan Perez and Pamela Brown, "Federal criminal investi-

gation into Hunter Biden focuses on his business dealings in China," CNN.com, December 10, 2020, https://www.cnn.com/2020/12/09/politics/hunter-biden-tax-investigtation/index.html.

9. Paul Bedard, "Media's hiding of Hunter Biden scandal robbed Trump of clear win: Poll," MSN.com, November 13, 2020, https://www.msn.com/en-us/news/politics/media-s-hiding-of-hunter-biden-scandal-robbed-trump-of-clear-win-poll/ar-BB1aZGcF.

10. Benjamin Hart, "Twitter Backs Down After Squelching New York Post's Hunter Biden Story," NYMag.com, October 16, 2020, https://nymag.com/intelligencer/2020/10/twitter-facebook-block-ny-post-hunter-biden-article.html.

11. Audrey Conklin, "Facebook official who said platform is reducing distribution of Hunter Biden has worked for top Dems," FoxNews.com, October 14, 2020, https://www.foxnews.com/politics/facebook-spokesperson-top-democrats-new-york-post.

12. https://twitter.com/andymstone/status/1316395902479872000.

13. https://twitter.com/andymstone/status/1316423671314026496.

14. Alex Hern, "Facebook leak reveals policies on restricting New York Post's Biden story," TheGuardian.com, October 30, 2020, https://www.theguardian.com/technology/2020/oct/30/facebook-leak-reveals-policies-restricting-new-york-post-biden-story.

15. 47 U.S. Code §230.

16. "Section 230 of the Communications Decency Act," EFF .org, https://www.eff.org/issues/cda230.

17. "CDA 230: Legislative History," EFF.org, https://www .eff.org/issues/cda230/legislative-history.

18. 47 U.S. Code §230.

19. Mark Zuckerberg, "Bring the World Closer Together," Facebook.com, June 22, 2017, https://techcrunch.com /2017/06/22/bring-the-world-closer-together/.

20. Justin Fox, "Why Twitter's Mission Statement Matters," HBR.org, November 13, 2014, https://hbr.org/2014/11 /why-twitters-mission-statement-matters.

21. Angie Drobnic Holan, "2016 Lie of the Year: Fake news," Politifact.com, December 13, 2016, https://www.politifact .com/article/2016/dec/13/2016-lie-year-fake-news/.

22. David Remnick, "Obama Reckons with a Trump Presidency," NewYorker.com, November 18, 2016, https://www .newyorker.com/magazine/2016/11/28/obama-reckons -with-a-trump-presidency.

23. Scott Shackford, "Senator Feinstein's Threat to 'Do Something' to Social Media Companies Is a Bigger Danger to Democracy Than Russia," Reason.com, November 3, 2017, https://reason.com/2017/11/03/sen-feinsteins-threat -to-do-something-to/.

24. Kurt Wagner, "Mark Zuckerberg says it's 'crazy' to think fake news stories got Trump elected," Vox.com, November 11, 2016, https://www.vox.com/2016/11/11/13596792 /facebook-fake-news-mark-zuckerberg-donald-trump.

25. Mark Zuckerberg, "Building Global Community," Facebook.com, February 16, 2017, https://www.facebook.com/notes/mark-zuckerberg/building-global-community/10103508221158471/?pnref=story.

26. "Transcript of Mark Zuckerberg's Senate hearing," WashingtonPost.com, April 10, 2018, https://www.washingtonpost.com/news/the-switch/wp/2018/04/10/transcript-of-mark-zuckerbergs-senate-hearing/.

27. Tony Romm, "Zuckerberg: Standing for Voice and Expression," WashingtonPost.com, October 17, 2019, https://www.washingtonpost.com/technology/2019/10/17/zuckerberg-standing-voice-free-expression/.

28. Alison Durkee, "Jack Dorsey Sees a 'Major Gap and Flaw' in Mark Zuckerberg's Free Speech Argument," VanityFair.com, October 25, 2019, https://www.vanityfair.com/news/2019/10/jack-dorsey-mark-zuckerberg-free-speech-political-ads-facebook.

29. Sara Rimer, "Jack Dorsey, Twitter and Square Cofounder, Donates $10 Million to BU Center for Antiracist Research," BU.edu, August 20, 2020, https://www.bu.edu/articles/2020/jack-dorsey-bu-center-for-antiracist-research-gift/.

30. Kara Swisher, "Zuckerberg's Free Speech Bubble," NYTimes.com, June 3, 2020, https://www.nytimes.com/2020/06/03/opinion/facebook-trump-free-speech.html.

31. Alison Durkee, " 'So You Won't Take Down Lies?' AOC Blasts Mark Zuckerberg in Testy House Hearing," VanityFair.com, October 24, 2019, https://www.vanityfair

.com/news/2019/10/mark-zuckerberg-facebook-house
-testimony-aoc.

32. Cecilia Kang, "Biden Prepares Attack on Facebook's
Speech Policies," NYTimes.com, June 11, 2020, https://
www.nytimes.com/2020/06/11/technology/biden
-facebook-misinformation.html.

33. "Report of the Select Committee on Intelligence on Russian Active Measures Campaigns and Interference in the
2016 Election, Volume 2: Russia's Use of Social Media
with Additional Views," Intelligence.senate.gov, https://
www.intelligence.senate.gov/sites/default/files/documents
/Report_Volume2.pdf.

34. Nicholas Thompson and Issie Lapowsky, "How Russian
Trolls Used Meme Warfare to Divide America," Wired
.com, December 17, 2018, https://www.wired.com/story
/russia-ira-propaganda-senate-report/.

35. Molly Ball, "The Secret History of the Shadow Campaign
That Saved the 2020 Election," Time.com, February 4,
2021, https://time.com/5936036/secret-2020-election-cam
paign/.

36. Eliza Shearer and Elizabeth Grieco, "Americans Are
Wary of the Role Social Media Sites Play in Delivering
the News," Journalism.org, October 2, 2019, https://www
.journalism.org/2019/10/02/americans-are-wary-of-the
-role-social-media-sites-play-in-delivering-the-news/.

37. Kevin Roose, "The Making of a YouTube Radical," NY
Times.com, June 8, 2019, https://www.nytimes.com
/interactive/2019/06/08/technology/youtube-radical.html.

38. Lesley Stahl, "How Does YouTube Handle the Site's Misinformation, Conspiracy Theories, and Hate?," CBSNews.com, December 1, 2019, https://www.cbsnews.com/news/is-youtube-doing-enough-to-fight-hate-speech-and-conspiracy-theories-60-minutes-2019-12-01/.

39. Josh Constine, "Facebook will change algorithm to demote 'borderline content' that almost violates policies," Tech Crunch.com, November 15, 2018, https://techcrunch.com/2018/11/15/facebook-borderline-content/?guccounter=1.

40. Kevin Roose, Mike Isaac, and Sheera Frankel, "Facebook Struggles to Balance Civility and Growth," NYTimes.com, November 24, 2020, https://www.nytimes.com/2020/11/24/technology/facebook-election-misinformation.html.

41. Ben Shapiro, "Facebook Unveils Plan to Defeat 'Fake News': Rely on leftist Fact-Checkers," DailyWire.com, December 15, 2016, https://www.dailywire.com/news/facebook-unveils-plan-defeat-fake-news-rely-ben-shapiro.

42. Bethania Palma, "Did AOC Exaggerate the Danger She Was in During Capitol Riot?," Snopes.com, February 3, 2021, https://www.snopes.com/fact-check/aoc-capitol-attack/.

43. Stephen J. Ceci, "The Psychology of Fact-Checking," ScientificAmerican.com, October 25, 2020, https://www.scientificamerican.com/article/the-psychology-of-fact-checking1/.

44. Elizabeth Dwoskin, Nitasha Tiku, and Heather Kelly, "Facebook to start policing anti-Black hate speech more aggressively than anti-White comments, documents show,"

WashingtonPost.com, December 3, 2020, https://www
.washingtonpost.com/technology/2020/12/03/facebook
-hate-speech/.

45. Emine Saner, "YouTube's Susan Wojcicki: 'Where's the
line of free speech—are you removing voices that should
be heard?,'" TheGuardian.com, August 10, 2019, https://
www.theguardian.com/technology/2019/aug/10/youtube
-susan-wojcicki-ceo-where-line-removing-voices-heard.

46. https://www.facebook.com/communitystandards/hate
_speech/.

47. Tony Romm and Elizabeth Dwoskin, "Trump banned
from Facebook indefinitely, CEO Mark Zuckerberg says,"
WashingtonPost.com, January 7, 2021, https://www
.washingtonpost.com/technology/2021/01/07/trump-twitter
-ban/.

48. "Permanent suspension of @realDonaldTrump," Twitter
.com, January 8, 2021, https://blog.twitter.com/en_us
/topics/company/2020/suspension.html.

49. "Yann LeCun Quits Twitter Amid Acrimonious Ex-
changes on AI Bias," SyncedReview.com, June 30, 2020,
https://syncedreview.com/2020/06/30/yann-lecun-quits
-twitter-amid-acrimonious-exchanges-on-ai-bias/.

50. Dan Levin, "A Racial Slur, a Viral Video, and a Reckoning," NYTimes.com, December 26, 2020, https://
www.nytimes.com/2020/12/26/us/mimi-groves-jimmy
-galligan-racial-slurs.html.

51. Jon Ronson, "How One Stupid Tweet Blew Up Justine
Sacco's Life," NYTimes.com, February 12, 2015, https://

www.nytimes.com/2015/02/15/magazine/how-one-stupid
-tweet-ruined-justine-saccos-life.html.

52. Ari Levy, "Trump fans are flocking to the social media app
Parler—its CEO is begging liberals to join them," CNBC
.com, June 27, 2020, https://www.cnbc.com/2020/06/27
/parler-ceo-wants-liberal-to-join-the-pro-trump-crowd
-on-the-app.html.

53. Brian Fung, "Parler has now been booted by Amazon,
Apple and Google," CNN.com, January 11, 2021, https://
www.cnn.com/2021/01/09/tech/parler-suspended-apple
-app-store/index.html.

54. https://twitter.com/jason_kint/status/135846779332325
7857.

55. Brian X. Chen and Kevin Roose, "Are Private Messaging Apps the Next Misinformation Hot Spot?," NY
Times.com, February 3, 2021, https://www.nytimes
.com/2021/02/03/technology/personaltech/telegram
-signal-misinformation.html?smtyp=cur&smid=tw
-nytimes.

56. Eliza Shearer and Elizabeth Grieco, "Americans Are
Wary of the Role Social Media Sites Play in Delivering
the News," Journalism.org, October 2, 2019, https://www
.journalism.org/2019/10/02/americans-are-wary-of-the
-role-social-media-sites-play-in-delivering-the-news/.

57. H. Tankovska, "Facebook: Number of monthly active
users worldwide 2008–2020", https://www.statista.com
/statistics/264810/number-of-monthly-active-facebook
-users-worldwide/#:~:text=With%20roughly%202

.8%20billion%20monthly,network%20ever%20to%20do%20so.

58. Jeff Desjardins, "How Google retains more than 90% of market share," BusinessInsider.com, April 23, 2018, https://www.businessinsider.com/how-google-retains-more-than-90-of-market-share-2018-4.

59. Greg Stirling, "Almost 70% of digital ad spending going to Google, Facebook, Amazon, says analyst firm," Marketing Land.com, June 17, 2019, https://marketingland.com/almost-70-of-digital-ad-spending-going-to-google-facebook-amazon-says-analyst-firm-262565#:~:text=However%2C%20eMarketer%20revised%20downward%20its,nearly%2050%25%20to%2038%25.&text=Google%2C%20Facebook%20and%20Amazon%20are,dollars%20spent%20according%20to%20eMarketer.

The Choice Before Us

1. Emma Nolan, "What Did Gina Carano Say? 'The Mandalorian' Star Fired after Instagram Holocaust Post," Newsweek.com, February 11, 2021, https://www.newsweek.com/what-gina-carano-said-about-holocaust-mandalorian-fired-1568539.

2. " 'The Mandalorian' Star Gina Carano Fired Amid Social Media Controversy," THR.com, February 10, 2021, https://www.hollywoodreporter.com/news/the-mandalorian-star-gina-carano-fired-amid-social-media-controversy.

3. Emma Nolan, "What Did Gina Carano Say? 'The Mandalorian' Star Fired after Instagram Holocaust Post," Newsweek.com, February 11, 2021, https://www.newsweek.com/what-gina-carano-said-about-holocaust-mandalorian-fired-1568539.

4. " 'The Mandalorian' Star Gina Carano Fired Amid Social Media Controversy," THR.com, February 10, 2021, https://www.hollywoodreporter.com/news/the-mandalorian-star-gina-carano-fired-amid-social-media-controversy.

5. https://twitter.com/benshapiro/status/1359833571075227648.

6. Andreas Wiseman, "Carano Hits Back, Announces New Movie Project with Ben Shapiro's Daily Wire: 'They Can't Cancel Us If We Don't Let Them,' " Deadline.com, February 12, 2021, https://deadline.com/2021/02/gina-carano-mandalorian-ben-shapiro-hits-back-cancel-culture-1234692971/.

7. Marc Tracy, "Two Journalists Exit New York Times After Criticism of Past Behavior," NYTimes.com, February 5, 2021, https://www.nytimes.com/2021/02/05/business/media/donald-mcneil-andy-mills-leave-nyt.html.

8. Dylan Byers, "New York Times editor walks back statement on racial slurs," NBCNews.com, February 11, 2021, https://www.nbcnews.com/news/all/new-york-times-editor-walks-back-statement-racial-slurs-n1257482.

9. Joe Pompeo, " 'It's Chaos': Behind the Scenes of Donald McNeil's *New York Times* Exit," VanityFair.com, Febru-

ary 11, 2021, https://www.vanityfair.com/news/2021/02/behind-the-scenes-of-donald-mcneils-new-york-times-exit.

10. Pedro Domingos, "Beating Back Cancel Culture: A Case Study from the Field of Artificial Intelligence," January 27, 2021, https://quillette.com/2021/01/27/beating-back-cancel-culture-a-case-study-from-the-field-of-artificial-intelligence/.

About the Author

BEN SHAPIRO is founding editor in chief and editor emeritus of the Daily Wire and host of *The Ben Shapiro Show*, the top conservative podcast in the nation. A three-time *New York Times* bestselling author, Shapiro is a graduate of Harvard Law School and an Orthodox Jew. He is widely considered one of the most influential conservative voices in America.

Praise for *Father Abraham:*
Lincoln's Relentless Struggle to End Slavery

"In contrast to historians and biographers who emphasize Lincoln's pragmatism at the expense of his idealism, or claim that he was a conservative on racial issues who was pushed against his will toward emancipation, Richard Striner presents him as an idealist who employed his superb political skills to further the cause of freedom. The fresh and provocative insights in this book demonstrate that despite all that has been written about Lincoln, there is still something new to learn."

—James M. McPherson,
author of *Battle Cry of Freedom*

"Striner's nuanced exploration of Lincoln's words and deeds makes a stimulating case for the greatness of his conscience—resolutely practical, but ever attuned to the better angels of his nature."—*Publishers Weekly*

"In this estimable volume, Richard Striner effectively demolishes the fashionable myths of Lincoln the Reluctant Emancipator and Lincoln the White Supremacist. . . . Striner's readable account is not aimed at specialists, who will discover little new in it, but at the general reader, who will be impressed by the relentless way the author shows how relentless was Lincoln's struggle to end slavery."

—Michael Burlingame, *Washington Times*

"A provocative, richly detailed and exhaustively researched portrait of Lincoln as a zealous and lifelong opponent of slavery. Richard Striner presents a compelling counter-argument to those historians who claim Lincoln was a reluctant emancipator, and demonstrates convincingly that the fate of freedom was very much undecided until the North re-elected Lincoln."—Harold Holzer, author of *Lincoln at Cooper Union: The Speech That Made Him President*

"Compellingly argued. . . . A worthy contribution to the ongoing debates about the life and work of Abraham Lincoln."—Myron A. Marty, *St. Louis Post-Dispatch*

"A superb study of the Machiavellian Abraham Lincoln. Lincoln was shrewd, political and disingenuous. This excellent volume stands on its head the view that Lincoln argued re-Union first, Emancipation second. Richard Striner's analysis demonstrates that Lincoln was more than a moderate in word and action."

—Frank J. Williams,
Chief Justice of the Rhode Island Supreme Court
and Chair of The Lincoln Forum

"A brilliant and compelling account which reminds us that history, at its best, is a literary art. Reflecting deep understanding of the American political tradition, Striner's masterly study of Lincoln's statesmanship defies the conventions both of contemporary academic scholarship and political culture."—Herman Belz, Professor of History, University of Maryland

ALSO BY RICHARD STRINER

Washington Past and Present: A Guide to Our Nation's Capital
(with Donald R. Kennon)

Art Deco

The Civic Deal: Re-Empowering Our Great Republic

FATHER ABRAHAM

LINCOLN'S RELENTLESS STRUGGLE TO END SLAVERY

RICHARD STRINER

OXFORD
UNIVERSITY PRESS

OXFORD
UNIVERSITY PRESS

Oxford University Press, Inc., publishes works that
further Oxford University's objective of excellence
in research, scholarship, and education.

Oxford New York
Auckland Cape Town Dar es Salaam Hong Kong Karachi
Kuala Lumpur Madrid Melbourne Mexico City Nairobi
New Delhi Shanghai Taipei Toronto

With offices in
Argentina Austria Brazil Chile Czech Republic France Greece
Guatemala Hungary Italy Japan Poland Portugal Singapore
South Korea Switzerland Thailand Turkey Ukraine Vietnam

Copyright © 2006 by Richard Striner

First published by Oxford University Press, Inc., 2006
198 Madison Avenue, New York, NY 10016
www.oup.com

First issued as an Oxford University Press paperback, 2007
ISBN 978-0-19-532539-3

Oxford is a registered trademark of Oxford University Press

The Library of Congress has catalogued the hardcover edition as follows:
Striner, Richard, 1950–
Father Abraham : Lincoln's relentless struggle to end slavery / Richard Striner.
p. cm.
Includes bibliographical references and index.
ISBN-13: 978-0-19-518306-1
ISBN-10: 0-19-518306-1
1. Lincoln, Abraham, 1809–1865—Views on slavery.
2. Lincoln, Abraham, 1809–1865—Relations with African Americans.
3. Slaves—Emancipation—United States. I. Title.
E457.2.S89 2006
973.7'092—dc22
2005023083

1 3 5 7 9 8 6 4 2
Printed in the United States of America
on acid-free paper

To my wife, Sara Jane, and all my family

Contents

Acknowledgments

I WISH TO THANK the following people for their contributions to the book. I am deeply grateful to James M. McPherson, Eric Foner, David Grimsted, Harold Holzer, Michael Burlingame, Herman Belz, Robert Cleary, and my wife, Sara Striner, for their willingness to review the manuscript in whole or in part. I am especially indebted to my literary agent, John W. Wright, for his many helpful suggestions. At Oxford University Press, I will always be grateful to my editor, Peter Ginna, his assistant, Laura Stickney, and senior production editor Joellyn Ausanka for their many outstanding contributions to this book. I will always remember the encouragement provided by my family (especially my parents) and my friends Richard Berryman, Avis Black, Joan Nicolaysen, Jann Hoag, Laura Lieberman, Henry McKinney, and Carl Reddel. I will always be grateful to my graduate student Kevin Fields for his research assistance. Any errors in the book are my own.

FATHER ABRAHAM

Introduction

TO WHAT EXTENT should Abraham Lincoln be regarded as our nation's "Great Emancipator"?

This book will show that Lincoln was a masterful anti-slavery leader. A moral visionary, Lincoln was also blessed with extraordinary talent in the orchestration of power. *Father Abraham* will argue that this rare combination of gifts in the leadership of Lincoln played a vital role in the extinction of American slavery. This book will challenge portrayals of Lincoln that misunderstand his character and therefore misunderstand what his leadership achieved.

For a long time, a significant number of historians have argued that Lincoln was a cautious or emotionally tepid man, who was driven by outside pressures and events into anti-slavery leadership. A host of recent commentators have suggested that Lincoln's contributions to the anti-slavery movement were almost unintentional.

Several years ago, historian Allen C. Guelzo contended in *The Washington Post* that Lincoln was a "reluctant recruit to the abolitionist cause," a "restrained" and "emotionally chilly" politician whose "unblinking eye for compromise" created an "ambiguous shadow" of a legacy.[1]

In his best-selling 1995 biography of Lincoln, historian David Herbert Donald talked of an "essential passivity" in Lincoln's nature, an alleged personality quirk that resulted in "reluctance to take the initiative and make bold plans." He contended that this "basic trait of character" was "evident throughout Lincoln's life."[2]

In Ken Burns's 1989 documentary television series *The Civil War*, historian Barbara Fields expressed impatient disdain for the reputation

1

of Lincoln as the Great Emancipator. Fields dismissed the Emancipation Proclamation as a gesture of moral catch-up: "The people most affected by the Emancipation Proclamation," she said, "obviously did not receive it as news because they knew before Lincoln knew that the war was about emancipation."[3]

To be sure, there are millions of Americans who continue to venerate Lincoln for patriotic reasons. Moreover, some prominent historians continue to defend Lincoln's record as an anti-slavery leader. James M. McPherson, for example, credits Lincoln's "superb leadership, strategy, and sense of timing as president, commander in chief, and head of the Republican Party" with the liberation of millions.[4]

But for many Americans, Lincoln these days is a strikingly ambiguous figure: a moody, strange, and mysterious sort of politician.

Even worse, he seemed to be *tricky* now and then—a mere vote-grubbing "pol"—and Americans are not very keen nowadays about "tricky" politicians in the White House. In the 1984 novel *Lincoln*, Gore Vidal portrayed Lincoln as a consummate power broker whose real motivations were elusive. And a steady outpouring of scholarly books depicts Lincoln as a "practical" man who was driven into acts of moral leadership by others.[5]

In contrast, according to public affairs scholar William Lee Miller, Lincoln was a *virtuous* leader on all the major issues of the day, and a leader of the highest ideals.[6]

In my own view, Abraham Lincoln was a great moral leader. But I believe we must acknowledge that the ethical politics of Lincoln depended on some very crafty methods. Moreover, the ethics and the tricky maneuverings of Lincoln were essentially harmonious—paradoxical as this may seem—and they should not be detached from one another as we analyze his politics.

This book will show that Lincoln was a rare man indeed: a fervent idealist endowed with a remarkable gift for strategy. An ethicist, Lincoln was also an artist in the Machiavellian uses of power. It was this combination of qualities that made Lincoln's contribution to the anti-slavery movement so fundamental, and, it may be argued, so demonstrably *necessary*.

Building upon the work of scholars such as Harry V. Jaffa, Don E. Fehrenbacher, LaWanda Cox, James M. McPherson, and William Lee Miller, *Father Abraham* argues that the qualities that some regard as problematical in Lincoln in no way detract from his greatness. To the contrary—they *establish* his greatness. A few other observations are in order in regard to the book. First, I approach Lincoln's rise to greatness as a story of expanding audacity; though he learned from other people, his genius developed as an ongoing process of mental self-discovery. His goals kept expanding as he tested how far he might go in his attempt to change history.

Second, Lincoln scholars are continuously confronted with a problem of source analysis. The sheer *craft* of Lincoln's ways demands critical analysis, even to the point of asking questions about his veracity. Historian LaWanda Cox has observed that "in striving for consent," Lincoln "would tailor an argument to fit his hearer. To develop public support or outflank opposition, he would at times conceal his hand or dissemble. . . ."[7] Indeed, Cox has argued that "Lincoln's style of presidential leadership was as often devious as forthright."[8] The challenge for historians is to find and analyze the overall pattern in which Lincoln's ploys were merely parts within a whole.

Third, chapters 4 through 7, devoted to the war years, address Lincoln's overlapping of political and military strategy. This extensive examination of military issues is important for two reasons: If, as the German military theorist Carl von Clausewitz argued so famously, the waging of war is a direct extension of politics, the Civil War is fraught with validation of his point. Much of Lincoln's moral strategy in politics, especially concerning the issue of slavery, was connected to his prosecution of the war. Furthermore, Lincoln's genius in power orchestration can never be fully understood if his military and civilian stratagems are separated. His sheer capacity to *visualize* power, and his artistry in simultaneous best-case and worst-case contingency planning, will appear across the board in his presidential leadership.

Perhaps some words about my title—*Father Abraham*—are also in order. "We Are Coming, Father Abraham, Three Hundred Thousand More" was the title of a Union recruiting poem. It was later set to music by Stephen Foster and others. As the title of the poem made the rounds, "Father Abraham" took its place among the various nicknames for Lincoln. The derivation of the nickname was biblical: many hymns had long referred to the patriarch, the "father" of the Hebrew nation, as "Father Abraham." And when Lincoln's supporters began to compare him to Washington—as the second "Father of his Country"—the paternal theme deepened in its cultural resonance.

There is, of course, an extremely ironic difference in the fate of Abraham Lincoln and the fate of his biblical namesake. God tested the patriarch Abraham by telling him to sacrifice Isaac, his son. As Abraham prepared for the deed, God relented and spared him the sacrifice. "Venerable Father Abraham," wrote Søren Kierkegaard in 1843, "thou didst gain all and didst retain Isaac."[9] Though Lincoln "gained all," in a sense, he had to make a horrible sacrifice. Six hundred thousand were killed in the Civil War—including Lincoln himself—in a scourging of the nation that Lincoln, in his second Inaugural Address, proclaimed a wrathful judgment of the Lord.

Lincoln took responsibility for those in his charge: like a father, he sought to protect them, even (on occasion) from themselves. But alas, he could not forestall the sacrifice.

ONE

Lincoln and Slavery: The Problem

THEY HAD COME FROM ALL OVER the city of Chicago and vicinity to gather at the Tremont House hotel on the evening of July 10, 1858. They had come to hear the candidate, Lincoln.

Transcripts of the speech that he delivered that evening—and the newspaper texts included audience response—make it clear that his listeners were almost in a frenzy as he roused their turbulent emotions. While the speech was officially a kick-off address in his campaign for the United States Senate, its subjects were slavery and race.

Using patriotic and religious themes, Lincoln channeled his thoughts into searing incantations as he argued that white supremacy was poisoning the soul of America by slow degrees. White Americans were feasting on evil fruit, he declared, if they convinced themselves that their black fellow countrymen deserved nothing better than enslavement. What do such arguments amount to, Lincoln demanded, but "the arguments that kings have made for enslaving the people in all ages of the world?" Tyrants, he added sarcastically, "always bestrode the necks of the people, not that they wanted to do it, but because the people were better off for being ridden."

This was the argument, Lincoln said, of all the white supremacists who advocated slavery or said they didn't care about the issue. It was a vile, seductive, hypocritical, and sinful argument, Lincoln insisted. It was nothing less than "the same old serpent that says you work and I eat, you toil and I will enjoy the fruits of it. Turn [it] in whatever way you will—whether it come from the mouth of a King, as an excuse for enslaving the people of his country, or from the mouth of men of one race as a reason for enslaving the men of another race, it is all the same old serpent. . . ."

And where will it end, Lincoln asked—will it stop with the blacks? If Americans should choose to back away from "this old Declaration of Independence, which declares that all men are equal upon principle," if Americans indulged and abetted tyrannical behavior in violation of the principle, "it does not stop with the negro." Not at all: "If one man says it does not mean a negro, why [may] not another say it does not mean some other man?" And so the degradation would spread—the American Republic would degenerate.

Enough of such apostasy, Lincoln proclaimed as he worked his spell upon the crowd; if it comes to such a pass, it might be better to abandon the American experiment, to trash the Declaration and its eloquent phrases altogether if they stood for nothing.

"If that declaration is not the truth," Lincoln cried out at the speech's climax, "let us get the Statute book, in which we find it and tear it out! Who is so bold to do it! (Voices—'me' and 'no one,' etc.) If it is not true let us tear it out! (cries of 'no, no')."[1]

This is hardly the Lincoln that millions of Americans know from their schoolbook history. This is not the sort of Lincolnesque oratory chosen by a later generation for carving and enshrining on the walls of the Lincoln Memorial. Even Lincoln's extraordinary second Inaugural Address, with its stark Old Testament passages, renders but a muted distillation of the anger, the insistent vehemence, the sheer imperious brilliance of the Lincoln who could work those crowds with such impatient and charismatic fervor in the 1850s.[2]

People sanctify a very different Abraham Lincoln: the sorrowful and saintly "moderate" who put preservation of the Union first and who embraced anti-slavery goals as a means to that end. This Lincoln stereotype is quite pervasive in its influence. Even among academic scholars it remains influential. It is embraced by Lincoln admirers and Lincoln detractors alike.

Admirers praise Lincoln's wise "moderation," which could triumph over "extremism." Detractors (at least left-of-center detractors) revile Lincoln's "moderate" ways as pusillanimous compared to the anti-slavery militance of abolitionists like William Lloyd Garrison and Frederick Douglass.

Many believe that Lincoln "only wanted to save the Union" when the guns blazed away at Fort Sumter. They believe that he gradually came to "realize" how deeply the slavery issue was embroiled in the sectional tragedy—the tragedy that he had presumably tried to avert in his "House Divided" speech, the supposedly sorrowful, patient, and healing plea to de-escalate the tensions that were leading toward civil war.

But it was not so. Those who regard Lincoln's 1858 "House Divided" speech in this manner have probably never read much of it. If they did, they would swiftly encounter a sharp, insistent, and urgent warning that America's divided House was re-uniting in the worst possible way. The "House Divided" speech was a warning that the slavery system was on its way North unless Americans prevented the uniting of their "House" along pro-slavery lines.

By itself, preservation of the Union was an empty concept to Lincoln, unless the Union remained dedicated—or could forcibly be re-dedicated—to its founding principle that all men are created equal. If America *could* be re-dedicated to this fundamental principle, as Lincoln so fervently hoped, then there was justification for defending the Union's permanence. But if the nation should ever lose or repudiate that founding principle, the Union would become a monstrosity, better abandoned than patched up with "moderate" evasions or compromises of appeasement.

In fact, it might be better for decent men to leave the United States, Lincoln ruminated in the 1850s, if pro-slavery forces succeeded in uniting the nation their way. "Our progress in degeneracy appears to me to be pretty rapid," he wrote to a close friend in 1855. "As a nation, we began by declaring that '*all men are created equal.*' We now practically read it, 'all men are created equal, *except negroes.*'" Soon enough "it will read 'all men are created equal, except negroes, *and foreigners and Catholics.*' When it comes to this I should prefer emigrating to some country where they make no pretense of loving liberty—to Russia, for instance, where despotism can be taken pure, and without the base alloy of hypocracy [*sic*]."[3]

Right up to the outbreak of the Civil War, Lincoln talked this way and followed up with appropriate actions. Indeed, it was Lincoln's election itself that sparked the secession proclamations in the winter of 1860–61. The reason was clear to almost everyone: Lincoln had promised to support legislation that would stop the expansion of slavery. If Lincoln and his fellow Republicans succeeded in carrying out this promise—if Congress prevented the creation of new slave states in the West—the existing slave states would eventually be locked into permanent minority status in the Union, unable to block abolitionist legislation in Congress or stop an anti-slavery amendment of the Constitution.

Though Lincoln did not (until December 1861) reveal any plans that would push beyond the goal of slavery containment, there might be nothing to stop a Republican *successor* from adopting such a course of action, once the groundwork had been laid and the basic conditions were locked in place. After all, this was clearly a long-term struggle. Strategists on both sides of the issue engaged in long-term contingency planning, and they framed their short-term positions accordingly.

This was the reason, as the leaders in the slave states knew very well, why the strategy of slavery containment was a near-fatal threat to the "peculiar institution" of slavery. For as soon as the slave states were finally reduced to a minority faction in Congress and the nation at large, there might be nothing—nothing but the force of arms—that could hold abolitionism back from eventual victory.

Ever since the 1820s, American advocates of slavery had been keeping careful track of this political arithmetic, maintaining a vigilant and fearful watch upon the balance of the free and slave states. For years, Southern militants had threatened secession if the free states placed them in a "one-down" power position.

Lincoln resolutely stood up to these threats of secession and proposed to let the chips fall where they might. He would not back down one inch from his program of slavery containment. And this was merely the beginning of what Lincoln had in mind for America.

Lincoln fully intended to contain the institution of slavery as a prelude to phasing it out over time, perhaps through a gradual "buy-out" program. He hoped that the leverage provided by containing the slavery system would gradually soften resistance in the South to an offer of money in return for the liberation of slaves. He meant to place the institution of slavery "where the public mind shall rest in the belief that it is in [the] course of . . . extinction," as he said in his "House Divided" speech.[4] Preservation of the Union was entirely subsumed in this overriding objective. Nothing was to stand in the way of it.

In December 1860, Lincoln killed a sectional compromise designed to preserve the Union and to stall the momentum of secession. This compromise (the Crittenden Compromise) would have permitted the continued expansion of slavery. Lincoln shot down this compromise to save the Union by instructing his fellow Republicans to "entertain no proposition for a compromise in regard to the *extension* of slavery.

The instant you do, they have us under again; all our labor is lost, and sooner or later must be done over. . . . Have none of it. The tug has to come & better now than later."[5] So the war began.

Concurrently, he took a fresh look at his options for phasing out slavery. Within a year, he took advantage of political moods and got Congress to authorize federal funds to encourage the gradual liberation of slaves. As a test case, Lincoln offered this voluntary phaseout package to the handful of border slave states that had not attempted secession.

What he hoped to achieve was the creation of a voluntary pilot program that would demonstrate, in embryonic form, the overall feasibility of phasing out slavery. But the border states turned him down.

Whereupon, Lincoln promptly and drastically revised his whole approach to the problem and accelerated his anti-slavery strategy.

Specifically, he turned from the border states to the slave states comprising the rebellious Confederate States, and there, in the name of preserving the Union, he instituted sweeping and immediate emancipation with no compensation for the rebels. This plan, as announced in the Preliminary Emancipation Proclamation of September 22, 1862, would take effect just as soon as his armies took control of rebellious territory (provided the Confederate States were still in a state of rebellion as of January 1, 1863). There was no turning back from this sacred commitment, Lincoln told both Houses of Congress in his annual message of December 1862.

Lincoln critics deride these achievements as "gradualism," suggesting his commitment to equality was tepid or equivocal. But consider the achievement of Lincoln-style gradualism in context.

It amounted to nothing less than this: Lincoln forced the United States, North and South, to turn the fundamental corner on slavery. His anti-slavery gradualism was flexible enough for very fast acceleration when the turbulent give-and-take of political and military strategy made it possible. It was also backed up with a heroic commitment on the order of six hundred thousand killed, including Lincoln himself, by the time the Civil War had ended.

In light of this, it behooves us to take a very serious look at the stereotype of Lincoln as a "moderate" who "only wanted to preserve the Union." In the first place, how could such a one-sided stereotype have developed at all?

If the written Lincoln record were consistently clear, then the stereotype would not have developed. It must now be admitted, however, that Lincoln made some statements in the course of the Civil War, especially in a famous open letter that he wrote to political journalist Horace Greeley in 1862, in which he explicitly declared that preservation of the Union was indeed his paramount goal in the struggle. Moreover, in the course of the Lincoln-Douglas debates of 1858, Lincoln even made statements (under pressure from Douglas) denying that he advocated social equality for blacks.

The "moderate" stereotype of Lincoln has elements of truth: his politics were surely different, for example, from those of the Radical Republicans, even though the Radicals and Lincoln had a great deal more in common than people might suppose.

The politics of Lincoln were complex and multifaceted. There was clearly a moderate *side* to Lincoln, just as there was clearly a *sense* in which his commitment to saving the Union was genuine, indeed quite passionate.

So the Lincoln record could be regarded plausibly as murky or even contradictory, at least on the surface. No wonder that distinguished historian Richard N. Current once consigned the seeming contradictions in Lincoln's career to the enigmatic nature of "the Lincoln nobody knows."

But such apparent contradictions in the record of Lincoln are not enigmatic. They are part of an extraordinary pattern of statecraft, one that Americans should now understand on its merits.

Pioneering research and interpretation by scholars in the past half-century—especially the work of Harry V. Jaffa, Don E. Fehrenbacher, James M. McPherson, LaWanda Cox, and William Lee Miller—has cleared away a vast amount of confusion spawned by the "moderate" Lincoln stereotype.

Lincoln was that rarest of all great men, a political ethicist who was also an extraordinary natural genius in the Machiavellian orchestration of power.[6] Lincoln forged a brilliant plan to propel abolitionism forward into gradual and incremental victory, to roll back the evil of slavery, to make it recoil upon itself until it died. But the strategy entailed a certain tactical cost that might pain many Lincoln admirers.

The fact should not be evaded: Lincoln chose sometimes to obscure the full truth about his mission in the Civil War years. Like any political virtuoso, he weighed both the content and tone of what he said at different places and times. When it served his purpose, he was capable of generating lawyerly hair-splitting rhetoric, at times to the brink of pettifoggery. He deliberately played up the constitutional case for preserving the Union while playing down his anti-slavery mission whenever he believed that the realities of politics and power made it necessary.

Lincoln gave a very misleading impression now and then to the effect that his wartime anti-slavery acts should be understood *only* as ploys with which to save the Union. To be sure, he was careful to phrase the proposition as a matter of constitutional law—as a matter of the constitutional *justification* for his anti-slavery actions, a justification that was certainly true enough on its level but surely not the *whole* truth—and to write key statements in a cunningly legalistic way.

He did this to pacify opponents of his anti-slavery program, opponents whose support he needed to win the Civil War and to achieve his full objectives for America. So he talked to them in terms they would respect.

In this manner, an enduring cult built up around the notion that "Lincoln only wanted to preserve the Union" in the Civil War. This is how the "moderate" stereotype of Lincoln developed and grew, notwithstanding the fact that it was after all Lincoln's own insistence on containing the institution of slavery that *triggered* the secession crisis (thereby jeopardizing the Union) in the first place.

If Lincoln only wanted to preserve the Union, then why did he oppose the Crittenden Compromise in 1860? Preservation of the Union (at least until the outbreak of secession) was relatively easy: just appease the slave-holding states and let slavery continue to expand. But Lincoln refused. Yet posterity regards him as primarily a Unionist, who freed the slaves in his endeavor to save the Union.

Such were the arts of this master politician who would use the necessity of saving the Union as a justification for saving the Union *his way*. It is obvious enough that if Lincoln had been willing to compromise on the issue of slavery expansion, the Union might very well have "held." But with the Union placed in serious peril, an occasion was provided for a very tough policy against the rebellious slave states.

This policy, of course, would develop into outright emancipation, thus extending the Republican anti-slavery agenda that had *caused* the Confederates to put the Union in peril. The logic of the Lincoln policies came full circle.

It is no special pleading, however, to observe that such behavior can be morally defensible in certain situations. Few politicians choose to blurt out their deepest intentions to everyone all the time. They may even choose on occasion to mask their full intentions to avert catastrophic possibilities.

Consider the case of Franklin Delano Roosevelt, who told an isolationist-leaning American public in 1939 and 1940 that America could stay out of World War II when in fact he believed the reverse and needed time to shape public opinion.

Were the tactical methods of Lincoln and FDR mere studies in guile? Or were they nothing less than grand demonstrations of the ethical calculus that strategists must always confront as they weigh lesser evils with greater?

However dismaying it may seem to admirers of Lincoln to acknowledge that he didn't always tell the "whole truth," his case must be judged not only in the context of moral ends that may justify otherwise questionable means but also in a clear-headed, wide-awake realization of the risks and the dangers Lincoln faced as he struggled to keep white supremacy at bay while phasing out slavery.

A powerful segment of Northern public opinion regarded Lincoln as a "nigger lover." The hate campaigns that were waged against Lincoln's policies were fearsome and ugly. The heart of Lincoln's strategy was simple and stunning: having captured the White House on terms that plunged the slave states into secession, Lincoln used the battle cry of saving the Union as a method for building a political and military power coalition that would break the power of the slaveholding states forever. This coalition extended necessarily beyond the Republican Party. It included white supremacist Democrats who would *only* support the Republican administration in a war over principles of Union.

But to keep that Union devoted to the principles essential to its highest meaning, Lincoln used a remarkable tactic that is far too little understood: he embraced the cause of saving the Union on two different levels at once.

At the highest level, Lincoln's mission to save the Union was a heartfelt imperative. For so long as the Union continued to embody the principles enshrined in the Declaration of Independence, it was for Lincoln a sacred vessel, a channel through which, as he said in his 1858

Chicago address, Americans could feel themselves to be "blood of the blood, and flesh of the flesh of the men who wrote that Declaration."[7]

Nonetheless, the mission of saving the Union would always be contingent for Lincoln on America's success in putting slavery "on the downhill," as he phrased it. The Union cried out for preservation as long as it stood for its founding ideals.

Lincoln's wartime rhetoric of saving the Union was intended on this highest level for those who agreed already with his anti-slavery ideals or for those who could at least be touched by his moral principles.

At a lower level—at the level of tactical dealings with those who supported slavery—Lincoln's Unionism was employed for a very different purpose, an essentially Machiavellian purpose, an ingeniously calculated strategy of transformation, a strategy that forced its own opponents into limited cooperation by dint of a patriotic cause that transcended their bigotry.

And this was the level at which Lincoln insisted, as he did in his 1862 letter, that his wartime anti-slavery measures were *only* designed to preserve the Union, a point which, though true as a justification, begged the larger question of what that Union would stand for in years to come.

This strategy was neither "insincere" nor "sincere" in conventional terms. It was political artistry developed for transcendent and practical purposes, artistry that was morally consistent, ethically justified, and paradoxically grounded in the craft of juxtaposing half-truth and truth for simultaneous transmission to very different groups of "players."

The genius behind all this—the orchestration of ideas and passion and power—has no real equal in American history. Call it moderate, conservative, radical, or liberal, as prompted by your own sensibilities. Call it any combination of personal or ideological principles that strike your fancy. It was nothing less than a *tour de force* of power in the service of freedom.

Moreover, as Lincoln strove in this high-risk manner to assure the success of his cause through the strategy of slavery containment, he worked experimentally to craft the best possible deal for American blacks in a post-Emancipation epoch. But he remained ever mindful that a white supremacist backlash could wipe away all the moral progress he had gained.

The backlash occurred in 1862 (in reaction to Lincoln's Emancipation Proclamation), and it recurred periodically until the Civil War was over. While it almost cost him the presidency in 1864, it cost him his life the next year. By then, the transformation he had wrought was irreversible in its essentials. But what "might have been" if he had lived is a very different matter, as we shall see.

To UNDERSTAND LINCOLN, some historical background is in order. For in many respects Lincoln's anti-slavery strategy built upon some older ideas that emerged in the age of the Founding Fathers, a number of whom viewed slavery as one of the fundamental issues that confronted the new nation.

At the Constitutional Convention, for example, James Madison acknowledged that "the States were divided into different interests not by their difference of size, but by other circumstances; the most material of which resulted partly from climate, but principally from [the effects of] their having or not having slaves."[8]

Well before the American Revolution, abolitionism had been taken up by Quakers. But in the Revolutionary and early National periods, it was "in the air" across the nation. The idealism unleashed by the American Revolution prompted most of the Northern states to embark upon abolishing or phasing out slavery between 1777 and 1804.

In the upper South as well, the anti-slavery cause made an impact. Indeed, one of the most famous expositors of anti-slavery principles in Revolutionary America was the Virginian Thomas Jefferson.

Many recent historians have indicted Jefferson-the-slaveholder on the charge of hypocrisy, a charge containing strong elements of truth. For present purposes, though, it behooves us to acknowledge that Jefferson, as the preeminent oracle of American freedom, made a powerful impact on Lincoln and many others.

The Jefferson who wrote the extraordinary lines of the Declaration of Independence was the Jefferson whom Lincoln revered. This was the Jefferson who proclaimed in a famous letter written just before he died that "the mass of mankind has not been born with saddles on their backs, nor a favored few booted and spurred, ready to ride them legitimately by the grace of God."[9]

This was the Jefferson who proposed a new constitution for Virginia in 1783, a constitution that would have forbidden the importation of "any more slaves to reside in this State, or the continuance of slavery beyond the generation which shall be living on the thirty-first day of December, one thousand eight hundred; all persons born after that day being hereby declared free."[10]

Other Virginians such as George Mason and George Washington hoped that the state of Virginia would phase out slavery. Washington worked behind the scenes in the 1790s to get the work started; meanwhile, he developed a plan to convert Mount Vernon to a well-rounded farm to be worked by free tenants. When his plans for Mount Vernon came to nought, he determined to free his slaves in his will. He predicted in private that the nation would have to face up to the issue and decide in favor of freedom, universal freedom. According to one reminiscence, he told a British visitor in conversations at Mount Vernon in 1797, "I can clearly foresee that nothing but the rooting out of slavery can perpetuate the existence of our union, by consolidating it in a common bond of principle."[11]

Washington also told Edmund Randolph—if notes of this second-hand account as set forth in the papers of Jefferson can be believed—that if North and South should ever divide on the issue of slavery during his lifetime, "he had made up his mind to move and be of the northern."[12]

The anti-slavery Founding Fathers were men of diverse sensibilities. Some of them were white supremacists, who nonetheless condemned slavery. A few regarded blacks as their equals. But most of them agreed that a phaseout program was the only realistic way to end slavery in light of the widespread prevalence of racial prejudice, combined with the enormous amount of money invested in slaves. So they did what they could on the national level to begin such a phaseout. The preliminary step was containment.[13]

Anti-Slavery Measures in the New American Nation

In 1784, Jefferson tried to lay the groundwork for such a policy in Congress (still meeting under the Articles of Confederation) when he introduced legislation setting forth the process whereby states would be created out of territory west of the Appalachians. Several states possessed colonial charters without a western boundary. Such states were expected by many to cede their western lands to the Union, and Virginia, while retaining Kentucky, had already ceded its western territories north of the

Ohio River to the Union. Other states, such as Georgia and the Carolinas, had not yet taken action on the issue.

In Jefferson's text for the Ordinance of 1784 slavery would have been forbidden in *all* common territories west of the Appalachians after 1800. This was deleted from the ordinance (it lost in Congress by the margin of one vote), but an anti-slavery provision was adopted in the stronger Northwest Ordinance of 1787. It bears noting, however, that the Northwest Ordinance was limited to the former Colonial lands above the Ohio River.

Another significant step was taken in 1787 to prevent the expansion of slavery. The Federal Constitution, which was being drafted at this time, gave the Federal Congress the power to shut off the importation of slaves after twenty years. Together, the Northwest Ordinance and the Constitution's importation cut-off provision were twin features of a policy hammered out piecemeal to contain the institution of slavery—a prelude to long-term phaseout. But a counter-movement against this policy had started already.

In 1790, the Federal Congress passed the Southwest Ordinance, covering western lands to be ceded by the states below Virginia. This ordinance did *not* forbid slavery below the Ohio River. In the same year, 1790, North Carolina ceded its western territories. Kentucky broke away from Virginia in 1792, and was admitted to the Union with a slave state constitution. Tennessee (created out of former North Carolina lands) was admitted as a slave state in 1796. Georgia ceded its western lands in 1802. The western lands of Georgia went the same way: Mississippi was admitted as a slave state in 1817, and Alabama was admitted as a slave state in 1819.

The expansion of slavery below the Ohio River was driven in part by "economics," that is, by visions of prodigious fortunes to be made through the cultivation and harvesting of cotton using Eli Whitney's new "gin." The movement to contain the evil of slavery was obviously hampered by the powerful appeal of the riches to be gained by expanding it.

There was, however, a different side to the pro-slavery movement of the 1790s: a fear that anti-slavery talk could incite a slave insurrection that would lead to a catastrophic race war. Events in the Caribbean convinced a great many owners of slaves in the United States that even casual talk of a long-term slavery phaseout was tantamount to playing with matches, as we would say, in the presence of gasoline.

The Caribbean events in question took place at "St. Dominique" (Santo Domingo), the island of Hispaniola comprising the present-day Dominican Republic and Haiti. From 1791 to 1804, a bloody slave insurrection ravaged the island, alarming scores of American slave owners. Nervous alarms pervaded Southern American ports, and the discovery in 1800 of an incipient slave revolt in Virginia (the Gabriel Prosser revolt) added to the scare.

For these reasons, pro-slavery leaders at the time viewed talk of a long-term anti-slavery program in the United States as dangerous folly. They argued that the presence of freed blacks was a permanent incitement to rebellion among the enslaved, for which reason a number of them proposed sending former slaves out of the country if their masters chose to free them.

Even before these tensions of the 1790s, Jefferson had expressed his belief that a long-term separation of the races was the only real scenario for abolition. He avowed that "deep-rooted prejudices entertained by the whites; ten thousand recollections, by the blacks, of the injuries they have sustained; new provocations; the real distinctions that nature has made; and many other circumstances, will divide us into parties, and produce convulsions, which will probably never end but in the extermination of the one or the other race," unless blacks and whites agreed to seek separate destinies in separate countries.[14]

This package of presuppositions was sufficiently widespread to influence the founding (in 1816) of the American Colonization Society, an anti-slavery group that proposed to repatriate thousands of slaves to Africa, the continent of their ancestors. Within a few years the nation of Liberia was founded as a promised land for former slaves.

This was the America into which Abraham Lincoln was born on February 12, 1809, in the slave state of Kentucky, a nation poised between advocates of slavery containment and advocates of slavery expansion. The two philosophies were reflected in rival formulae for state constitutions: free states above the Mason-Dixon and Ohio River border and slave states below the border. On each side of the line, Americans argued about the morality of enslavement. But the anti-slavery movement was generally centered on the strategy of colonization. Such was the overall situation before the great Missouri crisis broke out in 1819, when Lincoln was ten years old.

The Missouri Crisis and Its Aftermath

The state of Louisiana had been admitted to the Union as a slave state in 1812. But the rest of the Louisiana Purchase, which the United States had acquired from France in 1803, was in a state of limbo regarding slavery. Congress had not yet addressed the issue as to whether or not slavery should exist in the future states that would be created in the vast Louisiana Territory.

Still, the westward spread of American slavery continued. In 1819, a majority of voters and leaders of the territory of Missouri (whose population was 16 percent enslaved) petitioned Congress for admission as a slave state. In response, Congressman James Tallmadge, Jr., of New York proposed to amend the Missouri statehood bill by prohibiting the introduction of any more slaves into the state and by requiring the emancipation of slaves who were born in Missouri, after its statehood had been granted, when they reached the age of twenty-five. The Tallmadge amendments were passed in the House of Representatives but defeated in the Senate.

Almost immediately, the sectional difference over slavery erupted into fury, with Southern denunciations of the amendments as unconstitutional, and with threats of secession if the free states attempted to stop the institution of slavery from expanding.

In March 1820, Speaker of the House Henry Clay engineered the passage of a series of measures that would constitute the famous Missouri Compromise. Missouri would be admitted as a slave state, but some northern counties of Massachusetts would be organized into the new free state of Maine.

In 1820, the geopolitical balance of the free and slave states was even: eleven apiece. With the admission of Missouri and Maine into the Union, the delicate balance of power between the free states and the slave states would be preserved.

Or would it? In a critical development, Senator Jesse Thomas of Illinois proposed that Congress establish a dividing line that would run from east to west across the remainder of the Louisiana Territory, a line that would stipulate the outermost limit beyond which slavery would be prohibited.

This boundary line would extend due west from the *southern*, rather than the northern, border of the new state of Missouri. What this meant was that the free-state system got the lion's share of all the land that remained in the Louisiana Purchase. The free-state system would gradually overwhelm the slave-state system in its geographical magnitude, and hence in its representation in Congress. The Thomas Proviso passed, and the boundary line was established.

Thus the political war over slavery expansion began with the Missouri crisis, with the slave states emerging from the war's first engagement with their long-term power at risk. Though some politicians thought the compromise had settled the issue "forever," by the end of the decade pro-slavery leaders began to think about the worst-case picture if the free-state bloc should outnumber the slave states.

To be sure, pro-slavery Americans kept working to encourage the expansion of slavery where the Thomas Proviso permitted it: into Arkansas territory, for instance, just below the new state of Missouri, and into the newly independent nation of Mexico, whose province of Texas received a heavy new influx of American settlers, many of whom brought their slave property with them. But when Mexico abolished and prohibited slavery in 1829, the American settlers resisted all Mexican attempts to bring them into compliance. The importance of Texas to American struggles over slavery would soon be apparent.

Pro-slavery theorists were troubled by the prospect of being outnumbered by the free states. They worried about the growing abolitionist movement, fearing that a militant and abolitionist North might begin to wield the power of the federal government in ways that would insinuate an anti-slavery agenda into slave states by measured degrees.

These fears propelled one of the most spectacular ideological turnabouts in American history, the transformation of South Carolina's preeminent political leader John C. Calhoun from an ardent supporter of broad construction of the Constitution for the purpose of creating magnificent public works (a program he supported when he served as secretary of war under James Monroe) into a militant strict constructionist and states-rights advocate, shrilly committed to the platform that federal tariffs to finance internal improvements were an abrogation of the rights of the sovereign states. Such was the justification of the famous "nullification" campaign against the Tariff of 1828. This controversy, which erupted when Lincoln was about to turn twenty years old, was settled by another compromise brokered by Henry Clay in 1833.

The nullification controversy—a controversy over taxes, the rights of states, and the subtleties of constitutional logic—is generally offered as "Exhibit A" by the people who argue that the controversy over slavery could not possibly in and of itself have caused the Civil War, and that other issues, mostly economic and constitutional issues, were more fundamental.

But slavery *was* the central issue all the while, as the nullification leaders admitted. The nullification episode was largely a pretext—a symbolic rallying point—a flashpoint for agitation by which to generate leverage against the much larger formations of power that the agitators envisioned just over the horizon.

Calhoun admitted as much in his private correspondence. Notwithstanding his denunciation of the so-called Tariff of Abominations, in 1830 Calhoun confided: "I consider the Tariff, but as the occasion, rather than the real cause of the present unhappy state of things. . . . The truth can no longer be disguised, that the peculiar domestick institutions of the Southern States . . . [have] placed them in regard to taxation and appropriation in opposite relation to the majority of the Union; against the danger of which, if there be no protective power in the reserved rights of the states, they must in the end be forced to rebel, or submit to have . . . their domestick institutions exhausted by Colonization and other schemes, and themselves & children reduced to wretchedness."[15]

A fellow South Carolina "nullifier" named James Hamilton, Jr., made the same point: "I have always looked upon the present contest with the government, on the part of the Southern States, as a battle at the outposts, by which, if we succeeded in repulsing the enemy, *the citadel would be safe*. The same doctrines 'of the general welfare' which enable the general government to . . . appropriate the common treasure to make roads and canals . . . would authorize the federal government to erect the *peaceful* standard of servile revolt, to give the bounties for Emancipation here, and transportation to Liberia afterwards."[16]

The point was this: in light of the majority status that the free-state bloc had been gaining, the most militant slave-state leaders decided to prevent any sizable concentration of power—including the power to raise significant amounts of revenue—at the federal level, lest a newly powerful federal government fall into the hands of abolitionists, who would use their power to strike at the slavery system in all of the slave states. Historian William W. Freehling put it succinctly; the nullifiers feared that "the 'general welfare' clause would serve abolitionists as well as road builders."[17]

The most extreme Southern militants were dubious even of nullification. In 1830, a South Carolinian named John Richardson proclaimed the "absurdity of assuming the right to nullify Federal laws, *as a sovereign right reserved to the State*," when the rights of any state could be easily trumped through the power of a constitutional amendment, as soon as three-quarters of the states had chosen to ratify one. The sovereign powers of a state, he argued, could in turn be "controlled by three-fourths of the States."[18]

The 1830s

Slaveowners' fears became greater in the 1830s with the emergence of a radical new generation of abolitionists such as William Lloyd Garrison. And the outbreak at last of a full-fledged slave revolt—the 1831 Nat Turner Revolt in Virginia—quickened fears that had haunted the proslavery mind since the 1790s. Consequently, opinions on both sides of the issue became more militant during the 1830s, when Lincoln was beginning his political career.

The new abolitionists were militant in different degrees and in different ways. Some of them followed the philosophic lead of Garrison, who gradually expanded his anti-slavery principles to encompass a complete renunciation of force in human relationships, a radical and in many ways utopian worldview. Garrisonian abolitionists were increasingly non-political and even anti-political. But others, following the leadership of Theodore Dwight Weld, believed that the slavery system should be challenged not only through moral agitation but also political action.[19]

Weld, it bears noting, was happily married to an abolitionist woman from Charleston, South Carolina: Angelina Grimké, whose sister Sarah Grimké was also an abolitionist.

Many of the new abolitionists were sincere advocates of racial equality. They were therefore highly unpopular figures at a time in American history when mainstream culture was pervaded by the notions of white supremacy.

The idealism of the abolitionist movement grew steadily. The movement was augmented significantly by the participation of people such as Frederick Douglass, an escaped slave who became an important abolitionist leader in the 1840s and afterward. Free blacks (such as David Walker) had played a fundamental role in the abolitionist movement for a while.[20] But the leadership provided by former slaves was even more dramatic.

Foreign events, moreover, played a role in the issue once again: in 1833, British abolitionists succeeded in convincing Parliament to end the institution of slavery throughout the Empire. The goal was achieved through a program of gradual and compensated emancipation. This decisive event inspired the creation of the American Anti-Slavery Society.

Yet throughout the 1830s, the militance of the new abolitionist radicals was matched by a growing pro-slavery militance, such that John C. Calhoun declared in his notorious "Positive Good" speech of 1837 that the greatness of every superior civilization was grounded in the existence of a mud-sill class of degraded workers.[21] It was a militance that prompted several slave-holding states to pass laws against abolitionist speeches and rallies, against the publishing of abolitionist books, and against the possession of abolitionist literature. (It should be noted that nineteenth-century jurisprudence viewed the Bill of Rights as a bulwark against actions by the federal government, and not against actions by the states.)[22] It was a militance that prompted Southern postmasters to search and censor the mails in order to destroy abolitionist tracts. It was a militance that foisted a "Gag Rule" upon the Congress, a rule that from 1836 to 1844 prevented congressional discussion of abolitionist petitions by automatically tabling them.

In the South, the establishment of this new authoritarian "Cordon Sanitaire" forced the anti-slavery movement into hiding or out of existence.[23] In the North, the anti-slavery movement was approaching a crossroads. This was the political world in which Lincoln was rising in the state of Illinois as he approached the age of thirty.

In 1836, Texas achieved its independence from Mexico. Texas petitioned Congress for admission to the Union as a state—as potentially the largest state in the Union—and as a huge new bastion of slavery. Texas annexation hung in limbo for the next nine years, and the reason was obvious.

The 1840s

The sectional dispute over slavery continued in the 1840s, when Lincoln was elected to Congress. By the end of the decade the slavery issue was dominating the political life of the United States, and pro-slavery militants were threatening to break up the Union unless the abolitionist threat could be removed on a permanent basis.

The abolitionists themselves had become increasingly politicized. Some of them joined the new Liberty Party, whose nominee for the presidency in 1840 and again in 1844 was James G. Birney, a former slave owner. The Liberty Party succeeded in electing only one of its members to Congress (Gerrit Smith of New York). And yet a growing number of congressmen owed their elections to anti-slavery voters. For that reason, an anti-slavery bloc was emerging in Congress.

The most urgent dispute about slavery during the early 1840s was the issue of Texas. The issue had festered since 1836, when the Texans had broken away from Mexico and proclaimed their country an independent republic, at least until annexation to the United States could be achieved. In 1843, President John Tyler, a pro-slavery Virginian, appointed John C. Calhoun as his secretary of state, and the two of them forced the Texas issue by submitting an annexation treaty to the Senate. The Senate rejected this treaty, and the Texas question became a major source of controversy in the 1844 presidential election.

In 1844, the voters of the United States elected James K. Polk of Tennessee. Polk supported the annexation of Texas. But he believed that he could pacify the anti-Texas opposition by the time-honored methods of regional compromise. In a bid to appease anti-slavery sentiment, Polk suggested that the annexation of Texas be linked to the acquisition of the Oregon country, which the United States and Great Britain had occupied jointly pursuant to an 1818 treaty. Once again, the accession of additional land for the institution of slavery would be counter-balanced by an augmentation of land in which slavery would probably never take root—or so it seemed to conventional wisdom.

Upon Polk's election, lame-duck President Tyler proclaimed that a mandate for Texas annexation had been given. Through adroit maneuvering in Congress, Tyler was able to invite the Republic of Texas to join the United States in 1845.

Simultaneously, Florida, another slave state, joined the Union, and in quick succession, two more free states: Iowa, admitted to statehood in 1846, and Wisconsin, in 1847.

The years in which the old techniques of territorial balance could contain the slavery dispute were drawing to a close. A fundamental change had overtaken the anti-slavery movement, a change of over-powering magnitude. More and more, the movement's political power was centered in a broad coalition of anti-slavery whites who were not necessarily abolitionists at all, a coalition whose members often denied any interest in promoting racial equality. On the contrary, many of them were white supremacists, who saw slavery as an infringement of the liberties of *whites*.

It abridged white liberties by keeping poor whites from the best agricultural lands in the Southern states. It preempted the choicest plantations for the use of a selfish and arrogant elite. It abridged white liberties by spreading this system to the West, by sending out scores of would-be plantation nabobs, with thousands of enslaved black drudges in tow, to monopolize the great new Western empire and keep it from "the common man."

It abridged white liberties by censoring the words of Southern citizens who challenged the system, by stifling the voices of white representatives in Congress, by threatening murder and torture to any poor lout who presumed to think himself man enough to challenge the self-proclaimed lords and masters of Dixie. This, said the leaders of the "Free-Soil movement," was a threat to the liberties of all.[24]

It was something un-American, they said, and it threatened to pull the United States backward into Old World social conditions, back to medieval misery with lords of the manor in control, and their wretched vassals down below. Having started down the path to autocracy by tyrannizing blacks, the leaders of America's "Slave Power" were beginning to tyrannize whites. More and more, the militant protection of the slavery system was suppressing white freedom of speech, curtailing white freedom of the press, and threatening vocal white opponents of the system with beatings, whippings, and death.

In 1847, a dramatic development in Richmond, Virginia increased these fears even more. White workers at the Tredegar Iron Works called a strike for better hours and wages. The owner of the factory proceeded to fire them all and then rented—actually *rented*—enough slaves to run his factory effectively. American slavery was suddenly proven effective in industrial settings. And it had taken the jobs of white workers.[25]

Because of these fears and concerns, the anti-slavery bloc in Congress grew apace. And the Polk administration collided with its leaders when the president chose to pick a new territorial fight with Mexico.

Polk was indeed a believer in America's "Empire of Liberty." He meant to expand it to continental size by acquiring not only the Oregon country, but the Mexican province of California as well. His attempt to buy California from Mexico was quickly rebuffed. Unfazed, he proceeded to agitate relations with Mexico, ordering American troops onto land that was disputed by the Texans and Mexicans.

As the Mexican War erupted in 1846, the anti-slavery leaders in Congress took action. A Free-Soil Democrat from Pennsylvania named David Wilmot proposed a proviso to a war appropriations bill on August 8, 1846. The Wilmot Proviso declared "that, as an express and fundamental condition of the acquisition of any territory from the Republic of Mexico . . . neither slavery nor involuntary servitude shall ever exist in any part of said territory." The proviso was passed by the House of Representatives but killed in the Senate.

Once again, the territorial issue put slavery at the center of American politics. Southern newspapers praised California as a natural extension of Dixie and claimed that California was perfect for slavery.

But no sooner had Mexico consented to sell California and New Mexico in 1848 than gold was discovered in the streams of California, bringing in swarms of feisty "forty-niners." They got to California fast, most frequently in clipper ships racing south "around the Horn" and then up the west coast of South America. Before slave owners could make their way to California, the settlers applied for admission to the Union as a free state, and pro-slavery Southerners cried foul.

There had not been sufficient time, they protested, to give the South a real chance in California. Events had moved too quickly. Slave owners needed time to extend and to stabilize their Cordon Sanitaire. They needed time to convince a territorial legislature to pass a tough and effective slave code in order to prevent or suppress any slave insurrections and to catch any fugitive slaves.[26] The South was being pushed around, they declared—preempted in a fight for supremacy.

All the while, the slavery issue was tearing away at America's political parties. The Free-Soil movement was furious, its leaders reviling the Polk administration and its infamous "war to expand slavery." The

Wilmot Proviso was revived; over fifty different versions were passed
by the House of Representatives between 1846 and 1850. But all of
them were killed in the Senate, because the votes between the free-
and slave-state blocs were equal.

To break the impasse, Polk suggested extending the Missouri
Compromise line to the Pacific, which would turn California into
two states. But most of the Free-Soil leaders and slave-state leaders
wanted none of it.

In 1848, the Democratic Party nominated Senator Lewis Cass of
Michigan for president. Cass tried to play it safe on the territorial problem by espousing "Popular Sovereignty," a policy that would allow
white settlers to decide about the slavery issue themselves on a case-
by-case basis. But the doctrine of Popular Sovereignty begged the crucial question as to *when* these settlers would have their say: *before* the
institution of slavery had entered a territory (thus angering the owners
of slaves), or *afterward*, when the institution might be very hard to
dislodge, thus offending Free-Soilers?

Because of widespread contempt for this policy among the members of the Free-Soil movement, renegade Democrats bolted and joined
with anti-slavery citizens across party lines to form a "Free-Soil Party"
under the leadership of former President Martin Van Buren.

The other major party, the Whigs, selected a military hero as their
candidate in 1848: General Zachary Taylor, "Old Rough and Ready."
While Taylor belonged to neither party and had never even voted, he
did own slaves, along with some large plantations in Mississippi and
Louisiana, and his daughter (by that time deceased) had been married
to Senator Jefferson Davis of Mississippi.

Free-Soil Whigs ("Conscience Whigs," as they called themselves)
were sufficiently troubled by the nomination of Taylor to bolt from
their party to the Free-Soil Party of Van Buren. But Taylor won the
election, and he promptly astonished both Northerners and Southerners by siding with the Free-Soil movement.

Though Taylor owned slaves, he selected a prominent congressional
anti-slavery leader, Senator William H. Seward of New York, as his
adviser. Taylor proposed that California and New Mexico skip the territorial stage and be admitted as states—free states—immediately. The
South was in an uproar.

In 1849 and 1850, Senator John C. Calhoun made it clear that the
Union was in grave jeopardy. It was the slavery issue that threatened

destruction of the Union, he warned. "I have, Senators," he thundered, "believed from the first that the agitation of the subject of slavery would, if not prevented by some timely and effective measure, end in disunion." In the current crisis, he predicted, "California will become the test question. If you admit her, under all the difficulties that oppose her admission, you compel us to infer that you intend to exclude us from the whole of the acquired territories, with the intention of destroying, irretrievably, the equilibrium between the two sections."[27]

Calhoun, like his fellow Southern "Fire Eaters," felt pushed to the brink by two related circumstances: first, the presidential power of Taylor, a military hero, a determined leader, and a newly revealed (or newly unmasked) adherent of the Free-Soil movement; and second, the loss to the slave-state bloc of the entire West Coast of North America. This situation prompted Calhoun to call for new and permanent measures to protect the interests of slavery. He warned that only an amendment of the Constitution for the permanent protection of slavery would appease Southern fears about the abolitionist threat.

Calhoun had barely a month to live when, on March 4, 1850, he called upon the North to agree to drafting the amendment. But the Constitution was not to be amended that year. Instead, Senator Henry Clay took his final bow as America's "Great Pacificator." He crafted yet another big regional compromise for passage by Congress.

1850

The Compromise of 1850, however, was a mess, and it satisfied no one. California would enter the Union as a new free state, but the slave-state system remained a possibility in all the newly acquired lands between Texas and California, which would henceforth be settled on the basis of "Popular Sovereignty."

To satisfy anti-slavery proponents, the slave trade would be ended in Washington, D.C. But to appease pro-slavery sentiment, a tough new Fugitive Slave Law would be passed to empower the federal government to catch runaway slaves.[28] This latter provision, importantly, showed that the defenders of slavery could jettison the doctrine of "states' rights" whenever they perceived the possibility of using the federal government's power to police their system.

President Taylor opposed this compromise, and urged its rejection emphatically. But then Taylor suddenly died of a digestive illness, and Vice President Millard Fillmore, his successor, supported the compromise. Congress passed it as a package of measures in August and September of 1850, after months of fiery debate.

But the sectional tensions emerged more powerfully than ever when a staunch pro-slavery Democrat, Franklin Pierce, won the presidency in 1852. Concurrently, the advocates of slavery began an audacious new counterattack on the Free-Soil movement. They attempted to expand the territorial reach of slavery to unheard-of dimensions. It was this campaign that propelled Lincoln into the maelstrom.

For over thirty years, the geopolitical struggle of the slave-state bloc and the free-state bloc had swerved back and forth, with each side probing and grasping for a method that would somehow guarantee protection to its own social system and preempt the menace of the other. Through most of this period, the intermittent struggles kept returning to a tense "equilibrium." But, by the 1850s, the days of equilibrium were over.

As THE STRUGGLE OVER SLAVERY DEVELOPED, young Lincoln was a novice politician. He was quiet on the issue of slavery. But within him were tremendous reserves of audacity—and a powerful capacity for outrage. These qualities emerged full-blown after many years of reflection.

In the multitudinous studies of Lincoln produced since his death— all of the biographies and monographs, specialized studies, and assessments of his words and deeds—the complexities of Lincoln's personality continue to challenge us. He was the awkward-looking yokel from the backwoods who had a brilliant and penetrating mind. He was the blithe and gregarious spinner of yarns, the best raconteur in his surroundings, possessing a rich and boundless repertoire of earthy stories. But he was also a man who could suddenly withdraw into reveries, sinking at times into profoundly morbid spells, which he called "the hypos."

He was precocious, rebelling at a very early age against farm life and all of its tedium. He read constantly, absorbing Shakespearean drama, the works of Euclid, the poems of Byron and Robert Burns, and the Bible—though mostly to refute it at first, since his early religious views were decidedly skeptical.[29]

He taught himself surveying and law. He ran for public office in his twenties. An ardent follower of Henry Clay, he believed in heroic government. He advocated for public works and "internal improvements" that would build up the nation and provide its people with employment. In 1834 he was elected to the Illinois legislature at age twenty-five.

His political techniques could vary from conciliation and reason to the use of merciless ridicule (which led in one case to a challenge to a duel) to the droll and self-deprecating humor for which he would later become quite famous to the stirring and electrifying oratory that he put to such important use in later years.

His first public stance on the slavery issue took the form of a negative vote. Some slavery supporters had sent to the Illinois legislature a package of provocative resolutions affirming the constitutionality of slavery in states that permitted it while condemning anti-slavery agitation by abolitionists. Lincoln joined a small minority in voting "no" to these resolutions when the issue was considered in January 1837.

The minority was small because the attitudes of white supremacy were rampant in frontier America. Abolitionists were often reviled in the 1830s as the vanguard of "mongrelization." In November 1837, a pro-slavery mob in the town of Alton, Illinois, had murdered an abolitionist editor named Elijah Lovejoy.

This incident served as the backdrop to one Lincoln's most important early speeches, his address to the Young Men's Lyceum of Springfield, Illinois, on January 27, 1838, almost two months after Lovejoy's murder. Without mentioning the incident directly, Lincoln condemned mob rule, which he singled out as the greatest existing threat to the United States. But his speech went on to identify other potential threats to republics that might very well threaten America in days to come. Many of these threats were inherent in human nature, Lincoln observed.

The worst of them all was an emerging spirit of autocracy, whatever its symptoms. Throughout history, Lincoln observed, most republics had succumbed to the machinations of power mongers, to Napoleonic and Caesarian figures whose audacious ambition "thirsts and burns for distinction, and, if possible . . . will have it, whether at the expense of emancipating slaves, or enslaving freemen."

Consequently, asked Lincoln, is it really far-fetched for Americans "to expect, that some man possessed of the loftiest genius, coupled with ambition sufficient to push it to the utmost stretch, will at some time, spring up among us? And when it does, it will require the people to be united with each other, attached to the government and laws . . . to successfully frustrate his designs."[30]

It was the wide-ranging critic and novelist Edmund Wilson who perceived, in the early 1950s, that Lincoln's Lyceum Speech might have
been something truly extraordinary: that Lincoln might well have been
using this occasion to imagine for himself his own future role in American history, while doing it in terms that were *negative*, at least in part.

The towering "genius" envisioned by Lincoln, the ambitious leader
who imagined both the possibility of emancipating slaves and of enslaving free men, was an image as it seemed to Wilson that in some
ways attracted but also troubled the young politician.[31] In Wilson's
opinion, as Lincoln gave the speech he was in all probability conjuring
with his own inner urge to greatness.

On an obvious level, the Lyceum Speech was an oratorical set piece,
a reiteration of familiar political proverbs, which, since Napoleon's
rise and fall, had revived all the ancient warnings against the "Caesarian" threat to republics. On this level, certainly, the Lyceum Speech
was not unusual.

But if Wilson's observations have real psychological validity, the
Lyceum Speech was quite remarkable. It was nothing less, perhaps,
than a channel through which Lincoln poured out a secret knowledge
of his own latent talents in gathering and orchestrating power, while
expressing a guilt-ridden fear that these abilities amounted to hubris.

Writing several years after Edmund Wilson, political philosopher
Harry V. Jaffa examined the same speech and concurred on its importance. Indeed, said Jaffa, Lincoln "seems to have concentrated his whole
inner life upon preparing for the crisis foretold in the Lyceum speech."[32]

But for Jaffa, this speech was a philosophic "teaching," a warning by
an upcoming statesman that all truly free societies should ask of their
citizens a basic control of their passions. Republics, in order to protect
their inner nature, must require of their people an ethical restraint
against the surging projections of ego that could otherwise verge into
tyranny—whether it amounted to the tyranny that slave owners showed
to their slaves, or the tyranny of mobs lashing out against their helpless
victims, or the tyranny of would-be emancipating geniuses, believers
in heroic government, who, above all, must always remember to summon and wield their power in a manner that preserves their republic
instead of undermining its substance.

Whatever the meaning of this thought-provoking speech, Lincoln
resolutely continued to support the philosophy of Henry Clay, that
consummate believer in energetic government. Lincoln also supported

the Whig Party's national agenda for "internal improvements" and economic expansion.

In the economic depression that followed the Panic of 1837, for instance, Lincoln pushed for the creation of extensive public works to turn the economy around and ease unemployment, even if that meant financing them through deficit spending on occasion. By the end of the 1830s, Lincoln had risen to membership in the leadership "Junto" controlling his state's Whig organization.

Lincoln's service in the Illinois legislature ended in 1842. Shortly thereafter he began to prepare for a congressional career, and his efforts paid off with his election in 1846 to the House of Representatives. His service in Congress, which lasted from 1847 to 1849, coincided with his party's opposition to the Polk administration's foreign policy. Not only did Lincoln oppose the Mexican War as an act of shameful aggression, he also supported the Wilmot Proviso in its various incarnations.

Lincoln, like many Americans, had been turning his thoughts to the slavery issue more intensely in the 1840s. Moreover, an experience in 1841 affected his feelings on the issue profoundly. Traveling aboard an Ohio River steamer, he saw twelve slaves being shipped to the Deep South; they were chained together, he observed, "like so many fish upon a trot-line."[33] Years later, he said that the experience was "a continual torment to me," and that the slavery issue "had the power of making me miserable."[34]

By 1846, he had joined the Free-Soil movement within the Whig Party, and his opposition to slavery became more pronounced. In January 1849, he informed the House of Representatives that he would introduce legislation to abolish the institution of slavery in Washington, D.C. But when Lincoln sized up the prospects for passing such a bill, he gave up the venture as futile.

In his political orientation, Lincoln still remained devoted to the levelheaded principles of Henry Clay, his mentor. And Clay, in addition to supporting active government, took special pride in his role as the nation's impresario of sectional compromise, the orchestrator of the great Missouri Compromise of 1820 and the Compromise of 1850.

While Clay was an opponent of slavery, he was truly a *moderate* one. He had served for a very long time as president of the cautious American Colonization Society, for which reason he was often denounced by abolitionist militants.

After a long and illustrious career, Clay died in 1852. Lincoln's eulogy, delivered in Springfield, demonstrates the steady influence that Clay's anti-slavery precepts continued to exert upon his thought. Since the days of the Missouri Compromise, Lincoln observed, Americans had rightly regarded Henry Clay as "*the* man" in periods of national crisis, and especially in crises over slavery.

Clay had saved his country on several occasions, said Lincoln, and he hoped to see America flourish more and more as a land of universal freedom. Clay supported the eventual abolition of slavery, and he did so throughout his life as a matter of fundamental conviction, according to Lincoln. "He was, on principle and feeling, opposed to slavery," Lincoln observed. "The very earliest, and one of the latest public efforts of his life . . . were both made in favor of gradual emancipation of slaves in Kentucky. He did not perceive, that on a question of human right, the negroes were to be excepted from the human race."

Yet Clay was also a gradualist who thought that the two "extremes" in the great dispute over slavery were both misguided. Clay opposed the sorts of abolitionists, Lincoln said, "who would shiver into fragments the Union of these states; tear to tatters its now venerated constitution; and even burn the last copy of the Bible, rather than slavery should continue a single hour. . . ." Such people, said Lincoln, "have received, and are receiving their just execration. . . ."

But Clay, added Lincoln, was also opposed to the other extreme in the slavery debate, the Southern militants who, "for the sake of perpetuating slavery, are beginning to assail and to ridicule the white-man's charter of freedom—the declaration that 'all men are created free and equal.'"

Clay fervently hoped to resolve the problem of slavery through colonization, and Lincoln went on to commend this vision, citing images from Scripture as he did so:

Pharaoh's country was cursed with plagues, and his hosts were drowned in the Red Sea for striving to retain a captive people who had already served them more than four hundred years. May like disasters never befall us! If as the friends of colonization hope, the present and coming generations of our countrymen shall . . . succeed in freeing our land from the dangerous presence of slavery; and, at the same time, in restoring a captive people to their long-lost fatherland, with bright prospects for the future; and this too, so gradually, that neither races nor individuals shall have suffered by the change, it will indeed be a glorious consummation. And if, to such a consummation, the efforts of Mr.

Clay shall have contributed . . . none of his labors will have been more valuable to his country. . . .[35]

It is striking to observe at this point the degree to which passages such as the above appear to vindicate all of the conventional views about Lincoln as a moderate Unionist, a man who had pledged himself to the rule of sweet reason and its corollary ethics of compromise, a man who scorned both extremes in the American slavery dispute, and who advocated mild and gradual measures to resolve the problem over time. Here, if anywhere, the evidence presents us with a very clear portrait of the Lincoln who is currently praised (or attacked) for his steady ways of "moderation."

Look closely at the picture while it lasts. For the Lincoln who had eulogized Henry Clay was about to change his precepts forever.

An event just beyond the historical horizon as he eulogized his hero, an event that would burst upon the nation only two years later—an event so completely disgusting to Lincoln as to catalyze his inner potential through the force of irrepressible outrage—was about to cause Lincoln to transform himself into a very different kind of politician.

He would swiftly abandon the principles of Clay and embrace, in effect, the more determined politics of Zachary Taylor as he launched a new phase of his career, a phase that would quickly propel him to the head of the Free-Soil movement and beyond, to his presidential destiny.

This was the Lincoln who would start to denounce any further appeasement on slavery. This was the Lincoln who prepared to use federal force in the struggle.

This was the Lincoln who avowed, as the crisis of secession was approaching, that "the tug" between the advocates and foes of American slavery expansion should come, and "better now than later." This was the Lincoln who would cast aside doubts and push his gifts to the "utmost stretch"—not to dominate his country like Napoleon or Caesar, but to realize the hopes of its Founders.

He aspired to be America's executive commander of the free in their greatest ordeal. And he was only beginning to discover the extent of his powers.

TWO

Lincoln and Free Soil, 1854–1858

L INCOLN'S SURGE into national prominence began with a series of speeches that he gave in the autumn of 1854. By the end of the decade, he emerged as a forceful new leader of the Free-Soil movement and the new Republican Party. It started with his angry reaction to a cataclysmic development in the early part of 1854.

After months of impassioned debate, Congress voted to repeal the Missouri Compromise of 1820. What this meant for the ongoing sectional struggle over slavery remained to be seen. But for people like Abraham Lincoln, what it meant was almost unbelievable. It meant that all the unorganized lands that still remained in the Louisiana Territory would be opened again to slavery.

The move resulted in a wave of anger and loathing that electrified the Free-Soil movement. For Lincoln, the repeal of the Missouri Compromise was nothing short of an obscenity. And it was largely the work of an old political rival, Stephen A. Douglas.

The advocates of slavery had been taking the offensive since 1852. They were clearly emboldened by the fact that a pro-slavery Democrat had won the presidency in that year. He was a "northern man of southern principles," Franklin Pierce of New Hampshire. To a certain extent, the Democrats had won because the Whigs were so bitterly divided in regard to the Compromise of 1850. While the Democratic Party was also divided into Free-Soil and pro-slavery factions, the old belief in Manifest Destiny—the belief that the expansion of American territory would unify whites, both North and South, as they joined together in the great adventure of building the "Empire of

Liberty"—died hard in the Democratic Party, notwithstanding the fact that its use by the Polk administration had intensified the slavery dispute instead of quieting it.

In 1850, Governor John A. Quitman of Mississippi tried to help a Venezuelan soldier of fortune named Narciso Lopez in fomenting a revolt by the Cuban people against their imperial overlord, Spain. Lopez, Quitman, and others were indicted by the federal government (under the Fillmore administration) for violating American neutrality laws. Quitman resigned as governor to defend himself against the charges.[1]

No sooner had Pierce won the presidency, however, than Quitman was at it again: he tried to organize an American "filibustering" expedition that would "liberate" Cuba and annex it to the Union as a slave state. Other "filibusterers"—a Spanish-derived term for pirates or desperadoes—began to call for a second Mexican War to create more expansion room for slavery. In 1853, a Tennessean named William Walker invaded Mexico with a band of followers. But the Mexicans overpowered his forces and ejected him.

In 1854, under the leadership of a Virginian named George Bickley, a secret organization called the "Knights of the Golden Circle" was founded in Kentucky. Its members dreamed of a "Golden Circle" of rule by the white master race, a tropical empire for slavery that would take in the whole Caribbean rim, including upper South America.[2]

Throughout the 1850s, this "filibustering" spirit generated one provocation after another in Latin America. Senator Albert Gallatin Brown of Mississippi pushed for annexation of Cuba along with additional conquests in Mexico and Central America. He wanted "Cuba . . . and one or two other Mexican States; and I want them all for the same reason—for the planting or spreading of slavery."[3]

In 1854, at the request of Pierce's secretary of state, three diplomats, Pierre Soulé of Louisiana, John Y. Mason of Virginia, and James Buchanan of Pennsylvania—another "northern man of southern principles," as well as the next man to occupy the White House—met in Ostend, Belgium to confer about the Cuba "issue." Their aim was to trigger a sequence of events that would lead to American seizure of the island. They proclaimed, in their soon-to-be notorious "Ostend Manifesto," that if Spain refused to sell Cuba, Americans would be perfectly justified in taking it over.

These attempts to expand the slavery system through additional sei-
zures of territory were prompted by the widespread desire in the slave-
holding states to "keep up" with the free-state bloc in numerical power.
But the need to maintain the Southern "Cordon Sanitaire" was also
important. Congressman Thomas L. Clingman of North Carolina said
that Northerners were surely too intelligent to think "that humanity,
either to the slave or the master, requires that they should be pent up
within a territory which after a time will be insufficient for their subsistence, and where they must perish from want, or from collision that
would occur between the races."[4]

Collision that would occur between the races: the old Southern fear
of slave insurrections was as powerful a theme in the 1850s as it was in
previous decades. According to pro-slavery theorists, the expansion of
slavery amounted to the operation of a salutary pressure valve that would
siphon off the "excess" black population in the interest of public safety.
The fear was that the blacks would outnumber the whites and endanger white supremacist control.

So the advocates of American slavery were pushing more fervently
than ever in the early 1850s to expand their system. They did it without apology. They did it, indeed, with an air of self-conscious bravado.
This was the context of sectional politics in which Senator Stephen A.
Douglas of Illinois ignited a firestorm in 1854.

Like many Americans, Douglas was advocating the construction of
a transcontinental railroad to hasten the flow of people and goods between the new state of California and the rest of America. Moreover,
Douglas was committed to a northerly route that would extend due
west from Chicago, his state's greatest city. It seemed imperative to
Douglas that the western lands along this route be settled and admitted to the Union quickly.

In 1853, at the behest of Douglas, the Pierce administration took
steps to remove all the Indian peoples who were living in Nebraska, a
territorial subdivision of the Louisiana Territory. Nebraska lay immediately north and west of the slave state of Missouri.

After Indian removal was completed, the next precondition for construction of the railroad was the preparation of Nebraska for statehood.
To this end, Douglas crafted and introduced legislation that was passed
by the House of Representatives in February 1853. But then the slave
state leaders objected when the measure was sent to the Senate.

Because of the Missouri Compromise, they reminded Douglas and his supporters, the territory of Nebraska was forbidden to slavery. Nebraska lay beyond the great dividing line that ran across the Louisiana Purchase, the dividing line that began at the southern border of Missouri and forbade the introduction of slavery both to the north and west of the state.

Senator David Atchison of Missouri declared that he would sooner see Nebraska "sink in hell" than he would ever consent to the creation of any more free states near Missouri. Most of the Senators from slaveholding states took a similar position.

Then, pro-slavery leaders began to see a more interesting angle in the issue of Nebraska statehood. They began to see a chance to convert their initially defensive reaction to Douglas's bill into a new and decisive opportunity to launch a pro-slavery offensive. Led by David Atchison of Missouri, Robert M.T. Hunter of Virginia, Andrew Butler of South Carolina, and others, the slave-state bloc leaders saw a chance in Douglas's predicament to open another geographical front for the expansion of slavery. They decided to hold the Nebraska bill hostage until Douglas consented to repeal the old dividing line established in the Missouri Compromise.

By the end of 1853, Stephen Douglas began to come around. And on January 4, 1854, he introduced legislation to create a new Nebraska policy. His bill, which he introduced on January 4, consigned the slavery issue in Nebraska to the principles of "Popular Sovereignty." His bill stipulated that Congress would vote on Nebraska statehood "with or without slavery as her constitution may prescribe."

But this tremendous concession was still not enough for pro-slavery leaders. Senator Archibald Dixon of Kentucky introduced an amendment to the Nebraska bill that explicitly repealed the section of the Missouri Compromise (the Thomas Proviso) that established the anti-slavery dividing line.

Douglas capitulated: on January 23, 1854, he revised his Nebraska bill to incorporate the Dixon amendment. He also consented to divide Nebraska into northern and southern segments. The northern portion would retain the name of Nebraska while the southern portion would bear the name of Kansas.

And since Kansas was situated right next door to Missouri, it was widely presumed at the time that it would enter the Union as a slave state, just like its older neighbor to the east. For whatever it was worth,

Douglas struggled to remind his constituents that settlers in Kansas and Nebraska would certainly decide the matter for themselves.

The Free-Soil movement was livid. *An Appeal of the Independent Democrats*, written by Salmon P. Chase and Joshua R. Giddings, accused Stephen Douglas of a "gross violation of a sacred pledge" in repealing the Missouri Compromise. Nonetheless, with crucial support from President Pierce, the Kansas-Nebraska Bill was passed by Congress in May 1854 and signed into law. In theory, all the unorganized lands in the Louisiana Territory were open to slavery. No one could be sure of where the owners of slaves might settle.

All through the summer of 1854, the backlash against this series of events began to shake the foundations of the two-party system in the North. Free-Soil Democrats and Conscience Whigs began abandoning their parties and joining together in hopes of creating a "fusion" movement that would put the Free-Soil issue at the center of its national agenda. The new Republican Party emerged rather quickly as the clear frontrunner in the movement.

As anti-slavery leaders looked back upon the shattering events of that spring, they were aghast: was there nothing too audacious for the leaders of the slave-state bloc to foist upon the nation? At this critical juncture, a provocative book was published in Virginia. While its audience was limited at first to the regional vicinity, it was triggering reactions by the end of the year from as far away as New York City, where Horace Greeley, editor of the *New York Tribune*, condemned it.[5]

The book was entitled *Sociology for the South*, and its author was a Virginia planter named George Fitzhugh. Ever since the forthright defense of slavery by John C. Calhoun, pro-slavery literature in the United States was common. What set this new book apart from the others, however, was its astonishing radicalism.

Fitzhugh argued that slavery was such an obviously wise and justified social institution that its benefits ought to extend across the race line. Indirectly, he seemed to be recommending the enslavement of "inferior" whites.

Fitzhugh took direct aim at America's iconic fountainhead of anti-slavery ideals, his fellow Virginian Thomas Jefferson. With sarcastic verve, he took on the man who had stated in the final year of his life, "the mass of mankind has not been born with saddles on their backs, nor a favored few booted and spurred, ready to ride them legitimately by the grace of God."

Quite wrong, said Fitzhugh, for precisely the reverse was true. It was a clear and self-evident truth, he insisted, that inferior people are suited by their nature to the status of dependent livestock: "It would be nearer the truth to say," he continued with relish, "that some were born with saddles on their backs, and others booted and spurred to ride them; and the riding does them good." "Slavery," he continued, "is the natural and normal condition of the working man, whether white or black."[6]

And there it was: the spectre that had energized the leaders of the Free-Soil movement since the early 1840s, the threat that American slavery would gradually erode the liberty of whites just as surely as it stole away the liberties of blacks.

The Fitzhugh book began to penetrate the North about the same time that Senator Stephen Douglas came back to Chicago, Illinois, to explain himself to his constituents, to mend some fences if he could. But he was greeted at home with rage. As he looked out the window of his train, he saw his own burning effigy in cities across the state.

When he arrived in Chicago, he lost his temper and cursed at a hostile crowd. Afterward, he was hounded by "Anti-Nebraska" speakers who followed him, pelting him with ridicule and vilifying the Kansas-Nebraska Act.

In a series of speeches throughout Illinois, Douglas answered his Free-Soil critics. His application of the principle of Popular Sovereignty to Kansas and Nebraska, he said, was merely an extension of the Compromise of 1850, which adopted the very same policy in all of the newly acquired lands between Texas and California. Besides, he boasted, the principle of letting the people in every new territory choose for themselves by majority vote about the presence of slavery was nothing less than American democracy at work. And the principle of letting American whites decide the fate of American blacks was also quite natural and wholesome, he said.

In any case, he contended, the chance that slavery would root itself in Kansas and Nebraska was negligible. The climate and soil of the plains, he theorized, were clearly unsuited to slavery.

Some of his listeners began to be convinced by these nimble arguments. But others, like Lincoln, were even more enraged at Douglas than before.

For Lincoln, these weeks and months became the great turning point of his career. Not only the developments themselves but also the se-

ductive perversities of Douglas caused Lincoln to abandon any previous restraints or inhibitions in asserting his Free-Soil convictions.

But Lincoln did not choose to join the new Republican Party right
away. He was not at all certain that the situation of the old Whig Party
was hopeless. What he did, however, was to take to the stump against
Douglas in the autumn months of 1854.

In the city of Bloomington, Illinois, he accosted Douglas in mid-to-
late September. But the angry Douglas refused to debate him. So Lincoln gave speeches by himself on September 12 and September 26. These
two speeches in Bloomington were published only in summary form.

Then Lincoln followed Douglas to Springfield. On October 3, as
Douglas gave his usual remarks of prepared self-justification, Lincoln
paced back and forth in the hall. He then announced to the crowd that
he would answer Douglas point for point on the very next day and in
the very same location. Like the Bloomington speeches, the text of his
October 4, Springfield address has survived only in summary. But when
he gave the same speech on October 16, in Peoria, newspapers published it in full.

His "Peoria Speech," as we have known it ever since, was both a
legal brief against Douglas and a charismatic statement of ideals. It was
one of Lincoln's earliest attempts to get an audience aroused not only
by the menace of slavery toward whites but also by its subjugation of
blacks.

By pre-arrangement, Lincoln and Douglas gave sequential speeches
that amounted to a veritable debate. Douglas was the first to speak.
Then Lincoln followed up with some tactical ploys that were aimed at
both sides of his audience. His use of wry humor in these opening
remarks went beyond mere forensic technique. It exemplified a shrewd
psychological strategy. It is therefore worth sharing at length:

> I do not arise to speak now, if I can stipulate with the audience to meet me here
> at half past 6 or at 7 o'clock. It is now several minutes past five, and Judge
> Douglas [a reference to Douglas's earlier service on the Illinois Supreme Court]
> has spoken over three hours. . . . Now every one of you who can remain that
> long, can just as well get his supper, meet me at seven, and remain one hour or
> two later. The Judge has already informed you that he is to have an hour to
> reply to me. I doubt not but you have been a little surprised to learn that I have
> consented to give one of his high reputation and known ability, this advantage
> of me. Indeed, my consenting to it, though reluctant, was not wholly unselfish;
> for I suspected if it were understood, that the Judge was entirely done, you
> democrats would leave, and not hear me; but by giving him the close, I felt
> confident you would stay for the fun of hearing him skin me.[7]

Quite a package: self-deprecating humor, concern for the comfort of his audience, an open confession of a very sly purpose, all delivered in a manner that would soften his opponents' hostility while treating his friends to bonhomie.

When the audience gathered once again that evening, his tone became different. With razor-sharp analysis, he passionately attacked every one of his opponent's contentions with regard to the subject of slavery.

For instance, he took up the issue of the Compromise of 1850 as compared to the Kansas-Nebraska Act. Did the fact that the 1850 Compromise applied the principle of Popular Sovereignty to lands between Texas and California mean, as Douglas asserted, that Congress had somehow given that principle its blessing in every open territory? Ridiculous, Lincoln said; the Compromise of 1850 was merely an expedient hodge-podge of balancing elements, a deal that was struck at an urgent point of tension in the ongoing struggle over slavery.

"I insist," he said, that the Popular Sovereignty provision of the Compromise of 1850 was "made for Utah and New Mexico, and for no other place whatsoever. It had no more direct reference to Nebraska than it had to the territories of the moon. . . . The North consented to this provision, not because they considered it right in itself; but because they were compensated—paid for it. They, at the same time, got California into the Union as a free State. . . . Also, they got the slave trade abolished in the District of Columbia."[8]

But what of Douglas's larger contention that the principle of Popular Sovereignty amounted to a "sacred" distillation of American democracy by giving "the people" of every new territory—specifically the white people, of course—full power to decide about the slavery issue for themselves? In Lincoln's opinion, this assertion was wrong to the point of indecency.

That Douglas even dared to offer this argument, Lincoln said, "shows that the Judge has no very vivid impression that the negro is a human; and consequently has no idea that there can be any moral question in legislating about him. In his view, the question of whether a new country shall be slave or free, is a matter of as utter indifference, as it is whether his neighbor shall plant his farm with tobacco, or stock it with horned cattle."[9]

Citing Douglas's frequent use of white supremacist slogans, Lincoln challenged his audience, including his very own supporters, to reject white supremacist thinking when it came to the fundamentals of freedom. "Judge Douglas," he said, "frequently . . . paraphrases our argument by saying 'The white people of Nebraska are good enough to govern themselves, *but they are not good enough to govern a few miserable negroes!!'* Well," said Lincoln, "I doubt not that the people of Nebraska are, and will continue to be as good as the average of people elsewhere. I do not say the contrary. What I do say is, that no man is good enough to govern another man, *without that other's consent.* I say this is the leading principle—the sheet anchor of American republicanism."[10]

Lincoln pressed the argument further, using logic and analogies to hammer home a point that many racists would never concede, the point that blacks should be regarded as human, and not subhuman:

> Equal justice to the south, it is said, requires us to consent to the extending of slavery to new countries. That is to say, inasmuch as you do not object to my taking my hog to Nebraska, therefore I must not object to you taking your slave. Now, I admit this is perfectly logical, if there is no difference beween hogs and negroes. But while you thus require me to deny the humanity of the negro, I wish to ask whether you of the south yourselves, have ever been willing to do as much?[11]

Every slave owner who ever freed some or all of his human "property" was clearly unable to accept the proposition that blacks were mere beasts of burden. "There are in the United States and territories," Lincoln pointed out, "433,643 free blacks." How could such a situation exist if black Americans were little more than livestock? "How comes this vast amount of property to be running around without owners," Lincoln asked. "We do not see free horses or free cattle running at large. How is this? All these free blacks are the descendants of slaves, or have been slaves themselves, and they would be slaves now, but for SOMETHING which has operated on their white owners, inducing them, at vast pecuniary sacrifices, to liberate them."

Lincoln pressed the point harder: "What is that SOMETHING? Is there any mistaking it? In all these cases it is your sense of justice, and human sympathy, continually telling you, that the poor negro has some natural right to himself—that those who deny it, and make mere merchandise of him, deserve kickings, contempt and death."[12]

And clearly, said Lincoln, "if the negro *is* a man," is it not indecent and grotesque "to say that he too shall not govern *himself*? . . . If the negro is a *man*, why then my ancient faith teaches me that 'all men are created equal'. . . ."[13]

But what of Douglas's contention that American slavery would stay away from Kansas and Nebraska due to inauspicious conditions—that slavery was such a distinctive feature of the very Deep South that it was laughable to think that the system would flourish on the Great Plains?

Wrong again, said Lincoln, and American experience proved it. Experience showed that the American system of slavery would root itself in any locale in which involuntary labor could be put to any use, and where public opinion would condone it. "A glance at the map," Lincoln said, "shows that there are five slave states—Delaware, Maryland, Virginia, Kentucky, and Missouri—and also the District of Columbia, all north of the Missouri Compromise line," at the same latitude or even further north than Kansas.

So what was to keep the institution of slavery from coming into Kansas from Missouri, the state next door? "Missouri adjoins these territories," Lincoln observed, "by her entire western boundary, and slavery is already within every one of her western counties. . . . Slavery pressed entirely up to the old western boundary of the State, and when, rather recently, a part of that boundary, at the north-west was moved a little farther west, slavery followed on quite up to the new line. Now, when the restriction is removed, what is to prevent it from going still further? Climate will not. No peculiarity of the country will. . . ."[14]

Indeed, Lincoln asked his midwestern audience, what kind of geographical difference kept slavery away from Illinois, when the state of Missouri lay directly to the west of it, just across the Mississippi River? "What was it," he asked, "that made the difference between Illinois and Missouri? They lie side by side, the Mississippi river only dividing them." One thing only, he contended, had prevented the institution of slavery from coming right into Illinois: the prior prohibition put in place by the founding generation in the Northwest Ordinance of 1787.

The founding generation, Lincoln said, had done its best to keep slavery contained. Most of the Founding Fathers had known that the institution was wrong, but they could not get rid of it at once. So they blocked it and hemmed it in; they even shunned the very name of slavery, as if to avoid the rhetorical pollution of the nation's great charter of law with the mention of an unclean thing. "At the framing and adoption of the constitution," Lincoln said, the Founding Fathers "forebore so much as to mention the word 'slave' or 'slavery' in the whole instrument. In the provision for the recovery of fugitives, the slave is spoken of as a 'PERSON HELD TO SERVICE OR LABOR'. . . . Thus, the thing is hid away, in the constitution, just as an afflicted man hides away a wen or a cancer, which he dares not cut to the bone at once, lest he bleed to death; with the promise, nevertheless, that the cutting may begin at the end of a given time."[15]

The "cutting," however, was opposed in the South, and so slavery had spread, notwithstanding the fact that the greatest of the Founding Fathers had wanted to contain and shrink it over time.

And now, politicians like Stephen Douglas were telling the American people that they ought to be indifferent to the spread of unfreedom, that the fate of American blacks did not matter. "This *declared* indifference," Lincoln said, was nothing less than a thinly veiled zeal for slavery.[16] "Nearly eighty years ago we began by declaring that all men are created equal; but now . . . we have run down to the other declaration that for SOME men to enslave OTHERS is a 'sacred right of self-government.'" Unfreedom was on the rise, and people like Douglas were helping it along. "Nebraska brings it forth, places it on the high road to extension and perpetuity; and, with a pat on its back, says to it, 'Go and God speed you.'"[17]

But the forces of freedom and slavery were too fundamentally at war for Senator Stephen Douglas or anyone like him to keep them from collision. "Slavery," said Lincoln, "is founded in the selfishness of man's nature—opposition to it in his love of justice. These principles are an eternal antagonism. . . . Repeal the Missouri Compromise—repeal all compromises—repeal the declaration of independence—repeal all past history, you still cannot repeal human nature. It still will be the abundance of man's heart, that slavery extension is wrong; and out of the abundance of his heart, his mouth will continue to speak."[18]

And his hands would continue to act in response to his heart. Lincoln predicted that warfare and bloodshed would probably break out in Kansas. The mechanics of the Kansas-Nebraska Act made this prospect nearly inevitable. "The people are to decide the question of slavery for themselves," Lincoln acknowledged, but the questions as to "WHEN they are to decide; or HOW they are to decide; or whether, when the question is once decided, it is to remain so . . . the law does not say. Is it to be decided by the first dozen settlers who arrive there? Or is it to await the arrival of a hundred? Is it to be decided by a vote of the people? Or a vote of the legislature? Or, indeed, by a vote of any sort?"

The situation was made to order for a violent showdown, he predicted: "Some Yankees are sending emigrants to Nebraska, to exclude slavery from it; and, so far as I can judge, they expect the question to be decided by voting, in some way or other. But the Missourians are awake too. They are within a stone's throw of the contested ground. . . . They resolve . . . that abolitionists shall be hung, or driven away. Through all this, bowie-knives and six-shooters are seen plainly enough."[19]

Maybe peaceful measures would somehow avert the threat of violence, Lincoln mused. But for this to happen, the leaders of America's Free-Soil movement had to summon forth the spirit to oppose Stephen Douglas and his politics of sleazy "indifference" on the subject of slavery. And surely they would do so.

Be not complacent, Lincoln warned the supporters of Douglas, regarding the temporary disarray of the "Anti-Nebraska" movement. Douglas "should remember that he took us by surprise—astounded us—by this measure. We were thunderstruck and stunned; and we reeled and fell in utter confusion. But we rose each fighting, grasping whatever he could first reach—a scythe—a pitchfork—a chopping axe, or a butcher's cleaver. We struck in the direction of the sound; and we are rapidly closing in upon him."[20]

Such was the "Peoria Speech," the most vivid demonstration of the change in the political outlook of Lincoln that began in 1854. It heralded the fiery orations that would blaze his path to the White House. And it established the moral fundamentals of his whole political creed.

But in the view of certain latter-day detractors, the Peoria Speech was something else: it was clear and unambiguous proof of Lincoln's racism.

Why? Because Lincoln demurred about extending civil rights to former slaves after slavery had ended. This is the offending passage:

> If all earthly power were given me, I should not know what to do, as to the existing institution [of slavery]. My first impulse would be to free all the slaves, and send them to Liberia,—to their own native land. But a moment's reflection would convince me, that whatever of high hope, (as I think there is) there may be in this, in the long run, its sudden execution is impossible. If they were all landed there in a day, they would all perish in the next ten days; and there are not surplus shipping and surplus money enough in the world to carry them there in many times ten days. What then? Free them all, and keep them among us as underlings? Is it quite certain that this betters their condition? I think I would not hold one in slavery, at any rate; yet the point is not clear enough for me to denounce people upon. What next? Free them, and make them politi-

cally and socially, our equals? My own feelings will not admit of this; and if mine would, we well know that those of the great mass of white people will not. Whether this feeling accords with justice and sound judgment, is not the sole question, if indeed, it is any part of it. A universal feeling, whether well or ill-founded, can not be safely disregarded.[21]

What are we to make of such words as applied to the issue of black civil rights? "My own feelings," Lincoln said, "will not admit of this." What "feelings" did he mean in particular?

The conventional wisdom these days is that Lincoln shared many of the bigoted notions that were common in nineteenth-century America. Possibly, he did. He proclaimed, for instance, just a few years later—if indeed we can be sure that he was telling the truth and not fending off racist attacks by Douglas with expedient verbiage—that he disapproved of racial intermarriage.

Perhaps so. Or perhaps, for the moment, he decided to surrender to the passions of his white supremacist audience to nullify the arguments of Douglas on race and thus prevail in the fight against slavery. Douglas, after all, was a virulent racist, and his snide denigrations of blacks were delivered with gusto, much to his supporters' delight.

"I do not believe that the Almighty ever intended the Negro to be the equal of the white man," Douglas told his supporters on one occasion. "If he did, he has been a long time demonstrating the fact. (Cheers) For thousands of years, the negro has been a race upon the earth, and during all that time, in all latitudes and climates, wherever he has wandered or been taken, he has been inferior to the race which he has there met. He belongs to an inferior race, and must always occupy an inferior position."[22]

White supremacy attitudes were rampant in this milieu. Free blacks had been barred under Illinois law from setting foot in the state, and there was even a law on the books against racial intermarriage. Historian James M. McPherson has confirmed that Illinois was "one of the most race-conscious of the free states" in the 1850s.[23] William Lee Miller is a bit more severe: in Miller's opinion, Illinois was "probably the most racially prejudiced free state in the Union" during this period.[24] Such was the political atmosphere in which Lincoln had to work.

Why did Lincoln, if he were nothing but a racist politician, argue so fervently that blacks were fully human and their feelings had the utmost importance? Why shoulder such a burden at all when the easiest way for him to attack Stephen Douglas in front of an audience composed of a great many other white supremacists was perfectly obvious? The most crowd-pleasing move would be to sound the hue-and-cry that kept resounding in the Free-Soil movement: the tried-and-true message that the slavery system was a threat to all working-class *whites*.

Why on earth would a racist politician try to tell a white audience that blacks and their feelings really mattered? Why invoke "human sympathy" for every "poor negro" who desired the "right to himself?" Lincoln did this again and again.

Lincoln said that black Americans possessed the basic right to freedom. He said his personal preference on the issue of slavery was full emancipation, over time if conditions should require it. When it came to political and social equality, his feelings, he said, did not "admit of this." He did not say *why* this was the case. Yet he added that when and if his feelings *should* "admit of it," he feared that "universal" feelings, which could never be safely ignored, would oppose him overwhelmingly.

Harry V. Jaffa has observed of this speech that while Lincoln said his feelings were unable to support the proposition of black civil rights, "he immediately introduced, as a hypothetical possibility, that his own feelings might not be against it. Why? The sentence, taken as a whole, is an equivocation."[25]

It was hardly white supremacist chatter by a bigot. It seemed to be the struggle of a man who knew perfectly well that his principles of universal freedom led in practice beyond emancipation.

But it was also the talk of a man who knew equally well that if he came out openly for black civil rights because of principles that overrode "feeling"—if he contended that the widespread visceral dynamics of racial aversion were stupid, unworthy, and vile—the white supremacists would jeer him off the stage.

Lincoln's present-day detractors say his anti-slavery politics fail to measure up to the morally uncompromising stand of the boldest abolitionists, those who consistently supported civil rights for all Americans. But abolitionists *by themselves* could not summon the power to eliminate so deeply entrenched an institution as slavery.

The summoning of power requires strategy as well as ideals. This leads to the frequently thankless political task of balancing the lesser evils with the greater.

What alternative really existed to the power manipulations of Lincoln and his fellow politicians? What strategy to overcome the South—a region that was armed to the teeth with militias, and weapons, and first-rate military schools, a region that suppressed the abolitionists and made their movement *illegal* under many state laws—did the morally advanced abolitionists offer to the slaves?

The most forceful of them—John Brown, for example—tried to start the kind of war between the races that the slaveholders feared the most. But what chances did a fragmented slave insurrection really have? Consider a comparison: when *political* action caused the Union to split, it took four long years for the powerful North to beat the South in the Civil War, and the South came very close to winning on a number of occasions.

This is not to dismiss the abolitionists, whose work was both vital and heroic.[26] But they could simply not destroy the power of slavery without assistance. It took a great *coalition* of power that was centered in the Northern states.

The inescapable fact is that the power of the North could be channeled in one way alone: through the work of politics. And any working politician who ignored the force of white supremacy, either within or beyond his own political base, was too naïve for the work that lay before him.

For the rest of their political rivalry, Douglas would attempt to bait Lincoln with the charge that he favored the "mongrelization" of the races. Lincoln sensed this intention as he faced Stephen Douglas in October 1854. He would face it again, and from a great many others, in the years of campaigning ahead of him. He would face it right down to the very last week of his life when he supported black voting rights explicitly—for which John Wilkes Booth would shoot him dead.

IN THE NEXT FEW YEARS, Lincoln's reputation spread as he continued to excoriate Douglas. And his angry response to an outrageous judicial decision kept his name in the public eye.

As political events grew worse for the principles he championed, Lincoln's mood in the final months of 1854 became bitter. He tried to run for the Senate, where he hoped to undo the work of Douglas. Since the Constitution still provided for the election of Senators by the legislatures of the states, he worked the back-room politics of Springfield. He came close, but the seat in the United States Senate eluded him.[27]

Concurrently, the leaders of the slave-state bloc were on the move. In the middle of 1855, the Tennessean William Walker and his followers, who called him the "grey-eyed man of destiny," embarked for Nicaragua. Intervening in a civil war, they seized control of the country. After instituting slavery, they ran Nicaragua despotically for several years.[28]

Meanwhile, settlers had poured across the border into Kansas from Missouri, just as Lincoln had warned. Early in 1855, they elected a territorial legislature. Some of these settlers were long-term residents, but others were "border ruffians," Missourians who crossed the border into Kansas, cast illegal votes, and then returned to their homes in Missouri.

The legislature passed some pro-slavery laws that were draconian. Any aid to a fugitive slave in the territory of Kansas would be punished by death. Abolitionist speeches would be felonies.

Anti-slavery settlers poured into Kansas as well, and by the autumn of 1855 a civil war had broken out. That summer, Lincoln told a politician in Kentucky he had given up hope for any peaceful resolution of America's slavery crisis. "There is no peaceful extinction of slavery in prospect for us," he said.[29]

He asked another correspondent in Kentucky to consider how Northerners "crucify their feelings" on slavery. He said that he hated the existing institution as much as he hated its extension to the west. The fate of fugitive slaves, above all, made him miserable: "I hate to see the poor creatures hunted down, and caught," Lincoln wrote, "and carried back to their stripes, and unrewarded toils; but I bite my lip, and keep quiet." Attacks against the Fugitive Slave Law were probably hopeless.

He was deeply pessimistic in the short run. "Kansas," he said, "will form a Slave constitution, and, with it, will ask to be admitted to the Union." And though Lincoln and his friends would oppose such a move, "we may be beaten," he admitted.[30]

In the final months of 1855, the Free-Soilers decided to establish a legitimate territorial legislature in Kansas. All the credible evidence shows that these settlers were in the majority.[31] But the Pierce administration, predictably, supported the old pro-slavery legislature.

The fighting in Kansas reached a climax in 1856. Artillery barrages were directed at Lawrence, a Free-Soil settlement. On May 21, seven hundred pro-slavery men attacked the town, burning buildings and wreaking havoc. The anti-slavery zealot John Brown led a raid of retaliation with help from his sons and some angry Free-Soilers. They attacked Pottawatomie Creek, where they split the skulls of pro-slavery victims and slashed them to death with swords. All of these events took place on the eve of the 1856 presidential election.

The Democrats spurned both their controversial incumbent, Pierce, and the controversial Stephen A. Douglas, who had long since begun to entertain presidential ambitions. Instead, they nominated Pennsylvania's James Buchanan—one of the Ostend Manifesto's framers. In spite of this latter notoriety, Buchanan was perceived to be "safe" because he was conveniently out of the country in Britain when the Kansas-Nebraska drama began to unfold. But he was just as sympathetic to the South as his Democratic predecessor Pierce.

The Republicans were just as decisively anti-slavery. Lincoln at last made the move to the Republican Party; the whole structure of the old Whig Party was a shambles and the Whigs had all but ceased to exist. He gave the keynote speech at the Bloomington Convention that established the Republican Party in the state of Illinois.

John C. Frémont, an explorer and military hero who endorsed the cause of free soil, was nominated by the Republicans. The new Republican Party did reasonably well, in light of the facts that it was only two years old and its first campaign was unfortunately blunted by a third-party presence: the short-lived American Party whose stock-in-trade was its resistance to the influence in politics of Catholics and non-Anglo-Saxons. It drew off some of the white working-class vote that would have supported free-soil policies.

Lincoln stumped Illinois and other midwestern states for Frémont, responding to some shrill pro-slavery warnings that a Frémont victory would trigger the secession of the slave states. Lincoln ridiculed Buchanan as an agent of the South, like Pierce, Douglas, and the rest of the Northern politicians whose political self-damnation had reduced them to lackeys of the slave-holding interests.

Southern strategy, Lincoln claimed, was to operate by proxy using Northern political agents whenever it was feasible. In notes for a campaign speech, he addressed this issue with sarcastic anger. "If a Southern man aspires to be president," he wrote, "they choke him down instantly, in order that the glittering prize of the presidency, may be held up, on Southern terms, to the greedy eyes of Northern ambition. . . . The democratic party, in 1844, elected a Southern president. Since then, they have neither had a Southern candidate for *election*, or *nomination*. Their Conventions of 1848, 1852 and 1856, have been struggles exclusively among *Northern* men, each vieing [*sic*] to out-bid the other for the Southern vote—the South standing calmly by to finally cry going, going, gone to the highest bidder; and, at the same time, to make its power more distinctly seen, and thereby to secure a still higher bid at the next succeeding struggle."[32]

If the offer of political rewards should ever fail them, the leaders of the South would use blackmail, he said, to maintain their domination of the North. The form of this blackmail was obvious: the threat of secession. But if Frémont should win and the Free-Soil movement should prevail, Lincoln vowed, any threat of secession would be stamped out swiftly and sternly. Overwhelming force would be used. He warned the "fire-eating" leaders of the South who had started to advocate a new Southern nation that the Union "won't be dissolved. We don't want to dissolve it, and if you attempt it, *we won't let you*. With the purse and the sword, the army and navy and treasury in our hands and at our command, you *couldn't do it*. This Government would be very weak, indeed, if a majority, with a disciplined army and navy, and a well-filled treasury, could not preserve itself, when attacked by an unarmed, undisciplined, unorganized minority. All this talk about the dissolution of the Union is humbug—nothing but folly. *We* WON'T dissolve the Union, and *you* SHAN'T."[33]

This was confident defiance of the enemy, the talk of a man who was roused to a very high pitch by the heat of the campaign. Yet Buchanan won the election.

Additional reasons for gloom had arisen from the white supremacist attitudes that Lincoln encountered that year while campaigning. Even though his speeches in the 1856 campaign drew thunderous applause from his fellow Republicans, Lincoln had been booed and jeered on the hustings by Democrats and bigots when he argued that blacks deserved freedom.

These events, however, were trifling compared to a major new disaster for the Free-Soil movement that was brewing in the federal judiciary, one so wretched that it surpassed the worst crimes of the Nebraska-Kansas crisis.

A slave from Missouri, Dred Scott, had been seeking his freedom in court. He claimed that his master unwittingly gave him his freedom when he took him to places where slavery was barred under law. In the

1830s, when his master had lived in Illinois, he had taken Scott along as his servant. Afterward, his master had taken him into the territory of Wisconsin, well above the anti-slavery dividing line of the Missouri Compromise.[34]

The Dred Scott case had gone through several appeals to the United States Supreme Court. The arguments began on February 11, 1856. Of the nine Supreme Court justices, five were pro-slavery Democrats.

The significance of this case went far beyond the status of Scott (and his wife, who had signed on as co-plaintiff). The issues of the case could set precedents determining some fundamental questions of law. Could slaves, for example, bring lawsuits? Did residence, if only for a time, in any of the free states or territories liberate "sojourning" slaves? How far did the power of Congress extend when it came to the regulation of slavery in federal territories?

At first glance, the power of Congress appeared to be obvious. In clear and extremely open-ended language, the Constitution (Article IV, Section 3) gave Congress the "Power to dispose of and make all needful Rules and Regulations respecting the Territory" of the United States before statehood was granted to a territory.

Since the 1840s, however, the issue had been clouded by interpretation. Two reverse-logic schools of thought—one of them pro-slavery and one of them anti-slavery—maintained that the above-cited language was forever superceded by the language of the Constitution's Fifth Amendment, which states, in part, "No person shall be . . . deprived of life, liberty, or property, without due process of law. . . ."

John C. Calhoun had invoked the Fifth Amendment as he argued that congressional attempts to prevent the owners of slaves from bringing their slaves into federal territories amounted to depriving them of their property without due process.[35]

Salmon P. Chase, however, had developed an opposite interpretation: if Congress should *permit* slave owners to bring their slaves into federal lands, he argued, it would thus deprive the *slaves* of their *liberty* without due process, since slavery was merely a *state*-sanctioned institution.[36]

All of these issues were intrinsic to the Dred Scott case. The Supreme Court delayed its decision as election year events played out. In his final message to Congress, President Pierce endorsed the imminent decision and urged all American citizens to obey it.

The Supreme Court's decision was about to be issued as President-elect Buchanan took the oath of office and delivered his Inaugural Address in 1857. He announced in his speech that the Supreme Court would issue a ruling very shortly that would settle the issue of slavery in the territories once and for all. Like Pierce, he urged the public to accept this decision, whatever it turned out to be. He did not, however, tell the public that he and two justices were busily engaged in a detailed and secret correspondence about the decision.[37]

On March 6, 1857, the Supreme Court issued its ruling. It was not unanimous. Every justice wrote a separate opinion, and those in the majority differed in a number of respects. But an overall majority decision was written by Chief Justice Roger Brooke Taney.

Taney said that this particular case should not have been in court at all: Scott, he observed, was quite obviously black, and blacks, proclaimed Taney, were "inferior . . . beings," who had absolutely "no rights . . . the white man was bound to respect." At the time the Constitution was written, said Taney, this view was universal.

In any case, Taney continued, Scott's sojourn in Illinois did nothing to free him, since precedents of interstate comity required that the laws of Missouri should govern his status on trips beyond the boundaries of the state.

Finally, Scott's sojourn in Wisconsin did nothing to free him, since Congress had *never* had the power—at least since the Fifth Amendment's ratification—to prohibit the owners of slaves from transporting their property wherever they wished in the federal domain.

In other words, long before Congress had chosen to repeal the Missouri Compromise, the Compromise was void since its contents violated the Fifth Amendment of the Constitution (as John C. Calhoun had construed it). Thus, by extension, the goals of the Republican Party and the Free-Soil movement were illegal. There was nothing any Congress could do to prevent the institution of slavery from spreading just as far and as wide in any federal lands as the owners of slaves could take it, said the justices who voted with Taney.

Furthermore, Taney contended, "if Congress itself cannot do this—if it is beyond the powers conferred on the Federal Government—it will be admitted, we presume, that it could not authorize a Territorial Government to exercise them."[38] This pronouncement was directly germane to the doctrine of Popular Sovereignty. If the territorial legislatures lacked jurisdiction on the slavery question, then how could the wishes of the territorial settlers be addressed?

The justices in the minority dissented as vigorously as they could. Justices John McLean and Benjamin Curtis, in particular, disputed Taney's version of history. Curtis showed that when the Constitution was drafted in 1787, several states allowed blacks the rights of citizenship; he added that the Constitution, in Article IV, Section 2, guarantees that "the Citizens of each State shall be entitled to all Privileges and Immunities of Citizens of the several States." So much for the argument that blacks were universally regarded as beings of an inferior order when the Constitution was written.

As to the Fifth Amendment, insofar as it figured in Taney's opinion, McLean and Curtis denounced the Court's decision as simplistic. They denied that exclusion of slavery from federal territories amounted to an actual deprivation of property or an abridgement of due process. In any case, Curtis contended, since Taney had argued that the case was improperly in court, the matter should have ended right there: the case should have been dismissed. Consequently, he said, the more sweeping pronouncement of the Court upon larger constitutional issues amounted to an *obiter dictum*, a comment in passing, of no legal force at all.

But the Dred Scott ruling held. White supremacists welcomed it, and Democrats demanded that Republicans obey it at the risk of being branded as outlaws if they did not. The Republicans—those who were told between the lines that their party might just as well disband, since the Free-Soil program at the center of its organizational mission was unconstitutional—denounced Taney as a viper and the Dred Scott decision as a virulent pack of lies.

They said its arguments were farcical and twisted. But they struggled to avoid the charge of lawlessness as they groped for some way to resist it. Many promised to abide by the Dred Scott decision in a minimal way, along the lines that Justice Curtis sketched out: by acknowledging the fact that Dred Scott was still a slave under law, while declaring that the larger constitutional pronouncements of the Court were not binding.

Stephen Douglas was in a very different sort of quandary. The decision placed his politics in serious jeopardy. The denial of Congress's power to bar slavery in federal territories was one thing—but the further denial of this power to the legislatures of the territories seemed fatal to the politics of Douglas. He had after all assured his supporters that whites would have a choice in the matter. But the logic of the Dred Scott decision raised serious doubts about his program.

And events in Kansas eroded his position even further in 1857. In February, the dubiously elected territorial legislature called a constitutional convention for Kansas. But the resulting constitution would not be presented to the voters for ratification.

The viability of Popular Sovereignty was slipping away, and for many of the reasons that Lincoln had predicted in 1854. He would naturally pounce upon the issue at the first opportunity, especially to counter Douglas in his reelection campaign of 1858.

Douglas pondered his reelection chances and foresaw his own vulnerabilities. So he decided to make a big speech to the voters, a speech that would give him a chance to react to the Dred Scott decision, to defend the vitality of Popular Sovereignty, and, most importantly of all, to taunt the Republicans with the issue of race. He spoke to his constituents in Springfield on June 7, 1857.

He acknowledged that the Dred Scott decision gave him pause the first time he read it. But he insisted that the principles of Popular Sovereignty were viable. If white settlers were bound and determined to keep slavery out of a territory, Douglas reasoned, the way to accomplish such a goal was easy: just refrain from either passing or enforcing the "police regulations and local legislation" that slaveholders always demanded before they would put their slave property at risk in an open territory. Then Douglas fell back upon the demagoguery of race.

He agreed with Taney's contention that blacks were regarded as inferior beings at the time of America's founding. He said political and social equality was intended for equals only, and blacks were not equal to whites.

Douglas viewed the Declaration of Independence in minimal terms: He said that it was merely an instrument by which to gain colonial freedom from Britain. In historical context, he argued, the statement that "all men are created equal" was simply shorthand for arguing that British Americans were equal to the British themselves. It was *not* a declaration, he insisted, that applied to inferior races.

He said Republicans were secret abolitionists or worse; he said they wanted the "amalgamation" of the races through black and white intermarriage. And he warned against indulging the Negro-loving affinities of "Black Republicans."

Upon the invitation of some Illinois Republicans, Lincoln answered Douglas on June 26, in Springfield. Excoriating the Dred Scott decision, Lincoln challenged its assertion that the Founding generation viewed blacks as "inferior beings." He cited all of the evidence amassed by Justice Curtis to demonstrate that blacks were in many ways far better off in the days of the early Republic than they were in the 1850s.

"In those days," he pointed out, "Legislatures held the unquestioned power to abolish slavery in their respective States; but now it is becoming quite fashionable for State Constitutions to withhold that power from the Legislatures. In those days, by common consent, the spread of the black man's bondage to new countries was prohibited; but now, Congress decides that it *will* not continue the prohibition, and the Supreme Court decides that it *could* not if it would. In those days, our Declaration of Independence was held sacred by all, and thought to include all; but now, to aid in making the bondage of the negro universal and eternal, it is assailed, and sneered at, and construed, and hawked at, and torn, till, if its framers could rise from their graves, they could not at all recognize it."[39]

Lincoln tried his very best to get his audience to empathize with slaves. He used picturesque imagery—the image, for example, of a man in a cage—to make his audience suffer as they listened. "All the powers of earth seem rapidly combining" against the slave in the United States, Lincoln said. "They have him in his prison house; they have searched his person, and left no prying instrument with him. One after another they have closed the heavy iron doors upon him, and now they have him, as it were, bolted in with a lock of a hundred keys, which can never be unlocked without the concurrence of every key; the keys are in the hands of a hundred different men, and they [have] scattered in a hundred different and distant places; and they stand musing as to what invention, in all the dominions of mind and matter, can be produced to make the impossibility of his escape more complete than it is."[40]

Stephen Douglas, said Lincoln, cared nothing for the suffering of slaves. He coldly assisted in expanding the vile institution that oppressed them. He was reckless and callous as he tried to deflect the public's anger by pandering to racial aversions; he sought to cover his tracks and change the subject politically by stirring up the "natural disgust in the minds of nearly all white people, to the idea of an indiscriminate amalgamation of the white and black races [racial intermarriage]." Douglas, said Lincoln, "evidently is basing his chief hope, upon the chances of being able to appropriate the benefit of this disgust" and thus beguile a white supremacist public:

> If he can, by much drumming and repeating, fasten the odium of that idea [racial "amalgamation"] upon his adversaries, he thinks he can struggle through the storm. He therefore clings to this hope, as a drowning man to the last plank. . . . He finds the Republicans insisting that the Declaration of Independence includes ALL men, black as well as white; and forthwith he boldly denies that it includes negroes at all, and proceeds to argue gravely that all who contend it does, do so only because they want to vote, and eat, and sleep, and marry with negroes! . . . Now I protest against the counterfeit logic which concludes that, because I do not want a black woman for a *slave* I must necessarily want her for a *wife*. I need not have her for either, I can just leave her alone. In some respects she certainly is not my equal; but in her natural right to eat the bread she earns with her own hands without asking leave of anyone else, she is my equal, and the equal of all others.[41]

"She is my equal," Lincoln said, in her right to freedom. Yet "in some respects she certainly is not my equal," Lincoln stated.

Here again, Lincoln's documented words provide his critics with evidence of bigotry. Indeed, there is more: in explicit terms, Lincoln put his opposition to racial intermarriage on the record in his Springfield speech.

It bears noting, however, that he crafted this statement on racial intermarriage in a way that came very close to satirizing white supremacist fears. He approached the point of tongue-in-cheek humor when he said there were fortunately "white men enough to marry all the white women, and black men enough to marry all the black women; and so let them be married. . . . On this point we fully agree with the Judge."[42]

Like Gilbert and Sullivan's Mikado, he strove to turn this evil into humor that was relatively harmless. Whereas Douglas warned against "mongrelization," Lincoln calmed and amused his touchy audience with visions of benign mass weddings.

Where does that put Lincoln? Did he oppose the "mixing" of the races? Lincoln uttered one sentence in his Springfield address that appears to support this view. "Judge Douglas," he said, "is especially horrified at the thought of the mixing of the blood by the white and black races: agreed for once—a thousand times agreed."[43]

Yet the statement in question makes very little sense if we compare it to Lincoln's *behavior*. Here, after all, was a man who alleged that he was "horrified" by the thought of racial intermarriage. But then he *joked* about the subject, and he sought to make light of it whenever Douglas raised the issue.

So again, we face the issue of candor: Was Lincoln really telling the truth? Did he really find the concept of racial intermarriage disgusting? Or did he deem it *unwise* to depart from the conventional views when the "near universal disgust" among whites with regard to this subject would distract them from the evil of slavery if Douglas succeeded in changing the subject from slavery to interracial sex? Were Lincoln's words a statement of *principle*? Or was he making expedient concessions?

Before we jump to any quick conclusions—if we can put the above-cited statements by Lincoln to the side, at least momentarily—it behooves us to read a very different statement by Lincoln in the course of the very same speech.

Lincoln used this occasion to unfold a great vision for America: the vision that America's equality principle should spread and expand its inner meaning over time to ever greater heights of moral fulfillment.

He began by refuting the perverse illogic that was used by Taney and Douglas when they spoke about the issue of "original intent" as it related to racial equality. Lincoln said: "Chief Justice Taney admits that the language of the Declaration is broad enough to include the whole human family, but he and Judge Douglas argue that the authors of that instrument did not intend to include negroes, by the fact that they did not at once, actually place them on an equality with the whites. Now this grave argument comes to just nothing at all, by the other fact, that they did not at once, *or ever afterwards*, actually place all white people on an equality with one another."

So what was the innermost meaning of the Declaration of Independence? Lincoln quickly asserted that the signers of the document intended "to include *all* men, but they did not intend to declare all men equal *in all respects*. They did not mean to say all were equal in color, size, intellect, moral developments, or social capacity. They defined with tolerable distinctness, in what respects they did consider all men created equal—equal in 'certain inalienable rights, among which are life, liberty, and the pursuit of happiness.' This they said, and this they meant."

They did *not* assert "the obvious untruth, that all were then actually enjoying that equality, nor yet, that they were about to confer it immediately upon them," said Lincoln. "In fact they had no power to confer such a boon. They meant simply to declare the *right*, so that the *enforcement* of it might follow as fast as circumstances should permit. They meant to set up a standard maxim for free society, which should be familiar to all, and revered by all; constantly looked to, constantly labored for, and even though never perfectly attained, constantly approximated, and thereby constantly spreading and deepening its influence, and augmenting the happiness and value of life to all people of all colors everywhere."[44]

How can we reconcile this eloquent manifesto with equivocal statements by Lincoln on the subject of race? In what manner did his wish to see a constant expansion of the "the happiness and value of life" for "all people everywhere" relate to his words about a hypothetical female black who was not to be regarded as his equal *in every respect*? Did the statement really mean what it implied? Or, was Lincoln playing games with his audience?

It all depends upon the meaning (or the multiple meanings) of "equal" as he used the term. Did he mean, in effect, that the hypothetical female black was less *worthy* than he? Or did he mean, without spelling it out, that she lacked the same *qualifications* (at the moment) for citizenship?

"Equal" could be used in three senses: to denote an "equality" in *abstract rights* such as freedom or liberty itself; an "equality" of *talent*, an issue of the sort that preoccupied gut-level racists; or an "equality" of *status* or *condition*, as when Lincoln referred to the Founders and the issue of their power to "place" certain people "on an equality" in terms of social standing. Which of these different definitions was Lincoln employing at any given time? Consider this problem in regard to the issue of voting.

Many of the states had put voting restrictions in place for *adult white males*. Even some Northern states had set property requirements for voting, and a few of them subjected their voters to literacy tests. Connecticut and Massachusetts, for example, had established such tests in the 1850s.[45]

It bears noting that when Lincoln came around to supporting black voting rights (in 1864), he intended to *phase in* the delicate reform so that whites would stay calm about the change and accept it peacefully. To that end, he proposed to give the vote to certain blacks who had impressive *credentials*—who were "equal" to the challenges of voting.

In the political culture of today, a great deal of this sounds absurd. Many take it for granted that American adults (with a few exceptions such as felons) are entitled automatically to vote. But this state of affairs has resulted from a long revolution in constitutional law. The Fifteenth Amendment to the Constitution, which Republicans drafted at the high tide of Reconstruction in 1869, was one of the first great national milestones in this revolution.

An amendment such as this was unthinkable before the Civil War. So we return to the middle of 1857, and the issue of "equality" vis-à-vis Lincoln and the female black. If she were not at the moment his "equal" either in her *power* or her *qualifications*, she could nonetheless *become* his equal over time. Lincoln, after all, had said America's Founders lacked the *power to confer* certain rights, notwithstanding the fact that a few of these rights were inherent—indeed, inalienable—in the human condition.

For which reason the rights would have to be *conferred* just "as fast as circumstances should permit." The first of the rights to be conferred was the right to be free. Then some other basic rights could be added in the fullness of time.

Some observers are impatient with attempts such as this to distinguish Lincoln's views on the subject of race from the bigotry of Douglas. It is easy enough to view Lincoln in a very bad light by our contemporary standards. It is possible to say that he was little more than a racist, and leave it at that.[46]

It is equally possible that Lincoln made concessions to the phobias and biases of mainstream America—on racial intermarriage, for example—in a defense against the crude demagoguery of Douglas. But he limited each of these concessions through the use of qualifying language, or else through the medium of clever ambiguities, the sort of thing he learned as a lawyer to concoct in tight situations.

He made statements on the subject of race that in many ways *sounded* like the sort of thing his audience demanded to hear. But these statements were often ambiguous. And perhaps that was Lincoln's intention. The very same Lincoln who could scrutinize a text for any secrets its author had encrypted—and he would demonstrate the art as he extracted hidden meanings or intentions from the Dred Scott decision—had the skill to encode special caveat provisions of his own.

He could craft a written speech in such a way that it contained *alternative* meanings. No less an observer than Stephen Douglas said that Lincoln excelled in this art. He paid Lincoln the backhanded compliment of crediting him with a "fertile genius in devising language to conceal his thoughts."[47]

Again, take the outwardly racist formulation on the female slave: "in some respects she certainly is not my equal." Plain language, it would seem—but murky enough if we subject it to a probing analysis. In *which* respects was Lincoln contending that the woman was "not his equal?"

And what *meaning* did he give the word "equal?" Was it "equal" in the sense of her *ability*? Or was it "equal" in the sense of *social standing*? Lincoln left this important matter vague, and perhaps deliberately.

We often chafe at ambiguities when issues such as this are on the line. We want to know the full truth about Lincoln's racial views, since the issue is central to his legacy. An easy resolution is impossible. But there remain some interesting clues about his racial feelings.

Some of them consist of memoranda that were written by Lincoln. In 1854, Lincoln jotted down the following reflections as he grappled with the arguments propounded by the advocates of slavery: "If A. can prove, however conclusively, that he may, of right, enslave B.," Lincoln reasoned, "why may not B. snatch the same argument, and prove equally, that he may enslave A?—You say A. is white, and B. is black. It is *color*, then; the lighter, having the right to enslave the darker? Take care. By this rule, you are to be the slave to the first man you meet, with a fairer skin than your own. You do not mean *color* exactly?—You mean the whites are *intellectually* the superior of the blacks, and, therefore, have the right to enslave them? Take care again. By this rule, you are to be slave to the first man you meet, with an intellect superior to your own."[48]

In other words, traits are diffused in such a very broad range across the races that the issue of racial identity is frequently pointless in individual instances. *Individual* traits are all-important, Lincoln seemed to be saying.

On another occasion, in 1858, Lincoln searched his soul in response to the incessant racial demagoguery of Douglas. What Lincoln told himself on this occasion was simple and clear: *he did not really know* whether blacks were inferior to whites in any crucial respect. In other words, he faced the issue honestly in private and without preconceptions. A most curious thing, by the way, for any knee-jerk racist to do.

But his instinct, regardless of the facts about the matter, was to err on the side of magnanimity. If, for the sake of the argument, he wrote, one hypothesized black inferiority, the ethical response, and indeed

the only decent response, was an attitude of kindliness and not malevolence: "*Suppose* [my emphasis] it is true, that the negro is inferior
to the white, in the gifts of nature; is it not the exact reverse [of] justice
that the white should, for that reason, take from the negro, any part of
the little which has been given him? '*Give* to him that is needy' is the
christian rule of charity; but 'Take from him that is needy' is the rule
of slavery."[49]

But the racist hypothesis was nothing but a vague conjecture. In the
Civil War years, Lincoln made this point to a white supremacist who
sent him a telegram of pushy admonitions that whites were the "first-
class" people of America and blacks were merely "second-class" detri-
tus. The method chosen by Lincoln to respond to this particular critic
was the method of tongue-in-cheek ridicule.

He had a secretary write to the critic and ask him to identify his own
race distinctly—white or black (as if Lincoln didn't know the answer)—
so the President could understand his point of view with maximum
clarity. But "in either case," Lincoln's secretary told the critic, the president believes "you cannot be regarded as an impartial judge. It may be
that you belong to a third or fourth class of *yellow* or *red* men, in which
case the impartiality of your judgment would be more apparent."[50]

Another clue to Lincoln's feelings on race can be found in the memoirs of blacks who encountered him in person. They, above all, were in
an excellent position to *sense* and to *feel* his racial attitudes. Frederick
Douglass, the black abolitionist, was in such a position.

Though Douglass concluded in a speech before a largely black audience in 1876 (presumably on the basis of Lincoln's public statements
in the 1850s) that Lincoln "was a white man and shared toward the
colored race the prejudices common to his countrymen," he reached a
very different conclusion in the summer of 1865—when the memory
of Lincoln was vivid.[51] Douglass stated that Lincoln was "emphatically
the black mans [*sic*] President: the first to show any respect for their
rights as men."[52]

Moreover, Douglass stated on a number of occasions that whenever
he had called upon Lincoln, he encountered no hint of racial tension.
"I was never more quickly or more completely put at ease in the presence
of a great man," Douglass stated, "than in that of Abraham Lincoln. . . .
In his company I was never in any way reminded of my humble origin,
or of my unpopular color."[53]

He recalled a particular visit to the White House early in 1865. Lincoln recognized him as he approached, and then, said Douglass, "he exclaimed, so that all around could hear him, 'Here comes my friend Douglass.' Taking me by the hand, he said, 'I am glad to see you.'"[54]

Historian David Grimsted has argued that Lincoln was struggling with a "self-admitted racism." In the course of this struggle, he would not allow his prejudice to "cloud his sense of blacks' full humanity." If such a theory is correct, then Lincoln's struggle, as Grimsted suggests, "has something of the transcending dignity of Huck Finn's."[55]

But there remains the possibility that *no* real prejudice existed in the mind of Lincoln. It is possible that Lincoln, under pressure and confronting a militantly white supremacist electorate, pretended to feelings he did not really have on the subject of race.

Whatever his innermost feelings on race, Lincoln's overall intention in the 1850s was apparent to all: to make whites disgusted with slavery, as much for its oppression of blacks as for its ancillary menace to themselves.

As events played out in the summer and autumn months of 1857, Lincoln made it clear that he intended to challenge Stephen Douglas for his seat in the United States Senate. Meanwhile, surprising events in Kansas drove a wedge between Douglas and Buchanan.

Because of widespread electoral fraud in Kansas, Free-Soilers decided to boycott the gerrymandered election for delegates to serve in the territory's constitutional convention. The convention, which met at Lecompton in September, wrote a slave-state constitution.

But Buchanan's new territorial governor, Robert J. Walker (a Mississippian), insisted that this constitution be submitted to the voters of Kansas in a referendum to be held in December. Furthermore, he guaranteed an honest election in October when the members of the territorial legislature had to face the voters. Because of Walker's oversight, the Free-Soilers gained a majority in the legislature.

After the October election, the pro-slavery convention reacted with a blatant and arrogant gambit to rig the referendum on the constitution. They decided to submit *two* options to the voters: (1) the draft constitution containing an unlimited slavery provision; (2) the same constitution with a special alternative provision that barred any future importation of slaves while permitting the slave-holding settlers of Kansas to keep the slaves they owned already, along with their progeny.

Either way, the institution of slavery would to some extent be legalized in Kansas. Either way, the slave-holding interests would win. Once again, the Free-Soilers in Kansas cried foul and they sat out the trick referendum, which was held in December. So the slave-state "Lecompton Constitution" was approved with the wide-open slavery provision.

But then the Free-Soil legislature called for a new and honest referendum: one in which the voters of Kansas would be given the option of rejecting the entire constitution if they wished to do so. They did so in January 1858.

And yet President Buchanan maintained that the first referendum was valid. He sent the Lecompton Constitution to Congress and proposed that Kansas be admitted to the Union as a slave state right away. Whereupon, Stephen Douglas broke relations with James Buchanan and declared an open war with his own party's leader in the White House.

The "Lecompton fraud" was a very real threat to Stephen Douglas. For if Popular Sovereignty, Douglas's rallying cry, appeared to be a sham, then he would probably fail in his upcoming bid for reelection to the Senate, and his presidential hopes would be destroyed. So he battled to the death against Buchanan and his "Buchaneers," as the Republicans watched in amazement.

The Douglas-Buchanan fight was so spectacular that certain Republican leaders and opinion makers (political journalist Horace Greeley, for example, and Senator William H. Seward) urged their Illinois counterparts to throw their full support behind Douglas in his reelection struggle.

Lincoln worried that Douglas and his politics of Popular Sovereignty would hijack the Free-Soil movement and ruin it, at least in Illinois. But he consoled himself when the United States House of Representatives rejected the Lecompton Constitution for Kansas in April 1858.

All the while, he was brooding on an issue that the Dred Scott case had left dangling. The Supreme Court had declared that the right of American whites to own slaves was constitutionally sacred. It denied that Congress or the territorial legislatures had power to prevent the spread of slavery in federal lands. But what about the power of the *states*?

What could stop Roger Taney or another Chief Justice from issuing a ruling sometime in the future claiming that *states* were just as impotent as Congress in regulating slavery? If Congress lacked the

power to prevent the spread of slavery, then how could any state claim
the power?

Maybe this was the last secret weapon of the South, the final trump
card for slavery expansion, the endgame of Southern domination that
its leaders had been planning all along. Perhaps the next outrageous
surprise from the South would be a ruling by Taney that would open
the floodgates for slavery expansion in the North. Was it possible?

IT WAS POSSIBLE INDEED: and the issue gave Lincoln the conceptual basis for his formal challenge to Douglas. In the course of the 1858 election campaign, his debates and confrontations with Douglas gained
national attention: indeed, by the end of the year, his political prospects were national.

Lincoln's genuine alarm about the prospect of slavery invading the
North was related to his sense of a slaveholders' scheme. The new
modus operandi of the schemers was to take Free-Soilers *by surprise* in an
escalating manner.

When the Compromise of 1850 was adopted, the Free-Soil strategists expected that the next great sectional battle would occur in New
Mexico territory. Then, surprise—the whole slavery issue was reopened
to the East, and all the federal lands that had for years been off-limits
to slavery were suddenly at risk. The great rollback of Free-Soil power
had begun: the battle had erupted in Kansas, and the outcome would
determine the fate of all the other open federal lands.

Then, surprise—the Dred Scott decision changed the rules of the
game and made the politics of Kansas almost moot. The slavery system could extend freely west, and there was nothing any Free-Soil
majority could do that would prevent it, said Chief Justice Taney.

The fact that Dred Scott had lived in an area cordoned off from
slavery—not as a *fugitive slave* but rather as a servant attending his
master—gave Taney no discomfort whatsoever. Scott's presence in
Wisconsin Territory did nothing to free him, since the rights of private property were sacred. In the aftermath of this ruling almost everyone seemed to be focused on its stark *territorial* component.

Perhaps another big surprise was now in store. For the presence of
Scott in *the state of Illinois* had done nothing to liberate him either. And
the logic of Taney was the same. Dred Scott, said Taney, was a slave
"sojourner" whose status outside of his owner's home state would be
controlled by the laws of that state.

Lincoln thought about the issue in the early months of 1858, and then it hit him: what could stop the Southern owners of slaves from bringing *thousands* of their slaves into the North on the very same basis?[56]

In a fragment of an undelivered speech, Lincoln gathered some preliminary thoughts about the fact that the "bringing of Dred Scott into Illinois by his master, and holding him there for a long time as a slave, did not operate his emancipation." This point, said Lincoln, was in all probability established by the Taney Court for some intended use in the future. It was "not to be pressed immediately; but if acquiesced in for a while, then to sustain the logical conclusion that what Dred Scott's master might lawfully do with Dred in the free State of Illinois, every other master may lawfully do with any other one or one hundred slaves in Illinois, or in any other free State."[57]

It would be easy: just rent them out to businessmen whose workers went out on strike. Slave "sojourners" would remain enslaved. There was nothing that the laws of any Northern state could do to free them, or even to remove them. The rights of private property were sacred, said Taney, and the Constitution—as interpreted by him along the lines that Calhoun recommended—was supreme.

This was the threat that Lincoln gradually perceived, and it should not be dismissed or shrugged away. As Harry V. Jaffa has observed, "There is no reason to suppose that, should slavery in the mines, foundries, factories, and fields of the free states have proved advantageous to powerful groups therein, new systems of discipline might not have been invented to make the exploitation of slave labor highly profitable there."[58]

Lincoln pondered these matters with increasing private rage as he wrote the big speech that he was planning to deliver in June. He was writing this speech for the Republican convention that would nominate him for the position of United States senator. He had worked through the spring with Republican leaders in the state (men such as Norman Judd, who chaired the Republican State Central Committee) to get the Senate nomination locked up before the convention.[59] He had fought against naifs who saw in Douglas a heroic contender against the "Buchaneers."

This was nonsense, Lincoln insisted. Douglas was waging the fight of his life because his policies exploded in his face. He had hoped to get ahead by appeasing the South and by lulling the opponents of slavery with Popular Sovereignty. But Buchanan was about to spoil everything by pushing the Lecompton Constitution too hard: the attempted rape of Kansas was sufficiently blatant to deprive Stephen Douglas of his very last shred of credibility.

So his schism with Buchanan was sensible. But it was hardly an act to be rewarded by Free-Soil Republicans. Douglas was a rogue, and if Republicans should "drop their own organization, fall into rank behind him, and form a great free-State Democratic Party," Lincoln warned, they would reap the grim results of such stupidity. "If they so fall in with Judge Douglas, and Kansas shall be secured as a free State," Lincoln wrote, "will not the Republicans stand ready, haltered and harnessed, to be handed over by him to the regular Democracy, to filibuster indefinitely for additional slave territory,—to carry slavery into all the States, as well as Territories, under the Dred Scott decision, construed and enlarged from time to time, according to the demands of the regular slave Democracy,—and to assist in reviving the African slave-trade in order that all may buy negroes where they can be bought the cheapest. . . ?"[60]

A revival of the African slave trade? Why not? Why not go farther and imagine the entire Western Hemisphere converted to a bastion for a tyranny of global dimensions? The pro-slavery movement was sufficiently shameless that nothing of the sort could be precluded.

It was all a matter of conviction, Lincoln said, and of conviction augmented by power. Those whose convictions held that slavery was right would keep pushing their repulsive system. And the push would go on until those whose convictions told them slavery was wrong could get the power to push the other way.

And when push came to shove, Lincoln said in the speech that he delivered in Springfield on June 16, the country's future would be settled one way—and one way alone. He cited Scripture in the famous invocation:

> "A house divided against itself cannot stand."
> I believe this government cannot endure, permanently half *slave* and half *free*.
> I do not expect the Union to be *dissolved*—I do not expect the house to *fall*—but I do expect it will cease to be divided. It will become *all* one thing, or *all* the other. Either the *opponents* of slavery, will arrest the further spread of it, and place it where the public mind shall rest in the belief that it is in course of ultimate extinction; or its *advocates* will push it forward, till it shall become alike lawful in *all* the States, old as well as *new*—*North* as well as *South*.
> Have we no *tendency* to the latter condition?[61]

The tendency toward slavery expansion was dominant, Lincoln said, and this was hardly an accident—hardly a fortuitous convergence of events or impersonal forces. It was nothing less than a *scheme* that was deliberate, willful, and shameless.

Stephen Douglas had helped the scheme along by opening the federal lands in the West to the spread of slavery. He helped it along by telling whites not to care, and that the fate of black slaves didn't matter. Franklin Pierce had provided some crucial leverage by using and abusing his presidential office to manipulate events in Kansas. James Buchanan had done the same thing.

Both Pierce and Buchanan paved the way for the Dred Scott decision by telling the public to obey it before it was even issued. Then Taney followed up with his judicial revolt against the Founding Fathers and their legacy.

And this was where matters then stood, Lincoln said, as he summarized the recent historical events in terms of *power* for the advocates of slavery. They perverted the law to gain power, he said, and their method was to build a political structure of enslavement through the following precedents of law:

> First, that no negro slave, imported as such from Africa, and no descendant of such slave can ever be a *citizen* of any State. . . .
>
> Secondly, that "subject to the Constitution of the United States," neither *Congress* nor a *Territorial Legislature* can exclude slavery from any United States Territory. . . .
>
> Thirdly, that whether the holding [of] a negro in actual slavery in a free State, makes him free, as against the holder, the United States courts will not decide, but will leave to be decided by the courts of any slave State the negro may be forced into by the master.
>
> This point is made, not to be pressed *immediately*; but, if acquiesced in for a while, and apparently *indorsed* [sic] by the people at an election, *then* to sustain the logical conclusion that what Dred Scott's master might lawfully do with Dred Scott, in the free State of Illinois, every other master may lawfully do with any other *one*, or one *thousand* slaves, in Illinois, or in any other free State.[62]

All the while, Stephen Douglas played a role in this despicable drama by urging white Americans to turn their thoughts away from the subject. He urged whites to "live and let live" when it came to the ownership of Negroes. He meant to lull the Northern public—including the Northern anti-slavery public—into quiet but maleficent sleep. "We shall *lie down* pleasantly dreaming that the people of *Mississippi* are on the verge of making their State *free*," said Lincoln, and then "we shall *awake* to the *reality*, instead, that the Supreme Court has made *Illinois* a *slave State*."[63]

It could happen in the blink of an eye. And the preparations had begun as far back as the Kansas-Nebraska Act. In a little-noticed passage of the act, Lincoln said, the law stated that "the people of a *State* as well as *Territory*, were to be left *'perfectly free'*" to decide about the issue of slavery, "*'subject only to the Constitution.'*"

But why, Lincoln asked, had there been mention of a *state* in the Nebraska legislation? "Why mention a *State*? They were legislating for *territories*, and not *for* or *about* States. Certainly the people of a State *are* and *ought to be* subject to the Constitution of the United States; but why is mention of this *lugged* into this merely *territorial* law? Why are the people of a *territory* and the people of a *state* therein *lumped* together, and their relation to the Constitution therein treated as being *precisely* the same?"[64]

The reason, said Lincoln, was to open up a path for a new interpretation—the Calhoun school-of-thought interpretation—of the United States Constitution in defining the *powers of a state*. "Put *that* and *that* together, and we have another nice little niche, which we may, ere long, see filled with another Supreme Court decision, declaring that the Constitution of the United States does not permit a *state* to exclude slavery from its limits."[65]

It was all a coordinated plan, Lincoln argued, a conspiracy to shrink away the power of the anti-slavery movement. The principal conspirators—Douglas, Pierce, Taney, and Buchanan—had been working from a kind of a strategic blueprint, a political schematic for gradually constructing a national edifice of slavery.

As if they were laborers, he called them by their first names—Stephen and Franklin and Roger and James—as he worked the Republican crowd at the Springfield convention. His logic was tinged with sarcastic anger as he argued that the busy machinations of the Democratic crew had been coordinated from the beginning. "We cannot absolutely *know* that all these exact adaptations are the result of preconcert," Lincoln admitted. "But when we see a lot of framed timbers, different portions of which we know have been gotten out at different times and places by different workmen—Stephen, Franklin, Roger, and James, for instance— and when we see these timbers joined together, and see they exactly make the frame of a house or mill, all the tenons and mortices exactly fitting, and all the lengths and proportions of the different pieces exactly adapted to their respective places, and not a piece too many or too few—not omitting even scaffolding—or, if a single piece be lacking, we can see the place in the frame exactly fitted and prepared to yet bring such piece in—in *such* a case, we find it impossible to not *believe* that Stephen and Franklin and Roger and James all understood one another from the beginning, and all worked upon a common *plan* or *draft* drawn up before the first lick was struck."[66]

But the edifice of slavery was still unfinished, and Republican crusaders could destroy the ugly thing if they rose to their challenge in time. "Two years ago the Republicans of the nation mustered over thirteen hundred thousand strong," Lincoln said, making reference to the 1856 election. This was done "under the single impulse of resistance to a common danger, with every external circumstance against us. Of *strange*, *discordant*, and even, *hostile* elements, we gathered from the four winds, and *formed* and fought the battle through, under the hot fire of a disciplined, proud, and pampered enemy. Did we brave all *then*, to falter now?—*now*—when that same enemy is *wavering*, dissevered and belligerent?"[67]

This "House Divided" speech—so completely the reverse in its feelings and intentions from the notions that "sound-bite" summaries suggest—was the prelude to Lincoln's great speech in Chicago the following month, the speech from the balcony of the Tremont House hotel.

As he readied his challenge to Douglas, Lincoln hoped to see the day when he could use his new position in the Senate to reverse the course of slavery expansion. The following reflections leave very little doubt that Lincoln hoped to usher in a long phaseout of slavery, one that was modeled as closely as possible on Britain's great achievement of the 1830s. "I have not allowed myself to forget," he wrote, "that the abolition of the Slave-trade by Great Brittain [*sic*], was agitated a hundred years before it was a final success; that the measure had its open fire-eating opponents; its stealthy 'don't care' opponents; its dollar and cent opponents; its inferior race opponents; its negro equality opponents; and its religion and good order opponents; that all these opponents got offices, and their adversaries got none." Nonetheless, he continued,

> I have also remembered that though they blazed, like tallow-candles for a century, at last they flickered in the socket, died out, stank in the dark for a brief

season, and were remembered no more, even by the smell. School-boys know that Wilbe[r]force, and Granville Sharpe, helped that cause forward; but who can now name a single man who labored to retard it? Remembering these things I can not but regard it as possible that the higher object of this contest may not be completely attained within the term of my natural life. But I can not doubt either that it will come in due time. Even in this view, I am proud, in my passing speck of time, to contribute an humble mite to that glorious consummation. . . .[68]

Douglas—one of those men who were currently blazing like candles but whose fate was to flicker out and stink in the dark for a time—charged that Lincoln was calling for a war between the sections in his "House Divided" speech. He said that Popular Sovereignty worked—indeed, he even claimed paramount credit for defeating the Lecompton Constitution. And he told his constituents again and again that a vote for Lincoln was a vote for mongrelization.

He did it in his kick-off address in Chicago, delivered from a window balcony at Tremont House hotel. On the very next evening, however, Lincoln occupied the very same balcony. As we heard in chapter one, he roused the crowd with passionate oratory, striking back hard at Douglas. It was Douglas, after all, said Lincoln, who had opened up Kansas to slavery. It was Douglas who said he didn't care whether slavery spread. He parted company with James Buchanan over matters of *procedure*.

But it was Republican anti-slavery men who had done the real work to stop slavery expansion in Kansas. It was anti-slavery Republicans who stopped the Lecompton fraud in the House of Representatives. Douglas and his Democratic allies furnished "some twenty votes," said Lincoln, "and the Republicans furnished *ninety odd*. [Loud applause] Now who was it who did the work?"[69]

Lincoln denied Douglas's charge that he was fomenting war between the sections. His "House Divided" speech, he observed, was a *prediction* that America's struggle over slavery would resolve itself in one way alone: "If you will carefully read that passage over," he said, "I did not say that I was in favor of anything in it. I only said what I expected to take place. . . . I did not even say that I desired that slavery should be put in course of ultimate extinction."[70]

But now, said Lincoln, since Douglas forced the question, he was ready to declare that the extinction of slavery was precisely what he *did* wish to see: "I do say so now, however [great applause] so there need be no longer any difficulty about that. It may be written down . . . [Applause and laughter]."[71]

Still, said Lincoln, he had never proposed any short-term action that would interfere with slavery in states that permitted it: "I believe there is no right, and ought to be no inclination on the part of the people of the free States to enter into the slave States, and interfere with the question of slavery at all."[72] Instead, Lincoln wanted the *containment* of slavery, so that others could extinguish its evil in the future.

But when Taney, Pierce, Buchanan, and Douglas tried to force the *expansion* of slavery, Lincoln said that he would fight them to the end, to the point of ignoring the Dred Scott decision. He would not so much *resist* the decision as ignore it completely. "If I were in Congress," he proclaimed, "and a vote should come up on a question whether slavery should be prohibited in a new territory, in spite of that Dred Scott decision, I would vote that it should. [Applause; 'good for you;' 'we hope to see it;' 'that's right.']"[73]

Lincoln worked this audience in ways that we have seen already; he invoked the recent pageant of the Fourth of July as he spoke to the descendants of people who had come from all over Europe, telling them that they and their kind were quite right to feel kinship with America's Founding Fathers. It was a kinship based upon a principle transcending ethnicity and race; people like themselves had "a right to claim it as though they were blood of the blood, and flesh of the flesh of the men who wrote that Declaration, (loud and long continued applause) and so they are."[74] He continued:

> Now, sirs, for the purpose of squaring things with this idea of "don't care if slavery is voted up or down," for sustaining the Dred Scott decision [A voice— "Hit him again"], for holding that the Declaration of Independence did not mean anything at all, we have Judge Douglas giving his exposition of what the Declaration of Independence means, and we have him saying that the people of America are equal to the people of England. According to his construction, you Germans are not connected with it. Now I ask in all soberness, if all these things, if indulged in, if ratified, if confirmed and endorsed, if taught to our children, and repeated to them, do not tend to rub out the sentiment of liberty in this country, and to transform this Government into a government of some other form. Those arguments that are made, that the inferior race are to be treated with as much allowance as they are capable of enjoying; that as much is to be done for them as their condition will allow. What are these arguments? They are the arguments that kings have made for enslaving the people in all ages of the world.[75]

We have heard the climax of the speech:

> I should like to know if taking this old Declaration of Independence, which
> declares that all men are equal upon principle and making exceptions to it where
> will it stop. If one man says it does not mean a negro, why not another say it
> does not mean some other man? If that declaration is not the truth, let us get
> the Statute book, in which we find it and tear it out![76]

As he concluded, Lincoln urged his supporters to "discard all this quibbling about this man and the other man—this race and that race and
the other race being inferior, and therefore they must be placed in an
inferior position. . . . Let us discard all these things, and unite as one
people. . . ."[77]

But Douglas meant to sabotage Lincoln on race, and he continued
to agitate the issue by dwelling on interracial sex. So Lincoln crafted a
lawyer-like position that he hoped would be of use throughout the
weeks and months of campaigning. He tried it out on a Springfield
audience a week after issuing his plea in Chicago.

"Last night," he said, "Judge Douglas tormented himself with hor-
rors about my disposition to makes negroes perfectly equal with white
men in social and political relations. He did not stop to show that I
have said any such thing, or that it legitimately follows from any thing
I have said, but he rushes in with his assertions." Lincoln carefully
avoided *denying* that he wished to make blacks and whites socially and
politically equal; he just denied that he had actually *said* he wished to
make them equal.

He further tiptoed along the boundary of racial prejudice with more
careful language that echoed his earlier remarks about a "Negro wife":
"Certainly the negro is not our equal in color—perhaps not in other
respects; still, in the right to put into his mouth the bread that his own
hands have earned, he is the equal of every other man, white or black.
. . . All I ask for the negro is that if you do not like him, let him alone."[78]

To counter the racial demagoguery of Douglas, Lincoln temporized—
though on close inspection his formulations conceded very little. "Certainly the negro is not our equal in color," Lincoln said, and "perhaps
not in other respects." The only difference that was definite—Lincoln
used the word "certainly"—was difference in *color*.

But if blacks and whites were "unequal" in color—that is, they had
different amounts of pigmentation—this form of "inequality" was noth-

ing but a matter of taste with regard to the physical appearance of others. If one happened not to like the appearance of others, one could obviously leave them alone.

Though other forms of racial "inequality" *might* exist (Lincoln pointedly used the word "perhaps"), none had been *proven*. The only thing that could be proven on the subject of race was that blacks were the equals of whites when it came to their liberty.

Would the strategy work? The question had become more urgent since the speech in Chicago. Lincoln had challenged Stephen Douglas to a series of debates that would carry their struggle into every major section of the state. And this included southern Illinois ("Egypt," as its natives dubbed it), where the sentiments of white supremacy were near universal.

Though Illinois voters lacked the power to elect their senators, they did vote for the members of the state legislature, who in turn voted for the senators. The Lincoln-Douglas debates made the senatorial choice the big issue in the statewide elections.

The first debate took place on August 21, 1858, in Ottawa, in northern Illinois. Over twelve thousand people had jammed the public square to hear Lincoln and Douglas debate. Republican sentiment prevailed in this town, but Douglas used the occasion for all it was worth to get Lincoln on the record in a number of ways that would damage his chances in "Egypt," where white supremacy was stronger.

Douglas started with assertions that America's "divided House" could stand forever in a state of division. He said the Founding Fathers had intended this state of affairs. In their wisdom, said Douglas, the Founders left the people to decide about the issue for themselves—state by state. The Founding Fathers, in effect, were thus the earliest practitioners and advocates of Popular Sovereignty.

Then Douglas launched into his white supremacy routine. He began with some questions for the audience. "I ask you," said Douglas, "are you in favor of conferring upon the negro the rights and privileges of citizenship? ('No, no.') Do you desire to strike out of our State Constitution that clause which keeps slaves and free negroes out of the State, and allow the free negroes to flow in, ('never') and cover your prairies with black settlements? Do you desire to turn this beautiful State into a free negro colony, ('no, no') in order that when Missouri abolishes slavery she can send one hundred thousand emancipated slaves into Illinois, to become citizens and voters, on an equality with your-selves? ('Never,' 'no.') If you desire negro citizenship . . . then support Mr. Lincoln and the Black Republican party. . . . For one, I am op-posed to negro citizenship in any and every form. (Cheers.) I believe this government was made on the white basis. ('Good.') I believe it was made by white men, for the benefit of white men and their posterity for ever. . . ."[79]

Then he twisted the knife a bit more: "I do not question Mr. Lincoln's conscientious belief that the negro was made his equal, and hence is his brother, (laughter) but for my own part, I do not regard the negro as my equal, and positively deny that he is my brother or any kin to me whatever. ('Never.' 'Hit him again,' and cheers)."[80]

Douglas challenged Lincoln to reply to a series of questions regard-ing the Republican Party's doctrines—did Lincoln, for example, stand pledged to prevent the admission of any more slave states to the Union, "even if the people want them?" Did Lincoln stand pledged to bar slavery from all the open territories of the United States? Did he op-pose the acquisition of any more American territory unless it was for-bidden to slavery?

"I ask Abraham Lincoln to answer these questions," said Douglas, "in order that when I trot him down to lower Egypt I may put the same questions to him. (Enthusiastic applause.) My principles are the same everywhere. (Cheers, and 'hark.') I can proclaim them alike in the North, the South, the East, and the West. . . . I desire to know whether Mr. Lincoln's principles will bear transplanting from Ottawa to Jonesboro."[81]

Lincoln was on the defensive. He avoided quick answers to the ques-tions, and he tried to defuse the racial issue by employing some new formulations—carefully composed, with all the qualifying language he could manage—that would sound good enough when he was forced to "trot down" to "lower Egypt": "I have no purpose to introduce politi-cal and social equality between the white and the black races," he said. "There is a physical difference between the two, which in my judg-ment will probably forever forbid their living together upon the foot-ing of perfect equality, and inasmuch as it becomes a necessity that there must be a difference [in the power positions of the races], I, as well as Judge Douglas, am in favor of the race to which I belong, hav-ing the superior position."[82]

A tricky disclaimer: though it *sounded* like a racist manifesto, Lincoln carefully restricted its moral implications, as a critical analysis reveals. Lincoln said that he had *no intention at the moment* ("no purpose") of pursuing full equality for blacks *in light of the existing political reality*: the reality that blacks and whites were so deeply divided due to hatred arising from their "physical difference" that the politics of racial equality were probably impossible, at least in America. All attempts to place the races on the "footing" of perfect equality would probably fail, for political reasons.

If, therefore, a choice should ever have to be made between subjection and domination—then Lincoln, for obvious reasons, would not choose subjection.[83]

But the choice between subjection and total domination was gratuitous, in Lincoln's estimation. Lincoln firmly denied that any such choice was predestined when it came to the issue of *freedom*.

Lincoln then struck back at Douglas on the issue of Popular Sovereignty vis-à-vis the Dred Scott decision. He demanded to know the real meaning of Popular Sovereignty: "Is it the right of the people to have Slavery or not have it, as they see fit, in the territories? . . . My understanding is that Popular Sovereignty . . . does allow the people of a Territory to have Slavery if they want to, but does not allow them *not* to have it if they *do not* want it. [Applause and laughter.]" According to the Dred Scott decision, he said, if a single settler should make up his mind to hold slaves, then the rest of the settlers would have "no way of keeping that one man from holding them."[84]

He then returned to his charge from the House Divided Speech: Douglas was complicit with Pierce, Buchanan, and Taney in extending the reach of the slavery system with intentions of making it national. He reminded his listeners that Douglas had placed the word "state" in the Kansas-Nebraska Bill, for what reason one could gradually infer: "I have always been puzzled to know what business the word 'State' had in that connection. Judge Douglas knows. *He put it there.* . . . This law they were passing was not about States, and was not making provisions for States." But after "seeing the Dred Scott decision, which holds that the people cannot exclude slavery from a *Territory*, if another Dred Scott decision shall come, holding that they cannot exclude it from a *State*, we shall discover that when the word was originally put there, it was in view of something which was to come in due time. . . ."[85]

And Douglas, said Lincoln, was a cheerleader *par excellence* for the Dred Scott decision—even though it gutted his supposedly sacred principles of Popular Sovereignty. So what were his real convictions? "This man," said Lincoln, "sticks to a decision which forbids the people of a Territory from excluding slavery, and he does so not because he says it is right in itself—he does not give any opinion on that—but because it has been *decided by the court. . . .*"[86]

Yet this same Stephen Douglas held Supreme Court opinions in contempt when his interests had demanded it. Decades earlier, Lincoln pointed out, both Douglas and his Democratic colleagues refused to go along with a Supreme Court ruling on the charter of a National Bank. But now, they insisted that the Dred Scott decision was sacrosanct, a holy pronouncement.

Douglas, in the course of his rebuttal, called immediate attention to the fact that Lincoln failed to respond to his questions, which he called "interrogatories." For his own part, Douglas shrugged away the charges that Lincoln had made with respect to what Douglas called "that nonsense about Stephen, and Franklin, and Roger, and Bob, and James." The conspiracy charges were hardly worth rebutting, said Douglas. It was all a mere political conceit by Lincoln, a ploy to call attention to himself:

> He studied that out, prepared that one sentence with the greatest care, committed it to memory, and put it in his first Springfield speech, and now he carries that speech around and reads that sentence to show how pretty it is. (Laughter.) His vanity is wounded because I will not go into that beautiful figure of his about the building of a house. (Renewed laughter.) All I have to say is, that I am not green enough to let him make a charge which he acknowledges he does not know to be true, and then take up my time in answering it, when I know it to be false and nobody else knows it to be true. . . . Let him prove it if he can.[87]

As to the insertion of "state" into the language of the Kansas-Nebraska Act, Douglas claimed that his intentions were innocuous: "Mr. Lincoln wants to know why the word 'state,' as well as 'territory,' was put into the Nebraska Bill! I will tell him. It was put there to meet just such false arguments as he had been adducing. (Laughter.) That first, not only the people of the territories should do as they pleased, but that when they come to be admitted as States, they should come into the Union with or without slavery, as the people determined. I meant to knock in the head this Abolition doctrine of Mr. Lincoln's, that there shall be no more slave States, even if the people want them. (Tremendous applause.)"[88]

In the aftermath of the Ottawa debate, Lincoln urgently sought the advice of his fellow Republicans. He met with Norman Judd and the members of the Republican State Central Committee. He met with Joseph Medill of the *Chicago Tribune*, who advised him to hit back at Douglas with embarrassing questions of his own.

He did so at Freeport, in northern Illinois, where some fifteen thousand people turned out for the second of the Lincoln-Douglas debates on August 27. Lincoln struck back at Douglas by proclaiming he would gladly "answer any of the interrogatories" Douglas had framed "upon condition that he will answer questions from me not exceeding the same number." Lincoln paused for the effects of one-upmanship: "I give him an opportunity to respond. The Judge remains silent. I now say to you that I will answer his interrogatories, whether he answers mine or not; [applause] and that after I have done so, I shall propound mine to him."[89]

Lincoln's answers took advantage of the way in which Douglas posed the questions: he had asked whether Lincoln at the time "stood pledged" to key Republican doctrines. One should bear this distinctly in mind in making sense of Lincoln's responses; the mere fact that he denied being "pledged" to certain goals *at the moment* meant nothing when it came to his possible actions in the *future*: it never stopped him from embracing the very same goals later on, when conditions had improved. Here are a few of his answers: "I do not now, nor ever did, stand pledged against the admission of any more slave States into the Union. . . . I do not stand to-day pledged to the abolition of slavery in the District of Columbia. . . . I do not stand pledged to the prohibition of the slave trade between the different States."[90]

One of his answers, however, was a pledge he meant everyone to hear: "I am impliedly, if not expressly, pledged to a belief in the *right* and *duty* of Congress to prohibit slavery in all the United States Territories. [Great applause]"[91]

He pointed out quickly that his answers to Douglas were deliberately legalistic: "Now my friends, it will be perceived upon an examination of these questions and answers, that so far I have only answered that I was not *pledged* to this, that or the other. The Judge has not framed his interrogatories to ask me anything more than this, and I have answered in strict accordance with the interrogatories. . . . But I am not disposed to hang upon the exact form of the interrogatory. I am rather disposed to take up at least some of these questions, and state what I really think upon them."[92]

Lincoln stated his belief that if Congress kept slavery from federal lands it was extremely unlikely the settlers there would write slave-state constitutions. Hence the issue of whether he was "pledged" to oppose the admission of any more slave states was probably moot if his policies prevailed.

Then he turned to his personal *wishes*. Even though he had never been "pledged" to abolishing slavery in Washington, D.C., he announced that he heartily endorsed the idea, with a few stipulations: "I should be exceedingly glad to see slavery abolished in the District of Columbia. [Cries of 'good, good.'] . . . Yet as a member of Congress, I should not with my present views, be in favor of *endeavoring* to abolish slavery in the District of Columbia, unless it would be upon these conditions. *First*, that the abolition should be gradual. *Second*, that it should be on a vote of the majority of qualified voters in the District, and *third*, that compensation should be made to unwilling owners."[93]

It should be noted that the very same principles Lincoln set forth in this speech for abolition in the nation's capital—gradual emancipation, with full compensation to the owners—were an embryonic version of the principles he sought to apply later on across the country.

Then Lincoln asked Douglas to respond to some questions of his own. "Can the people of a United States Territory, in any lawful way, against the wish of any citizen of the United States, exclude slavery from its limits prior to the formation of a State Constitution," he inquired. Then he asked a more painful question: "If the Supreme Court of the United States shall decide that States can not exclude slavery from their limits, are you in favor of acquiescing in, adopting and following such decision as a rule of political action?"[94]

Douglas answered these questions energetically. As Lincoln had heard him proclaim many times, he exclaimed, it was his settled opinion that "the people of a territory can, by lawful means, exclude slavery from their limits . . . for the reason that slavery cannot exist a day or an hour anywhere, unless it is supported by local police regulations." Hence "if the people are opposed to slavery they will elect representatives" to their territorial legislature "who will by unfriendly legislation effectually prevent the introduction of it in their midst."[95]

As to a Supreme Court decision overturning all the free-state constitutions, Douglas said, "I am amazed that Lincoln should ask such a
question. . . . He casts an imputation upon the Supreme Court of the
United States by supposing that they would violate the Constitution of
the United States. I tell him that such a thing is not possible. (Cheers.)
It would be an act of moral treason that no man on the bench would
ever descend to."[96]

Then Douglas reverted to his warnings about racial equality. "The
last time I came here to make a speech," he intoned, "while talking
from the stand to you, people of Freeport, as I am doing to-day, I saw
a carriage and a magnificent one it was, drive up and take a position
outside the crowd; a beautiful young lady was sitting on the box seat,
whilst Fred. Douglass and her mother reclined inside, and the owner
of the carriage acted as driver. (Laughter, cheers, cries of right, what
have you to say against it, &c.) I saw this in your own town. ('What of
it.') All I have to say of it is this, that if you, Black Republicans, think
that the negro ought to be on a social equality with your wives and
daughters, and ride in a carriage with your wife, whilst you drive the
team, you have a perfect right to do so."[97]

This was a Republican crowd, and Douglas knew it perfectly well.
He was baiting both Lincoln and the crowd not so much for its immediate effect as for its use later on in the campaign—so he could brag
about speaking in the very same language all over the state as he dished
out his bigoted opinions. He would strive to contrast his own forthright behavior with the difference in tone that he expected from Lincoln when the two of them went down to "Egypt."

In mid-September, the scene of the debates began to shift in
Douglas's favor: it shifted to the South. On September 15, the third
Lincoln-Douglas debate was held in Jonesboro, Illinois. Douglas used
the same anecdote that rattled the crowd at Freeport. But the reactions
in southern Illinois were very different.

"In the extreme northern counties," Douglas said, "they brought
out men to canvass the State whose complexion suited their political
creed, and hence Fred Douglass, the negro, was to be found there. . . .
Why, they brought Fred Douglass to Freeport when I was addressing a
meeting there in a carriage driven by the white owner, the negro sitting
inside with the white lady and her daughter. (Shame.) When I got through
canvassing the northern counties that year [1854] and progressed as far
south as Springfield, I was met and opposed in discussion by Lincoln,

Lovejoy, Trumbull, and Sidney Breese, who were on one side. (Laughter.) Father Giddings, the high priest of abolitionism, had just been there, and Chase came about the time I left. ('Why didn't you shoot him?') I did take a running shot at them, but as I was single-handed against the white, black and mixed drove, I had to use a short gun and fire into the crowd instead of taking them off singly with a rifle. (Great laughter and cheers.)"[98]

Douglas then presented all his standard declarations of white supremacy; he said that "I hold that a negro is not and never ought to be a citizen of the United States. (Good, good, and tremendous cheers.) . . . I do not believe that the Almighty made the negro capable of self-government."[99] As to the Declaration of Independence, "in my opinion the signers of the Declaration had no reference to the negro whatever when they declared all men to be created equal. They desired to express by that phrase, white men, men of European birth and European descent, and had no reference either to the negro, the savage Indians, the Fejee, the Malay, or any other inferior and degraded race. . . ."[100]

Lincoln decided not to rise to this bait "down in Egypt." Instead, he used folksy humor in an effort to change the subject—he sought to shift attention to himself. He made sport of his opponent's attempt to depict him as fearful of the voters in Egypt; Douglas let it be known that "I would not come to Egypt unless he forced me—that I could not be got down here, unless he, giant-like, had hauled me down here. [Laughter.] . . . Judge Douglas, when he made that statement must have been crazy, and wholly out of his sober senses, or else he would have known that when he got me down here—that promise—that windy promise—of his powers to annihilate me, wouldn't amount to anything. Now, how little do I look like being carried away trembling? . . . Did the Judge talk of trotting me down to Egypt to scare me to death? Why, I know this people better than he does. I was raised just a little east of here. I am a part of this people. But the Judge was raised further north, and perhaps he has some horrid idea of what this people might be induced to do. [Roars of laughter and cheers.]"[101]

Lincoln avoided the subject of race as he launched new attacks against Douglas's positions, especially the doctrine that settlers could stop the spread of slavery in federal lands by "unfriendly" legislation. Lincoln said the proposition "that slavery cannot enter a new country without police regulations is historically false." How else could one account for the fact that Dred Scott had been taken into lands that were forbidden to slavery?

Besides, said Lincoln, if the views of Roger Taney set the tone for interpreting the Constitution, consider the effect this would have upon the territorial legislatures: "I will ask you my friends, if you were elected members of the Legislature, what would be the first thing you would have to do before entering upon your duties? *Swear to support the Constitution of the United States. . . .* How could you, having sworn to support the Constitution, and believing it guaranteed the right to hold slaves in the Territories, assist in legislation *intended to defeat that right?* . . . Not only so, but if you were to do so, how long would it take the courts to hold your votes unconstitutional and void? Not a moment."[102]

So far so good: notwithstanding the race-baiting tactics of Douglas, the Jonesboro clash was bereft of any lurid confrontations on the racial issue. But Douglas kept taunting both Lincoln and his fellow Republicans to get a rise on the subject. He told the crowd that Lincoln's "party in the northern part of the State hold to that abolition platform, and . . . if they do not in the south and in the centre they present the extraordinary spectacle of a house divided against itself. . . ."[103]

Douglas said the very same thing in his next debate with Lincoln on September 18, in Charleston, central Illinois. Douglas charged that the Republicans deliberately altered their rhetoric and principles in different parts of the state: "Their principles in the North are jet black, (laughter), in the centre they are in color a decent mulatto, (renewed laughter), and in lower Egypt they are almost white. (Shouts of laughter.)"[104]

Lincoln countered Douglas with a strong outpouring of ridicule. He began by restating his racial formulations from their very first debate in Ottawa. He challenged "every fair-minded man" to read his printed speeches from the Ottawa and Freeport debates and then compare them to what he said in Charleston that very day: "*I dare him to point out any difference between my printed speeches north and south.*"[105]

But there *were* great differences in *tone* between his "speeches north and south." The great plea in Chicago for cessation of racial animosities, the plea to discard racial consciousness entirely and stop the incessant "quibbling about this man and the other man—this race and that race and the other race being inferior," could not be used among voters in southern or central Illinois if Lincoln wanted to drive Stephen Douglas from office in 1858.

Politics had forced the racial issue on Lincoln. And there were limits to the number of times he could get away with changing the subject.
So Lincoln seized upon the issue in the Charleston debate and turned
it back upon Douglas in a manner that he hoped would make his enemy look like a fool.

Once again, he took aim at the phobia of racial intermarriage, and
he treated it in ways that made his audience laugh it off. He observed
that racial intermarriage was illegal in the state of Illinois. Even so, "I
have never had the least apprehension," he said, "that I or my friends
would marry negroes if there was no law to keep them from it."

But Judge Douglas kept bringing up the issue. Very well: since it
seemed to preoccupy the mind of Stephen Douglas, it would probably
be best if he retired from the Senate to devote his full energies to su-
pervising Illinois mores. "I do not understand [that] there is any place
where an alteration of the social and political relations of the negro
and the white man can be made except in the State Legislature," Lincoln said, and most certainly "not in the Congress of the United States."
Inasmuch "as Judge Douglas seems to be in constant horror that some
such danger is rapidly approaching, I propose as the best means to
prevent it that the Judge be kept at home and placed in the State Legislature to fight the measure. [Uproarious laughter and applause.] I do
not propose dwelling any longer at this time on the subject."[106]

Douglas, of course, chose to dwell upon the subject continually. His
speeches in the Charleston debate contained the regular nasty fare:
snide quips about Frederick Douglass in the coach at Freeport, warnings about the insidious measures that whites could expect the Republicans to foist upon the people, and allusions to the interest that "the
colored brethren felt in the success of their brother Abe."[107]

On October 7, the debates between Lincoln and Douglas moved
north to the city of Galesburg. Douglas was slightly more civil. He
asked the audience to think about the dire implications if a Lincoln-
type "House Divided" doctrine had prevailed at the founding of the
nation: "When this government was made," he said, "there were twelve
slaveholding States and one free State in this Union. . . . Suppose Mr.
Lincoln himself had been a member of the convention which framed
the constitution, and that he had risen in that august body, and addressing the father of his country, had said as he did at Springfield: A
house divided against itself cannot stand. . . ." If the issue had been
forced at the Constitutional Convention, said Douglas, the "House

Divided" doctrine would have caused the twelve slave states to over-whelm the isolated free state:

> Would not the twelve slaveholding States have outvoted the one free State, and under his doctrine have fastened slavery by an irrevocable constitutional provision upon every inch of the American Republic? Thus you see that the doctrine he now advocates, if proclaimed at the beginning of the government, would have established slavery everywhere throughout the American continent, and are you willing, now that we have the majority section, to exercise a power which we never would have submitted to when we were in the minority?[108]

This was clever, said Lincoln, but the tricks of Stephen Douglas all flowed from his stark amorality. For he would never say that slavery was *wrong*.

And that was the difference, not only in the choice between Lincoln and Douglas but also in the choice between their two parties: "Everything that emanates from him or his coadjutors in their course of policy, carefully excludes the thought that there is anything wrong with Slavery," Lincoln pointed out.[109]

And that was the reason why the Dred Scott decision, if accepted as the binding law of the land, was positioning the South to export its great evil to the North:

> The essence of the Dred Scott case is compressed into the sentence which I will now read . . . "The right of property in a slave is distinctly and expressly affirmed in the Constitution!" What is it to be "affirmed" in the Constitution? Made firm in the Constitution—so made that it cannot be separated from the Constitution without breaking the Constitution—durable as the Constitution, and part of the Constitution. Now, remembering the provision of the Constitution which I have read, affirming that the instrument is the supreme law of the land; that the Judges of every State shall be bound by it, any law or Constitution of any State to the contrary notwithstanding; that the right of property in a slave is affirmed in that Constitution, is made, formed into and cannot be separated from it without breaking it; durable as the instrument; part of the instrument;—what follows . . . ?[110]

What followed was the overthrow of Northern institutions, just as soon as the electorate was ready.

Stephen Douglas was working night and day to prepare Northern public opinion. He told the Northern public not to *care* about blacks and that reducing a slave to the status of a beast of the field was in no way morally *wrong*. He told them that any community of whites who wished to have the institution of slavery should certainly have it. He told them to obey the decisions of Taney and his court without worrying about the *rightness* of such decisions.

Douglas's adherence to the Dred Scott decision, said Lincoln, "commits him to the next decision, whenever it comes, as being as obligatory as this one, since he . . . won't inquire whether this opinion is right or wrong. So he takes the next one without inquiring whether *it* is right or wrong. [Applause.] He teaches men this doctrine, and in so doing prepares the public mind to take the next decision when it comes, without any inquiry."[111]

Perhaps, said Lincoln, this was not what Stephen Douglas intended, but "I call upon your minds to inquire, if you were going to get the best instrument you could, and then set it to work in the most ingenious way, to prepare the public mind for this movement, operating in the free States, where there is now an abhorrence of the institution of Slavery, could you find an instrument so capable of doing it as Judge Douglas? or one employed in so apt a way to do it? [Great cheering. Cries of 'Hit him again,' 'That's the doctrine.']"[112]

The campaign was drawing to an end. On October 13, the penultimate debate occurred in Quincy, a town in the south-central portion of the state. Douglas challenged Lincoln to present a good Republican way in which America's people could unite along *peaceful* lines. Precisely *how*, he asked, would Lincoln put slavery on course for an ultimate extinction in the states that already permitted it? "How can he extinguish it in Kentucky, in Virginia, in all the slave States by his policy, if he will not pursue a policy which will interfere with it in the States where it exists?"[113]

This was a very good question, but Lincoln passed over it in silence. Furthermore, asked Douglas, how did Lincoln envision overturning the Dred Scott decision? "By what tribunal will he reverse it? Will he

Abraham Lincoln as he looked a few weeks before his final debate with Stephen Douglas in 1858. Photograph by Calvin Jackson. (Library of Congress, Meserve Collection #12)

appeal to a mob? Does he intend to appeal to violence, to Lynch law? Will he stir up strife and rebellion in the land and overthrow the Court by violence?"[114]

Lincoln was fomenting war between the states, Douglas said, and the voters should prevent him from succeeding in his plans. "Let each State mind its own business and let its neighbors alone, and there will be no trouble on this question. If we will stand by that principle, then Mr. Lincoln will find that this republic can exist forever divided into free and slave States. . . ."[115]

Lincoln replied: "I wish to return Judge Douglas my profound thanks for his public annunciation here to-day, to be put on record, that his system of policy in regard to the institution of slavery *contemplates that it shall last forever*. [Great cheers, and cries of 'Hit him again.']"[116]

As to reversing the Dred Scott decision, Lincoln ridiculed Douglas by reminding him of all the many times in the past when he had overturned decisions of the courts: "He is desirous of knowing how we are going to reverse the Dred Scott decision. Judge Douglas ought to know how. Did not he and his political friends find a way to reverse the decision of that same Court in favor of the constitutionality of the National Bank? [Cheers and laughter.] . . . And let me ask you, didn't Judge Douglas find a way to reverse the decision of our [Illinois] Supreme Court, when it decided that Carlin's old father—old Governor Carlin—had not the constitutional power to remove a Secretary of State? [Great cheering and laughter.] Did he not appeal to the 'MOBS' as he calls them? Did he not make speeches in the lobby to show how villainous that decision was, and how it ought to be overthrown? Did he not succeed too in getting an act passed by the Legislature to have it overthrown? And didn't he himself sit down on the bench as one of the five added judges, who were to overslaugh the four old ones—getting his name of 'Judge' in that way and no other? [Thundering cheers and laughter.]"[117]

In the final debate held in Alton, Illinois, down in "Egypt"—the very same place in which Elijah Lovejoy had been murdered almost twenty years earlier—Lincoln decried the Democrats' tendency to "dehumanize the negro—to take away from him the right of ever striving to be a man. I combat it as being one of the thousand things constantly done in these days to prepare the public mind to make property, and nothing but property of the *negro in all the States of this Union*."[118]

Lincoln was confident of victory, so long as the Illinois Democrats refrained from any frauds or hoaxes at the polls.[119] The Illinois electorate voted on November 7. Lincoln's candidates for the legislature got approximately 125,000 votes to 121,000 for the candidates pledged to Douglas.[120]

But that was not enough. Because Douglas had carried more *counties* statewide, the Democratic Party retained its existing control of the legislature.[121] The reelection of Stephen Douglas was thereby assured.

Lincoln's supporters were distraught. And Lincoln was depressed, but he tried to view the matter philosophically. "I am glad that I made the late race," he told supporters on a wistful note. "It gave me a hearing on the great and durable question of the age, which I could have had in no other way; and though I now sink out of view, and shall be forgotten, I believe that I have made some marks which will tell for the cause of liberty long after I am gone."[122]

His spirits would revive soon enough. To one supporter he wrote: "I hope and believe that the seed has been sown that will yet produce fruit. . . . Douglas managed to be supported both as the best means to *break down* and to *uphold* the slave power. No ingenuity can long keep those opposing elements in harmony. Another explosion will come before a great while."[123]

In fact, the Kansas-Nebraska and Dred Scott issues had inflicted great damage on the presidential prospects of Douglas. And the 1858 debates would make the name of Lincoln better known far beyond Illinois. His speeches were eventually reprinted all over the country in books and political pamphlets.

To another supporter he imparted an impish consolation: "I believe . . . [that] you are 'feeling like h—ll yet.' Quit that. You will soon feel better. Another 'blow-up' is coming; and we shall have fun again."[124]

But it was something very different that Lincoln and his followers would have when the blowup occurred. They would have a great war between the states, just as Douglas, perverse and bombastic though he was, had predicted so forcefully to Lincoln.

And with war, Lincoln gradually learned something new about his talents as a strategist. He knew better than most of his generals the way to destroy the power of the South. And this would lead to the destruction of the slavery system much faster than he ever thought possible—if he won.

THREE

Lincoln and Slavery: Containment, 1859–1861

Lincoln captured the White House in spite of his defeat for a Senate seat in 1858. And his politics quickly unleashed a secessionist movement in the South.

American politics were nothing short of explosive in 1860. For if Republicans won a clean sweep—if they managed to secure the White House and take control of Congress as well—the slave-holding interest would be jeopardized.

The expansion of slavery was halted in Kansas by the U.S. House of Representatives in 1858. The free-state majority was growing, and the Northern population was surpassing the Southern by a greater margin every year. Republican strategists determined early on that if they could take just the *Northern* states that had been lost to Buchanan in 1856, they would win the presidential election of 1860 decisively.

The power of the presidency had been vested since 1852 in the hands of pro-slavery leaders who endeavored to "save the Union" by appeasing slave-holding interest. As late as 1859, Buchanan's party was still continuing its near-relentless push for the expansion of slavery. He had reopened the issue of Cuban annexation and had attempted to bribe the government of Spain into acquiescence.[1] Meanwhile, pro-slavery leaders created a brand-new lobbying group to force repeal of the old Jeffersonian-era prohibition on the importation of slaves from Africa. The new "African Labor Supply Organization" was launched in 1859.[2]

In the early months of that year, some Republican friends began suggesting to Lincoln that he think about a race for the White House.

At first, Lincoln dismissed the presidential possibility. After all, some impressive Republicans of national stature had already assembled in the wings for the 1860 nomination struggle: Salmon P. Chase of Ohio, for example, and William H. Seward of New York. Both of them had been leaders of the Free-Soil movement for a great many years before Lincoln was known by voters beyond Illinois.

And the prominence of Seward had increased dramatically. In the very same year that Lincoln's "House Divided" speech had gained national attention, Seward made a similar and widely publicized speech about America's "irrepressible conflict" over slavery.

Yet before long, Lincoln took a fresh view of his political future. He began to imagine himself as an *executive* leader instead of a mere parliamentary figure. As historian Don E. Fehrenbacher has observed, "a change gradually came over Lincoln in 1859; this was his year of self-discovery."[3]

Lincoln kept criticizing Stephen Douglas in a way that made the latter's presidential ambitions an occasion for advancing his own. Fehrenbacher has argued that throughout the 1850s Douglas was "unquestionably . . . the most vibrant and controversial public figure of his time." Accordingly, "Lincoln achieved prominence without election to office by making a career of opposing the famous Little Giant. His speeches throughout [the 1850s] constituted one long running rebuttal to what Douglas said and what Douglas did. And when the latter was compelled in 1858 to acknowledge him formally as a rival, Lincoln at last began to acquire a national reputation. Indeed, it is no great exaggeration to say that Douglas for a number of years was unwittingly engaged in clearing Lincoln's path to the White House."[4]

By 1859, Douglas's political position was increasingly fragile. His attempts to reinvigorate his doctrine of Popular Sovereignty caused trouble for his presidential chances in the South. In the eyes of a significant number of Southerners, Douglas was far too entangled with the Free-Soil movement. His resistance to Buchanan's Lecompton policy had impeded the accession of Kansas as a slave state.

And his attempt to assure his constituents that settlers could halt the spread of slavery by means of "unfriendly" territorial laws prompted several pro-slavery leaders to demand the enactment of a territorial slave code—a code to be created by Congress and enforced by the federal government. But Douglas's stated philosophy of federal non-interference with slavery in federal territories made such a code an impossible pill for him to swallow.

In December 1858, Lincoln wrote to a political ally, Senator Lyman Trumbull of Illinois, in regard to Douglas's predicament, along with its flip-side threat to the Republicans. If Douglas, whom Lincoln regarded as the South's greatest hope, were ironically rejected by an overwrought South, he could still win the White House with Northern electoral votes by seducing the Republican Party. "Since you left," Lincoln wrote, "Douglas has gone South, making characteristic speeches, and seeking to re-instate himself in that section. The majority of the democratic politicians of the nation mean to kill him; but I doubt whether they will adopt the aptest way to do it."

Lincoln said that the best course of action for the Democratic enemies of Douglas would be "to present him with no new test, let him into the Charleston Convention [in 1860], and then outvote him, and nominate another. In that case, he will have no pretext for bolting the nomination, and will be as powerless as they can wish. On the other hand, if they push a Slave code upon him, as a test, he will bolt at once, turn upon us, as in the case of Lecompton, and claim that all Northern men shall make common cause in electing him President as the best means of breaking down the Slave power. In that case, the democratic party go into a minority inevitably; and the struggle in the whole North will be, as it was in Illinois last summer and fall, whether the Republican party can maintain its identity, or be broken up to form the tail of Douglas's new kite."[5]

In 1859, Lincoln sent out warnings to his fellow Republicans—warnings of the trickery of Douglas. If Republicans were ever seduced by the "Little Giant," Lincoln said, the Republican Party would be ruined and its cause would be set back, perhaps for a whole generation. On March 1, 1859, Lincoln told a Republican rally in Chicago that "if we, the Republicans of this State, had made Judge Douglas our candidate for the Senate of the United States last year and had elected him, there would to-day be no Republican Party in this Union." While the "principles around which we have rallied and organized would live" and "reproduce" in "another party in the future . . . in the meantime all the labor that has been done to build up the present Republican party would be entirely lost, and perhaps twenty years of time" would elapse "before we would again have formed around that principle" of containing slavery.[6]

In April, he wrote to the organizers of a Jefferson birthday celebration in Boston and warned that the great Jeffersonian maxims of liberty were slowly succumbing to the kinds of politicians who were really "the van-guard—the miners, and sappers—of returning despotism."

"It is now no child's play to save the principles of Jefferson from total overthrow in this nation," Lincoln wrote. "They are denied, and evaded, with no small show of success. One dashingly calls them 'glittering generalities'; another bluntly calls them 'self-evident lies'; and still others insidiously argue that they apply only to 'superior races.'" But since "this is a world of compensations," Lincoln argued, "he who would *be* no slave, must consent to *have* no slave. Those who deny freedom to others, deserve it not for themselves; and, under a just God, can not long retain it. All honor to Jefferson—to the man who . . . had the coolness, forecast, and capacity to introduce into a merely revolutionary document, an abstract truth, and so to embalm it there, that to-day, and in all coming days, it shall be a rebuke and a stumbling block to the very harbingers of re-appearing tyrany [*sic*] and oppression."[7]

In July, he warned Schuyler Colfax, a Republican Congressman from Ohio, that there were "three substantial objections" to Republican dalliance with Douglas and Popular Sovereignty: "First, no party can command respect which sustains this year, what it opposed last. Second, Douglas, (who is the most dangerous enemy of liberty, because the most insidious one) would have little support in the North, and by consequence, no capital to trade on in the South, if it were not for our friends thus magnifying him and his humbug. But lastly, and chiefly, Douglas's popular sovereignty, accepted by the public mind, as a just principle, nationalizes slavery, and revives the African Slave-trade, inevitably. . . ." After all, Lincoln reasoned, "taking slaves into new territories, and buying slaves in Africa, are identical things—identical *rights* or identical *wrongs*—and the argument which establishes one will establish the other. Try a thousand years for a sound reason why congress shall not hinder the people of Kansas from having slaves, and when you have found it, it will be an equally good one why congress should not hinder the people of Georgia from importing slaves from Africa."[8]

As Lincoln strove to counteract Republican apostasy, he also warned Republicans to limit themselves to the doctrine of slavery containment and avoid the more divisive proposals and platforms on the subject of slavery. Divisions over issues like repeal of the Fugitive Slave Law,

Lincoln said, could "explode" the Republican Party and play into the hands of the Democrats. In July, he told Schuyler Colfax that "the point of danger is the temptation in different localities to 'platform' there for something which will be popular just there, but which, nevertheless, will be a firebrand elsewhere, and especially in a National convention."[9]

Above all, the free-soil principle had to be championed. In a letter that he wrote to Republican Senator Thomas Corwin of Ohio on October 9, 1859—a long-lost letter that was purchased by a manuscript dealer in 2004—Lincoln stated that Republicans "must have . . . a man who recognizes that Slavery issue as being the living issue of the day; who does not hesitate to declare slavery a wrong, nor to deal with it as such; who believes in the power, and duty of Congress to prevent the spread of it."[10]

In all of these speeches and letters, which so shrewdly analyzed the political calculus on a national scale, Lincoln sought to advise the Republicans in ways that implicitly suggested his fitness to *lead* the Republican Party. As Fehrenbacher has observed, by the autumn of 1859, Lincoln "was fast becoming, without acknowledging it, a presidential candidate in earnest."[11]

As a candidate, he familiarized himself with the electoral college and its crucial arithmetic for presidential victory in 1860. Republicans would have to win all or most of the lower Northern states that were lost to Buchanan in 1856 if they meant to win the presidency. This included Lincoln's own state of Illinois. Whomever the Republicans should nominate in 1860 would have to be "centrist" enough to attract the swing votes in all of the lower Northern border states.

Lincoln began a series of speaking engagements in the middle of August 1859. The tour was designed to show Republicans that Lincoln—a favorite son of the swing-state Illinois—had the qualities the party would need to win the White House. A charismatic leader for the principles of free soil, he nonetheless appeared to be "moderate" compared to both Seward and Chase. Moreover, he had out-polled Douglas in the 1858 senatorial race, notwithstanding the latter's reelection by a state legislature dominated by his party.

In preliminary notes for some mid-September speeches, Lincoln set forth the themes that he intended to develop in his swing through the border-state cities north of the Ohio River. The most fundamental theme was the danger of Douglas's white supremacist appeal.

If Douglas convinced Northern whites to view blacks as subhuman, said Lincoln, it was only a matter of time before the South would try to use the doctrine of Popular Sovereignty to overturn the free-state system in the North. Lincoln cited recent statements by Douglas that appeared to classify blacks as a different species. "At Memphis," Lincoln wrote, "Douglas told his audience that he was for the negro against the crocodile, but for the white man against the negro. This was not a sudden thought spontaneously thrown off at Memphis. He said the same thing many times in Illinois last summer and autumn, though I am not sure it was reported then. It is a carefully framed illustration of the estimate he places on the negro and the manner in which he would have him dealt with. It is a sort of proposition in proportion. '*As* the negro is to the crocodile, *so* the white man is to the negro.' As the negro ought to treat the crocodile as a beast, so the white man ought to treat the negro as a beast."[12]

The corollary to this crude suggestion of black inhumanity was simple. It was the proposition that the legal status of blacks should be determined by majority votes of all the whites in every territory or state. This, said Lincoln—in phonetic imitation of his rival's bombastic manner—was the substance of that "gur-reat pur-rinciple" that Douglas called Popular Sovereignty.[13]

Republicans should never succumb to such poison, Lincoln warned: "Republicans believe that slavery is wrong," he said, "and they insist, and will continue to insist upon a national policy which recognizes it, and deals with it, *as a wrong*. There *can* be no letting down about this."[14]

As the Illinois Republicans had warded off Douglas in 1858 by nominating Lincoln, the fight should be extended, Lincoln said. Though "Douglas is back in the Senate in spite of us," Lincoln observed, "we are *clear* of *him*, and *his* principles; and, we are uncrippled and ready to fight both him and them straight along till they shall finally be 'closed out.' Had we followed the advice [of people like Seward and Greeley, who had urged Illinois Republicans to re-elect Douglas] there would now be no Republican party in Illinois, and none, to speak of, anywhere else. The whole thing would now be floundering along after Douglas, upon the Dred Scott and crocodile theory. It would have been the grandest '*haul*' for slavery, ever yet made."[15]

The Republicans' duties were clear, Lincoln wrote: "We must, by a national policy, prevent the spread of slavery into new territories, or free states, because the constitution does not forbid us, and the general welfare does demand such prevention. We must prevent the revival of the African slave trade, because the constitution does not forbid us, and the general welfare does require the prevention. We must prevent these things being done by either *congresses* or *courts*. The people—the people—are the rightful masters of both congresses, and courts—not to overthrow the constitution, but to overthrow the *men* who pervert it."[16]

Lincoln's opening speech in the campaign was an address he had delivered in August on a trip to Council Bluffs, Iowa. Only newspaper summaries of this speech survive. But the speech that Lincoln gave on September 16, in Columbus, Ohio, was reported verbatim.

He began with a statement designed to show his "moderate" credentials in the swing states. The "chief and real purpose of the Republican party," Lincoln asserted, "is eminently conservative. It proposes nothing save and except to restore this government to its original tone in regard to this element of slavery," in other words to roll back the drive for the expansion of slavery and bring back a policy that looked to its termination.[17]

But then, Lincoln's "moderate" stance gave way to a manner very close to his 1858 fervor. Lincoln warned that the schemers pushing slavery expansion were active. While their endgame strategy was still in abeyance, their short-term tactics were as stealthy as they were effective. "The chief danger to this purpose of the Republican party," Lincoln said, "is not just now the revival of the African slave trade, or the passage of a Congressional slave code, or the declaring of a second Dred Scott decision, making slavery lawful in all the States. These are not pressing us just now. . . . The authors of these measures know that we are too strong for them; but they will be upon us in due time, and we will be grappling with them hand to hand, if they are not now headed off. They are not now the chief danger to the purpose of the Republican organization; but the most imminent danger that now threatens that purpose is that insidious Douglas Popular Sovereignty."[18]

Lincoln turned his attention to an article that Douglas had written, a piece that was hot off the press in the September 1859 issue of *Harper's Magazine*. It provided the occasion for Douglas to revise his claims about Popular Sovereignty.[19]

While playing down the issue as much as he could, Douglas modified his earlier boasts that under Popular Sovereignty the legislatures of the territories could bar the institution of slavery by means of "unfriendly legislation." Instead, Douglas limited himself to the assertion that territories could *control* the institution of slavery as regulated property.

Lincoln ridiculed this article in several ways. He began by stating that its author "has had a good deal of trouble with his popular sovereignty. His explanations explanatory of explanations explained are interminable. [Laughter]"[20]

After paraphrasing Douglas's claims about the Founding Fathers, Lincoln asked how Douglas could possibly ignore what the anti-slavery Founders had accomplished in the Northwest Ordinance of 1787, which successfully stopped the institution of slavery from spreading right into Ohio and the states next door. "Under that ordinance we live," Lincoln argued. "First here in Ohio you were a territory, then an enabling act was passed authorizing you to form a constitution and State government, provided it was . . . not in conflict with the ordinance of '87."

Lincoln pointed out that "the Constitution of the United States was in process of being framed when that ordinance was made by the Congress of the Confederation; and one of the first acts of Congress itself under the new Constitution itself was to give force to that ordinance by putting power to carry it out into the hands of the new officers under the Constitution." Lincoln then observed that "Indiana once or twice, if not Ohio, petitioned the general government for the privilege of suspending that provision and allowing them to have slaves. A report made by Mr. Randolph [Edmund J. Randolph] of Virginia, himself a slaveholder, was directly against it, and the action was to refuse them the privilege of violating the ordinance of '87."[21]

Having demonstrated the degree of anti-slavery feelings among the Founders, Lincoln turned to the counter-revolution that Roger Taney and his fellow pro-slavery schemers were trying to initiate.

"The Dred Scott decision expressly gives every citizen of the United States a right to carry his slaves into the United States' Territories," Lincoln said, reiterating his critique of the Scott ruling.[22]

Yet Douglas kept claiming that a territorial legislature could fulfill the wishes of an anti-slavery majority. This was nonsense, Lincoln contended: "When all the trash, the words, the collateral matter was cleared away from it; all the chaff was fanned out of it," Douglas's claim was "a bare absurdity—*no less than a thing may be lawfully driven away from where it has a lawful right to be.* [Cheers and laughter.] Clear away all the verbiage, and that is the naked truth of his proposition."[23]

Observe, Lincoln said, that the nimble Douglas "does not say any longer that the people [can] exclude slavery. . . . What he says now is different in language, and we will consider whether it is not different in sense too. It is now that the Dred Scott decision, or rather the Constitution under that decision, does not carry slavery into the Territories beyond the power of the people in the territories *to control it as other property*."[24] Lincoln made sport of this language with a lengthy barnyard analogy:

> Driving a horse out of this lot, is too plain a proposition to be mistaken about; it is putting him on the other side of the fence. [Laughter] Or it might be a sort of exclusion of him from the lot if you were to kill him and let the worms devour him; but neither of these things is the same as "controlling him as other property." That would be to feed him, pamper him, to ride him, to use and abuse him, to make the most money out of him "as other property"; but, please you, what do the men who are in favor of slavery want more than this? [Laughter and applause] . . . I know the Judge sometimes squints at the argument that in controlling [slavery] as other property by unfriendly legislation they may control it to death, as you might in the case of a horse, perhaps, feed him so lightly and ride him so much that he would die. [Cheers and laughter] . . . But I undertake to give the opinion, at least, that if the territories attempt by any direct legislation to drive the man with his slave out of the territory, or to decide that his slave is free because of his being taken in there, or to tax him to such an extent that he cannot keep him there, the Supreme Court will unhesitatingly decide all such legislation unconstitutional, as long as that Supreme Court is constructed as the Dred Scott Supreme Court is.[25]

But such issues were *secondary*, argued Lincoln, to the ugly contention of Douglas that the fate of black slaves should be regarded by whites as a matter of very little importance. He warned that "if this principle is established, that there is no wrong in slavery, and whoever wants it has a right to have it, is a matter of dollars and cents, a sort of question as to how they shall deal with brutes, that between us and the negro here there is no sort of question, but that at the South the question is between the negro and the crocodile. . . . where this doctrine prevails, the miners and sappers will have formed public opinion for the slave trade. They will be ready for Jeff. Davis and Stephens and other leaders of that company, to sound the bugle for the revival of the slave trade, for the second Dred Scott decision, for the flood of slavery to be poured over the free States, while we shall be here tied down and helpless and run over like sheep."[26]

Just look at the erosion, said Lincoln, in the state of Northern public opinion since the Kansas-Nebraska Act and the launching of

Douglas's quest for the presidency: "Did you ever five years ago, hear of anybody in the world saying that the negro had no share in the Declaration of National Independence; that it did not mean negroes at all; and when 'all men' were spoken of negroes were not included? . . . I have been unable at any time to find a man in an audience who would declare that he had ever known any body saying so five years ago. But last year there was not a Douglas popular sovereign in Illinois who did not say it."[27]

How far, asked Lincoln, had this sinister change in opinion proceeded in Ohio? Surely many a man in Ohio "declares his firm belief that the Declaration of Independence did not mean negroes at all," said Lincoln, but how many of them had believed such a thing only five years earlier? Something fundamental had changed. "If you think that now," he observed, "and did not think it then, the next thing that strikes me is to remark that there has been a *change* wrought in you (laughter and applause), and a very significant change it was, being no less than changing the negro, in your estimation, from the rank of a man to that of a brute. They are taking him down, and placing him, when spoken of, among reptiles and crocodiles, as Judge Douglas himself expresses it. . . . I ask you to note that fact, and the like of which is to follow, to be plastered on, layer after layer, until very soon you are prepared to deal with the negro everywhere as with the brute. If public sentiment has not been debauched already to this point, a new turn of the screw in that direction is all that is wanting; and this is constantly being done by the teachers of this insidious popular sovereignty."[28]

On the very next day after giving this speech in Columbus, Lincoln gave another speech in Cincinnati. "I should not wonder," Lincoln ventured to say, "that there are some Kentuckians about this audience; we are close to Kentucky; and . . . we are on elevated ground, and by speaking distinctly, I should not wonder if some of the Kentuckians would hear me on the other side of the river. [Laughter.]"[29]

He told the residents of slave-state Kentucky that they ought to view Douglas as their perfect presidential candidate. Regardless of Southern discontent with some of the positions that Douglas had taken, Lincoln told the Kentuckians to look at the larger picture: "he is as sincerely for you, and more wisely for you, than you are for yourselves." He followed up with pointed questions: "What do you want more than anything else to make successful your views on Slavery, to advance the outspread of it, and to secure and perpetuate the nationality of it? . . .

What is indispensable to you? Why! if I may be allowed to answer the question, it is to retain a hold upon the North—it is to retain support and strength from the Free States. If you can get this support and strength from the Free States, you can succeed. If you do not get this support and strength from the Free States, you are in the minority, and you are beaten at once."[30]

Lincoln told the Kentuckians that Douglas was their very best advocate because he was *sneaky*: "I lay down the proposition that Douglas is not only the man that promises you in advance a hold upon the North, and support in the North, but that he constantly moulds public opinion to your ends . . . and if there are a few things in which he seems to be against you—a few things which he says that appear to be against you, and a few that he forbears to say which you would like to have him say—you ought to remember that the saying of the one, or the forbearing to say the other, would loose his hold upon the North, and, by consequence, would lose his capacity to serve you. (A Voice, 'That is so.')"[31]

For example, Douglas refused to state clearly his belief about the rightness or wrongness of slavery. Many Southerners were angered by this, and they demanded that Douglas endorse "the Southern way of life."

But he served Southern interests far better, said Lincoln, by evading and dodging the issue: "Upon this subject of moulding public opinion, I call your attention to the fact . . . that the Judge never says your institution of Slavery is wrong; he never says it is right, to be sure, but he never says it is wrong. [Laughter] . . . He leaves himself at perfect liberty to do all in your favor which he would be hindered from doing if he were to declare the thing to be wrong. . . . This you ought to set down to his credit. [Laughter.] . . . He said upon the floor of the United States Senate . . . that he does not care whether Slavery is 'voted up or voted down.' This again shows you, or ought to show you, if you would reason upon it, that he does not believe it to be wrong, for . . . no man can logically say that he cares not whether a thing goes up or goes down, which to him appears to be wrong. You therefore have a demonstration in this, that to Douglas' mind your favorite institution which you would have spread out, and made perpetual, is no wrong."[32]

Lincoln finally abandoned this tone and spoke directly to the men of Ohio, but not without a final sally at his absent but handy Kentuckians. He advised them about their own prospects in resisting the

Free-Soil movement. "You will surely be beaten," he said, "if you do not take him [Douglas]. We, the Republicans and others forming the Opposition of this country, intend to 'stand by our guns,' to be patient and firm, and in the long run to beat you whether you take him or not. [Applause.] We know that before we fairly beat you, we have to beat you both together. We know that you are 'all of a feather,' [loud applause,] and that we have to beat you altogether, and we expect to do it. [Applause.]"[33]

Yet Lincoln was careful to qualify the taunts with some assurances of fair treatment. "When we do as we say, beat you," he told the Kentuckians, "you perhaps want to know what we will do with you. [Laughter] . . . We mean to treat you as near as we possibly can, like Washington, Jefferson and Madison treated you. [Cheers] We mean to leave you alone, and in no way to interfere with your institution; to abide by all and every compromise of the constitution. . . . We mean to recognize and bear in mind that you have as good hearts in your bosoms as other people. . . ."[34]

But if Northern magnanimity were not reciprocated by the South— if Southern militants attempted to break up the Union if the Free-Soil movement prevailed—then the South would be totally defeated. "I have told you what we mean to do," Lincoln said, and "I want to know, now, when that thing takes place, what you mean to do. I often hear it intimated that you mean to divide the Union whenever a Republican, or anything like it, is elected President of the United States. [A voice, 'That is so.'] 'That is so,' one of them says. I wonder if he is a Kentuckian? [A voice, 'He is a Douglas man.'] Well, then, I want to know what you are going to do with your half of it? [Applause and laughter] Are you going to split the Ohio down through, and push your half off a piece? Or are you going to keep it right alongside of us outrageous fellows? Or are you going to build up a wall some way between your country and ours, by which that movable property of yours can't come over here any more, to the danger of your losing it?"

Lincoln said that if the Union was successfully divided, and the people of the North "cease to be under obligations to do anything for you, how much better off do you think you will be? Will you make war upon us and kill us all? Why, gentlemen, I think you are as gallant and as brave men as live . . . but, man for man, you are not better than we are, and there are not so many of you as there are of us. [Loud cheering.]"[35] It bears noting, of course, that Lincoln continued to regard the secession talk at this point as essentially bluff.

Two days after his Cincinnati speech, Lincoln went to Indiana to address a crowd in Indianapolis. Then he traveled to Milwaukee to address the Wisconsin State Agricultural Society. He talked about the virtues of the free labor system: "the just and generous, and prosperous system, which opens the way for all."[36]

Just after he gave these speeches, some electrifying news arrived: on October 16, John Brown and his supporters seized the federal arsenal at Harpers Ferry, Virginia, in a bid to initiate a full-scale slave revolt. After Brown was arrested and tried for treason, all over the South arose a chorus of militant voices condemning "Black Republicans" and warning that the Union would break if the voters elected a Republican president in 1860.

Lincoln answered these threats in December, when he traveled to Kansas. He made this pilgrimage to praise the Free-Soilers and to celebrate the imminent admission of Kansas to statehood. At Leavenworth, he aimed some remarks at Southern militants, much as he had done in Cincinnati when he talked to pro-slavery Kentuckians *in absentia*. He spoke of their threats to dissolve the Union: "Your own statement of it is, that if the Black Republicans elect a President, you won't stand it. You will break up the Union. That will be your act, not ours. . . ."[37]

He bade Southern militants reflect upon the way in which Republicans put up with the likes of Buchanan and Pierce without trying to break up the Union. "While you elect [the] President," he argued, "we submit, neither breaking nor attempting to break up the Union. If we shall constitutionally elect a President, it will be our duty to see that you submit. Old John Brown has just been executed for treason against a state. We cannot object, even though he agreed with us in thinking slavery wrong. That cannot excuse violence, bloodshed, and treason. It could avail him nothing that he might think himself right. So, if constitutionally we elect a President, and therefore you undertake to destroy the Union, it will be our duty to deal with you as old John Brown has been dealt with."[38]

Lincoln could afford to talk tough about secession in December, 1859. Southern anger over Harpers Ferry was directed less at Lincoln than it was at his Republican rival, William H. Seward. Seward's "irrepressible conflict" slogan appeared to be a call to arms—an incitement to abolitionist militants like John Brown.

Lincoln's managers were quick to make the most of this. They argued that the "radical" tone of Seward's speech made the nomination of Lincoln advisable in light of the importance of the lower-Northern swing votes. They said much the same thing about Chase, who had fought against the Fugitive Slave Law.

Lincoln's managers were largely self-appointed. They included such Illinois Republican movers and shakers as David Davis, Norman Judd, Jesse Fell, and more than half a dozen others. In December, as Lincoln was speaking in Kansas, Judd struck a blow for his nomination chances. Judd nonchalantly suggested at a meeting of the Republican National Committee that the 1860 Republican convention be held in Chicago, a "neutral" location for the nomination struggle. The Committee agreed— so the Republican convention would be held in Lincoln's own state.

Meanwhile, Lincoln took advantage of a speaking offer from New York. Several months before, he had received an invitation from illustrious clergyman Henry Ward Beecher to speak at the famous Plymouth Church in Brooklyn. The location for the speech was then changed to the Cooper Institute (or "Cooper Union") in downtown New York City.

Here was Lincoln's chance to the show Republican leaders— and to show them in Seward's home state—that he was fit to lead the Republican Party. Moreover, as Lincoln scholar Harold Holzer has observed, this speech, if successful, might complete the transformation of Lincoln "from a regional phenomenon to a national figure. Lincoln knew it, and rose to the occasion."[39] He traveled to New York in late February 1860.

Lincoln in New York City just before his Cooper Institute address in 1860. Photograph by Matthew Brady. (Library of Congress, Meserve Collection #20)

Seward's local enemies pounced upon the chance to boost Lincoln to the detriment of Seward. They set up a gala reception for Lincoln at Astor House and got an audience of over a thousand to travel to hear Lincoln speak on the night of February 27.

Lincoln's Cooper Institute address was a turning point in his quest for the Republican nomination. The major point of his address was to link the Republican program to the Founding Fathers and their anti-slavery legacy.

He devoted the first portion of the speech to historical evidence, beginning with the thirty-nine men who had signed the Constitution in 1787. Most of these men, he argued, took part in creating or supporting the creation of policies designed to prevent the spread of slavery.

He showed that three of the thirty-nine had voted for the bill in the Confederation Congress that was introduced by Jefferson in 1784: the bill that would have banned the institution of slavery from any Western territory. Two more of the thirty-nine, he said, had voted in Congress later on for the anti-slavery Northwest Ordinance of 1787.

In 1789, when the Federal Congress convened under the newly-ratified Constitution, "an act was passed to enforce the Ordinance of '87, including the prohibition of slavery in the Northwestern Territory. The bill for this act was reported by one of the 'thirty-nine,' Thomas Fitzsimmons, then a member of the House of Representatives from Pennsylvania. It went through all its stages without a word of opposition, and finally passed both branches without yeas or nays, which is equivalent to an unanimous passage. In this Congress there were sixteen of the thirty-nine fathers who framed the original Constitution."[40]

Moreover, "George Washington, another of the 'thirty-nine,' was then President of the United States, and, as such, approved and signed the bill; thus completing its validity as a law, and thus showing that, in his understanding, no line dividing local from federal authority, nor anything in the Constitution, forbade the Federal Government, to control as to slavery in federal territory."[41]

Then Lincoln took aim at Roger Taney and his use of the Fifth Amendment in the Dred Scott decision. He also took aim at the analogous use of the Tenth Amendment (which states that "the powers not delegated to the United States by the Constitution . . . are reserved to the States respectively, or to the people").

Both of these amendments, Lincoln pointed out, had been passed by the very same people who had done what Roger Taney was calling outrageous and unconstitutional. "Now it so happens," he observed, "that these amendments were framed by the first Congress which sat under the Constitution—the identical Congress which passed the act already mentioned, enforcing the prohibition of slavery in the North-western Territory. Not only was it the same Congress, but they were the identical, same individual men who, at the same session, had under consideration, and in progress toward maturity, these Constitutional amendments, and this act prohibiting slavery in all the territory the nation then owned. The Constitutional amendments were introduced before, and passed after the act enforcing the Ordinance of '87, so that, during the whole pendency of the act to enforce the Ordinance, the Constitutional amendments were also pending."

In light of these facts, Lincoln argued, "is it not a little presumptu-ous in any one at this day to affirm that the two things which that Congress deliberately framed, and carried to maturity at the same time, are absolutely inconsistent with each other?"[42] Clearly, he said, a great number of the framers of the Constitution had supported the premise of the Free-Soil movement and believed it constitutional.

As he finished expounding this theme, Lincoln chose once again to lecture "fire-eating" Southerners in ways that would please a North-ern audience. He reminded the South that George Washington had hoped for the eventual extinction of slavery: "Some of you delight to flaunt in our faces the warning against sectional parties given by Wash-ington in his Farewell Address. Less than eight years before Washing-ton gave that warning, he had, as President of the United States, approved and signed an act of Congress, enforcing the prohibition of slavery in the Northwestern Territory . . . and about one year after he had penned it [the warning] he wrote La Fayette that he considered the prohibition a wise measure, expressing in that same connection his hope that we should at some time have a confederacy of free states."

"Bearing this in mind," Lincoln said, "and seeing that sectionalism has since arisen upon this same subject, is that warning a weapon in your hands against us, or in our hands against you? Could Washington himself speak, would he cast the blame of that sectionalism upon us, who sustain his policy, or upon you who repudiate it?"[43]

Turning to current events, Lincoln talked about Harpers Ferry. "You charge that we stir up insurrections among your slaves," he said. "We deny it; and what is your proof? Harpers Ferry! John Brown! John

Brown was no Republican; and you have failed to implicate a single Republican in his Harpers Ferry enterprise. If any member of our party is guilty in that matter, you know it or you do not know it. If you do know it, you are inexcusable for not designating the man and proving the fact. If you do not know it, you are inexcusable for asserting it."[44]

Lincoln chided Southern militants for warning they would break up the Union "unless you be allowed to construe and enforce the Constitution as you please, on all points in dispute between you and us. You will rule or ruin in all events."[45] Indeed, "you will not abide the election of a Republican President! In that supposed event, you say, you will destroy the Union; and then, you say, the great crime of having destroyed it will be upon us! That is cool. A highwayman holds a pistol to my ear, and mutters through his teeth, 'Stand and deliver, or I shall kill you, and then you will be a murderer!'"[46]

Lincoln finished this speech with a clarion call to the Republicans. He told them that the South would never be satisfied with anything less than Republican capitulation. What on earth would convince Southern militants that "black Republicans" deserved a fair hearing? Lincoln said: we must "cease to call slavery wrong, and join them in calling it right. . . . Silence will not be tolerated—we must place ourselves avowedly with them. . . . We must arrest and return their fugitive slaves with greedy pleasure. We must pull down our Free State constitutions. The whole atmosphere must be disinfected from all taint of opposition to slavery, before they will cease to believe that all their troubles proceed from us."[47]

All this, said Lincoln, "we could readily grant" if we thought that slavery was right. And yet "thinking it wrong, as we do, can we yield to them? . . . If our sense of duty forbids this," he said, "let us stand by our duty. . . ."

> Let us be diverted by none of those sophistical contrivances wherewith we are so industriously plied and belabored—contrivances such as groping for some middle ground between the right and the wrong, vain as the search for a man who should be neither a living man nor a dead man—such as a policy of "don't care" on a question about which all true men do care—such as Union appeals beseeching true Union men to yield to Disunionists, reversing the divine rule, and calling, not the sinners, but the righteous to repentance—such as invocations to Washington, imploring men to unsay what Washington said, and undo what Washington did.
>
> Neither let us be slandered from our duty by false accusations against us, nor frightened from it by menaces of destruction to the Government nor of

dungeons to ourselves. LET US HAVE THE FAITH THAT RIGHT MAKES MIGHT, AND IN THAT FAITH, LET US, TO THE END, DARE TO DO OUR DUTY AS WE UNDERSTAND IT.[48]

Lincoln's audience rose to a standing ovation as he finished: cheer upon cheer rang out through the hall as people waved their hats and Lincoln bowed. Newspapers published the speech the next day, and more speaking invitations began to pour in from other cities. Consequently, in the weeks that followed, Lincoln spoke in Rhode Island, New Hampshire, and Connecticut.

Since the anti-slavery movement was strong in New England, Lincoln's moderate stance required appeals for abolitionist prudence. He used a new metaphor in some of the speeches: to convince anti-slavery militants to limit their goals to free soil—to eschew the more radical short-term goals that lacked a firm constitutional basis and would lead to political defeat—he likened slavery to a poisonous serpent that threatened his children.

> If I saw a venomous snake crawling in the road, any man might say I might seize the nearest stick and kill it; but if I found that snake in bed with my children, that would be another question. [Laughter.] I might hurt the children more than the snake, and it might bite them. [Applause.] Much more, if I found it in bed with my neighbor's children, and I had bound myself by a solemn compact not to meddle with his children under any circumstances, it would become me to let that particular mode of getting rid of the gentleman alone. [Great laughter.] But if there was a bed newly made up, to which the children were to be taken, and it was proposed to take a batch of young snakes and put them there with them, I take it no man in the world would say there was any question how I ought to decide! [Prolonged applause and cheers.] That is just the case! The new Territories are the newly made bed to which our children are to go, and it lies with the nation to say whether they shall have snakes mixed up with them or not.[49]

As Lincoln built up his national following, Douglas prepared for the Democratic National Convention that was scheduled for April in Charleston, South Carolina. The results of that convention would ruin the Democrats' chances in 1860.

A two-thirds vote was required for the Democratic nomination; Douglas failed to get it. But he controlled a simple majority of delegates. And by this simple majority, his delegates voted down the territorial slave-code plank that Southern delegates demanded for the Democratic Party platform. Whereupon, the delegates from seven Southern states walked out: no one had been nominated.

The "fire-eating" Southerner who orchestrated this move was William Lowndes Yancey of Alabama. Yancey had berated Douglas from the podium. He condemned the unwillingness of Douglas to side with the "legitimate" rights of the South in unequivocal terms: "If you had taken the position directly that slavery was right," Yancey thundered, "you could have triumphed, and anti-slavery would now be dead in your midst."[50] Yancey had worked out a prearranged plan—the "Alabama Platform," they called it—for a Southern walk-out if Douglas and his delegates defeated the slave-code plank. The Democrats agreed to re-assemble that June for another convention in Baltimore.

The Republican convention was scheduled for May. Seward was still the front-runner. Lincoln confided to a friend that his strategy was watchful waiting. "My name is new in the field," he admitted, "and I suppose I am not the *first* choice of a very great many. Our policy, then, is to give no offense to others—leave them in a mood to come to us, if they shall be compelled to give up their first love."[51] He also confided to an ally that "the taste *is* in my mouth a little."[52]

Once Lincoln had secured the support of the Illinois delegation, his managers set up his convention headquarters at Tremont House hotel. As Fehrenbacher has observed, "when they arrived on the scene and sounded out certain key delegations, the Lincoln men discovered that their prospects were brighter than anyone had dreamed."[53] And when the first ballot started, "it became apparent that Seward was weaker and Lincoln stronger than anyone had expected."[54]

His managers counseled him to keep a level head. One of them wrote to him as follows: "Things are working; keep a good nerve—be not surprised at any result—but I tell you that your chances are not the worst. . . . We are dealing tenderly with delegates, taking them in de-tail, and making no fuss. Be not too expectant, but rely upon our dis-cretion. Again I say brace your nerves for any result."[55]

Seward failed to gain the Republican nomination on the first ballot. His support became weaker on the second. A massive shift to Lincoln began to take place, and the mood of the convention, in Fehrenbacher's opinion, revealed "a hard-headed decision that the leading candidate could not win and must give way to someone who could. Yet in nomi-nating the more 'available' Lincoln, the Republicans did not compro-mise themselves or their principles. In fact, without fully realizing it, they had selected a man whose moral fibre was tougher than Seward's."[56]

Along the range of "conservative" to "moderate" to "radical" Republicans, Lincoln was closest to the Radicals in spite of all the "moderate" stances that his short-term strategy required. As historian Eric Foner has pointed out, "at the time of his nomination, Lincoln's political outlook more closely resembled that of the radicals than of the conservatives in his party." Though his short-term stance required a promise of non-interference with slavery in existing slave slaves, "his ultimate goal was not merely the non-extension of slavery . . . but its 'ultimate extinction.'"[57]

In June, Lincoln's chances of winning the election increased because the Democrats' schism got worse. Some of the seceders from the Charleston convention refused to go to Baltimore and tangle with the Douglas men. This group of pro-slavery seceders met in Richmond while another group of fire-eating Southerners went to Baltimore. When they got there, the chairman of the Democratic Party Convention ruled that a majority of two-thirds *present* could select the nominee. Douglas was quickly selected.

Once again, the Southern militants bolted: they regrouped in a rump convention, passed a platform demanding a tough territorial slave code, and nominated John C. Breckinridge of Kentucky. Their colleagues in Richmond approved. And so the Democratic Party split in two. To make matters trickier, a new "Constitutional Union Party" was created by some former Whigs who proceeded to nominate John Bell of Tennessee.

Lincoln, following a time-honored code for presidential elections, declined to make speeches that summer or fall.

But Douglas, approaching desperation, tried to barnstorm the country.

It did him little good, for the voters of the deep South were stampeding to Breckinridge. All over the South, predictions of Northern aggression, of slave insurrections, of war between the races made voters view Lincoln's election as a veritable doomsday event. In most Southern states the name of Lincoln would be kept off the ballot.

Lincoln listened to advisers who told him that the threat of disunion from the South was probably bluster. In August, he wrote that "the people of the South have too much of good sense, and good temper, to attempt the ruin of the government, rather than see it administered as it was administered by the men who made it. At least, so I hope and believe."[58]

The Republicans were sweeping the North. All over the region Republican "Wide-Awake" clubs were parading through the streets by torchlight. "A Political Earthquake—THE PRAIRIES ON FIRE FOR LINCOLN," cried Republican editors and pundits.[59] It was more than propaganda: in October, the Republicans captured state offices in two of the lower-Northern states that would be crucial in the electoral college. Douglas was doomed.

The alternately proud and self-effacing manners of the "two-faced" Lincoln: an 1860 cartoon by an unknown artist. (Library of Congress)

Certificate of membership in the 1860 Republican "Wide-Awake" marching club—"wide awake" to the tricky machinations of the pro-slavery Democrats. (Library of Congress)

A pro-Lincoln cartoon that was published by Currier & Ives in the election of 1860: wearing "Wide-Awake" garb, Lincoln proudly declares that he will not be caught napping by his various opponents, including the incumbent president, Buchanan. This print has been attributed to artist Louis Maurer. (Library of Congress)

An anti-Lincoln cartoon that was published by Currier & Ives in the election of 1860: Republican editor Horace Greeley tries to play down the anti-slavery content of Lincoln's platform. But the racist skeptic can nonetheless perceive the grinning "nigger in the woodpile." The print has been attributed to Louis Maurer. (Library of Congress)

"THE NIGGER" IN THE WOODPILE.

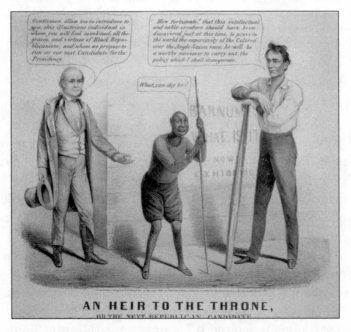

AN HEIR TO THE THRONE,
OR THE NEXT REPUBLICAN CANDIDATE

Another racist cartoon attacking Lincoln that was published by Currier & Ives in 1860. The artist portrayed the most likely Republican successor to Lincoln if the latter should capture the White House: a deformed black man who had been recently featured at P. T. Barnum's Museum as the "What-is-it." The print has been attributed to Louis Maurer. (Library of Congress)

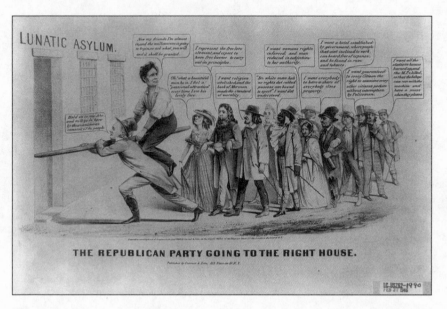

THE REPUBLICAN PARTY GOING TO THE RIGHT HOUSE.

One more anti-Lincoln cartoon from the presses of Currier & Ives in 1860. The artist shows Lincoln on his way to an insane asylum with his various followers, including a black who mutters, "De white man hab no rights dat cullud pussons am bound to spect. . . ." The print has been attributed to Louis Maurer. (Library of Congress)

He went South, making speeches that would put him on record as a Unionist. He urged Southerners to keep their cool and reject secession. On November 6, Lincoln carried every Northern state except New Jersey. He won 173 electoral votes compared to 72 for Breckinridge, 39 for Bell, and just 12 for Douglas.

Abraham Lincoln had become the highest magistrate in the land. He would soon have the power—the enormous power—to start controlling the evil of slavery.

He would clamp a firm lid upon the South. The Southern black population would continue to grow and yet the "safety valve" would start to close. And how long would it take for the fear of revolution to persuade Southern leaders to reform? Thirty years? Forty?

Southern militants determined not to wait. Fire-eating South Carolinians demanded a secession convention in December. The convention made its logic very clear:

We affirm that . . . [the] ends for which this Government was instituted have been defeated, and the Government itself has been destructive of them by the action of the non-slaveholding States. Those States have . . . denounced as sinful the institution of Slavery; they have permitted the open establishment among them of societies, whose avowed object is to disturb the peace of and eloin [*sic*] the property of the citizens of other States. They have encouraged and assisted thousands of our slaves to leave their homes; and those who remain have been incited by emissaries, books, and pictures, to servile insurrection. . . .

On the 4th of March next . . . [a sectional] party will take possession of the Government. It has announced that the South shall be excluded from the common territory, that the Judicial tribunal shall be made sectional, and that a war must be waged against Slavery until it shall cease throughout the United States.

Their preference was to leave at once: "We, therefore, the people of South Carolina, by our delegates in Convention assembled, appealing to the Supreme Judge of the world for the rectitude of our intentions, have solemnly declared that the Union heretofore existing between this State and the other States of North America is dissolved, and that the State of South Carolina has resumed her position among the Nations of the world. . . ."[60]

The election of President Lincoln had broken up the Union.

LINCOLN ROSE TO THE CHALLENGE when secession broke out: he refused to back down on his policies. And he resisted all attempts at appeasement.

As the South Carolina convention did its work—and as other secession conventions started meeting— congressional leaders took action. Both the House and the Senate formed special committees to explore the possibility of measures to avert secession.

Senator John J. Crittenden of Kentucky suggested a series of constitutional amendments. One would revive and extend the Missouri Compromise line: slavery could spread in all the territories "now held, or hereafter acquired" by the United States below the latitude of 36° 30'.

Other amendments would have bolstered the Fugitive Slave Law, indemnified the owners of runaway slaves, and protected the interstate slave trade. The capstone amendment would forbid any future attempts by Congress to abolish slavery. These amendments would be unamendable.

Lincoln lashed out quickly at the deal. He dashed off letters marked "Private & confidential" to congressional Republicans. "Entertain no proposition for a compromise in regard to the *extension* of slavery," he told one of them. "The instant you do, they have us under again; all our labor is lost, and sooner or later must be done over. . . . Have none of it. The tug has to come & better now than later."[61]

He told another Republican to spread the word that there was "no possible compromise" on slavery extension. Extend the Missouri Compromise line, he warned, and "immediately filibustering and extending slavery recommences. On that point hold firm, as with a chain of steel."[62]

He told Senator Lyman Trumbull that "if any of our friends do prove false, and fix up a compromise on the territorial question, I am for fighting again—that is all."[63] As to the amendment to prevent abolition legislation in Congress, Lincoln was silent. After all, his plans for the ultimate extinction of slavery appeared to envision a *voluntary*, compensated phaseout rather than compulsion.

He did, however, tell an emissary of the lame-duck President Buchanan that he found the idea of constitutional amendments distasteful. "I do not desire any amendment of the Constitution," he said. Nonetheless, as he was willing to acknowledge "that questions of such amendment rightfully belong to the American People, I should not feel justified, or inclined, to withhold from them, if I could, a fair opportunity of expressing their will thereon."[64]

Buchanan urged Lincoln to agree to some plan that would slow the drive for secession. Lincoln drafted a statement supporting "the maintenance inviolate of the rights of the States" and condemning "the lawless invasion, by armed force, of the soil of any State or Territory, no matter under what pretext."

But this was as far as he would go in December 1860. "I am greatly averse to writing anything for the public at this time," he stated, "and I consent to the publication of this, only upon the condition that six of the twelve United States Senators for the States of Georgia, Alabama, Mississippi, Louisiana, Florida, and Texas [all of which had summoned secession conventions] shall sign their names to what is written on this sheet below my name, and allow the whole to be published together."[65] Below his signature, Lincoln wrote the following: "We recommend to the people of the States we represent respectively, to suspend all action for dismemberment of the Union, at least, until some act, deemed to be violative of our rights, shall be done by the incoming administration."[66]

He was angry. He asked a Southerner who pleaded for concessions whether people expected him to grovel for the fire-eating militants: "Is it desired that I shall shift the ground upon which I have been elected? I can not do it. . . . It would make me appear as if I repented for the crime of having been elected, and was anxious to apologize and beg forgiveness."[67]

He was firm about secession as well. In mid-December he wrote to Thurlow Weed, a Republican leader in New York as well as an erstwhile Seward supporter, telling him that "no state can, in any way lawfully, get out of the Union, without the consent of the others" and that "it is the duty of the President, and other government functionaries to run the machine as it is."[68]

He instructed a political ally, Elihu Washburne, to "present my respects to General [Winfield Scott, the general in chief of the United States Army], and tell him, confidentially, I shall be obliged to him to be as well prepared as he can to either *hold*, or *retake*" any federal forts that secessionists might attack and to be ready to swing into action "after the inaugeration [*sic*]."[69]

As Republicans voted down the Crittenden Compromise, secessionist fervor was sweeping through the lower South. South Carolina's convention proclaimed secession on December 20. The following states joined the exodus: Mississippi on January 9, Florida on January 10, Alabama on January 11, Georgia on January 19, Louisiana on January 26, and Texas on February 1.

In the city of Montgomery, Alabama, on February 4, commissioners from all of these states came together to draft a preliminary constitution for a confederacy of slave states and to elect provisional officers. Jefferson Davis of Mississippi was elected provisional president of the Confederate States of America.

The leaders of upper-Southern states like Virginia, Tennessee, and North Carolina were divided about joining the Confederacy. So were the leaders of the border slave states like Maryland, Kentucky, and Missouri. Unionists in the Virginia legislature called for a "peace convention" of all the states to meet in Washington, D.C., on February 4. The convention was held, and yet the seven self-proclaimed Confederate states ignored it.

William H. Seward, whom Lincoln had invited to be secretary of state—Seward, whom the militant South had regarded as a war-crazed abolitionist—began to show his true colors by advising Lincoln to indulge the Virginia conference, which was generating compromise proposals very similar in spirit and substance to the Crittenden Compromise.

Lincoln brought Seward into line. On the question of slavery extension, he repeated, "I am inflexible. I am for no compromise which *as-
sists* or *permits* the extension of the institution on soil owned by the
nation. And any trick by which the nation is to acquire territory, and
then allow some local authority to spread slavery over it, is as obnoxious as any other. I take it that to effect some such result as this, and to
put us again on the high-road to a slave empire is the object of all these
proposed compromises. I am against it. . . ."

Nonetheless, he continued, "as to fugitive slaves, District of Columbia, slave trade among the slave states, and whatever springs of
necessity from the fact that the institution is amongst us, I care but
little, so that what is done is comely, and not altogether outrageous.
Nor do I care much about New-Mexico, if further extension were
hedged against."[70]

He told another Republican leader to look upon secessionist politics as blackmail: "We have just carried an election on principles fairly
stated to the people. Now we are told in advance, the government shall
be broken up, unless we surrender to those we have beaten, before we
take the offices. In this they are either attempting to play upon us, or
they are in dead earnest. Either way, if we surrender, it is the end of us,
and of the government. They will repeat the experiment upon us *ad
libitum*. A year will not pass, till we shall have to take Cuba as a condition upon which they will stay in the Union."[71] Thus Lincoln made it
clear that the principles of free soil must never be surrendered.

Yet the days in which the Free-Soil struggle was his *primary* challenge were ending. If he meant to block *secession* as well as the extension of slavery, a whole new arena lay before him.

All through the 1850s, Lincoln's powers had been focused on preventing the expansion of slavery. The loathsome scenario of slavery's
extension to the North was his worst-case projection. Secession he regarded as in all probability a bluff, since the North could so easily
resist it. Surely Southern strategists would know this, Lincoln had presumed, for which reason they would stop before the brink.

But it was suddenly clear in the early months of 1861 that the secessionists had not been bluffing. So it was time for an urgent game of
catch-up. It was time to get better information on the state of Southern
politics and public opinion. It was time to make practical plans that would
use the approach to the prospect of war that Lincoln had developed—
the overwhelming use of Northern power—and convert that vision

into action. Most importantly, it was time for the president-elect to turn his thoughts to the defense of the Union. It was time for him to craft some manifestos to use against secession.

Like millions of Americans, Lincoln regarded the Union as sacred. But with him there was always a caveat: the worth of the Union was dependent for Lincoln on the strength of its founding principles.

Like many of his fellow Americans, Lincoln had always regarded the Union as a way of refuting the age-old notion that the weakness and depravity of human nature made governance by despots imperative. Yet again, Lincoln added a caveat: human weakness and depravity were *real*. They would manifest themselves in a will for domination that could ruin and degrade the lives of others. Individuals, minorities, and even majorities could act in this despicable manner.

The test for free institutions was "self-government"—not only in the obvious sense of majority rule but also in the *governance of selfish instincts*. "Those who deny freedom to others," he had written in 1859, "deserve it not for themselves." This negative version of the golden rule—a positive form being Jefferson's assertion that "All men are created equal"—was a watchword for guarding the republic through mutual control.

Just as men were essentially equal in their right to basic liberty, Lincoln seemed to believe, they were equal in tyrannical potential. For this reason, the people must restrain one another through legitimate powers of governance. "Slavery is founded in the selfishness of man's nature—opposition to it in his love of justice," he declared in Peoria. "These principles are an eternal antagonism."

Strong governance was needed to suppress the human instinct for tyranny. Strong magistrates were needed to restrain the wolfish tendencies of people. In free institutions, these magistrates must come from the people and answer to the people. Lincoln was determined to be forceful, conscientious, and clever in his role as a magistrate. He would have to be clever enough to prevail without abusing his power, but prevail he must.

If he failed, the nation would unravel or else lose its soul. "If destruction be our lot, we must ourselves be its author and finisher," Lincoln had warned in his Lyceum Speech years before. "As a nation of freemen, we must live through all time, or die by suicide."[72] The Founding Fathers had striven to carry out "a practical demonstration of the truth of a proposition, which had hitherto been considered, at best no better than problematical; namely, *the capability of a people to govern themselves.*"[73]

So the nation had to live—Lincoln had to keep his nation intact, with its definitive evil on the way to a slow termination. Such were his nonnegotiable purposes and goals on the eve of war.

But the constitutional basis for his policy was tricky. Like Daniel Webster and others before him, Lincoln argued that the Union was older than the Constitution, which was really the *second* constitution under which the United States had lived. The full title of the *first* constitution—the Articles of Confederation and Perpetual Union—made the argument for permanent Union appear to be obvious. It was easy for Lincoln to argue that the Union's permanence endured in the Federal Constitution, which, after all, was ordained and established to "form a more perfect Union." How could any perpetual Union become "more perfect" by losing its permanence?

But there remained a significant problem. The Constitution itself said nothing on the issue of permanence. Indeed, the method set forth for its very own ratification was a break in the nation's continuity.

The Constitution provided that as soon as *any nine* of the thirteen states had completed the process of ratification, the federal process would start *among the nine.* This meant that if any four of the original states had decided not to ratify the Constitution, they would *not have been included* in the Union.

The fact that all the states had been given a chance to opt out made the permanent Union effectively a nullity, at least in the view of the political metaphysicians of Confederate secession. What the states had agreed to, the Confederates said, could be voided any time at their discretion.

Historian Kenneth M. Stampp has contended that "the Philadelphia Convention made the historical argument for perpetuity invalid, because the Convention and the ratifying states destroyed the existing Union. Every state had the option of *not* ratifying, and as many as four might have remained independent (as two did for a time) while the other nine entered a new union. . . . The preamble to the Constitution, be it noted, does not propose to make the old Union more perfect but to '*form* a more perfect Union'—that is, to create a new and better one."[74]

Lincoln would insist until the very last days of the war that the Union remained unbroken. He would never refer to "Confederates" as such—they were Confederates "so-called." In his own view, all of them were "rebels"—part of a huge and illegal insurrection that usurped state power in the Southern region of the Union.

A crusade to preserve the Union was a powerful weapon in a number of ways. It could serve as a basis for uniting Republicans and Democrats. But the Democrats could always insist and complain that the Republicans had *caused* the problem—that Republicans were really *to blame* for the crisis of the Union—because they pushed the South into rebellion.

If the war became costly, Democratic support would be essential, especially in Congress. And yet Republican policies and needs would put a very real limit on the politics of coalition.

There were also concerns about the border states. If Maryland proclaimed secession, then the national capital of Washington, D.C., would be surrounded and would have to be abandoned. If Virginia should proclaim secession, a tremendous array of assets would fall into the laps of the Confederates. For all of the undecided slave states, the issue of "coercion" by the federal government was fraught with emotional significance.

As historian Richard N. Current has described the situation, Lincoln faced an apparent dilemma: "If he took a stand, he would run the risk of antagonizing and losing Virginia and other still-loyal slave states. But if he declined to take a stand, he would still risk losing those states, though conferring new prestige and attractiveness upon the Confederacy. And, besides, he would surely alienate many of his adherents in the North."[75]

But he knew what he was going to do. And he knew what he would not allow. He would not allow secession to unravel the American nation. He would not allow secessionists to form a powerful slave-holding nation that would spread its institutions any further in the Western Hemisphere. And, in immediate terms, he would not allow Confederates to take over federal functions in the Southern states. Indeed, he would draw the line *there*. But he would try to play for time as he considered all the military options.

Moreover, he would pick the best ground on which to fight. He would try to force the enemy to fire the first shot, thus arousing and uniting the North.

Lincoln left his home in Springfield, Illinois, on February 11, 1861. The journey by train that would take him from Springfield to Washington, D.C., would take a "winding way," as Lincoln put it, in response to some speaking invitations from a number of Northern cities. When his train reached Indianapolis, Lincoln strove to make fun of the secessionists. He asked "by what principle of original right is it that one-fiftieth or one-ninetieth of a great nation, by calling themselves a State, have the right to break up and ruin that nation as a matter of original principle? Now, I ask the question—I am not deciding anything—[laughter,] . . . where is the mysterious, original right, from principle, for a certain district of the country with inhabitants, by merely being called a State, to play tyrant over all its own citizens, and deny the authority of everything greater than itself. [Laughter.]"[76]

On February 12, in Cincinnati, he recalled the very statements he had aimed across the river to Kentucky less than two years before, "in a playful manner," he admitted, "but with sincere words." He assured the Kentuckians in 1859 that Republicans would always treat them fairly—we will treat you as "Washington, Jefferson, and Madison treated you," Lincoln had said—and he now reaffirmed those sentiments.[77]

In New York City—which harbored a significant amount of Southern sympathy along with considerable Democratic strength—Lincoln made a very interesting statement. The Union was designed for a *purpose*, he reminded the city's Democratic Mayor, Fernando Wood: "There is nothing that can ever bring me willingly to consent to the destruction of this Union . . . unless it were to be that thing for which the Union itself was made. I understand a ship to be made for the carrying and preservation of the cargo, and so long as the ship can be saved, with the cargo, it should never be abandoned. This Union should likewise never be abandoned unless it fails and the probability of its preservation shall cease to exist without throwing the passengers and cargo overboard."[78] In other words, the Union would be saved *Lincoln's way*, and with its fundamental principles preserved. But Lincoln would never sacrifice these principles to preserve the union.

At Trenton, New Jersey, after speaking of the valor of Washington's troops in the American Revolution, he became more emphatic and decisive. "I shall do all that may be in my power to promote a peaceful settlement of all our difficulties," he said. "The man does not live who is more devoted to peace than I am. [Cheers.] None who would do more to preserve it. But it may be necessary to put the foot down firmly. [Here the audience broke out into cheers so loud and long that for some moments it was impossible to hear Mr. L's voice.] He continued:

And if I do my duty, and do right, you will sustain me, will you not? [Loud cheers, and cries of 'Yes,' 'Yes,' 'We will.']"[79]

In Philadelphia, he spoke about war and made it clear that he would wait for Southern violence before he used force. "There will be no blood shed unless it be forced upon the Government," he promised his audience. "The Government will not use force unless force is used against it."[80]

He also spoke of his personal feelings when he first beheld Independence Hall. "I have never asked anything," he said, "that does not breathe from those walls. All my political warfare has been in favor of the teachings coming forth from that sacred hall. May my right hand forget its cunning and my tongue cleave to the roof of my mouth, if ever I prove false to those teachings."[81]

He made a longer speech the next day in Independence Hall: he said that he had "never had a feeling politically that did not spring from the sentiments embodied in the Declaration of Independence," a document, he added, whose purpose "was not the mere matter of the separation of the colonies from the mother land." No, it was "something in that Declaration giving liberty, not alone to the people of this country, but hope to the world for all future time," a promise that "the weights should be lifted from the shoulders of all men, and that *all* should have an equal chance."

Then he made a most stunning declaration: "If this country cannot be saved without giving up that principle," Lincoln proclaimed, "I would rather be assassinated on the spot than to surrender it."[82] The threat was very much upon his mind. Southern hate mail had flooded his home since the election, and it frequently threatened his life.[83] Indeed, sudden news of a plot to murder him had been uncovered just the day before.[84] The killing ground would be Baltimore—the goal was to kill him before he could take his presidential oath—and the killers were a bevy of secessionists who knew he would have to change trains on the trip to Washington, D.C.

So he agreed to employ a disguise, accept the protection of bodyguards, and take a special nighttime train that would arrive in Washington secretly, well ahead of schedule. At dawn on February 23, he arrived in the nation's capital and checked in at Willard's Hotel. His family arrived the next day.

Awaiting his arrival was Secretary of State-designate William H. Seward, the senior member of his cabinet. Other cabinet appointments had been worked out slowly and carefully. Lincoln strove for a nominal "unity" cabinet including former Democrats and Whigs. Salmon P. Chase would be the secretary of the treasury. Montgomery Blair—son of Francis Preston Blair, the old anti-secessionist Democrat who served as a member of Andrew Jackson's "kitchen cabinet" back in the 1830s—would be postmaster general. Gideon Welles, a Connecticut Republican, would head the Department of the Navy. Simon Cameron, a wily machine politician from Pennsylvania would, by dint of a political bargain, be the secretary of war. Seward had continued his dalliance with Virginia's "peace convention," which was meeting in a dance hall adjacent to Willard's Hotel. And while the peace convention was meeting in Washington, another Virginia convention—a secession convention—was meeting in Richmond.

Seward tried to convince his new chief to back down, to negotiate a deal. But the peace convention kept insisting on a package of warmed-over Crittenden measures that would never be acceptable to Lincoln.

Rumor had it that some peace convention delegates had broached a very different deal. They allegedly hinted to Lincoln that if South Carolina secessionists were permitted to occupy the federal fort in the middle of Charleston Harbor—Fort Sumter—it would strengthen the Unionists' hand in the Virginia secession convention.

Most of the federal forts and coastal defenses in the lower-Southern states had been seized already by secessionists. A few held out: Fort Sumter in Charleston, South Carolina, and Fort Pickens in Pensacola, Florida. In January, President Buchanan tried to send a ship with reinforcements to Fort Sumter. But Confederate batteries had fired upon the ship and turned it back.

At Seward's behest, Lincoln had a few talks with some peace convention delegates at Willard's. And yet a "Sumter-for-Virginia" bargain proved to be impossible. None of the Virginia delegates was authorized to bind Virginia to a deal or to adjourn its secession convention.[85]

The most substantive attempt to avert the threat of war was the passage by Congress of a constitutional amendment that would tie the hands of Congress forever on the question of abolishing slavery. This amendment was never ratified, but it demonstrated exactly how far the congressional Republicans and Democrats were willing to go to put an end to the crisis of secession in the early months of 1861.

Lincoln was obliged to respond to this important new development. Importantly—and unbelievably, to some—he accepted the amendment in principle on the day of his inauguration. It behooves us to ask why.

Answers to the question must to some extent remain conjectural: Lincoln never made his reasons for the move clear to anyone, at least so far as we can tell. And yet the reasons can be easily inferred.

In light of everything that Lincoln ever said or did, his acceptance of a measure such as this would be a grudging acceptance at best. But he confronted a genuine conundrum. For years he had predicted that the institution of slavery would wither and die if Americans could manage to contain it.

Especially after the election, he tried to reassure the white South that this containment of slavery would never be a threat to their safety, their property, their interests. Abolition would be left up to them. And so he urged Southern whites to keep calm and reject the secessionist movement—while the nation put a quarantine around them.

Now, if Lincoln had *opposed* this amendment that would guarantee his promise of non-interference with the slave-holding South, then what, may we ask, would have happened? Southern militants would claim that Lincoln's promise was a trick—a guileful and *temporary* promise, not binding on Republican successors, since he fought against a measure that would guarantee a permanent policy. Thus the politics of secession forced a painful decision on Lincoln with regard to this amendment.

Yet Lincoln really seemed to believe that the evil of slavery would die if the nation contained it. He appeared to believe that it was only a matter of time before Southerners would listen to the logic of a voluntary phaseout.

Why should this have been the case? One reason, perhaps, was the fear that had been haunting the South—the fear that became so unbearable after Harpers Ferry. Once the South lost control of the executive branch, an Alabama writer ventured to predict in 1860, "what social monstrosities, what desolated fields, what civil broils, what robberies, rapes, and murders of the poorer whites by the emancipated blacks would then disfigure the whole fair face of this prosperous, smiling, and happy Southern land [?]"[86]

The great fear of the blacks in the South might become so horrific—the great fear of the ever-growing black population that could not be channeled any longer into lands beyond the great quarantine—that it could break down the Southern police state. White Southerners might come to their senses over time and demand a new politics of change.

This particular freedom scenario could never be averted by a constitutional amendment to tie the hands of *Congress*. Lincoln's hope for the "ultimate extinction" of slavery was premised on a *voluntary* phase-out. The *compulsion* that would break the Southern system would arise within the South itself.

And Southern militants feared this scenario. In October 1860, the *Charleston Mercury* warned that if Republicans should capture the executive branch, a dark chain of events would divide the Southern people into factions. With the Republican Party "enthroned at Washington," declared the *Mercury*,

> the *under*-ground railroad will become an over-ground railroad. The tenure of slave property will be felt to be weakened; and the slaves will be sent down to the Cotton States for sale, and the Frontier States *enter on the policy of making themselves Free States*.
>
> With the control of the Government of the United States, and an organized and triumphant North to sustain them, the Abolitionists will renew their operations upon the South with increased courage. . . . They will have an Abolition Party in the South, of Southern men. The contest for slavery will no longer be one between the North and the South. It will be in the South, between the people of the South. . . .
>
> If, in our present position of power and unitedness, we have the raid of John Brown . . . what will be the measures of insurrection and incendiarism, which must follow our notorious and abject prostration to Abolition rule at Washington, with all the patronage of the Federal Government, and a Union organization in the South to support it? . . . Already there is uneasiness in the South, as to the stability of its institution of slavery. But with a submission to the rule of abolitionists at Washington, thousands of slaveholders will despair of the institution. While the condition of things in the Frontier States will force their slaves on the markets of the Cotton States, the timid in the Cotton States, will also sell their slaves. The general distrust, must affect purchasers. The consequence must be, slave property must be greatly depreciated.[87]

Which of course could make a voluntary buyout—perhaps by a new and more powerful American colonization society—financially feasible.

Under cloudy skies, Lincoln rode to his inauguration at the U.S. Capitol on March 4, 1861. He would receive his presidential oath from the lips of Chief Justice Taney.

His Inaugural Address had been revised after numerous reviews by advisors such as Seward and the Blairs. It would stand for all time as a conventional-wisdom exhibit of "Lincoln the moderate," regardless of the numerous strategic issues that affected its contents—and dated its message.

He began by promising the slave states that he would commit no actions that would harm them. "Apprehension seems to exist among the people of the Southern States," he said, "that by the accession of a Republican Administration, their property, and their peace, and personal security, are to be endangered. There has never been any reasonable cause for such apprehension. Indeed, the most ample evidence to the contrary has all the while existed, and been open to their inspection. It is found in nearly all the published speeches of him who now addresses you. I do but quote from one of these speeches when I declare that 'I have no purpose, directly or indirectly, to interfere with the institution of slavery in the States where it exists. I believe I have no lawful right to do so, and I have no inclination to do so.'"[88]

He contended that "the Union of these States is perpetual," asserting that "no government proper, ever had a provision in its organic law for its own termination." Even if the United States were regarded as "not a government proper, but an association of states in the nature of a contract merely, can it, as a contract, be peacefully unmade, by less than all the parties who made it?"[89]

He asserted that the Union was older than the Constitution, explaining that the permanence proclaimed in the Articles of Confederation carried over to the Federal sequel. So it follows, he continued, "that no State, upon its own mere motion, can lawfully get out of the Union,—that *resolves* and *ordinances* to that effect are legally void."[90]

He called secession "the essence of anarchy," contending that majority rule, with appropriate restraints, was the only possible method for governing republics: "a majority, held in restraint by constitutional checks, and limitations, and always changing easily, with deliberate changes of popular opinions and sentiments, is the only true sovereign of a free people. . . . Unanimity is impossible; the rule of a minority, as a permanent arrangement, is wholly inadmissible; so that, rejecting the majority principle, anarchy, or despotism in some form, is all that is left."[91]

With regard to Supreme Court decisions, Lincoln challenged the doctrine of unlimited judicial review. "I do not forget the position assumed by some, that constitutional questions are to be decided by the Supreme Court," Lincoln explained, "nor do I deny that such decisions must be binding in any case, upon the parties to a suit, as to the object of that suit, while they are also entitled to very high respect and consideration, in all paralel [sic] cases, by all other departments of the government." Nonetheless, Lincoln reasoned, "at the same time the candid citizen must confess that if the policy of the government, upon vital questions, affecting the whole people, is to be irrevocably fixed by decisions of the Supreme Court, the instant they are made . . . the people will have ceased, to be their own rulers, having, to that extent, practically resigned their government, into the hands of that worthy tribunal."[92]

Lincoln acknowledged that the Free-Soil leaders and the slave-state leaders held different constitutional views about slavery's expansion. But he challenged the South to consider whether separation in merely *political* terms would achieve their objectives. "Physically speaking, we cannot separate," Lincoln said. "We cannot remove our respective sections from each other, nor build an impassible wall between them. A husband and wife may be divorced, and go out of the presence, and beyond the reach of the other; but the different parts of our country cannot do this. They cannot but remain face to face; and intercourse, either amicable or hostile, must continue between them."

In light of this, Lincoln asked, "can treaties be more faithfully enforced between aliens, than laws can among friends? Suppose you go to war, you cannot fight always; and when, after much loss on both sides, and no gain on either, you cease fighting, the identical old questions, as to terms of intercourse, are again upon you."[93]

Lincoln turned to the recent work of Congress; he acknowledged that the sovereign will of the people could approve constitutional amendments. "I can not be ignorant of the fact that many worthy, and patriotic citizens are desirous of having the national constitution amended," he acknowledged. "While I make no recommendation of amendments, I fully recognize the rightful authority of the people over the whole subject . . . and I should, under existing circumstances, favor, rather than oppose, a fair oppertunity [sic] being afforded the people to act upon it."

Moreover, he continued, "I understand a proposed amendment to the Constitution—which amendment, however, I have not seen, has passed Congress, to the effect that the federal government, shall never interfere with the domestic institutions of the States, including that of persons held to service. . . . Holding such a provision to now be implied constitutional law, I have no objection to its being made express, and irrevocable."[94]

Nonetheless, he had taken an oath to uphold the *existing* laws, and the people had never conferred an authority "to fix terms for the separation of the States." He urged Southerners to take their time, but made it clear that he awaited their decision on the use of force, and would respond accordingly: "In *your* hands, my dissatisfied fellow countrymen, and not in *mine*, is the momentous issue of civil war. The government will not assail *you*. You can have no conflict, without being yourselves the aggressors. You have no oath registered in Heaven to destroy the government, while *I* shall have the most solemn one to 'preserve, protect, and defend' it."[95]

At Seward's suggestion, Lincoln closed with some conciliatory words: "I am loth to close. We are not enemies, but friends. We must not be enemies. Though passion may have strained, it must not break our bonds of affection. The mystic chords of memory, streching [*sic*] from every battle-field, and patriot grave, to every living heart and hearthstone, all over this broad land, will yet swell the chorus of the Union, when again touched, as surely they will be, by the better angels of our nature."[96]

On his very first day in the White House, Lincoln received bad news. The supplies at Fort Sumter in Charleston were running out.

Fort Pickens down in Florida was better provisioned, and Lincoln ordered it held and defended. But Fort Sumter was in peril. Lincoln, in the course of his inaugural address, had made a promise to "hold, occupy, and possess the property, and places belonging to the government. . . ."[97] So what was to be done about Sumter?

Lincoln asked for the advice of his top-ranking military officer, General Winfield Scott. He also sought advice from his cabinet.

Scott was extremely pessimistic. Seward was convinced that the fort should be evacuated. He started to spread some unauthorized rumors to Confederate agents that the fort would be abandoned very soon.

But Montgomery Blair was committed to holding the fort and he introduced Lincoln to a relative—a retired naval officer named Gustavus Vasa Fox—who had a plan to reinforce and provision Fort Sumter by means of a small flotilla.

A slim majority of Lincoln's cabinet opposed this move. Nevertheless, Lincoln quietly granted Fox approval to travel to the fort at night and assess the situation.

Lincoln also sent an agent of his own into South Carolina to report on public opinion. This agent was a friend named Stephen S. Hurlbut, an Illinois colleague who was born in South Carolina. After visiting Charleston, Hurlbut bluntly told Lincoln there was "no attachment to the Union" in South Carolina. He said that even "a ship known to contain *only provisions* for Sumpter [*sic*]"—in other words a ship containing food but no troops—"would be stopped & refused admittance." He said that an evacuation of the fort would be "followed by a demand for Pickens and the Keys of the Gulf," and that "the attempt to fulfill the duties of the Executive Office in enforcing the laws & authority of the U.S." within the limits of the so-called Confederate States "will be War."[98]

Lincoln called another meeting of his cabinet on March 29. He suggested a modified proposal: He would send an expedition to Sumter and *announce his intention* to secessionists. He would tell them that the fort would be *peacefully* provisioned as long as the Confederates held their fire. The ships would be delivering *food* to feed some hungry men. It almost sounded like a mercy mission. The cabinet supported this proposal, with Seward in dissent.

The sheer cunning of the move has elicited praise and condemnation down the years. For Lincoln's message to the South could be read in very different ways. In the North it sounded mild and innocuous. In the South it was an act of defiance. Lincoln knew from his agent what the South Carolinians would think when he told them of his plans. And he knew what they would do in return. But it was *Northern* opinion that he wanted to bring into line with his Sumter policy.

Historian James M. McPherson has observed that "if Confederates opened fire on the unarmed boats carrying 'food for hungry men,' the South would stand convicted of an aggressive act. . . . This would unite the North and, perhaps, keep the South divided. If southerners allowed the supplies to go through, peace and the status quo at Sumter could be preserved and the Union government would have won an important symbolic victory. Lincoln's new conception of the resupply undertaking was a stroke of genius. In effect he was telling Jefferson Davis, 'Heads I win, Tails you lose.' It was the first sign of the mastery that would mark Lincoln's presidency."[99]

Oblivious to this mastery was Seward, whose judgment had been yielding to a very strange flight from reality. On April 1, he sent Lincoln a presumptuous and pushy memorandum entitled "Some thoughts for the President's consideration." Seward complained that, after drifting for a month, the administration was "without a policy either domestic or foreign."

He counseled the abandonment of Fort Sumter and urged that Fort Pickens alone be defended. He urged Lincoln to rally Union sentiment in Southern states through a naked jingoistic ploy: he should try to pick a quarrel with France or Spain, since both of those nations were asserting their interests in the Western Hemisphere.

Surely, Seward argued, this quarrel could be fanned into a war. And such a war might cancel out secessionist fervor and revive the old patriotic bond between the North and South. The *pièce de résistance* was the suggestion by Seward that Lincoln choose "some member of his Cabinet" to supervise the policy.

Once again, Lincoln had to put Seward quite firmly in his place. He carefully responded to Seward's allegation that the president and cabinet had drifted for a month, and that they lacked a coherent policy. "At the *beginning* of that month," he reminded Seward, he announced in his Inaugural Address:

> "The power confided in me will be used to hold, occupy and possess the property and places belonging to the government, and to collect the duties and imposts." This had your distinct approval at the time; and, taken in connection with the order I immediately gave General Scott, directing him to employ every means in his power to strengthen and hold the forts, comprises the exact domestic policy you now urge, with the single exception, that it does not propose to abandon Fort Sumpter [*sic*]. . . .
>
> Upon your closing propositions, that "whatever policy we adopt, there must be an energetic prossecution [*sic*] of it"
>
> "For this purpose it must be somebody's business to pursue and direct it incessantly"
>
> "Either the President must do it himself, and be all the while active in it, or"
>
> "Devolve it on some member of his cabinet"
>
> I remark that if this must be done, *I* must do it.[100]

Lincoln could have rid himself of Seward. Indeed, Seward had offered in a moody and petulant manner to resign on an earlier occasion. But Lincoln kept him on—and his reason for doing so was probably to keep him *on a very tight leash*, thus containing his potential for mischief.

On April 4, Lincoln met with Fox to put the finishing touches on their plan. Lincoln would notify the governor of South Carolina that a peaceful supply expedition was heading to Sumter. The first boats into the harbor would indeed be unarmed. But if Confederates should fire upon the boats, then some warships held in reserve beyond the harbor would return the fire. Having done so, they would escort the expedition to the fort.

On April 6, Lincoln sent off his message to the governor of South Carolina by courier. He also permitted some leaks to the press with regard to the mission and the peaceful intentions behind it.[101]

South Carolina Governor Francis W. Pickens received Lincoln's message on April 8. At once, the Confederates' military commander in Charleston, General P.G.T. Beauregard, cabled Jefferson Davis in Montgomery, Alabama, and reported the news. Davis's response was immediate: he had a telegram sent to Beauregard commanding him to fire on the Lincoln expedition as soon as the ships arrived.[102]

On April 10, an old friend and colleague of Davis's suggested that he act preemptively. "No one doubts that Lincoln intends war," cabled Louis Wigfall of Texas, who was staying in Charleston. "The delay on his part is only to complete his preparations. All here is ready on our side. Our delay is therefore to his advantage, and our disadvantage. Let us take Fort Sumter before we have to fight the fleet and the fort."[103]

Davis amended his orders to Beauregard, instructing his general to issue an ultimatum to Fort Sumter: evacuate or else. The bombardment of Fort Sumter began on April 12, before Lincoln's ships reached the harbor.

The Union troops at Fort Sumter were finally obliged to evacuate, but the response in the North was almost everything that Lincoln could have wished. Even some of the most flagrantly partisan Democrats were clamoring for war against secessionist traitors. On April 15, Lincoln issued a proclamation calling for seventy-five thousand troops from the state militias to suppress the insurrection in the South. They would serve for a ninety-day term.[104] In the same proclamation, he called a special session of Congress that would start on the Fourth of July.

The militia call tipped the uneasy balance in Virginia's secession convention, which proceeded to vote for secession on April 17. Arkansas proclaimed secession on May 6, with North Carolina following on May 20. Tennessee proclaimed secession in the following month.

Pro-slavery leaders exulted in this turn of events; moreover, they dedicated themselves and their Confederate nation-in-the-making to the triumph of white supremacy. Confederate Vice President Alexander Stephens, for example, had declared in March that the Confederacy has put at rest forever all the agitating questions relating to our peculiar institution—African slavery as it exists among us—the proper status of the negro in our form of civilization. This was the immediate cause of the late rupture and present revolution. Jefferson, in his forecast, had anticipated this, as the "rock upon which the old Union would split." He was right. . . . But . . . the prevailing ideas entertained by him and most of the leading statesmen at the time of the formation of the old Constitution were, that the enslavement of the African was in violation of the laws of nature. . . . It was an evil they knew not well how to deal with; but the general opinion of the men of that day was, that, somehow or other, in the order of Providence, the institution would be evanescent and pass away. . . . Those ideas, however, were fundamentally wrong. They rested upon an assumption of the equality of the races. This was an error. It was a sandy foundation, and the idea of a Government built upon it—when the "storm came and the wind blew, it fell."

Our new Government is founded upon exactly the opposite ideas; its foundations are laid, its cornerstone rests, upon the great truth that the negro is not equal to the white man; that slavery, subordination to the superior race, is his natural and moral condition. This, our new Government, is the first, in the history of the world, based upon this great physical, philosophical, and moral truth.[105]

Many Southerners who fought for the Confederacy would fight to defend their communities, their families, their homes. Nonetheless, it is absolutely clear—and the point demands very strong emphasis—that the impetus for secession had arisen in the slave-holding class of the South.

Many slave-holding Southerners were ever more intent upon expansion. As early as February 1860, the *Charleston Mercury* had spoken of "Mexico and the Tropics" as ripe for the plucking and asked whether any prescient observer could possibly deny that "as in the past, so in the future, the Anglo-Saxon race will, in the course of years, occupy and absorb the whole of that splendid but ill-peopled country, and . . . remove by a gradual process, before them, the worthless mongrel races that now inhabit and curse the land[.]"[106]

The place to begin was New Mexico, the *Mercury* suggested: even though this region was regarded by some as "too barren and arid for Southern occupation or settlement," it nonetheless "teems with mineral resources." For this reason the South should remember that "there is no vocation in the world in which slavery can be more useful or profitable than in mining."[107]

In the summer of 1861, the Confederate States sent military forces to New Mexico. Indeed, as historian Eugene D. Genovese has pointed out, "Confederate troops marched into New Mexico with the intention of proceeding to Tucson and then swinging south to take Sonora, Chihuahua, Durango, and Tamaulipas. . . . Juárez was so alarmed that he was ready to go to great lengths to help the Union put down the rebellion."[108]

The long-term scope of an empire for Southern slavery appeared unlimited. Alexander Stephens had declared that the Confederate States comprised "the nucleus of a growing power, which, if we are true to ourselves, our destiny, and high mission, will become the controlling power on this continent."[109]

But the short-term Confederate challenge—indeed, the short-term Confederate imperative—was to unify the slave-state bloc. With Virginia in Confederate hands, the state of Maryland should come soon enough. And then Lincoln could sit in his surrounded city to await his capture and its sequel.

"We are prepared to fight," exulted the *Mobile Advertiser*, "and the enemy is not. . . . Now is the time for action, while he is yet unprepared. Let . . . a hundred thousand men . . . get over the border as quickly as they can. Let a division enter every Northern border state, destroy railroad connections to prevent concentration of the enemy, and the desperate strait of these States, the body of Lincoln's country, will compel him to a peace—or compel his successor, should Virginia not suffer him to escape from his doomed capital."[110]

Lincoln was alert to the threat of invasion and he took urgent action to preempt it. In the first week of April he secretly advised Pennsylvania's governor, Andrew G. Curtin, that militia troops would be needed to defend the nation's capital. On April 8, he told Curtin, "I think the necessity of being *ready* increases. Look to it."[111]

A few army and volunteer companies defended the capital when Lincoln issued his militia call on April 15. And more were on the way—a few hundred troops arrived from Pennsylvania on April 18.

The next day, a large mob of secessionists in Baltimore attacked the Sixth Regiment of Massachusetts Volunteers on their way to Washington. Richard N. Current has observed that "many Baltimoreans, including city officials, though not the Mayor, were determined secessionists, and so were most members of the Maryland legislature. In the city, and in the counties adjacent to Washington, there was a secret organization with the ultimate aim of seizing the national capital and setting up a provisional government to serve the interests of the Confederacy." In the aftermath of the Baltimore riot, the "conspirators sent to Richmond for a supply of arms. Responding with alacrity, the

Virginia governor forwarded two thousand muskets and promised twenty heavy guns. President Davis encouraged [Virginia] Governor Letcher. 'Sustain Baltimore, if practicable,' Davis telegraphed to him."[112]

On the night of April 19, some railroad bridges in Baltimore were burned at the order of the city's own officials. This would make the reinforcement of Washington much more difficult.

These events must be clearly understood to make sense of Lincoln's policy in Maryland. On April 19, Lincoln asked his attorney general, Edward Bates, to give him an opinion on declaring martial law in the state. On the same day, he declared a naval blockade of the Confederate states.

On April 25, as more Northern regiments arrived to defend the capital city, he wrote to General Scott with regard to the Maryland legislature. The governor of Maryland, under public pressure, had convened the state's General Assembly. Lincoln worried that they might attempt secession:

> The Maryland legislature assembles to-morrow at Anapolis [sic]; and, not improbably, will take action to arm the people of that State against the United States. The question has been submitted to, and considered by me, whether it would not be justifiable, upon the ground of necessary defense, for you, as commander in Chief of the United States Army, to arrest, or disperse the members of that body. I think it would *not* be justifiable; nor, efficient for the desired object.
>
> First, they have a clearly legal right to assemble; and, we can not know in advance, that their action will not be lawful, and peaceful. And if we wait until they shall *have* acted, their arrest, or dispersion, will not lessen the effect of their action.
>
> Secondly, we *can* not permanently prevent their action. If we arrest them, we can not long hold them as prisoners; and when liberated, they will immediately re-assemble, and take their action. And, precisely the same if we simply disperse them. They will immediately re-assemble in some other place.
>
> I therefore conclude that it is only left to the Commanding General to watch, and await their action, which, if it shall be to arm their people against the United States, he is to adopt the most prompt, and efficient means to counteract, even, if necessary, to the bombardment of their cities—and in the extremest necessity, the suspension of the writ of habeas corpus.[113]

The bombardment of their cities: already, the supposedly "moderate" Lincoln was beginning to move toward the policies we call "total war."

Though the legislature of Maryland did not attempt secession, Lincoln nonetheless authorized Scott to suspend the writ of habeas corpus in Maryland on April 27. Two days later he instructed the secretary of the navy to "have as strong a War Steamer as you can conveniently put on that duty, to cruise upon the Potomac, and to look in upon, and, if practicable, examine the Bluff and vicinity, at what is called the White House, once or twice per day; and, in any case of an attempt to erect a battery there, to drive away the party attempting it. . . ."[114]

The city appeared to be safe by the first week of May. But Lincoln's thoughts had been moving very quickly from defensive to offensive options. On May 3, he issued another militia call for forty-two thousand more troops. These troops, however, were required to sign up for *three years*. He expanded the size of the regular army and navy. Congress would be called upon to ratify all of these actions in the special session that Lincoln had summoned for the Fourth of July.

Above all, Lincoln sought to devise an appropriate war plan. As McPherson has noted, Lincoln was "painfully aware that his Confederate counterpart . . . was better qualified than he as a military leader. Jefferson Davis had graduated from West Point, commanded a regiment in the Mexican War, and served four years (1853–1857) as an outstanding U.S. secretary of war. To remedy his deficiencies, Lincoln borrowed books on military strategy from the Library of Congress and burned the midnight oil reading them. His experience as a self-taught lawyer and his analytical mind (for mental exercise he had mastered Euclidian geometry on his own) stood him in good stead."[115]

Indeed, his mental powers were architectonic: he could grasp in a moment the relationship of parts to whole. He could visualize surges of power as they flowed along lines of force. In this way he would quickly surpass the outmoded thinking that was frequently instilled in young military men—thinking that regarded the troops of the enemy as *barriers* standing in the way of proper *targets* like the enemy's capital city. With all due respect to the importance of fixed geographical assets in war—the Confederate capital, for instance, which was moved to Richmond, Virginia, in the latter part of May—Lincoln quickly came to view the Confederate armies as *targets in their own right*. They were *sources of power* that his armies had to conquer or destroy.

Historian T. Harry Williams has said that Lincoln was "a better natural strategist than were most of the trained soldiers. He saw the big picture of war from the start. The policy of the government was to restore the Union by force; the strategy perforce had to be offensive. Lincoln knew that numbers, material resources, and sea power were on his side. . . . He grasped immediately the advantage that numbers gave the North and urged his generals to keep up a constant pressure on the whole strategic line of the Confederacy until a weak spot was found—and a break-through could be made."[116]

In late April, he requested a strategic plan from General Scott. Scott proposed to seal off the rebel states through a naval blockade augmented by control of the Mississippi River. When this had been accomplished, in Scott's opinion, the government should then let the steady pressure of containment impel the Confederate leaders to desist. This "Anaconda Plan," he suggested, would squeeze the life out of the rebellion.

The containment approach came naturally to Lincoln, for it built upon his policy for slavery. Indeed, he had issued his orders for a naval blockade already. But for military purposes, containment was not enough. Williams has argued that "even if the Anaconda worked, it would take years to make its effect felt, and [Lincoln] wanted quicker results. The defect in the thinking of Scott, the military man, was the idea that the war could be won by a single effort of some kind. Lincoln, the civilian strategist, knew better; he knew that many efforts of different kinds would be required."[117]

As military forces came pouring into Washington and elsewhere, he weighed his many options for attacking the Confederate forces. He prepared for the congressional session in July that would commit the nation to the war. The times had become revolutionary. Lincoln tested and exercised his powers of command as the flow of events rushed along.

In June he received some poignant news. Stephen Douglas, "the most dangerous enemy of liberty because the most insidious one," as Lincoln had once called him, had succumbed to a "rheumatic fever." He was dead.

He had visited Lincoln at the White House and offered to help build support for the war, for he had always been a patriotic unionist. But now, like a candle that had "flickered in the socket," he was gone.

Yet his legacy would linger in the form of a white supremacy consensus. This would curb Lincoln's actions for a time, as we shall see—but it could not constrain them forever. A great decision would be coming in a year: the decision to liberate.

FOUR

Lincoln and Emancipation, 1861–1862

LINCOLN'S INSTINCTS appeared to be "moderate" as war began. But in the very first year of the war against secession, he extended his plans to kill slavery. He found a way to move beyond the first step of his moral strategy—containment—to the process of long-term phaseout.

In immediate terms, Lincoln needed three things to beat the rebels: full access to Northern resources, the continued support of a Northern majority, and brilliant commanders in the field. Winfield Scott made it very clear to Lincoln that a younger man should be offered command of the army on the fields of battle. In April, he suggested that Lincoln consider Colonel Robert E. Lee of Virginia. On April 18, Lincoln offered the position to Lee through an emissary, Francis Preston Blair, Sr.

Lee turned down the offer. At the same time, an impressive number of other West Pointers from the South chose to serve the Confederate cause. Lincoln, however, had very little time in which to brood upon the loss of such a large group of capable commanders. In May, two more of the slave states, Arkansas and North Carolina, succumbed to secession. And a lethal fight was beginning in Missouri, as Governor Claiborne Jackson and former Governor Sterling Price tried to take the state out of the Union.

Another border slave state was hanging in the balance: Kentucky's pro-Confederate governor faced off against a determined Unionist majority in the legislature. The legislature managed to hold off secession by proclaiming "neutrality": both Confederate and Union forces were warned to stay out of the state.

Lincoln did his best to support the loyal Kentuckians. He authorized Major Robert Anderson, the commander-to-the-end at Fort
Sumter, to establish a recruiting office in Ohio for Kentucky Unionists. But he avoided any short-term actions that could play into the
hands of the governor.

When politics permitted fast action, however, Lincoln seized the
opportunity and acted. In the western counties of Virginia, the secessionist cause was unpopular. Some leaders in the area began to talk
openly of plans for seceding from Virginia. When Confederate troops
were dispatched to the region in the latter part of May, Lincoln sent
Union troops from Ohio. Just a few weeks later, on June 19, a Unionist convention met at Wheeling, Virginia to begin the slow process
that would gradually result in the new state of West Virginia.

So it went, as the Confederates and Unionists scrambled for position not only in the border states but also in the global arena. Robert
Toombs, who served as the Confederates' first secretary of state, commenced a major campaign to win big-power allies abroad. One of the
Confederates' tactics took over a year to become effective: they proclaimed an embargo on the exportation of cotton in the hope that by
withholding a commodity that Europeans needed they could force diplomatic recognition or even make alliances. But the British had a back-
log of cotton in their warehouses.

Some other tactical ploys of the Confederates, however, were effective right away. They invoked the great principle of self-determination
to project their cause to the world in a favorable light. They tried to
cultivate certain aristocrats who viewed the Southern planter class with
sympathetic eyes. Viscount Palmerston, the British prime minister, appeared to be receptive.

On May 13, the Confederates won a major skirmish on the diplomatic front. Due to Lincoln's blockade of the rebellious states, the
British government declared that the Confederate States should have
"belligerent" status under international law. Emperor Napoleon III of
France took the cue and declared the same thing.

The conventions of international law regarded naval blockades as
acts of war between sovereign nations. In other words, Lincoln's attempt to contain the rebellion was ironically assisting the Confederate
claim to nationhood. Working closely with Seward and with Charles
Francis Adams, whom Lincoln had appointed as ambassador to Britain, the president struggled with the difficult problem.

As all of these events unfolded, Lincoln found himself compelled to make some very careful choices as he pondered how best to deploy his many forces in the months of May and June. He strove to fine-tune his decisions, paying careful heed to all the micro-politics in each of the distinctive arenas. But he was also careful to relate the variations to the overall strategic picture.

Above all, he used the most powerful theme of bipartisan consensus— Unionism—for all it was worth in terms of money and troops and votes to make war upon secession. His Free-Soil principles were kept under cover as he wrote the long message he intended to deliver to Congress on the Fourth of July. The last thing he needed was to lose Democratic support that was essential for the war.

Lincoln would never retreat from his pledge to keep slavery contained; indeed, his insistence on the gradual extinction of slavery was a non-negotiable element in his Unionism, even in the summer of 1861. For obvious reasons, however, the next phase of his struggle with the slave states demanded an insistently Unionist politics. After all, if the Confederates won their independence, then his plans for the long-term phaseout of slavery were obviously dead.

So any overlap in patriotic feelings that existed in the minds of Republicans and Democrats demanded cultivation. This meant, in effect, that most partisan differences regarding the slavery issue would have to be minimized in Lincoln's politics, at least for the season.

To be sure, the developing circumstances of war began to force the issue of slavery back into prominence. On May 23, a politician who applied for a Union military command, General Benjamin Butler—a Massachusetts Democrat who would gradually become a Republican— issued very significant orders. Butler and his troops were in Fortress Monroe, a United States installation on the southern Virginia coastline. Some slaves had escaped from their masters and crossed into Butler's lines. The General refused to return them, proclaiming they were "contraband of war." Lincoln let Butler's orders stand. But he did not propose going further: there was too much at risk.

On the Fourth of July, Lincoln sent his special message to Congress, a message that requested retroactive approval of the measures he had taken to suppress the insurrection since the fall of Fort Sumter. In addition, he requested authority to raise at least 400,000 more soldiers; he also asked for a congressional authorization of $400 million to finance the war.

Lincoln ridiculed the logic of secession; he argued that statehood, *per se*, was impossible outside of the Union. "The States," he argued, "have their *status* IN the Union, and they have no other *legal status*. . . . The Union is older than any of the States; and, in fact, it created them as States."[1]

The Confederate cause was not secession at all; it was treason pure and simple—even though the rebels tried to cloak their crimes against the nation in the rhetoric of states' rights. Confederates, said Lincoln, "knew that they could never raise their treason to any respectable magnitude, by any name which implies *violation* of law. . . . Accordingly, they commenced . . . an insidious debauching of the public mind" by means of the doctrine of state sovereignty. "With rebellion thus sugar-coated," Lincoln said, "they have been drugging the public mind in their section for more than thirty years . . . until at length, they have brought many good men to a willingness to take up arms against the government the day *after* some assemblage of men have enacted the farcical pretense of taking their State out of the Union."[2] The Confederate cause should be viewed as a "giant insurrection," Lincoln said.[3]

Gigantic though it was, it was led by a despotic minority, according to Lincoln. "It may well be questioned," he argued, "whether there is, to-day, a majority of the legally qualified voters of any State, except perhaps South Carolina, in favor of disunion." To the contrary, he continued, "there is much reason to believe the Union men are the majority in many . . . of the so-called seceded States." Even in Virginia and Tennessee, which submitted their acts of secession to the voters for ratification, the results were suspicious, Lincoln claimed. "The result of an election, held in military camps, where the bayonets are all on one side of the question voted upon, can scarcely be considered as demonstrating popular sentiment," Lincoln said. In both of these states, there was reason to believe that the voters were "coerced to vote against the Union."[4]

The seceders cared nothing for the will of the people, or the rights of the people, or the *cause* of the people, Lincoln charged. He pointed out that in their draft Confederate Constitution "they omit 'We, the People,' and substitute 'We, the deputies of the sovereign and independent States.' Why? Why this deliberate pressing out of view [of] the rights of men, and the authority of the people?"

Essentially, Lincoln argued, this war was "a People's contest. On the side of the Union, it is a struggle for maintaining in the world, that form, and substance of government, whose leading object is, to elevate the condition of men—to lift artificial weights from all shoulders—to clear the paths of laudable pursuit for all—to afford all, an *unfettered* start, and a fair chance, in the race of life [my emphasis]."[5]

Regarding those who rebelled against a people's government, the duty of patriots was clear. Their duty was to "demonstrate to the world, that those who fairly carry an election, can also suppress a rebellion— that ballots are the rightful, and peaceful, successors to bullets; and that when ballots have fairly, and constitutionally, decided, there can be no successful appeal, back to bullets; that there can be no successful appeal, except to ballots themselves, at succeeding elections."[6]

At this point he made a brief and elliptical reference to his Free-Soil program. He treated it as almost incidental to the issue of putting down secessionist treason. "No popular government," he said, "can long survive a marked precedent, that those who carry an election, can only save the government from immediate destruction, by giving up the main point, upon which the people gave the election. The people themselves, and not their servants, can safely reverse their own deliberate decisions."[7] This was not a *Republican* war, he told the Democratic members of Congress in so many words. It was a fight to protect the very principle of popular rule through elections.

Surely Congress had to judge the propriety of what he had done, but he urged bipartisan unity to save the nation. Referring to himself in the third-person, he said "the Executive . . . has, so far, done what he has deemed his duty," adding that the members of Congress must clearly perform their own duty in whatever way they chose. He concluded by urging all American patriots to swiftly "go forward without fear, and with manly hearts."[8]

Congress gave him everything he asked for; indeed, they exceeded his financial request by approving the immense sum of *$500* million for the war. Most of the money would be raised through the sale of bonds—deficit spending—though Congress went on to approve the first direct tax on incomes in American history (deferring its collection until 1863).

Thus armed with congressional authorization, Lincoln turned his mind to fast victory: he would aim a decisive blow at the political heart of the rebellion. In his message to Congress he had singled out Virginia for its offer to allow the Confederate government to move its capital to Richmond.[9]

On June 29, Lincoln made initial plans for a Virginia campaign in a meeting with General Winfield Scott and Irvin McDowell, the general in tactical command of the Union forces in the National Capital region. Lincoln wanted to attack the Confederate troops who were gathered at Manassas railway junction near the banks of a stream known as Bull Run, only twenty-five miles southwest of Washington, D.C.

As McDowell got ready to attack, there was good news from western Virginia: Generals George B. McClellan and William S. Rosecrans defeated the Confederates on July 11 in the battle of Rich Mountain. In Washington, a mood of triumphalism reigned and the battle cry of "On to Richmond" was heard through the city. McDowell and his men marched off to Manassas, and they crossed Bull Run on Sunday, July 21. Much of official Washington decided to tag along in carriages.

Their hopes would be shattered when McDowell's forces were driven from the battlefield in panic. The first battle of Manassas was a tactical disaster for the North, and its shock effects in Washington and elsewhere were profound.

But it only made Lincoln more determined. Two days after the battle, he wrote a list of private "Memoranda of Military Policy Suggested by the Bull Run Defeat." Among their other provisions, the memoranda proposed to "let the forces late before Manassas . . . be reorganized as rapidly as possible." He also proposed further action in other theatres.[10]

Lincoln promptly demoted McDowell and summoned George B. McClellan, the victorious commander from western Virginia, to take command of the army in Washington, the army that was soon to be christened the "Army of the Potomac."

In the aftermath of the defeat at Manassas, congressional politics were churning. The Democrats pushed through some stark resolutions on July 22 and July 25 that were aimed at preventing the Republican Party from expanding the war's rationale and political objectives. The Crittenden-Johnson Resolutions, named for John J. Crittenden of Kentucky (the author of the failed Crittenden Compromise of December, 1860) and Andrew Johnson of Tennessee (the only Senator from a Confederate state who refused to resign from his seat in the United States Senate), declared that the war was definitely not to be fought for the purpose of "overthrowing or interfering with the rights or established institutions" of any state, but "to defend and maintain the supremacy of the Constitution and to preserve the Union with all the dignity, equality, and rights of the several States unimpaired."[11] In other words, slavery was not to be molested in any of the states that permitted it, even in the so-called Confederate states.

The politics of war were so delicate that most of the Republicans supported this action, however faint-heartedly. But a few weeks later, Republicans infuriated Crittenden and other pro-slavery Democrats by pushing through a daring new counter-measure. On August 6, Congress passed a new law that would permit the confiscation of any property—including slaves—that Confederates used in their rebellion. Lincoln signed this law, which in many ways built upon the precedent that Benjamin Butler had set through the orders that he issued at Fortress Monroe back in May. Confiscation was not emancipation: the "contraband" slaves who were seized by the army were in no way given their freedom on a permanent basis. But they would not be returned to their owners.

Many anti-slavery leaders were eager to move much farther and to do it quickly. One of them was John C. Frémont, the Republicans' nominee for president in 1856. Frémont had served as an explorer for the Army, and he asked for a commission as a Union general. Lincoln gave him the command of the "Western Department," with his headquarters at St. Louis. To him would be given the challenge of defeating the Confederate forces in Missouri.

The fighting in Missouri was bitter, and Frémont used the occasion to assert his anti-slavery leadership. On August 30, he issued a military proclamation declaring that the slaves of all the rebels in Missouri were henceforth free.

Three days later, Lincoln sent off a message to Frémont advising him to pay closer heed to all the short-term ramifications of his action. "I think there is great danger," Lincoln said, "that the closing paragraph" of Frémont's proclamation "in relation to the confiscation of property, and the liberating slaves of traiterous owners, will alarm our Southern Union friends, and turn them against us—perhaps ruin our rather fair prospect in Kentucky. Allow me therefore to ask, that you will as of your own motion, modify that paragraph so as to conform to the . . . act of Congress, entitled 'An Act to confiscate property used for insurrectionary purposes,' approved August 6th, 1861, and a copy of which I herewith send you. This letter is written in a spirit of caution and not of censure."[12]

Frémont told the president to *order* him to change the proclamation. Lincoln did so, observing to the general (and also for the record) that since Frémont expressed "the preference . . . that I should make an open order for the modification . . . I cheerfully do."[13] Lincoln began to have serious doubts about the soundness of Frémont's judgment. And since the military efforts of Frémont had been failures, the president relieved him of command.

The Frémont affair prompted further agitation by Republicans who sought to expand the anti-slavery dimensions of the war. Even Senator Orville Browning, an Illinois friend of the president's, was critical of Lincoln's response to Frémont.

In his answer to a letter from Browning, Lincoln said that he would stay within the strictest limits of the law unless Congress *changed* the law. "Genl. Fremont's proclamation," Lincoln wrote, "is purely *political*, and not within the range of *military* law, or necessity." With regard to the military seizure of slaves, Lincoln wrote, "if the General needs them, he can seize them, and use them; but when the need is past, it is not for him to fix their permanent future condition. That must be settled according to laws made by law-makers, and not by military proclamations."

Lincoln then applied the same stipulation to himself: "I do not say Congress might not with propriety pass a law, on the point, just such as General Fremont proclaimed. I do not say I might not, as a member of Congress, vote for it. What I object to, is, that I as President, shall expressly or impliedly seize and exercise the permanent legislative functions of the government."

Lincoln then took time to review the political issues that pertained to Frémont's action. He told Browning that when news of the proclamation by Frémont had reached Kentucky, "a whole company of our Volunteers threw down their arms and disbanded." And to lose Kentucky, Lincoln warned, "is nearly the same as to lose the whole game. Kentucky gone, we can not hold Missouri, nor, as I think, Maryland. These all against us, and the job on our hands is too large for us. We would as well consent to separation at once, including the surrender of this capitol." But if Browning and other Republicans would only be patient, "give up your restlessness for new positions, and back me manfully on the grounds upon which you and other kind friends gave me the election . . . we shall go through triumphantly."[14]

Lincoln had some very pressing reasons to be careful in regard to Kentucky. On September 3, Confederate forces under General Leonidas Polk had occupied Columbus, Kentucky on the Mississippi River. Kentucky Unionists were quick to seize the opportunity afforded by this breach of their "neutrality": through the Unionist legislature, they appealed to Washington for help in repelling the "invaders." Union troops under General Ulysses S. Grant were dispatched to Kentucky only three days later.

On the eastern front, the political pressure in Washington was building for a fast and decisive return to the attack in Virginia. But George B. McClellan, the commander of the Army of the Potomac, was slow to move. He was gradually taking the remnants of the army that was beaten at Manassas and was trying to shape them, along with many thousands of new recruits, into a large and mighty force. This work was McClellan's forte: he was excellent at training and preparation. McClellan was by temperament and experience a military engineer.

He was also a Democratic white supremacist who had voted for Stephen Douglas. Supporting the war in the manner of Douglas, he had no intention of moving in Frémont's direction. In fact, he asked a Democratic confidante to "help me dodge the nigger—we want nothing to do with him."[15] McClellan made no secret of his views on the "negro question." Republicans worried that he might be treacherous, but Lincoln was prepared to give him time. After all, the troops seemed to worship McClellan: they called him "little Mac." Others—especially Democrats—called him the "young Napoleon" and talked to him of presidential prospects.

It went to his head in a manner that elicited arrogance. "I seem to have become *the* power in the land," he wrote to his wife. "I almost think that were I to win some small success now, I could become Dictator or anything else that might please me—but nothing of the kind would please me—*therefore I won't* be Dictator. Admirable self denial!"[16]

This foolish demeanor was linked to some character flaws. McClellan possessed two crippling vices that would doom him to failure as a general. First, his bravado was nothing more than a brittle veneer to conceal a major weakness of will. When the bloodshed started and the casualties rose, this military man would prove weak to the point of timidity. Second, when he lost a battle, he would blame it on his superiors. Ironically, his victories in western Virginia that summer had been won to some extent by the skill of his subordinates.[17]

Lincoln had yet to discover these problems in early October when he wrote a memorandum on military strategy envisioning the next campaigns. His intention was to work for simultaneous, coordinated action in all theatres.[18] But McClellan was still inactive, and congressional

Republicans were starting to suggest that he malingered due to "softness"—perhaps a *Democratic* softness toward the South.

Lincoln suggested that McClellan accelerate his plans, and the general's response was revealing. He said that Winfield Scott, the old general in chief, was to blame for most of the delays. Perhaps retirement for Scott would be the answer, suggested McClellan.[19]

The old general, ill and fatigued, was more than ready to retire and McClellan was appointed on November 1 to command all the Union armies. Early in November, he rearranged some theatre commands. He appointed a military bureaucrat, Henry Halleck, to command a large "Western Department," consisting of Missouri and the western portion of Kentucky. He created a "Department of the Ohio," comprising eastern Kentucky and all of Tennessee, appointing Don Carlos Buell, an officer who shared a great many of his own personal foibles, to command it. McClellan himself would retain direct command of the Army of the Potomac.

All through November, Lincoln visited McClellan at his headquarters, sharing ideas, encouraging action, and attempting to build up rapport with the "young Napoleon." In mid-November, he tried to get McClellan enthused about a new proposal from the Navy Department to attack New Orleans and move up the Mississippi River. McClellan was not impressed.

Lincoln had some other issues to contend with. It was time for him to write his long annual message to Congress, a message transmitted in writing at the end of the calendar year. As December approached, it was beginning to look as if the war might last a long time. For this reason, the politics of war were changing.

For Lincoln, the outlook was guardedly hopeful as winter arrived. Notwithstanding the bitter disappointment at Manassas, the Confederate menace was preliminarily contained. The British held back from any open or decisive recognition of Confederate independence. The Unionist position in the border states had been slowly but dramatically improving. Bipartisan unity in Congress remained when it came to the issue of the *Union*.

But the slavery issue had caused a clear schism when Republicans had pushed through their confiscation bill on an obvious party-line basis—a bill that Lincoln promptly signed. Lincoln's strategy concerning slavery had been weighing on his mind since summer.

After pondering the matter, Lincoln came to a decision in the closing days of 1861: he would use the Civil War as a fitting and perhaps
providential occasion to launch the second phase of his anti-slavery
strategy. With slavery's *containment* on the way to accomplishment—
and the Republicans in Congress were fully intent upon pushing through
a free-soil measure just as soon as the timing seemed right—perhaps
the *phaseout* of slavery could also be pushed if the president could catalyze the process.

The politics, of course, would be tricky, but perhaps it could be
done through coordinated legislative action at the federal and state
levels. The thirteenth amendment to the Constitution that Congress
had passed that spring—the amendment that would tie the hands of
Congress forever on the subject of slavery within the states—had not
been ratified. And so the coast was clear, at least in legal terms, to
launch a gradual phaseout of slavery, propelled with federal funding.

As historian Allen C. Guelzo has suggested, Lincoln truly believed
"from the first" that he should "not leave office without some form of
legislative emancipation policy in place. By his design, the burden would
have to rest mainly on the state legislatures, largely because Lincoln
mistrusted the federal judiciary and expected that any emancipation
initiatives that came directly from his hand would be struck down in
the courts."[20]

Lincoln secretly drafted some plans in late November for a bill to be
passed by the legislature of Delaware—tiny Delaware, whose Unionist
politics and small population of slaves made it seemingly the perfect
place from which to launch emancipation in the border states. Lincoln's
bill, if adopted by the state of Delaware, would *ask* for congressional
financial assistance to rid the state of slavery. "Be it enacted by the
State of Delaware," Lincoln's draft proclaimed, "that on condition the
United States of America will, at the present session of Congress, engage by law to pay . . . in the six per cent bonds of the said United
States, the sum of seven hundred and nineteen thousand and two hundred dollars, in five equal annual instalments [*sic*], there shall be neither
slavery nor involuntary servitude, at any time after the first day of January in the year of our Lord one thousand, eight hundred and sixty-seven,
within the said State of Delaware. . . ."[21] A second version of the plan
would extend the process over thirty years. Lincoln intended to work
behind the scenes for the Delaware bill as he helped the Republicans

in Congress to be ready for the moment when the state would apply for assistance. He would work both ends of the process simultaneously.

As he drafted these proposals, he put the final touches on his message to Congress, which he sent on December 3. While the message restated some points he had made in July, it included some important new proposals.

Lincoln hurled some new barbs against Confederate autocracy, repeating his earlier warnings that Confederate power was a threat to free government itself, observing that the power of the Southern electorate seemed to be shrinking in Confederate states.[22]

Lincoln spoke once again of the free-labor system as "the just, and generous, and prosperous system, which opens the way to all." Regardless of the rights of capital, he said, human "labor is the superior of capital, and deserves much the higher consideration."[23] Property rights, said Lincoln, flowed directly from the efforts of the people, and were grounded in the aspirations of the people. But Confederates meant to invert this principle and make human rights subservient to property.

The great war to suppress the insurrection, said Lincoln, was proceeding rather well, but coordination was essential. And in that regard, Lincoln mentioned McClellan's new position as general in chief, observing that "the nation seemed to give a unanimous concurrence" to the appointment. And yet he added a statement that seemed to imply that he was hedging his bets about McClellan. There was a saying, said Lincoln, that "one bad general is better than two good ones; and the saying is true, if taken to mean no more than that an army is better directed by a single mind, though inferior, than by two superior ones, at . . . cross-purposes with each other."[24] A curious thing for a commander in chief to observe in a message to Congress—unless the actual purpose was to seed the record with expressions of doubt that might be useful later on if McClellan turned out to be incompetent.

Turning to the slavery issue, Lincoln noted his own strict adherence to the letter of the confiscation law. His behavior had been prudent and legal to a fault: "In considering the policy to be adopted for suppressing the insurrection," he declared, "I have been anxious and careful that the inevitable conflict for this purpose shall not degenerate into a violent and remorseless revolutionary struggle. I have, therefore, in every case, thought it proper to keep the integrity of the Union prominent as the primary object of the contest on our part, leaving all questions which are not of vital military importance to the more deliberate action of the legislature." But then Lincoln made a statement that could plausibly be read as a come-on to fellow Republicans: "If a new law upon the same subject shall be proposed," Lincoln said, "its propriety will be duly considered."[25]

And in that connection, he added, it would probably be best to start planning right away *for the freedom of the confiscated slaves*. The slaves who had been seized by the army since Butler's proclamation were "already dependent on the United States, and must be provided for in some way," Lincoln said. Besides, he continued, it was "not impossible that some of the States will pass similar enactments for their own benefit respectively." Consequently, he continued, "I recommend that Congress provide for accepting such persons from such States, according to some mode of valuation, in lieu, *pro tanto*, of direct taxes, or upon some other plan to be agreed on with such States respectively; that such persons, on acceptance by the general government, be at once deemed free."[26]

"Deemed free." There it was—the thin end of the wedge that would open up a path for emancipation. No mention by Lincoln of the embryonic Delaware plan was included in this message to Congress. He was playing a doubled-handed game.

To appease white supremacist Democrats, not only in Congress, not only in the border states, but also in places such as "Egypt" in southern Illinois, Lincoln quickly endorsed the old colonization approach that would send former slaves to other countries when their freedom was granted. He recommended that "steps be taken for colonizing" contraband slaves "at some place, or places . . . congenial to them," adding that "it might be well to consider, too—whether the free colored people already in the United States could not, so far as individuals may desire, be included in such colonization."[27]

Here again, Lincoln's latter-day critics see a white supremacist at work. But the overall sense of his anti-slavery program makes the allegation weak. Lincoln's motive for colonization—at least until he changed his mind about the subject in 1864—was his fear that racial prejudice would undermine the cause of liberation unless, somehow, the racial issue could be gradually defused. He would make this explicit to a group of black leaders later on. Moreover, his concept of colonization was that of a *voluntary* haven—"so far as individuals may desire," had been his words.

There were even a few black leaders at the time who found the vision attractive, in light of the pervasiveness of American white supremacy—though it has to be admitted that blacks as a rule found the colonization idea to be insulting.[28]

Regardless of its feasibility (an open question), the concept of colonization was an obvious device to defuse white supremacist resistance to emancipation. Pennsylvania Congressman Charles Biddle, for example, confided that the "alarm [about emancipation] would spread to every man of my constituents who loves his country and his race if the public mind was not lulled and put to sleep with the word 'colonization.'"[29]

Lincoln's phaseout strategy for slavery was launched in December 1861. And he would push the experiment hard. He concluded his annual message by observing that "the struggle of today, is not altogether for today" but "for a vast future also."[30]

Congressional Republicans were suitably emboldened in December: they showed new strength by reversing their previous action on the Crittenden-Johnson Resolutions, which protected slavery. Fifty-three Republican congressmen changed their position when the issue came up in December. And so the Crittenden-Johnson Resolutions were repealed, and it was no longer possible for anyone to say how far or how fast the anti-slavery cause might propel the next actions of Republicans.

LINCOLN TOOK SOME UNPRECEDENTED ACTIONS to extend his anti-slavery program during the first six months of 1862. And he became more demanding of his generals.

The new year of 1862 dawned angrily and bitterly in Washington. The Army of the Potomac was still on the sidelines, and no one could predict when it would move. Indeed, the war seemed almost at a standstill. Early in December, McClellan came down with typhoid fever and was bed-ridden. Lincoln was left uninformed as to what (if anything) McClellan had been doing to stimulate coordinated action in the other military theatres. At this point, as T. Harry Williams has observed, Lincoln "took over the function of general in chief" until McClellan recovered.[31]

Lincoln wrote to Halleck and Buell, the two western commanders, asking questions and urging action.[32] Buell replied that he could not be optimistic in regard to ambitious attacks in the near future. Lincoln wrote that he was deeply disappointed; he instructed Buell and Halleck to "name as early a day as you safely can, on, or before which you can be ready to move Southward. . . ."[33]

Neither man complied. Indeed, Halleck told Lincoln he was not in a position to commence any action that would really be of benefit to Buell. Lincoln sent off a copy of the message from Halleck to the secretary of war, observing that in Halleck's department, "as everywhere else, nothing can be done."[34]

The secretary of war, Simon Cameron, was another of Lincoln's problems. Cameron was coming under fire by critics who accused him of financial and political impropriety, perhaps to the point of real crookedness. He had also been issuing statements on the slavery issue that were totally at odds with the statements of Lincoln.

Lincoln decided to ease him out of office, and appointed him Minister to Russia. To succeed Cameron, Lincoln promoted the chief legal advisor for the War Department, an attorney named Edwin M. Stanton. Stanton was a Unionist Democrat who had served for a time as attorney general under President James Buchanan—hardly a service to commend him in the eyes of Lincoln. Even earlier than that, he had clashed with Lincoln in a bitter courtroom battle. But Lincoln looked beyond these negative factors, perceiving all the benefits that Stanton could bring to the executive branch: a militant Unionist, Stanton was extremely intelligent and also familiar with the War Department's routine.

Stanton would become a very useful advisor to Lincoln, much as William H. Seward, notwithstanding his earlier lapses, began to be useful to Lincoln in a great many ways when he learned that the president was fully intent upon running his own administration.

As Lincoln made arrangements to remove Simon Cameron, he met with selected generals to get their advice and work around the absent McClellan. By January 13, McClellan was well enough—indeed, he was angry enough when he heard about these meetings behind his back—to attend a council of war with other generals, members of the cabinet, and Lincoln.

McClellan's behavior at this meeting was sulky and disdainful. He said his plans for Virginia were not quite ready, and he had no intention of revealing them unless Lincoln ordered him to do it. But he did acquiesce in the proposition that the forces of Buell should be goaded into action.

On the same day, Lincoln seized the opportunity of writing to Buell for the purpose of offering "encouragement," along with some pointed

strategic advice. He sent a copy of this letter to Halleck. He said his
"general idea of this war," his grand vision of the gatherings of force
that were currently in play on the battlefield, was his insight that "we
have the *greater* numbers, and the enemy has the *greater* facility of con-
centrating forces upon points of collision." Consequently, the Union
"must fail . . . unless we can find some way of making *our* advantage an
over-match for *his*." The way to do this, Lincoln suggested, was "by
menacing him with superior forces at *different* points, at the *same* time;
so that we can safely attack, one, or both, if he makes no change; and if
he *weakens* one to *strengthen* the other, forbear to attack the strengthened one, but seize, and hold the weakened one."[35] In other words,
Lincoln was telling his generals to stretch out the enemy's forces as
thin as they could and then smash their way through the weakest point
in the enemy's lines.

Though Lincoln was preoccupied with military matters in January
1862, his attention to the slavery issue was keen. Abolitionists and Radical Republicans were much more demanding. Around January 20, two
anti-slavery leaders paid a call on Lincoln at the White House. One of
them—an abolitionist Virginian named Moncure Daniel Conway—
wrote a long account of the meeting years later when he published his
memoirs. The account is both convincing and instructive.

Conway was joined at the meeting by William Ellery Channing, a
nephew of the great Unitarian clergyman of the same name. Their
purpose in meeting with Lincoln was to push him toward emancipation. What Lincoln allegedly revealed to them was extraordinary.

In Conway's account, Channing opened the discussion by declaring
"his belief that the opportunity of the nation to rid itself of slavery had
arrived." Lincoln responded by asking, "how he thought they might
avail themselves of it. . . . Channing suggested emancipation with compensation for the slaves." Lincoln "said he had for years been in favour
of that plan."

Then, wrote Conway, "when the President turned to me, I asked
whether we might not look to him as the coming Deliverer of the Nation from its one great evil. . . . He said, 'Perhaps we may be better able
to do something in that direction after a while than we are now.'"

Conway pressed the point harder. He asked Lincoln whether "the
masses of the American people would hail you as their deliverer if, at
the end of this war, the Union should be surviving and slavery still in

it?'" Yes, said Lincoln, "if they were to see that slavery was on the downhill."

Conway would not let up: he told Lincoln that "our fathers compromised with slavery because they thought it on the downhill; hence war to-day." At this point Lincoln confided some strategic ploys in a manner that deserves a full quotation:

> "I think the country grows in this direction daily, and I am not without hope that something of the desire of you and your friends may be accomplished. Perhaps it may be in the way suggested by a thirsty soul in Maine who found he could only get liquor from a druggist; as his robust appearance forebade the plea of sickness, he called for a soda, and whispered, 'Couldn't you put a drop o' the creeter into it unbeknownst to yourself?'" Turning to me the President said, "In working in the antislavery movement you may naturally come in contact with a great many people who agree with you, and possibly may overestimate the number in the country who hold such views. But the position in which I am placed brings me into some knowledge of opinions in all parts of the country and of many different kinds of people; and it appears to me that the great masses of this country care comparatively little about the negro, and are anxious only for military successes." We had, I think, risen to leave and had thanked him for his friendly reception when he said, "We shall need all the anti-slavery feeling in the country, and more; you can go home and try to bring the people to your views; and you may say anything you like about me, if that will help. Don't spare me!" This was said with a laugh. Then he said very gravely, "When the hour comes for dealing with slavery I trust I will be willing to do my duty though it cost my life. And, gentlemen, lives will be lost."[36]

"You may say anything you like about me, if that will help. Don't spare me!" How often in American politics have we seen a president encouraging others to besmirch his own reputation—to call him names, when it came right down to it—to increase public pressure for actions that he secretly favored but could not yet espouse? Where else in American history does such a remarkable spectacle present itself?

Until public sentiment was ready, Lincoln hinted, he would work toward emancipation by phasing it in, through deception if he felt that it was needed. He would play the role of a *Unionist only* and expand his agenda by cunning, like the druggist who connived to spike a soda for his friend in Maine—"unbeknownst to himself."

This account suggests that Lincoln envisioned his work with abolitionist militants as something of a *synergistic* process. His strategy amounted to an insider/outsider orchestration, with the "outsider" militants building up pressure in a manner that the wily "insider" used. Consider this scenario in light of the account set forth by Senator

Charles Sumner—a Radical Republican who came to believe in Lincoln's judgment—in regard to a meeting with Lincoln in December 1861. Sumner's purpose was very much the same as Conway and Channing's: to push for emancipation measures. According to Sumner, Lincoln told him that their only major difference when it came to the subject was the difference of "a month or six weeks."[37] He was probably alluding to his secret Delaware plan.

On the military front, Lincoln's patience with McClellan was slipping. On January 27 he issued an order designed to be as simple and clear as he could make it, beginning with its title, "President's General War Order No. 1." He commanded a "general movement of the Land and Naval forces of the United States" no later than "the 22nd day of February, 1862."[38]

It worked: at last McClellan unveiled his big scheme for Virginia when the Lincoln orders forced his hand. And in the Western Department, the bureaucratic Halleck permitted a subordinate, Ulysses S. Grant, to attack the Confederates.

The Confederates had been establishing a line in Kentucky with a fallback line to protect Tennessee. In February, Grant destroyed this fallback line; he attacked the Confederate defenses, moving up the Tennessee River with gunboats, attacking the Confederate bastion Fort Henry on February 6. Having captured Fort Henry, Grant moved up the Cumberland River and attacked Fort Donelson, which likewise surrendered to his forces on February 16. With the fall of Forts Henry and Donelson, the rebels' position fell apart. They withdrew not only from Kentucky but also from most of Tennessee and then fled to Mississippi.

In the East, it was a different story. McClellan decided it was time to reveal his grand design, and he did, first to Stanton and then to Lincoln. His plan was to execute a flanking maneuver, to bypass the rebels at Manassas by sending his army on boats down the Chesapeake Bay and then landing his men *in between* the rebel forces at Manassas and the city of Richmond. He would flush the Confederates out of Manassas by threatening their capital city. He proposed to land his army at Urbana, Virginia, on the Rappahannock River.

Lincoln didn't like the scheme at all. He was worried that the plan would leave Washington defenseless, that a gap in the Federal lines would be opened that would give the Confederates a chance to strike at Washington before McClellan hit Richmond. He thought that an overland attack against Manassas would be safer, since it would permit McClellan to switch back and forth from offensive to defensive measures if necessary.

McClellan begged for a chance to make a case for his plan, and Lincoln agreed. But on February 3, Lincoln dashed off a letter to McClellan with a series of questions. "If you will give me satisfactory answers," he told McClellan, "I shall gladly yield my plan to yours." The last of Lincoln's questions was a worst-case contingency issue: "In case of disaster," Lincoln wrote, "would not a safe retreat be more difficult by your plan than by mine?"[39]

McClellan defended his plan in a lengthy report that he sent via Stanton to Lincoln.[40] And so, with tremendous misgivings, Lincoln gave him a preliminary go-ahead. There is very little doubt that in the next six months Lincoln came to regret this decision. But he had no intention of allowing McClellan to behave as if he had a blank check. Indeed, Lincoln supervised the planning for the whole operation.

In February, Lincoln was preoccupied with several other issues, not least of all the fast-breaking action in the West. In addition, two depressing developments haunted him, one of them profoundly disappointing and the other one deeply tragic. In the first place, his Delaware plan was going nowhere. In the second place, on February 20, the Lincolns' next-to-youngest child, William Wallace Lincoln ("Willie") took sick and then died of a fever.

Mary Todd Lincoln was hysterical with grief and the president was terribly shaken. Of all the Lincoln children, young Willie was the closest to Lincoln himself in his personal qualities. Though a number of men who were near and dear to the Lincolns had been perishing in battle, the death of little Willie was a foretaste of all the morbid feelings and events that were soon to engulf both Lincoln and the nation in 1862 and beyond.

Early in March, Lincoln felt a greater urgency than ever on the slavery front. He had to prove to himself that his vision—his long-cherished vision of the gradual phaseout of slavery—would come into being. The emotional imperative was nothing less than this: he had to *force* the great vision into being.

His attempt to begin indirectly was a failure: even Delaware was too far-gone in the ways of the slavery system for hints or behind-the-scene promptings to have an effect. But what if a direct legislative approach by Congress—a direct and official offer of federal funding—could be put on the table? As long as it was framed as a measure to suppress the insurrection, such a measure might withstand the resistance of bigots.

On March 6, Lincoln sent Congress an unprecedented presidential message recommending "a Joint Resolution . . . as follows: 'Resolved that the United States ought to co-operate with any state which may adopt gradual abolishment of slavery, giving to such state pecuniary aid, to be used by such state in it's [sic] discretion. . . .'" Lincoln said that such a measure could weaken the Confederate rebellion: it could sever the link between the slave-holding border states and the cotton-belt states that comprised the Confederate nucleus. "The point is not that *all* the states tolerating slavery would very soon, if at all, initiate emancipation," Lincoln said. Yet the process of offering the deal to all the slave states could start a great chain reaction that could split the Southern bloc in two.

"While the offer is equally made to all," explained Lincoln, "the more Northern [of the slave states] shall, by such initiation, make it certain to the more Southern, that in no event, will the former join the latter, in their proposed confederacy." Why should states that were phasing out slavery attempt to secede?

The cost of the plan, said Lincoln, was an issue of money well spent: "In the mere financial or pecuniary view," he argued, "any member of Congress, with the census-tables and Treasury-reports before him, can readily see for himself how very soon the current expenditures of this war would purchase, at fair valuation, all the slaves in any named State."

Lincoln stressed that the plan should be "a matter of perfectly free choice." The decision would remain with the voters in each of the slave states, Lincoln insisted. But he warned that if rebel resistance should continue, "the war must also continue; and it is impossible to foresee all the incidents, which may attend and the ruin which may follow it." In other words, Lincoln was telling the supporters of slavery to take up his offer while it lasted, since sterner measures might follow. In view of "my great responsibility to my God, and to my country," Lincoln said in his conclusion, "I earnestly beg the attention of Congress and the people to the subject."[41]

Three days later, Lincoln dashed off a private letter to the editor of the *New York Times* pointing out that "one half-day's cost of this war would pay for all the slaves in Delaware, at four hundred dollars per head." Indeed, "eighty-seven days cost of this war would pay for all in Delaware, Maryland, District of Columbia, Kentucky, and Missouri at the same price."[42]

The Republicans in Congress proceeded to pass this measure in a near-straight party-line vote. But many Democrats denounced the very concept of "taxes to buy negroes." A new slogan in the North began to make the rounds of white supremacist Democrats: "The Constitution as it is and the Union as it was."

On March 13, the Republicans in Congress passed another anti-slavery measure. It forbade Union military men from returning any slaves who had crossed Union lines. Lincoln signed the new bill into law.

As all of these events unfolded in March, Lincoln's doubts about McClellan kept nagging him. He issued new orders on March 8 to the effect that the Army of the Potomac should not make a move "without leaving in, and about Washington, such a force as, in the opinion of the General-in-chief, and the commanders of all the Army corps, shall leave said City entirely secure."[43]

On the following day, the Confederates forces at Manassas abandoned their position and relocated farther south. This movement was fatal to McClellan's existing plans: the Confederates had moved too close to Urbana for his army to take them by surprise or to get between them and Richmond.

Lincoln seized the opportunity to cut back McClellan's authority: considering the work that was in store for him, Lincoln said, it was fitting to relieve him from his duties as general in chief so he could turn his mind wholly to Virginia. Lincoln did this on March 11.

Lincoln also consolidated the western armies in a new and greatly expanded "Department of the Mississippi," to be commanded by Halleck. Moreover, he created a "Mountain Department" in the Appalachians from western Virginia to the uplands of Unionist East Tennessee, which were still in Confederate hands. At the behest of some powerful congressional Republicans, Lincoln guardedly agreed to give Frémont a chance to redeem himself in this theatre and win a victory. The position of "general in chief" was left vacant for the time being.

While McClellan was chagrined by his demotion, he was all the more determined to revive his Virginia scheme and thus prove himself. So he shifted his landing point southward: his army, he decided, could be landed at Fortress Monroe at the tip of the peninsula created by the York and James Rivers. He would then proceed to take Richmond and end the war.

On March 13, he persuaded his subordinate commanders to endorse this scheme, which he promptly dispatched to Stanton. Lincoln approved it, with some new stipulations, and at last McClellan was ready: his troops began departing on March 17 and McClellan embarked for the peninsula on April 1.

As he left, he sent a letter to the War Department explaining the deployment of his troops. But as McClellan and his army sailed down the Potomac, a furor was developing in Washington: it seemed that McClellan had made some mistakes, or had juggled some numbers, in reporting on the troop deployments. Lincoln and others were worried that the troops who were left in the Washington defense perimeter were far too few. Indeed, the commander of the Washington defenses said as much to the secretary of war. So Lincoln held back a large number of troops—a corps of over thirty thousand commanded by General Irvin McDowell—in the first week of April.

As McClellan's campaign was launched, there were very few people who imagined that the war was approaching a horrific new crisis: that murderous battles would soon be unleashed that would surpass any previous slaughters in American history.

In the western theatre, the armies of Grant and Buell were pursuing the Confederate troops who had fled to Mississippi. Then on April 6, at the crack of dawn, an audacious Confederate counterattack was unleashed against Grant's army at a place called Shiloh Church near the southern Tennessee border. On the first day of battle, the Confederates seemed to be winning. But their commander, General Albert Sidney Johnston, was killed in action. On the second day, Grant succeeded in pushing the Confederates back with assistance from reinforcements he received overnight from Buell.

The fighting at Shiloh was savage; moreover, the death toll was staggering compared to the experience of 1861. The political and personal shock effects of this carnage began to change the atmosphere and politics of war both in Washington and Richmond. The Confederates were prompted to initiate a military draft, and the Union did the same thing a few months later—though the federal draft would be deferred in its direct operations until 1863.

The battle of Shiloh threw a cloud over Grant's reputation that would last for the better part of a year. It almost looked for a while as if Grant were another false hope—another "flash in the pan" whose beginner's luck had run out.

But Union victories resumed in the West. Some Union forces commanded by General John Pope put a major Confederate fortification on the Mississippi River near the border of Kentucky and Tennessee—Island # 10—out of action on the day after Shiloh.

Then, at the end of April, a combined sea-and-land operation carried out by Admiral David Farragut and General Benjamin Butler ventured up the Mississippi River and seized New Orleans. Farragut continued up the river: he captured Baton Rouge, the Louisiana capital, and occupied Natchez. The Confederates' position in the West was unraveling quickly.

In the East, however, it was merely the same old story. As McClellan got ready for his march upon Richmond, his forces at the edge of the Virginia peninsula confronted some Confederate troops who were waiting in the fortifications of Yorktown. The Confederates, commanded by General John B. Magruder, numbered only seventeen thousand. McClellan's own troop strength was somewhere in the eighty- to ninety-thousand range. But he believed himself vastly outnumbered and concluded that a frontal attack on the Confederate position would be suicide.

Lincoln wrote to McClellan on April 6; he told him that in light of the fact that he was currently supplied with "over one hundred thousand troops . . . I think you had better break the enemies' line from York-town to Warwick River, at once. They will probably use *time*, as advantageously as you can."[44]

Three days later Lincoln urged McClellan once again to attack the enemy quickly. This is "the precise time for you to strike a blow," Lincoln said. "By delay the enemy will relatively gain upon you—that is, he will gain faster, by *fortifications* and *re-inforcements*, than you can by re-inforcements alone." The enemy had to be attacked, Lincoln said, and it was no good trying to evade that fact by maneuvering to stave off a battle. "Going down the Bay in search of a field, instead of fighting at or near Manassas," said Lincoln, "was only shifting, and not surmounting, a difficulty. . . . The country will not fail to note—is now noting—that the present hesitation to move forward upon an intrenched enemy, is but the story of Manassas repeated."[45]

Lincoln was also disturbed at the time by the fact that the border-state initiative for phasing out slavery was facing resistance. Political reactions from the border-state leaders had been sullen and defiant. In contrast, Republicans in Congress took another step against slavery. They passed a new law to abolish it forever in Washington, D.C., with provision to compensate the owners and to set aside funds for the purpose of colonization, as Lincoln recommended. Lincoln signed this new anti-slavery measure on April 16.

At the end of the month, the great army of McClellan remained inactive. Lincoln was very angry: on May 1, he wrote that a request by McClellan for some more heavy siege guns "argues indefinite procrastination. Is anything to be done?"[46]

Something was done: the Confederates abandoned their Yorktown position on May 3 and withdrew their forces to Richmond, where General Joseph Johnston was preparing a last-ditch defense of the city. To stiffen the resolve of McClellan, Lincoln worked up a plan to send McDowell's corps to the vicinity of Richmond by land, thus achieving two goals: reinforcing McClellan while positioning McDowell and his men to be available to fend off Confederate attacks upon Washington, if any should develop.[47]

But Confederate authorities in Richmond ordered Stonewall Jackson to stir up some trouble in the Shenandoah Valley, and the onset of Jackson's Valley campaign made a mess of these plans for McDowell. This campaign, which commenced on May 8 and concluded on June 9, was a *tour de force*. In lightning-fast moves, Jackson fell upon the Union forces in the area commanded by Frémont and also by Nathaniel Banks (another political general), prompting Lincoln to re-route McDowell and his men to assist in the fighting.

Lincoln's purpose, however, was more than defensive: what he wanted was to use his military forces to converge upon Jackson and *destroy* him. Accordingly, he goaded his generals and urged them on by telegraph. On May 24, he cabled Frémont to "put the utmost speed into it. Do not lose a minute."[48] He also goaded McClellan. When it looked as if Jackson might cross the Potomac, Lincoln telegraphed McClellan that "the time is near when you must either attack Richmond or give up the job and come to the defense of Washington. Let me hear from you instantly."[49]

Jackson, however, kept his forces in Virginia, so Lincoln kept working to trap him. On May 30 he demanded of Frémont, "Where *is* your force? You ought this minute to be near Strasburg. Answer at once."[50]

In the meantime, Confederate authorities decided to throw the full weight of their Richmond troops against McClellan. On May 31, the Confederate forces in Richmond under General Joseph Johnston lashed out against McClellan and his army. The result was the two-day battle of Fair Oaks or Seven Pines: a tactical standoff. But McClellan was sickened by the gore of this battle and his weakness on the field increased. The Confederate result was different: Joseph Johnston, the Confederate commander, was wounded and had to be replaced. His replacement was Robert E. Lee.

Lincoln's faith in his Virginia commanders—such as it was—was nearly gone by the middle of June. He had given up hope of catching Jackson and his army when Frémont, McDowell, and Banks were so maddeningly slow. His disgust with his Virginia commanders was prompting him to look for replacements. Perhaps it was time to transfer a western commander to Virginia—time to summon a real fighting general and give him a chance to get Virginia under control. Grant's reputation was under a cloud, but there remained the Union general who captured a fortified island: John Pope.

McClellan continued to reiterate his call for reinforcements. He warned Lincoln that the grim responsibility of "saving" his army should "rest where it belongs," in Washington.[51]

Why, one is tempted to ask at this point, did Lincoln tolerate this behavior? It was clear to many members of Congress, as well as to the greater part of the Lincoln inner circle, that McClellan was a prima donna. Even Stanton, who at first was on the friendliest of terms with McClellan, was beginning to loathe him. Why did Lincoln keep him in command?

It seems likely that Lincoln had little intention of retaining McClellan much longer. Yet Lincoln, after all, had been "burned" already by promoting some generals who looked like winners at first but revealed fatal weaknesses later. McClellan himself was such a man, and it appeared that Grant could be another. Lincoln was bringing John Pope to Virginia, but time—and time alone—would determine whether Pope should replace McClellan.

On June 26, Lincoln issued an order consolidating all "the forces under Major Generals Frémont, Banks, and McDowell" into "one army, to be called the Army of Virginia." The command of this army was "specially assigned to Major General John Pope." The Army of Virginia would proceed to "attack and overcome the rebel forces under

Jackson and Ewell, threaten the enemy in the direction of Charlottes-ville, and render the most effective aid to relieve General McClellan and capture Richmond."[52]

On June 26, Lee was ready for another attack: he unleashed a tre-mendous assault upon McClellan. Lee's forces were approximately ninety thousand strong, with McClellan's in the one hundred thou-sand range. But McClellan believed that he was vastly outnumbered, and he panicked as the onslaught grew. In a series of attacks—known forever after as the "Seven Days Battles"—Lee hurled his forces at McClellan. In every battle but one (Gaines's Mill), Lee's attacks were repulsed with heavy losses. Yet McClellan proceeded to retreat. He dashed off a cable to Stanton proclaiming, "I have lost this battle be-cause my force was too small. . . . The government must not and can-not hold me responsible for the result. . . . If I save this army now, I tell you plainly that I owe no thanks to you or to any other person in Wash-ington. You have done your best to sacrifice this army."[53]

Lee hammered at McClellan's men: he drove them ever farther from Richmond. Yet at Malvern Hill, Lee's forces were savaged by the broad-sides of Union artillery. Malvern Hill was a major Union victory, a vic-tory that could have been decisive. But McClellan refused to follow up.

In the midst of this fighting, Lincoln came to a major decision: he had to issue another call for troops. If McClellan really faced a gigantic Confederate army, it was time to do some worst-case analysis. Lincoln drafted a letter to be carried by Secretary Seward to a meeting of Union governors; he stated in the letter that the enemy had concentrated "too much force in Richmond for McClellan to successfully attack."

The best course of action, he said, "is to hold what we have in the West, open the Mississippi, and, take Chatanooga [*sic*] and East Ten-nessee, without more." Then, "let the country give us a hundred thou-sand new troops in the shortest possible time, which added to McClellan . . . will take Richmond, without endangering any other place which we now hold—and will substantially end the war."[54] When Seward reported to Lincoln that the governors were behind him, Lincoln tripled his call for volunteers: he sent out a volunteer call for another *three hundred thousand* troops on July 1.

All the while, he was working on the slavery issue. He was pushing, pleading, and cajoling the border-state leaders to assist him with the great second phase of his anti-slavery program. When another Union general muddied the waters for Lincoln by issuing an anti-slavery proclamation, Lincoln stopped him. General David Hunter had proclaimed emancipation in Georgia, Florida, and South Carolina on May 9; his anti-slavery proclamation had been issued from his base in the Sea Islands off the coast.

Ten days later, Lincoln countermanded this order, observing that the question of "whether it be competent for me, as Commander-in-Chief of the Army and Navy, to declare the Slaves of any state or states, free, and whether at any time, in any case, it shall have become a necessity indispensable to the maintenance of the government, to exercise such supposed power, are questions which . . . I reserve to myself." Between the lines of this message was a big revelation: Lincoln at last might be willing to consider some direct form of presidential action that would strike at slavery.

In the same proclamation, Lincoln added an "appeal" to the leaders of the border states. "I beseech you," Lincoln said, to consider the financial offer that Congress extended in March. "You can not if you would," he argued, "be blind to the signs of the times. . . . This proposal makes common cause for a common object, casting no reproaches on any. It acts not the pharisee. The change it contemplates would come gently as the dews of heaven, not rending or wrecking anything. Will you not embrace it? . . . May the vast future not have to lament that you have neglected it."[55] But they *did* neglect it.

Conversely, the Republicans in Congress passed more anti-slavery laws: in June, the congressional Republicans enacted a free-soil measure barring slavery from federal lands. Moreover, on June 7, the Republican Congress passed a law for the collection of taxes in rebel states, with the stipulation of a lien on the physical property of rebel tax dodgers. Then, the congressional Republicans drafted a stronger confiscation act, as Lincoln had invited them to do in his annual message of December 1861. This act was designed to give freedom to the contraband slaves under certain conditions.

Lincoln's thoughts about the slavery issue were expanding—expanding from the ethical plane to the frankly religious realm. Lincoln was a scoffer in his youth: he had ridiculed the Bible as a hodge-podge of myths.[56] Nonetheless, in the 1850s he had used a number of quotations from Scripture as he sought to express his position on the slavery issue in the language of the golden rule.

Then, after Willie's death, he found himself turning to Scripture more often, not only to console his wife, who in the deepest phase of her depression had locked herself in her room for a great many days, but also to console himself.

In addition, the cost of this war, the great toll in human life that was constantly forced upon Lincoln by the death of his friends—Elmer Ephraim Ellsworth, for instance, who had worked with Lincoln in his law office back in Springfield, and Edward Baker, who had served with Lincoln in the Illinois legislature many years earlier (both of whom were killed in Virginia)—played over his mind as he ordered his generals to *fight* the Confederates, to overcome squeamishness, to smash and annihilate the armies of the rebels—to deal out death without mercy.

He thought about the flickering and transient nature of our life: about the "passing speck of time" he had been given. The enormity of thoughts such as these began to move his vision in a starkly Old Testament direction. In June, he responded to a visit by some anti-slavery leaders who hoped that he "might, under divine guidance, be led to free the slaves." Lincoln told them "he had sometime thought that perhaps he might be an instrument in God's hands" and was "not unwilling to be."[57]

His great purpose in life became clear in the 1850s: he would dedicate himself and his political talents to the gradual elimination of slavery. When his policies had triggered secession, then the fight to save the Union was *added*. To this work in its totality he swore to dedicate his life.

In appealing for hundreds of thousands of additional troops, Lincoln pledged to "maintain this contest until successful, or till I die, or am conquered, or my term expires, or Congress or the country forsakes me. . . ."[58]

Until he died—or was "conquered" or forsaken by the country. What would happen if one (or more) of these gloomy latter visions came to pass? What would happen, for example, if Lincoln should die, by assassination or by illness? His vice president, Hannibal Hamlin, would be forced to cope with the terrible crisis of the nation as best he could.

What would happen if the Union should lose? A successful Confederate republic of slave states would then be positioned for a wave of aggressive conquest. The "golden circle" of white supremacist rule in Latin America could be the result.

What would happen if Lincoln's support in the Northern states were to plummet—what would happen, indeed, if he were voted out of office in the next presidential election? Would the backlash against him be sufficiently great as to wreck the Republican Party, at least for a while? Would the Democrats be willing to terminate the war and then patch things up with the South? Would this development set back the anti-slavery movement for decades on end?

He had vowed to "maintain this contest until successful, or till I die." But could he contemplate the prospect of death without knowing for certain that his country was safely on the proper course for the eventual phaseout of slavery? If his strategy were not in the cards—if the border-state leaders refused to listen to his pleading—then perhaps it would be time for something drastic.

He would make a last appeal to the border states. He would make a final effort on behalf of his gradual plan. But if the border-state leaders continued to be willfully obstinate—if it proved to be impossible for Lincoln to *pay* them to do the right thing—then he would start to handle matters very differently. He would make the great decision very quickly in the month of July.

LINCOLN'S ANTI-SLAVERY STRATEGY would reach the point of radical measures as the second year of war continued. In the summer, he decided on a short-term gamble of extraordinary scope: he would start to free the slaves of the rebels.

Charles Sumner, the Radical Republican senator, was urging Lincoln on. The Union should proceed to attack the real source of the rebellion, he advised the president: put the axe to the root and strike directly at the evil of slavery, Sumner urged.

For months, certain Radical Republicans had argued, in Congress and elsewhere, a case for the war that was profoundly different from Lincoln's. In February 1862, Sumner introduced in the Senate a series of resolutions on the status of the rebel states. In contrast to Lincoln's assertion that the so-called Confederate states were still functional units of the nation (albeit under temporary criminal rule until secessionist treason could be crushed), Sumner, Thaddeus Stevens, and a number of others in the Radical camp began claiming that the rebel states were no longer real states at all: by dint of their treason, the Radicals argued, these Southern jurisdictions had committed a kind of "state suicide." Such states had reverted to the status of federal territories. They were soon to be conquered provinces—richly deserving of whatever new rules the Republican majority in Congress might impose for their political and social reconstruction. Emancipation was just the beginning.[59]

This impatient agenda caused a number of the Radicals to speak in rather hostile or even contemptuous terms when it came to Lincoln's incremental methods. But Sumner, in particular, was firmly convinced that Lincoln's strategy was good for their own. In a letter to a Radical Republican colleague (whose name was deleted from the published correspondence), Sumner claimed that the president agreed with the Radicals on many fundamental issues. He revealed, moreover, he had met with the president on numerous occasions for behind-the-scenes talks at the White House.

Consequently, he told his correspondent on June 5, 1862, "your criticism of the President" was altogether "hasty." If you knew the president, Sumner continued, "you would feel the sincerity of his purpose to do what he can to carry forward the principles of the Declaration of Independence," a course that in Lincoln's estimation "promised the sure end of slavery." In Sumner's opinion, Lincoln's strategy was well worth pursuing. In fact, his invitation to the border states to initiate a gradual emancipation program was a wedge in the door for the anti-slavery movement. Importantly, Sumner himself had once suggested a financial phaseout program for slavery and still supported the concept: "To me, who had already proposed a Bridge of Gold for the retreating Fiend," he explained, the proposal of Lincoln was "welcome." Indeed, "proceeding from the President, it must take its place among the great events of history."

Sumner told his colleague to reflect upon everything that Lincoln had "done in a brief period," and then, "from the past," go on to "discern the sure promise of the future." "If you knew the President," Sumner admonished in closing, you would surely "be grateful that he is so true to all you have at heart."[60]

A month later, however, on the Fourth of July, Sumner called upon Lincoln and told him it was time to escalate his strategy: time to issue a strong presidential decree that would strike at the institution of slavery for military reasons. "You need more men," Sumner told the president, "not only at the North, but at the South, in the rear of the Rebels: you need the slaves." Lincoln told his supporter he was deeply concerned about the backlash that such a decree could provoke: "half the officers would fling down their arms and three more States would rise," Lincoln told the senator.[61]

Perhaps Sumner could sense that the president was secretly receptive to what he was suggesting, as indeed Lincoln was. Yet the president continued to be wary of a white supremacist backlash that, in the event of a worst-case political scenario—defeat on the battlefield, foreign intervention, electoral revolt in the North—could destroy almost everything that Lincoln had achieved thus far.

So he resolved to try again to convince the border-state leaders to go along with his gradual liberation plan. At the same time, of course, he would have to keep his mind almost constantly engaged with the ongoing military challenge.

On July 1, Lincoln issued his call for three hundred thousand more troops. Two days later, McClellan demanded fifty thousand reinforcements—as a minimal condition for resuming the battle with Lee. He later raised that number to one hundred thousand more troops.

Such demands were impossible to meet in the short run: reinforcements on the order that McClellan was demanding could not be delivered for months. Though a large new recruiting drive was getting started in the North—an abolitionist named James S. Gibbons had written a patriotic poem (to be set to music later on by composers such as Stephen Foster) entitled, "We are Coming, Father Abraham, Three Hundred Thousand More"—the lead time for training new recruits would remain considerable.

On July 17, Congress strengthened Lincoln's hand by passing the Militia Act. This law permitted the Department of War to set recruiting quotas for the states. If the states were unable to meet these quotas, a "militia draft" would be created by the federal government.

And yet the troops were only part of the problem. As Commander-in-Chief, Lincoln had to decide how to *use* the new troops, in Virginia most of all. He had to decide what to do about McClellan and his army, at least until General Pope had been tested in battle.

On July 7, Lincoln traveled to McClellan's new James River base at Harrison's Landing near Richmond to inspect his army. As Lincoln departed, he was handed a letter by McClellan. This letter contained some outspoken political advice: ignore the Radical Republicans, McClellan recommended, and keep the emancipation issue out of the war. Lincoln thanked McClellan and left without further comment.

As soon as he returned to Washington, Lincoln summoned Henry Halleck, the theatre commander whose armies had won the big victories out West. Lincoln had decided to elevate this theatre commander to the post of general in chief. He did this upon the strong recommendation of the secretary of war. On July 11, Lincoln ordered Halleck to Washington.

On the very next day, Lincoln turned his attention to the slavery issue again. He met with over two-dozen border-state leaders, imploring them to take up the government's offer of assistance with the gradual phaseout of slavery. "Let the states which are in rebellion see," he told them, "that, in no event, will the states you represent ever join their proposed Confederacy." It was time, Lincoln said, to break the lever of power that the rebels can use in your states: "Break that lever before their faces, and they can shake you no more forever."

After all, Lincoln warned them, the war itself might destroy the institution of slavery through "friction and abrasion—by the mere incidents of war." If so, he suggested, then the capital investment in slaves would be "gone, and you will have nothing valuable in lieu of it." Already, he continued, the pressure to emancipate was strong; by rescinding the orders of General Hunter in May, he confided, "I gave dissatisfaction, if not offense, to many whose support the country cannot afford to lose. And this is not the end of it. The pressure, in this direction, is still upon me, and is increasing."

Therefore, seize the moment, Lincoln told them: it could all be easy in light of the fact that there was "room in South America for colonization." Moreover, "the freed people will not be so reluctant to go" when their "numbers shall be large enough to be company and encouragement for one another."[62] Once again, however, the border-state leaders turned him down.

So he made the great decision at last—the decision to liberate. His feelings at the moment are all too easy to imagine. In all likelihood, the president was angry, supremely angry.

The sheer moral banality of slave owners, coupled with the escalating battlefield carnage, prompted him to raise the moral stakes for which so many lives were being lost. If even the offer of money made no impression on slave owners, so much the worse for them.

The next afternoon, in the course of a carriage ride with William H. Seward and Gideon Welles, Lincoln told the two cabinet members he would issue a decree against slavery in all of the rebellious states. He would do it for military reasons.[63]

This was *not*, however, a decision to abandon his voluntary method in the border states: a decree that was aimed at the slaves of the Confederates could never apply in any slave states fighting for the Union.

So Lincoln kept his offer wide open: indeed, on July 14, he sent Congress a bill that contained a more specific new method for its implementation.

But his secret new decision was a radical addition to his plans. His whole *modus operandi* would be changed: in light of his earlier objection to the notion that he (or any president) should "seize and exercise the permanent legislative functions of the government," as he put it in his letter to Browning, his new decision took him straight to the brink of a political and personal Rubicon.

To be sure, he was counting on some new legislative authority as "cover" for his move: he was writing the decree to be viewed as an *enforcement measure* that he meant to be related—at least in the public mind—to the new and more powerful confiscation act that congressional Republicans were drafting.

The decision by Lincoln in July was important for another reason: it amounted to a mid-course correction in his overall emancipation strategy, a *drastic* correction. His preliminary plan had been to use the border states to demonstrate his program, while hoping their achievement in phasing out slavery would serve as a model for the rebel states later.

Lincoln's choice in July was to reverse this sequence: the *rebel* states would now commence the emancipation process, under federal coercion.

The new confiscation act, which reached Lincoln's desk on July 14, made provision for the permanent forfeiture of property, including, most importantly, the slaves of the rebel traitors. Lincoln read this bill over carefully, and then, on July 17, drafted a long message to Congress on the constitutional issues pertaining to it.

In the message that he sent to the Congress, he made a number of important suggestions for strengthening the bill. For example, he identified a serious problem in the portions of the act that provided for the liberation of slaves belonging to the rebels. Slavery, he hastened to observe, was a state-sanctioned institution. For this reason, he suggested, "it is startling to say that congress can free a slave within a state." Nonetheless, the problem could be solved very quickly through insertion of an intermediate step: "if," the president proposed, "it were said that the ownership of the slave had first been transferred to the nation, and that congress had then liberated him, the difficulty would at once vanish."

Furthermore, Lincoln suggested, the bill contained a problem in regard to enforcement: since only those slaves who belonged to the rebels would fall within the act's jurisdiction, he argued, some procedure would have to be created for determining their status.

Finally, Lincoln objected to the permanent forfeiture of *real estate*. In the president's opinion, this provision was a bill for permanent attainder, which the constitution forbids.

But he quickly reaffirmed that congressional action in regard to the freedom of *slaves* could indeed be permanent: the constitutional ban on such bills of attainder, he continued, "applies only in this country . . . to real, or landed estate."[64] Consequently, any slaves who belonged to the rebels could be freed forever.

When congressional Republicans received Lincoln's message, they revised the new law very quickly. In its final version, it warned that the slaves of individual rebels would be freed if the rebellion should continue more than sixty days. Judicial proceedings would be used to enforce this threat. Moreover, any slaves who escaped to Union lines would be classified as "captives of war," and deemed "forever free." Indeed, such liberated slaves were invited to enlist in the United States Army and fight for the Union. Finally, federal funds were provided for the voluntary colonization of blacks who wished to leave the country. This act was a major transitional step in the radicalization of the war.

In secret, however, the president was drafting a document far more radical than anything the act contained. Lincoln's Emancipation Proclamation would extend the power of the federal government in ways that were far more controversial.

Lincoln presented his secret decree to the cabinet on July 22. It began with legalistic probity:

> In pursuance of the sixth section of the act of congress entitled "An act to suppress insurrection and to punish treason and rebellion, to seize and confiscate property of rebels . . . I, Abraham Lincoln, President of the United States, do hereby proclaim to, and warn all persons within the contemplation of said sixth section to cease participating in, aiding, countenancing, or abetting the existing rebellion . . . on pain of the forfeitures and seizures, as within and by said sixth section provided.

So far, the proclamation was grounded in congressional actions. At the end of the document, however, the president extended his executive authority in bold and unprecedented terms. In addition to the previous warnings and threats, he continued

I, as Commander-in-Chief of the Army and Navy of the United States, do order and declare that on the first day of January in the year of Our Lord one thousand, eight hundred, and sixty-three, all persons held as slaves within any state or states, wherein the constitutional authority of the United States shall not then be practically recognized, submitted to, and maintained, shall then, thenceforward, and forever, be free.[65]

This was nothing less than a revolutionary action: a revolution in the name of maintaining the established legal order. Lincoln was explicitly warning the rebels, both leaders and followers, to lay down their arms by the end of the year or face sweeping, irreversible sanctions. Every slave in a rebellious state—regardless of whether a particular slave could be proven to belong to a rebel—would be freed in the following year just as soon as the armies of Lincoln could reach him, the proclamation warned.

Lincoln's announcement at the cabinet meeting drew very mixed reactions indeed. Montgomery Blair, as a former Democrat, could not support the proclamation; he warned of the political backlash that such a decree might provoke in the congressional elections that fall. Stanton, the former attorney general under Buchanan, supported the measure wholeheartedly. Chase, the antebellum Free-Soiler, was somewhat ambivalent. And Seward, most famously of all, recommended to Lincoln that he wait for a battlefield victory: he should issue his decree from a platform of obvious strength. Lincoln chose to take Seward's advice. But he did tell the public on July 25 that he would implement the new confiscation law in sixty days.

The threat of a white supremacist backlash was real that summer. White supremacists throughout the North began howling as soon as Lincoln had signed the second confiscation act. Democratic editorials warned that millions of "semi-savages" would pour into Northern cities when emancipation started. They would flood the job market. They would perpetrate horrendous crimes. They would pant for political and social equality and lust for racial intermarriage.

A New York headline was typical: "Can Niggers Conquer Americans?" Midwestern opinions were also inflamed: Indiana Congressman George Julian, a prominent Radical Republican, wrote, "our people hate the Negro with a perfect if not a supreme hatred."[66] Racial violence—urban riots against free blacks—broke out in Northern cities that summer.

So the political risk for the Republican Party was clear: if the Republicans should lose their majority in Congress because of a white supremacist backlash during the autumn elections, the Democrats would probably (indeed, almost certainly) repeal the anti-slavery laws that the Republicans had recently passed. The confiscation acts, of course, would be the first to go, but the threat was even bigger than that: the Free-Soil measure that Republicans had passed in defiance of the Dred Scott decision could be wiped off the books as well. This was the tremendous gamble that Republicans had taken in the summer of 1862. Lincoln's secret proclamation would of course raise the ante even more.

Moreover, the political threat to the Republicans' program was broadened when the danger of foreign intervention resurfaced in the early weeks of July. To observers in Paris, London, and elsewhere, the failure of McClellan to capture Richmond had improved the Confederates' prospects. Accordingly, Napoleon III sent a query to the British in regard to the wisdom of recognizing the Confederate States of America as a new nation. Parliament considered the issue on July 18, though without taking action. The prime minister was cautious: he wanted more assurance of Confederate military victory.

But the cotton embargo of the South was beginning to succeed in the summer of 1862: the British warehouse supplies were exhausted and a major "cotton famine" was creating unemployment in the British textile industry. Pro-Confederate sentiment was growing in parliament, and one thing alone held it back: the long-standing anti-slavery feelings of the British electorate. Lincoln's Emancipation Proclamation— so politically risky at home—could bring tremendous benefits abroad. But, would the moment arrive soon enough to avert a Confederate diplomatic coup?

In mid– to late July, Lincoln faced the following challenges: to stave off foreign intervention, to stimulate military action in Virginia, and— most challenging of all—to prepare Northern public opinion for his secret liberation decree.

On July 23, the new general in chief, Henry Halleck, arrived in Washington. Lincoln sent him off promptly with a message for George McClellan: if McClellan would agree to renew the campaign against Lee, then the president could offer him twenty thousand more troops. If McClellan should decline to proceed, then the president intended to withdraw McClellan's army from Richmond and merge it into Pope's.

On July 25, Halleck stated these terms to McClellan and suggested that he put the issue to a vote among his corps commanders. Lincoln's offer was accepted very quickly.

But when Halleck returned to Washington, a message from McClellan was waiting. The general had changed his mind: at least *forty thousand* more troops would be needed to renew the campaign against Lee.

For Lincoln this message was decisive: McClellan was hopeless. The campaign in Virginia, the president decided, would use the army of Pope as its spearhead. McClellan's forces would be siphoned away from the vicinity of Richmond—with stealth, by water, in a manner that would shield the gigantic maneuver from the eyes of Confederate scouts—and then fed in a continuous-flow operation into Pope's new Army of Virginia. Already, John Pope was on the move: he had crossed the Rappahannock and was moving toward Richmond by land.

On the fourth of August, Lincoln ordered McClellan to withdraw from the Virginia peninsula. The general, however, was sulking. He decided to take his own time about withdrawing his troops. In the meantime, as Pope was advancing, the Confederates in Richmond guessed the truth about Lincoln's intentions. Lee decided to attack Pope's army and defeat it as McClellan took his time. He ordered twenty-three thousand Confederate troops under Stonewall Jackson to attack Pope's Army of Virginia.

As the battlefield struggle heated up in Virginia, Lincoln turned his mind to the challenge of preparing the North for his secret decree. In light of the anti-black hatred that was glaringly apparent that summer—hatred that was leading to anti-black violence—Lincoln tried to get his colonization program started in the hope of reducing racial tension.

On August 14, he invited a small delegation of blacks to the White House for the purpose of discussing the concept of colonization with them frankly. He was seeking black leaders to be colonizing pioneers—to join with him in founding a haven for expatriate blacks.

He began by acknowledging the racial evils of America. "Your race," Lincoln told his black visitors, "are suffering the greatest wrong inflicted on any people." Beyond the evil of enslavement, blacks were systematically oppressed all over the country, Lincoln acknowledged. "On this broad continent, not a single man of your race is made the equal of a single man of ours."

In guarded language, Lincoln made it clear to his guests that he shared their emotions with regard to this sordid oppression: it was a "fact, about which we all think and feel alike, I and you." Yet, it was "a fact with which we have to deal," for "I cannot alter it."

Consequently, Lincoln urged his black listeners to start life over in another country—to savor the rest of their lives undiminished by oppression and cruelty. The obvious hardship of starting life over, he said, should be weighed very carefully indeed with the dubious merits of staying in a land that was familiar but relentlessly harsh. Compare yourselves, Lincoln urged them, to General Washington as founders of a nation: "Gen. Washington himself endured greater physical hardships" in fighting for the fullness of his own human freedom "than if he had remained" in the comparative comfort of being "a British subject," Lincoln reasoned. Nonetheless, "he was a happy man"—happier by far in embracing the struggle—because he and his fellow revolutionaries were "cheered by the future."

Moreover, a venture in colonization could facilitate emancipation, Lincoln argued. Free blacks like you, Lincoln told them, "ought to do something to help those who are not so fortunate"—that is, they ought to help free the slaves in the South. In light of the "unwillingness on the part of our people, harsh as it may be, for you free colored people to remain with us," Lincoln continued, a vanguard of free black emigrants could, by starting a triumphant exodus, "open a wide door for many to be made free." Leave the house of bondage, he bade them, put it quickly behind you so that others could follow and flourish.

Consider a move to Liberia, Lincoln suggested, or—if something in the Western Hemisphere were more attractive—in Central America, Lincoln continued, there were excellent places for a colony. "The particular place I have in view is to be a great highway from the Atlantic or Caribbean Sea to the Pacific Ocean," he explained, "and this particular place has all the advantages for a colony." Lincoln promised to support the first colonists with federal funding: "I shall, if I get a sufficient number of you engaged, have provisions made that you shall not be wronged."

Above all, Lincoln told them, he hoped they would free themselves from the constant persecution in white supremacist America. "To your colored race," Lincoln said, the inhabitants of Central America "have no objection," and besides, he continued, "I would endeavor to have you made equals, and have the best assurance that you should be the equals of the best."

Take your time, Lincoln said, and consider this matter with care, for "these are subjects of very great importance, worthy of a month's study, [instead] of a speech delivered in an hour."[67]

As he tried to persuade black leaders to think about colonization, Lincoln looked for corresponding opportunities to soften white resistance to emancipation. He dropped hints that much stronger measures would be coming if Confederate resistance continued. In response to some complaints about the Union occupation tactics in Louisiana, Lincoln warned that such measures were just the beginning.

To Cuthbert Bullitt, a New Orleans attorney, he was blunt and defiant. Regarding complaints about the ways in which "the relation of master and slave is disturbed by the presence of our Army," Lincoln posed some questions for the malcontents of New Orleans. "What would you do in my position," he demanded: "Would you drop the war where it is? Or, would you prosecute it in future, with elder-stalk squirts, charged with rose water? Would you deal lighter blows rather than heavier ones? Would you give up the contest, leaving any available means unapplied[?]"[68]

In a letter to financier August Belmont, he warned, "broken eggs cannot be mended. . . . This government cannot much longer play a game in which it stakes all, and its enemies stake nothing. Those enemies must understand that they cannot experiment for ten years trying to destroy the government, and if they fail still come back into the Union unhurt."[69]

Above all, he pounced upon an editorial by Horace Greeley in the *New York Tribune*. Greeley's editorial, "The Prayer of Twenty Millions," accused the president of weakness on the issue of slavery.

Lincoln's famous answer to Greeley, which he wrote as an open letter to the editor, is central to the "moderate" Lincoln legend. Dated August 22, his letter to the editor ignored the specifics of Greeley's complaints; instead, Lincoln offered propositions of his own that would be useful in preparing Northern public opinion for emancipation.

Lincoln posed as a commander-in-chief who was *solely* devoted to the cause of saving the Union, at least in his official capacity as president. "My paramount object in this struggle," he wrote, "*is* to save the Union, and is *not* either to save or to destroy slavery. If I could save the Union without freeing *any* slave I would do it, and if I could save it by freeing *all* the slaves I would do it; and if I could save it by freeing some and leaving others alone I would also do that. . . . I have here stated my purpose according to my view of my *official* duty; and I intend no modification of my oft-expressed *personal* wish that all men every where could be free."[70]

For years these lines have been read with only minimal comprehension by those who argue that "Lincoln only wanted to save the Union."

But—as we have seen—his entire career as a national leader makes the proposition untenable. Right up to his inauguration, he scorned the notion of saving a Union that was not *worth* saving. He killed the Crittenden Compromise for saving the Union by refusing to engage in any further appeasement on the issue of slavery expansion. It was, after all, Lincoln's Free-Soil platform that *caused* the secession crisis in the first place.

No, the famous letter to Greeley is *not* proof that Lincoln "only wanted to save the Union" in the Civil War. It is rather a stunning demonstration of Lincoln the tactician.

Observe his rhetorical manner: *if* he could save the Union without freeing slaves, then he would do it as an act of duty. This was close to the truth in political and constitutional terms—it was an obvious statement of his constitutional constraints—but it was surely not the whole truth for Lincoln. For he chose not to mention the important fact that he intended to do much more than merely save the Union. He would force a great change in the Union, putting slavery "on the downhill."

Moreover, he chose not to mention the fact that there were things he would refuse to do—back down on the issue of slavery expansion, for example—in his struggle to save the Union.

But observe: in the midst of expressing his commitment to saving the Union by doing whatever it took on the issue of slavery—a commitment so strong that it supposedly trumped any other commitments of his own—Lincoln stated that he might free some slaves.

He was softening public opinion. He was getting things ready for his big and risky revelation. To establish his patriotic platform, to pose as a presidential leader who was far above the fray when it came to the slavery issue, he implied that he was still undecided on the merits of emancipation.

Perhaps, he implied, he would *not* free the slaves at all. He was weighing all his options very carefully. But whatever he did—rest assured, white supremacist voters!—he would do it for the sake of the Union.

This deception has been swallowed by millions of readers who encounter Lincoln's letter to Greeley by itself, and without any knowledge of the president's overall purposes.

Meanwhile, the battlefield struggle in Virginia was approaching a disaster. Lee decided to send Jackson's corps on a march to Manassas, which was serving as a Union supply base. Jackson raided Manassas on August 26, and Pope quickly turned north to pursue him.

Pope's initial assaults upon Jackson were inconclusive. Then, when the rest of Lee's army arrived, Lee was able to conceal the presence of his forces. A surprise attack was in the making. On August 30, Lee gave the order to unleash a tremendous assault upon Pope's unprotected left flank. The Union line crumbled and was driven from the field in rout.

Pope was out-generaled at "Second Manassas," without a doubt. Nonetheless, there was plenty of blame to go around for this Union defeat. As the battle was raging, Henry Halleck did a miserable job in his attempts to coordinate the armies of Pope and McClellan. Halleck was beginning to demonstrate his own kind of weakness in the post of general in chief. According to John Hay, Lincoln's secretary, the dispatches that Halleck wrote to Lincoln at the time of the battle were "weak, whiney [and] vague."[71]

McClellan, moreover, bore a huge amount of the blame for the Manassas disaster. He deliberately dragged his heels when Halleck had asked him to send reinforcements to Pope. In the midst of the battle he had telegraphed Lincoln and suggested that the president "leave Pope to get out of his own scrape."[72]

Lincoln at first was inclined to give Pope a second chance. "We must hurt this enemy before it gets away," he declared. On September 1, Hay recorded in his diary that Lincoln was "singularly defiant" in the aftermath of the battle. After Hay had incautiously "made a remark in regard to the bad look of things," Lincoln quickly rebuked him, saying, "'No, Mr. Hay, we must whip these people now. Pope must fight them.'"[73]

But when Lincoln found out that the troops in Pope's army despised him, he decided that McClellan, at least for a while, was the better man to reorganize the army and restore its faltering morale. Strange and perverse as it seems, the troops continued to worship "Little Mac," whom they regarded as a life-saving friend—a commander who would never sacrifice his troops without a very good reason.

Then a new emergency developed: Lee's army crossed into Maryland. A Confederate invasion had begun, and it looked for a time as if Washington itself could be the target. Here again, resignedly, Lincoln turned to McClellan, the defensive commander and fortifier *par excellence*. He confided to Hay that "we must use the tools we have. . . . There is no man in the Army who can man these fortifications and lick these troops of ours into shape half as well as he. . . . He is too useful just now to sacrifice."[74] Since McClellan and Pope were on the angriest of terms, Pope was sent back out to the West (to fight Indians in Minnesota). The new Army of Virginia was disbanded and merged back into the Army of the Potomac.

But the McClellan arrangement would clearly not last. As historian T. Harry Williams has observed, the president "was determined that McClellan's command would be temporary because he believed the General was incapable of offensive warfare."[75]

Since no attack upon Washington occurred, Lee's army would have to be pursued. Lincoln quietly attempted to recruit a successor to McClellan—a *fighting* general to lead the army into battle. Early in September, the president offered the command to General Ambrose E. Burnside, who had made a name for himself by his capture of Roanoke Island and much of the "outer banks" of North Carolina six months earlier.[76]

But Burnside declined, and so, *again* with tremendous misgivings, Lincoln had to give the field command to McClellan. It would take well over another year for the president to find some commanders whose thinking was similar to his and whose battlefield prowess was equivalent to that of the enemy.

Lee's invasion of Maryland was part of a multi-pronged counteroffensive, a coordinated effort by Confederate armies to pull Union forces out of occupied states and bring war to the Northern people. Confederate victories on Northern soil could tip the balance in the international arena. Southern victories could bring recognition, mediation, *intervention* by the British and French.[77] They could even bring an end to the Republican control of Congress. In a message to Jefferson Davis on September 8, Lee expressed high hope that a successful invasion would enable "the people of the United States to determine at their coming elections whether they will support those who favor a prolongation of the war, or those who wish to bring it to a termination."[78] As

Lee headed north into Maryland, Confederate forces in East Tennessee headed northward into Kentucky. And Confederate troops in Mississippi prepared to strike north.

This tremendous crisis moved Lincoln to reflect once again upon religious themes. If indeed he were called to be an agent of Providence, perhaps he should see the Manassas disaster and the crisis of invasion as goads toward a higher moral outcome. Sometime during the month of September, Lincoln penned the following reflections:

> The will of God prevails. In great contests each party claims to act in accordance with the will of God. Both *may* be, and one *must* be wrong. God can not be *for*, and *against* the same thing at the same time. In the present civil war it is quite possible that God's purpose is different from the purpose of either party—and yet the human instrumentalities, working just as they do, are of the best adaptation to effect His purpose. I am almost ready to say this is probably true—that God wills this contest, and wills that it shall not end yet. By his mere quiet power, on the minds of the now contestants, He could have either *saved* or *destroyed* the Union without a human contest. Yet the contest began. And having begun He could give the final victory to either side any day. Yet the contest proceeds.[79]

In early September, Lincoln made a personal vow: he promised to regard a Union victory in Maryland as nothing less than "an indication of Divine Will" concerning the higher meaning of the war. Indeed, Lincoln vowed to interpret such a victory as a providential sign to "move forward in the cause of emancipation." On September 22, he revealed this vow to his cabinet.[80]

Until victory, however, he would have to keep playing for time. He would have to keep pretending he had not yet decided on emancipation policy. He even chose to play the role of devil's advocate in mid-September and floated a series of arguments *against* the proclamation to achieve this political deception. On September 13, a Chicago delegation of Christian abolitionists called upon Lincoln at the White House. He talked with the group for the better part of an hour in the following manner.

"What *good* would a proclamation of emancipation from me do," he inquired, "especially as we are now situated? . . . Would *my* word free the slaves, when I cannot even enforce the Constitution in the rebel states?" Besides, he continued, if the proclamation turned out to be successful, "how can we feed and care for such a multitude?" Lincoln treated his guests to a dazzling display of mock perplexity.

Mind you, the president continued, he was raising "no objections" at all against a proclamation such as this "on legal or constitutional grounds; for, as commander-in-chief of the army and navy, in time of war, I suppose I have a right to take any measure which may best subdue the enemy." This, of course, was a complete reversal of the constitutional views he expressed to his friend Senator Orville Browning just a year before.

At the end of the discourse the president concluded in a reassuring manner: "I have not decided against a proclamation of liberty to the slaves . . . but hold the matter under advisement."[81] Under advisement indeed! The only matter that was really uncertain in his mind was the *timing* of the great proclamation. And what a devious way of half-revealing/half-concealing the truth in this case through the use of a sly double negative—he had not decided *against* the proclamation, he stated—thus concealing the fact that a positive decision had been made, for the liberating document was written already and was waiting in his desk drawer.

As McClellan moved off into Maryland, he wasted several chances to destroy the Confederate army. Lee, on the march, had divided his army into fragments. On September 13, a most extraordinary windfall was given to George McClellan: a Union private had stumbled by chance upon a copy of Lee's secret orders.

An intelligence coup of this sort must be used very quickly, but McClellan, of course, took his time. An audacious commander—a Stonewall Jackson, for instance—would have pounced upon the isolated pieces of his enemy's army and crushed them before they could unite. But McClellan was fretful and obtuse. When he finally caught Lee at Sharpsburg, Maryland, to the west of Antietam Creek, Lee had almost succeeded in pulling his army together. Even so, a determined attack at this point could have dealt Lee a staggering blow. Yet McClellan continued to hesitate. And so, by the time that he finally attacked, he confronted a consolidated enemy.

Lee's forces, however, were meager when compared to McClellan's: at seventy-five thousand, the Army of the Potomac continued to outnumber the Army of Northern Virginia, which was down to forty-five thousand.

The battle of Antietam, on September 17, was the bloodiest day of the war. The Confederates had not been able to entrench. Consequently, the bloodbath was out in the open, with little more than cornfields, fences, and sunken lanes to provide any cover for the troops. By the end of the day, over twenty-three thousand soldiers had fallen, either dead or wounded.

The battle almost ended the war. At one point, a significant gap was created in the center of Lee's position. At that moment, as T. Harry Williams has observed, "McClellan had victory in his grasp." He had a full corps of troops in reserve. If, in the opinion of Williams, he "had sent this force against the weakened Confederate right, he would have swept Lee from the field. He was at the crisis of his career, and he fumbled the moment completely.... He halted the attack for the day."[82]

Lee's army retreated to Virginia, and McClellan simply let it go. He did nothing to harass the retreat of the Confederates' principal army—nothing to finish off the army of Lee when it was ready for the *coup de grace*.

But this victory appeared strong enough to give Lincoln the occasion for which he was praying. On September 22, Lincoln issued the Preliminary Emancipation Proclamation. The proclamation was labeled *preliminary* because it was framed as a *warning*. *If*, the president warned, the rebellion continued into 1863, then a *final* proclamation would be issued to carry out the threat of emancipation.

"I, Abraham Lincoln, President of the United States of America, and Commander-in-chief of the Army and Navy thereof, do hereby proclaim and declare that hereafter, as heretofore, the war will be prosecuted for the object of practically restoring the constitutional relation between the United States, and each of the states, and the people thereof, in which states that relation is, or may be suspended, or disturbed." Lincoln launched his revolutionary plan by assuring the public that the war remained a fight to save the Union.

Before proceeding any further, he attempted to prepare Northern racists for the imminent freeing of slaves. As always, Lincoln used the formula of colonization in hopes of staving off a backlash: "the effort to colonize persons of African descent, with their consent, upon this continent, or elsewhere, with the previously obtained consent of the Governments existing there, will be continued," Lincoln affirmed.

Then, without more ado, the great lines were delivered to the nation:

> On the first day of January in the year of our Lord, one thousand eight hundred and sixty-three, all persons held as slaves within any state, or designated part of a state, the people whereof shall then be in rebellion against the United

States shall be then, thenceforward, and forever free; and the executive government of the United States, including the military and naval authority thereof,
will recognize and maintain the freedom of such persons, and will do no act or
acts to repress such persons, or any of them, in any efforts they may make for
their actual freedom.

"*Maintain* the freedom of such persons," here was a promise to use
all the might of the nation to *assist* those slaves seeking freedom in
Confederate states if the war continued after 1862. Lincoln warned
the rebels that "on the first day of January" he would "designate the
States, or parts of states" in which rebellion continued to be active.
Lincoln closed with a promise to support the idea of compensation for
loyal masters in rebellious states who had lost their slaves in the war.[83]

On September 24, a group of admirers arrived at the White House
and serenaded Lincoln. Afterward, a crowd of administration revelers
gathered at the home of Salmon Chase to continue the festivities. As
Lincoln's young secretary John Hay reflected in his diary, "they all seemed
to feel a sort of new and exhilarated [*sic*] life; they breathed freer." The
new proclamation "had freed them as well as the slaves. They gleefully
and merrily called each other and themselves abolitionists. . . ."[84]

Lincoln issued yet another proclamation on the same day invoking
martial law against "all Rebels and Insurgents, their aiders and abettors
within the United States, and all persons discouraging volunteer enlist-
ments, resisting militia drafts, or guilty of any disloyal practice. . . ."
Habeas corpus was suspended for anyone arrested pursuant to the
policy.[85] "Stronger measures" were arriving indeed.

There was plenty of reason for the Lincoln entourage to celebrate:
Lee's invasion of Maryland was stopped and his army had been forced
to retreat. The threat of foreign intervention had subsided, at least for
a while. And the revolutionary step had been taken that would elevate
the war into a national crusade for liberation.

But there were also causes for brooding in the Lincoln inner circle.
If the Northern electorate turned upon Lincoln, then Republicans could
lose control of Congress. And while Lee's invasion of Maryland was
thwarted, there remained the Confederate invasion attempts in Mississippi and Kentucky.

As it happened, the Confederate attack in Mississippi would be easily
stopped. Union forces under Ulysses S. Grant—who had succeeded
Henry Halleck as commander in the Mississippi theatre—and William

S. Rosecrans vanquished two Confederate armies in the battles of Iuka on September 19, and Corinth on October 3–4, both in Mississippi.

But the Confederate invasion of Kentucky under Generals Braxton Bragg and Edmund Kirby Smith had been gathering momentum since August. From East Tennessee, these Confederates had slashed through Kentucky, seizing one city after another: Richmond, August 30, Lexington, September 2, and Frankfort, the state capital, September 3. The Union army of Buell was unable to stop them and alarm bells were ringing in the North. Cincinnati was directly in the path of the Confederate invasion.

Moreover, thousands of "contraband" slaves had been seized in Kentucky by the Southern invaders and shipped off to slavery again. Lee's army did the very same thing.[86]

On October 8, Buell finally managed to stop the Confederate invasion in the battle of Perryville, Kentucky. But like McClellan in the aftermath of Antietam, he allowed the Confederate forces to fight another day and gain strength. He refused to deliver the knockout blow that the president demanded.

Lincoln's patience with generals like Buell and McClellan was running out. The only reason he had kept them in command, as he confided a month or so later, was his fear that he "would not find successors to them, who would do better."[87]

Lincoln visited McClellan and inspected his army at Antietam in the first week of October. Then he issued an order, through Halleck, on October 6: McClellan was to cross the Potomac and attack the army of Lee as rapidly as possible. McClellan made the usual excuses as he fumbled and dithered. On October 13, Lincoln wrote him: "You remember my speaking to you of your over-cautiousness. Are you not over-cautious when you assume that you can not do what the enemy is constantly doing?"

The best strategy, the president argued, was to strike in the direction of Richmond in order to force Lee into a battle on favorable ground. Lee's forces were largely in or near the Shenandoah; consequently, "you are now nearer to Richmond than the enemy is. . . . Why can you not reach there before him. . . [?] His route is the arc of a circle, while yours is the chord." Consequently, "to beat him to Richmond on the inside track" should be "easy . . . if our troops march as well as the enemy; and it is unmanly to say they can not do it."[88]

Meanwhile, on October 23, Lincoln fired Buell and replaced him with William S. Rosecrans. And though McClellan at last gave the order to cross the Potomac, his fate with the president was sealed. Lincoln finally relieved him of command on November 5, and replaced him with Ambrose Burnside.

When the Northern electorate voted, the Republicans retained control of Congress. But their margin of control was reduced in the House of Representatives: the Democrats gained thirty-two seats. Moreover, the Democrats took control of the Illinois and Indiana legislatures; they also captured the governorships of New Jersey and New York. Though the outcome could have been worse by far (the Republicans actually gained five seats in the Senate), it had a morbid effect upon Lincoln. "We have lost the elections," the president lamented, and "the ill-success of the war had much to do with it."[89]

But he would not back down from his new emancipation commitment. According to a story in the *New York Tribune*, he told a delegation of "unconditional Union Kentuckians" in late November that "he would rather die than take back one word of the Proclamation of Freedom."[90] Moreover, as he wrote his long message to Congress, he conferred with General Burnside regarding a new campaign against Lee.

Burnside was almost McClellan's opposite. Where McClellan was arrogant, Burnside was modest; where McClellan was cautious to the point of occasional cowardice, Burnside—and here was the rub—would pit his troops against hopeless odds.

Burnside proposed to take the Army of the Potomac toward Richmond as the president wanted. But he preferred to move his forces much farther away from Lee's position near Virginia's Blue Ridge. He proposed to take his army all the way to Fredericksburg, east on the Rappahannock River. Having crossed the Rappahannock, he would move his army toward Richmond. Lincoln approved this scheme, with the proviso that the movement should be fast.

But when Burnside arrived in the Fredericksburg vicinity, the bridges he had ordered for the crossing of the river had not yet arrived. And so he waited. By the time the bridges finally arrived, so had Lee's army.

On November 26, Lincoln traveled by boat to Acquia Creek for an urgent conference with Burnside. In a memorandum of the meeting, Lincoln put it on record that Burnside "thinks he can cross the river in the face of the enemy and drive him away, but that, to use his own expression, it is somewhat risky." These odds were not good enough for Lincoln. Consequently, the president urged a new plan to bring forces to the south of Lee's army in order to engage it as Burnside crossed the river. To Lincoln's chagrin, both Burnside and Halleck rejected the plan as unrealistic.[91]

As planning for the Fredericksburg attack continued, Lincoln sent his long annual message to Congress. In a startling move, he urged Congress to write every feature of his presidential anti-slavery program, both the short-term measures and long-term measures, into law as constitutional amendments.

What better strategic hedge could he have had against the worst-case scenarios that haunted him night and day? After all, if the public were to throw him out of office in the next presidential election, the amended Constitution might nonetheless permit the anti-slavery movement to resume in another generation.

Lincoln advocated three amendments: (1) "Every state, wherein slavery now exists, which shall abolish the same therein, at any time, or times, before the first day of January, in the year of our Lord one thousand and nine hundred, shall receive compensation from the United States. . . ." (2) "All slaves who shall have enjoyed actual freedom by the chances of the war, at any time before the end of the rebellion, shall be forever free; but all owners of such, who shall not have been disloyal, shall be compensated for them. . . ." (3) "Congress may appropriate money, and otherwise provide, for colonizing free colored persons, with their own consent, at any place or places without the United States."[92]

In proposing these amendments, Lincoln was trying to give an anti-slavery thrust to the Constitution itself. The cost of paying for the slaves would be paid through the sale of bonds: through deficit spending. Lincoln argued that prosperity resulting from national growth would make the economic burden acceptable. By the turn of the twentieth century, he reasoned, "we shall probably have a hundred millions of people to share the burden, instead of thirty one millions, as now. . . ."[93]

To assuage racist critics, Lincoln emphasized colonization. But he also decided to challenge American racism. Since his program called for colonization as a *voluntary* venture, he considered the case of free blacks who might insist upon staying. Consequently, he criticized racists who objected to the presence of blacks as free neighbors in America. What was it that the racists were afraid of, Lincoln demanded. They seemed to dread "that the freed people will swarm forth, and cover the whole land." But, Lincoln asked, "are they not already in the land?" If the entire population of American blacks were "distributed among the whites of the whole country . . . there would be but one colored to seven whites," Lincoln observed. Moreover, "there are many communities now, having more than one free colored person, to seven whites; and this, without any apparent consciousness of evil from it."[94]

The real question, he said, was a simple formulation for America: "can we all do better?" "The dogmas of the quiet past," he continued, "are inadequate to the stormy present. The occasion is piled high with difficulty, and we must rise with the occasion. As our case is new, so we must think anew, and act anew. We must disenthrall ourselves, and then we shall save our country."

"Fellow citizens," Lincoln concluded, "*we* cannot escape history. . . . The fiery trial through which we pass, will light us down, in honor or dishonor, to the latest generation. . . . In *giving* freedom to the *slave*, we *assure* freedom to the *free*." And so, in the end, "we shall nobly save, or meanly lose, the last best hope of earth."[95]

On December 13, the war's "fiery trial" continued in the eastern theatre. Burnside was ready at Fredericksburg, or so he thought. He ordered his men to attack the Confederates, without the support from subsidiary Union forces that Lincoln had suggested. The result was horrible. Lee's men were entrenched along impregnable heights behind the town. And so the Union army was mauled. Wave after wave tried to storm Lee's position. They were all cut down and slaughtered. The Army of the Potomac suffered 12,600 casualties that day, compared to less than 5,000 Confederate losses.

The casualties at Shiloh back in April (both Union and Confederate) came close to the 20,000 mark; at Fair Oaks, 11,000; in the Seven Days Battles, the Union and Confederate losses had been roughly 31,000; at Second Manassas, close to 25,000; Antietam had cost over 23,000; at Perryville, 7,600. Then at Fredericksburg, on December 13, over 17,000 more.

Lincoln would not back down. As New Year's Day was approaching, people speculated about the president's commitment, both to the Union and to liberation. Would his threat against the rebels hold good? Would the final proclamation be delivered on January 1? Frederick Douglass, the black abolitionist, a critic of Lincoln since the very beginning of the war, was in Boston on New Year's Day. He recalled the occasion in his memoirs: "Eight, nine, ten o'clock came and went, and still no word. . . . At last, when patience was well-nigh exhausted . . . a man (I think it was Judge Russell) with hasty step advanced through the crowd, and with a face fairly illuminated with the news he bore, exclaimed in tones that thrilled all hearts, 'It is coming! It is on the wires!' . . . My old friend Rue, a colored preacher, a man of wonderful vocal power . . . led all voices in the anthem, 'Sound the loud timbrel o'er Egypt's dark sea, Jehovah hath triumphed, his people are free.'"

Though inspection of the document chagrined certain people who expected it to lash out at slavery everywhere at once, Douglass "saw in its spirit, a life and power far beyond its letter. Its meaning to me was the entire abolition of slavery, wherever the evil could be reached by the Federal arm, and I saw that its moral power would extend much further."[96]

Thus, as the new year began, the war for Union had become a war for freedom. The president who guided the soldiers had two years remaining in his term. But he would have to face the voters again—win or lose on the bloody fields of combat. And only *one* year remained before the critical election year of 1864.

FIVE

Lincoln and the War to the Death, 1863

I N 1863, Lincoln mobilized himself for a political race against time. As he carried out his pledge to free the slaves of the rebels, he was keenly aware of the white supremacist backlash this would provoke. Only one year remained before the next presidential election would be getting under way. And so, as he liberated blacks, he tried desperately to win the Civil War before the end of his presidential term.

On January 1, he put the finishing touches on his final and definitive Emancipation Proclamation. To allay Democratic accusations that he meant to start a war between the races by unchaining Southern blacks, he urged slaves "to abstain from all violence, unless in necessary self-defense." But he also declared that black force would be welcomed and encouraged in the *federal uniform*: freedmen "of suitable condition," he declared, would "be received into the armed service of the United States."[1] In other words, Lincoln had decided to turn the former slaves into soldiers.

The Democrats were shrill as they reviled this "wicked abolition crusade" of the "black Republicans." The so-called "Peace Democrats" or "Copperheads"—the anti-war faction of the party—called for measures to restore the "old Union" as it was in the decades before the Civil War. There was even furtive talk of a new midwestern Confederacy.

As emancipation started, the political question for the president recurred with new intensity: how deep were the racial animosities of Northern whites? Lincoln carefully pondered both the best-case options and the worst-case options for his fragile politics of freedom. It was characteristic of Lincoln that he tried to make concurrent provision for the best-case and worst-case scenarios. But the tension of his mood was unmistakable in 1863. His sense that time was running out would reveal the inner anger that had always been a driving force in his attacks upon slavery.

His best-case plan on the racial issue was to extend as many opportunities to freedmen as politics permitted. But he continued to assuage the white supremacist voters by promoting the concept of voluntary colonization, at least until the middle of the year. He insisted on working both ends of the range of possibility: as he tried to use the valor of blacks as they fought for the Union to silence or shame white supremacists, he carefully retained his old fall-back position on the racial problem as a hedge in case his strategies should fail.

His worst-case strategy—in anticipation of a possible Democratic victory in 1864—was to lock in as many of his anti-slavery achievements as he possibly could. He was striving for a way to force a national commitment to his long-term plan for liberation. He was striving, indeed, to force an irreversible commitment to eliminate slavery. His proposed constitutional amendments, for instance, if enacted and ratified quickly, would serve to protect the great "beach-head" that he and the congressional Republicans had gained for the anti-slavery movement.

One of these proposed amendments would guarantee permanent protection to his wartime emancipation policy: no Democratic judges would be able to challenge the legality of what he had done to emancipate blacks if the Constitution were amended. Another amendment would establish his voluntary program for the non-Confederate slave states as permanent policy.

But if the Lincoln amendments were to founder in Congress (which indeed would be the case during 1863), only military victory could rescue both Lincoln and the nation from the worst-case future: the election of a racist, pro-slavery Democrat in 1864. So Lincoln pushed his commanders to defeat the Confederate armies with ever-greater vehemence.

On the last day of 1862, an important battle began in Tennessee. Union forces under General William S. Rosecrans were fighting the Confederate troops under Braxton Bragg near the town of Murfreesboro. The battle of Murfreesboro (or Stone's River) raged from December 31 until January 2, when Bragg and his army, unable to break the Union lines, gave up and withdrew.

Ever since the failure of the three-prong Confederate counterof-fensive in the autumn of 1862, Lincoln strove to regain the initiative in all major theatres of war. In each major theatre, Lincoln's goal was two-fold: he sought to wipe out Confederate armies (or to force their surrender) and to seize geographical assets. In the Tennessee theatre, he urged Rosecrans to do what his predecessor, Don Carlos Buell, had repeatedly failed to do: destroy the Confederate presence in the state and capture Unionist-tending East Tennessee with its transportation hub, Chattanooga.

In Virginia, the promotion of Ambrose Burnside had led to disaster. Lincoln found some other duties for Burnside—he sent him to Ohio to build a new army that would operate in pincer-fashion with Rosecrans in East Tennessee—as he turned his mind to the task of selecting yet another commander for the ill-starred Army of the Potomac. Lincoln turned to a corps commander, Joseph Hooker.

In the third major theatre—the Mississippi Valley theatre—Lincoln's goal, in addition to defeating rebel armies, was to open up the Missis-sippi River. To do this, his armies had to seize the rebel-held and for-tified cities of Vicksburg, Mississippi, and Port Hudson, Louisiana.

With the Mississippi River in Union hands, the Confederacy would be split: both Arkansas and Texas would be severed from the other rebel states. Moreover, the control of the river would facilitate Union transportation and tighten the Union's blockade. Lastly, with the state of Mississippi under Union bayonets, a great Union-occupied zone would be established all the way from the southern border of the state of Illinois to the Gulf of Mexico.

Union forces would be mustered for this western campaign just as soon as the Confederate offensive had been stopped in the battles of Corinth and Iuka, Mississippi in the autumn of 1862. From the South, Union forces under General Nathaniel Banks (the political general who had served in the Virginia theatre in 1862) would move north along the Mississippi River and attack Port Hudson, Louisiana. Simulta-neously, from the north, Union forces commanded by General John A. McClernand, a Unionist Democrat (and therefore a political gen-eral with very strong value to Lincoln), would lead the attack upon Vicksburg.

Though Ulysses S. Grant was in nominal command of this depart-ment, he was left uninformed about the nature of McClernand's expe-dition in the earliest weeks of its development. Perhaps Grant, to a certain extent, was still "under a cloud" in the mind of Lincoln. But as soon as Grant learned about the turn of events, he took action to ensure his authority. Indeed, Grant had plans of his own for the capture of Vicksburg.

In December, Grant ordered a two-pronged attack upon the city. But all of the attacks in the Mississippi theatre came to grief in the final weeks of 1862. Banks was unable to fight his way farther up the river than Baton Rouge, Louisiana. Meanwhile, Grant had been forced to turn back and regroup because of rebel raiders who attacked and destroyed his supply lines. And Grant's trusted lieutenant William Tecumseh Sherman discovered that the swampy topography north of the city made direct assault upon Confederate defensive positions almost hopeless. Vicksburg appeared unassailable.

Grant's strategy was to move his men around the city by the opposite bank of the river. But he quickly discovered that the opposite shore was just another impenetrable swamp. So he tried to dig *canals* farther inland on the other side of the river—canals he could use to send gunboats, transports, and troops around Vicksburg to approach it from the southern side. He would then bring his men across the river for a final attack upon Vicksburg from good dry land.

On the sociopolitical front, as emancipation policy went into effect, many thousands of slaves began flocking to the armies of Rosecrans and Grant, thus belying the lame but extremely influential statement of historian Richard Hofstadter, who complained years ago that the Proclamation "did not free any slaves. . . . It simply declared free all slaves in 'the States and parts of States' where the people were in rebellion—that is to say, precisely where its effect could not reach."[2] This observation is frequently repeated by determined critics of Lincoln. But Lincoln's Emancipation Proclamation was a deadly serious announcement, not only that the slaves in rebel states (and certain parts of rebel states) were deemed free but that the armies of Lincoln would promptly set them free just as soon as those armies took control of the areas in question. Within months, moreover, this threat became a demonstrated deed. And with the actual freeing of slaves in the Confederate states, the great question of the freedmen's status was thrust upon the nation.

For a while, Lincoln kept alive his colonization proposal, shifting its point of destination from Central America—where his vision of a colony settled in the Chiriqui coal region met stiff resistance from the governments of Honduras and Nicaragua—to an island off the coast of Haiti: Isle-a-Vache.[3] In December 1862, Lincoln signed a contract with entrepreneurs to resettle five thousand black volunteers, and the project began in the early months of 1863.

Nonetheless, Lincoln pushed the recruitment of blacks for Union armies at the very same time. What he wanted was a group of black army veterans whose help in preserving the nation would deserve an appropriate level of patriotic glory in the years to come. On March 26, he wrote to Andrew Johnson—who had left the United States Senate to serve as appointed civilian governor of occupied Tennessee—as follows: "I am told you have at least *thought* of raising a negro military force. In my opinion the country now needs no specific thing so much as some man of your ability, and position, to go to this work. When I speak of your position, I mean that of an eminent citizen of a slave-state, and himself a slave-holder. The colored population is the great *available* and yet *unavailed* of, force for restoring the Union. The bare sight of fifty thousand armed, and drilled Black soldiers on the banks of the Mississippi, would end the rebellion at once."[4]

As Lincoln used this logic to prevail upon Johnson, he turned to other methods of assisting the slaves whom his armies were beginning to liberate. He supported the creation of policies to offer them jobs on seized plantations. This policy was launched in the early spring of 1863. Specifically, in March he issued orders to Adjutant General Lorenzo Thomas to create a new "refugee" policy for occupied parts of the rebellious Mississippi Valley. Thomas organized a work-for-wages program that was promising in Lincoln's eyes.

Moreover, in the Sea Islands off the coast of South Carolina, yet another important experiment was starting in the early months of 1863. The tax act that congressional Republicans had passed in the summer of 1862 provided for the confiscation of real estate belonging to tax evaders in the occupied rebel states. This particular procedure for the confiscation of land in the South—for non-payment of taxes—was immune from the constitutional problems involved in the effort to seize rebel land as a punishment for *treason*.

Tax commissioners were duly dispatched to the South Carolina Sea Islands in October 1862. On February 6, 1863, Congress passed an important amendment to the tax/confiscation law that allowed these federal agents to reserve a certain portion of the seized lands—which were slated to be sold at auction—as a special "reserve" for educational and charitable purposes. This was euphemistic language for a potent idea: the lands would be sold to the very same slaves who had been tilling the soil for their masters. Accordingly, almost two thousand acres in the South Carolina Sea Islands were purchased by freedmen in 1863. Lincoln took direct action to ensure that these "homesteads" for blacks would be delivered. The rest of the lands in question were sold to investors, who instituted programs of wage employment very similar to those underway in the Mississippi Valley.[5]

Moreover, as all of these events unfolded, the executive branch was at work upon a comprehensive policy for aiding the newly freed slaves. As historian LaWanda Cox has observed, "Secretary of War Stanton established the Freedmen's Inquiry Commission shortly after Lincoln issued the Emancipation Proclamation; it is highly unlikely that he did so without the president's sanction." The members of this commission were "staunchly antislavery men." Their reports during 1863 "went beyond emancipation to outline what has been characterized as a 'Blueprint for Radical Reconstruction.' The blueprint included citizenship, suffrage, and landownership for the freedmen."[6] Moreover, certain Radical Republicans demanded the creation by Congress of a stronger "Freedmen's Bureau" to assist the freed slaves more efficiently. But Congress failed to pass such a law during 1863.

The white supremacist backlash against Lincoln's liberation program grew apace in the Northern states in 1863. Copperhead Democrats were urging white resistance to the Negro-loving "tyrant" or "dictator," Lincoln. They called for "peace"—peace with Southern brethren whose pride and "decency" rebelled against the abolitionists who wished to unleash "semi-savages." The resistance of Copperheads was sure to increase as Congress extended its plans to initiate a federal draft, since recruitment was beginning to falter.

Insofar as racist advocates of "peace" could be charged with interference in federal recruitment or enrollment efforts, Lincoln took strong measures against them. In May, new military forces being mustered in the state of Ohio under Burnside arrested the important Democratic Copperhead Clement L. Vallandigham, who was seeking the Democratic gubernatorial nomination. His prison term, handed down by a military tribunal, was commuted by Lincoln to banishment to the Confederacy.

But strong measures such as these against Copperheads led to even stronger appeals to a war-weary Northern public by Democratic critics.[7] Above all, it was the racial issue that the Democrats, working in the mode of Stephen Douglas, kept using for maximum effect. Accordingly, Lincoln continued to promote his plans for voluntary colonization to calm the racists down.

By May, Lincoln's colonization venture near Haiti was beginning in earnest. Over four hundred Blacks took a chance on the venture and departed for the Caribbean. But the project would prove to be a failure as corruption, disease, and squalor took their toll on the relocated community. When news of this reached Lincoln, he gradually began to move away from the colonization idea. After all, he had promised black leaders that the volunteers for colonization would not be "wronged."

Meanwhile, the war raged on. Early in April, Lincoln visited the army of Hooker, which was still in winter camp across the Rappahannock River from Fredericksburg. The army of Lee had not moved.

Lincoln talked at great length with Hooker, who assured his commander that he would dedicate himself to the speedy capture of Richmond. But Lincoln made it very clear to Hooker that Richmond, at least for a time, was but a secondary goal for the army. He observed that "just now, with the enemy directly ahead of us, there is no eligible route for us into Richmond." Consequently, "our prime object is the enemies' [sic] army in front of us." Lincoln also counseled Hooker to avoid the gross mistake of Burnside: "While he [Lee's army] remains in tact," he suggested, "I do not think we should take the disadvantage of attacking him in his entrenchments; but we should continually harrass [sic] and menace him. . . . If he weakens himself, then pitch into him."[8]

Hooker proposed that his army should cross the Rappahannock at a point far above Lee's position and attack Lee's army from the rear. Lincoln approved this proposal. On April 27, Hooker modified his plan to be a pincer movement: he would leave a Union force across the river from Lee and then move a separate force upriver to hit him from the rear. If Lee abandoned his position, Union forces would converge and destroy him.

Lee's response was the greatest single masterpiece of strategy that he and Stonewall Jackson devised in their Civil War partnership. Lee mimicked Hooker's action: He divided his forces, leaving troops under General Jubal Early to man the Confederate lines behind the city of Fredericksburg. He then marched with the bulk of his men to parry Hooker's thrust near the tiny country crossroads of Chancellorsville.

As soon as he encountered Lee's army, Hooker started to panic. He ordered a withdrawal to defensive positions as the fighting began on May 1. Lee sensed Hooker's weakness, and divided his army yet again, sending Jackson on a sweeping flank maneuver that erupted in a storm-like attack upon Hooker's exposed right flank on the evening of May 2. A Union rout began and Hooker was completely stunned.

Hooker's weakness gave Lee a free hand. When the Union forces that were stationed on the opposite side of the Rappahannock River crossed over and stormed up the heights behind Fredericksburg, Lee divided his army *yet again*. He led a separate detachment from the center of battle to suppress this Union drive.

It was all too much for Joseph Hooker, who withdrew his forces from the battle and re-crossed the Rappahannock on May 6. Chancellorsville was yet another major triumph for Lee. But it came at a terrible cost: Stonewall Jackson was mortally wounded by the "friendly fire" of his troops, who mistook him in the gathering twilight for an enemy scout.

In the Mississippi Valley the news was much better for the Union. Grant finally abandoned his canal-building scheme and took a calculated risk to get his troops below the guns of Vicksburg. He would send his flotilla of transports and gunboats straight below Vicksburg under cover of darkness; he would do it so quickly as to thwart the Confederate gunners who were always on alert. On a moonless night he succeeded; his ships ran the gauntlet on the evening of April 16. With his ships below the city, he could ferry his troops across the river and move to the attack.

His army now in place, Grant decided on another surprise. Instead of moving directly on Vicksburg, he moved his army rapidly inland. The Confederate defenders of Vicksburg—commanded by General John C. Pemberton and numbering thirty-two thousand—had been recently augmented by another rebel force that was assembled under General Joseph Johnston. Johnston had been gathering an army at Jackson, the Mississippi capital. Grant decided to lunge at these forces and defeat them as the first order of business. He would thereby rid himself of threats to his rear as he turned to the capture of Vicksburg.

At this point the military leadership of Grant began to rise to the level of Lee: with speed and audacity, he severed his supply lines and lived completely off the land. Within weeks he defeated the forces of Johnston, sacked the city of Jackson, turned westward to confront the

Confederate forces of Pemberton, beat them in open engagements, chased them back into Vicksburg, and started a siege of the city. His endgame was simple: he would starve them into submission. Well before the surrender of Vicksburg, Lincoln called this whirlwind campaign "the most brilliant in the world."[9]

Conversely, in the aftermath of Hooker's lamentable performance in Virginia, Lincoln tried to size up the situation. He counseled temporary caution as he played for more time to form a clearer impression of Hooker.

This interlude, however, was drawing to a close, for in the weeks after beating Hooker's army, Lee proposed to stage another invasion of the Northern states. Such a move, he suggested in Richmond, would ease the pressure on Vicksburg, strengthen the Democratic Copperheads, reopen the issue of foreign recognition, and aid the Confederate cause across the board. The Confederate cabinet agreed, and the Gettysburg campaign began. Lee gathered his forces and began to move north in early June.

As he did so, the president reversed his recent guidance to Hooker: instead of caution, Lincoln wanted fast *action* to destroy the rebel army. When Hooker suggested that he try to take Richmond, Lincoln overruled him completely. "I think *Lee's* Army, and not *Richmond*, is your true objective point," Lincoln wrote.[10]

Hooker's army attempted to harass Lee's men as they moved through northern Virginia. An encounter on June 9 at Brandy Station turned into the largest single cavalry battle of the war. Notwithstanding, Lee continued his march. So Lincoln prodded Hooker again: "If the head of Lee's army is at Martinsburg and the tail of it on the Plank road between Fredericksburg and Chancellorsville," Lincoln cabled on June 14, then "the animal must be very slim somewhere. Could you not break him?"[11]

Once again, it was too much for Hooker to bear, and he resigned his command. On June 28, Lincoln quickly promoted General George Gordon Meade, another corps commander of the Army of the Potomac, to succeed him.

Lee's troops had reached Pennsylvania. They were seizing supplies (and also blacks, whom they shipped down their lines into slavery, just as they had done in the Antietam campaign). Their preliminary goal was to destroy and disrupt the important Pennsylvania Railroad line between Harrisburg and Lancaster. On the first of July, a Confederate foraging party ran into some cavalry units from the Army of the Potomac near the town of Gettysburg. The clash widened. By dusk it became a great vortex that drew both armies into battle.

Lee tried to seize the best strategic ground—a line of hills and ridges that stretched like a fishhook below the town—on the first day of battle, and he ordered Richard Ewell, who had succeeded in command of Stonewall Jackson's old corps, to assault the Union-held Cemetery Hill. But Ewell proved overly cautious and he missed this crucial opportunity.

By the second day of battle Meade's army had occupied the hill and the long ridge below it. Lee occupied a parallel ridge and prepared to attack: his plan was to hit both ends of the Union line and then to "enfilade" the line from the tallest hills at the ends. A Confederate attack against the southernmost Union position came close to succeeding, but a desperate series of Union counterattacks on a hill known as "Little Round Top" gradually repulsed it. The lines of Meade's army held firm as the second day of battle played out.

On the third and most fateful day, Lee took a great gamble and unleashed an assault—Pickett's charge—against the center of the Union line, which he mistakenly believed to be weakened. The result was catastrophic for Lee: his forces were slaughtered in a hopeless and wasteful assault. Moreover, on the very next day, which was also the Fourth of July, Grant succeeded in capturing Vicksburg. All Confederate troops in the city surrendered, and a few days later the Confederate defenders of the other major fortified city down the river, Port Hudson, surrendered to the army of Nathaniel Banks. The news of these triumphs took several days to reach the White House.

On the Fourth of July, bearing news of the Gettysburg victory, Lincoln sent to the nation a hymn of thanksgiving, announcing that "the highest honor" had been won by the Army of the Potomac. Lincoln called for the "profoundest gratitude" not only to the army of General Meade but to God, "whose will, not ours," should be done.[12]

Though Lincoln continued to express such feelings in public, he was privately disturbed about the *aftermath* of Gettysburg. Meade was allowing Lee's army to escape, just as George McClellan had done in the aftermath of Antietam. On July 6, Lincoln wrote to Halleck, "I left the telegraph office a good deal dissatisfied." He suspected Meade's intention was to "get the enemy across the river again without a further collision," rather than "prevent his crossing and . . . destroy him."[13] Indeed, Lee and his army crossed into Virginia on the night of July 13.

Lincoln was enraged: to John Hay he exclaimed that "we had them within our grasp. We had only to stretch forth our hands & they were ours."[14] According to Hay, "the Tycoon"—a private nickname that Hay had been using for Lincoln—had gone so far as to say that he "'could have whipped them myself.'"[15] On July 14, Lincoln wrote a long letter to Meade—a letter that he never signed or sent. In this letter Lincoln made it emphatically clear that this war was nothing less than a war to be fought to the death unless the enemy surrendered. "I do not believe," Lincoln concluded, that "you appreciate the magnitude of the misfortune involved in Lee's escape. He was within your easy grasp, and to have closed upon him would, in connection with our other late successes, have ended the war. As it is, the war will be prolonged indefinitely. . . . Your golden opportunity is gone, and I am distressed immeasureably [sic] because of it."[16]

Despite the fact that Lincoln kept this letter to himself, Meade began to get wind of the president's mood and he offered to submit his resignation. But Lincoln kept him in command. Many Northerners regarded George Meade as a hero, and dismissing him might have seemed absurd. So Lincoln kept him on, but in a deeply pessimistic frame of mind. The fight to the death was not succeeding in the summer of 1863. In another brief year, the political conventions would launch the next race for the White House.

IN THE SECOND HALF OF 1863, Lincoln turned his attention more and more to the issue of race. The black troops of Lincoln's armies won distinction in two different battles. Blacks participated in the capture of Port Hudson, Louisiana. And near Charleston, South Carolina, blacks fought a gallant but suicidal action in assaulting a Confederate bastion known as Fort Wagner.

Yet military heroism notwithstanding, whites had still not accepted African Americans as equal citizens. As the Union draft went into effect in July, white mobs turned their wrath upon blacks. The biggest and worst of all the riots took place in New York City, where Democratic mobs went berserk on July 13. As James M. McPherson has observed, "the mob's chief target was the black population. Chanting 'kill the naygers' [many of the rioters were Irish immigrants], they lynched at least a dozen blacks and burned down the Colored Orphan Asylum. Because most of the militia had gone to Pennsylvania for the Gettysburg campaign, the city was especially vulnerable. . . . On the fourth day of rioting, the police and several regiments of soldiers that had been rushed to New York finally brought the city under control."[17] Throughout the riots, according to John Hay, Lincoln was a pillar of strength. A few weeks after the riots, Hay set down the following reflections: "The Tycoon is in fine whack. . . . He is managing this war, the draft, foreign relations, and planning a reconstruction of the Union, all at once. I never knew with what tyrannous authority he rules the Cabinet, till now. The most important things he decides, and there is no cavil."[18]

In August, an angry Lincoln wrote a letter intended to shame the white supremacist Northerners. This public letter was dispatched to a very old acquaintance in Springfield, Illinois: James C. Conkling. This letter to Conkling is a striking example of the methods Lincoln used to dragoon white supremacists by means of patriotic imperatives. It is also an excellent example of the methods Lincoln used to make heroes of the Union's black troops.

"There are those who are dissatisfied with me," Lincoln wrote. "To such I would say: You desire peace; and you blame me that we do not have it. But how can we attain it? There are but three conceivable ways. First, to suppress the rebellion by force of arms. This, I am trying to do. Are you for it? If you are, so far we are agreed. If you are not for it, a second way is to give up the Union. I am against this. Are you for it? If you are, you should say so plainly. If you are not for *force*, not yet for *dissolution*, there only remains some imaginable *compromise*. I do not believe any compromise, embracing the maintenance of the Union, is now possible."

Lincoln tried to make the case that a negotiated Unionist settlement appeared to be impossible as long as the Confederates remained unrepentant and their armies kept fighting. "The strength of the rebellion," he continued, "is its military—its army. That army dominates all the country, and all the people, within its range. Any offer of terms made by any man or men within that range, in opposition to that army, is simply nothing for the present; because such man or men, have no power whatever to enforce their side of a compromise. . . . No paper compromise, to which the controllers of Lee's army are not agreed, can, at all, affect that army. In an effort at such compromise we should waste time, which the enemy would use to our disadvantage; and that would be all."

Lincoln then grabbed the bull by the horns: "But, to be plain, you are dissatisfied with me about the negro. Quite likely there is a difference of opinion between you and myself upon that subject. I certainly wish that all men could be free, while I suppose you do not. Yet I have neither adopted, nor proposed any measure, which is not consistent with even your view, provided you are for the Union. I suggested compensated emancipation; to which you replied you wished not to be taxed to buy negroes. But I had not asked you to be taxed to buy negroes, except in such way, as to save you from greater taxation to save the Union exclusively by other means."

Lincoln turned to the Emancipation Proclamation. This too, he insisted, was imperative to save the Union. "You dislike the emancipation proclamation," he continued, "and, perhaps, would have it retracted. You say it is unconstitutional—I think differently. I think the constitution invests its commander-in-chief, with the law of war, in time of war. . . . Is there—has there ever been—any question that by the law of war, property, both of enemies and friends, may be taken when needed? And is it not needed whenever taking it, helps us, or hurts the enemy? . . . Some of our commanders of our armies in the field who have given us our most important successes, believe the emancipation policy, and the use of colored troops, constitute the heaviest blow yet dealt to the rebellion; and that, at least one of those important successes [Port Hudson, presumably], could not have been achieved when it was, but for the aid of black soldiers. Among the commanders holding these views are some who have never had any affinity with what is called abolitionism, or with republican party politics; but who hold them purely as military opinions."

Like a cross before the face of a vampire, the president brandished the emblem of "Union" in the faces of his white supremacist detractors. "You say you will not fight to free negroes. Some of them seem willing to fight for you; but, no matter. Fight you, then, exclusively, to save the Union. I issued the proclamation on purpose to aid you in saving the Union. Whenever you shall have conquered all resistance to the Union, if I shall urge you to continue fighting, it will be an apt time, then, for you to declare you will not fight to free negroes."

By the end of the letter, Lincoln's deep inner anger was emerging. "Peace," he concluded, "does not appear so distant as it did. I hope it will come soon, and come to stay; and so come as to be worth the keeping in all future time. . . . And then, there will be some black men who can remember that, with silent tongue, and clenched teeth, and steady eye, and well-poised bayonet, they have helped mankind on to this great consummation; while, I fear, there will be some white ones, unable to forget that, with malignant heart, and deceitful speech, they have strove to hinder it."[19]

At the risk of repetition, our question must be asked once again: is it possible to read such a letter as the statement of a racist politician who intended nothing more than preservation of the Union?

To the contrary—Lincoln sought to use every practical means at his disposal to reduce the power of slavery. Consistent with that, he would cautiously elevate the status of the newly freed slaves—either by placing them out of harm's reach beyond the borders of the country or by giving them the rudiments of status (the status, for example, of combat veterans and landowners)—while protecting his program from the backlash that might ruin everything.

He continued to be haunted by a number of worst-case scenarios. Around the time that he sent his long letter to Conkling, he penned the following reflections: "Suppose those now in rebellion should say: 'We cease fighting: re-establish the national authority amongst us— customs, courts, mails, land-offices,—all as before the rebellion—we claiming to send members to both branches of Congress, as of yore, and to hold our slaves according to our State laws, notwithstanding anything or all things which has [sic] occurred during the rebellion.'"

Lincoln was fearful and candid as he contemplated this scenario: "I shall dread, and I think we all should dread, to see 'the disturbing element' so brought back into the government. . . . During my continuance here, the government will return no person to slavery who is free according to the proclamation, or to any of the acts of congress, unless such return shall be held to be a legal duty, by the proper court of final resort. . . ."[20]

As LaWanda Cox has observed, Lincoln was "deeply troubled for the future of his emancipation policy" in 1863.[21] He was not alone; Cox has confirmed that "during 1863 and 1864 antislavery men feared the battle against the South's peculiar institution might yet be lost or compromised. However inevitable slavery's end may appear in retrospect, contemporary concern was real, and not without cause."[22]

So much for the worst-case scenarios: what of the best-case? In the summer of 1863, Frederick Douglass came to Washington to meet with the president concerning the status of blacks who were serving in uniform. This was the first time Frederick Douglass had met Lincoln, and his rich account of the event in his memoirs deserves to be quoted in detail.

"I was induced to go to Washington," Douglass remembered, "and lay the complaints of my people before President Lincoln and the secretary of war; and to urge upon them such action as should secure to the colored troops then fighting for the country, a reasonable degree of fair play." He did not know what to expect: "The distance then between the black man and the white American citizen, was immeasurable. . . . I was an ex-slave, identified with a despised race; and yet I was to meet the most exalted person in this great republic. . . . I could not know what kind of a reception would be accorded me. I might be told to go home and mind my business . . . or I might be refused an interview altogether."

But Douglass was admitted to an interview with Lincoln on August 10. The president "was seated, when I entered, in a low arm chair, with his feet extended on the floor, surrounded by a large number of documents, and several busy secretaries. The room bore the marks of business, and the persons in it, the president included, appeared to be much over-worked and tired. Long lines of care were already deeply written in Mr. Lincoln's brow; . . . his strong face . . . lighted up as soon as my name was mentioned. As I approached and was introduced to him, he rose and extended his hand, and bade me welcome."

Douglass stated his mission; the president responded by asking him to "state particulars." Douglass did so:

> I replied that there were three particulars which I wished to bring to his attention. First, that colored soldiers ought to receive the same wages as those paid to white soldiers. Second, that colored soldiers ought to receive the same protection when taken prisoners, and be exchanged as readily, and on the same terms, as any other prisoners, and if Jefferson Davis should shoot or hang colored soldiers in cold blood, the United States government should retaliate in kind and degree. . . . Third, when colored soldiers, seeking the "bauble-reputation at the cannon's mouth," performed great and uncommon service on the battle-field, they would be rewarded by distinction and promotion. . . .

The president "listened with patience and silence to all I had to say. He was serious and even troubled by what I had said, and by what he had evidently thought himself before on the same points." Lincoln then replied:

He began by saying that the employment of colored troops at all was a great gain to the colored people; that the measure could not have been successfully adopted at the beginning of the war; that the wisdom of making colored men into soldiers was still doubted; that their enlistment was a serious offense to popular prejudice; that they had larger motives for being soldiers than white men . . . that the fact that they were not to receive the same pay as white soldiers, seemed a necessary concession to smooth the way to their employment at all as soldiers; but that ultimately they would receive the same.

"They would receive the same" in due time: Lincoln quietly stated his intention to phase-in equality in wages. As to black promotions, Lincoln left the matter open, while deferring to the secretary of war. Lastly, in regard to Confederate crimes and atrocities against black soldiers, Lincoln said that he feared retaliation was a "terrible remedy," one which, "if once begun, there was no telling where it would end."[23]

Once again, however, Lincoln chose to conceal his hand for some reason. For he had signed precisely the sort of directive on war crimes that Douglass recommended. On July 30, Lincoln signed an order that was drafted by the War Department proclaiming it "the duty of every government to give protection to its citizens, of whatever class, color, or condition. . . . To sell or enslave any captured person, on account of his color, and for no offense against the laws of war, is a relapse into barbarism and a crime against the civilization of the age. . . ." Consequently, Lincoln's order continued, "If the enemy shall sell or enslave anyone because of his color, the offense shall be punished by retaliation upon the enemy's prisoners in our possession. It is therefore ordered that for every soldier of the United States killed in violation of the laws of war, a rebel soldier shall be executed; and for every one enslaved by the enemy or sold into slavery, a rebel soldier shall be placed at hard labor. . . ."[24]

Beyond military issues, the fate of black civilians and families was clearly on the minds of all anti-slavery Americans. As the Sea Island process of land confiscation by the federal tax commissioners continued off the South Carolina coast, Lincoln sent explicit orders to ensure that lots of twenty acres would be set aside for "heads of families of the African race, one only to each, preferring such as by their good conduct, meritorious services or exemplary character, will be examples of moral propriety and industry . . . for the charitable purpose of providing homes for such heads of families and their families respectively."[25]

At the same time, another experiment in black economic liberation was beginning to germinate. The scene was Davis Bend, Mississippi, which included the plantations of Jefferson Davis and his brother Joseph Davis. Both plantations had been seized and confiscated. Historian Eric Foner has described the outcome: "In 1863, General Grant decided that Davis Bend should become a 'negro paradise,' and the following year the entire area was set aside for the exclusive settlement of freedmen." Davis Bend became "a remarkable example of self-reliance, whose laborers raised nearly 2,000 bales of cotton and earned a profit of $160,000. The community had its own system of government, complete with elected judges and sheriffs."[26]

Elsewhere, however, the freedmen encountered some neglect, which Lincoln tried to mitigate. In August, Lincoln wrote to his friend Stephen Hurlbut, who had recently been commissioned as a Union general in occupied Mississippi. Lincoln expressed his concern that while "the able bodied male contrabands are already employed by the Army," the other freed slaves were "in confusion and destitution." Hence, "if there be plantations near you," Lincoln instructed, "which are abandoned by their owners, first put as many contrabands on such, as they will hold—that is, as can draw subsistence from them. If some still remain, get loyal men, of character in the vicinity, to take them temporarily on wages, to be paid to the contrabands themselves—such men obliging themselves to not let the contrabands be kidnapped, or forcibly taken away. Of course, if any voluntarily make arrangements to work for their living, you will not hinder them."[27]

In occupied Louisiana, General Nathaniel Banks issued labor regulations in 1863. These regulations, as Foner has stated, "bore a marked resemblance to slavery. The former slaves, [Banks] announced, must avoid vagrancy and idleness and enter into yearly contracts with loyal planters. . . . Once hired, the blacks were forbidden to leave the plantations without permission of their employers."[28] It is not at all clear as to when (or even whether) Lincoln knew the specific provisions of the code that Banks had developed. But Lincoln knew about the code's existence. And it is true that the president had special reasons to be cautious in Louisiana, reasons to be set forth momentarily.

Nonetheless, he made it clear in a letter to Banks that he wanted arrangements such as labor codes to be "probationary"—that is, temporary. He agreed with the short-term proposition that the state should "adopt some practical system by which the two races could gradually live themselves out of their old relation to each other, and both come out better prepared for the new." Some emphasis is needed: the president said that he wanted the races to live themselves *out* of their previous relation. By the end of summer, this vision was decisively replacing his preference for voluntary colonization. He then continued: "Education for young blacks should be included in this plan."[29]

Lincoln's reasons for exercising caution in Louisiana were complex, but the gist of his reasoning was simple: Lincoln had reason to believe in the summer and early fall of 1863 that Louisiana Unionists stood a good chance of redrafting the state's constitution *to make it a free state*. The new state of West Virginia was admitted to the Union on June 20, 1863. In terms of constitutional politics, the growth of the free-state bloc was of paramount importance to Lincoln. If Louisiana should succeed in redrafting its state constitution to abolish slavery, a new free state would be added to the Union and the slave states accordingly weakened. Indeed, Louisiana might set a new precedent that other occupied Confederate states could be induced, albeit under military pressure, to copy.

Moreover, in terms of Lincoln's worst-case analysis, the abolition of slavery by action of the loyal citizens state by state could be another important strategic hedge against the politics of Democratic victory in 1864. As Cox has observed, "beginning quietly in the spring of 1863, [Lincoln] moved to obtain emancipation in occupied states through state action, a piecemeal but constitutionally unchallengeable solution."[30]

As Cox has elaborated, the supporters of slavery were quick to try to hinder this action. On May 1, 1863, a group of pro-slavery Louisiana Unionists convened in New Orleans. They proceeded to send "a delegation to ask Lincoln for 'full recognition of all the rights of the State, as they existed previous to the passage of the act of secession, upon the principle of the existence of the State Constitution unimpaired.'"[31] They were obviously trying to cut their losses and return to allegiance with their system of slavery intact. But the president was playing for much higher stakes by the summer of 1863. And since a group of Louisiana Unionists led by Thomas J. Durant, Michael Hahn, and Benjamin Flanders were planning a constitutional convention to repudiate secession on a "free state" basis, Lincoln told the pro-slavery Louisiana Unionists on June 19 that since "reliable information has reached me that a respectable portion of the Louisiana people, desire to amend their State constitution, and contemplate holding a convention for that object," the fact of such a project seemed "sufficient reason why the general government should not give the committal you seek, to the existing State constitution."[32]

Since Banks was an active participant in pushing the project, Lincoln was probably averse to making much of an issue of his labor code, at least for a while. Indeed, Lincoln wished to make his role in Louisiana politics appear to be minimal in order that the free-state movement should appear to be a massive insurgency, which it was not. Lincoln summarized the matter in an August 5 letter to Banks: "While I very well know what I would be glad for Louisiana to do, it is quite a different thing for me to assume direction of the matter. I would be glad for her to make a new Constitution recognizing the emancipation proclamation, and adopting emancipation in those parts of the state to which the proclamation does not apply. . . . If these views can be of any advantage in giving shape, impetus, and action there, I shall be glad for you to use them prudently for that object. Of course you will confer with intelligent and trusty citizens of the State, among whom I would suggest Messrs. Flanders, Hahn, and Durant."[33]

In September, Lincoln turned to reconstruction efforts in occupied Tennessee; once again, he encouraged his allies and agents to redraft the state constitution to abolish slavery. Due to different political circumstances, however, he was far more direct than he had been in his Louisiana dealings. To Governor Andrew Johnson he wrote that "not a moment should be lost. . . . I see that you have declared in favor of emancipation in Tennessee, for which, may God bless you. Get emancipation into your new State government—Constitution—and there will be no such word as fail for your case." Do it quickly, Lincoln added, for "it can not be known who is next to occupy the position I now hold, nor what he will do."[34]

A free-state movement was also under way in the loyal slave state of Maryland. This movement, as Foner has explained, was "bolstered by loyalty oaths administered to voters by army provost marshals. . . . Voting was confined to those who took a strict loyalty oath, which included an avowal that one had never expressed a 'desire' for Confederate victory." With the Maryland electorate reduced in this manner, anti-slavery "Unionists committed to immediate and uncompensated emancipation swept the Maryland elections of 1863 and called a constitutional convention to reconstruct the state."[35]

In all, Lincoln's actions on slavery were heavily prioritized in 1863. He sought to do everything within his power to make emancipation permanent, to eliminate the legal underpinnings of slavery. His policies regarding the freedmen were, though extremely important, less urgent. As Cox has affirmed, both in this and other issues, "what becomes apparent in examining Lincoln's leadership role is his way of placing first things first."[36] And in 1863, the first issue was victory and permanent commitment to freedom, well before the next presidential election put everything at risk.

Though the war had fallen short of Lincoln's hopes in the critical theatre of Virginia, his armies in East Tennessee began moving toward victory late in the summer. Burnside and his newly formed army moved south from Ohio and occupied Knoxville in East Tennessee on September 3. More importantly, Rosecrans was able to flush the Confederates out of Chattanooga on September 9. Braxton Bragg's Confederate army retreated into Georgia, with Rosecrans in pursuit.

The Confederates, however, turned the tables and unleashed a ferocious assault upon the Union forces at Chickamauga Creek, about a dozen miles below Chattanooga, just across the Georgia line. The two-day battle of Chickamauga, which was fought from September 19 to September 20, was a tactical Union defeat. As Rosecrans began a retreat to Chattanooga, a subordinate Union commander of far greater bravery and presence of mind—General George Thomas, a loyalist Virginian—held Confederate attackers at bay and thus prevented the retreat from becoming a rout.

Then Bragg turned the tables again: he threw a siege around Chattanooga, turning Rosecrans and all of his troops into prisoners within the very city they had captured just a few weeks before. From Missionary Ridge and from Lookout Mountain, the Confederate gunners prevented any food or supplies from reaching the Union defenders.

In October, Lincoln sent a great infusion of troops from Mississippi and Virginia to break this Confederate siege. He placed Ulysses S. Grant in command of all Union armies in the West so he could supervise the whole operation. Grant went to Chattanooga himself: he promptly removed William Rosecrans from theatre command and appointed George Thomas in his place.

It bears noting that Lincoln's opinion of Meade was sufficiently low that he was quite nonchalant about reducing Union forces in Virginia. In early September, Meade asked for instructions as to how to proceed against Lee. Lincoln answered, via Halleck, that Meade should "move upon Lee in a manner of general attack, leaving to developments, whether he will make it a real attack."[37] Meade's reply (via Halleck) was extremely depressing to Lincoln. Meade claimed that Lee's defensive position (near the Rapidan River in Virginia) was almost unassailable. In other words, according to Meade, there was nothing whatsoever he could do against Lee—though his forces outnumbered Lee's army to a massive extent.

Lincoln dashed off a series of comments to Halleck in a mood of ill-suppressed disgust. "Let me say," Lincoln wrote, that "if our army can not fall upon the enemy and hurt him where he is, it is plain to me it can gain nothing by attempting to follow him over a succession of intrenched [sic] lines into a fortified city [i.e., Richmond]."[38]

On October 16, Lincoln tried once again to get Meade to consider an offensive. He sent a message to Meade via Halleck: "If Gen. Meade can now attack him on a field no worse than equal for us, and will do so with all the skill and courage, which he, his officers and men possess, the honor will be his if he succeeds, and the blame may be mine if he fails."[39] But Meade continued to demur.

So another Union general was proven quite useless for the total-war purposes of Lincoln. Grant, meanwhile—Lincoln's best fighting general—had his hands full out in Tennessee. So Lincoln drained away some troops from Meade's army and sent them off to Grant. He told Gideon Welles, secretary of the navy, that he regarded Meade as utterly hopeless. According to Welles, the president complained that in the autumn of 1863 it was still "the same old story with the Army of the Potomac. Imbecility, inefficiency—don't want to *do*. . . ."[40] It seemed that winning the war would have to wait until 1864, with all the risks of the election in the balance.

The war had been costly enough that year in terms of human losses: though the overall level of casualties had been light in the Vicksburg campaign, combined Union and Confederate casualties at Murfreesboro had been almost 25,000; at Gettysburg, almost 50,000; and at Chickamauga, almost 35,000.

In November, Lincoln made his famous trip to pay homage to the Union soldiers who were killed in the battle of Gettysburg. Their bodies were being slowly reinterred in the federal cemetery there. He who had commanded a war to the death with such anger and vehemence

Lincoln on November 8, 1863, with
his secretaries John Nicolay and
John Hay. Photograph by Alexander
Gardner. (Library of Congress,
Meserve Collection #56)

was privately tortured by the
news of each battle's cost. Morbid feelings were all too familiar
in the life of Abraham Lincoln.
Ever since his youth, his depres-
sive side had been haunted by the
death of his loved ones. The loss
of Ann Rutledge, his young
fiancée, drove him close to a
suicidal madness in the 1830s.
(This affair, long dismissed as a
romanticized legend, has been
recently validated by the historian Douglas L. Wilson.)[41] In 1850, he
lost a young son—Edward, or "Eddie," Lincoln. Then he lost little
Willie in the winter of 1862. He kept pondering the heart-breaking
cost of what his policies had forced upon the nation.

The worst-case future—the twisted future of America eaten away at
the core by the poison of white supremacy—was being averted. But
the price of averting such a sickening future for the nation was utterly
grievous: the *personal* futures of the troops who were falling in battle
were lost forever.

One thing alone could redeem all the death: a transcendent national
rebirth. Lincoln used the occasion of the Gettysburg Address to invoke his old vision from the 1850s—the vision for America he used in
his Peoria and Springfield addresses when he castigated Stephen Douglas. America's equality creed, as enshrined in its peerless Declaration
of Independence, must be rescued from those who would pervert it. It
must be lifted on high through a new infusion of spirit.

The Founders, Lincoln said, had conceived a new nation "dedicated
to the proposition that all men are created equal." This war was a test
to determine not only whether *this* particular nation but *any* nation "so
conceived, and so dedicated, can long endure." This hallowed field
would be a monument to those who "gave their lives, that the nation
might live."

His listeners were challenged by his solemn invocation of the human cycle and its turnings: conception, birth, endurance, the sorrow of death, and his visions of re-birth.

In the midst of the mourning, it is up to the living, he declared, to "be dedicated here to the unfinished work which they who fought here have thus far so nobly advanced." They must not have died in vain for their country. "The last full measure of devotion" played out upon the field must inspire in the hearts of all the living an "increased devotion" to the cause for which the sacrificed heroes gave everything they had. A "new birth of freedom" must result from the death: the Union, devoted to its quintessential creed, must triumph and triumph completely. If not, then all the dreams that America had stood for would "perish from the earth."[42]

As scholar Garry Wills has observed, the "audacity of Lincoln's undertaking" in the Gettysburg Address was to lift the Declaration of Independence and its ideals of freedom and equality far above the moral reputation of the United States Constitution. Lincoln's critics were quick to observe this. "Some people, looking on from a distance," according to Wills, "saw that a giant (if benign) swindle had been performed" by Lincoln in his Gettysburg speech—a "swindle" by the logic of their white supremacist standards. "The Chicago *Times* quoted the letter of the Constitution to Lincoln—noting its lack of reference to equality, its tolerance of slavery—and said that Lincoln was betraying the instrument he was on oath to defend." The editorial quoted by Wills—an openly white supremacist document—proceeded as follows: "It was to uphold this constitution, and the Union created by it, that our officers and soldiers gave their lives at Gettysburg. How dare he [Lincoln], then, standing on their graves, misstate the cause for which they died, and libel the statesmen who founded the government? They were men possessing too much self-respect to declare that negroes were their equals, or were entitled to equal privileges."[43]

As Lincoln gave the speech, the forces of Grant were preparing to defeat the Confederate besiegers of Chattanooga. On November 24, Joseph Hooker, dispatched from Virginia, took Lookout Mountain in the so-called "Battle Above the Clouds." (Hooker, who had fallen apart when he confronted the challenge of senior command in Virginia, seemed to do quite well when he was placed in subordinate positions). And on the very next day, George Thomas's troops performed the seemingly impossible feat of storming Missionary Ridge, driving Bragg and his Confederate troops to abandon their position on the heights and retreat across the Georgia state line.

As news of this great Union victory reached Lincoln, it was time once again for the president to write his long annual message to Congress. With the message, which he sent on December 8, came another presidential proclamation: a proclamation of amnesty and reconstruction.

Here is yet another major item in the orthodox legend of Lincoln the "moderate": his "lenient" plan for reconstruction. But Lincoln's earliest plan for reconstruction was clearly just a temporary ploy if we consider his position on the issue as it changed in the months before he died. His lenient offer in the closing days of 1863 was very closely related to his improvised "free-state" strategy.

As we have seen, Lincoln hoped to catalyze the drafting of anti-slavery constitutions in some of the occupied rebel states. He had particular hopes for Tennessee and Louisiana; he was heartened as well by some recent events in Arkansas. He was quietly encouraging the free-state movement in Maryland as well as a brand-new movement in the state of Missouri to eliminate slavery through gradual phaseout. It was vital to his plans to get the work done *quickly*, before the next national election.

But the politics were delicate and tricky. In Louisiana, for example, the drive to enroll a new electorate to frame an anti-slavery constitution had begun to break down. "This disappoints me bitterly," the president wrote to General Banks in early November. "There is danger, even now, that the adverse element seeks insidiously to pre-occupy the ground." Consider the danger, Lincoln warned, that would loom "if a few professedly loyal men shall draw the disloyal about them, and colorably set up a State government, repudiating the emancipation proclamation, and re-establishing slavery." Make haste, Lincoln pleaded with Banks: you should "lose no more time."

Then he turned to the issue of the labor code that Banks had developed. "I do not insist upon such temporary arrangement," the president wrote to Banks, "but only say such would not be objectionable to me." On the largest issue, however, the president was adamant in fighting for the status of Louisiana freedmen: "my word is out to be *for* and not *against* them on the question of their permanent freedom."[44]

In overall terms, Lincoln's "lenient" plan for reconstruction must be understood as a facilitating scheme for his plans to protect emancipation— a facilitating scheme to *speed the work* of redrafting some rebel state constitutions. It was also, of course, an experiment to see whether offers of federal pardon might weaken the grip of Confederate leaders and induce more rebel defections, thus shortening the war.

Lincoln's Proclamation of Amnesty and Reconstruction declared:

> whereas it is now desired by some persons heretofore engaged in . . . rebellion to resume their allegiance to the United States, and to reinaugurate loyal State governments . . . therefore, I, Abraham Lincoln, President of the United States, do proclaim, declare, and make known to all persons who have, directly or by implication, participated in the existing rebellion . . . that a full pardon is hereby granted to them and each of them, with restoration of all rights of property, except as to slaves, and in property cases where rights of third parties shall have intervened . . .

Presumably this was a reference to the properties sold to third parties through tax foreclosures.

Lincoln then insisted on an oath that would have to be sworn by the penitent rebels; not only would the rebels have to swear to support the Constitution and the federal government, but, the president ordered, they would also have to swear to "abide by and faithfully support all acts of Congress passed during the existing rebellion with reference to slaves, so long and so far as not repealed, modified or held void by Congress, or by decision of the Supreme Court. . . ." By the same token, they would have to support "all proclamations of the President made during the existing rebellion having reference to slaves."

In other words, the only whites who would vote in rebel states would be the ones who had sworn to uphold Lincoln's anti-slavery policies. They and they alone would have the power to redraft the state constitutions. A small group of such people would suffice—a mere 10 percent of the 1860 voting population, to be precise.

Lincoln pointedly excluded from the offer any persons who had served as Confederate leaders. Having done so, he offered the following terms for political reorganization state by state: in any rebel state, when a tenth of the voting population (as of 1860) took the loyalty oath and created a new state government "in no wise contravening said oath," that government would then be recognized by Lincoln as "the true government of the State." Moreover, Lincoln promised that if any "provision . . . may be adopted by such State government in relation to the freed people of such State, which shall recognize and declare their permanent freedom, provide for their education, and which may yet be consistent, as a temporary arrangement, with their present condition as a laboring, landless, and homeless class," it would "not be objected to by the national Executive."

Then he added some important disclaimers. "To avoid misunderstanding," the president continued, "it may be proper to . . . say that whether members sent to Congress from any State shall be admitted to seats, constitutionally rests exclusively with the respective Houses [of Congress], and not to any extent with the Executive." Moreover, while he stressed that his reconstruction plan of December 1863 was "the best the Executive can suggest, *with his present impressions*, it must not be understood that no other possible mode would be acceptable [my emphasis]."[45] Lincoln clearly implied that his offer of a "lenient" reconstruction *might very well change* if the *circumstances* changed. Lincoln emphasized the very same point in his message to Congress.[46]

Lincoln's message was replete with congratulations and praise for his Union commanders. He was also exultant on the new birth of freedom and its progress. His preliminary announcement of emancipation, the president recalled, "gave to the future a new aspect, about which hope, and fear, and doubt contended in uncertain conflict." Indeed, when the final proclamation had been issued, "it was followed by dark and doubtful days." But now, with the passage of a year, Lincoln wrote, the whole prospect for freedom was changed, triumphantly changed. A new spirit was sweeping the land.

Lincoln wrote that "the movements, by State action, for emancipation in several of the States, not included in the emancipation proclamation, are matters of profound congratulation."[47] As examples, he cited the states of Maryland and Missouri. "Three years ago," Lincoln wrote, neither one of these states "would tolerate any restraint upon the extension of slavery into new territories." But now, it seemed that the only dispute about slavery in each of these states was "as to the best mode of removing it within their own limits." Moreover, in occupied states, some examples could be given of a movement to embrace emancipation under law and make it permanent: "Tennessee and Arkansas have been substantially cleared of insurgent control, and influential citizens in each, owners of slaves and advocates of slavery at the beginning of the rebellion, now declare openly for emancipation in their respective States."[48]

Turning to his scheme for reconstruction, he defended his reconstruction oath and its attempt to force allegiance to the policies of the president and Congress on the issue of emancipation. "Those laws and proclamations," the president reasoned, "were enacted and put forth for the purpose of aiding in the suppression of the rebellion. To give them their fullest effect, there had to be a pledge for their maintenance. . . . To now abandon them would be not only to relinquish a lever of power, but would also be a cruel and astounding breach of faith. . . ." He continued: "I may add at this point, that while I remain in my present position I shall not attempt to retract or modify the emancipation proclamation; nor shall I return to slavery any person who is free by the terms of that proclamation, or by any of the acts of Congress. For these and other reasons it is thought best that support of these measures shall be included in the oath; and it is believed that the Executive may lawfully claim it in return for pardon and restoration of forfeited rights, which he has clear constitutional power to withhold altogether, or grant upon the terms which he shall deem wisest for the public interest."[49]

Lincoln tried to maintain a brave front in this message as he pondered the political prospects for what he had achieved. He told Congress that the nation's anti-slavery measures were enjoying broad public support, both at home and abroad. "These measures have been much discussed in foreign countries, and . . . the tone of public sentiment there is much improved," he stated. "At home the same measures have been fully discussed, supported, criticized, and denounced, and the annual elections . . . [presumably Lincoln was referring to the off-year elections held in 1863] are highly encouraging to those whose official duty it is to bear the country through this great trial. Thus we have the new reckoning. The crisis which threatened to divide the friends of the Union is past."[50]

The crisis was past? Surely Lincoln knew better when he made the assertion: he was obviously seeking to rally his supporters in Congress and the nation at large. He was clearly aware of the ordeal that was in all probability awaiting him.

Lincoln's war would be resumed in the spring with the hope of preempting the results of the 1864 election. But if victory eluded him, the worst-case future was looming, and the president knew it. Everything he had struggled to achieve for the nation could be lost if the politics were wrong. And the Confederates knew it as well. If he ever felt the need for providential assistance, he would feel it to the point of despair in the horrid months ahead.

SIX

Lincoln and the Worst-Case Future, 1864

I N 1864, almost everything that Lincoln had been dreading in regard to the next presidential election began to come true: by the end of the summer, he was certain he would lose the presidency. The election of 1864 would be one of the most decisive in American history—and potentially the most catastrophic.[1]

His very renomination was disputed by Republican dissenters: certain Radical Republicans began to court Salmon Chase, Lincoln's secretary of the treasury. Chase, of course, had been a major contender for the 1860 nomination. His supporters were urging him to risk an open breach with the president. In January and February 1864, the growing "Chase boom" flourished in Washington, and Chase encouraged it. On February 22, Senator Samuel Pomeroy of Kansas sent a circular to newspapers: the statement, signed by a number of influential Republicans, declared that Lincoln's reelection was all but impossible and advocated the nomination of Chase.

The "Pomeroy Circular" backfired. Lincoln's supporters swung quickly into action to counteract it: in both local and state Republican conventions, Lincoln's renomination was urged in the strongest of terms. The Republican National Committee followed suit and support for Chase declined in early March. Yet the damage to Lincoln was significant.

Radical Republicans were angry with Lincoln, in large part because of the provisions of his Reconstruction plan. They were especially angry in regard to Louisiana. In late December, Lincoln wrote to General Nathaniel Banks and instructed him to "give us a free-state reorganization of Louisiana, in the shortest possible time."[2] Since the drive to amend the Louisiana state constitution had been stalling, Banks forced abolition on the state through a faster method. As LaWanda Cox has explained, Banks decided to skip the constitutional convention temporarily and "order an election for governor and other state officials under the antebellum constitution with its slavery provisions declared inoperative and void by military authority. . . . A convention for the revision of the state constitution would be held after the government was organized. . . ."[3]

The elections were held on February 22, and Michael Hahn, the Free State leader, was elected as Louisiana's governor. Per Banks's arrangement, the constitutional convention was scheduled for April.

Blacks were not allowed to vote in these Louisiana elections and a number of them chose to protest. As Eric Foner has explained, "In New Orleans lived the largest free black community of the Deep South. Its wealth, social standing, education, and unique history set it apart not only from the slaves but from free persons of color elsewhere. Most were the descendants of unions between French settlers and black women or of wealthy mulatto emigrants from Haiti. Although denied suffrage, they enjoyed far more rights than free blacks in other states, including the ability to travel freely and testify in court against whites."[4]

On March 12, two leaders of this black community, Arnold Bertonneau and Jean-Baptiste Roudanez, came to Washington and met with the president: they protested the fact that they had not been allowed to cast votes in the Louisiana elections. On the very next day, Lincoln wrote to Hahn and encouraged him to think about the phase-in of voting rights for blacks. "I congratulate you on having fixed your name in history as the first free-state Governor of Louisiana," Lincoln wrote. "Now you are about to have a Convention which, among other things, will probably define the elective franchise." Then he made his secret suggestion: "I barely suggest for your private consideration, whether some of the colored people may not be let in—as, for instance, the very intelligent, and especially those who have fought gallantly in our ranks. They would probably help, in some trying time to come, to keep the jewel of liberty within the family of freedom. But this is only a suggestion, not to the public, but to you alone."[5]

It is hard to overstate the importance of this letter: Lincoln clearly supported giving voting rights to blacks incrementally. This experiment could lead toward the gradual achievement of political equality for blacks all over the nation. Many Northern states also denied blacks the right to vote at the time Lincoln made his suggestion, and the issue was explosive with the electorate.

Lincoln had reached another major milestone: in concept at least, he was moving toward the goal of political equality for blacks.[6] As LaWanda Cox has affirmed, "there is ample evidence to conclude that Lincoln's conception of freedom was expansive and that his personal racial feelings constituted no barrier to pushing the boundaries between slavery and freedom to whatever limit could be sustained by public consent and law."[7]

There was no more talk about colonization by Lincoln in 1864. The brief experiment with black volunteers on Isle-a-Vache had ended. In March, Lincoln sent a Navy vessel to bring back the colonists.

His concern about the fate of freed blacks continued to develop. In the previous October, Lincoln had directed General James S. Wadsworth to investigate conditions for blacks in the Mississippi Valley. In February, Lincoln sent another general, Daniel Sickles, to "make a tour for me . . . by way of Cairo and New-Orleans, and returning by the Gulf and Ocean" to determine "what is being done, if anything, for reconstruction. . . ." Then, the president continued, "learn what you can as to the colored people—how they get along as soldiers, as laborers in our service, on leased plantations, and as hired laborers with their old masters, if there be such cases. Also learn what you can about the colored people within the rebel lines."[8]

Lincoln cared about the fate of these blacks: in a speech that he delivered in Baltimore on April 18, 1864, he likened himself to a shepherd protecting his flock from the fangs of the wolves. "The world has never had a good definition of the word liberty," the president observed, "and the American people, just now, are much in want of one. . . . With some the word liberty may mean for each man to do as he pleases with himself, and the product of his labor; while with others the same word may mean for some men to do as they please with other men, and the product of other men's labor. . . . The shepherd drives the wolf from the sheep's throat, for which the sheep thanks the shepherd as a *liberator*, while the wolf denounces him for the same act as a destroyer of liberty, especially as the sheep was a black one."[9]

At the time that Lincoln gave this speech, the new Louisiana constitution was being drafted. It would later be ratified on September 5, 1864, by the 10 percent electorate permitted under Lincoln's plan.

This new constitution ended slavery in Louisiana. Emancipation would be permanent—at least if this new constitution were upheld as binding and legitimate. It provided for a system of public schools that would be open to blacks as well as whites. And it empowered the Louisiana legislature to confer voting rights upon blacks.

In the view of certain Radical Republicans, however, such results were woefully inadequate. The 10 percent plan was too easy on the South in the view of leading Radical Republicans like Thaddeus Stevens and Benjamin Wade. Many prominent abolitionists such as Wendell Phillips gave angry speeches denouncing Lincoln's plan. Even Lincoln's Radical friend in the Senate, Charles Sumner, was angry: a new breach between Lincoln and Sumner was starting to develop.

The Radicals apparently failed to perceive the way in which Lincoln used his 10 percent plan to push *fast abolition* by tiny *minorities* in each rebel state. By allowing only 10 percent of the 1860 electorate to start Reconstruction, Lincoln made it easy for his agents like Banks to foist emancipation on the racist (and rebel) majority. This was a clever trick. Under Lincoln's scheme, a mere 10 percent of each rebel state's electorate could change the state's constitution and make it a free state.

In the spring of 1864, Lincoln privately pushed his emancipationist free-state agenda in Arkansas. He worked with General Frederick Steele, the military governor, to sponsor elections under the antebellum constitution with its slavery provisions held void. On January 27, the president instructed Steele to force unity among the various political factions in the state, and at the same time to "be sure to retain the free State constitutional provision in some unquestionable form."[10] The Arkansas elections were held in March, and the state's constitution was redrafted months later on the president's free-state principles.

Lincoln also intervened in the free-state politics of Maryland, though the Unionist state was exempt from the provisions of his 10 percent plan. Lincoln wrote that he was "anxious for emancipation to be effected in Maryland in some substantial form." As to gradual versus immediate emancipation, he explained to a supporter that his earlier expressions of a "preference for *gradual* over *immediate* emancipation, are misunderstood. I had thought that *gradual* would produce less confusion, and destitution . . . but if those who are better acquainted with the subject . . . prefer the *immediate*, most certainly I have no objection to their judgment prevailing. My wish is that all who are for emancipation *in any form*, shall co-operate. . . ."[11]

Lincoln's work behind the scenes on behalf of the free-state movement cut very little ice with the Radicals. In addition to all of their complaints about the "leniency" of his Reconstruction offer, they had reasons to protest against his offer to return all confiscated property to penitent rebels, except for their slaves. Indeed, the Radical Republican Congressman George Julian of Indiana introduced a bill in the early months of 1864 to extend the provisions of the 1862 Homestead Act to cover confiscated lands in the South. His intention was to offer such confiscated lands to the freedmen and Union soldiers. While Julian's bill passed the House of Representatives on May 12, it was buried in the Senate by the time that Congress adjourned.

As we have seen, Lincoln firmly supported the redistribution of confiscated lands when they were seized for non-payment of taxes. Nonetheless, we have also seen that he opposed the redistribution of lands that were seized as a penalty for treason. He believed this to be unconstitutional. Congress had deferred to his position by attaching a joint declaration in support of his views to the second confiscation act.

But evidence suggests that Lincoln started to rethink his position on the issue of land redistribution by the spring of 1864. Historian James M. McPherson has suggested that the publication of a book entitled *War Powers Under the Constitution of the United States*, written by a widely respected legal scholar named William Whiting (who was serving at the time in the War Department as solicitor), might have influenced Lincoln on the matter of "bills of attainder." Whiting "argued learnedly that the constitutional prohibition of bills of attainder did not debar Congress from confiscating property permanently by separate legislative act as a punishment for treason."[12] Moreover, Congressman Julian claimed that Whiting's arguments had changed Lincoln's mind.

As McPherson recounts the story, "Julian went to see Lincoln on July 2 [1864], hoping to convince the President of the constitutionality of permanent confiscation. Lincoln admitted

Lincoln in 1864. Photograph by Matthew Brady. (Library of Congress, Meserve Collection #81)

that when he had forced Congress to adopt the joint resolution in 1862 he had not examined the question thoroughly. William Whiting's written and spoken arguments, the President said, had since convinced him of his error, and he was now ready to sign a bill repealing the joint resolution of 1862."[13]

Important subsequent events (in the early months of 1865) lend strong circumstantial support to this theory that the president was coming around to the position of across-the-board land redistribution. In short, Lincoln and his Radical Republican critics were closer on a number of issues in 1864 than appeared on the surface. Indeed, Radicals embraced the rather daring proposal that *Lincoln* introduced in Congress many months earlier: the amendment of the Constitution to protect emancipation.

Instead of the three-amendment package as proposed by Lincoln in his annual message of December 1862, however, the Thirteenth Amendment, as the Radical Republicans drafted it, eliminated slavery nationwide—and all at once. While this powerful amendment was passed by the Senate in April, the Democratic gains in the elections of 1862 kept it stalled in the House of Representatives.

Moreover, Lincoln worked with the Radicals on early civil rights legislation in the spring of 1864. He signed a series of bills that permitted blacks to testify in Federal courts, forbade discrimination in the streetcar system of the District of Columbia, and (in fulfillment of his pledge to Frederick Douglass) raised the level of pay for black troops.[14]

So much for the common positions of Lincoln and the Radicals in 1864: what about the breach? The Radicals' growing discontent with the president's Reconstruction program prompted Senator Benjamin Wade of Ohio and Representative Henry Winter Davis of Maryland to draft an alternative congressional plan for Reconstruction. The Wade-Davis Bill, as it was called, was more demanding than the Lincoln plan. Instead of permitting only 10 percent of the 1860 electorate to start Reconstruction (after taking a loyalty oath), the Wade-Davis Bill demanded that a minimum of 50 percent should take the oath before the process of Reconstruction could start in any rebel state. Moreover, a constitutional convention was *required* in the Wade-Davis Bill. This was clearly an expression of the Radicals' long-standing theory of "state suicide": Congress, in the Radicals' view, possessed unlimited power to reconstruct any state that had forfeited its statehood.

In its earliest version, the Wade-Davis Bill permitted "loyal" men to vote in rebel states, regardless of their race. In its final version, however, the right to vote was limited to whites. Wade and Davis consented to this latter provision so as not to "sacrifice the bill."[15] (Like Lincoln, in other words, these Radical Republicans were willing to modify their tempo of reform in a manner that was mindful of political realities, especially the danger of a backlash.)

On the other side of the political spectrum, the white supremacist Democrats could hardly wait for their chance to oust both Lincoln and the Radicals from power. In preparing himself for a Democratic backlash, the president was careful to maintain his position as a patriotic Unionist above all else—as a president who put the preservation of the Union *first* in every one of his actions. To a Kentuckian he wrote in early April that his "private" convictions on slavery had never affected his judgment in his struggle to protect the Constitution while saving the Union. He admitted he was "naturally anti-slavery," for "if slavery is not wrong, nothing is wrong." But he had "never understood that the Presidency conferred upon me an unrestricted right to act officially upon this judgment and feeling." He continued: "I aver that, to this day, I have done no official act in mere deference"—note the qualifier, "mere" deference—"to my abstract judgment and feeling." He went on to admit that the national emergency had sometimes convinced him "that measures, otherwise unconstitutional, might become lawful, by becoming indispensable to the preservation of the constitution, through the preservation of the nation." Emancipation, Lincoln argued, had become an "indispensable necessity."

Near the close of his letter, he wrote a famous line, often used as evidence of Lincoln's moderate side: "I claim not to have controlled events," Lincoln wrote, "but confess plainly that events have controlled me."

Like so much of his writing, this "confession" must be read on two levels. At the tactical level, the statement was a calculated ploy. For those who knew him best, for those who watched him in action, such a statement would in all probability have seemed like a "put-on." And one is tempted to compare it to the "foxy" maneuverings of Franklin Delano Roosevelt many years later. The "Tycoon," it appeared, was in "fine whack" again: he was crafty in denying any craftiness, ascribing all his actions to "events." We know better: his unremitting efforts to direct, to rechannel, to coordinate events—his brilliance in strategy, his talent for behind-the-scenes orchestration ("give us a free-state re-organization . . . in the shortest possible time"), his peremptory tone with subordinates who flouted his will ("Answer at once")—make a mockery of any such political "confession" that events had somehow "controlled" him. On this level, surely, Lincoln's statement was a palpable deception. He was making such statements to inoculate himself against attacks by the Copperheads who claimed he was acting like a "tyrant." He was posing as a paragon of probity, responding to events as they happened to occur: just a servant of the people who had pledged himself to save the nation.

On a deeper level, however, there is reason to articulate a very different meaning in the statement. We are forced to acknowledge here a different kind of truth: for events *had indeed* been overriding Lincoln's plans since the onset of war. The coming of secession and the coming of the war had been written off by Lincoln as improbable before they occurred, and yet they *did* occur. The carnage of the war had been appalling and surprising to Lincoln. And the worst-case contingencies were threatening to wipe out all of his achievements if his luck should take a turn for the worse in the coming election.

Even geniuses succumb to the vastness of events: the contingencies determine the outcomes they try to control. The wisest will acknowledge it is all "in God's hands" when they have finished. On this level, surely, the statement by Lincoln was an invocation of Providence: it was a prayer that the Lord would sustain him.

Lincoln made this clear at the end of his letter, while expressing guarded hope that his interpretation of Providence would prove to be prophetic. "Now, at the end of three years struggle," Lincoln wrote, the condition of the nation "is not what either party, or any man devised, or expected. God alone can claim it. Whither it is tending seems plain. If God now wills the removal of a great wrong, and wills also that we of the North as well as you of the South, shall pay fairly for our complicity in that wrong, impartial history will find therein new cause to attest and revere the justice and goodness of God."[16] The theme he would use for his second Inaugural Address was taking shape in his mind already—if God granted him a second term in office.

The key to a second term was victory in the war, and Lincoln had reason to hope that a final major military effort could defeat the Confederate armies before the election. Early in the year, he had made his big decision to promote Ulysses S. Grant to the position of general in chief, and to demote Henry Halleck. "[A]t his own request," as Lincoln put it, Halleck opted for the newly created position of Chief of Staff, the senior clerk who would arrange Grant's paperwork.[17]

Legend has it that when Grant took over as general in chief, Lincoln faded as a military strategist. Such was not the case. Grant's initial strategic conceptions were at odds with the views of Lincoln, and the president was called upon to take some remedial action. In January—just after Grant's victory at Chattanooga and before his promotion to the post of general in chief—he took the liberty of sending the president, by way of Halleck, some important strategic suggestions. Lincoln found them to be deeply flawed.

Grant initially proposed to take the Union forces in East Tennessee and divide them into two smaller armies. One of these armies would pursue the retreating Confederates deep into Georgia; the other would be sent on a mission to the Gulf of Mexico to strike against Mobile, Alabama. Historian T. Harry Williams's research has made it clear that Lincoln forced a change in this plan since he believed, as Williams has interpreted the record, that "the government did not have enough troops in the West to constitute two major striking forces." In particular, according to Williams, Lincoln feared that "if the army at Chattanooga was weakened to build up the force destined for Mobile, there was always the possibility that the Confederates might be able to recover East Tennessee. . . . Lincoln saw the weakness in the plan and vetoed it."[18]

Lincoln's *modus operandi*, both in politics and war, was his constant preparation for the best-case and worst-case contingencies—*both of them at once*. He wanted armies that were poised to attack while positioned to defend. He wanted generals who thought in these terms, but too often what he got were "uneven" commanders who were strong on the one side but pitifully weak on the other. None of the president's commanders, as yet, gave *equal* attention to offensive and defensive positioning.

Grant's suggestion for a new campaign in the eastern theatre was worse than his proposal for the West: he proposed to drain troops from the Army of the Potomac and send them by sea into North Carolina to disrupt the Confederate railroads that serviced Richmond. There was no need for Lincoln to veto this plan, since Halleck took care of it for him. Williams elaborates: "When Halleck read Grant's plan, he knew

Lincoln would not like it. Halleck was so familiar with Lincoln's strategic ideas that he could tell how the President would react to almost any proposal. He informed Grant that he would lay the scheme before Lincoln but that the President would disapprove it. Using almost the same words that Lincoln had employed in several letters to Meade, Halleck emphasized that Lee's army, not Richmond, should be the objective of the Potomac Army. . . ." Moreover, Halleck explained, "when Lee learned that the army facing him had been depleted he would move on Washington, forcing the government to recall the whole Carolina expedition for the defense of the capital."[19]

After Grant had been summoned to Washington and given his command, he and Lincoln had a number of conferences. These conferences led to an overall plan, which Williams describes: "After he talked to Lincoln in Washington, Grant dropped completely his scheme to send an army into North Carolina. His new plan was to make Lee's army the objective and to go after it in Virginia and destroy it. In words that Lincoln might have written, Grant instructed Meade: 'Wherever Lee goes, there you will go also.'"[20]

To ensure the compliance of Meade, Grant would ride along and supervise his army in the field. Consequently, in his new post as general in chief, Grant also assumed the *de facto* command of the Army of the Potomac.

The endgame strategy as Lincoln and Grant worked it up was to send the Union forces in Chattanooga to pursue the Confederate army (now commanded by General Joseph Johnston) into central Georgia. These Union forces would be led by William Tecumseh Sherman. In Virginia, Grant and Meade would go after Lee's army—with a number of peripheral forces adding pressure from the Shenandoah Valley and along the James River.

Late in April, everything was ready, and the armies of Lincoln went to work. John Hay was optimistically expectant. At last, Lincoln's macro-strategic ideas would be used for their maximum effect. "The President," Hay wrote in his diary, "has been powerfully reminded, by General Grant's present movements and plans, of his (President's) old suggestion so constantly made and as constantly neglected, to Buell & Halleck, et al., to move at once upon the enemy's whole line so as to bring into action to our advantage our great superiority in numbers."[21] This would now be the case in all theatres. Lincoln too was expectant.

Early in May, he remarked that the conqueror of Vicksburg and Chattanooga could be trusted to destroy Lee's army. "It is the dogged pertinacity of Grant that wins," the president declared.[22] Grant crossed the Rapidan River on May 4.

BUT IT ALL WENT WRONG, and disaster spread out like a rotten abyss in the summer of 1864.

Grant's army collided with the rebels very close to the battlefield of Chancellorsville in a thick forest called "the Wilderness" by locals. The battle of the Wilderness lasted from May 5 to May 7, and it ended in a tactical draw. It was an ugly and terrifying battle that cost almost twenty-eight thousand causalities (Union and Confederate). An unfazed Grant moved quickly around the flank of Lee's army to flush the Confederates out into the open for the showdown.

But then Confederate strategy changed: Lee decided to entrench with the aim of *denying* his attacker (whom he knew to be his equal) any chance for a wide-open battle. Lee's men dug trenches overnight, so quickly that they were ready for Grant's onslaught *the next day*. The battle of Spotsylvania Court House, which lasted from May 8 to May 19, took the lives of approximately twenty-nine thousand men. It ended in a tactical draw.

For the rest of the month, Grant tried again to move around the flank of Lee's army and force the rebels into the open for the blow that would destroy them. Yet, each time Lee entrenched just ahead of Grant and blocked him. Lee and his army were too fast to be caught in the open.

Grant was leery of attacking these Confederate trenches because Civil War weaponry gave the defenders of fortified positions tremendous advantages. He wanted a wide-open battle, and dreaded the prospect of driving Lee back into the formidable defenses of Richmond. A siege of the Richmond defenses could last a long time, and Grant's army was terribly depleted by the recent casualties. Besides, the president wanted fast action to end the war decisively.

Lee entrenched once again at Cold Harbor, very close to the Richmond fortifications. Grant was running out of time. So at last he gave the order for a frontal attack on June 3. The result was a hideous failure—a slaughter that shocked Grant. The troops themselves had a grim premonition before the charge: many of them had pinned notes to their backs or made final entries in their diaries recording the date as their last day on earth. They were dead men, and most of them knew it. They remembered Pickett's charge; they remembered the troops who attacked the impregnable heights behind Fredericksburg. Now it was their turn. Seven thousand Union casualties occurred within the first half hour. By the end of Cold Harbor, Grant had lost about a third of his army in only a month.

As the news of these casualties began to pour back to the home front, the Copperheads were jubilant. Even Grant's admirers began to deplore his latest actions; his detractors began to call him names like "the Butcher." "The immense slaughter of our brave men," wrote Gideon Welles, "chills and sickens us all."[23]

This suited the Confederates perfectly. It was perfectly in line with their new strategy: bog things down and let the clock run out on Lincoln's presidency. McPherson has criticized the various historians who claim that Grant's intention was to wage a war of attrition against Lee. In truth, he contends, "it was Lee who turned it into a war of attrition. . . . The Confederates could no longer hope to 'win' the war with the tactics or strategy of Chancellorsville or Gettysburg. By remaining on the defensive, however, they could hope to hang on long enough and inflict losses enough on the Yankees to make *them* give up trying to win. This strategy was beginning to work in June 1864."[24]

The Confederates used the same strategy down in Georgia: as Sherman's troops tried to force an open battle, the Confederate army under General Joseph Johnston fell back through successive lines of trenches.

The Republican National Convention was held just four days after Cold Harbor. The party was running very scared. Moreover, a schism had occurred: a group of Radical Republicans had joined with some free-lancing Democrats and they held their own convention in Cleveland. They dubbed themselves the "Radical Democratic Party," and proceeded to nominate John C. Frémont as their presidential candidate. Frémont, the political general, had also been the Republicans' first nominee for the presidency in 1856.

Many of the Radical Republicans who flocked to the banner of Frémont had dabbled in the "Chase boom" a few months before. But the "independent" Democrats who helped out the "Radical Democratic Party" were a very different breed. A number of observers at the time, such as William Lloyd Garrison (the venerable abolitionist), concluded that Frémont was nothing but a dupe—or as McPherson has put it, a "catspaw of wily War Democrats hoping to divide and conquer the Republicans."[25]

The convention of the regular Republican Party was held in Baltimore on June 7. Lincoln, of course, was renominated, but the delegates were seriously worried. Consequently, they changed the party's name for the season to the National Union Party. And they decided to replace Vice President Hannibal Hamlin (a staunchly anti-slavery man) with a Democratic running mate for Lincoln. They selected Andrew Johnson, the Tennessee Democrat who served under Lincoln's supervision as the occupation governor. Johnson had also been the cosponsor of the old pro-slavery Crittenden-Johnson resolutions in 1861. Indeed, he had owned five slaves before the war.

He had changed since then, of course: he had come to support emancipation. But Johnson's reasons for "conversion" were selfish, at least psychologically. As a self-made man from the hills—as a "poor boy" who nursed class resentments—he had loathed the plantation aristocrats who ran the South. Freeing their slaves would be a blow to them, humbling their power, in Johnson's estimation. Years earlier, Johnson had declared that he would "show the stuck-up aristocrats who is running the country."[26]

But Johnson was no friend to the slaves: he was virulently racist. He declared later on that blacks possessed less "capacity for government than any other race of people."[27] Here was Lincoln's new running mate for 1864, and it was definitely not his idea.

Lincoln made no attempt to intervene in the work of this convention, with one exception: he strongly suggested its formal endorsement of the anti-slavery amendment to the Constitution. According to LaWanda Cox, "Lincoln made certain that the Republican national convention held in June 1864 would include a plank calling for the 'utter and complete extirpation' of slavery through constitutional amendment. He called in the Republican national chairman to ask that it be made the core of the chairman's keynote address."[28]

After the convention, Lincoln's problems with his fellow Republicans worsened. His relations with Salmon P. Chase had reached the breaking point at last: Chase became terminally quarrelsome. He petulantly offered to resign, and Lincoln accepted. "Of all I have said in commendation of your ability and fidelity," Lincoln wrote, "I have nothing to unsay; and yet you and I have reached a point of mutual embarrassment in our official relation which it seems cannot be over-come, or longer sustained. . . ."[29] Lincoln's Radical Republican critics started screaming: Chase was one of their cabinet icons.

They screamed even louder after Lincoln decided to pocket veto the Wade-Davis Bill, which Congress passed on the second of July. Six days later, Lincoln offered a terse proclamation. He insisted once again that he was *not* "inflexibly committed to any single plan of restora-tion." But he was "unprepared to declare" at the moment that his free-state regimes in Louisiana and Arkansas should be "set aside and held for nought," as the Wade-Davis Bill would surely do.[30] The Radical Republicans were livid.

To add to the president's woes, faint-hearted Republicans were urg-ing him to think about negotiating peace with the Confederates. The ever-mercurial Horace Greeley wrote to Lincoln in early July. He im-plored him to try negotiations. "Our bleeding, bankrupt, almost dying country," wrote Greeley, "longs for peace" and "shudders at the pros-pect of fresh conscriptions, of further wholesale devastations, and of new rivers of human blood. And a widespread conviction that the Gov-ernment [is] not anxious for Peace . . . is doing great harm now, and is morally certain, if not removed, to do far greater in the approaching Elections. . . . I entreat you, in your own time and manner, to submit overtures for pacification to the Southern insurgents. . . ."[31]

These divisions among the Republicans played into the hands of the Democratic Copperheads. The Democratic Party had scheduled its convention for August.

In the middle of June, Grant finally managed to surprise the Con-federates by shifting the bulk of his forces across the James River in a carefully concealed maneuver. Grant's purpose was to strike at Peters-burg, a railroad hub below Richmond. He aimed to cut off the rail-roads supporting both Richmond and Lee, thus forcing Lee to come and attack him.

But the corps commanders of the Union army made a mess of the attack when they arrived in the vicinity of Petersburg. The town had its own defensive perimeter: a thin line of troops under P.G.T. Beauregard was manning these Confederate trenches. The Union troops who arrived on the scene were afraid to attack—they were suf-fering from "Cold Harbor syndrome." By the time Grant arrived with the bulk of his army, Lee's troops had been given all the time that they needed to arrive in force and man the trenches.

Then Lee found a way to twist the knife. He dispatched a Confederate force under General Jubal Early to accomplish what Lincoln had feared in the first two years of war: a raid against Washington, D.C. Lincoln's capital, protected by its own ring of forts, had been stripped of its garrison by Grant.

Jubal Early and his troops crossed over the Potomac on July 5, and just a few days later they were marching toward the Washington defenses. From Petersburg help was on the way: Grant dispatched a whole corps. But would the troops relieve Washington in time?

As the rebels arrived at the Washington defenses, only boys and some local militia were manning the guns of the forts surrounding the city. On July 11, Lincoln anxiously rode to the scene of the battle at a bastion known as Fort Stevens. In the nick of time, Grant's veterans arrived and put an end to the Confederate attack. But in the midst of the battle something very peculiar occurred: Lincoln stood upon the parapet with bullets flying all around him. A young officer—none other than the future Supreme Court Justice Oliver Wendell Holmes, Jr.— looked up at his commander in chief and shouted, "Get down, you damn fool" before he knew what he was doing or saying. Lincoln obliged and got down.[32]

This episode is easy to dismiss as an odd and momentary aberration, or as a fleeting illustration of the Lincoln eccentricities. But in light of what was really at stake (a successful Confederate attack upon Washington might truly have been the last straw for the administration's credibility that summer), and in light of the increasing inclination of Lincoln to regard such events as providential, it might have been something more serious. Consider the emotional pressure that the president was feeling in the aftermath of the casualty reports from Virginia. He lamented in a speech in mid-June that the war had "carried mourning into every home," that it could "almost be said that the 'heavens are hung with black.'"[33] Was there possibly a reason why Lincoln risked his life under fire? According to historian Gabor S. Boritt, who has mused upon the spectacle of Lincoln on the Fort Stevens parapet, here was "this tall man, six-foot four, with a top hat on to exaggerate his height further, recognizable to all on both sides. He stands there, bullets whistle by, an officer falls close to him, but he just stands there— looking at the enemy." Boritt's thesis? "I see a man standing there looking not at the Confederates, but [at] God, saying silently: if I am wrong, God, strike me down."[34]

At Petersburg, Grant began a siege. But his army was so greatly diminished in size—he had lost almost sixty-four thousand men from the Wilderness to Petersburg—that his options were severely limited. He could not throw a ring around the city and starve it out, as he had done in the case of Vicksburg: his forces would be stretched too thin. And the loss of the corps that he had sent back to Washington diminished his army even further.

In July, some clever troops from the Pennsylvania coal-mining country thought up a new stratagem: they would tunnel right under the Confederate trenches and blow a huge hole in their lines with an enormous charge of gunpowder. At first the attack was a stunning success: the explosives went off in the predawn darkness of July 30. The explosion was horrific, and Confederates fled from their positions in hysteria. But the Union attack through "the Crater" bogged down, and by the time that Grant's troops had been reorganized, the rebels were entrenched once again, to the rear of the Crater.

Grant vowed to keep the pressure on Lee. In mid-August Lincoln telegraphed Grant as follows: "I have seen your dispatch expressing your unwillingness to break your hold where you are. Neither am I willing. Hold on with a bull-dog gripe [*sic*], and chew & choke, as much as possible."[35]

Lincoln and Grant then developed a plan to destroy the Confederate troops who had tried to raid Washington. The soldiers who had saved the city would be sent to pursue its attackers. Their leader would be Grant's great cavalry commander, Philip Sheridan. Lincoln told Grant to make sure that Early's troops were wiped out. "I have seen your despatch [*sic*] in which you say 'I want Sheridan put in command of all the troops in the field, with instructions to put himself South of the enemy, and follow him to the death. . . .' This, I think, is exactly right." Lincoln also admonished Grant to check on the progress himself; he wanted no mistakes. "I repeat to you," Lincoln wrote to Grant, that the war to the death "will neither be done nor attempted unless you watch it every day, and hour, and force it."[36]

"Force it": here again, we remember the double-sided meaning of the Lincoln remark that he had not "controlled events." Maybe not, but he was constantly *trying* to control them.

Early's army had been causing more mischief. The Confederate raiders had blackmailed the cities of Frederick and Hagerstown, Maryland, extorting two hundred thousand dollars in "protection money" in return for their promise to spare the two cities from the torch. They made a quick lunge into Pennsylvania and burned the town of Chambersburg. Then they faded back into Virginia. Hunting them down would take time. As Sheridan prepared for this task, Grant worked with his limited forces. He kept tightening the pressure on Lee with continued bombardments, tightening his grip upon Petersburg. This, too, would take a very long time if Lee were clever enough to hold out. And in Georgia, Sherman had pursued the Confederates right to the gates of Atlanta; he had started a siege, which of course would take time.

The pressure was becoming excruciating. Horace Greeley had heard about the presence of some Confederate agents in Niagara Falls (on the Canadian side). He urged the president to sound out the agents as the first step to possible peace talks. Lincoln knew the real purpose of the agents; he knew that they were working with the Democratic Party. So he told Horace Greeley to investigate the matter in person. When Greeley demurred, Lincoln sent John Hay to convince him.

When Greeley conferred with the agents, he learned for himself that they had *not* been sent to negotiate. Lincoln made this information public. To another journalist, Abram Wakeman, Lincoln wrote, "the men of the South, recently (and perhaps still) at Niagara Falls, tell us distinctly that they *are* in the confidential employment of the rebellion; and they tell us as distinctly that they are *not* empowered to offer terms of peace. Does any one doubt that what they *are* empowered to do, is to assist in selecting and arranging a candidate and a platform for the Chicago [Democratic] convention?"[37]

Lincoln even obtained a copy of text that these agents had drafted for the Copperheads. In a private memorandum, Lincoln jotted down some notes from the document. In particular, the president copied down the following lines of abuse that were directed at himself: "The stupid tyrant who now disgraces the Chair of Washington and Jackson could, any day, have peace . . . only that he persists in the war merely to free the slaves."[38]

This anti-Lincoln rhetoric was mild when compared to the abuse that was directed at Lincoln by the Democratic presses in August 1864. Democratic editors vilified the "negro-loving, negro-hugging worshippers of old Abe." One Democratic voice proclaimed, "Abe Lincoln—passing the question as to his taint of Negro blood . . . is altogether an imbecile. . . . He is brutal in all his habits. . . . He is filthy. He is obscene. . . . He is an animal!"[39]

Henry J. Raymond, who was serving as the chairman of the Republican National Committee (he was also the editor of the *New York Times*), wrote to Lincoln on August 22 in a state of despair. "I feel compelled to drop you a line concerning the political condition of the country," Raymond wrote. "I am in active correspondence with your staunchest friends in every state and from them all I hear but one report. The tide is setting against us." He continued: "Two special causes are assigned to this great reaction in public sentiment,—the want of military successes, and the impression in some minds, the fear and suspicion in others, that we are not to have peace *in any event* under this administration until Slavery is abandoned. In some way or other the suspicion is widely diffused that we *can* have peace with Union if we would. It is idle to reason with this belief—still more idle to denounce it. It can only be expelled by some authoritative act . . . bold enough to fix attention and distinct enough to defy incredulity & challenge respect."

Then Raymond suggested his stratagem: "Would it not be wise," he wrote, "under these circumstances, to appoint a Commissioner, in due form, *to make distinct proffers of peace to Davis, as the head of the rebel armies, on the sole condition of acknowledging the supremacy of the constitution,*—all other questions to be settled in convention of the people of all the states?"

The chairman of the Republican National Committee was suggesting that Lincoln offer the Confederates peace *with Union only*—that he abandon his emancipation promise.

Raymond, to be sure, was suggesting the measure as a trick. "If the proffer were *accepted*," wrote Raymond, "(which I presume it would not be,) the country would never consent to place the practical execution of its details in any but loyal hands, and in those we should be safe. If it should be *rejected*, (as it would be,) it would . . . dispel all the delusions about peace that prevail in the North. . . ."[40]

It is a stunning measure of the agony that Lincoln was suffering in August that he briefly considered this suggestion. On August 24, the president drafted a letter to Raymond, authorizing him to proceed.[41] But Lincoln never sent this letter.

At the same time he drafted a letter to a Democratic editor, stating, "if Jefferson Davis wishes, for himself, or for the benefit of his friends at the North, to know what I would do if he were to offer peace and reunion, saying nothing about slavery, let him try me."[42]

But Lincoln never sent this letter either. On August 25, he met with Raymond (in the presence of his cabinet) and told him that the course of action he had recommended would be "worse than losing the presidential contest—it would be ignominiously surrendering it in advance."[43] To some Wisconsin Republicans Lincoln remarked that "there have been men who have proposed to me to return to slavery the black warriors of Port Hudson . . . to conciliate the South. I should be damned in time & in eternity for so doing. The world shall know that I will keep my faith to friends & enemies, come what will."[44]

But he was deeply convinced that he would lose the election in the fall: "I am going to be beaten," he said, "and unless some great change takes place *badly* beaten."[45] On August 23, he wrote a strange memorandum, which he then folded over and sealed. He asked his cabinet members to sign their names on the back, without having read it. The memorandum read as follows: "This morning, as for some days past, it seems exceedingly probable that this Administration will not be re-elected. Then it will be my duty to so co-operate with the President elect, as to save the Union between the election and the inauguration; as he will have secured his election on such ground that he can not possibly save it afterwards."[46]

Lincoln secretly invited Frederick Douglass to call at the White House. "I went most gladly," the black abolitionist remembered. Lincoln's purpose was to start a black exodus—to figure out a method "to induce the slaves in the rebel States to come within the Federal lines. The increasing opposition to the war, in the north, and the mad cry against it . . . alarmed Mr. Lincoln, and made him apprehensive that a peace might be forced upon him which would leave still in slavery all who had not come within our lines."

Douglass continued as follows: "I listened with the deepest interest and profoundest satisfaction" to what Lincoln had to say, "and, at his suggestion, agreed to undertake the organizing of a band of scouts, composed of colored men, whose business should be . . . to go into the rebel States, beyond the lines of our armies, and carry the news of emancipation, and urge the slaves to come within our boundaries."[47] The scouts would relay a simple message: escape from your masters as quickly as you can, so that President Lincoln can free you while he still has the power.

Regarding the freedmen, some bad news arrived that month. John Eaton, an army chaplain who was working with the contrabands in Mississippi, paid a visit to Lincoln in August to tell him that some of them were being mistreated. "Mr. Lincoln's keen face sharpened with indignation," Eaton recalled. Exasperated, the president "exclaimed more than once" that he had "signed no regulations authorizing that!"[48]

Could anything else go wrong in this horrible summer? Yes: on August 30, a group of Republicans demanded a second convention to get rid of Lincoln entirely. This convention, they suggested, should meet in Cincinnati on September 28. After dumping Lincoln, they reasoned, the party might still find a way to pull through. Meanwhile, out in Chicago, the Democrats were gathering in full expectation of triumph. And their candidate: George B. McClellan.

Yes, *McClellan*—the man of the hour. McClellan, who had wanted to "dodge the nigger," and who viewed Lincoln's freedom proclamation as a wicked act.

To his followers, McClellan was a prophet in 1864. Had he not, after all, taken steps to avoid needless bloodshed when he was in command? Had he not advised Lincoln to resist the abolitionists and keep this a war for Union only? All right, then: just look at what had happened to the country after Lincoln had relieved George McClellan.

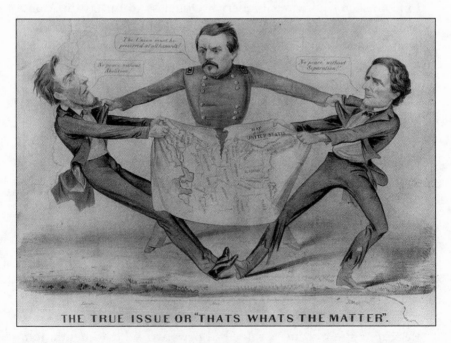

THE TRUE ISSUE OR "THATS WHATS THE MATTER".

An anti-Lincoln cartoon that was published by Currier & Ives in the election of 1864: the wise and patriotic McClellan tries to mediate between the petulant rivals, Lincoln and Davis. (Library of Congress)

A pro-Lincoln cartoon from the election of 1864: as Lincoln shakes hands with a dignified workman—with the image of a racially integrated school in the background—McClellan shakes hands with Jefferson Davis with a slave auction in the background. This cartoon was published by printer M. W. Siebert. (Library of Congress)

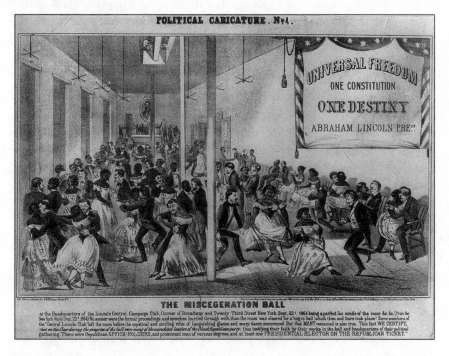

"The Miscegenation Ball": an anti-Lincoln cartoon from the election of 1864 depicting white male Lincoln supporters embracing black women at a dance. This cartoon was published by the printer Bromley & Company. (Library of Congress)

Was Ulysses S. Grant any closer to defeating the rebels after losing almost half of his army?

So it went for Lincoln as he faced the disgusting future in the summer of this year. It appeared that McClellan would win. Like the blowhard he was, he would promise the country to fight for the Union, but his swaggering would probably yield to his deep inner cowardice before very long. He would not have the stomach to fight. A political advisor to McClellan contended that "the General is for peace, not war."[49]

But what kind of peace would he negotiate? Would McClellan abandon the Union and allow the Confederates to build their great empire for slavery? The *Charleston Mercury* predicted that McClellan's election "must lead to peace and our independence . . . [if] for the next two months *we hold our own. . . .*"[50] Alexander Stephens wrote that McClellan's nomination "presents . . . the first ray of real light I have seen since the war began."[51]

If McClellan held out for preservation of the Union, the Confederates would drive a hard bargain. They would play to his obvious weakness— and to his prejudice. They would naturally demand a pro-slavery nation, a nation of the sort that Calhoun or Taney would approve of. Emancipation would be rescinded, and, perhaps, even the free-state regimes in Louisiana and elsewhere would be overturned. The Emancipation Proclamation itself would be discarded.

This wretched scenario was indeed possible, since as Frederick Douglass would later reflect, the institution of slavery was only "wounded and crippled" by 1864, "not disabled and killed."[52]

And what would happen to the thousands of freedmen if McClellan should win? Would he try to send them right back to bondage? Would the blacks troops resist or flee to Canada? Would they riot in the streets, thus inducing McClellan to repress them, or even shoot them down? Would a race war start that would discredit anti-slavery politics for many generations? Would this set back the cause of abolition in America for fifty or a hundred years or longer?

As Harry V. Jaffa has suggested, the wrong resolution of the slavery issue could have happened very easily in nineteenth-century America. The result could have been a long nightmare in which a white minority "would be engulfed in the swirling tides of hatred of an unprivileged majority of a different complexion." Only naked repression could maintain such a system for long: "It is almost inconceivable," Jaffa continues, "that democratic processes could have survived such complications. And we can only shudder to think what the twentieth century would be like if the United States had entered it as first and foremost of totalitarian powers."[53] Does this appear to be "impossible" as well?

Many people recoil at such examples of "what-if" history, dismissing it as "mere" speculation or worse. But as Donald Kagan has argued, "anyone who tries to write history . . . must consider what might have happened; the only question is how explicitly he reveals what he is doing."[54] So let me be very clear: if Lincoln had lost the election of 1864, the United States might very well have lost its last chance to remain a decent country. Everything was hanging in the balance: Lincoln's flickering chances were dependent on the flickering fortunes of his armies. James M. McPherson has emphasized the shifting "contingency that hung over every campaign, every battle, every election during the war."[55] It could all have been disastrously different.

If Lincoln lost the election, then the suffering and sacrifice of hundreds of thousands of Americans would have been in vain. The antislavery movement would be weakened and its mission discredited, perhaps for many years to come. Lincoln's brilliance would all have been for nothing. Was there no way out?

SEVEN

Lincoln and the Best-Case Future, 1864–1865

L

INCOLN'S FORTUNES took a sudden and spectacular turn for the better in the first few days of September 1864: Sherman captured the city of Atlanta. With extraordinary speed, Lincoln's popularity surged as he raced toward an easy reelection. McClellan sounded more and more like the puling defeatist that he was. The power of the Copperheads was broken.

As Lincoln's luck began to change for the better, so did prospects for African Americans. By the time of his death, Lincoln hovered at the brink of endorsing and leading a true civil rights revolution. He never burned his bridges with the Radical Republicans; he frequently agreed with their intentions, even in the miserable summer of 1864. His chief difference with them was a different sense of timing and worst-case risk. As Lincoln's second term began, things had changed: he decided it was time for him to advocate the phase-in of voting rights for blacks, and he did this in public—quite fervently. And he did it in a manner that was carefully chosen to encourage the movement and to soften up public opinion.

The fall of Atlanta made it possible for Lincoln both to win the election and to start his second term auspiciously. Since the capture of Atlanta was the key to all this, it was the military genius of William Tecumseh Sherman that rescued the nation from McClellan and re-empowered Lincoln.

Jefferson Davis had helped in an inadvertent manner. Early in the summer of 1864, the Confederate tactics in Georgia were similar to Lee's. Joseph Johnston (the Confederate commander in Georgia) had been stalling and delaying in the trenches. Delay was inimical to Lincoln in the summer of 1864. With Sherman bogged down in his Georgia campaign and with Grant bogged down in his Petersburg siege, the Confederate logic was obvious: hang on, hurt Northern morale as much as possible, and then cut a deal with McClellan right after the election.

But the pressure on Davis in the summer of 1864 was as brutal as the pressure on Lincoln. Lincoln bent under pressure, in ways that we have seen: he was tempted by others to rescue his party by abandoning his mission on slavery. He had bent under pressure, but he pulled himself together right away: he would rather lose his power, he said, than be "damned in time and eternity."

Davis, on the other hand, broke when the strain was unbearable. The Confederate war of attrition was wearing down Confederate nerves just as surely as it wore down the Yankees. Here was Grant at the outer defenses of Richmond; here was Sherman approaching Atlanta. The pressure on Davis was tremendous. His political enemies attacked him that summer, complaining that Confederates had lost their will to fight when they needed it the most. Of course Robert E. Lee was immune from such attack, for he was almost a saint in the minds of most loyal Confederates. But Johnston cut a very different figure, so Davis relieved him of command on July 17 and replaced him with John Bell Hood, an impetuous fighter.

The result was exactly what Sherman and Grant had been hoping for: battles in the open where the North could use all of its advantages in men and supplies. Hood's attacks upon Sherman were disasters: even Davis sent him orders to call the thing off and get back in place behind the trenches. In the aftermath of these battles, Sherman used his superiority in numbers—he had suffered few casualties, compared with Grant's catastrophe in Virginia—to make his siege of Atlanta effective. Late in August, his raiders struck twenty miles south of the city to cut its railroad links, thus threatening to cut off its food. Hood tried but failed to reopen these lines, and so he had to evacuate the city. Sherman's men marched into the streets of Atlanta on September 3. The result in the North was immediate jubilation.

Lincoln quickly congratulated Sherman and called for a day of thanksgiving and prayer to thank God for "His mercy in preserving our national existence. . . ."[1]

As always, these religious reflections of Lincoln were undoubtedly sincere. On the very next day Lincoln wrote to a Quaker who had visited him at the White House two years earlier, thanking her for helping him to strengthen his "reliance on God." "The purposes of the Almighty are perfect," Lincoln wrote, "and must prevail, though we erring mortals may fail to accurately perceive them in advance. We had hoped for a happy termination to this terrible war long before this; but God knows best, and has ruled otherwise." But Lincoln said he was certain that God "intends some great good to follow this mighty convulsion."[2]

Union victories multiplied: In the Shenandoah Valley, Union forces commanded by General Philip Sheridan attacked Jubal Early's Confederates. In superb displays of battlefield prowess, Sheridan beat the Confederates at Winchester, Virginia on September 19, and again at Fisher's Hill only three days later. As Early's forces retreated, the Union troops began a massive campaign of destruction. Under "total war" directives from Grant, they began to destroy all the farms in the Shenandoah Valley, thus depriving the Confederates of food and other provisions.

In October, as Sheridan prepared to return a great number of his soldiers to Grant—who could use them at Petersburg—he went to Washington to talk about his plans. In his absence, Early struck at his forces in a daring attack at Cedar Creek.

It is interesting to note that Lincoln feared such a move and warned against it. "I hope it will lay no constraint upon you," he had written to Grant in September, "for me to say I am a little afraid lest Lee sends re-enforcements to Early, and thus enables him to turn upon Sheridan."[3]

On October 19, Philip Sheridan was riding back from Washington; approaching Cedar Creek, he heard the sounds of cannon. He spurred his horse, and he encountered his own retreating troops. They cheered him, but he urged them to return to the front. The result was remarkable. Sheridan turned the tide of battle through the force of charisma alone. As McPherson has written, "the effect of this man's presence on the beaten army was extraordinary. By midafternoon, Sheridan had gotten the stragglers into line and organized a counterattack. . . . By nightfall, the blue tide had not only washed back over the four miles lost in the morning but had driven the enemy eight miles farther south. Early's army, thrice routed in a month, virtually ceased to exist as a fighting force."[4]

Lincoln issued another proclamation on the following day, urging citizens to set aside the "last Thursday in November" as a time to thank

God for inspiring their country "with fortitude, courage and resolution sufficient for the great trial of civil war into which we have been brought by our adherence as a nation to the cause of Freedom and Humanity." He also urged Americans to "humble themselves in the dust" as they offered these thanks.[5]

The legend-like details of what Sheridan achieved made the candidacy of McClellan appear almost pitiful in late October. Moreover, McClellan had managed to unify most of the Republicans: he was viewed throughout the party as an odious figure, and the party came together in response. Meanwhile, the "Radical Democratic Party" of Frémont withered away.

The election of 1864 was a tremendous victory for Lincoln. McClellan carried only three states: Kentucky, New Jersey, and Delaware. The vote in the electoral college was overwhelming: 212 for Lincoln and 21 for McClellan.

On election night, Lincoln made an impromptu speech to some cheering serenaders. He seemed to be supremely happy; he said that "the consequences of this day's work . . . will be to the lasting advantage, if not to the very salvation, of the country. . . . All who have labored to-day in behalf of the Union organization, have wrought for the best interests of their country and the world, not only for the present, but for all future ages. I am thankful to God for this approval of the people." He added, however, that his gratitude was "free from any taint of personal triumph . . . if I know my heart."[6]

In response to another group of serenaders, he sought once again to discourage any gloating by the victors. "It adds nothing to my satisfaction," he explained, "that any other men may be disappointed or pained by the result. . . . So long as I have been here I have not willingly planted a thorn in any man's bosom." He urged Americans to use the Civil War as "philosophy to learn wisdom from," adding that "in any future great national trial, compared with the men of this, we shall have as weak, and as strong; as silly and as wise; as bad and as good."[7]

If Lincoln tried to disavow any sense of vainglorious triumph, the elections were nonetheless a triumph for Republicans, a triumph of extraordinary magnitude. The Republicans won everything they lost in the elections of 1862, with some abundant dividends. They would dominate the House of Representatives by a margin of 145 votes to only 40. They would dominate the Senate by a margin of 42 to 10.

There was another big reason for Republican satisfaction: Roger Taney, the belligerent racist of "Dred Scott" infamy, had died, thus ridding the United States Supreme Court of a shrill and reactionary enemy. Lincoln nominated Salmon P. Chase as the new chief justice. Moreover, in October the free-state constitution of Maryland was ratified. On this particular occasion, Lincoln *did* permit himself some gloating; when the serenaders called, he was unabashedly righteous: "Most heartily do I congratulate you, and Maryland, and the nation, and the world, upon the event. . . . I sincerely hope it's [*sic*] friends may fully realize all their anticipations of good from it; and that it's opponents may, by it's [*sic*] effects, be agreeably and profitably, disappointed."[8]

After the election, a daring proposal from Sherman came across Lincoln's desk. The general proposed to divide his forces and move them away from Atlanta. Sherman wanted to destroy the Confederate army of John Bell Hood. He also wanted to strike a great blow that would cripple Confederate morale. His proposal was twofold: from his army of ninety thousand, he would send a detachment of thirty thousand to protect Tennessee if Hood should make any moves in that direction. This force would be commanded by General George Thomas. Sherman then proposed to take the other sixty thousand men and march through Georgia while destroying almost everything of value in his path.

T. Harry Williams has shown that both Grant and Lincoln had doubts about the wisdom of the plan. "The general in chief feared that if Sherman set out for the coast the Confederate field army in Georgia would invade Tennessee, and he well knew how Lincoln would react to a movement that might weaken the defenses of the bastion of the West. Grant wanted Sherman to defeat the Confederate army before he left Atlanta. Sherman, however, insisted that he could never destroy the enemy from Atlanta but if he smashed across Georgia the Confederates would have to follow him or attack Thomas in Tennessee. Whichever course the Confederates took, Sherman was sure they would be defeated."[9]

With assurances from Sherman that the Tennessee line would be defended, both Lincoln and Grant approved his "March to the Sea": Sherman left Atlanta on November 15, after ordering the whole population of the city to flee as he torched everything his enemies could possibly use. (The fire destroyed about a third of what remained of the city.) Thomas took his thirty thousand men to Tennessee, where he started to recruit reinforcements.

The next move was up to the Confederates. Hood decided to invade Tennessee, and Thomas readied himself for this blow.

Because of Hood's decision, Sherman was able to march from Atlanta to Savannah almost totally unopposed. His men "lived off the land," and after eating their fill, they put the torch to whatever might be left. Plantation houses, livestock, and crops were all consumed, and many thousands of slaves were set free. They followed Sherman's army by the thousands. The famous Union song that was inspired by the Georgia campaign—"Marching Through Georgia"—contained a message of joyous liberation; "Hoorah," rang the lyrics of the song—"Hoorah! We bring the Jubilee! Hoorah! Hoorah! The flag that makes you free." And it was Lincoln's flag—rededicated by him to its original and founding proposition—that was setting people free.

As Sherman marched to Savannah, Lincoln sent his long annual message to Congress on December 6. He promised war to the bitter end. Judging by the recent election, Lincoln wrote, "The purpose of the people, within the loyal States, to maintain the integrity of the Union, was never more firm, nor more nearly unanimous, than now." Moreover, the *power* to wage war was never stronger. "We have *more* men *now* than we had when the war *began*," Lincoln wrote. "We are not exhausted, nor in process of exhaustion;" indeed, "we are *gaining* strength, and may, if need be, maintain the contest indefinitely."[10] Under these conditions, Union victory was inevitable.

That being the case, he continued, it was time to revisit Reconstruction. Just a year before, he had offered some "lenient" terms to the rebels. "The door has been, for a full year, open to all," the president reflected, "except such as were not in condition to make free choice—that is, such as were in custody or under constraint." But now, he continued, it was time to consider how long that door should stay open. "The time may come—probably will come—when public duty shall demand that it be closed; and that, in lieu, more rigorous measures than heretofore shall be adopted."[11] Lincoln's message was very clear: he was ready to patch up his differences with Radical Republicans.

Lincoln turned to the Thirteenth Amendment—the amendment to abolish slavery everywhere, all at once—which was stalled in the House of Representatives. He exhorted the Congress to pass it and to do so immediately: "At the last session of Congress a proposed amendment of the Constitution abolishing slavery throughout the United States, passed the Senate, but failed for lack of the requisite two-thirds vote in the House of Representatives. Although the present is the same Congress [meeting in lame-duck session], and nearly the same members . . . I venture to recommend the reconsideration and passage of the measure at the present session." Lincoln argued that the very next Congress would pass the amendment, so why not do so at once? "The intervening election," Lincoln wrote, "shows, almost certainly, that the next Congress will pass the measure if this does not. Hence, there is only a question of *time* as to when the proposed amendment will go to the States for their action. And as it is to so go, at all events, may we not agree that the sooner the better?"[12]

Soon after Lincoln sent this message to Congress, the Confederate invasion of Tennessee ended in disaster. Already, a Confederate attack upon a strongly entrenched Union force had been smashed at Franklin, Tennessee, on the last day of November. But Hood persisted. He took his weakened force all the way to the Union defenses of Nashville, where Thomas was waiting. On December 15, Thomas ordered an assault that hit the rebel forces front and rear. McPherson has called the resulting battle "one of the most crushing Union victories of the war."[13] Hood's army was all but destroyed, and its remnants fled toward Mississippi. Lincoln ordered Thomas to pursue them: "Please accept for yourself, officers, and men, the nation's thanks for your good work of yesterday," the president wrote. "You made a magnificent beginning. A grand consummation is within your easy grasp. Do not let it slip."[14]

Thomas made certain he did not "let it slip"; he pursued the fleeing Confederates. Williams summarizes the eventual results: "Only remnants of Hood's army escaped, and it was never an army again."[15]

Then Sherman reached Savannah on December 21; in a message to Lincoln, he offered him the city as a Christmas present. He then proposed to march north, joining forces with Grant to administer the final blow to Lee and Richmond.

In the meantime, Lincoln worked tirelessly to convince the old Congress to approve the new Thirteenth Amendment before it adjourned. As historian Michael Vorenberg has written, "no piece of legislation during Lincoln's presidency received more of his attention than the Thirteenth Amendment."[16] He worked behind the scenes, twisting arms, making deals, and assembling his winning coalition. He even threatened to call the new Congress into special session in March. His tactics worked: on the last day of January 1865, the great anti-slavery amendment was passed, and a huge celebration broke out in the House of Representatives. Republicans began to cheer wildly, and visiting blacks in the galleries—a new rule to admit them had been passed in 1864—cheered and wept.

When a group of serenaders paid a call upon Lincoln, he exulted that the passage of the Thirteenth Amendment was the "King's cure for all the evils." It would settle any lingering disputes about the scope and the validity of what he had achieved with his Emancipation Proclamation. "That proclamation," the president acknowledged, "falls far short of what the amendment will be when fully consummated. A question might be raised whether the proclamation was legally valid. It might be added that it only aided those who came into our lines and that it was inoperative as to those who did not give themselves up, or that it would have no effect upon the children of the slaves." Such arguments would soon be moot forever. The occasion, Lincoln said, was "one of congratulation to the country and to the whole world."[17]

To increase the chances that the Thirteenth Amendment would be ratified, Lincoln actually suggested that the federal government should pay all the slave states to ratify. On February 5, he recommended a joint resolution affirming that

> the President of the United States is hereby empowered, at his discretion, to pay four hundred millions of dollars to the States of Alabama, Arkansas, Delaware, Florida, Georgia, Kentucky, Louisiana, Maryland, Mississippi, Missouri, North Carolina, South Carolina, Tennessee, Texas, Virginia, and West-Virginia . . . on the conditions following, towit: . . . [that] all resistance to the national authority shall be abandoned and cease, on or before the first day of April next; and upon such abandonment and ceasing of resistance, one half of said sum to be paid . . . and the remaining half to be paid only upon the amendment of the national constitution recently proposed by congress, becoming valid law, on or before the first day of July next, by the action thereon of the requisite number of States.[18]

Lincoln's cabinet, however, disapproved of this proposal, so the president quietly retracted it.

In the meantime, as Sherman prepared to move north and turn his wrath upon South Carolina, he decided to do something drastic in order to relieve the pressing needs of the slaves who were following his army. On January 12, he held a conference with a group of black leaders (most of them Methodist and Baptist ministers) from Savannah. It bears noting that Edwin Stanton, Lincoln's secretary of war, attended this meeting. A few days later Sherman issued an extraordinary order— Special Field Order Number 15—granting freedmen "possessory" title to a vast tract of seized rebel lands that would extend from Charleston to Jacksonville. Forty acres would be given to each black family; their titles to the land would be deemed "possessory" until such time as congressional action "shall regulate the title."[19]

Lincoln never countermanded this order, as he clearly had the power to do. It is almost impossible to think that he was ignorant of Sherman's decision, for his secretary of war had been present in Savannah when Sherman had developed the plan. Lincoln probably supported Sherman's order to redistribute this land. It appears that George Julian was telling the truth about his meeting with Lincoln in the previous summer to discuss the constitutional issue of bills of attainder. It seems the president had finally agreed to the redistribution of lands as punishment for treason.

On March 4, Lincoln delivered his second Inaugural Address. As he took the rostrum at the Capitol, a group of the conspirators led by John Wilkes Booth were lurking very close to where he stood. His address was a vision out of Scripture, a vision of a chosen people who had broken their covenant with God. Divine Providence had brought about the war, Lincoln said, and would determine its results in a manner transcending the actions of any participants, including himself. "Neither party expected for the war, the magnitude, or the duration, which it has already attained," Lincoln pointed out. "Each looked for an easier triumph, and a result less fundamental and astounding. Both read the same Bible, and pray to the same God; and each invokes his aid against the other."

Lincoln paused to reflect upon the difference between the two sides: "It may seem strange," he observed, "that any men should dare to ask a just God's assistance in wringing their bread from the sweat of other men's faces." But—he checked himself quickly as he said it—"let us judge not that we be not judged."

"That we be not judged": maybe Lincoln was reflecting on the deeper human sins of which slavery was only a symptom. Perhaps he meant that the sin of forcing others into bondage was a sign of a very deep flaw that lurks secretly in every human heart. It was the quintessential sin of wicked pride.

This sense of Lincoln's message is confirmed in the lines that followed, in which he visualized the war was a punishment designed for the Northern people as well as for the people of the South. God was punishing the nation as a whole.

We must remember that in Lincoln's estimation America was founded as a world-significant experiment in golden-rule ethics. All men were declared to be *equal*, and deserved to be regarded as equal in their rights—treated reciprocally. But Americans continued to *break* that rule by allowing in their midst a vicious social system that reduced other people to the status of beasts of the field. Indirectly or directly, they had done to these suffering people what they obviously wished to avoid having done to themselves. (About a week after giving this Inaugural Address, Lincoln quipped, "Whenever I hear anyone arguing for slavery I feel a strong inclination to see it tried on him personally.")[20]

Now the moment of reckoning had come for the nation of hypocrites. The president continued: "If we shall suppose that American Slavery is one of those offenses which, in the providence of God, must needs come, but which, having continued through His appointed time, He now wills to remove, and that He gives to both North and South this terrible war, as the woe due to those by whom the offense came, shall we discern therein any departure from those divine attributes which the believers in a Living God always ascribe to him?"

Americans should therefore submit to the lash, Lincoln warned, notwithstanding their hopes for God's speedy pardon of their sins. "Fondly do we hope—fervently do we pray—that this mighty scourge of war may speedily pass away." (Note carefully: a scourge is a whip.) "Yet, if God wills that it continue, until all the wealth piled by the bond-man's two hundred and fifty years of unrequited toil shall be sunk, and until every drop of blood drawn with the lash, shall be paid by another drawn with the sword, as was said three thousand years ago, so still it must be said 'the judgments of the Lord are true and righteous altogether.'"[21]

God was *whipping* the American land with a scourge to make it run with the blood of atonement. Every drop of slave's blood that was drawn by a whip would be paid by the blood of fighting soldiers. It was *after* he presented this vision that Lincoln saw fit to deliver those immortal lines about "malice toward none" and "charity for all," about binding up the wounds of the nation and caring for the orphans.

Lincoln supplemented this sermon-like address in an interesting but private letter. New York politician Thurlow Weed had written him a letter in praise of the Inaugural Address. Lincoln replied to him thus: "Every one likes a compliment. Thank you for yours on my . . . recent Inaugeral [*sic*] Address. I expect the latter to wear as well as—perhaps better than—any thing I have produced; but I believe it is not immediately popular. Men are not flattered by being shown that there has been a difference of purpose between the Almighty and them. To deny it, however, in this case, is to deny that there is a God governing the world. It is a truth which I thought needed to be told; and as whatever of humiliation there is in it, falls most directly on myself, I thought others might afford for me to tell it."[22] The "humiliation" of his sermon, wrote Lincoln, fell "directly" on himself more than others.

But Lincoln's awe in the face of what he took to be the Providence of God placed no inhibitions whatsoever on his penchant for using all the wits that God gave him to improve the lot of others through the arts and skills of politics. In the previous month, he had worked with the Radical Republicans. On March 3, he signed a new bill that established the federal Freedmen's Bureau, an unprecedented social welfare agency. The bureau was designed to give direct assistance to the freedmen: educational, medical, and legal assistance most of all. On the issue of land redistribution, moreover, the bureau was authorized to hold and survey "abandoned" lands and to lease them, in forty-acre tracts, with an option to purchase after three years' time with "such title thereto as the United States can convey." Lincoln signed this bill, which established the bureau on a one-year experimental basis.

Many Radical Republicans were scornful and impatient in regard to the free-state regimes in Louisiana and Arkansas. They refused to admit any members of Congress from these and other Southern states. But Lincoln came to an agreement with some of them: if they would compromise with him and support the regimes he had established already in those two states, he would agree to work closely with them to establish stronger policies elsewhere. According to historian Herman Belz, negotiations between Lincoln and the Radical Republican leader James Ashley began as early as December 1864.[23] McPherson has confirmed that in the months that followed "the President and House Republicans worked out a compromise whereby Congress would recognize the Lincoln-nurtured governments of Louisiana and Arkansas in return for presidential approval of legislation for the rest of the

Confederacy similar to the Wade-Davis Bill vetoed the previous July. This compromise measure initially enacted Black suffrage in the remaining Southern states, but moderates modified it to enfranchise only black army veterans and literate blacks."[24] No bill of this sort could be passed before Congress adjourned. But the newly elected Congress would probably approve such a measure in the autumn of 1865.

The Civil War approached its conclusion as Congress adjourned. Sherman's army of sixty thousand—now augmented to the level of ninety thousand by some troops from the Carolina coast—was storming through North Carolina. The Confederates had managed to assemble a force (of only twenty-two thousand) under General Joseph Johnston to oppose this juggernaut of Sherman. It was no use. And yet a desperate Confederate stratagem was being worked out: if Lee could somehow escape from the Petersburg trenches, swing South, join forces with Johnston, beat Sherman, and then turn to face Grant's army again, perhaps the rebels would still have a chance. A chance of one in a million, no doubt, but a chance all the same.

It was not to be. When Lee attempted his breakout on March 25, Grant counterattacked and forced him back. Then, with Sheridan's cavalry (newly returned from the Shenandoah Valley), Grant threatened to cut the last railroad to Petersburg and Richmond. He sent Sheridan to turn the rebel flank to the south and west of Petersburg. Lee countered this move, and the resulting battle on April 1 at a crossroads known as Five Forks was a massive Union victory. The Confederates abandoned both Petersburg and Richmond: they set their capital ablaze to destroy as many records as they possibly could when they left.

Lincoln was almost on the scene, for he was visiting Grant at his base of operations at City Point, Virginia. From the edge of battle, Lincoln sent back letters that described the sounds of the fighting. To Stanton, the president wrote that on the previous night he had listened to a "furious cannonade" and watched "the flashes of guns upon the clouds."[25] When Richmond was abandoned, Lincoln made up his mind that he would visit the city right away: "I think I will go there tomorrow," he wrote back to Stanton.[26]

As Grant pursued Lee to the west (Union cavalry blocked every one of Lee's attempts to turn south and join forces with Johnston), Lincoln entered the smoldering ruins of the Confederate capital. Black troops escorted him, and Richmond slaves turned out to kneel in his presence. "I know I am free," shouted one of them, "for I have seen Father

Abraham and felt him."[27] Lincoln entered the "Confederate White House," and sat at the desk of Jefferson Davis.

Grant hounded and hammered Lee's troops as he drove them farther to the west, farther toward the mountains. By April 9, it was over: surrounded, outnumbered by a factor of five or six to one, his supplies exhausted and his men nearly dead on their feet, Lee surrendered at Appomattox Court House.

On April 10, an immense cheering crowd asked Lincoln to address them at the White House. Lincoln briefly appeared and requested that they reappear the next evening: "I would much prefer having this demonstration take place to-morrow evening," he explained, when he promised to be better prepared to "say what I have to say."[28] He would give them a speech on Reconstruction.

On the following evening, he began the last speech of his life by acknowledging the joyous tidings from the front. "We meet this evening, not in sorrow, but in gladness of heart. The evacuation of Petersburg and Richmond, and the surrender of the principal insurgent army, give hope of a righteous and speedy peace whose joyous expression can not be restrained."

Then he got down to business very quickly: the business of politics. "By these recent successes the re-inauguration of the national authority— reconstruction—. . . is pressed much more closely upon our attention," the president said. "It is fraught with great difficulty."

He talked about Louisiana: he said that it had come to his attention that he was "much censured for some supposed agency in setting up, and seeking to sustain, the new State Government of Louisiana. In this I have done just so much as, and no more than, the public knows." Of course he did much more behind the scenes than the public would know for many years. But he continued: "In the Annual Message of Dec. 1863 and accompanying Proclamation, I presented *a* plan of reconstruction (as the phrase goes) which, I promised, if adopted by any State, should be acceptable to, and sustained by, the Executive government of the nation. I distinctly stated that this was not the only plan which might possibly be acceptable; and I also distinctly protested that the Executive claimed no right to say when, or whether members should be admitted to seats in Congress from such States."

His own role in the matter was minimal, Lincoln asserted: "When the Message of 1863, with the plan before mentioned, reached New-Orleans, Gen. Banks wrote me that he was confident the people, with his military co-operation, would reconstruct, substantially on that plan. I wrote him, and some of them to try it; they tried it, and the result is known. Such only has been my agency in getting up the Louisiana government. As to sustaining it, my promise is out."

Then he suddenly released upon his audience a sentence that was riveting—almost breathtaking—in its sheer monumental audacity: "But, as bad promises are better broken than kept, I shall treat this as a bad promise, and break it, whenever I shall be convinced that keeping it is adverse to the public interest. But I have not yet been so convinced."

The audacity increased, and the duplicity thickened, as the president digressed to consider some larger issues that pertained to the ex-rebel states. "I have been shown a letter," the president said, "supposed to be an able one, in which the writer expresses regret that my mind has not seemed to be definitely fixed on the question whether the seceded States, so called, are in the Union or out of it. It would perhaps, add astonishment to his regret, were he to learn that . . . I have *purposely* forborne any public expression upon it."

Can we figuratively believe our ears? How on earth could Lincoln deliver such a statement with a straight face? Ever since the beginning of secession the president insisted—in his first Inaugural Address, for example, and his message to Congress on July 4, 1861—that the rebel states were definitely *in* the Union, not "out" of it. Confederate claims of secession, he insisted, were delusions, illegalities, and treason. ("The States," he had written, "have their status IN the Union, and they have no other legal status.") But now Lincoln was saying (or pretending) that he never committed himself on the issue, that he had *purposely* refused to address it. What, may we ask, was Lincoln up to?

In all probability he uttered these words to send a message to the Radical Republicans, a message that he placed between the lines of this address. He was letting them know that if they wished to pursue their old tactic of claiming the Confederates committed "state suicide," he was ready at last to accept their logic and would no longer stand in their way. Listen to his words: "We all agree that the seceded States, so called, are out of their proper practical relation with the Union; and that the sole object of the government, civil and military, in regard to those States is to again get them into that proper practical relation. I believe it is not only possible, but in fact, easier, to do this, without deciding, or even considering, whether these states have even been out of the Union, than with it. . . . Let us all join in doing the acts necessary to restoring the proper practical relations between these states and the Union; and each forever after, innocently indulge his own opinion whether, in doing the acts, he brought the States from without, into the Union, or only gave them proper assistance, they never having been out of it."

Lincoln told the American people to indulge their own "opinions" on a matter of colossal urgency! But this was *not* just a matter of opinion to be privately "indulged" in a state of sweet "innocence." For if Congress should declare that the Confederate states had been *out* of the Union, then the terms of their eventual readmission—or their re-creation as states—could be severe. Lincoln opened up the door to a harsh and demanding Reconstruction in the guise of dismissing an abstract problem that was trivial and almost irrelevant.

Still, Lincoln turned once again to his Louisiana program, and he tried to make the case for retaining it. "Some twelve thousand voters in the heretofore slave-state of Louisiana have sworn allegiance to the Union," Lincoln pointed out; they had "held elections, organized a State government, adopted a free-state constitution, giving the benefit of public schools equally to black and white, and empowered the Legislature to confer the elective franchise upon the colored man. Their Legislature has already voted to ratify the constitutional amendment recently passed by Congress, abolishing slavery throughout the nation. These twelve thousand persons are thus fully committed to the Union, and to perpetual freedom in the state—committed to the very things, and nearly all the things the nation wants—and they ask the nations [*sic*] recognition, and its assistance to make good their committal."

The president admitted there was room for improvement, to be sure; he acknowledged it was "unsatisfactory to some that the elective franchise is not [already] given to the colored man. I would myself prefer that it were now conferred on the very intelligent, and on those who serve our cause as soldiers." Lincoln made the big announcement at last, in a low-key manner—he would favor the extension of voting rights to blacks on an incremental basis. He went on: "Still the question is not whether the Louisiana government, as it stands, is quite all that is desirable. The question is 'Would it be wiser to take it as it is, and help to improve it; or to reject, and disperse it?'"

Lincoln shifted in a moment to a charismatic tone in regard to the issue of voting rights; he said that if the nation should accept the Louisiana achievement, "we encourage the hearts, and nerve the arms of

the twelve thousand to adhere to their work, and argue for it, and pros-
elyte for it, and fight for it, and feed it, and grow it, and ripen it to a
complete success. The colored man, too, in seeing all united for him,
is inspired with vigilance, and energy, and daring to the same end.
Grant that he desires the elective franchise, will he not attain it sooner
by saving the already advanced steps toward it, than by running backward over them?" Could this message be in any way misread? He was
urging all blacks to show vigilance and energy and daring in their fight
to win the vote.

But then, Lincoln took a different tack. He admitted that his 10 percent plan might have to be discarded in the very near future. He observed that "so great peculiarities pertain to each state; and such important
and sudden changes occur in the same state; and, withal, so new and
unprecedented is the whole case, that no exclusive, and inflexible plan
can safely be prescribed as to details and colatterals [sic]. Such exclusive,
and inflexible plan, would surely become a new entanglement."

He closed with a hint of some dramatic new policies to come. "In
the present 'situation' as the phrase goes, it may be my duty to make
some new announcement to the people of the South. I am considering," he pointedly warned, "and shall not fail to act, when satisfied that
action will be proper."[29]

In the audience was John Wilkes Booth. "That means nigger citizenship," Booth hissed to his companions as the president concluded
his speech. "Now, by God, I'll put him through. That is the last speech
he will ever make."[30]

KNOWING AS WE DO the great direction of his life, the cruel murder of
Lincoln by a racist is all the more outrageous—all the more grievous.
Lincoln's plans for Reconstruction would in all probability have led to a
partnership with most, if not all, of the Radicals, a partnership to work
for black civil rights. Success was entirely possible: the times were auspi-
cious for a social revolution in the months that followed Appomattox.

McPherson has conjectured that the "Southern whites might have
submitted to almost any terms of reconstruction the government had
seen fit to impose"; such was the mood of despondency and shock
throughout the South after Lee had surrendered.[31] A South Carolinian lamented that "the conqueror has the right to make the terms, and
we must submit."[32]

The possibilities were outstanding. McPherson has reasoned that "if Lincoln had lived through his second term, the polarization of Executive and Congress after 1865 that turned Reconstruction into a bitter confrontation would not have occurred and the postwar transition from slavery to freedom might have been grounded in firmer and longer-lasting principles of justice and equity."[33] We can only imagine what a like-minded president and Congress could have done to make a civil rights revolution begin after Appomattox.

As it was, crucial months and years went to waste after Lincoln's death, as Andrew Johnson and the Radicals began their political war. Once Johnson took over, he tried to end Reconstruction quickly. He rescinded Sherman's order to set aside the vast "reservation" of confiscated lands for black settlement. He looked the other way in the autumn of 1865 as ex-Confederate states passed a series of "black codes" reducing former slaves to the status of peons. When blacks were shot down as they attempted to vote, Johnson washed his hands of the matter in the name of states' rights and strict construction. When the Radicals voted to extend the existence of the Freedmen's Bureau, Johnson vetoed the bill and condemned it as unconstitutional.

The Radicals forced their way to power and reversed some of Johnson's most flagrant derelictions of duty. By super-majorities, they overturned his presidential vetoes. They renewed the Freedmen's Bureau over Johnson's determined opposition. They passed a civil rights law, pushed through the Fourteenth and Fifteenth Amendments (civil rights and voting rights amendments) to the Constitution, and—for a while—seized control of the army and forced an upheaval in the South that brought blacks into state and local offices, and even into Congress. But the gains were short-lived: a counterrevolution overturned almost all of these advances in the following decades.

By the time the Republicans recaptured the White House in 1869 (with Ulysses S. Grant as president), the public was repelled by the "mess in Washington." The downhill slide was beginning, and the basis for continued Reconstruction would be gone before very long. By the turn of the twentieth century, Americans had come to regard Reconstruction as a "failure," an "age of corruption." The Jim Crow South was the result. It endured until challenged by the "second Reconstruction" of the 1950s and 1960s.

If Lincoln had lived, perhaps the first Reconstruction would have worked. With Lincoln at the helm for another four years—with the savior of the Union working closely with the Radical members of his party—a lasting consensus for black civil rights might have formed in the 1860s.

With such knowledge of the history that *might* have occurred, what form of consolation can we have? For that, we are forced to return to an earlier installment of conjectural or "what-if" history: the history consisting of the danger that Lincoln invoked when he challenged Stephen Douglas in the 1850s, when he warned about the danger of slavery invading the North. By opposing Douglas, by destroying the Crittenden Compromise, by forcing the geographical containment of slavery, Lincoln sought to make certain that the nightmare future of blacks being shipped to the North in stinking cattle cars or in chain gangs—shipped to the North to break strikes in Chicago, in Pittsburgh, and elsewhere—would never come to pass. As political philosopher Jaffa has said, it is "simply unhistorical to say that such a thing *couldn't* have happened because it *didn't* happen. It didn't happen because Lincoln was resolved that it *shouldn't* happen. And nothing but his implacable will made it impossible."[34]

Lincoln stopped such a worst-case future. Then he launched the alternative best-case future: he led the anti-slavery movement to its great consummation, and he did it through his sheer virtuosity in channeling and orchestrating power. He must have felt a secret thrill as he manipulated power in its various forms: political, military, moral, psychological, literary.[35] Perhaps he felt within himself the potential to become a great catalytic force many years before his leadership talent began to blaze forth.

But a discussion of his genius in the uses of power must also force discussion of his fatal lapse in judgment near the end of his life. Lincoln was repeatedly and maddeningly "fatalistic" when it came to the issue of his safety. Assassination threats had increased in the early months of 1865; Lincoln even suffered an eerie premonition through a dream of the White House in mourning. But he tended to dismiss all suggestions for tightening security, asserting that if anyone were truly determined to kill him, they could probably do it regardless of any precautions.

This was nonsense, and Lincoln must have known it. While total security is obviously out of the question, it can be greatly improved through intelligent precautions, and Lincoln was smart enough to know this well: indeed, we *know* that he knew it in the early years of the war.

It is crucial to observe at this point that Lincoln's attitude regarding his personal safety had *changed*. For just consider: he had listened to the warnings back in 1861 when he learned of the assassins in Baltimore. He had traveled, we remember, under cover of darkness, changing trains and wearing a disguise. Months later, when he feared that the Confederates would try to raid Washington, he told his secretary of the navy to "have as strong a War Steamer as you can conveniently put on that duty, to cruise upon the Potomac, and to look in upon, and, if practicable, examine the Bluff and vicinity, at what is called the White House, once or twice per day; and, in any case of an attempt to erect a battery there, to drive away the party attempting it. . . ."[36]

The prudent leader who issued these instructions presents a striking contrast to the spectacle of Lincoln under fire at Fort Stevens, exposing himself to Confederate bullets.

And now a terrible thought begins to dawn—does it not?—the thought that Lincoln under fire at Fort Stevens was a prelude to Booth and Ford's Theater. There is no way to prove such a thing. But one cannot help wondering about it: was the rashness of Lincoln in dismissing the security issue a way for him to somehow "offer himself"—unconsciously, perhaps—to an avenging Lord? Was he offering himself as a gesture in golden-rule ethics—offering to prove to his Maker he was willing to pay the same price as all the hundreds of thousands of soldiers whom his policies had forced to their premature deaths?[37] Remember the tone of Lincoln's lamentations in the previous summer: the war, he reflected, "carried mourning into every home."

We can never pursue any psychological theory in regard to Lincoln's death beyond the limits of a sketchy hypothesis. But we can certainly critique the behavior of Lincoln in regard to his personal safety, behavior that constitutes the greatest single lapse in his career. And we can use this occasion for a more explicit look at Lincoln's spiritual side and what it meant to him.

Theologian Reinhold Niebuhr once wrote that Lincoln's "combination of moral resoluteness about the immediate issues with a religious awareness of another dimension of meaning and judgment must be regarded as almost a perfect model of the difficult but not impossible task of remaining loyal and responsible toward the moral treasures of a free civilization on the one hand while yet having some religious vantage point over the struggle. Surely it was this double attitude that made the spirit of Lincoln's, 'with malice toward none; with

Lincoln as he looked a few days before his assassination. Photograph by Alexander
Gardner. (Library of Congress, Meserve Collection #97)

charity for all' possible. There can be no other basis for true charity;
for charity cannot be induced by lessons from copybook texts. It can
proceed only from a 'broken spirit, and a contrite heart.'"[38]

"A broken spirit and a contrite heart": Niebuhr, of course, is not
referring to a state of *despair* in this phrase but to the spiritual *humbling
of pride* that is essential to most, if not all, forms of Christian spirituality. Lincoln's keen understanding of the dangers of pride can be traced
all the way to the 1830s. Well before he embraced Christian piety,

Lincoln expressed his fear of hubris in his address to the Young Men's Lyceum of Springfield in 1838. He warned that "some man possessed of the loftiest genius, coupled with ambition sufficient to push it to its utmost stretch, will at some time, spring up among us." And he reflected that the people would have to be "united with each other" to "successfully frustrate his designs."[39]

It can certainly be argued that Lincoln's great career as a strategist contained a deep tension: a tension between his awareness of his gifts and his fear that they could lead him into hubris—into sinful pride. But if it led him unconsciously to put himself at risk in a manner that is wholly indefensible except as a gesture of tragic self-sacrifice—if it led him to lay upon the altar of the nation nothing less than his future potential to advance the new birth of freedom—then we are justified in asking whether Lincoln, in the end, reached the point of *excessive* self-effacement that critics of the Christian tradition as diverse in their views and sensibilities as Machiavelli, Hobbes, Gibbon, and Nietzsche have complained about over the centuries. There are, after all, situations where a strong and healthy self-regard is essential to moral accomplishment.

At his best, however, Lincoln reconciled the tension of humility and ego in a manner that Harry V. Jaffa has described in an admirable way: in Lincoln, Jaffa wrote a half-century ago, a man of genius discovered "that the highest ambition can be conceived as consummated only in the highest service, that egotism and altruism ultimately coincide in that consciousness of superiority which is superiority in the ability to benefit others."[40]

In what did this superiority of Lincoln truly consist? It is futile to ascribe it all to Lincoln's sense of "practicality." No less an observer than Theodore Roosevelt attempted to describe it this way and fell sadly short of the mark. Lincoln, said Roosevelt, "did not war with phantoms; he did not struggle among the clouds; he faced facts; he endeavored to get the best results he could out of the warring forces with which he had to deal . . . [And] when he could not get the best he was forced to content himself and did content himself with the best possible."[41]

No, indeed—Lincoln *never* contented himself with the best results he could attain unless they passed a certain threshold of *decency*. And this point is absolutely essential. Lincoln weighed lesser evils with greater, to be sure; he weighed the opportunities of history with countervailing hazards. And he would choose the lesser evil, as Roosevelt has said, but he would do this *only at times when that choice advanced a greater good.* He insisted that the overall "package" of moral results should be good enough to make the subsidiary choices worthwhile. Below a certain level, any "compromise" to Lincoln was worthless or positively evil.

It is only when seen in this light of moral value that the gifts of Lincoln as a strategist can really be considered. But when seen in this light, Lincoln's gifts amounted to the following: (1) His capacity to view the large picture in a flash and to relate the subsidiary parts of a problem to the whole; (2) his capacity to visualize surges of power as they moved along dynamic lines of force; (3) his gift for doing best-case and worst-case contingency planning simultaneously; (4) his ability to develop his plans incrementally, expanding his power by degrees as he diminished the power of his enemies; (5) his ability to practice deception as a ploy within a context of honesty.

All of these abilities were channeled by Lincoln in the following manner when it came to the problem of slavery: (1) He believed it was impossible for him to deal with the institution unless he *condemned* it as an unambiguous evil; (2) however, knowing and saying that slavery was wrong was just a prelude to strong civic *action*; (3) the great challenge for the anti-slavery movement was to deal with the evil *effectively*; (4) the best incremental plan was to revive the early national creed that was inimical to human enslavement: "all men are created equal"; (5) in so doing, one should summon all available power to manipulate the flow of events in this general direction while fighting to prevent any further *erosion* of the national creed.

Harry V. Jaffa has seen in this work an application of "prudential" morality conceived in the Aristotelian tradition. He has suggested that "Lincoln understood the task of statesmanship" as "to know what is good or right, and how much of that good is attainable."[42]

Jaffa's application of Aristotelian principles to Lincoln's moral statecraft is justified. For in his *Nicomachean Ethics*, Aristotle wrote that the challenge of ethical life is essentially the challenge of determining the moral *excellence* or *fitness* of our various responses to the situations we encounter.

In the case of Lincoln, however, one particular issue that figures in the ethics of Aristotle—and especially so if we choose to contrast it to its treatment in the ethics of Kant, who would not condone deception—is deeply provocative: the problem of *honesty*.[43] It is, after all, Lincoln's use of *crafty methods* that appears paradoxical or even inconsistent to some in light of his morality.

Aristotle praises the honest man's nature in no uncertain terms: "falsehood," he writes, is "by its own nature bad and reprehensible." Consequently, "truth [is] a fine and laudable thing."[44] Yet certain key exceptions are presented in the *Nicomachean Ethics*. At one point, for instance, Aristotle speaks in great praise of sincerity, but nonetheless cautions, "by the 'sincere' man I do not mean one who, when he enters into a contract or agreement, puts all his cards on the table."[45] At another point Aristotle states that "the superior man is bound to be open in his likes and dislikes, and to care more for truth than for what people think, and to be straightforward in word or deed." But then he adds this worldly-wise caveat: "His language will be sincere, *unless when he has recourse to irony, which will be his tone in addressing the generality of men* [my emphasis]."[46]

The relationship of truth to untruth in the tactics of Lincoln is a problem that may give the reader pause. But his uses of deception were frequently justified, disturbing though this may seem to be. So let's be *honest*: let us really "put our cards on the table." Most of us demand an inner honesty in those whom we trust. We teach our children to honor the truth, and we teach them to *tell* the truth as well. But do we not, on occasion, teach our children to be wary of the complicated ways of this world? Do we not, as they grow, acknowledge more and more that the problem of honesty relates to situational ethics?

Intellectual historian Jacques Barzun asked the fundamental questions long ago as he reflected on the challenges of twentieth-century "relativism" in relation to the problem of behavior: "Is a man honest who does not always tell the truth? Certainly not! Well then, is he to tell the homicidal maniac where his victim has just gone? Certainly not again. The casuist laboriously works out a rationale: he relates the rule to the circumstance. But if we admit this exception to truth telling, are not people going to hide dishonesty under the name of conditional judgment? No doubt." And the upshot? A *perfect* resolution of the problem is morally impossible. In Barzun's opinion, "there has been no way yet discovered of preventing either absolute or relative rules from . . . cloaking hypocrisies. The only safeguard is in the conscience."[47]

In the conscience. And is there any doubt that Lincoln's conscience controlled his deceptions to achieve moral ends?

Let us leave it at this: Lincoln's genius—in addition to his mastery in shaping historical events—was to force upon those who paid attention to his teachings a "civic religion" that transcended his occasional deceptions.[48] And the message of his creed was as follows: Most of us—even those of gentle nature, it would seem—can be tyrants if our conscience goes to seed. Many of us can be seduced into breaches of morality, some of them minor, to be sure, but some of them as gross as the evil of enslavement. Only principles of self-restraint that are based upon a power of human empathy, a power transcending the self—"all men created equal"—give decency to government of, by, and for the people. Only principles transcending the self can make a free society possible and worth the cost of saving.

Lincoln did much more than merely "save the Union," and he did much more than "free the slaves." At the cost of some occasional deception—and at the cost of some six hundred thousand lives that were lost to the nation, including his own—it can be said that he saved our nation's soul. He was an indispensable genius such as no other figure in our past.

On the day after Lincoln had died, a great banner was stretched across Broadway. The message was powerful and brief. It is a message this book has sought to prove. "The great person," it read, "the great man, is the miracle of history."[49]

Notes

INTRODUCTION

1. Allen C. Guelzo, "A Reluctant Recruit to the Abolitionist Cause," *The Washington Post*, February 11, 2001, "Outlook," B-3. Guelzo's important recent books about Lincoln include *Abraham Lincoln: Redeemer President* (Grand Rapids, Mich.: William B. Eerdmans Publishing Company, 1999) and *Lincoln's Emancipation Proclamation: The End of Slavery in America* (New York: Simon & Schuster, 2004). The former book is an intellectual biography with special emphasis on Lincoln's religious views. The latter is a study of the Emancipation Proclamation, which Guelzo regards as a definitive event in American history, an act both "sincere and profound," and the product of effective "prudential" morality on Lincoln's part. This book conveys a higher estimation of Lincoln by Guelzo than the views he expressed in the above-cited article in the *Washington Post*. Nonetheless, though Guelzo appears to be a great deal more impressed at this writing with the qualities of Lincoln as a moral strategist, he continues to understate or even underestimate the radical side of Lincoln's temperament. Though Guelzo concedes that "Lincoln was not exaggerating in 1858 that he 'hated' slavery," he nonetheless argues that Lincoln was "not enough moved by American slavery's singular injustice to their African captives to call for their immediate emancipation" at the time, as did the full-fledged abolitionists (*Lincoln's Emancipation Proclamation*, 4, 22). While of course it is true that Lincoln called in the 1850s for an incremental emancipation, it hardly follows that his stance in this matter is proof that he was "not enough moved" about slavery's effect upon the slaves. Witness Lincoln's private statements in 1855, in a letter that he wrote to one of his oldest and closest friends, Joshua Speed, to the effect that the status of slaves was "a continual torment to me," that he and many other anti-slavery Northerners "crucify their feelings" on the issue of slavery, and, most directly of all, that "I hate to see the poor creatures [fugitive slaves] hunted down, and caught, and carried back to their stripes, and unrewarded toil" (Lincoln to Joshua F. Speed, August 24, 1855). It is strangely ironic that Guelzo cites the statements quoted above, though without, apparently, being moved by their emotional force.

2. David Herbert Donald, *Lincoln* (New York: Simon & Schuster, 1995), 14–15. For a polite but very strong rebuttal of Donald, see James M. McPherson's book review "A Passive President?" *Atlantic Monthly*, November 1995, 134–40.
3. Statement by Barbara Fields, in Ken Burns et al., *The Civil War* (Florentine Films and WETA-TV, 1989), Episode Four, "Simply Murder (1863)." This particular variation of the argument that Lincoln was shallow or opportunistic may be traced back at least as far as the 1948 essay by Richard Hofstadter, "Abraham Lincoln and the Self-Made Myth." See Richard Hofstadter, *The American Political Tradition and the Men Who Made It* (New York: Alfred A. Knopf, 1948), chapt. 5.
4. James M. McPherson, *Abraham Lincoln and the Second American Revolution* (New York: Oxford University Press, 1991), 42.
5. See, for example: Gore Vidal, *Lincoln* (New York: Random House, 1984) and William K. Klingaman, *Abraham Lincoln and the Road to Emancipation: 1861–1865* (New York: Viking Press, 2001).
6. William Lee Miller, *Lincoln's Virtues: An Ethical Biography* (New York: Alfred A. Knopf, 2002). Miller's book expands upon the writings of political philosopher Harry V. Jaffa, who has analyzed the politics of Lincoln from the philosophic standpoint of ethics, and especially Aristotelian ethics, for half a century. Jaffa's most recent book is *A New Birth of Freedom: Abraham Lincoln and the Coming of the Civil War* (Lanham, Md.: Rowman & Littlefield, 2000).
7. LaWanda Cox, *Lincoln and Black Freedom: A Study in Presidential Leadership* (Columbia: University of South Carolina Press, 1981), 1994 ed., 7.
8. Ibid., 43.
9. Søren Kierkegaard, *Fear and Trembling* (1843), in *Fear and Trembling and The Sickness Unto Death*, trans. Walter Lowrie (Princeton: Princeton University Press, 1941; repr., New York: Doubleday, 1945), 37.

CHAPTER ONE

1. Abraham Lincoln, "Speech at Chicago," July 10, 1858, in *Collected Works of Abraham Lincoln*, ed. Roy P. Basler (New Brunswick, N.J.: Rutgers University Press, 1953), II, 500–501.
2. See Harold Holzer's observations, which are based upon a number of authoritative primary-source descriptions, with regard to the charismatic power of Lincoln as a speaker. Holzer writes of "Lincoln's hypnotic manner. . . . his power to amuse and enthrall with a jolt of the head or the flash of an eye." Harold Holzer, *Lincoln at Cooper Union: The Speech That Made Abraham Lincoln President* (New York: Simon & Schuster, 2004), 173. For a persuasive analysis of the role that anger played in the emotional dynamics of Lincoln, see Michael Burlingame, *The Inner World of Abraham Lincoln* (Urbana: University of Illinois Press, 1994).
3. Abraham Lincoln to Joshua F. Speed, August 24, 1855, in *Collected Works*, II, 323.
4. Abraham Lincoln, "'A House Divided,' Speech at Springfield, Illinois," June 16, 1858, in *Collected Works*, II, 461–62.
5. Abraham Lincoln to William Kellogg, December 11, 1860, in *Collected Works*, IV, 150.

6. For those who presume that "Machiavellian" implies an autocratic outlook, a reading of Machiavelli's *Discourses on the First Ten Books of Titus Livy* is a good antidote. Machiavelli preferred republics to monarchies.

7. Abraham Lincoln, "Speech at Chicago," July 10, 1858, in *Collected Works*, II, 500.

8. James Madison, in ed. Max Farrand, *The Records of the Federal Convention* (New Haven: Yale University Press, 1966), I, 486.

9. Thomas Jefferson to Roger C. Weightman, June 24, 1826, in *The Writings of Thomas Jefferson*, ed. Paul Leicester Ford (New York: G. P. Putnam's Sons, 1892–99), X, 390–92. Jefferson's statement was a reiteration of words that were spoken in a 1685 speech on the gallows by Colonel Richard Rumbold, an English Puritan.

10. Thomas Jefferson, "Proposed Constitution for Virginia," (June 1783), in *Writings*, ed. Ford, III, 320–33.

11. John Bernard, *Retrospections of America, 1797–1811* (New York: Harper and Brothers, 1887; repr. New York: Benjamin Blom, 1969) 91.

12. Thomas Jefferson, "Heads of Information given me by E. Randolph," n.d., Library of Congress, M, III, n. 297.

13. The best general interpretations of the role of the Founding Fathers vis-à-vis slavery can be found in William W. Freehling, "The Founding Fathers and Slavery," in *American Negro Slavery*, ed. Allen Weinstein and Frank Otto Gatell (New York: Oxford University Press, 1973), and William W. Freehling, *The Road to Disunion: Secessionists at Bay, 1776–1854* (New York: Oxford University Press, 1990), especially chapt. 7; and Winthrop D. Jordan, *White Over Black: American Attitudes Toward the Negro, 1550–1812* (Chapel Hill: University of North Carolina Press, 1968), parts 3 and 4.

14. Jefferson, *Notes on the State of Virginia* (1785), Harper Torchbook Edition (New York: Harper & Row, 1964), 138, 132–33.

15. John C. Calhoun to Virgil Maxcy, September 11, 1830, Galloway-Maxcy-Markoe Papers, Library of Congress, cited in William W. Freehling, *Prelude to Civil War: The Nullification Controversy in South Carolina, 1816–1836* (New York: Harper & Row, 1965), 257.

16. James Hamilton, Jr., to John Taylor et al., September 14, 1830, *Charleston Mercury*, cited in Freehling, *Prelude to Civil War*, 256.

17. William W. Freehling, *Prelude to Civil War*, 127.

18. *City Gazette and Commercial Daily Advertiser* (Charleston, S.C.), September 14, 1830, and *Proceedings of the States Rights Meeting in Columbia, S.C. on the Twentieth of September, 1830*, 18–42, cited in Freehling, *Prelude to Civil War*, 168.

19. Weld, in addition to his charismatic anti-slavery speeches, assisted several drives to send anti-slavery petitions to Congress. He served in the early 1840s as advisor to the anti-slavery Whigs who were fighting the "Gag Rule."

20. David Walker published an *Appeal to the Colored Citizens of the World* in 1829. Both free black leaders of the North and the black insurrectionaries who hoped to trigger slave revolts were active in the anti-slavery cause before the growth of white militance during the 1830s. In 1817, black leaders met at Philadelphia's Bethel Church to protest the strategy of colonization among white anti-slavery leaders. The first black American newspaper, *Freedom's Journal*, was established in 1827. Its editors were Samuel Cornish and John Russwurm. Over fifty abolition societies were founded by free blacks.

21. See John C. Calhoun, "Remarks on Receiving Abolition Petitions (Revised Report), in the Senate, February 6, 1837," in *The Papers of John C. Calhoun*, ed. Clyde N. Wilson (Columbia: University of South Carolina Press, 1980), XIII, especially 395–96:

> The relation now existing in the slave-holding States between the two [races] is, instead of an evil, a good—a positive good. . . . I hold then, that there never has yet existed a wealthy and civilized society in which one portion of the community did not, in point of fact, live on the labor of the other. . . . It would not be difficult to trace the various devices by which the wealth of all civilized communities has been so unequally divided, and to show by what means so small a share has been allotted to those by whose labor it was produced. . . .

22. See Kenneth Stampp, *The Peculiar Institution: Slavery in the Ante-Bellum South* (New York: Alfred A. Knopf, 1956), Vintage edition, 211:

> Every slave state made it a felony to say or write anything that might lead, directly or indirectly, to discontent or rebellion. In 1837, the Missouri legislature passed an act "to prohibit the publication, circulation, and promulgation of the abolition doctrines." The Virginia code of 1849 provided a fine and imprisonment for any person who maintained "that owners have not right of property in their slaves." Louisiana made it a capital offense to use "language in any public discourse, from the bar, the bench, the stage, the pulpit, or in any place whatsoever" that might produce "insubordination among the slaves."

23. See John Hope Franklin, *The Militant South, 1800–1861* (Cambridge: Harvard University Press, 1956), and David Grimsted, *American Mobbing, 1828–1861: Toward Civil War* (New York: Oxford University Press, 1998).

24. The best work to date on the Free-Soil movement remains Eric Foner's *Free Soil, Free Labor, Free Men: The Ideology of the Republican Party Before the Civil War* (New York: Oxford University Press, 1970).

25. For more information on the use of slaves as rented strikebreakers in Southern industry, see Eugene D. Genovese, *The Political Economy of Slavery* (New York: Random House, 1965), 199, 233, and Robert S. Starobin, *Industrial Slavery in the Old South* (New York: Oxford University Press, 1970).

26. Representative Thomas L. Clingman of North Carolina declared in a speech before the House of Representatives on January 22, 1850, that Southerners would have utilized their slaves in California gold mines if slavery had been given a fair chance to establish itself. (*Selections from Writings and Speeches of Hon. Thomas L. Clingman, of North Carolina* [Raleigh: J. Nichols, printer, 1877], 239). J. D. B. De Bow, in his influential Southern journal *De Bow's Review*, declared in 1850 that it was solely the lack of a protective slave code that deterred Southern owners of slaves from bringing them to California and making it a slave state: "Such is the strength and power of Northern opposition that property, which is ever timid, and will seek no hazards, is excluded from the country in the person of the slave, and Southerners are forced, willingly or not, to remain at home." (J. D. B. De Bow, "California—The New American El Dorado," *De Bow's Review*, VIII, June 1850, 540).

27. Speech by John C. Calhoun in the United States Senate, March 4, 1850, in *Calhoun: Basic Documents*, ed. John M. Anderson (State College, Pa.: Bald Eagle Press, 1952), 298–324.

28. The original Fugitive Slave Law, passed by Congress in 1793, had proven unsatisfactory to slave owners. This law had permitted the owners of escaped slaves to appear in any state or federal court with their captured human property and

then provide legal proof of their ownership. But free-state officials often proved uncooperative. Later, the Supreme Court ruled in *Prigg vs. Pennsylvania* (1842) that enforcement of the Fugitive Slave Law was entirely the federal government's responsibility. Thereafter, a number of free state legislatures passed "personal liberty laws" that interfered with the operations of slave catchers. The stronger Fugitive Slave Law of 1850 attempted to override the personal liberty laws.

29. The most authoritative recent accounts of Lincoln's self-education and early psychological development are Douglas L. Wilson, *Honor's Voice: The Transformation of Abraham Lincoln* (New York: Alfred A. Knopf, 1998), 1999 Vintage edition, especially chapt. 2, and Michael Burlingame, *The Inner World of Abraham Lincoln*.

30. Abraham Lincoln, "Address Before the Young Men's Lyceum of Springfield, Illinois, 'The Perpetuation of Our Political Institutions,'" January 27, 1838, *Collected Works*, I, 114.

31. Edmund Wilson, "Abraham Lincoln: The Union as Religious Mysticism," in *Eight Essays* (New York: Doubleday and Anchor Books, 1954), 190–91, 202.

32. Harry V. Jaffa, *Crisis of the House Divided: An Interpretation of the Lincoln-Douglas Debates* (Chicago: The University of Chicago Press, 1959), 219, passim, chapt. IX.

33. Abraham Lincoln to Mary Speed, September 27, 1841, in *Collected Works*, I, 260.

34. Abraham Lincoln to Joshua Speed, August 24, 1855, in *Collected Works*, II, 320.

35. Abraham Lincoln, "Eulogy on Henry Clay," July 6, 1852, in *Collected Works*, II, 129, 126, 130, 132.

CHAPTER TWO

1. For further information on Quitman and the "filibusterers," see John Hope Franklin, *The Militant South, 1800–1861* (Cambridge: Harvard University Press, 1956), 103–14.

2. See Robert E. May, *The Southern Dream of a Caribbean Empire, 1854–1861* (Baton Rouge: Louisiana State University Press, 1973).

3. M. W. McCluskey, ed., *Speeches, Messages, and Other Writings of the Hon. Albert G. Brown, a Senator in Congress from the State of Mississippi* (Philadelphia: J. B. Smith & Co., 1859), 588–99.

4. *Selections from Writings and Speeches of Hon. Thomas L. Clingman, of North Carolina* (Raleigh: J. Nichols, printer, 1877), 239.

5. On the influence of Fitzhugh's *Sociology for the South*, see Harvey Wish, *Ante-Bellum: Writings of George Fitzhugh and Hinton Rowan Helper on Slavery* (New York: G. P. Putnam's Sons, 1960), 6–8.

6. George Fitzhugh, *Sociology for the South—Or, the Failure of Free Society* (Richmond: A. Morris, Publisher, 1854), Burt Franklin Research and Source Book Series No.102, 179.

7. Abraham Lincoln, "Speech at Peoria, Illinois," October 16, 1854, in *Collected Works of Abraham Lincoln*, ed. Roy P. Basler (New Brunswick, N.J.: Rutgers University Press, 1953), II, 247–48.

8. Ibid., 259.

9. Ibid., 281.

10. Ibid., 266.

11. Ibid., 264.

12. Ibid., 265.

13. Ibid., 266.

14. Ibid., 262.

15. Ibid., 274.

16. Ibid., 255.

17. Ibid., 275.

18. Ibid., 271.

19. Ibid., 271. On the issue of Lincoln and race, see: Benjamin Quarles, *Lincoln and the Negro* (New York: Oxford University Press, 1962); Don E. Fehrenbacher, "Only His Stepchildren: Lincoln and the Negro," *Civil War History* 20 (December 1974): 293–310; and LaWanda Cox, *Lincoln and Black Freedom: A Study in Presidential Leadership* (Columbia: University of South Carolina Press, 1981), 1994 ed., 19–26. Almost fifty years ago, David Herbert Donald came to the conclusion that "the President himself was color-blind . . . and he thought of the black man first of all as a man." (David Herbert Donald, *Lincoln Reconsidered: Essays on the Civil War Era* [New York: Alfred A. Knopf, 1956], 135.)

20. Ibid., 282.

21. Ibid., 255–56.

22. Stephen A. Douglas, "Mr. Douglas's Speech," in "First Debate with Stephen A. Douglas at Ottawa, Illinois," August 21, 1858, *Collected Works*, III, 10.

23. James M. McPherson, *Ordeal By Fire: The Civil War and Reconstruction* (New York: McGraw-Hill, 1982, 1992), 111.

24. William Lee Miller, *Lincoln's Virtues: An Ethical Biography* (New York: Alfred A. Knopf, 2002), 358.

25. Harry V. Jaffa, *Crisis of the House Divided: An Interpretation of the Lincoln-Douglas Debates* (Chicago: The University of Chicago Press, 1959), 383.

26. The "peripheral" status of the abolitionists in no way diminishes their vital catalytic role in the anti-slavery movement. As theologian Reinhold Niebuhr once observed, "Through the whole course of history mankind has . . . reserved its highest admiration for those heroes who resisted evil at the risk or price of fortune and without too much hope of success. Sometimes their very indifference to the issue of success or failure provided the stamina which made success possible." Niebuhr went on to analyze the "paradoxical relation between the possible and the impossible in history." See Reinhold Niebuhr, *The Irony of American History* (New York: Charles Scribner's Sons, 1952), 144–45, passim.

27. For a detailed analysis of the politics behind the 1854 senatorial nomination struggle in Illinois, see Don E. Fehrenbacher, *Prelude to Greatness: Lincoln in the 1850's* (Stanford, Calif.: Stanford University Press, 1962), 37–39.

28. Walker and his government were overthrown in 1857. Three years later, the "grey-eyed man of destiny" met his death—by firing squad—in Honduras.

29. Abraham Lincoln to George Robertson, August 15, 1855, in *Collected Works*, II, 318.

30. Abraham Lincoln to Joshua F. Speed, August 24, 1855, in *Collected Works*, II, 320–22.

31. For a convincing summation of the evidence, see James M. McPherson, *Ordeal by Fire*, 96.

32. Abraham Lincoln, "Fragment on Sectionalism," ca. July 23, 1856, in *Collected Works*, II, 352.

33. Abraham Lincoln, "Speech at Galena, Illinois," July 23, 1856, in *Collected Works*, II, 355.

34. For an excellent and detailed account of the Dred Scott case, see Kenneth M. Stampp, *America in 1857: A Nation on the Brink* (New York: Oxford University Press, 1990), chapt. 4. See also Don E. Fehrenbacher, *The Dred Scott Case: Its Significance in American Law and Politics* (New York: Oxford University Press, 1978).

35. Calhoun expounded this position in a series of resolutions introduced in the Senate in 1847. See James M. McPherson, *Ordeal by Fire*, 64, 104.

36. See Eric Foner, *Free Soil, Free Labor, Free Men: The Ideology of the Republican Party Before the Civil War* (New York: Oxford University Press, 1970), chapt. 3.

37. Ibid., 91–92.

38. Ibid., 96.

39. Abraham Lincoln, "Speech at Springfield, Illinois," June 26, 1857, *Collected Works*, II, 404.

40. Ibid., 404.

41. Ibid., 405.

42. Ibid., 408.

43. Ibid., 407.

44. Ibid., 405–6. See Garry Wills, *Lincoln at Gettysburg: The Words That Remade America* (New York: Simon & Schuster, 1992), 108–10, for an exposition regarding the possible antecedents of this vision in the transcendentalism of Theodore Parker. Parker, in turn, was probably indebted to the international influence of Hegel, whose *Philosophy of History* expounded the doctrine that Absolute Spirit puts forth, as an embryonic "notion," the "idea" of freedom, which develops itself through progressive stages of history. For further development of the Parker-Lincoln connection, see Carl F. Wieck, *Lincoln's Quest for Equality: The Road to Gettysburg* (DeKalb, Ill.: Northern Illinois University Press, 2002).

45. See Alexander Keyssar, *The Right to Vote: The Contested History of Democracy in the United States* (New York: Basic Books, 2000), 142.

46. See Lerone Bennett, Jr., *Forced Into Glory: Abraham Lincoln's White Dream* (Chicago: Johnson Publishing Co., 2000) for a simplistic treatment of the issue based upon erratic skimming of the evidence. For an indirect rebuttal of Bennett, see William Lee Miller, *Lincoln's Virtues*, 353–63.

47. Stephen A. Douglas, "Senator Douglas's Reply," in "Sixth Debate with Stephen A. Douglas at Quincy, Illinois, October 13, 1858," in *Collected Works*, III, 261.

48. Abraham Lincoln, "Fragment on Slavery," ca. July 1, 1854, in *Collected Works*, II, 222–23.

49. Abraham Lincoln, "Fragment on Pro-Slavery Theology," ca. October 1, 1858, in *Collected Works*, III, 204.

50. John Nicolay to John McMahon, August 6, 1864, in *Collected Works*, VII, 483.

51. Frederick Douglass, "Oration by Frederick Douglass, Delivered on the Occasion of the Unveiling of the Freedmen's Monument, in Memory of Abraham Lincoln," in Lincoln Park, Washington, D.C., April 14, 1876," in Frederick Douglass, *Life and Times of Frederick Douglass, written by himself* (Hartford, Conn.: Park Publishing Co., 1881, facsimile edition, Secaucus, N.J.: Citadel Press, 1983), 921.

52. Frederick Douglass, "Draft of Speech," June 1, 1865, Frederick Douglass Papers, Library of Congress.

53. Ibid., 351, 365.

54. Ibid., 373.

55. David Grimsted, letter to the author, January 31, 2002.

56. Lincoln was hardly the first Free-Soiler to perceive the danger, as others have pointed out. As early as March 10, 1857, the Bloomington, Illinois *Pantagraph* reacted to the Dred Scott decision in the following manner: "One little step only remains, to decide all *State* prohibitions of slavery to be void." (See Fehrenbacher, *Prelude to Greatness* 80, 92–93). On November 17, 1857, the *Washington Union* (a pro-slavery Democratic newspaper) ran an editorial condemning as unconstitutional every state law that deprived slave owners of their right to take their slaves with them anywhere in the Union. On March 22, 1858, Stephen Douglas denounced this editorial. At some point Lincoln found out about the matter, for he used it in the Lincoln-Douglas debates to show that Douglas in reality acknowledged the danger that slavery could spread into the North. In so doing, Lincoln modified his charges in the House Divided Speech; he acknowledged that Douglas was perhaps nothing more than a *dupe* of the conspirators Pierce, Buchanan, and Taney.

57. Abraham Lincoln, "Fragment of a Speech," ca. May 18, 1858, *Collected Works*, II, 453.

58. Harry V. Jaffa, *Crisis of the House Divided*, 395. Jaffa continues:

> Even if it were true that the productivity of a system based on free labor is greater than one based on slave labor, it does not follow that it is more *profitable to the men who run it*. A large portion of a smaller sum may still be more than a small portion of a larger one. All we know of the fierce struggles, the long uphill climb, of free labor in the grip of the industrial revolution that followed the Civil War suggests that it never could have succeeded, as it has, if in addition to all the other handicaps the incubus of slavery could have been placed in the scales against it. If the great corporations, the "robber barons" who came to dominate the state legislatures in the postbellum period, had wanted to import slaves as strikebreakers, *then* it would not have required even another Dred Scott decision to spread slavery to the free states.

59. The nomination of a candidate for the United States Senate by a state political convention was audacious and unprecedented. For an illuminating discussion of the politics surrounding the Springfield convention, see Fehrenbacher, *Prelude to Greatness*, chapt. 3.

60. Ibid., 448–49.

61. Abraham Lincoln, "'A House Divided,' Speech at Springfield, Illinois," June 16, 1858, *Collected Works*, II, 461.

62. Ibid., 464–65.

63. Ibid., 467.

64. Ibid., 466.

65. Ibid., 466–67.

66. Ibid., 465–66.

67. Ibid., 468.

68. Abraham Lincoln, "Fragment on the Struggle Against Slavery," ca. July 1858, in *Collected Works*, 482.

69. Abraham Lincoln, "Speech at Chicago, Illinois," July 10, 1858, in *Collected Works*, 489.

70. Ibid., 491.
71. Ibid.
72. Ibid., 492.
73. Ibid., 495.
74. Ibid., 500.
75. Ibid.
76. Ibid., 500–501.
77. Ibid., 501.
78. Abraham Lincoln, "Speech at Springfield, Illinois," July 17, 1858, in *Collected Works*, 519–20.
79. Stephen A. Douglas, "Mr. Douglas's Speech," in "First Debate with Stephen A. Douglas at Ottawa, Illinois," August 21, 1858, in *Collected Works*, III, 9.
80. Ibid., 10.
81. Ibid., 5.
82. Abraham Lincoln, "Mr. Lincoln's Reply," in *Collected Works*, 16.
83. A few years later, Lincoln openly denied that any fight for racial supremacy was truly at stake, while reserving his judgment with regard to the likelihood of such a development in the future. On March 5, 1860, he declared that "the proposition that there is a struggle between the white man and the negro contains a falsehood. There *is* no struggle. *If* there was, I should be for the white man. If two men are adrift at sea on a plank which will bear up but one, the law justifies either in pushing the other off. I never had to struggle to keep a negro from enslaving me, nor did a negro ever have to fight to keep me from enslaving him." "Speech at Hartford, Connecticut," March 5, 1860, *Collected Works*, 10.
84. Ibid., 18–19.
85. Ibid., 23–24.
86. Ibid., 27.
87. Stephen A. Douglas, "Mr. Douglas's Reply," in *Collected Works*, 35.
88. Ibid., 36.
89. Abraham Lincoln, "Mr. Lincoln's Speech," in "Second Debate with Stephen A. Douglas at Freeport, Illinois," August 27, 1858, in *Collected Works*, 39.
90. Ibid., 40.
91. Ibid.
92. Ibid., 40–41.
93. Ibid., 41–42.
94. Ibid., 43.
95. Stephen A. Douglas, "Mr. Douglas's Speech," August 27, 1858, in *Collected Works*, 51–52. For a very long time, historians regarded this response to Lincoln's question as the "Freeport Doctrine" of Douglas. They argued that Lincoln had extracted this answer from Douglas in a clever bid to drive a wedge between Douglas and his Southern supporters. But as Douglas himself pointed out, he had said the same thing many times before, most notably in his reaction to the Dred Scott decision on June 7, 1857. For a good discussion of the issue, see Fehrenbacher, *Prelude to Greatness*, Chapt. 6.
96. Ibid., 53–54.
97. Ibid., 55–56.
98. Stephen A. Douglas, "Mr. Douglas's Speech" in "Third Debate with Stephen A. Douglas at Jonesboro, Illinois," September 15, 1858, in *Collected Works*, 105.
99. Ibid., 112.

100. Ibid., 113.
101. Abraham Lincoln, "Mr. Lincoln's Speech," September 15, 1858, in *Collected Works*, 134–35.
102. Ibid., 130–31.
103. Stephen A. Douglas, "Mr. Douglas's Reply," in *Collected Works*, 140.
104. Stephen A. Douglas, "Senator Douglas's Speech," in "Fourth Debate with Stephen A. Douglas at Charleston, Illinois, September 18, 1858," in *Collected Works*, 176.
105. Abraham Lincoln, "Mr. Lincoln's Rejoinder," September 18, 1858, in *Collected Works*, 179.
106. Abraham Lincoln, "Mr. Lincoln's Speech," September 18, 1858, in *Collected Works*, 146.
107. Stephen A. Douglas, "Senator Douglas's Speech," in *Collected Works*, 171.
108. Stephen A. Douglas, "Mr. Douglas's Speech," in "Fifth Debate with Stephen A. Douglas at Galesburg, Illinois, October 7, 1858," in *Collected Works*, 218–19.
109. Abraham Lincoln, "Mr. Lincoln's Reply," October 7, 1858, in *Collected Works*, 225.
110. Ibid., 230–31.
111. Ibid., 233.
112. Ibid.
113. "Senator Douglas's Reply," in "Sixth Debate with Stephen A. Douglas at Quincy, Illinois, October 13, 1858," in *Collected Works*, 265.
114. Ibid., 267.
115. Ibid., 274.
116. "Mr. Lincoln's Rejoinder," October 13, 1858, in *Collected Works*, 276.
117. Ibid., 278.
118. "Mr. Lincoln's Reply," in "Seventh and Last Debate with Stephen A. Douglas at Alton, Illinois, October 15, 1858," in *Collected Works*, 304.
119. Abraham Lincoln to Norman B. Judd, October 20, 1858, in *Collected Works*, 329–30.
120. James M. McPherson, *Ordeal by Fire*, 111.
121. Ibid., 111–12.
122. Abraham Lincoln to Anson G. Henry, November 19, 1858, in *Collected Works*, 339.
123. Abraham Lincoln to Anson S. Miller, November 19, 1858, in *Collected Works*, 340.
124. Abraham Lincoln to Charles H. Ray, November 20, 1858, in *Collected Works*, 342.

CHAPTER THREE

1. James M. McPherson, *Ordeal by Fire: The Civil War and Reconstruction* (New York: McGraw-Hill, 1982, 1992), 112.
2. Ibid., 113.
3. Don E. Fehrenbacher, *Prelude to Greatness: Lincoln in the 1850's* (Stanford, Calif.: Stanford University Press, 1962), 143.
4. Ibid., 17–18.

5. Abraham Lincoln to Lyman Trumbull, December 11, 1858, in *Collected Works of Abraham Lincoln*, ed. Roy P. Basler (New Brunswick, N.J.: Rutgers University Press, 1953), III, 345.

6. Abraham Lincoln, "Speech at Chicago, Illinois," March 1, 1859, in *Collected Works*, III, 367.

7. Abraham Lincoln, to Henry L. Pierce and Others, April 6, 1859, in *Collected Works*, III, 375–76.

8. Abraham Lincoln, to Samuel Galloway, July 28, 1859, in *Collected Works*, III, 394–95.

9. Abraham Lincoln, to Schuyler Colfax, July 6, 1859, in *Collected Works*, III, 390–91.

10. Abraham Lincoln to Thomas Corwin, October 9, 1859. The discovery and authentication of this long-lost letter from Lincoln was reported by Harold Holzer in the February/March 2005 issue of *American Heritage*. The letter was purchased from the Corwin heirs in 2004 by the Abraham Lincoln Book Shop in Chicago.

11. Fehrenbacher, *Prelude to Greatness*, 144.

12. Abraham Lincoln, "Notes for Speeches at Columbus and Cincinnati, Ohio," September 16, 17, 1859, *Collected Works*, III, 431–32.

13. Ibid., 434.

14. Ibid., 433.

15. Ibid., 434.

16. Ibid., 435.

17. Abraham Lincoln, "Speech at Columbus, Ohio," September 16, 1859, in *Collected Works*, 404.

18. Ibid., 404–405.

19. The complete text of Douglas's article may be found in *In the Name of the People: Speeches and Writings of Lincoln and Douglas in the Ohio Campaign of 1859*, ed. Harry V. Jaffa and Robert W. Johannsen (Columbus: Ohio State University Press, 1959), 58–125.

20. Abraham Lincoln, "Speech at Columbus, Ohio," September 16, 1859, *Collected Works*, 405.

21. Ibid., 414–15.

22. Ibid., 417.

23. Ibid., 417.

24. Ibid., 418.

25. Ibid., 418–19.

26. Ibid., 423.

27. Ibid., 423–24.

28. Ibid., 424.

29. Abraham Lincoln, "Speech at Cincinnati, Ohio," September 17, 1859, *Collected Works*, 440.

30. Ibid., 441.

31. Ibid., 442.

32. Ibid.

33. Ibid., 453.

34. Ibid.

35. Ibid., 453–54.

36. Abraham Lincoln, "Address before the Wisconsin State Agricultural Society, Milwaukee, Wisconsin," September 30, 1859, *Collected Works*, 479.
37. Abraham Lincoln, "Speech at Leavenworth, Kansas," December 3, 1859, *Collected Works*, 502.
38. Ibid, 502.
39. Harold Holzer, *Lincoln at Cooper Union*, 5.
40. Abraham Lincoln, "Address at Cooper Institute, New York City," February 27, 1860, *Collected Works*, 527.
41. Ibid., 527.
42. Ibid., 533–34.
43. Ibid., 536–37.
44. Ibid., 538.
45. Ibid., 543.
46. Ibid., 546–47.
47. Ibid., 547–48.
48. Ibid., 549–50.
49. Abraham Lincoln, "Speech at New Haven, Connecticut," March 6, 1860, *Collected Works*, IV, 18.
50. Quoted in Benjamin P. Thomas, *Abraham Lincoln* (New York: Alfred A. Knopf, 1952), 218.
51. Abraham Lincoln to Samuel Galloway, March 24, 1860, *Collected Works*, op. cit., IV, 34.
52. Abraham Lincoln to Lyman Trumbull, April 29, 1860, *Collected Works*, IV, 45.
53. Don E. Fehrenbacher, *Prelude to Greatness*, 154.
54. Ibid., 157–58.
55. Nathan M. Knapp to Abraham Lincoln, quoted in Thomas, *Abraham Lincoln*, 210.
56. Fehrenbacher, *Prelude to Greatness*, 159.
57. Eric Foner, *Free Soil, Free Labor, Free Men: The Ideology of the Republican Party Before the Civil War* (New York: Oxford University Press, 1970), 215–16.
58. Abraham Lincoln to John B. Fry, August 15, 1860, in *Collected Works*, IV, 95.
59. *Illinois State Journal*, August 9, 1860, quoted in *Collected Works*, IV, 91–92, n. 1.
60. South Carolina's "Declaration of the Causes of Secession," in *The Causes of the Civil War*, ed. Kenneth M. Stampp (New York: Simon & Schuster/Touchstone, 1974), 44–45.
61. Abraham Lincoln to William Kellogg, December 11, 1860, *Collected Works*, IV, 150.
62. Abraham Lincoln to Elihu B. Washburne, December 13, 1860, in *Collected Works*, IV, 151.
63. Abraham Lincoln to Lyman Trumbull, December 17, 1860, in *Collected Works*, IV, 153.
64. Abraham Lincoln to Duff Green, December 28, 1860, in *Collected Works*, IV, 162.
65. Ibid., 162.
66. Ibid., 163.
67. Abraham Lincoln to John A. Gilmer, December 15, 1860, in *Collected Works*, IV, 151–152.
68. Abraham Lincoln to Thurlow Weed, December 17, 1860, in *Collected Works*, IV, 154.

69. Abraham Lincoln to Elihu B. Washburne, December 21, 1860, in *Collected Works*, IV, 159.

70. Abraham Lincoln to William H. Seward, February 1, 1861, in *Collected Works*, IV, 183.

71. Abraham Lincoln to James T. Hale, January 11, 1861, in *Collected Works*, IV, 172.

72. Abraham Lincoln, "Address Before the Young Men's Lyceum of Springfield, Illinois," January 27, 1838, *Collected Works*, I, 109.

73. Ibid., 113.

74. Kenneth M. Stampp, "The Concept of a Perpetual Union," *Journal of American History*, Vol. 65, no. 1, June 1978, 7-8. For a different though problematical interpretation, see Daniel Farber, *Lincoln's Constitution* (Chicago: University of Chicago Press, 2003), 84, 196.

75. Richard N. Current, *Lincoln and the First Shot* (New York: Harper & Row, 1963), Waveland Press edition, 1990, 203.

76. Abraham Lincoln, "Speech from the Balcony of the Bates House at Indianapolis, Indiana," February 11, 1861, *Collected Works*, IV, 195-96.

77. Abraham Lincoln, "Speech at Cincinnati, Ohio," February 12, 1861, in *Collected Works*, IV, 199.

78. Abraham Lincoln, "Reply to Mayor Fernando Wood, at New York City," February 20, 1861, in *Collected Works*, IV, 233.

79. Abraham Lincoln, "Address to the New Jersey General Assembly at Trenton, New Jersey," February 21, 1861, in *Collected Works*, IV, 237.

80. Abraham Lincoln, "Speech in Independence Hall, Philadelphia, Pennsylvania," February 22, 1861, in *Collected Works*, IV, 241.

81. Abraham Lincoln, "Reply to Mayor Alexander Henry at Philadelphia, Pennsylvania," February 21, 1861, in *Collected Works*, IV, 239.

82. Abraham Lincoln, "Speech in Independence Hall, Philadelphia, Pennsylvania," February 22, 1861, in *Collected Works*, IV, 240.

83. See Stephen B. Oates, *With Malice Toward None: The Life of Abraham Lincoln* (New York: Harper & Row, 1977), 195-96.

84. See Benjamin P. Thomas, *Abraham Lincoln*, 242-44.

85. See Richard N. Current, *Lincoln and the First Shot*, 33-35.

86. *Southern Advocate*, December 12, 1860, cited in Stephen B. Oates, *With Malice Toward None*, 188. See also James M. McPherson, *Battle Cry of Freedom: The Civil War Era* (New York: Oxford University Press, 1988), 228-29, and Ollinger Crenshaw, *The Slave States in the Presidential Election of 1860* (Baltimore: Johns Hopkins University Press, 1945).

87. *Charleston Mercury*, October 11, 1860, cited in *The Causes of the Civil War*, ed. Kenneth M. Stampp, 114-15.

88. Abraham Lincoln, "First Inaugural Address—Final Text," March 4, 1861, *Collected Works*, IV, 262-63.

89. Ibid., 264-65.

90. Ibid., 265.

91. Ibid., 267-68.

92. Ibid., 268.

93. Ibid., 269.

94. Ibid., 269-70.

95. Ibid., 271.

96. Ibid.

97. Ibid., 266.

98. See Richard N. Current, *Lincoln and the First Shot*, 72–73.

99. James M. McPherson, *Battle Cry of Freedom*, 271–72.

100. Abraham Lincoln to William H. Seward, April 1, 1861, in *Collected Works*, IV, 316–17.

101. See Richard N. Current, *Lincoln and the First Shot*, 120–21.

102. Ibid., 148.

103. Ibid., 151.

104. Abraham Lincoln, "Proclamation Calling Militia and Convening Congress," April 15, 1861, in *Collected Works*, IV, 331–32.

105. Alexander Stephens, Speech at Savannah, March 21, 1861, in *The Causes of the Civil War*, ed. Kenneth M. Stampp, 116. Jefferson Davis said much the same thing in a speech to the Confederate Congress on April 29, 1861, in *The Causes of the Civil War*, 117–18.

106. *Charleston Mercury*, February 28, 1860, in *The Causes of the Civil War*, 113.

107. Ibid.

108. Eugene D. Genovese, *The Political Economy of Slavery* (New York: Random House, 1965), 258. The penultimate section of Genovese's book, "The Origins of Slavery Expansionism," is a capable refutation of a famous but preposterous 1929 article, "The Natural Limits of Slavery Expansion," by Charles W. Ramsdell.

109. Cited in Richard N. Current, *Lincoln and the First Shot*, 131.

110. Ibid., 160–61.

111. Abraham Lincoln to Andrew G. Curtin, April 8, 1861, in *Collected Works*, IV, 324.

112. Richard N. Current, *Lincoln and the First Shot*, 165.

113. Abraham Lincoln to Winfield Scott, April 25, 1861, in *Collected Works*, IV, 344. Historian Mark E. Neely, Jr., has addressed the apparent incongruity of this letter's closing priorities—specifically, the letter's seeming implication that the bombardment of cities was less momentous than suspension of habeas corpus—as a matter of hasty editing. See Mark E. Neely, Jr., *The Fate of Liberty: Abraham Lincoln and Civil Liberties* (New York and Oxford: Oxford University Press, 1991), 7.

114. Abraham Lincoln to Gideon Welles, April 29, 1861, in *Collected Works*, 348.

115. James M. McPherson, "Tried by War: Lincoln as Self-Taught Strategist," *Civil War Times Illustrated*, November/December 1995, repr. in *Major Problems in the Civil War and Reconstruction*, ed. Michael Perman (New York: Houghton Mifflin Company, 1998), 177.

116. T. Harry Williams, *Lincoln and His Generals* (New York: Alfred A. Knopf, 1952), Vintage edition, 7–8.

117. Ibid., 18.

CHAPTER FOUR

1. Abraham Lincoln, "Message to Congress in Special Session," July 4, 1861, in *Collected Works of Abraham Lincoln*, ed. Roy P. Basler (New Brunswick, N.J.: Rutgers University Press, 1953), IV, 434–35.

2. Ibid., 432–33.

3. Ibid., 427.

4. Ibid., 437.
5. Ibid., 438.
6. Ibid., 439.
7. Ibid., 440.
8. Ibid., 440–41.
9. Ibid., 427.
10. Ibid., 457–58.
11. *Congressional Globe*, 37th Congress, First Session, 222–23, 258–62.
12. Abraham Lincoln to John C. Frémont, September 2, 1861, in *Collected Works*, IV, 506.
13. Abraham Lincoln to John C. Frémont, September 11, 1861, in *Collected Works*, IV, 518.
14. Abraham Lincoln to Orville H. Browning, September 22, 1861, in *Collected Works*, IV, 531–32.
15. George B. McClellan to Samuel L. M. Barlow, November 1, 1861, S. L. M. Barlow Papers, Henry E. Huntington Library.
16. George B. McClellan to Ellen Marcy McClellan, cited in George B. McClellan, *McClellan's Own Story* (New York: Webster & Company, 1887), 82–83.
17. See James M. McPherson, *Ordeal by Fire: The Civil War and Reconstruction* (New York: McGraw-Hill, 1982, 1992), 164. As to McClellan's character flaws, see Stephen W. Sears, *George B. McClellan: The Young Napoleon* (New York: Ticknor & Fields, 1988), xii, 103, 104, 133, 134, 201, passim, in which the biographer, though writing dispassionately, calls McClellan "inarguably the worst" commander of the Army of the Potomac and a man warped by arrogance and self-deception. See also Kenneth P. Williams, *Lincoln Finds a General: A Military Study of the Civil War*, 5 volumes (New York: Macmillan, 1949–1959) and T. Harry Williams, *McClellan, Sherman, and Grant* (New Brunswick, N.J.: Rutgers University Press, 1962).
18. See Abraham Lincoln, "Memorandum for a Plan of Campaign," ca. October 1, 1861, in *Collected Works*, IV, 544–45.
19. See T. Harry Williams, *Lincoln and His Generals* (New York: Alfred A. Knopf, 1952), Vintage edition, 42–43.
20. Allen C. Guelzo, *Lincoln's Emancipation Proclamation: The End of Slavery in America* (New York: Simon & Schuster, 2004) 5.
21. Abraham Lincoln, "Drafts of a Bill for Compensated Emancipation in Delaware," ca. November 26, 1861, in *Collected Works*, V, 29–30.
22. Abraham Lincoln, "Annual Message to Congress," December 3, 1861, in *Collected Works*, V, 51.
23. Ibid., 52.
24. Ibid., 51.
25. Ibid., 48–49.
26. Ibid., 48.
27. Ibid.
28. For a good discussion of divided black opinions on the issue of colonization in the decade preceding the Civil War, see Ira Berlin, *Slaves Without Masters: The Free Negro in the Antebellum South* (New York: Oxford University Press, 1974), 356–62, passim.
29. *Congressional Globe*, June 2, 1862, 37th Congress, Third Session, 2504.

30. Abraham Lincoln, "Annual Message to Congress," December 3, 1861, in *Collected Works*, V, 53.
31. T. Harry Williams, *Lincoln and His Generals*, 53.
32. Abraham Lincoln to Henry W. Halleck and Don C. Buell, December 31, 1861, *Collected Works*, V, 84.
33. Abraham Lincoln to Don C. Buell, January 7, 1862, in *Collected Works*, V, 91.
34. Abraham Lincoln to Simon Cameron, January 10, 1862, in *Collected Works*, V, 95.
35. Abraham Lincoln to Don C. Buell, January 13, 1862, in *Collected Works*, V, 98.
36. Moncure Daniel Conway, *Autobiography, Memories and Experiences* (New York: Houghton Mifflin Company, 1904), I, 345–46. The plausibility of Conway's story is increased by another account of a meeting with Lincoln when the very same "drop o' the creeter" joke—and in the very same connection vis-à-vis emancipation—was used only two months later. In her 1981 book *Lincoln and Black Freedom*, historian LaWanda Cox referred to "a letter of Wendell Phillips which has only recently come to light." It seems that in March, 1862 Lincoln met with Phillips at the White House. The president urged the abolitionist to give him more credit for his anti-slavery initiatives. He told a story to illustrate his point by way of a metaphor. As Cox has paraphrased the letter, "the story was of an Irishman in legally dry Maine who asked for a glass of soda with a 'drop of the crathur [put] into it *unbeknown to myself.*' Lincoln made his point explicit: he 'meant it [slavery] to die.'" See LaWanda Cox, *Lincoln and Black Freedom: A Study in Presidential Leadership* (Columbia: University of South Carolina Press, 1981), 8.
37. Charles Sumner, "Letter to Governor Andrew, of Massachusetts, December 27, 1861," *The Works of Charles Sumner* (Boston: Lee and Shepard, 1870–1873), VI, 152.
38. Abraham Lincoln, "President's General War Order No. 1," January 27, 1862, in *Collected Works*, V, 111–12.
39. Abraham Lincoln to George B. McClellan, February 3, 1862, in *Collected Works*, V, 118–19.
40. For a lengthy documentary account of the written give-and-take between Lincoln and McClellan from January 31 to ca. February 3, 1862, see *Collected Works*, V, 119–25, n. 1.
41. Abraham Lincoln, "Message to Congress," March 6, 1862, in *Collected Works*, V, 144–46.
42. Abraham Lincoln to Henry J. Raymond, March 9, 1862, in *Collected Works*, V, 152–53.
43. Abraham Lincoln, "President's General War Order No. 3," March 8, 1862, in *Collected Works*, V, 151.
44. Abraham Lincoln to George B. McClellan, April 6, 1862, in *Collected Works*, V, 182.
45. Abraham Lincoln to George B. McClellan, April 9, 1862, in *Collected Works*, V, 184–85.
46. Abraham Lincoln to George B. McClellan, May 1, 1862, in *Collected Works*, V, 203.
47. Abraham Lincoln to Irvin McDowell, May 17, 1862, in *Collected Works*, V, 219.
48. Abraham Lincoln to John C. Frémont, May 24, 1862, in *Collected Works*, V, 231.
49. Abraham Lincoln to George B. McClellan, May 25, 1862, in *Collected Works*, V, 235–36.

50. Abraham Lincoln to John C. Frémont, May 30, 1862, in *Collected Works*, V, 250.

51. George B. McClellan to Abraham Lincoln, June 25, 1862, cited in McClellan, *McClellan's Own Story*, 392–93.

52. Abraham Lincoln, "Order Constituting the Army of Virginia," June 26, 1862, in *Collected Works*, V, 287.

53. *War of the Rebellion: A Compilation of the Official Records of the Union and Confederate Armies* (Washington, D.C.: Government Printing Office, 1880–1901), Series 1, Volume 11, Part 1, 61. The last two sentences of this dispatch were deleted by a telegraph officer.

54. Abraham Lincoln to William H. Seward, June 28, 1862, in *Collected Works*, V, 291–92.

55. Abraham Lincoln, "Proclamation Revoking General Hunter's Order of Military Emancipation of May 9, 1862," May 19, 1862, in *Collected Works*, V, 222–23.

56. See Douglas L. Wilson, *Honor's Voice: The Transformation of Abraham Lincoln* (New York: Alfred A. Knopf, 1998), 1999 Vintage edition, 76–85, 186–87, 334–35.

57. Abraham Lincoln, "Remarks to a Delegation of Progressive Friends," June 20, 1862, *Collected Works*, V, 278–79. For studies of Lincoln's evolving sense of spirituality, see: William E. Barton, *The Soul of Abraham Lincoln* (New York: George H. Doran Co., 1920); William J. Wolf, *The Almost Chosen People: A Study of the Religion of Abraham Lincoln* (Garden City: Doubleday & Co., 1959); Elton Trueblood, *Abraham Lincoln: Theologian of American Anguish* (New York: Harper & Row, 1973); Allen C. Guelzo, *Abraham Lincoln: Redeemer President* (Grand Rapids, Mich.: William B. Eerdmans Publishing Company, 1999); Lucas Morel, *Lincoln's Sacred Effort: Defining Religion's Role in American Self-Government* (New York, Oxford: Lexington Books, 2000); and Joseph R. Fornieri, *Abraham Lincoln's Political Faith* (DeKalb: Northern Illinois University Press, 2003).

58. Abraham Lincoln to William H. Seward, June 28, 1862, in *Collected Works*, V, 292.

59. See James M. McPherson, "The Ballot and Land for the Freedmen, 1861–1865," in *Reconstruction: An Anthology of Revisionist Writings*, ed. Kenneth Stampp and Leon F. Litwack (Baton Rouge: Louisiana State University Press, 1969), 133. See also David Herbert Donald, *Charles Sumner and the Rights of Man* (New York: Alfred A. Knopf, 1970), 54–57.

60. Charles Sumner, "'Stand by the Administration,' Letter to _____, June 5, 1862," in *The Works of Charles Sumner*, VII, 116–18.

61. Charles Sumner to John Bright, August 5, 1862, Bright MSS, British Museum, London, cited in David Herbert Donald, *Charles Sumner and the Rights of Man*, 60.

62. Abraham Lincoln, "Appeal to Border State Representatives to Favor Compensated Emancipation," July 12, 1862, in *Collected Works*, V, 317–19.

63. Gideon Welles, *Diary of Gideon Welles, Secretary of the Navy Under Lincoln and Johnson* (New York: Houghton Mifflin Company, 1911), I, 70–71. See also Gideon Welles, "History of Emancipation," *Galaxy* (December, 1872), 842–43.

64. Abraham Lincoln, "To the Senate and House of Representatives," July 17, 1862, in *Collected Works*, V, 329–31.

65. Abraham Lincoln, "Emancipation Proclamation—First Draft," July 22, 1862, in *Collected Works*, V, 336–37.

66. See: V. Jacque Voegeli, *Free But Not Equal: The Midwest and the Negro During the Civil War* (Chicago: University of Chicago Press, 1967), 6; Forrest G. Wood, *Black Scare: The Racist Response to Emancipation and Reconstruction* (Berkeley: University of California Press, 1968), 35; and Frank L. Klement, *The Copperheads in the Middle West* (Chicago: University of Chicago Press, 1960), 14.

67. Abraham Lincoln, "Address on Colonization to a Deputation of Negroes," August 14, 1862, *Collected Works*, V, 370–75.

68. Abraham Lincoln to Cuthbert Bullitt, July 28, 1862, in *Collected Works*, 345–46.

69. Abraham Lincoln to August Belmont, July 31, 1862, in *Collected Works*, 350.

70. Abraham Lincoln to Horace Greeley, August 22, 1862, in *Collected Works*, 388–89.

71. Tyler Dennett, ed., *Lincoln and the Civil War in the Diaries and Letters of John Hay* (New York: Dodd, Mead, 1939), 46.

72. Ibid., 45.

73. Ibid., 46.

74. Ibid., 47.

75. T. Harry Williams, *Lincoln and His Generals*, 161.

76. Ibid., 164.

77. For analysis of the international stakes of the Antietam campaign, see Howard Jones, *Union in Peril: The Crisis over British Intervention in the Civil War* (Chapel Hill: University of North Carolina Press, 1992) and James M. McPherson, *Crossroads of Freedom: Antietam* (New York: Oxford University Press, 2002), 93–94.

78. Robert E. Lee to Jefferson Davis, September 8, 1862, in eds. Clifford Dowdey and Louis H. Manarin, *The Wartime Papers of R.E. Lee* (New York: Bramhall House, 1961), 301.

79. Abraham Lincoln, "Meditation on the Divine Will," ca. September 2, 1862, in *Collected Works*, V, 403–404.

80. Welles, *Diary of Gideon Welles*, I, 143.

81. Abraham Lincoln, "Reply to Emancipation Memorial Presented by Chicago Christians of All Denominations," September 13, 1862, in *Collected Works*, V, 420, 421, 425.

82. T. Harry Williams, *Lincoln and His Generals*, 168.

83. Abraham Lincoln, "Preliminary Emancipation Proclamation," September 22, 1862, in *Collected Works*, V, 433–36.

84. Tyler Dennett, ed., *Lincoln and the Civil War in the Diaries and Letters of John Hay*, 50.

85. Abraham Lincoln, "Proclamation Suspending the Writ of Habeas Corpus," September 24, 1862, in *Collected Works*, V, 436–37.

86. See James M. McPherson, *Crossroads of Freedom*, 77, 114.

87. Abraham Lincoln to Carl Schurz, November 24, 1862, in *Collected Works*, V, 509.

88. Abraham Lincoln to George B. McClellan, October 13, 1862, 460–61.

89. Abraham Lincoln to Carl Schurz, November 10, 1862, in *Collected Works*, V, 493–94.

90. Abraham Lincoln, "Remarks to Kentucky Unionists," November 21, 1862, in *Collected Works*, V, 503.

91. Abraham Lincoln to Henry Halleck, November 27, 1862, in *Collected Works*, V, 514–15.

92. Abraham Lincoln, "Annual Message to Congress," December 1, 1862, in *Collected Works*, V, 530.

93. Ibid., 532.

94. Ibid., 535.

95. Ibid., 537.

96. Frederick Douglass, *Life and Times of Frederick Douglass, written by himself* (Hartford, Conn.: Park Publishing Co., 1881, facsimile edition, Secaucus, N.J.: Citadel Press, 1983), 359–60.

CHAPTER FIVE

1. Abraham Lincoln, "Emancipation Proclamation," January 1, 1863, in *Collected Works of Abraham Lincoln*, ed. Roy P. Basler (New Brunswick, N.J.: Rutgers University Press, 1953), VI, 29–30.

2. Richard Hofstadter, *The American Political Tradition and the Men Who Made It* (New York: Alfred A. Knopf, 1948), 132. Hofstadter's essay on Lincoln is in many ways the worst of all the cameo portraits in this clever but uneven book. His quip about the Emancipation Proclamation was drawn, in part, from a sardonic remark that was attributed to William Seward. See Allen C. Guelzo, *Lincoln's Emancipation Proclamation: The End of Slavery in America* (New York: Simon & Schuster, 2004), 221–22.

3. For an account of the Chiriqui colonization project, from its origins in October 1861 to its termination at the close of 1862, see *Collected Works*, V, 370–371, n. 1.

4. Abraham Lincoln to Andrew Johnson, March 26, 1863, in *Collected Works*, VI, 149–50.

5. See James M. McPherson, "The Ballot and Land for the Freedmen, 1861–1865," in *Reconstruction: An Anthology of Revisionist Writings*, ed. Stampp and Litwack (Baton Rouge: Louisiana State University Press, 1969), 146–47.

6. LaWanda Cox, *Lincoln and Black Freedom: A Study in Presidential Leadership* (Columbia: University of South Carolina Press, 1981), 1994 ed., 30–31.

7. For a full treatment of this issue, see Mark Neely, Jr., *The Fate of Liberty: Abraham Lincoln and Civil Liberties* (New York: Oxford University Press, 1991).

8. Abraham Lincoln, "Memorandum on Joseph Hooker's Plan of Campaign Against Richmond," ca. April 6–10, 1863, in *Collected Works*, VI, 164–65.

9. Abraham Lincoln to Isaac N. Arnold, May 26, 1863, in *Collected Works*, VI, 230.

10. Abraham Lincoln to Joseph Hooker, June 10, 1863, in *Collected Works*, VI, 257.

11. Abraham Lincoln to Joseph Hooker, June 14, 1863, in *Collected Works*, VI, 273.

12. Abraham Lincoln, "Announcement of News From Gettysburg," July 4, 1863, in *Collected Works*, VI, 314.

13. Abraham Lincoln to Henry Halleck, July 6, 1863, in *Collected Works*, VI, 318.

14. Tyler Dennett, ed., *Lincoln and the Civil War in the Diaries and Letters of John Hay* (New York: Dodd, Mead, 1939), 67.

15. Ibid., 67. "Tycoon," a word that was a brand-new addition to American slang, was an anglicized version of a Japanese term that referred to the Shogun.

16. Abraham Lincoln to George G. Meade, July 14, 1863, in *Collected Works*, VI, 318.

17. James M. McPherson, *Ordeal by Fire: The Civil War and Reconstruction* (New York: McGraw-Hill, 1982, 1992), 357–58.

18. Tyler Dennett, ed., *Lincoln and the Civil War in the Diaries and Letters of John Hay*, 76.

19. Abraham Lincoln to James C. Conkling, August 26, 1863, in *Collected Works*, VI, 406–10. Conkling orchestrated the release of this letter to the newspapers. See Lincoln-Conkling correspondence, in *Collected Works*, VI, 430.

20. Abraham Lincoln, "Fragment," ca. August 26, 1863, in *Collected Works*, VI, 410–11.

21. LaWanda Cox, *Lincoln and Black Freedom*, 64.

22. Ibid., 4.

23. Frederick Douglass, *Life and Times of Frederick Douglass* (Hartford, Conn.: Park Publishing Co., 1881, facsimile edition, Secaucus, N.J.: Citadel Press, 1983), 350–53.

24. Abraham Lincoln, "Order of Retaliation," July 30, 1863, in *Collected Works*, VI, 357. Lincoln found it hard to carry out the order. On April 12, 1864, Confederate troops under General Nathan Bedford Forrest murdered several dozen black soldiers who surrendered at Fort Pillow, Tennessee, on the Mississippi River. According to James M. McPherson (*Battle Cry of Freedom: The Civil War Era* [New York: Oxford University Press, 1988], 748, n. 48), the facts in this case are "well established and generally accepted." This Confederate action was more than worthy of Hitler's SS, which machine-gunned a contingent of American troops in the Battle of the Bulge after they had surrendered. On May 17, Lincoln sent a letter to the secretary of war in which he seemed unwilling to pursue retaliation in this particular case; "blood cannot restore blood," he stated, and "government should not act for revenge." (*Collected Works*, VII, 345–46.)

25. Abraham Lincoln, "Instructions to Tax Commissioners in South Carolina," September 16, 1863, in *Collected Works*, VI, 457.

26. Eric Foner, *A Short History of Reconstruction, 1863–1877* (New York: Harper & Row, 1990), 27.

27. Abraham Lincoln to Stephen A. Hurlbut, ca. August 15, 1863, in *Collected Works*, VI, 387.

28. Eric Foner, *Short History of Reconstruction*, 26–27.

29. Abraham Lincoln to Nathaniel P. Banks, August 5, 1863, in *Collected Works*, VI, 365.

30. LaWanda Cox, *Lincoln and Black Freedom*, 15.

31. Ibid, 52–53.

32. Abraham Lincoln to E.E. Malhiot, Bradish Johnson, and Thomas Cottman, June 19, 1863, in *Collected Works*, VI, 288.

33. Abraham Lincoln to Nathaniel Banks, August 5, 1863, in *Collected Works*, VI, 364–65.

34. Abraham Lincoln to Andrew Johnson, September 11, 1863, in *Collected Works*, VI, 440.

35. Eric Foner, *Short History of Reconstruction*, 18–19. For Lincoln's justification of this action to the Governor of Maryland, see Abraham Lincoln to Augustus W. Bradford, November 2, 1863, in *Collected Works*, VI, 556–57.

36. LaWanda Cox, *Lincoln and Black Freedom*, 35.

37. Abraham Lincoln to Henry Halleck, September 15, 1863, in *Collected Works*, VI, 450.

38. Abraham Lincoln to Henry Halleck, September 19, 1863, in *Collected Works*, VI, 466–67.

39. Abraham Lincoln to Henry Halleck, October 16, 1863, in *Collected Works*, VI, 518.

40. Gideon Welles, *Diary of Gideon Welles, Secretary of the Navy Under Lincoln and Johnson* (New York: Houghton Mifflin Company, 1911), I, 438–40.

41. See Douglas L. Wilson, *Honor's Voice: The Transformation of Abraham Lincoln* (New York: Alfred A. Knopf, 1998), 114–26.

42. Abraham Lincoln, "Address Delivered at the Dedication of the Cemetery at Gettysburg," November 19, 1863, "Final Text," in *Collected Works*, VII, 23.

43. Garry Wills, *Lincoln at Gettysburg: The Words That Remade America* (New York: Simon & Schuster, 1992), 38–39.

44. Abraham Lincoln to Nathaniel Banks, November 5, 1863, in *Collected Works*, VII, 1–2.

45. Abraham Lincoln, "Proclamation of Amnesty and Reconstruction," December 8, 1863, in *Collected Works*, VII, 53–56.

46. Abraham Lincoln, "Annual Message to Congress," December 8, 1863, in *Collected Works*, VII, 52.

47. Ibid., 52.

48. Ibid., 49.

49. Ibid., 51.

50. Ibid., 50.

CHAPTER SIX

1. For a book-length analysis of this election, see David E. Long, *The Jewel of Liberty: Abraham Lincoln's Re-Election and the End of Slavery* (Mechanicsburg, Pa.: Stackpole Books, 1994).

2. Abraham Lincoln to Nathaniel Banks, December 24, 1863, in *Collected Works of Abraham Lincoln*, ed. Roy P. Basler (New Brunswick, N.J.: Rutgers University Press, 1953), VII, 90.

3. LaWanda Cox, *Lincoln and Black Freedom: A Study in Presidential Leadership* (Columbia: University of South Carolina Press, 1981), 1994 ed., 70.

4. Eric Foner, *Short History of Reconstruction, 1863–1877* (New York: Harper & Row, 1990), 21.

5. Abraham Lincoln to Michael Hahn, March 13, 1864, in *Collected Works*, VII, 243.

6. LaWanda Cox has argued that Lincoln indirectly endorsed black voting rights as early as August 1863 via orders through the secretary of war. His "permission" for enrollment of blacks as voters in occupied Louisiana "was embodied in the order which Secretary of War Stanton gave at the President's express direction to Governor Shepley August 24, 1863. The relevant portion read: 'you will cause a registration to be made in each parish in the State of Louisiana of *all the loyal citizens of the United States.*'" (LaWanda Cox, *Lincoln and Black Freedom*, 77).

On another matter, historians have long disagreed with regard to the authenticity of a letter that Lincoln supposedly wrote to General James S. Wadsworth ca. January 1864 on the subject of black voting rights that was included in the *Collected Works* edited by Basler et al. For commentary on the issue of this document's authenticity, see Ludwell H. Johnson, "Lincoln and Equal Rights: The Authenticity of the Wadsworth Letter," *Journal of Southern History*

32 (February 1966): 83–87, and Harold M. Hyman, "Lincoln and Equal Rights for Negroes: The Irrelevancy of the 'Wadsworth Letter,'" *Civil War History* 12 (September 1966): 258–66.

7. LaWanda Cox, *Lincoln and Black Freedom*, 36.

8. Abraham Lincoln to Daniel E. Sickles, February 15, 1864, in *Collected Works*, VII, 185.

9. Abraham Lincoln, "Address at Sanitary Fair, Baltimore, Maryland," April 18, 1864, in *Collected Works*, VII, 301–302.

10. Abraham Lincoln to Frederick Steele, January 27, 1864, in *Collected Works*, VII, 155.

11. Abraham Lincoln to John A. J. Creswell, March 7, 1864, in *Collected Works*, VII, 226.

12. James M. McPherson, "The Ballot and Land for the Freedmen, 1861–1865," in *Reconstruction: An Anthology of Revisionist Writings*, ed. Stampp and Litwack (Baton Rouge: Louisiana State University Press, 1969), 143.

13. Ibid., 151–52.

14. See James M. McPherson, *Ordeal by Fire: The Civil War and Reconstruction* (New York: McGraw-Hill, 1982, 1992), 467.

15. Ibid., 141.

16. Abraham Lincoln to Albert G. Hodges, April 4, 1864, in *Collected Works*, VII, 281–82. Another dress rehearsal for the Second Inaugural Address may be found in a letter by Lincoln to a Baptist religious committee. On May 30, 1864, Lincoln wrote the following:

> To read in the Bible, as the word of God himself, that "In the sweat of *thy* face shalt thou eat bread,["] and to preach therefrom that, "In the sweat of *other mans* [sic] faces shalt thou eat bread," to my mind can scarcely be reconciled with honest sincerity. When brought to my final reckoning, may I have to answer for robbing no man of his goods; yet more tolerable even this, than for robbing one of himself, and all that was his. When, a year or two ago, those professedly holy men of the South, met in the semblance of prayer and devotion, and, in the name of Him who said "As ye would all men should do unto you, do ye even so unto them" appealed to the christian world to aid them in doing to a whole race of men, as they would have no man do unto themselves, to my thinking, they contemned and insulted God and His church, far more than did Satan when he tempted the Saviour with the Kingdoms of the earth. . . . But let me forebear, remembering it is also written "Judge not, lest ye be judged."

Abraham Lincoln to George B. Ide, James R. Doolittle, and A. Hubbell, May 30, 1864, in *Collected Works*, VII, 368.

17. Abraham Lincoln, "General Orders No. 98," March 12, 1864, in *Collected Works*, VII, 239.

18. T. Harry Williams, *Lincoln and His Generals* (New York: Alfred A. Knopf, 1952), Vintage edition, 295.

19. Ibid., 296–97.

20. Ibid, 304–306.

21. Tyler Dennett, ed., *Lincoln and the Civil War in the Diaries and Letters of John Hay*, 178.

22. Ibid, 180.

23. Gideon Welles, *Diary of Gideon Welles, Secretary of the Navy Under Lincoln and Johnson* (New York: Houghton Mifflin Company, 1911), II, 44–45.

24. James M. McPherson, *Ordeal by Fire*, 423–24.

25. Ibid, 409.
26. Andrew Johnson, quoted in Robert W. Winston, *Andrew Johnson, Plebeian and Patriot* (New York: Henry Holt, 1928), 83.
27. These excerpts from Johnson's annual message to Congress of December 1867, are quoted by Eric Foner, *Short History of Reconstruction*, 84.
28. LaWanda Cox, *Lincoln and Black Freedom*, 18.
29. Abraham Lincoln to Salmon P. Chase, June 30, 1864, in *Collected Works*, VII, 419.
30. Abraham Lincoln, "Proclamation Concerning Reconstruction," July 8, 1864, in *Collected Works*, VII, 433.
31. Horace Greeley to Abraham Lincoln, July 7, 1864, in *Collected Works*, VII, 435, n. 1.
32. See John Henry Cramer, *Lincoln Under Enemy Fire: The Complete Account of His Experiences During Early's Attack on Washington* (Baton Rouge: Louisiana State University Press, 1948).
33. Abraham Lincoln, "Speech at Great Central Sanitary Fair, Philadelphia, Pennsylvania," June 16, 1864, in *Collected Works*, VII, 394. The latter phrase in the quotation was adapted by Lincoln from the first line of Shakespeare's *Henry VI, Part I*.
34. Gabor S. Boritt, "War Opponent and War President," in *Lincoln the War President: The Gettysburg Lectures*, ed. Gabor S. Boritt (New York: Oxford University Press, 1992), 205, 208.
35. Abraham Lincoln to Ulysses S. Grant, August 17, 1864, in *Collected Works*, VII, 499.
36. Abraham Lincoln to Ulysses S. Grant, August 3, 1864, in *Collected Works*, VII, 476.
37. Abraham Lincoln to Abram Wakeman, July 25, 1864, in *Collected Works*, VII, 461.
38. Abraham Lincoln, "Memorandum on Clement C. Clay," ca. July 25, 1864, in *Collected Works*, VII, 459. Clay was one of the Confederate agents in Niagara Falls.
39. *Columbus Crisis*, August 3, 1864, and *Freeman's Journal*, August 20, 1864, quoted in James M. McPherson, *Ordeal by Fire*, 438, 449. See also Forrest G. Wood, *Black Scare: The Racist Response to Emancipation and Reconstruction* (Berkeley: University of California Press, 1968), 53–79.
40. Henry J. Raymond to Abraham Lincoln, August 22, 1864, in *Collected Works*, VII, 517–18, n. 1.
41. Abraham Lincoln to Henry J. Raymond, August 24, 1864, in *Collected Works*, VII, 517.
42. Abraham Lincoln to Charles D. Robinson, August 17, 1864, in *Collected Works*, VII, 501.
43. Quoted by John G. Nicolay, in *Collected Works*, VII, 518, n.1.
44. "Interview with Alexander W. Randall and Joseph T. Mills," in *Collected Works*, VII, 507.
45. Quoted in James M. McPherson, *Battle Cry of Freedom: The Civil War Era* (New York: Oxford University Press, 1988), 771.
46. Abraham Lincoln, "Memorandum Concerning His Probable Failure of Reelection," August 23, 1864, in *Collected Works*, VII, 514.
47. Frederick Douglass, *Life and Times of Frederick Douglass*, 363–64.

48. John Eaton, *Grant, Lincoln, and the Freedmen* (New York: Longmans, Green & Co., 1907), 167–76.
49. Samuel L.M. Barlow to Manton Marble, August 24, 1864, S.L.M. Barlow Papers, Henry E. Huntington Library, quoted in James M. McPherson, *Battle Cry of Freedom*, 771.
50. *Charleston Mercury*, September 5, 1864, quoted in McPherson, *Battle Cry of Freedom*, 772.
51. Alexander Stephens to Herschel V. Johnson, September 5, 1864, in *Battle Cry of Freedom*, 772.
52. Frederick Douglass, *Life and Times of Frederick Douglass*, 360–61.
53. Harry V. Jaffa, *Crisis of the House Divided*, 408.
54. Donald Kagan, *Pericles of Athens and the Birth of Democracy* (New York: Touchstone/Simon & Schuster, 1991), xiii–xiv.
55. James M. McPherson, *Battle Cry of Freedom*, 858.

CHAPTER SEVEN

1. Abraham Lincoln, "Proclamation of Thanksgiving and Prayer," September 3, 1864, in *Collected Works of Abraham Lincoln*, ed. Roy P. Basler (New Brunswick, N.J.: Rutgers University Press, 1953), VII, 533.
2. Abraham Lincoln to Eliza P. Gurney, September 4, 1864, in *Collected Works*, VII, 535.
3. Abraham Lincoln to Ulysses S. Grant, September 29, 1864, in *Collected Works*, VIII, 29.
4. James M. McPherson, *Ordeal By Fire: The Civil War and Reconstruction* (New York: McGraw-Hill, 1982, 1992), 444–46.
5. Abraham Lincoln, "Proclamation of Thanksgiving," October 20, 1864, in *Collected Works*, VIII, 55.
6. Abraham Lincoln, "Response to a Serenade," November 8, 1864, in *Collected Works*, VIII, 96.
7. Abraham Lincoln, "Response to a Serenade," November 10, 1864, in *Collected Works*, VIII, 100–101.
8. Abraham Lincoln, "Response to a Serenade," October 19, 1864, in *Collected Works*, VIII, 52.
9. T. Harry Williams, *Lincoln and His Generals* (New York: Alfred A. Knopf, 1952), Vintage edition, 339.
10. Abraham Lincoln, "Annual Message to Congress," December 6, 1864, in *Collected Works*, VIII, 149, 151.
11. Ibid., 152.
12. Ibid., 149.
13. James M. McPherson, *Ordeal by Fire*, 466.
14. Abraham Lincoln to George H. Thomas, December 16, 1864, in *Collected Works*, VIII, 169.
15. T. Harry Williams, *Lincoln and His Generals*, 344.
16. Michael Vorenberg, *Final Freedom: The Civil War, the Abolition of Slavery, and the Thirteenth Amendment* (Cambridge: Cambridge University Press, 2001), 180.
17. Abraham Lincoln, "Response to a Serenade," February 1, 1865, in *Collected Works*, VIII, 254.

18. Abraham Lincoln, "To the Senate and House of Representatives," February 5, 1865, in *Collected Works*, VIII, 260.

19. James M. McPherson, "The Ballot and Land for the Freedmen, 1861–1865," in *Reconstruction: An Anthology of Revisionist Writings*, ed. Kenneth Stampp and Leon F. Litwack (Baton Rouge: Louisiana State University Press, 1969), 152–53.

20. Abraham Lincoln, "Speech to One Hundred Fortieth Indiana Regiment," March 17, 1865, in *Collected Works*, VIII, 361.

21. Abraham Lincoln, "Second Inaugural Address," March 4, 1865, in *Collected Works*, VIII, 332–33.

22. Abraham Lincoln to Thurlow Weed, March 15, 1865, in *Collected Works*, VIII, 356.

23. Herman Belz, *Reconstructing the Union: Theory and Policy During the Civil War* (Ithaca, N.Y.: Cornell University Press, 1969), 251–76.

24. James M. McPherson, *Ordeal by Fire*, 476.

25. Abraham Lincoln to Edwin M. Stanton, March 30, 1865, in *Collected Works*, VIII, 377.

26. Abraham Lincoln to Edwin M. Stanton, April 3, 1865, in *Collected Works*, VIII, 385.

27. James M. McPherson, *Battle Cry of Freedom: The Civil War Era* (New York: Oxford University Press, 1988), 847.

28. Abraham Lincoln, "Response to Serenade," April 10, 1865, in *Collected Works*, VIII, 394.

29. Abraham Lincoln, "Last Public Address," April 11, 1865, in *Collected Works*, VIII, 399–405.

30. William Hanchett, *The Lincoln Murder Conspiracies* (Urbana: University of Illinois Press, 1983), 37, and Edward Steers, Jr., *Blood on the Moon: The Assassination of Abraham Lincoln* (Lexington: University Press of Kentucky, 2001), 91. Booth made these remarks to coconspirators Lewis Paine and David Herold.

31. James M. McPherson, *Ordeal by Fire*, 493.

32. Ibid., 493.

33. James M. McPherson, "Foreword," in LaWanda Cox, *Lincoln and Black Freedom*, x. In light of Lincoln's audacious actions in the spring of 1865, and in light of the *tone* of his final public address, it is hard to agree with the contention of historian William C. Harris that Lincoln, right down to the end, "sought to restore the South as it existed before the conflict, shorn, however, of the spirit of disunion and the institution of slavery. . . ." See William C. Harris, *With Charity for All: Lincoln and the Restoration of the Union* (Lexington: University Press of Kentucky, 1997), 4. Harris's reading of the evidence betrays the ever-powerful influence exerted by the school of thought that views Lincoln as a consummate moderate. Harris, for example, writes that Lincoln's support for the Freedmen's Bureau was in truth lukewarm in light of his alleged "deep reservations regarding the extension of federal power" (*With Charity for All*, 253–54), a most questionable presupposition in light of the Hamiltonian streak that pervaded the statecraft of Lincoln from his earliest days as a disciple of Henry Clay to the very last weeks of his life.

34. Harry V. Jaffa, *Crisis of the House Divided: An Interpretation of the Lincoln-Douglas Debates* (Chicago: The University of Chicago Press, 1959), 395.

35. Lincoln's interest in the uses and abuses of power—considered as raw and elemental *energy*—was often made explicit. Consider his response to a skeptic in

1864: "Drive back to the support of the rebellion the physical force which the colored people now give . . . and neither the present, nor any coming administration *can* save the Union. . . . It is not a question of sentiment or taste, but one of physical force, which may be measured, and estimated as horse-power, and steam-power, are measured and estimated." (Abraham Lincoln to Charles D. Robinson, August 17, 1864, *Collected Works*, VII, 500). Lincoln said much the same thing in his letter to Isaac M. Schermerhorn, September 12, 1864 (*Collected Works*, VIII, 2).

36. Abraham Lincoln to Gideon Welles, April 29, 1861, in *Collected Works*, IV, 348.

37. Edmund Wilson offers similar speculation with regard to the idea that "this prophet who had overruled opposition and sent thousands of men to their deaths should finally attest his good faith by laying down his own life with theirs" in "Abraham Lincoln: The Union as Religious Mysticism," in *Eight Essays* (New York: Doubleday and Anchor Books, 1954), 202.

38. Reinhold Niebuhr, *The Irony of American History* (New York: Charles Scribner's Sons, 1952), 172.

39. Abraham Lincoln, "Address Before the Young Men's Lyceum of Springfield, Ill.," January 27, 1838, in *Collected Works*, I, 114.

40. Harry V. Jaffa, *Crisis of the House Divided*, 306.

41. Theodore Roosevelt, Speech at Omaha, Nebraska, April 27, 1903, in *Presidential Addresses and State Papers* (New York: The Review of Reviews Company, 1904), I, 331. Theodore Roosevelt's appreciation for Lincoln became more profound in the decade that followed this particular speech.

42. Harry V. Jaffa, *Crisis of the House Divided*, 370.

43. Kant insisted again and again that one's moral *intent* is all-important, regardless of any results that one's moral behavior might deliver, or fail to deliver. "Practical [moral] laws," he proclaimed in his second great critique, the *Critique of Practical Reason*, "refer only to the will, irrespective of what is attained." See Kant's *Critique of Practical Reason* (1788), trans. Lewis White Beck (New York: Macmillan, 1985), 19. For this reason, Kant seemed to allow no exceptions to the moral imperative of truth telling. It bears noting that the ethical system of Kant flowed directly from his underlying metaphysical system, which is highly problematical, especially as he attempted to expand and elaborate it in his second critique.

With regard to Lincoln's moral casuistry, a useful comparison between the statecraft of Lincoln and the later teachings of sociologist Max Weber has been offered by William Lee Miller in his book *Lincoln's Virtues*. Miller emphasized Weber's distinction in his essay "Politics as a Vocation" between the ethic of perfect virtue and the "ethic of responsibility." See William Lee Miller, *Lincoln's Virtues: An Ethical Biography* (New York: Alfred A. Knopf, 2002), 195, 219, 225–26, 483, n. 195. See also Jacques Barzun, "Lincoln's Philosophic Vision," 21st Annual Robert Fortenbaugh Memorial Lecture, Gettysburg College, 1982.

44. Aristotle, *Nichomachean Ethics*, Book 4, chapt. 7, in *The Ethics of Aristotle*, trans. J. A. K. Thomson (Baltimore: Penguin Classics, 1953), 132.

45. Ibid.

46. Ibid., Book 4, chapt. 3, 124.

47. Jacques Barzun, *Darwin, Marx, Wagner: Critique of a Heritage* (New York: Little, Brown & Co., 1941; second revised edition, Garden City, N.Y.: Doubleday Anchor Books, 1958), 348–49.

48. In Lincoln's 1838 Lyceum address, he spoke about the need for a "political religion" to protect America's creed.

49. Carl Sandburg, *Abraham Lincoln, The War Years* (New York: Harcourt, Brace & Company, 1939), Vol. 4, 357.

Select Bibliography

As the corpus of writings on the subject of Abraham Lincoln is vast, this select bibliography is limited to work that was produced in the past half-century.

Anastaplo, George. "Abraham Lincoln's Emancipation Proclamation." In *Constitutional Government in America*, ed. Ronald L.K. Collins. Durham, N.C.: Carolina Academic Press, 1980.

Barzun, Jacques. "Lincoln's Philosophic Vision." 21st Annual Robert Fortenbaugh Memorial Lecture, Gettysburg College, Gettysburg, Pa., 1982.

Belz, Herman. *Reconstructing the Union: Theory and Policy During the Civil War.* Ithaca, N.Y.: Cornell University Press, 1969.

———. "Abraham Lincoln and American Constitutionalism." *The Review of Politics* 50 (Spring 1988): 169–97.

———. *Abraham Lincoln, Constitutionalism, and Equal Rights in the Civil War Era.* New York: Fordham University Press, 1998.

Bennett, Lerone, Jr. *Forced Into Glory: Abraham Lincoln's White Dream.* Chicago: Johnson Publishing Company, 2000.

Boritt, Gabor, ed. *Lincoln the War President: The Gettysburg Lectures.* New York: Oxford University Press, 1992.

———. *The Lincoln Enigma: The Changing Faces of an American Icon.* New York: Oxford University Press, 2001.

Burlingame, Michael. *The Inner World of Abraham Lincoln.* Urbana: University of Illinois Press, 1994.

Carwardine, Richard J. *Lincoln: Profiles in Power.* London: Longman Publishers, 2003.

Cox, LaWanda. *Lincoln and Black Freedom: A Study in Presidential Leadership.* Columbia: University of South Carolina Press, 1981.

Current, Richard N. *Lincoln and the First Shot.* New York: Harper & Row, 1963.

Davis, Collum, ed. *The Public and Private Lincoln: Contemporary Perspectives.* Carbondale: University of Southern Illinois Press, 1979.

Diggins, John Patrick. *On Hallowed Ground: Abraham Lincoln and the Foundations of American History.* New Haven: Yale University Press, 2000.

Dilorenzo, Thomas. *The Real Lincoln: A New Look at Abraham Lincoln, His Agenda, and an Unnecessary War.* New York: Crown Publishing Group, 2002.

Donald, David Herbert. *Lincoln Reconsidered: Essays on the Civil War Era.* New York: Alfred A. Knopf, 1956.

———. *Lincoln.* New York: Simon & Schuster, 1995.

———. *We Are Lincoln Men: Abraham Lincoln and His Friends.* New York: Simon & Schuster, 2003.

Farber, Daniel. *Lincoln's Constitution.* Chicago: University of Chicago Press, 2003.

Fehrenbacher, Don E. *Prelude to Greatness: Lincoln in the 1850's.* Stanford, Calif.: Stanford University Press, 1962.

———. "Only His Stepchildren: Lincoln and the Negro," *Civil War History* 20 (December 1974): 293–310.

Fletcher, George P. *Our Secret Constitution: How Lincoln Redefined American Democracy.* New York: Oxford University Press, 2001.

Foner, Eric. *Free Soil, Free Labor, Free Men: The Ideology of the Republican Party Before the Civil War.* New York: Oxford University Press, 1970.

Fornieri, Joseph R. *Abraham Lincoln's Political Faith.* DeKalb: Northern Illinois University Press, 2003.

Gienapp, William E. *Abraham Lincoln and Civil War America.* New York: Oxford University Press, 2002.

Greenstone, J. David. *The Lincoln Persuasion: Re-Making American Liberalism.* Princeton: Princeton University Press, 1993.

Guelzo, Allen C. *Abraham Lincoln: Redeemer President.* Grand Rapids, Mich.: Eerdmans, 1999.

———. *Lincoln's Emancipation Proclamation: The End of Slavery in America.* New York: Simon & Schuster, 2004.

Hanchett, William. *The Lincoln Murder Conspiracies.* Urbana: University of Illinois Press, 1983.

Harris, William C. *With Charity for All: Lincoln and the Restoration of the Union.* Lexington, Ky.: University Press of Kentucky, 1997.

Holzer, Harold. *Lincoln at Cooper Union: The Speech that Made Abraham Lincoln President.* New York: Simon & Schuster, 2004.

Jacobsohn, Gary L. "Abraham Lincoln 'On This Question of Judicial Authority': The Theory of Constitutional Aspiration." *Western Political Quarterly* 36 (March 1983): 52–70.

Jaffa, Harry V. *Crisis of the House Divided: An Interpretation of the Lincoln-Douglas Debates.* Chicago: The University of Chicago Press, 1959.

———. *A New Birth of Freedom: Abraham Lincoln and the Coming of the Civil War.* Lanham, Md.: Rowman & Littlefield, 2000.

Johannsen, Robert Walter. *Lincoln, the South, and Slavery: The Political Dimension.* Baton Rouge: Louisiana State University Press, 1991.

Klingaman, William K. *Abraham Lincoln and The Road to Emancipation: 1861–1865.* New York: Viking Press, 2001.

Long, David E. *The Jewel of Liberty: Abraham Lincoln's Re-Election and the End of Slavery.* Mechanicsburg, Pa.: Stackpole Books, 1994.

McPherson, James M. *Battle Cry of Freedom: The Civil War Era.* New York: Oxford University Press, 1988.

———. *Abraham Lincoln and the Second American Revolution.* New York: Oxford University Press, 1991.

Miller, William Lee. *Lincoln's Virtues: An Ethical Biography.* New York: Alfred A. Knopf, 2002.

Morel, Lucas. *Lincoln's Sacred Effort: Defining Religion's Role in American Self-Government.* New York: Lexington Books, 2000.

Neely, Mark E., Jr. *The Fate of Liberty: Abraham Lincoln and Civil Liberties.* New York: Oxford University Press, 1991.

———. *The Last Best Hope of Earth: Abraham Lincoln and the Promise of America.* Cambridge, Mass.: Harvard University Press, 1993.

Oates, Stephen B. *With Malice Toward None: The Life of Abraham Lincoln.* New York: Harper & Row, 1977.

Paludan, Phillip Shaw. "Lincoln, the Rule of Law, and the American Revolution." *Journal of the Illinois State Historical Society* 70 (February 1977): 10–17.

———. *The Presidency of Abraham Lincoln.* Lawrence: University Press of Kansas, 1994.

Pressly, Thomas J. "Bullets and Ballots: Lincoln and the 'Right of Revolution.'" *American Historical Review* 67 (April 1962): 661–62.

Quarles, Benjamin. *Lincoln and the Negro.* New York: Oxford University Press, 1962.

Steers, Edward, Jr. *Blood on the Moon: The Assassination of Abraham Lincoln.* Lexington: University Press of Kentucky, 2001.

Strozier, Charles B. *Lincoln's Quest for Union: Public and Private Meanings.* New York: Basic Books, 1982.

Thomas, Benjamin P. *Abraham Lincoln.* New York: Alfred A. Knopf, 1952.

Thomas, John L., ed. *Abraham Lincoln and the American Political Tradition.* Amherst: University of Massachusetts Press, 1986.

Thompson, Kenneth W., ed. *Essays on Lincoln's Faith and Politics.* Lanham, Md.: University Press of America, 1983.

Trueblood, Elton. *Abraham Lincoln: Theologian of American Anguish.* New York: Harper & Row, 1973.

Vorenberg, Michael. *Final Freedom: The Civil War, the Abolition of Slavery, and the Thirteenth Amendment.* Cambridge: Cambridge University Press, 2001.

Wieck, Carl F. *Lincoln's Quest for Equality: The Road to Gettysburg.* DeKalb, Ill.: Northern Illinois University Press, 2002.

Williams, T. Harry. *Lincoln and His Generals.* New York: Alfred A. Knopf, 1952.

Wills, Garry. *Lincoln at Gettysburg: The Words That Remade America.* New York: Simon & Schuster, 1992.

Wilson, Douglas L. *Honor's Voice: The Transformation of Abraham Lincoln.* New York: Alfred A. Knopf, 1998.

Wilson, Major L. "Lincoln and Van Buren in the Steps of the Fathers: Another Look at the Lyceum Address." *Civil War History* 29 (September 1983): 197–211.

Wolf, William J. *The Almost Chosen People: A Study of the Religion of Abraham Lincoln.* Garden City: Doubleday & Co., 1959.

Index